Lecture Notes in Computer Science   15889

Founding Editors

Gerhard Goos
Juris Hartmanis

Editorial Board Members

Elisa Bertino, *Purdue University, West Lafayette, IN, USA*
Wen Gao, *Peking University, Beijing, China*
Bernhard Steffen, *TU Dortmund University, Dortmund, Germany*
Moti Yung, *Columbia University, New York, NY, USA*

The series Lecture Notes in Computer Science (LNCS), including its subseries Lecture Notes in Artificial Intelligence (LNAI) and Lecture Notes in Bioinformatics (LNBI), has established itself as a medium for the publication of new developments in computer science and information technology research, teaching, and education.

LNCS enjoys close cooperation with the computer science R & D community, the series counts many renowned academics among its volume editors and paper authors, and collaborates with prestigious societies. Its mission is to serve this international community by providing an invaluable service, mainly focused on the publication of conference and workshop proceedings and postproceedings. LNCS commenced publication in 1973.

Osvaldo Gervasi · Beniamino Murgante ·
Chiara Garau · Yeliz Karaca ·
Maria Noelia Faginas Lago · Francesco Scorza ·
Ana Cristina Braga
Editors

Computational Science and Its Applications – ICCSA 2025 Workshops

Istanbul, Turkey, June 30 – July 3, 2025
Proceedings, Part IV

Editors
Osvaldo Gervasi
University of Perugia
Perugia, Italy

Beniamino Murgante
University of Basilicata
Potenza, Italy

Chiara Garau
University of Cagliari
Cagliari, Italy

Yeliz Karaca
University of Massachusetts
Worcester, MA, USA

Maria Noelia Faginas Lago
University of Perugia
Perugia, Italy

Francesco Scorza
University of Basilicata
Potenza, Italy

Ana Cristina Braga
University of Minho
Braga, Portugal

ISSN 0302-9743   ISSN 1611-3349 (electronic)
Lecture Notes in Computer Science
ISBN 978-3-031-97602-5   ISBN 978-3-031-97603-2 (eBook)
https://doi.org/10.1007/978-3-031-97603-2

© The Editor(s) (if applicable) and The Author(s), under exclusive license
to Springer Nature Switzerland AG 2026

This work is subject to copyright. All rights are solely and exclusively licensed by the Publisher, whether the whole or part of the material is concerned, specifically the rights of translation, reprinting, reuse of illustrations, recitation, broadcasting, reproduction on microfilms or in any other physical way, and transmission or information storage and retrieval, electronic adaptation, computer software, or by similar or dissimilar methodology now known or hereafter developed.
The use of general descriptive names, registered names, trademarks, service marks, etc. in this publication does not imply, even in the absence of a specific statement, that such names are exempt from the relevant protective laws and regulations and therefore free for general use.
The publisher, the authors and the editors are safe to assume that the advice and information in this book are believed to be true and accurate at the date of publication. Neither the publisher nor the authors or the editors give a warranty, expressed or implied, with respect to the material contained herein or for any errors or omissions that may have been made. The publisher remains neutral with regard to jurisdictional claims in published maps and institutional affiliations.

This Springer imprint is published by the registered company Springer Nature Switzerland AG
The registered company address is: Gewerbestrasse 11, 6330 Cham, Switzerland

If disposing of this product, please recycle the paper.

Preface

The compiled 14 volumes (LNCS volumes 15886–15899) consist of the peer-reviewed papers from the 68 Workshops of the 2025 International Conference on Computational Science and Its Applications (ICCSA 2025), which was held between June 30 – July 3, 2025 in Istanbul (Türkiye). The peer-reviewed papers of the main conference tracks are published in a separate set made up of three volumes (LNCS 15648–15650).

The conference was held in a hybrid form, with the large majority of participants in presence, hosted by Galatasaray University, Istanbul, Türkiye. We enabled virtual participation for those who did not attend the event in person due to logistical, political and economic problems, by adopting a technological infrastructure via open-source software (jitsi + riot) and a commercial Cloud infrastructure.

With the 2025 edition, ICCSA celebrated its 25th anniversary, a quarter of a century as a memorable moment that is harmoniously aligned with Istanbul, an extraordinary city located at the crossroads and acting as a bridge connecting Asia and Europe, representing different cultures, beliefs as well as lifestyles, which highlights its intercultural fabric.

ICCSA 2025 marked another fruitful and thought-provoking academic event in the International Conferences on Computational Science and Its Applications (ICCSA) conference series, previously held in Hanoi, Vietnam (2024), Athens, Greece (2023), Málaga, Spain (2022), Cagliari, Italy (hybrid with a few participants in presence in 2021 and completely online in 2020), whilst earlier editions took place in Saint Petersburg, Russia (2019), Melbourne, Australia (2018), Trieste, Italy (2017), Beijing, China (2016), Banff, Canada (2015), Guimaraes, Portugal (2014), Ho Chi Minh City, Vietnam (2013), Salvador, Brazil (2012), Santander, Spain (2011), Fukuoka, Japan (2010), Suwon, South Korea (2009), Perugia, Italy (2008), Kuala Lumpur, Malaysia (2007), Glasgow, UK (2006), Singapore (2005), Assisi, Italy (2004), Montreal, Canada (2003), and (as ICCS) Amsterdam, the Netherlands (2002) and San Francisco, USA (2001).

Computational Science constitutes the main pillar of most present research, industrial and commercial applications, and plays a unique role in exploiting ICT innovative technologies, and the ICCSA conference series has, accordingly, provided ample opportunities to researchers and industry practitioners to discuss new ideas, to share complex problems and their solutions, and to shape new trends in Computational Science. As the conference mirrors society from a scientific point of view, this year's undoubtedly dominant theme was large language models, machine learning and Artificial Intelligence (AI) and their applications in the most diverse technological, economic and industrial fields, amongst the others.

The ICCSA 2025 conference was structured in six general tracks covering the fields of computational science and its applications: Computational Methods, Algorithms and Scientific Applications – High Performance Computing and Networks – Geometric Modeling, Graphics and Visualization – Advanced and Emerging Applications – Information Systems and Technologies – Urban and Regional Planning. In addition, the conference consisted of 68 workshops, focusing on topical issues of utmost importance to science, technology and society: from new computational approaches for earth science, to mathematical methods for image processing, new statistical and optimization methods, several Artificial Intelligence approaches, sustainability issues, smart cities and related technologies, to name some.

In the Workshops' proceedings, we accepted 362 full papers, 37 short papers and 2 Ph.D. Showcase papers from total of 1043 submissions (Acceptance rate 38.4%). In the Main Conference Proceedings, we accepted 71 full papers, 6 short papers and 1 Ph.D. Showcase paper from 269 submissions to the General Tracks of the Conference (with an acceptance rate of 29.9%). We would like to convey our sincere appreciation to the workshops' chairs and co-chairs and program committee members for their diligent work, commitment and dedication.

The success and consistent maintenance of the ICCSA conference series in general, and of ICCSA 2025 in particular, rely upon the support of many people: authors, presenters, participants, keynote speakers, workshop chairs, session chairs, organizing committee members, student volunteers, Program Committee members, Advisory Committee members, International Liaison chairs, reviewers and other individuals in various roles. Thus, we take this opportunity to wholahartedly thank each and everyone.

We additionally wish to thank publisher Springer for their agreement to publish the proceedings, besides sponsoring part of the best papers awards and for their kind assistance and cooperation during the editing process.

We would cordially like to invite you to refer to the ICCSA website https://iccsa.org, where you can find the relevant details regarding this academic endeavor and event of ours.

June 2025

Osvaldo Gervasi
Yeliz Karaca
Beniamino Murgante
Chiara Garau

A Welcome Message from the Organizers

The International Conference on Computational Science and Its Applications (ICCSA) reflects a culmination of meticulous and dedicated efforts and academic endeavors toward the progress of science and technology.

One of the most noteworthy aspects of ICCSA is its fostering of a collective spirit, bringing together a plethora of participants from all over the world. Correspondingly, this merging power manifests itself in the 25th anniversary of ICCSA, which is a quarter of a century, in Istanbul, Türkiye, which connects and acts as a bridge between two continents, namely Asia and Europe. This unique location in the world hosts the 25th year of ICCSA at Galatasaray University, located on Çırağan Avenue by Istanbul's Bosphorus, which is an established international university bestowed with a distinctive past of teaching tradition, research and education exceeding five centuries.

Istanbul, having served as the capital city of four empires, namely the Roman Empire (330–395), the Byzantine Empire (395–1204 and 1261–1453), the Latin Empire (1204–1261) and the Ottoman Empire (1453–1922), is an exceptional city of the Republic of Türkiye founded by Mustafa Kemal Atatürk.

Situated at a strategic location along the historic Silk Road, Istanbul is at the core of extending rail networks which span across Europe and West Asia along with the only sea route between the Black Sea and the Mediterranean.

The cultural, historical and economic pulses of the country are evident in Istanbul whose rooted origins have embraced varying beliefs, lifestyles and populace, which highlights the city's mosaic quality with blended fabric in a constant harmonious flow. This has enabled cultures to grow and be nurtured, which is profoundly rooted in its urban culture.

Computational Science constitutes the main pillar of most present research, industrial and commercial activities besides manifesting a unique role in exploiting and addressing innovative Information and Communication Technologies. Thus, the 25-year-old ICCSA conference series provides remarkable opportunities to get acquainted with leading researchers, scientists, scholars, practitioners and many more while exchanging innovative ideas and initiating new partnerships, associations and bonds.

With the hosting of Galatasaray University, I would personally and on behalf of the Local Organizing Committee, with the members Emre Alptekin, Gülfem Işıklar Alptekin, Cengiz Kahraman, Abdullah Çağrı Tolga and Ayberk Zeytin, like to convey our sincere gratitude and thanks to everyone who exerted their efforts in and contributed to the realization of ICCSA 2025. With these notes and remarks, welcome to Istanbul!

Cordially yours,
On behalf of the Local Organizing Committee.

June 2025   Yeliz Karaca

Organization

Honorary General Chairs

Bernady O. Apduhan	Kyushu Sangyo University, Japan
Kenneth C. J. Tan	Sardina Systems, UK

General Chairs

Yeliz Karaca	University of Massachusetts, USA
Osvaldo Gervasi	University of Perugia, Italy
David Taniar	Monash University, Australia

Program Committee Chairs

Beniamino Murgante	University of Basilicata, Italy
Chiara Garau	University of Cagliari, Italy
Ana Maria A. C. Rocha	University of Minho, Portugal
A. Çağrı Tolga	Galatasaray University, Turkey

International Advisory Committee

Jemal Abawajy	Deakin University, Australia
Dharma P. Agarwal	University of Cincinnati, USA
Rajkumar Buyya	Melbourne University, Australia
Claudia Bauzer Medeiros	University of Campinas, Brazil
Manfred M. Fisher	Vienna University of Economics and Business, Austria
Pierre Frankhauser	University of Franche-Comté/CNRS, France
Marina L. Gavrilova	University of Calgary, Canada
Sumi Helal	University of Florida, USA & Lancaster University, UK
Bin Jiang	University of Gävle, Sweden
Yee Leung	Chinese University of Hong Kong, China

International Liaison Chairs

Ivan Blečić	University of Cagliari, Italy
Giuseppe Borruso	University of Trieste, Italy
Elise De Donker	Western Michigan University, USA
Maria Noelia Faginas Lago	University of Perugia, Italy
Maria Irene Falcão	University of Minho, Portugal
Robert C. H. Hsu	Chung Hua University, Taiwan
Yeliz Karaca	University of Massachusetts Chan Medical School, USA
Tae-Hoon Kim	Zhejiang University of Science and Technology, China
Vladimir Korkhov	Saint Petersburg University, Russia
Takashi Naka	Kyushu Sangyo University, Japan
Rafael D. C. Santos	National Institute for Space Research, Brazil
Maribel Yasmina Santos	University of Minho, Portugal
Anastasia Stratigea	National Technical University of Athens, Greece

Workshop and Session Organizing Chairs

Beniamino Murgante	University of Basilicata, Italy
Chiara Garau	University of Cagliari, Italy

Award Chair

Wenny Rahayu	La Trobe University, Australia

Publicity Committee Chairs

Elmer Dadios	De La Salle University, Philippines
Nataliia Kulabukhova	Saint Petersburg University, Russia
Daisuke Takahashi	Tsukuba University, Japan
Shangwang Wang	Beijing University of Posts and Telecommunications, China

Local Organizing Committee Chairs

Emre Alptekin	Galatasaray University, Turkey
Gülfem Işıklar Alptekin	Galatasaray University, Turkey
Cengiz Kahraman	İstanbul Technical University, Turkey
A. Çağrı Tolga	Galatasaray University, Turkey
Ayberk Zeytin	Galatasaray University, Turkey

Technology Chair

Damiano Perri	University of Perugia, Italy

Program Committee

Vera Afreixo	University of Aveiro, Portugal
Vladimir Alarcon	Northern Gulf Institute, USA
Filipe Alvelos	University of Minho, Portugal
Debora Anelli	Polytechnic University of Bari, Italy
Hartmut Asche	Hasso-Plattner-Institut für Digital Engineering Ggmbh, Germany
Nizamettin Aydın	İstanbul Technical University, Turkey
Ginevra Balletto	University of Cagliari, Italy
Nadia Balucani	University of Perugia, Italy
Socrates Basbas	Aristotle University of Thessaloniki, Greece
David Berti	ART SpA, Italy
Michela Bertolotto	University College Dublin, Ireland
Sandro Bimonte	CEMAGREF, TSCF, France
Ana Cristina Braga	University of Minho, Portugal
Tiziana Campisi	Kore University of Enna, Italy
Yves Caniou	Université Claude Bernard Lyon 1, France
Alessandra Capolupo	Polytechnic University of Bari, Italy
José A. Cardoso e Cunha	Universidade Nova de Lisboa, Portugal
Rui Cardoso	University of Beira Interior, Portugal
Leocadio G. Casado	University of Almería, Spain
Mete Celik	Erciyes University, Turkey
Maria Cerreta	University of Naples Federico II, Italy
Ta Quang Chieu	Thuyloi University, Vietnam
Rachel Chien-Sing Lee	Sunway University, Malaysia
Birol Ciloglugil	Ege University, Turkey
Mauro Coni	University of Cagliari, Italy

Florbela Maria da Cruz Domingues Correia	Polytechnic Institute of Viana do Castelo, Portugal
Alessandro Costantini	INFN, Italy
Roberto De Lotto	University of Pavia, Italy
Luiza De Macedo Mourelle	State University of Rio De Janeiro, Brazil
Marcelo De Paiva Guimaraes	Federal University of Sao Paulo, Brazil
Frank Devai	London South Bank University, UK
Joana Matos Dias	University of Coimbra, Portugal
Aziz Dursun	Virginia Tech University, USA
Laila El Ghandour	Heriot-Watt University, UK
Rafida M. Elobaid	Canadian University Dubai, United Arab Emirates
Maria Irene Falcao	University of Minho, Portugal
Florbela P. Fernandes	Polytechnic Institute of Bragança, Portugal
Paula Odete Fernandes	Polytechnic Institute of Bragança, Portugal
Adelaide de Fátima Baptista Valente Freitas	University of Aveiro, Portugal
Valentina Franzoni	University of Perugia, Italy
Andreas Fricke	University of Potsdam, Germany
Raffaele Garrisi	Centro Operativo per la Sicurezza Cibernetica, Italy
Ivan Gerace	University of Perugia, Italy
Maria Giaoutzi	National Technical University of Athens, Greece
Salvatore Giuffrida	University of Catania, Italy
Teresa Guarda	Universidad Estatal Peninsula de Santa Elena, Ecuador
Sevin Gümgüm	Izmir University of Economics, Turkey
Malgorzata Hanzl	Technical University of Lodz, Poland
Maulana Adhinugraha Kiki	Telkom University, Indonesia
Clement Ho Cheung Leung	Chinese University of Hong Kong, China
Andrea Lombardi	University of Perugia, Italy
Marcos Mandado Alonso	University of Vigo, Spain
Ernesto Marcheggiani	Katholieke Universiteit Leuven, Belgium
Antonino Marvuglia	Luxembourg Institute of Science and Technology, Luxembourg
Michele Mastroianni	University of Salerno, Italy
Hideo Matsufuru	High Energy Accelerator Research Organization, Japan
Fernando Miranda	Universidade do Minho, Portugal
Giuseppe Modica	University of Reggio Calabria, Italy
Majaz Moonis	University of Massachusetts, USA
Nadia Nedjah	State University of Rio de Janeiro, Brazil
Paolo Nesi	University of Florence, Italy

Suzan Obaiys	University of Malaya, Malaysia
Marcin Paprzycki	Polish Academy of Sciences, Poland
Eric Pardede	La Trobe University, Australia
Ana Isabel Pereira	Polytechnic Institute of Bragança, Portugal
Damiano Perri	University of Perugia, Italy
Massimiliano Petri	University of Pisa, Italy
Telmo Pinto	University of Coimbra, Portugal
Alessandro Plaisant	University of Sassari, Italy
Maurizio Pollino	ENEA, Italy
Alenka Poplin	Iowa State University, USA
Marcos Quiles	Federal University of São Paulo, Brazil
Nguyen Huu Quynh	Thuyloi University, Vietnam
Albert Rimola	Universitat Autònoma de Barcelona, Spain
Humberto Rocha	University of Coimbra, Portugal
Marzio Rosi	University of Perugia, Italy
Lucia Saganeiti	University of L'Aquila, Italy
Francesco Scorza	University of Basilicata, Italy
Marco Paulo Seabra dos Reis	University of Coimbra, Portugal
Jie Shen	University of Michigan, USA
Francesco Tajani	Sapienza University of Rome, Italy
Rodrigo Tapia Mcclung	Centro de Investigación en Ciencias de Información Geoespacial, Mexico
Eufemia Tarantino	Polytechnic University of Bari, Italy
Sergio Tasso	University of Perugia, Italy
Ana Paula Teixeira	Universidade do Minho, Portugal
Yiota Theodora	National Technical University of Athens, Greece
Giuseppe A. Trunfio	University of Sassari, Italy
Toshihiro Uchibayashi	Kyushu University, Japan
Marco Vizzari	University of Perugia, Italy
Frank Westad	Norwegian University of Science and Technology, Norway
Fukuko Yuasa	High Energy Accelerator Research Organization, Japan
Ljiljana Zivkovic	Republic Geodetic Authority, Serbia

Workshops

Workshop on Advancements in Applied Machine-Learning and Data Analytics (AAMDA 2025)

Workshop Organizers

Alessandro Costantini	INFN, Italy
Daniele Cesini	INFN, Italy
Elisabetta Ronchieri	INFN, Italy
Barbara Martelli	INFN, Italy

Workshop Program Committee Members

Alessandro Costantini	Istituto Nazionale di Fisica Nucleare (INFN), Italy
Daniele Cesini	Istituto Nazionale di Fisica Nucleare (INFN), Italy
Elisabetta Ronchieri	Istituto Nazionale di Fisica Nucleare (INFN), Italy
Barbara Martelli	Istituto Nazionale di Fisica Nucleare (INFN), Italy
Luca Dell'Agnello	Istituto Nazionale di Fisica Nucleare (INFN), Italy

Advanced and Innovative Web Apps 2025 (AIWA 2025)

Workshop Organizers

Damiano Perri	University of Perugia, Italy
Osvaldo Gervasi	University of Perugia, Italy
Stelios Kouzeleas	International Hellenic University, Greece
Sergio Tasso	University of Perugia, Italy

Workshop Program Committee Members

David Berti	ART SpA, Italy
JungYoon Kim	Gachon University, South Korea
TaiHoon Kim	Zhejiang University of Science and Technology, China

Advanced Processes of Mathematics and Computing Models in Complex Data-Intensive Computational Systems (AMCM 2025)

Workshop Organizers

Yeliz Karaca	University of Massachusetts Chan Medical School and Massachusetts Institute of Technology, USA
Dumitru Baleanu	Lebanese American University, Lebanon
Osvaldo Gervasi	University of Perugia, Italy
Yudong Zhang	University of Leicester, UK
Majaz Moonis	University of Massachusetts Chan Medical School and Massachusetts Institute of Technology, USA

Workshop Program Committee Members

TaeHoon Kim	Zhejiang University of Science and Technology, China
Martin Bohner	Missouri University of Science and Technology, USA
Shuihua Wang	University of Leicester, UK
Khan Muhammad	Sungkyunkwan University, South Korea
Mahmoud Abdel-Aty	Sohag University, Egypt
Aziz Dursun	Virginia Polytechnic Institute and State University, USA
Kemal Güven Gülen	Namık Kemal University, Turkey
Akif Akgül	Hitit Üniversitesi, Turkey

Advanced Numerical Approaches for Assessment and Design of No-Tension Masonry Structures (ANAMS 2025)

Workshop Organizers

Antonino Iannuzzo	Universitá degli studi del Sannio, Italy
Carlo Olivieri	Universitá Telematica Pegaso, Italy
Andrea Montanino	CIMNE, Spain
Elham Mousavian	University of Edinburgh, UK

Workshop Program Committee Members

Pietro Meriggi	Roma Tre University, Italy
Francesca Perelli	University of Naples Federico II, Italy
Marialuigia Sangirardi	University of Oxford, UK
Sam Cocking	University of Cambridge, UK

Matteo Salvalaggio — University of Minho, Portugal
Vittorio Paris — University of Bergamo, Italy
Luigi Sibille — Norwegian University of Science and Technology, Norway
Natalia Pingaro — Politecnico di Milano, Italy
Martina Buzzetti — Politecnico di Milano, Italy
Generoso Vaiano — Pegaso Telematic University, Italy
Alessandra Capolupo — Politecnico di Bari, Italy
Amal Gerges — Università degli Studi di Cagliari, Italy
Fabian Orozco — National Autonomous University of Mexico, Mexico
Nathanael Savalle — Polytech Clermont and Université Clermont Auvergne, France
Luca Umberto Argiento — University of Naples Federico II, Italy
Bartolomeo Pantó — Durham University, UK

Unveiling the Synergies Between Air Quality and Climate PlAnning (AQCliPA 2025)

Workshop Organizers

Angela Pilogallo — University of L'Aquila, Italy
Luigi Santopietro — University of Basilicata, Italy
Filomena Pietrapertosa — IMAA CNR, Italy
Monica Salvia — IMAA CNR, Italy
Carlo Trozzi — IMAA CNR, Italy
Valeria Scapini — Central University of Chile, Chile

Workshop Program Committee Members

Lucia Saganeiti — IMAA-CNR, Italy
Lorena Fiorini — University of L'Aquila, Italy
Antonio Mazza — IMAA-CNR, Italy
Gabriele Nolè — IMAA-CNR, Italy
Carmen Guida — University of Naples "Federico II", Italy
Floriana Zucaro — University of Naples "Federico II", Italy
Sabrina Lai — University of Cagliari, Italy
Chiara Garau — University of Cagliari, Italy

Advancements in Spatial assessment of Socio-Ecological SystemS (ASSESS 2025)

Workshop Organizers

Daniele Cannatella	TU Delft, The Netherlands
Giuliano Poli	University of Naples Federico II, Italy
Eugenio Muccio	TU Delft, The Netherlands
Claudiu Forgaci	TU Delft, The Netherlands

Workshop Program Committee Members

Daniele Cannatella	TU Delft, The Netherlands
Giuliano Poli	University of Naples Federico II, Italy
Eugenio Muccio	University of Naples Federico II, Italy
Claudiu Forgaci	TU Delft, The Netherlands
Maria Cerreta	University of Naples Federico II, Italy
Maria Somma	University of Naples Federico II, Italy
Laura Di Tommaso	University of Naples Federico II, Italy
Sabrina Sacco	Politecnico di Milano, Italy
Piero Zizzania	University of Naples Federico II, Italy
Gaia Daldanise	CNR IRISS, Italy
Benedetta Grieco	University of Naples Federico II, Italy
Giuseppe Ciciriello	University of Naples Federico II, Italy
Marta Dell'Ovo	Politecnico di Milano, Italy
Francesco Piras	University of Cagliari, Italy
Diana Rolando	Politecnico di Torino, Italy
Stefano Cuntò	University of Naples Federico II, Italy
Ludovica La Rocca	University of Naples Federico II, Italy

Blockchain and Distributed Ledgers: Technologies and Applications (BDLTA 2025)

Workshop Organizers

Vladimir Korkhov	Saint Petersburg State University, Russia
Elena Stankova	Saint Petersburg State University, Russia
Nataliia Kulabukhova	Saint Petersburg State University, Russia

Workshop Program Committee Members

Adam Belloum	University of Amsterdam, the Netherlands
Dmitrii Vasiunin	Deutsche Telekom Cloud Services E.P.E., Greece
Serob Balyan	Osensus Arm LLC, Armenia
Suren Abrahamyan	Osensus Arm LLC, Armenia
Ashot Sergey Gevorkyan	NAS of Armenia, Armenia

Michal Hnatic	Univerzita Pavla Jozefa Šafárika v Košiciach, Slovakia
Michail Panteleyev	Saint Petersburg Electrotecnical University, Russia
Martin Vala	Univerzita Pavla Jozefa Šafárika v Košiciach, Slovakia
Nodir Zaynalov	Tashkent University of Information Technologies named after Muhammad al Khwarizmi, Uzbekistan
Michail Panteleyev	Saint Petersburg Electrotecnical University, Russia
Alexander Degtyarev	Saint Petersburg University, Russia
Alexander Bogdanov	St. Petersburg State University, Russia

Bio and Neuro Inspired Computing and Applications (BIONCA 2025)

Workshop Organizers

Nadia Nedjah	State University of Rio de Janeiro, Brazil
Luiza de Macedo Mourelle	State University of Rio de Janeiro, Brazil

Workshop Program Committee Members

Nadia Nedjha	State University of Rio de Janeiro, Brazil
Luiza de Macedo Mourelle	State University of Rio de Janeiro, Brazil
Luigi Maciel Ribeiro	State University of Rio de Janeiro, Brazil
Joelmir Ramos	Federal University of Rio de Janeiro, Brazil
Rogério Moraes	Brazilian Navy, Brazil
Marcos Santana Farias	Institute of Nuclear Energy, Brazil
Luneque Silva Jr.	Federal University of ABC, Brazil
Alan Oliveira	University of Lisboa, Portugal
Brij Bhooshan Gupta	Asia University, Taiwan

Computational and Applied Mathematics (CAM 2025)

Workshop Organizers

Maria Irene Falcão	University of Minho, Portugal
Fernando Miranda	University of Minho, Portugal

Workshop Program Committee Members

Fernando Miranda	University of Minho, Portugal
Graça Tomaz	Polytechnic of Guarda, Portugal
Helmuth Malonek	University of Aveiro, Portugal

Isabel Cacao	University of Aveiro, Portugal
João Morais	Autonomous Technological Institute of Mexico, Mexico
Lidia Aceto	University of Eastern Piedmont, Italy
Luís Ferrás	University of Porto, Portugal
M. Irene Falcão	University of Minho, Portugal
Patrícia Beites	University of Beira Interior, Portugal
Paulo Amorim	FGV EMAp, Brazil
Regina de Almeida	University of Trás-os-Montes e Alto Douro, Portugal
Ricardo Severino	University of Minho, Portugal

Computational and Applied Statistics (CAS 2025)

Workshop Organizer

Ana Cristina Braga	ALGORITMI Research Centre, LASI, University of Minho, Portugal

Workshop Program Committee Members

Adelaide Freitas	University of Aveiro, Portugal
Andreas Futschik	Johannes Kepler University Linz, Austria
Ana Cristina Braga	University of Minho, Portugal
Ângela Silva	University of Minho, Portugal
Arminda Manuela Gonçalves	University of Minho, Portugal
Carina Silva	Polytechnic Intitute of Lisbon, Portugal
Elisete Correia	University of Trás-os-Montes e Alto Douro, Portugal
Frank Westad	Norwegian University of Science and Technology, Norway
Isabel Natario	New University of Lisbon, Portugal
Irene Oliveira	University of Trás-os-Montes e Alto Douro, Portugal
Ivan Rodriguez Conde	University of Vigo, Spain
Joaquim Gonçalves	Instituto Politécnico do Cávado e do Ave, Portugal
Lino Costa	University of Minho, Portugal
Marco Reis	University of Coimbra, Portugal
Maria Filipa Mourão	Polytechnic Institute of Viana do Castelo, Portugal
Maria João Polidoro	Polytechnic Institute of Porto, Portugal
Martin Perez Perez	University of Vigo, Spain
Michal Abrahamowicz	McGill University, Canada
Vera Afreixo	University of Aveiro, Portugal

Werner G. Müller — Johannes Kepler University Linz, Austria
Bruna Silva Ramos — University Lusiada de Famalicão, Portugal
Inês Sousa — University of Minho, Portugal
Luís Miguel Rocha Matos — University of Minho, Portugal
Manuel Carlos Figueiredo — University of Minho, Portugal

Cyber Intelligence and Applications (CIA 2025)

Workshop Organizer
Gianni D'Angelo — University of Salerno, Italy

Workshop Program Committee Members
Gianni D'Angelo — University of Salerno, Italy
Francesco Palmieri — University of Salerno, Italy
Massimo Ficco — University of Salerno, Italy
Arcangelo Castiglione — University of Salerno, Italy

Computational Methods for Business Analytics (CMBA 2025)

Workshop Organizers
Cláudio Alves — Universidade do Minho, Portugal
Telmo Pinto — Universidade do Minho, Portugal

Workshop Program Committee Members
Abdulrahim Shamayleh — American University of Sharjah, United Arab Emirates
Ana Rocha — University of Minho, Portugal
Angelo Sifaleras — University of Macedonia, Greece
Cristóvão Silva — University of Coimbra, Portugal
José Valério de Carvalho — University of Minho, Portugal
Miguel Vieira — Universidade Lusófona, Portugal
Rita Macedo — Université de Lille, France
Ana Moura — Universidade de Aveiro, Portugal
Cristina Lopes — ISCAP, Portugal
Eliana Costa e Silva — Instituto Politécnico do Porto, Portugal

Computational Methods, Statistics and Industrial Mathematics (CMSIM 2025)

Workshop Organizers

Maria Filomena Teodoro	IST ID, Instituto Superior Técnico, Portugal
Marina Alexandra Pedro Andrade	ISCTE – Lisbon University Institute, Portugal
Paula Simões	University of Lisbon, Portugal
Teresa A. Oliveira	IST ID, Instituto Superior Técnico, Portugal

Workshop Program Committee Members

Amilcar Oliveira	Universidade Aberta and Universidade de Lisboa, Portugal
Victor Lobo	Escola Naval and NOVA IMS Almada, Portugal
António Pacheco	IST Universidade de Lisboa, Portugal
Eliana Costa	Escola Superior de Tecnologia e Gestão IPPorto, Portugal
Aldina Correia	Escola Superior de Tecnologia e Gestão IPPorto, Portugal
Fernando Carapau	University of Évora, Portugal
Ricardo Moura	Portuguese Naval Academy, Portugal
Ana Borges	Escola Superior de Tecnologia e Gestão IPPorto, Portugal
Cristina Lopes	ISCAP IPPorto, Portugal
Fernanda Costa	University of Minho, Portugal
Cabrita Carlos	IPBeja, Portugal
Maria Luísa Morgado	University of Trás os Montes e Alto Douro and University of Lisboa, Portugal
Rosário Ramos	Universidade Aberta, Portugal
Sofia Rézio	Iscal, Instituto Politécnico de Lisboa, Portugal
Matteo Sacchet	University of Turin, Italy
Marina Marchisio Conte	University of Turin, Italy
António Seijas-Macias	University of Coruña, Spain
Luís F. A. Teodoro	University of Glasgow, UK and University of Oslo, Norway
Christos Kitsos	University of West Attica, Greece
M. Filomena Teodoro	Universidade de Lisboa, Portugal
Marina A. P. Andrade	Instituto Universitário de Lisboa, Portugal
Paula Simões	Military Academy and Universidade Nova de Lisboa, Portugal
Teresa Oliveira	Universidade Aberta and Universidade de Lisboa, Portugal

Computational Optimization and Applications (COA 2025)

Workshop Organizers

Ana Rocha	ALGORITMI Research Centre, LASI, University of Minho, Portugal, Portugal
Humberto Rocha	ALGORITMI Research Centre, LASI, University of Minho, Portugal, Portugal

Workshop Program Committee Members

Florbela Fernandes	Polytechnic Institute of Bragança, Portugal
Clara Vaz	Polytechnic Institute of Bragança, Portugal
Ana Pereira	Polytechnic Institute of Bragança, Portugal
Filipe Alvelos	University of Minho, Portugal
Joana Dias	University of Coimbra, Portugal
Eligius M. T. Hendrix	University of Málaga, Spain
Emerson José de Paiva	Federal University of Itajubá, Brazil
Ana Paula Teixeira	University of Trás-os-Montes and Alto Douro, Portugal
Lino Costa	Universidade do Minho, Portugal

Coastal Cities Versus Inland Areas. Hypotheses for Sustainable Regeneration Through Ecosystem Services of 'Hooking' and Rehabilitation of Brownfield Sites (CoastalCities_VS_InlandAreas 2025)

Workshop Organizers

Celestina Fazia	Università di Enna Kore, Italy
Angrilli Massimo	University of Chieti-Pescara, Italy
Valentina Ciuffreda	University of Chieti-Pescara, Italy
Maurizio Oddo	Università di Enna Kore, Italy
Marcello Sestito	Università di Enna Kore, Italy
Clara Stella Vicari Aversa	University of Reggio Calabria, Italy

Workshop Program Committee Members

Alessandro Camiz	Università d'Annunzio, Italy
Thowayeb Hassan	King Faisal University, Saudi Arabia
Alessandro Barracco	Università Kore di Enna, Italy
Mario Morrica	University of Urbino, Italy
Mariana Ratiu	University of Oradea, Romania
Alanda Akamana	Mohammed VI Polytechnic University, Morocco
Kaoutare Amini Alaoui	Mohammed VI Polytechnic University, Morocco

Computational Astrochemistry 2025 (CompAstro 2025)

Workshop Organizers

Marzio Rosi	University of Perugia, Italy
Daniela Ascenzi	University of Trento, Italy
Nadia Balucani	University of Perugia, Italy
Stefano Falcinelli	University of Perugia, Italy

Workshop Program Committee Members

Dario Campisi	Università degli Studi di Perugia, Italy
Giacomo Giorgi	Università degli Studi di Perugia, Italy
Andrea Giustini	Università degli Studi di Perugia, Italy
Luca Mancini	Università degli Studi di Perugia, Italy
Albert Rimola	Universitat Autònoma de Barcelona, Spain
Gianmarco Vanuzzo	Università degli Studi di Perugia, Italy
Dimitrios Skouteris	Master-Tec, Italy
Piero Ugliengo	Università degli Studi di Torino, Italy
Franco Vecchiocattivi	Università degli Sudi di Perugia, Italy
Giacomo Pannacci	Università degli Studi di Perugia, Italy
Costanza Borghesi	Università degli Studi di Perugia, Italy
Marco Parriani	Università degli Studi di Perugia, Italy
Marta Loletti	Università degli Studi di Perugia, Italy
Fernando Pirani	Università degli Studi di Perugia, Italy
Andrea Lombardi	Università degli Studi di Perugia, Italy
Noelia Faginas Lago	Università degli Studi di Perugia, Italy
Paolo Tosi	Università di Trento, Italy
Cecilia Coletti	Università degli Studi Chieti-Pescara, Italy
Nazzareno Re	Università degli Studi Chieti-Pescara, Italy
Linda Podio	Osservatorio Astrofisico di Arcetri INAF, Italy
Claudio Codella	Osservatorio Astrofisico di Arcetri INAF, Italy
Gabriella Di Genova	Università degli Studi di Perugia, Italy

Computational Methods for Porous Geomaterials (CompPor 2025)

Workshop Organizers

Vadim Lisitsa	IPGG SB RAS, Russia
Evgeniy Romenski	IPGG SB RAS, Russia

Workshop Program Committee Members

Vadim Lisitsa	Institute of Petroleum Geology and Geophysics SB RAS, Russia
Evgeniy Romenski	Sobolev Institute of Mathematics SB RAS, Russia
Vladimir Cheverda	Sobolev Institute of Mathematics SB RAS, Russia
Tatyana Khachkova	IPGG SB RAS, Russia
Dmitry Prokhorov	IPGG SB RAS, Russia
Mikhail Novikov	Sobolev Institute of Mathematics SB RAS, Russia
Sergey Solovyev	Sobolev Institute of Mathematics SB RAS, Russia
Kirill Gadylshin	LLC RNBashNIPIneft, Russia
Olga Stoyanovskaya	Lavrentev Institute of Hydrodynamics SB RAS, Russia
Yerlan Amanbek	Nazarbaev University, Kazakhstan

Workshop on Computational Science and HPC (CSHPC 2025)

Workshop Organizers

Elise de Doncker	Western Michigan University, USA
Hideo Matsufuru	High Energy Accelerator Research Organization, Japan

Workshop Program Committee Members

Elise de Doncker	Western Michigan University, USA
Hideo Matsufuru	High Energy Accelerator Research Organization (KEK), Japan
Fukuko Yuasa	KEK, Japan
Issaku Kanamori	RIKEN, Japan
Hiroshi Daisaka	Hitotsubashi University, Japan
Norikazu Yamada	KEK, Japan
Naohito Nakasato	University of Aizu, Japan
Robert Makin	Western Michigan University, USA

Cities, Technologies and Planning 2025 (CTP 2025)

Workshop Organizers

Giuseppe Borruso	University of Trieste, Italy
Beniamino Murgante	University of Basilicata, Italy
Malgorzata Hanzl	Lodz University of Technology, Poland
Anastasia Stratigea	National Technical University of Athens, Greece
Ljiljana Zivkovic	Republic Geodetic Authority, Serbia
Ginevra Balletto	University of Trieste, Italy

Workshop Program Committee Members

Giuseppe Borruso	University of Trieste, Italy
Beniamino Murgante	University of Basilicata, Italy
Malgorzata Hanzl	Lodz University of Technology, Poland
Anastasia Stratigea	National Technical University of Athens, Greece
Ljiljiana Zivkovic	Republic Geodetic Authority of Serbia, Serbia
Ginevra Balletto	University of Cagliari, Italy
Silvia Battino	University of Sassari, Italy
Mara Ladu	University of Cagliari, Italy
Maria del Mar Munoz Leonisio	University of Cádiz, Spain
Ahinoa Amaro Garcia	University of Las Palmas of Gran Canaria, Spain
Maria Attard	University of Malta, Malta
Enrico D'agostini	World Maritime University, Sweden
Francesca Krasna	University of Trieste, Italy
Brisol Garcia Garcia	Polytechnic University of Quintana Roo, Mexico
Tu Anh Trinh	UEH University, Vietnam
Giovanni Mauro	Università degli Studi della Campania, Italy
Maria Ronza	University of Naples Federico II, Italy
Massimiliano Bencardino	University of Salerno, Italy
Tomasz Bradecki	Silesian University of Technology, Poland
Dorota Kamrowska-Załuska	Gdańsk University of Technology, Poland
Iwona Jażdżewska	University of Lodz, Poland
Yiota Theodora	National Technical University of Athens, Greece
Apostolos Lagarias	University of Thessaly, Greece
George Tsilimigkas	University of the Aegean, Greece
Akrivi Leka	National Technical University of Athens, Greece
Maria Panagiotopoulou	National Technical University of Athens, Greece
Andrea Gallo	Ca' Foscari University of Venice, Italy
Francesca Sinatra	University of Trieste, Italy

Digital Transition: Effects on Housing Mobility, Market, Land Governance (DIGITRANS 2025)

Workshop Organizers

Fabrizio Battisti	University of Florence, Italy
Fabiana Forte	University of Campania, Italy
Orazio Campo	Sapienza University of Rome, Italy
Alessio Pino	Kore University of Enna, Italy
Carlo Pisano	University of Florence, Italy
Mariolina Grasso	Kore University of Enna, Italy

Workshop Program Committee Members

Fabrizio Battisti	University of Florence, Italy
Fabiana Forte	Università della Campania Luigi Vanvitelli, Italy
Orazio Campo	University of Rome "La Sapienza", Italy
Alessio Pino	Kore University of Enna, Italy
Carlo Pisano	University of Florence, Italy
Mariolina Grasso	Università Kore di Enna, Italy

Evaluating Inner Areas Potentials (EIAP 2025)

Workshop Organizers

Diana Rolando	Politecnico di Torino, Italy
Alice Barreca	Politecnico di Torino, Italy
Manuela Rebaudengo	Politecnico di Torino, Italy
Giorgia Malavasi	Politecnico di Torino, Italy

Workshop Program Committee Members

John Accordino	Virginia Commonwealth University, USA
Francesco Bruzzone	Università Iuav di Venezia, Italy
Maria Cerreta	Università degli Studi di Napoli Federico II, Italy
Maddalena Chimisso	Università degli Studi del Molise, Italy
Chiara Chioni	Università degli Studi di Trento, Italy
Annalisa Contato	Università degli Studi di Palermo, Italy
Cristina Coscia	Politecnico di Torino, Italy
Marta Dell'Ovo	Politecnico di Milano, Italy
Benedetta Di Leo	Università Politecnica delle Marche, Italy
Sara Favargiotti	Università degli Studi di Trento, Italy
Maddalena Ferretti	Università Politecnica delle Marche, Italy
Salvo Giuffrida	Università degli Studi di Palermo, Italy
Barbara Lino	Università degli Studi di Palermo, Italy
Umberto Mecca	Politecnico di Torino, Italy
Beatrice Mecca	Politecnico di Torino, Italy
Giuliano Poli	Università degli Studi di Napoli Federico II, Italy
Marco Rossitti	Politecnico di Milano, Italy
Alexandra Stankulova	Politecnico di Torino, Italy
Elena Todella	Politecnico di Torino, Italy
Asja Aulisio	Politecnico di Torino, Italy
Giulia Datola	Politecnico di Milano, Italy

Francesco Calabrò Università degli Studi Mediterranea di Reggio Calabria, Italy
Valeria Saiu Università degli Studi di Cagliari, Italy
Maria Rosa Trovato Università di Catania, Italy

Econometric and Multidimensional Evaluation in Urban Environment (EMEUE 2025)

Workshop Organizers

Maria Cerreta University of Naples Federico II, Italy
Carmelo Maria Torre Polytechnic University of Bari, Italy
Pierluigi Morano Polytechnic University of Bari, Italy
Simona Panaro University of Naples Federico II, Italy
Felicia Di Liddo University of Naples Federico II, Italy
Debora Anelli University of Naples Federico II, Italy

Workshop Program Committee Members

Carmelo Maria Torre Polytechnic University of Bari, Italy
Maria Cerreta University of Naples Federico II, Italy
Pierluigi Morano Polytechnic University of Bari, Italy
Francesco Tajani Sapienza University of Rome, Italy
Simona Panaro University of Naples Federico II, Italy
Felicia di Liddo Polytechnic University of Bari, Italy
Debora Anelli Sapienza University of Rome, Italy
Giuliano Poli University of Naples Federico II, Italy
Maria Somma University of Naples Federico II, Italy
Simona Panaro University of Campania Luigi Vanvitelli, Italy
Laura Di Tommaso University of Naples Federico II, Italy
Caterina Loffredo University of Naples Federico II, Italy
Ludovica La Rocca University of Naples Federico II, Italy
Sabrina Sacco Politecnico di Milano, Italy
Piero Zizzania University of Naples Federico II, Italy
Gaia Daldanise CNR IRISS, Italy
Benedetta Grieco University of Naples Federico II, Italy
Giuseppe Ciciriello University of Naples Federico II, Italy
Marta Dell'Ovo Politecnico di Milano, Italy
Daniele Cannatella TU Delft University, The Netherlands
Eugenio Muccio University of Naples Federico II, Italy
Sveva Ventre University of Naples Federico II, Italy

Governance of Energy Transition: Environmental, Landscape, Social and Spatial Planning (ENERGY_PLANNING 2025)

Workshop Organizers

Mara Ladu	University of Cagliari, Italy
Ginevra Balletto	University of Cagliari, Italy
Emilio Ghiani	University of Cagliari, Italy
Alessandra Marra	University of Salerno, Italy
Roberto De Lotto	University of Pavia, Italy
Balázs Kulcsár	Chalmers University of Technology, Sweden

Workshop Program Committee Members

Riccardo Trevisan	University of Cagliari, Italy
Marco Naseddu	University of Cagliari, Italy
Giuseppe Borruso	University of Trieste, Italy
Andrea Gallo	University of Trieste, Italy
Francesca Sinatra	University of Trieste, Italy
Maria Attard	University of Malta, Malta
Tu Anh Trinh	UEH University Ho Chi Minh City, Vietnam
Marcello Tadini	University of Eastern Piedmont, Italy
Luigi Mundula	University for Foreigners of Perugia, Italy
Silvia Battino	University of Sassari, Italy
Maria del Mar Munoz Leonisio	University of Cádiz, Spain
Anna Richiedei	University of Brescia, Italy
Michele Pezzagno	University of Brescia, Italy
Federico Mertellozzo	University of Firenze, Italy
Marco Mazzarino	IUAV University Venice, Italy

Ecosystem Services in Spatial Planning for Climate Neutral Urban and Rural Areas (ESSP 2025)

Workshop Organizers

Sabrina Lai	University of Cagliari, Italy
Francesco Scorza	University of Basilicata, Italy
Corrado Zoppi	University of Cagliari, Italy
Beniamino Murgante	University of Basilicata, Italy
Carmela Gargiulo	University of Naples Federico II, Italy
Floriana Zucaro	University of Naples Federico II, Italy

Workshop Program Committee Members

Alfonso Annunziata	University of Basilicata, Italy
Ginevra Balletto	University of Cagliari, Italy
Ivan Blečić	University of Cagliari, Italy
Giuseppe Borruso	University of Trieste, Italy
Barbara Caselli	University of Parma, Italy
Maria Cerreta	University of Naples Federico II, Italy
Chiara Garau	University of Cagliari, Italy
Carmen Guida	University of Naples Federico II, Italy
Federica Isola	University of Cagliari, Italy
Francesca Leccis	University of Cagliari, Italy
Federica Leone	University of Cagliari, Italy
Silvia Rossetti	University of Parma, Italy
Luigi Santopietro	University of Basilicata, Italy
Carmelo Torre	Polytechnic of Bari, Italy

The 15th International Workshop on Future Information System Technologies and Applications (FiSTA 2025)

Workshop Organizers

Bernady O. Apduhan	Kyushu Sangyo University, Japan
Rafael Santos	Brazilian National Institute for Space Research, Brazil

Workshop Program Committee Members

Agustinus Borgy Waluyo	Monash University, Australia
Andre Ricardo Abed Grégio	Federal University of Paraná, Brazil
Eric Pardede	La Trobe University, Australia
Kai Cheng	Kyushu Sangyo University, Japan
Ching-Hsien Hsu	Asia University, Taiwan
Fenghui Yao	Tennessee State University, USA
Yusuke Gotoh	Okayama University, Japan
Alvaro Fazenda	Federal University of São Paulo, Brazil
Kazuaki Tanaka	Kyushu Institute of Technology, Japan
Tengku Adil	MARA Technological University, Malaysia
Toshihiro Yamauchi	Okayama University, Japan
Yasuaki Sumida	Kyushu Sangyo University, Japan
Earl Ryan Aleluya	MSU-Iligan Institute of Technology, Philippines
Cherry Mae G. Villame	MSU-Iligan Institute of Technology, Philippines
Anton Louise De Ocampo	Batangas State University, Philippines
Krishnamoorthy Ranganthan	Chennai Institute of Technology, India

Flow Management in Urban Contexts (FMUC 2025)

Workshop Organizers

Alessio Pino	Kore University of Enna, Italy
Giovanna Acampa	Kore University of Enna, Italy

Workshop Program Committee Members

Giovanna Acampa	University of Florence, Italy
Alessio Pino	Kore University of Enna, Italy
Mariolina Grasso	Università Kore di Enna, Italy
Fabrizio Battisti	University of Florence, Italy
Fabrizio Finucci	Roma Tre University, Italy
Antonella G. Masanotti	Roma Tre University, Italy
Daniele Mazzoni	Roma Tre University, Italy

Geographical Analysis, Urban Modeling, Spatial Statistics 2025 (Geog-And-Mod 2025)

Workshop Organizers

Beniamino Murgante	University of Basilicata, Italy
Giuseppe Borruso	University of Trieste, Italy
Hartmut Asche	University of Potsdam, Germany
Rodrigo Tapia McClung	CentroGeo, Mexico
Andreas Fricke	University of Potsdam, Germany

Workshop Program Committee Members

Giuseppe Borruso	University of Trieste, Italy
Beniamino Murgante	University of Basilicata, Italy
Hartmut Asche	University of Potsdam, Germany
Rodrigo Tapia-McClung	Centro de Investigación en Ciencias de Información Geoespacial (CentroGeo), Mexico
Andreas Fricke	University of Potsdam, Germany
Malgorzata Hanzl	Lodz University of Technology, Poland
Anastasia Stratigea	National Technical University of Athens, Greece
Ljiljiana Zivkovic	Republic Geodetic Authority of Serbia, Serbia
Ginevra Balletto	University of Cagliari, Italy
Silvia Battino	University of Sassari, Italy
Mara Ladu	University of Cagliari, Italy
Maria del Mar Munoz Leonisio	University of Cádiz, Spain
Ahinoa Amaro Garcia	University of Las Palmas of Gran Canaria, Spain
Maria Attard	University of Malta, Malta

Enrico D'agostini	World Maritime University, Sweden
Francesca Krasna	University of Trieste, Italy
Brisol García García	Polytechnic University of Quintana Roo, Mexico
Tu Anh Trinh	UEH University, Vietnam
Giovanni Mauro	Università degli Studi della Campania, Italy
Maria Ronza	University of Naples Federico II, Italy
Massimiliano Bencardino	University of Salerno, Italy
Andrea Gallo	Ca' Foscari University of Venice, Italy
Francesca Sinatra	University of Trieste, Italy
Salvatore Dore	University of Trieste, Italy

Geogames for Sustainable Development (Geogames 2025)

Workshop Organizer

Alenka Poplin	Iowa State University, USA

Workshop Program Committee Members

Alenka Poplin	Iowa State University, USA
Bruno Amaral de Andrade	Portucalense University, Portugal
Brian Tomaszewski	Rochester Institute of Technology, USA
Deepak Marhatta	Tribhuvan University, Nepal
Alessandro Plaisant	University of Sassari, Italy
David Schwartz	Rochester Institute of Technology, USA
Silvia Rossetti	University of Parma, Italy
Floriana Zucaro	University of Naples Federico II, Italy
Alfonso Annunziata	University of Basilicata, Italy
Reza Askarizad	University of Cagliari, Italy
Chiara Garau	University of Cagliari, Italy
Tanja Congiu	University of Sassari, Italy

Geomatics for Resource Monitoring and Management (GRMM 2025)

Workshop Organizers

Alberico Sonnessa	Politecnico di Bari, Italy
Eufemia Tarantino	Politecnico di Bari, Italy
Alessandra Capolupo	Politecnico di Bari, Italy

Workshop Program Committee Members

Umberto Fratino	Politecnico di Bari, Italy
Valeria Monno	Politecnico di Bari, Italy

Antonino Maltese   Università degli studi di Palermo, Italy
Athos Agapiou   Cyprus University of Technology, Cyprus
Michele Mangiameli   Università di Catania, Italy
Angela Gorgoglione   Universidad de la República de Uruguay, Uruguay
Roberta Ravanelli   University of Liège, Belgium
Ester Scotto di Perta   Università degli studi di Napoli Federico II, Italy
Giacomo Caporusso   CNR, Italy
Andrea Montanino   International Centre for Numerical Methods in Engineering of Barcelona, Spain

Antonino Iannuzzo   Università degli studi del Sannio, Italy
Alessandro Pagano   Politecnico di Bari, Italy
Francesco Di Capua   Università degli Studi della Basilicata, Italy
Albertini Cinzia   CNR-IREA, Italy
Alessandra Saponieri   Università degli studi del Salento, Italy
PierFrancesco Recchi   Università degli studi di Napoli Federico II, Italy
Vincenzo Totaro   Politecnico di Bari, Italy
Stefania Santoro   CNR Water Research Institute, Italy
Francesco Bimbo   University of Foggia, Italy
Cristina Proietti   Istituto Nazionale di Geofisica e Vulcanologia, Italy

Carla Cavallo   University of Salerno, Italy
Gaetano Falcone   Università degli Studi di Napoli Federico II, Italy
Valeria Belloni   Sapienza University of Rome, Italy
Alessandra Mascitelli   University of Chieti-Pescara, Italy

HERitage and CLIMAte neutrality. Resilient approach for nature centered/based sustainable cities (HERCLIMA 2025)

Workshop Organizers

Celestina Fazia   Università di Enna Kore, Italy
Angrilli Massimo   University of Chieti-Pescara, Italy
Clara Stella Vicari Aversa   University of Reggio Calabria, Italy
Dorina Camelia Ilies   University of Oradea, Romania
Mariana Ratiu   University of Oradea, Romania

Workshop Program Committee Members

Alessandro Camiz   Università d'Annunzio, Italy
Mario Morrica   University of Urbino, Italy
Thowayeb Hassan   King Faisal University, Saudi Arabia
Alessandro Barracco   Università Kore di Enna, Italy
Kaoutare Amini Alaoui   Mohammed VI Polytechnic University (UM6P), Morocco

| Mariana Ratiu | University of Oradea, Romania |
| Valentina Ciuffreda | Università Chieti-Pescara, Italy |

International Workshop on Information and Knowledge in the Internet of Things (IKIT 2025)

Workshop Organizers
Teresa Guarda	Universidad Estatal Península de Santa Elena, Ecuador
Luis Enrique Chuquimarca Jimenez	Universidad Estatal Península de Santa Elena, Ecuador
Gustavo Gatica	Universidad Andrés Bello, Chile
Filipe Mota Pinto	Polytechnic Institute of Leiria, Portugal
Arnulfo Alanis	Instituto Tecnológico de Tijuana, Mexico
Luis Mazon	Universidad Estatal Península de Santa Elena, Spain

Workshop Program Committee Members
Arnulfo Alanis	Instituto Tecnológico de Tijuana, Mexico
Bruno Sousa	University of Coimbra, Portugal
Carlos Balsa	Instituto Politécnico de Bragança, Portugal
Filipe Mota Pinto	Instituto Politécnico de Leiria, Portugal
Gustavo Gatica	Universidad Andrés Bello, Chile
Isabel Lopes	Instituto Politécnico de Bragança, Portugal
José-María Díaz-Nafría	Universidad a Distancia, Spain
Maria Fernanda Augusto	BiTrum Research Group, Spain
Maria Isabel Ribeiro	Instituto Politécnico Bragança, Portugal
Modestos Stavrakis	University of the Aegean, Greece
Simone Belli	Universidad Complutense de Madrid, Spain
Walter Lopes Neto	Instituto Federal de Educação, Brazil

International Workshop on territorial Planning to integrate Risk prevention and urban Ontologies (IWPRO 2025)

Workshop Organizers
Beniamino Murgante	University of Basilicata, Italy
Roberto De Lotto	University of Pavia, Italy
Elisabetta Maria Venco	University of Pavia, Italy
Caterina Pietra	University of Pavia, Italy

Workshop Program Committee Members

Stefano Borgo	Consiglio Nazionale delle Ricerche ISTC, Italy
Valentina Costa	Università di Genova, Italy
Hamid Danesh Pajouh	Middle East Technical University, Turkey
Ilaria Delponte	Università di Genova, Italy
Lorena Fiorini	Università de L'Aquila, Italy
Veronica Gazzola	Politecnico di Milano, Italy
Ghazaleh Goodarzi	Islamic Azad University, Iran
Michele Grimaldi	Università degli Studi di Salerno, Italy
Alessandra Marra	Università degli Studi di Salerno, Italy
Naghmeh Mohammadpourlima	Åbo Akademi University, Finland
Francesca Pirlone	Università di Genova, Italy
Silvia Rossetti	Università di Parma, Italy
Bahareh Shahsavari	University of Minnesota, USA
Ilenia Spadaro	Università di Genova, Italy
Maria Rosaria Stufano Melone	Politecnico di Bari, Italy

Regional Connectivity, Spatial Accessibility and MaaS for Social Inclusion (MaaS 2025)

Workshop Organizers

Mara Ladu	University of Cagliari, Italy
Ginevra Balletto	University of Cagliari, Italy
Gianfranco Fancello	University of Cagliari, Italy
Tanja Congiu	University of Sassari, Italy
Patrizia Serra	University of Cagliari, Italy
Francesco Piras	University of Cagliari, Italy

Workshop Program Committee Members

Marco Naseddu	University of Cagliari, Italy
Italo Meloni	University of Cagliari, Italy
Giuseppe Borruso	University of Trieste, Italy
Andrea Gallo	University of Trieste, Italy
Francesca Sinatra	University of Trieste, Italy
Maria Attard	University of Malta, Malta
Tu Anh Trinh	UEH University, Vietnam
Marcello Tadini	University of Eastern Piedmont, Italy
Luigi Mundula	University for Foreigners of Perugia, Italy
Silvia Battino	University of Sassari, Italy
Brunella Brundu	University of Sassari, Italy
Veronica Camerada	University of Sassari, Italy

Maria del Mar Munoz Leonisio	University of Cádiz, Spain
Anna Richiedei	University of Brescia, Italy
Michele Pezzagno	University of Brescia, Italy
Marco Mazzarino	IUAV University Venice, Italy

The Development of Urban Mobility Management, Road Safety and Risk Assessment (MANTAIN 2025)

Workshop Organizers

Antonio Russo	Università degli Studi di Enna, Italy
Corrado Rindone	University of Reggio Calabria, Italy
Antonio Polimeni	University of Messina, Italy
Florin Rusca	Politehnica University of Bucharest, Romania
Grigorios Fountas	Aristotle University of Thessaloniki, Greece
Antonio Comi	University of Rome Tor Vergata, Italy

Workshop Program Committee Members

Massimo Di Gangi	University of Messina, Italy
Orlando Marco Belcore	University of Messina, Italy
Antonio Polimeni	University of Messina, Italy
Socrates Basbas	Aristotle University of Thessaloniki, Greece
Claudia Caballini	Polytechnic of Torino, Italy
Efstathios Bouhouras	Aristotle University of Thessaloniki, Greece
Stefano Ricci	Sapienza University of Rome, Italy
Marina Zanne	University of Lubljana, Slovenia
Kh Md Nahiduzzaman	Mohammed VI Polytechnic University, Morocco
Alexsandra Deluka Tibljaš	University of Rijeka, Croatia
Guilhermina Torrao	Aston University, UK

Multidimensional Evolutionary Evaluations for Transformative Approaches (MEETA 2025)

Workshop Organizers

Maria Cerreta	University of Naples Federico II, Italy
Giuliano Poli	University of Naples Federico II, Italy
Maria Somma	University of Naples Federico II, Italy
Gaia Daldanise	CNR IRISS, Italy
Ludovica La Rocca	University of Naples Federico II, Italy

Workshop Program Committee Members

Maria Cerreta	University of Naples Federico II, Italy
Giuliano Poli	University of Naples Federico II, Italy
Maria Somma	University of Naples Federico II, Italy
Laura Di Tommaso	University of Naples Federico II, Italy
Sabrina Sacco	Politecnico di Milano, Italy
Piero Zizzania	University of Naples Federico II, Italy
Gaia Daldanise	CNR IRISS, Italy
Benedetta Grieco	University of Naples Federico II, Italy
Giuseppe Ciciriello	University of Naples Federico II, Italy
Marta Dell'Ovo	Politecnico di Milano, Italy
Daniele Cannatella	TU Delft, The Netherlands
Eugenio Muccio	University of Naples Federico II, Italy
Francesco Piras	University of Cagliari, Italy
Diana Rolando	Politecnico di Torino, Italy
Sveva Ventre	University of Naples Federico II, Italy
Caterina Loffredo	University of Naples Federico II, Italy
Ludovica La Rocca	University of Naples Federico II, Italy
Simona Panaro	University of Campania Luigi Vanvitelli, Italy

Building Multi-dimensional Models for Assessing Complex Environmental Systems (MES 2025)

Workshop Organizers

Vanessa Assumma	University of Bologna, Italy
Caterina Caprioli	Politecnico di Torino, Italy
Giulia Datola	Politecnico di Milano, Italy
Federico Dell'Anna	University of Bologna, Italy
Marta Dell'Ovo	Politecnico di Milano, Italy
Marco Rossitti	Politecnico di Milano, Italy

Workshop Program Committee Members

Vanessa Assumma	Università di Bologna, Bologna
Caterina Caprioli	Politecnico di Torino, Italy
Giulia Datola	DAStU Politecnico di Milano, Italy
Federico Dell'Anna	Politecnico di Torino, Italy
Marta Dell'Ovo	Politecnico di Milano, Italy
Marco Rossitti	Politecnico di Milano, Italy
Francesca Torrieri	Politecnico di Milano, Italy
Mariarosaria Angrisano	Università Telematica Pegaso, Italy
Maksims Feofilovs	Riga Technical University, Latvia

Danny Caprini	Politecnico di Milano, Italy
Giulio Cavana	Politecnico di Torino, Italy
Sebastiano Barbieri	Politecnico di Torino, Italy
Marta Bottero	Politecnico di Torino, Italy
Francesco Cosentino	Politecnico di Milano, Italy
Silvia Ronchi	Politecnico di Milano, Italy
Chiara Mazzarella	TU Delft, Netherlands
Marco Volpatti	Politecnico di Torino, Italy
Chiara D'Alpaos	Università degli Studi di Padova, Italy
Alessandra Oppio	Politecnico di Milano, Italy
Alessia Crisopulli	Politecnico di Milano, Italy
Domenico D'Uva	Politecnico di Milano, Italy
Giorgia Malavasi	Politecnico di Torino, Italy
Rubina Canesi	Università degli Studi di Padova, Italy
Elena Todella	Politecnico di Torino, Italy
Beatrice Mecca	Politecnico di Torino, Italy
Giulia Marzani	University of Bologna, Italy
Isabella Giovanetti	University of Bologna, Italy
Lucia Petronio	University of Bologna, Italy
Franco Corti	University of Padova, Italy
Salvatore De Pascalis	Politecnico di Milano, Italy
Valeria Vitulano	Politecnico di Torino, Italy
Lorenzo Diana	Università degli studi di Napoli Federico II, Italy
Maksims Feofilovs	Riga Technical University, Latvia
Marco De Luca	Politecnico di Torino, Italy
Ilaria Cazzola	Politecnico di Torino, Italy
Andrea De Toni	Politecnico di Milano, Italy
Eugenio Muccio	University of Naples Federico II, Italy
Giuliano Poli	University of Naples Federico II, Italy
Francesco Sica	University "La Sapienza" of Rome, Italy
Elena Di Pirro	Università degli Studi del Molise, Italy
Riccardo Alba	Università di Torino, Italy
Irene Regaiolo	Università di Torino, Italy
Francesca Cochis	Università di Torino, Italy

Modelling Liveable Cities: Techniques, Methods, Challenges, and Perspectives Behind the 'X-Minute' City (MLC 2025)

Workshop Organizers

Federico Mara	University of Pisa, Italy
Valerio Cutini	University of Pisa, Italy
Alessandro Araldi	Université Côte d'Azur, France

Flávia Lopes — Chalmers University of Technology, Sweden
Giovanni Fusco — Université Côte d'Azur, France

Workshop Program Committee Members
Simone Rusci — University of Pisa, Italy
Lorena Fiorini — University of L'Aquila, Italy
Chiara Di Dato — University of L'Aquila, Italy
Francesco Zullo — University of L'Aquila, Italy
Alfonso Annunziata — University of Basilicata, Italy
Beniamino Murgante — University of Basilicata, Italy
Alessandro Araldi — Universitè Côte d'Azur, France
Chiara Garau — University of Cagliari, Italy
Giampiero Lombardini — Università di Genova, Italy
Flavia Lopes — Chalmers University of Technology, Sweden
Giovanni Fusco — Universitè Côte d'Azur, France

Mathematical Methods for Image Processing and Understanding 2025 (MMIPU 2025)

Workshop Organizers
Ivan Gerace — Università degli Studi di Perugia, Italy
Gianluca Vinti — Università degli Studi di Perugia, Italy
Arianna Travaglini — Università degli Studi della Basilicata, Italy

Workshop Program Committee Members
Ivan Gerace — University of Perugia, Italy
Gianluca Vinti — University of Perugia, Italy
Arianna Travaglini — University of Basilicata, Italy
Marco Baioletti — University of Perugia, Italy
Marco Donatelli — University of Insubria, Italy
Anna Tonazzini — C.N.R. Pisa, Italy
Muhammad Hanif — Ghulam Ishaq Khan Institute of Engineering Sciences and Technology, Pakistan
Francesco Marchetti — University of Padua, Italy
Wolfgang Erb — University of Padua, Italy
Danilo Costarelli — University of Perugia, Italy
Francesco Santini — University of Perugia, Italy
Valentina Giorgetti — University of Perugia, Italy

Mobility Opportunities Bridging Inequalities: Social Inclusion and Gender Equity Initiatives Strategies Against Fragmentation and Complexity of Mobility (MOBIL-EGI 2025)

Workshop Organizers

Tiziana Campisi	University of Enna Kore, Italy
Guilhermina Torrao	Aston University, UK
Socrates Basbas	Aristotle University of Thessaloniki, Greece
Tanja Congiu	University of Sassari, Italy
Stefanos Tsigdinos	National Technical University of Athens, Greece
Florin Nemtanu	Politehnica University of Bucharest, Romania

Workshop Program Committee Members

Massimo Di Gangi	University of Messina, Italy
Orlando Marco Belcore	University of Messina, Italy
Francesco Russo	Mediterranean University of Reggio Calabria, Italy
Alexandros Nikitas	University of Huddersfield, UK
Marilisa Nigro	Rome Tre University, Italy
Kh Md Nahiduzzaman	Mohammed VI Polytechnic University, Morocco
Efstathios Bouhouras	Aristotle University of Thessaloniki, Greece
Antonio Comi	University of Rome Tor Vergata, Italy
Edouard Ivanjko	University of Zagreb, Slovenia
Osvaldo Gervasi	University of Perugia, Italy
Beniamino Murgante	University of Basilicata, Italy
Chiara Garau	University of Cagliari, Italy

MOdels and indicators for assessing and measuring the urban settlement deVElopment in the view of NET ZERO by 2050 (MOVEto0 2025)

Workshop Organizers

Lorena Fiorini	University of L'Aquila, Italy
Lucia Saganeiti	CNR-IMAA, Italy
Angela Pilogallo	CNR-IMAA, Italy
Alessandro Marucci	University of L'Aquila, Italy
Francesco Zullo	University of L'Aquila, Italy

Workshop Program Committee Members

Ginevra Balletto	University of Cagliari, Italy
Giuseppe Borruso	University of Trieste, Italy
Chiara Garau	University of Cagliari, Italy

Beniamino Murgante	University of Basilicata, Italy
Giulia Desogus	University of Cagliari, Italy
Ljiljana Zivkovic	Republic Geodetic Authority, Serbia
Luigi Santopietro	University of Basilicata, Italy
Ilaria Delponte	University of Genoa, Italy
Carmen Guida	University of Naples Federico II, Italy
Chiara Di Dato	University of L'Aquila, Italy

5th Workshop on Privacy in the Cloud/Edge/IoT World (PCEIoT 2025)

Workshop Organizers

Lelio Campanile	Università degli Studi della Campania Luigi Vanvitelli, Italy
Mauro Iacono	Università degli Studi della Campania Luigi Vanvitelli, Italy
Michele Mastroianni	Università degli Studi di Foggia, Italy

Workshop Program Committee Members

Arcangelo Castiglione	Università degli Studi di Salerno, Italy
Maria Ganzha	Warsaw University of Technology, Poland
Daniel Grzonka	Cracow University of Technology, Poland
Antonio Iannuzzi	Università degli Studi Roma Tre, Italy
Armando Tacchella	Università degli Studi di Genova, Italy
Biagio Boi	University of Salerno, Italy
Marco De Santis	University of Salerno, Italy
Fiammetta Marulli	Università degli Studi della Campania "L. Vanvitelli", Italy
Christian Riccio	Università degli Studi della Campania "L. Vanvitelli", Italy
Luigi Piero Di Bonito	Università degli Studi di Napoli Federico II, Italy

Preserving Our Past: Spatial and Remote Sensing Technologies for Cultural Heritage in a Changing Climate (POP 2025)

Workshop Organizers

Maria Danese	CNR-ISPC, Italy
Nicola Masini	CNR-ISPC, Italy
Rosa Lasaponara	CNR-IMAA, Italy

Workshop Program Committee Members

Maria Danese	CNR-ISPC, Italy
Nicola Masini	CNR-ISPC, Italy
Rosa Lasaponara	CNR-IMAA, Italy
Dario Gioia	CNR-ISPC, Italy
Giuseppe Corrado	Università degli Studi della Basilicata, Italy
Canio Sabia	CNR-ISPC, Italy

Processes, methods and tools towards RESilient cities and cultural and historic sites prone to SOD and ROD disasters (RES 2025)

Workshop Organizers

Elena Cantatore	Polytechnic University of Bari, Italy
Dario Esposito	Polytechnic University of Bari, Italy
Alberico Sonnessa	Polytechnic University of Bari, Italy

Workshop Program Committee Members

Elena Cantatore	Politecnico di Bari, Italy
Dario Esposito	Politecnico di Bari, Italy
Alberico Sonnessa	Politecnico di Bari, Italy
Valeria Belloni	Sapienza University of Rome, Italy
Michela Ravanelli	Sapienza University of Rome, Italy
Silvano Dal Sasso	University of Basilicata, Italy
Francesco Chiaravalloti	CNR - IRPI, Italy
Roberta Ravanelli	University of Liège, Belgium
Alessandra Mascitelli	University of Chieti-Pescara, Italy
Francesco Di Capua	University of Basilicata, Italy
Gabriele Bernardini	Università Politecnica delle Marche, Italy
Vito Domenico Porcari	University of Basilicata, Italy
Carmen Rosa Fattore	University of Basilicata, Italy
Stefania Santoro	Water Research Institute, Italy

Scientific Computing Infrastructure (SCI 2025)

Workshop Organizers

Vladimir Korkhov	Saint Petersburg State University, Russia
Elena Stankova	Saint Petersburg State University, Russia
Nataliia Kulabukhova	Saint Petersburg State University, Russia

Workshop Program Committee Members

Adam Belloum	University of Amsterdam, the Netherlands
Dmitrii Vasiunin	Deutsche Telekom Cloud Services E.P.E., Greece
Serob Balyan	Osensus Arm LLC, Armenia
Suren Abrahamyan	Osensus Arm LLC, Armenia
Ashot Sergey Gevorkyan	NAS of Armenia, Armenia
Michal Hnatic	Univerzita Pavla Jozefa Šafárika v Košiciach, Slovakia
Michail Panteleyev	Saint Petersburg Electrotecnical University, Russia
Martin Vala	Univerzita Pavla Jozefa Šafárika v Košiciach, Slovakia
Nodir Zaynalov	Tashkent University of Information Technologies named after Muhammad al Khwarizmi, Uzbekistan
Michail Panteleyev	Saint Petersburg Electrotecnical University, Russia
Alexander Degtyarev	Saint Petersburg University, Russia
Alexander Bogdanov	St. Petersburg State University, Russia

Ports and Logistics of the Future - Smartness and Sustainability (SmartPorts 2025)

Workshop Organizers

Andrea Gallo	Università degli Studi di Trieste, Italy
Gianfranco Fancello	University of Cagliari, Italy
Giuseppe Borruso	Università degli Studi di Trieste, Italy
Enrico D'agostini	World Maritime University, Sweden
Silvia Battino	Università degli Studi di Sassari, Italy
Veronica Camerada	Università degli Studi di Sassari, Italy

Workshop Program Committee Members

Giuseppe Borruso	University of Trieste, Italy
Beniamino Murgante	University of Basilicata, Italy
Ginevra Balletto	University of Cagliari, Italy
Silvia Battino	University of Sassari, Italy
Mara Ladu	University of Cagliari, Italy
Maria del Mar Munoz Leonisio	University of Cádiz, Spain
Ahinoa Amaro Garcia	University of Las Palmas of Gran Canaria, Spain
Maria Attard	University of Malta, Malta
Enrico D'agostini	World Maritime University, Sweden
Francesca Krasna	University of Trieste, Italy

Tu Anh Trinh	UEH University - Ho Chi Minh City, Vietnam
Giovanni Mauro	Università degli Studi della Campania, Italy
Maria Ronza	University of Naples Federico II, Italy
Massimiliano Bencardino	University of Salerno, Italy
Andrea Gallo	Ca' Foscari University of Venice, Italy
Francesca Sinatra	University of Trieste, Italy
Salvatore Dore	University of Trieste, Italy
Veronica Camerada	University of Sassari, Italy
Brunella Brundu	University of Sassari, Italy
Gianfranco Fancello	University of Cagliari, Italy
Marcello Tadini	University of Eastern Piedmont, Italy
Marco Mazzarino	IUAV University Venice
José Ángel Hernández Luis	University of Las Palmas de Gran Canaria, Spain
Marco Naseddu	University of Cagliari, Italy
Maurizio Cociancich	Adriafer, Italy
Giovanni Longo	University of Trieste, Italy
Luca Toneatti	University of Trieste, Italy
Martina Sinatra	University of Cagliari, Italy
Enrico Vanino	University of Sheffield, UK
Patrizia Serra	University of Cagliari, Italy
Agostino Bruzzone	University of Genoa, Italy
Marco Petrelli	University of Roma 3, Italy

Smart Transport and Logistics - Smart Supply Chains (SmarTransLog 2025)

Workshop Organizers

Francesca Sinatra	University of Trieste, Italy
Maria del Mar Munoz	Universidad de Cádiz, Spain
Brunella Brundu	University of Sassari, Italy
Patrizia Serra	University of Cagliari, Italy
Salvatore Dore	University of Trieste, Italy
Marco Naseddu	University of Cagliari, Italy

Workshop Program Committee Members

Giuseppe Borruso	University of Trieste, Italy
Beniamino Murgante	University of Basilicata, Italy
Ginevra Balletto	University of Cagliari, Italy
Silvia Battino	University of Sassari, Italy
Mara Ladu	University of Cagliari, Italy
Maria del Mar Munoz Leonisio	University of Cádiz, Spain
Ahinoa Amaro Garcia	University of Las Palmas of Gran Canaria, Spain

Maria Attard	University of Malta, Malta
Enrico D'agostini	World Maritime University, Sweden
Francesca Krasna	University of Trieste, Italy
Tu Anh Trinh	UEH University, Vietnam
Giovanni Mauro	Università degli Studi della Campania, Italy
Maria Ronza	University of Naples Federico II, Italy
Massimiliano Bencardino	University of Salerno, Italy
Andrea Gallo	Ca' Foscari University of Venice, Italy
Francesca Sinatra	University of Trieste, Italy
Salvatore Dore	University of Trieste, Italy
Veronica Camerada	University of Sassari, Italy
Brunella Brundu	University of Sassari, Italy
Gianfranco Fancello	University of Cagliari, Italy
Marcello Tadini	University of Eastern Piedmont, Italy
Marco Mazzarino	IUAV University Venice
José Ángel Hernández Luis	University of Las Palmas de Gran Canaria, Spain
Marco Naseddu	University of Cagliari, Italy
Maurizio Cociancich	Adriafer, Italy
Giovanni Longo	University of Trieste, Italy
Luca Toneatti	University of Trieste, Italy
Martina Sinatra	University of Cagliari, Italy
Enrico Vanino	University of Sheffield, UK
Patrizia Serra	University of Cagliari, Italy
Agostino Bruzzone	University of Genoa, Italy
Marco Petrelli	University of Roma 3, Italy

Smart Tourism (SmartTourism 2025)

Workshop Organizers

Silvia Battino	University of Sassari, Italy
Francesca Krasna	University of Trieste, Italy
Ainhoa Amaro	University of Las Palmas de Gran Canaria, Spain
Maria del Mar Munoz	University of Cádiz, Spain
Brisol García García	Polytechnic University of Quintana Roo, Mexico
Marta Meleddu	University of Sassari, Italy

Workshop Program Committee Members

Giuseppe Borruso	University of Trieste, Italy
Beniamino Murgante	University of Basilicata, Italy
Gianfranco Fancello	University of Cagliari, Italy
Mara Ladu	University of Cagliari, Italy

Martina Sinatra	University of Cagliari, Italy
Salvatore Dore	University of Trieste, Italy
Marco Mazzarino	IUAV University Venice, Italy
Veronica Camerada	University of Sassari, Italy
Brunella Brundu	University of Sassari, Italy
Maria Attard	University of Malta, Malta
Ginevra Balletto	University of Cagliari, Italy
Giovanni Mauro	University degli Studi della Campania, Italy
Salvatore Lampreu	University of Sassari, Italy
Maria Ronza	University of Naples, Italy
Massimiliano Bencardino	University of Salerno, Italy

Sustainable evolution of long-Distance frEight and paSsenger Transport (SOLIDEST 2025)

Workshop Organizers

Francesco Russo	University of Reggio Calabria, Italy
Andreas Nikiforiadis	Democritus University of Thrace, Greece
Orlando Marco Belcore	University of Messina, Italy
Antonio Comi	University of Rome Tor Vergata, Italy
Tiziana Campisi	Kore University of Enna, Italy
Aura Rusca	Politehnica University of Bucharest, Romania

Workshop Program Committee Members

Massimo Di Gangi	University of Messina, Italy
Orlando Marco Belcore	University of Messina, Italy
Antonio Polimeni	University of Messina, Italy
Socrates Basbas	Aristotle University of Thessaloniki, Greece
Efstathios Bouhouras	Aristotle University of Thessaloniki, Greece
Marina Zanne	University of Lubljana, Slovenia
Marilisa Nigro	Rome Tre University, Italy
Edoardo Marcucci	Molde University College, Norway
Eugen Rosca	Polytechnic University of Bucharest, Romania
Kh Md Nahiduzzaman	Mohammed VI Polytechnic University, Morocco
Beniamino Murgante	University of Basilicata, Italy
Chiara Garau	University of Cagliari, Italy

Sustainability Performance Assessment: Models, Approaches, and Applications Toward Interdisciplinary and Integrated Solutions (SPA 2025)

Workshop Organizers

Francesco Scorza	University of Basilicata, Italy
Sabrina Lai	University of Cagliari, Italy
Francesco Rotondo	Università Politecnica delle Marche, Italy
Jolanta Dvarioniene	Kaunas University of Technology, Lithuania
Michele Campagna	University of Cagliari, Italy
Corrado Zoppi	University of Cagliari, Italy

Workshop Program Committee Members

Federico Amato	University of Lausanne, Switzerland
Ferdinando Di Carlo	University of Basilicata, Italy
Maddalena Floris	University of Cagliari, Italy
Federica Isola	University of Cagliari, Italy
Giuseppe Las Casas	University of Basilicata, Italy
Federica Leone	University of Cagliari, Italy
Giampiero Lombardini	University of Genoa, Italy
Federico Martellozzo	University of Florence, Italy
Alessandro Marucci	University of L'Aquila, Italy
Ana Clara Moura	Universidade Federal de Minas Gerais, Brazil
Beniamino Murgante	University of Basilicata, Italy
Silviu Nate	Lucian Blaga University of Sibiu, Romania
Anastasia Stratigea	National Technical University of Athens, Greece
Francesco Zullo	University of L'Aquila, Italy
Luigi Santopietro	University of Basilicata, Italy
Benedetto Manganelli	University of Basilicata, Italy

Specifics of Smart Cities Development in Europe (SPEED 2025)

Workshop Organizers

Chiara Garau	University of Cagliari, Italy
Katarína Vitálišová	Matej Bel University, Slovak Republic
Marco Fanfani	University of Florence, Italy
Anna Vaňová	Matej Bel University, Slovak Republic
Kamila Borsekova	Matej Bel University, Slovak Republic
Paola Zamperlin	University of Florence, Italy

Workshop Program Committee Members

Claudia Loggia	University of KwaZulu-Natal, South Africa
Francesca Maltinti	University of Cagliari, Italy
Alessandro Plaisant	University of Sassari, Italy
Alenka Poplin	Iowa State University, USA
Silvia Rossetti	University of Parma, Italy
Gerardo Carpentieri	University of Naples Federico II, Italy
Carmen Guida	University of Naples Federico II, Italy
Floriana Zucaro	University of Naples Federico II, Italy
Anastasia Stratigea	National Technical University of Athens, Greece
Yiota Theodora	National Technical University of Athens, Greece
Giovanna Concu	University of Cagliari, Italy
Paolo Nesi	University of Florence, Italy
Emanuele Bellini	University of Roma Tre, Italy
Mana Dastoum	Polytechnic University of Madrid, Spain
Barbara Caselli	University of Parma, Italy
Martina Carra	University of Brescia, Italy
Alfonso Annunziata	University of Basilicata, Italy
Elisabetta Venco	University of Pavia, Italy
Caterina Pietra	University of Pavia, Italy
Enrico Collini	University of Florence, Italy
Luciano Alessandro Ipsaro Palesi	University of Florence, Italy

Smart, Safe, and Healthy Cities (SSHC 2025)

Workshop Organizers

Chiara Garau	University of Cagliari, Italy
Gerardo Carpentieri	University of Naples Federico II, Italy
Carmen Guida	University of Naples Federico II, Italy
Tanja Congiu	University of Sassari, Italy
Martina Carra	University of Brescia, Italy
Alenka Poplin	Iowa State University, USA

Workshop Program Committee Members

Rosaria Battarra	Istituto di Studi sul Mediterraneo, Italy
Barbara Caselli	University of Parma, Italy
Francesca Maltinti	University of Cagliari, Italy
Romano Fistola	Università degli Studi di Napoli Federico II, Italy
Alessandro Plaisant	University of Sassari, Italy
Silvia Rossetti	University of Parma, Italy
Marco Fanfani	University of Florence, Italy
Reza Askarizad	University of Cagliari, Italy

Floriana Zucaro	University of Naples Federico II, Italy
Anastasia Stratigea	National Technical University of Athens, Greece
Yiota Theodora	National Technical University of Athens, Greece
Giovanna Concu	University of Cagliari, Italy
Francesco Zullo	University of L'Aquila, Italy
Paola Zamperlin	University of Florence, Italy
Vincenza Torrisi	University of Catania, Italy
Tiziana Campisi	University of Enna Kore, Italy
Katarína Vitálišová	Matej Bel University, Slovakia
Tazyeen Alam	University of Cagliari, Italy
Mana Dastoum	Polytechnic University of Madrid, Spain
Martina Carra	University of Brescia, Italy
Alfonso Annunziata	University of Basilicata, Italy
Elisabetta Venco	University of Pavia, Italy
Caterina Pietra	University of Pavia, Italy

Smart and Sustainable Island Communities (SSIC 2025)

Workshop Organizers

Chiara Garau	University of Cagliari, Italy
Anastasia Stratigea	National Technical University of Athens, Greece
Yiota Theodora	National Technical University of Athens, Greece
Giovanna Concu	University of Cagliari, Italy

Workshop Program Committee Members

Milena Metalkova-Markova	University of Portsmouth, UK
Tarek Teba	University of Portsmouth, UK
Alenka Poplin	Iowa State University, USA
Gerardo Carpentieri	University of Naples Federico II, Italy
Carmen Guida	University of Naples Federico II, Italy
Floriana Zucaro	University of Naples Federico II, Italy
Silvia Rossetti	University of Parma, Italy
Barbara Caselli	University of Parma, Italy
Martina Carra	University of Brescia, Italy
Alfonso Annunziata	University of Basilicata, Italy
Maria Panagiotopoulou	National Technical University of Athens, Greece
Apostolos Lagarias	University of Thessaly, Greece
Paola Zamperlin	University of Florence, Italy
Vincenza Torrisi	University of Catania, Italy
Giuseppina Vacca	University of Cagliari, Italy
Roberto Minunno	Curtin University, Australia
Marco Zucca	University of Cagliari, Italy

Elisabetta Venco	University of Pavia, Italy
Caterina Pietra	University of Pavia, Italy
Pietro Crespi	Politecnico di Milano, Italy

From STreet Experiments to Planned Solutions (STEPS 2025)

Workshop Organizers

Silvia Rossetti	Università degli Studi di Parma, Italy
Angela Ricciardello	Kore University of Enna, Italy
Francesco Pinna	Università degli Studi di Cagliari, Italy
Chiara Garau	Università degli Studi di Cagliari, Italy
Tiziana Campisi	Kore University of Enna, Italy
Vincenza Torrisi	University of Catania, Italy

Workshop Program Committee Members

Martina Carra	University of Brescia, Italy
Barbara Caselli	University of Parma, Italy
Tanja Congiu	University of Sassari, Italy
Gabriele D'Orso	University of Palermo, Italy
Matteo Ignaccolo	University of Catania, Italy
Md Kh Nahiduzzaman	Mohammed VI Polytechnic University, Morocco
Muhammad Ahmad Al-Rashid	University of Malaya, Malaysia
Alessandro Plaisant	University of Sassari, Italy
Marianna Ruggieri	University of Enna Kore, Italy
Michele Zazzi	University of Parma, Italy

Sustainable Tourism Evaluations: approaches, methods and indicators (STEva 2025)

Workshop Organizers

Mariolina Grasso	Università Kore di Enna, Italy
Fabrizio Finucci	Roma Tre University, Italy
Daniele Mazzoni	Roma Tre University, Italy
Antonella G. Masanotti	Roma Tre University, Italy
Giovanna Acampa	University of Florence, Italy

Workshop Program Committee Members

Giovanna Acampa	University of Florence, Italy
Fabrizio Finucci	Roma Tre University, Italy
Mariolina Grasso	"Kore" University of Enna, Italy

Alberto Marzo — Ministero della Cultura, Italy
Antonella G. Masanotti — Roma Tre University, Italy
Daniele Mazzoni — Roma Tre University, Italy
Rocco Murro — Sapienza University of Rome, Italy
Claudio Piferi — University of Florence, Italy
Alessio Pino — "Kore" University of Enna, Italy
Nicoletta Setola — University of Florence, Italy
Laura Calcagnini — Roma Tre University, Italy
Antonio Magarò — Roma Tre University, Italy
Janos Ghyerghyak — University of Pécs, Hungary
Ágnes Borsos — University of Pécs, Hungary
Fabrizio Battisti — University of Florence, Italy

Sustainable Development of Ports (SUSTAINABLEPORTS 2025)

Workshop Organizers
Tiziana Campisi — University of Enna KORE, Italy
Giuseppe Musolino — University of Reggio Calabria, Italy
Efstathios Bouhouras — Aristotle University of Thessaloniki, Greece
Elen Twrdy — University of Ljubljana, Slovenia
Elena Cocuzza — University of Catania, Italy
Aura Rusca — Politehnica University of Bucharest, Romania

Workshop Program Committee Members
Massimo Di Gangi — University of Messina, Italy
Orlando Marco Belcore — University of Messina, Italy
Antonio Polimeni — University of Messina, Italy
Claudia Caballini — Polytechnic of Torino, Italy
Gianfranco Fancello — University of Cagliari, Italy
Marina Zanne — University of Lubljana, Slovenia
Stefano Ricci — Sapienza University of Rome, Italy
Beniamino Murgante — University of Basilicata, Italy
Chiara Garau — University of Cagliari, Italy

Theoretical and Computational Chemistry and Its Applications (TCCMA 2025)

Workshop Organizers
Noelia Faginas Lago — Università di Perugia, Italy
Andrea Lombardi — Università di Perugia, Italy
Marcos Mandado Alonso — University of Vigo, Spain

Workshop Program Committee Members

Noelia Faginas-Lago	University of Perugia, Italy
Andrea Lombardi	University of Perugia, Italy
Marcos Mandado	University of Vigo, Spain
Angeles Peña	University of Vigo, Spain
Luca Mancini	Universiy of Perugia, Italy
Massimiliano Bartolomei	CSIC, Spain
Cecilia Coletti	University of Chieti-Pescara, Italy
Iñaki Tuñón	Universidad de Valencia, Spain
Albert Rimola Gilbert	Universitat Autònoma de Barcelona, Spain
Stefano Falcinelli	University of Perugia, Italy
Dario Campisi	University of Perugia, Italy
Ernesto García Para	University of the Basque Country, Spain
Giacomo Giorgi	University of Perugia, Italy
Tomás González Lezana	IFF CSIC, Spain
Enrique M. Cabaleiro Lago	Universidade de Santiago de Compostela, Spain
Aurora Costales	Universidad de Oviedo, Spain
Angel Martin	Universidad de Oviedo, Spain
Jose Manuel	University of Vigo, Spain
Annarita Laricchiuta	CNR ISTP Bari, Italy
Fernando Pirani	University of Perugia, Italy

Transport Infrastructures for Smart Cities (TISC 2025)

Workshop Organizers

Francesca Maltinti	University of Cagliari, Italy
Mauro Coni	University of Cagliari, Italy
Benedetto Barabino	University of Brescia, Italy
Nicoletta Rassu	University of Cagliari, Italy
James Rombi	University of Cagliari, Italy

Workshop Program Committee Members

Francesco Pinna	University of Cagliari, Italy
Chiara Garau	University of Cagliari, Italy
Mauro D'Apuzzo	University of Cassino, Italy
Roberto Minunno	Curtin University, Australia
Tiziana Campisi	University of Enna Kore, Italy
Roberto Ventura	University of Brescia, Italy
Alessandro Plaisant	University of Sassari, Italy
Massimo Di Francesco	University of Cagliari, Italy

Vincenza Torrisi — University of Catania, Italy
Paola Zamperlin — University of Florence, Italy

Transforming Urban Analytics: The Impact of Crowdsourced Mapping and Advanced AI Techniques on Future Cities (Tr-UrbAna 2025)

Workshop Organizers
Ayse Giz Gulnerman Gengec — Ankara Hacı Bayram Veli University, Turkey
Müslüm Hacar — Tildiz Technical University, Turkey
Himmet Karaman — Istanbul Technical University, Turkey

Workshop Program Committee Members
Beniamino Murgante — University of Basilicata, Italy
Abdulkadir Memduhoğlu — Harran University, Turkey
Zeynel Abidin Polat — İzmir Katip Çelebi University, Turkey
Güzide Miray Perihanoğlu — Van Yüzüncü Yıl University, Turkey
Tugba Memisoglu Baykal — Ankara Hacı Bayram Veli University, Turkey

From structural to TRAnsformative-change of City Environment: challenges and solutions and perspectives (TRACE 2025)

Workshop Organizers
Pierluigi Morano — Polytechnic University of Bari, Italy
Maria Rosaria Guarini — Sapienza University of Rome, Italy
Francesco Sica — Sapienza University of Rome, Italy
Francesco Tajani — Sapienza University of Rome, Italy
Marco Locurcio — Polytechnic University of Bari, Italy
Debora Anelli — Polytechnic University of Bari, Italy

Workshop Program Committee Members
Felicia di Liddo — Politecnico di Bari, Italia
Valeria Saiu — Università di Cagliari, Italia
Emma Sabatelli — Sapienza Università di Roma, Italia
Antonella Roma — Sapienza Università di Roma, Italia
Giuseppe Cerullo — Sapienza Università di Roma, Italia
Lucia della Spina — Università di Reggio Calabria, Italia
Alejandro Segura de la Cal — Politecnico di Madrid, Spain
Yilsy Nuñez — Politecnico di Madrid, Spain
Gabriella Maselli — Università di Salerno, Italy
Maria Rosa Trovato — Università di Catania, Italy

Manuela Rebaudengo	Politecnico di Torino, Italy
Pierfrancesco De Paola	Università di Napoli Federico II, Italy
Daniela Tavano	Università della Calabria, Italy
Maria Saez	University of Granada, Spain
Paola Amoruso	LUM "Giuseppe Degennaro" University, Italy

Temporary Real Estate management: Approaches and methods for Time-integrated impact assessments and evaluations (TREAT 2025)

Workshop Organizers

Chiara Mazzarella	TUDelft, The Netherlands
Hilde Remoy	TUDelft, The Netherlands
Maria Cerreta	University of Naples Federico II, Italy

Workshop Program Committee Members

Chiara Mazzarella	TU Delft, The Netherlands
Hilde Remoy	TU Delft, The Netherlands
Maria Cerreta	University of Naples Federico II, Italy
Maria Somma	University of Naples Federico II, Italy
Simona Panaro	University of Campania Luigi Vanvitelli, Italy
Laura Di Tommaso	University of Naples Federico II, Italy
Caterina Loffredo	University of Naples Federico II, Italy
Ludovica La Rocca	University of Naples Federico II, Italy
Sabrina Sacco	Politecnico di Milano, Italy
Piero Zizzania	University of Naples Federico II, Italy
Gaia Daldanise	CNR IRISS, Italy
Benedetta Grieco	University of Naples Federico II, Italy
Giuseppe Ciciriello	University of Naples Federico II, Italy
Marta Dell'Ovo	Politecnico di Milano, Italy
Daniele Cannatella	TU Delft, The Netherlands
Eugenio Muccio	University of Naples Federico II, Italy
Sveva Ventre	University of Naples Federico II, Italy

Supporting the Transition to Ecological Economy in Cities Regeneration: Circular Model Tools for Reusing Architecture and Infrastructures (TReE 2025)

Workshop Organizers

Mariarosaria Angrisano	Pegaso University, Italy
Giulio Cavana	Politecnico di Torino, Italy
Francesca Buglione	CNR-ISPC, Italy

Antonia Gravagnuolo	CNR-ISPC, Italy
Piera Della Morte	Pegaso University, Italy

Workshop Program Committee Members

Giulia Datola	Politecnico di Milano, Italy
Vanessa Assumma	University of Bologna, Italy
Marco Volpatti	Politecnico di Torino, Italy
Sebastiano Barbieri	Politecnico di Torino, Italy
Caterina Caprioli	Politecnico di Torino, Italy
Marta Dell'Ovo	Politecnico di Milano, Italy
Federico Dell'Anna	Politecnico di Torino, Italy
Elena Todella	Politecnico di Torino, Italy
Danny Casprini	Politecnico di Milano, Italy
Grazia Neglia	Università Telematica Pegaso, Italy
Francesca Nocca	Università degli Studi di Napoli Federico II, Italy
Giulio Cavana	Politecnico di Torino, Italy
Francesca Buglione	CNR-IPSC, Italy
Marco Rossitti	Politecnico di Milano, Italy
Jhon Escorcia	Politecnico di Torino, Italy
Beatrice Mecca	Politecnico di Torino, Italy
Sara Biancifiori	Politecnico di Torino, Italy

Urban Digital Twins and Data Spaces: Shaping the Future of Sustainable Cities (TwinAbleCities 2025)

Workshop Organizers

Dessislava Petrova Antonova	Sofia University, GATE Institute, Bulgaria
Beniamino Murgante	University of Basilicata, Italy
Senthil Rajendran	RMSI, Bahrain
Tiziana Campisi	Kore University of Enna, Italy
Mila Koeva	University of Twente, The Netherlands

Workshop Program Committee Members

Dessislava Petrova-Antonova	Sofia University, Bulgaria
Mila Koeva	The University of Twente, The Netherlands
Beniamino Murgante	University of Basilicata, Italy
Senthil Rajendran	RMSI, Bahrain
Tiziana Campisi	Kore University of Enna, Italy

Urban Regeneration: Innovative Tools and Evaluation Model (URITEM 2025)

Workshop Organizers
Fabrizio Battisti	University of Florence, Italy
Giovanna Acampa	University of Florence, Italy
Orazio Campo	Sapienza University of Rome, Italy
Melania Perdonò	University of Florence, Italy

Workshop Program Committee Members
Fabrizio Battisti	University of Florence, Italy
Giovanna Acampa	University of Florence, Italy
Orazio Campo	University of Rome "La Sapienza", Italy
Melania Perdonò	Università degli Studi di Firenze, Italy

Urban Space Accessibility and Mobilities (USAM 2025)

Workshop Organizers
Chiara Garau	DICAAR, University of Cagliari, Italy
Alessandro Plaisant	University of Sassari, Italy
Barbara Caselli	University of Parma, Italy
Mauro D'Apuzzo	University of Cassino and Southern Lazio, Italy
Gabriele D'Orso	University of Palermo, Italy
Matteo Ignaccolo	University of Catania, Italy

Workshop Program Committee Members
Mauro Coni	University of Cagliari, Italy
Martina Carra	University of Brescia, Italy
Tiziana Campisi	University of Enna Kore, Italy
Tanja Congiu	University of Sassari, Italy
Francesca Maltinti	University of Cagliari, Italy
Silvia Rossetti	University of Parma, Italy
Barbara Caselli	University of Parma, Italy
Angela Pilogallo	University of L'Aquila, Italy
Lorena Fiorini	University of L'Aquila, Italy
Reza Askarizad	University of Cagliari, Italy
Francesco Pinna	University of Cagliari, Italy
Aime Tsinda	University of Rwanda, Rwanda
Youssef El Ganadi	International University of Rabat, Morocco
Marco Migliore	University of Palermo, Italy
Alessio Salvatore	Italian National Research Council, Italy
Giuseppe Stecca	Italian National Research Council, Italy

Paola Zamperlin   University of Florence, Italy
Vincenza Torrisi   University of Catania, Italy
Gerardo Carpentieri   University of Naples Federico II, Italy
Carmen Guida   University of Naples Federico II, Italy
Floriana Zucaro   University of Naples Federico II, Italy
Alfonso Annunziata   University of Basilicata, Italy
Elisabetta Venco   University of Pavia, Italy
Caterina Pietra   University of Pavia, Italy
Tazyeen Alam   University of Cagliari, Italy
Valerio Cutini   University of Pisa, Italy

UX Mobility 2025: Placing User Experience at the Center of Urban Mobility: Methods and Frameworks (UXM 2025)

Workshop Organizers

Carmen Guida   Università degli Studi di Napoli Federico II, Italy
Gerardo Carpentieri   Università degli Studi di Napoli Federico II, Italy
Federico Messa   Systematica srl, Italy
Lamia Abdelfattah   Systematica srl, Italy

Workshop Program Committee Members

Rosaria Battarra   Istituto di Studi sul Mediterraneo CNR, Italy
Romano Fistola   Università degli Studi di Napoli Federico II, Italy
Lucia Saganeiti   IMAA-CNR, Italy

Virtual Reality and Augmented reality and applications (VRA 2025)

Workshop Organizers

Damiano Perri   University of Perugia, Italy
Osvaldo Gervasi   University of Perugia, Italy
Chau Ma Thi   University of Engineering and Technology, Vietnam National University, Hanoi, Vietnam
Paolo Nesi   University of Florence, Italy
Pierfrancesco Bellini   University of Florence, Italy

Workshop Program Committee Members

David Berti   ART SpA, Italy
JungYoon Kim   Gachon University, South Korea

TaiHoon Kim	Zhejiang University of Science and Technology, China
Marcelo de Paiva Guimares	Federal University of São Paulo, Brazil
Sergio Tasso	University of Perugia, Italy

Workshop on Advanced and Computational Methods for Earth Science Applications (WACM4ES 2025)

Workshop Organizers

Luca Piroddi	University of Cagliari, Italy
Patrizia Capizzi	University of Palermo, Italy
Marilena Cozzolino	University of Molise, Italy
Sebastiano D'Amico	University of Malta, Malta
Chiara Garau	University of Cagliari, Italy
Giuseppina Vacca	University of Cagliari, Italy

Workshop Program Committee Members

Andrea Angelini	CNR ISPC, Italy
Ilaria Barone	Università degli Studi di Padova, Italy
Patrizia Capizzi	University of Palermo, Italy
Luigi Capozzoli	CNR, Italy
Alberto Carletti	University of Cagliari, Italy
Emanuele Colica	University of Malta, Malta
Marilena Cozzolino	Università del Molise, Italy
Sebastiano D'Amico	University of Malta, Malta
Chiara Garau	University of Cagliari, Italy
Luciano Galone	University of Malta, Malta
Peter Iregbeyen	University of Malta, Malta
Mariano Lisi	Basilicata Aerospace Cluster CLAS, Italy
Raffaele Martorana	Università di Palermo, Italy
Paolo Mauriello	Università del Molise, Italy
Veronica Pazzi	University of Florence, Italy
Raffaele Persico	Università della Calabria, Italy
Luca Piroddi	University of Cagliari, Italy
Sina Saneiyan	Binghamton University, USA
Mercedes Solla	Universidade de Vigo, Spain
Deodato Tapete	ASI, Italy
Giuseppina Vacca	University of Cagliari, Italy
Enrica Vecchi	University of Cagliari, Italy

Sponsoring Organizations

ICCSA 2025 would not have been possible without the tremendous support of many organizations and institutions, for which all organizers and participants of ICCSA 2025 express their sincere gratitude:

Galatasaray University, Istanbul, Türkiye
(https://gsu.edu.tr/en)

African Mathematical Union
(https://www.africanmathunion.org/)

Springer Nature Switzerland AG, Switzerland
(https://www.springer.com)

The University of Massachusetts, USA
(https://www.umass.edu/)

University of Perugia, Italy
(https://www.unipg.it)

University of Basilicata, Italy
(http://www.unibas.it)

Monash University, Australia
(https://www.monash.edu/)

Kyushu Sangyo University, Japan
(https://www.kyusan-u.ac.jp/)

University of Minho, Portugal
(https://www.uminho.pt/)
Venue
ICCSA 2025 took place in: **Galatasaray University, Istanbul, Türkiye**

Additional Reviewers

Reviewers
The review tasks for each workshop have been carried out by the workshop Organizers and the members of the workshop Program Committee.

Plenary Lectures

Sky Safe with GAI and Post-quantum Computing

Elizabeth Chang

Professor of Cyber Security and Head of Discipline, University of the Sunshine Coast, Australia

Abstract. Professor Chang's talk in this presentation has two distinct parts. To start, she will introduce the landscape of cybersecurity development, attacks, threats, and vulnerabilities, as well as state-of-the-art cyber protection, cyber defence, and cyber incident prevention. This is followed by a discussion of the impact of Generative AI (GAI) and quantum-safe cryptographic computing, highlighting the major issues and challenges in research, education, and training. In conclusion, she will present a vision for Sky Safe solutions, aiming to achieve cyber resilience that supports business and economic stability, enhances human capabilities, and promotes environmental sustainability.

Disaster Preparedness and Risk Profiling in the Digital Era from Earth Observation Lens

Jagannath Aryal

Department of Infrastructure Engineering, University of Melbourne, Australia

Abstract. Natural hazards which turn into disasters result in severe losses of lives, infrastructure, and property. Disasters such as earthquakes and landslides and their impacts on transportation safety, infrastructure resilience, and displacement of people to new places are challenges. To address such challenges, earth observation data and intelligent methods can provide potential solutions in developing decision support systems. This talk will present the state of the art in Earth observation for disaster resilience using intelligent methods. In the Earth observation space, digitalisation has revolutionised the way we map, monitor, and develop decision support systems. Global case study examples covering earthquake-induced landslides from the Himalayan region will cover the digital capabilities. The digital capabilities will embrace object recognition, interpretation, and their accurate and precise capture to integrate into digital models. The developed digital models from representative case studies can be leveraged in other jurisdictions in profiling risks to protect lives and infrastructure and creating disaster preparedness in the era of digital age and digital economy.

Intelligent Image Enhancement for Real-World Applications in Adverse Atmospheric Conditions

Khan Muhammad

Department of Global Convergence, Sungkyunkwan University, South Korea

Abstract. The adverse impacts of atmospheric conditions such as haze, fog, and low-light environments pose significant challenges for real-world applications reliant on computer vision, including autonomous driving, surveillance, and remote sensing. This keynote explores cutting-edge advancements in intelligent image enhancement, drawing insights from two pivotal studies. The first introduces HazeSpace2M, a comprehensive dataset and novel classification-guided dehazing framework that improves image clarity across diverse atmospheric conditions, addressing the gap between synthetic and real-world dehazing performance. The second focuses on LoLI-Street, a benchmark for low-light image enhancement tailored to urban environments, extending beyond enhancement to enable robust object detection and scene understanding. Taken together, these contributions demonstrate how integrating domain-specific datasets, advanced algorithms, and performance benchmarks can significantly elevate the reliability of computer vision systems under challenging weather and lighting conditions. Attendees will gain valuable insights into the methodologies, datasets, and practical applications driving innovation in this field, with implications for research and industry alike.

In Memory of Carmelo Torre

Unfortunately, Professor Carmelo Torre, one of the cornerstones of the ICCSA Conference, passed away last December, leaving everyone stunned and deeply saddened. His loss has created a profound void within our academic community. Carmelo was not only a respected scholar and dedicated contributor to the success and growth of ICCSA, but also a generous colleague, mentor, and friend to many. His intellectual rigor, warm personality, and unwavering commitment to advancing research will be remembered with great admiration. As we continue the work he helped shape, we honor his legacy and the indelible mark he left on all of us. Carmelo Torre graduated in engineering at the Polytechnic of Bari with a thesis on urban planning under Dino Borri's guidance. He began his research career by collaborating with Franco Selicato. During his PhD at the University of Naples Federico II under Luigi Fusco Girard, he specialized in real estate market analysis and multi-criteria evaluation methods. He explored the social impacts of urban transformations with his lifelong friend Maria Cerreta. His first ICCSA participation was in Perugia in 2008, in the session Geographical Analysis, Urban Modeling, Spatial Statistics. Instantly captivated by the conference, his charisma enabled him to involve various Italian scientific communities, including those in real estate and statistics. ICCSA became a yearly commitment for him, where he valued the high editorial quality of the proceedings and the dynamic post-presentation discussions and debates he passionately and expertly enriched. In 2012, alongside Maria Cerreta and Paola Perchinunno, he organized the workshop Econometrics and Multidimensional Evaluation in the Urban Environment (EMEUE), fostering dialogue on critical topics. His influence steadily grew, drawing numerous research groups to ICCSA and establishing real estate and assessment as one of the conference's leading fields. A pillar of ICCSA, he was involved across all facets of the event. Torre's contributions to academic discourse were marked by intellectual rigor and innovative thinking. His conference interventions consistently challenged conventional wisdom, offering insights transcending disciplinary boundaries. Beyond the conference, he passionately advocated for equity and social justice. His left-leaning ideology, though firm, earned respect from those with differing views, thanks to his sincerity and loyalty. He was creative, generous, and always willing to help, even at a personal cost. Despite battling illness, he maintained his characteristic optimism, warmth, cheerfulness, and commitment, supported by his partner, Caterina Rinaldo. His legacy lives on in his ideas, dedication, and unmatched generosity.

Contents – Part IV

Cyber Intelligence and Applications (CIA 2025)

Detecting DDoS Attacks in Microservice Architectures via AI-Based Agents 3
   Giacomo Benedetti, Luca Caviglione, Alberto Falcone, Massimo Ficco, Massimo Guarascio, and Antonio Guerriero

Coastal Cities Versus Inland Areas. Hypotheses for Sustainable Regeneration Through Ecosystem Services of 'Hooking' and Rehabilitation of Brownfield Sites (CoastalCities_VS_InlandAreas 2025)

Disused Industrial Areas on the Waterfront. Between Sicily and Calabria 19
   Celestina Fazia, Kh Md Nahiduzzaman, Cristina Natoli, Federica Sortino, and Clarastella Vicari Aversa

Cities, Technologies and Planning 2025 (CTP 2025)

Communal Level Cybersecurity Incidents in the Slovak Republic 39
   Miroslav Fečko, Ondrej Mitaľ, and Silvia Ručinská

Decision Support System for Urban Road Safety: A Comparison Between Two Different City Size 54
   Michele Pinna, Gianfranco Fancello, Patrizia Serra, Sergio Useche, and Francisco Alonso

A Phygital Space-Related Storytelling of a Cultural Intangible and Social Experience. The *Telve Humanscape / Mappe del sentire* Application 72
   Letizia Bollini and Giulia Faccin

Methodologies for Wildland-Urban Interface (WUI) Fire Risk Assessment – Case Study North-Eastern Attica Region 88
   Angeliki Papazoglou, Apostolos Lagarias, and Anastasia Stratigea

Real-Time IoT with Edge Computing: Efficiency, Security, and Future Trends 106
   Teresa Guarda and Washington Torres

NET4SAFE: Network for Emergency and Safety Management. A Platform
for Emergency Management and Accessibility 117
  Annamaria Felli, Cristina Montaldi, Vanessa Tomei, Emilio Marziali,
  and Francesco Zullo

**Digital Transition: Effects on Housing Mobility, Market, Land
Governance (DIGITRANS 2025)**

The Subjective Dimension in Settlement Choices: Approaches and Tools
for Detecting Preferences 131
  Fabrizio Battisti and Melania Perdonò

Evaluating Inner Areas Potentials (EIAP 2025)

The Cultural Value of the *Tratturi* in Molise (Italy) 145
  Maddalena Chimisso

The Role of Cultural and Natural Heritage in a Place-Based Strategy
for Inner Peripheries 161
  Priscilla Sofia Dastoli and Francesco Scorza

Data-Driven AI Approach to Address Territorial Strategies. Why Investing
in Agri-Food Sector to Enhance the Valsesia Inner Area 177
  Diana Rolando, Alice Barreca, Giorgia Malavasi,
  and Manuela Rebaudengo

Renewable Energy Communities as a Tool for a Just Green Transition
in Inner Areas: A Pilot Project in Sardinia (Italy) 199
  Ivan Blečić, Alessandro Sebastiano Carrus, Eleonora Congiu,
  Giuseppe Desogus, and Valeria Saiu

Territorial Inequalities in Adaptive Reuse Opportunities: Evidence
from Lombardy Region (Italy) 216
  Marco Rossitti and Francesca Torrieri

Convergences Versus Gaps. Capital Axiology as a Cognitive Pattern
of Territorial Fragility 232
  Maria Rosa Trovato, Ludovica Nasca, Salvatore Giuffrida,
  and Vittoria Ventura

Decision-Making CIA Process (DeMaCIA) to Support SNAI Strategies:
The Case of Castelluccio Inferiore in Basilicata, Italy 250
  Cristina Coscia, Silvia Gron, and Enrico Vercellino

Mapping Vulnerability of Industrial Heritage for Adaptive Reuse:
A Spatial Multi-criteria Analysis Approach 268
    John Cullen Sayegh, Federica Cadamuro Morgante,
    Rossana Gabaglio, Oana Cristina Tiganea, and Marta Dell'Ovo

Undertourism and Destination Management in the Inner Areas. The Case
of Locride, Reggio Calabria 283
    Francesco Calabrò, Immacolata Lorè, Giovanna Emanuela Minniti,
    and Rosa Maria Staropoli

Econometric and Multidimensional Evaluation in Urban Environment (EMEUE 2025)

The Urban One Health Approach for the Planning of Effective
Interventions on Territory: A Systematic Analysis of the Scientific
Literature 303
    Pierluigi Morano, Felicia Di Liddo, Marco Locurcio,
    Francesca Fariello, and Debora Anelli

Urban Green Spaces and Housing Prices: The Impact of Metric Choice
on Econometric Models 320
    Pierluigi Morano, Debora Anelli, Francesca Fariello, Marco Locurcio,
    and Felicia Di Liddo

Reliable Evaluation Methods for Effective Urban Planning Initiatives: The
Case Study of the Agro-Food Center of Rome (Italy) 332
    Francesco Tajani, Pierluigi Morano, Debora Anelli, Giuseppe Cerullo,
    and Melania Arenas Morente

The Implementation of Multicriteria Analysis for Heritage Assets
Enhancement: An Application for the HBU Identification of a Historical
Building in an Italian Municipality 346
    Marco Locurcio, Felicia Di Liddo, Laura Tatulli, Pierluigi Morano,
    and Debora Anelli

Quantifying the Priceless: A Methodological Approach to the Evaluation
of Historical-Architectural Heritage 363
    Benedetto Manganelli, Francesco Tajani, Pierfrancesco De Paola,
    and Francesco Paolo Del Giudice

Environmental Impacts and Housing Deprivation: A Study of the Effects
of Industrial Polluting Sites in the Italian Context 381
    Debora Anelli, Pierluigi Morano, Francesco Tajani, Felicia Di Liddo,
    and Marco Locurcio

Student Housing Market: An Evaluation Model for the Identification
of the Investment Opportunities in the Major European Cities 393
  *Debora Anelli, Pierluigi Morano, Maria Rosaria Guarini,
  and Francesco Tajani*

Sustainable Real Estate in France: Impact of One-Stop Shop and Turnkey
Contract Models on Energy Efficiency 410
  Edda Donati and Dorothée Charlier

An SMCE Approach for Developing Integrated and Shared Strategies
for the Port City of Brindisi 429
  *Giuseppe Ciciriello, Benedetta Ettorre, Carlotta Grandis,
  Sabrina Sacco, and Maria Cerreta*

Marginal Costs of Building Energy Retrofit 447
  Sergio Copiello, Carlo Grillenzoni, and Pietro Bonifaci

Author Index 461

Cyber Intelligence and Applications (CIA 2025)

Detecting DDoS Attacks in Microservice Architectures via AI-Based Agents

Giacomo Benedetti[2], Luca Caviglione[2], Alberto Falcone[2], Massimo Ficco[1], Massimo Guarascio[2], and Antonio Guerriero[1](✉)

[1] Università degli Studi di Salerno, Via Giovanni Paolo II, 132, 84084 Fisciano, Italy
antguerriero@unisa.it
[2] National Research Council of Italy, Genova and Rende, Italy

Abstract. The widespread adoption of microservices captured the attention of attackers, mainly due to their distributed and dynamic nature. Unfortunately, traditional intrusion detection mechanisms may struggle to accurately and efficiently identify the most effective threats, for instance, DDoS campaigns. To advance in the security of modern microservice architectures, this paper presents an Intrusion Detection Agent (IDA) for the run-time identification and classification of DDoS campaigns. Specifically, the IDA takes advantage of AI to classify attacks in a multi-container environment. To prove the effectiveness of our approach, we collected data from a realistic testbed built on top of the Train Ticket framework. Then, a classification pipeline has been evaluated when used to identify four attack templates, *i.e.*, Standard DDoS, Slow DDoS, GET floods, and SYN floods. Obtained results showcased that the AI-based IDA can correctly handle the considered offensive templates, even when the data is scarce. For instance, when a decision tree is used, our IDA achieves an accuracy of ∼0.991 by considering only 4% of measurements capturing the behavior of containers (*e.g.*, the used RAM or the volume of network traffic).

Keywords: Machine Learning · Intrusion Detection · Denial of Service · Security benchmark · Microservices

1 Introduction

The rapid evolution of MicroService-based Architectures (MSAs) has facilitated the creation of modular, scalable, and resilient systems. As a consequence, they are responsible for the transformation of the development process at the basis of major software frameworks and Internet-wide platforms [4]. Unfortunately, MSAs are highly-distributed and characterized by a large attack surface, which attract the increasing attention of many malicious treat actors [3]. Among the various attack models that proven to be effective, MSAs exhibit an inherent vulnerability against Distributed Denial of Service (DDoS) attacks. In fact, the use of containerized software jointly with their decentralized flavor requires to extensively use inter-service communication paths, which inherently amplify the attack surface [11].

As a consequence, the research community doubled the efforts aimed at designing and evaluating automatic Intrusion Detection Systems (IDS) tailored for protecting MSAs [7]. Despite deploying heuristics may be a viable option, mitigation techniques leveraging AI proven their effectiveness. Specifically, AI-based solutions can take advantage of the monitoring infrastructure already integrated within MSAs, for instance to assess their performance or enforce service level agreements [9].

This paper presents an IDA endowed with AI capabilities for the run-time identification and classification of DDoS campaigns targeting MSAs. To prove the effectiveness of the proposed approach, we collected data from a realistic testbed implemented via the Train Ticket framework [31], which has been tested with various attack templates. In more detail, we considered a threat actor launching four types of DDoS offensive campaigns, *i.e.*, Standard DDoS, Slow DDoS, GET floods, and SYN floods. We point out that considering DoS-based threats is of major importance, since they can challenge the ability of MSAs of resorting to their intrinsic autoscaling mechanisms and cause major economical losses, for instance due to the over-provisioning of resources [1]. Obtained results showcased that the AI-based IDA can correctly detect and classify the considered DDoS attacks, even when the data is scarce. This aspect is of paramount importance, as effective IDA schemes should be able to balance their effectiveness with the overhead required to the monitoring infrastructure to make the detection possible (see, *e.g.*, [33] and the references therein).

Summing up, the contribution of this work is twofold: *i*) it confirms the effectiveness of the Train Ticket platform when used to experiment with container security, and *ii*) it proposes a prime IDA mechanism for demonstrating that the AI is a suitable tool for spotting DDoS-like attacks, even when in presence of scarce data.

The rest of the paper is structured as follows. Section 2 reviews past research on monitoring and security aspects of microservices, while Sect. 3 showcases the testbed for preparing the dataset used in our experiments. Section 4 describes the proposed AI-based IDA, Sect. 5 introduces the experimental setup, and Sect. 6 discusses numerical results. Lastly, Sect. 7 concludes the paper and outlines future research directions.

2 Related Work

The ability of microservices to handle complex software ecosystems promoted their adoption in several scenarios, such as artificial intelligence frameworks, massive IoT deployments, and cloud-native applications [26]. As a consequence, understanding the security properties of containers, orchestration mechanisms, and the overall deployments is an urgent need. In this vein, a vast amount of research has been done to enhance the security posture of microservices, for instance to make the development pipeline more robust, elaborate best practices, and enforce efficient static analysis mechanisms [13,16,29].

An important aspect concerns the ability of tracking the evolution of microservices both in terms of used hardware resources and software behaviors. Even if monitoring is an essential component to enforce the adherence to quality of service guarantees, it has been also extensively employed to detect anomalous patterns that may reveal an attack [21]. As possible examples, runtime monitoring techniques based on the collection of system calls have been used to spot the presence of Docker containers trying to exfiltrate sensitive data (*e.g.*, cryptographic keys) by means of information hiding techniques [25,32]. Moreover, data describing the evolution of containers (*e.g.*, the depletion of a specific hardware resource) can be mixed with more classical information (*e.g.*, logs) to tune proper heuristics able to spot anomalous behaviors [27]. More fine-grained behaviors (*e.g.*, volumes of syscalls or information on the execution flow) can be used to feed machine learning models or AI-based agents for detecting a wide-range of threats. Methods based on AI proven to be very effective in revealing the presence of stealth cryptomining software exploiting resources of a population of containers [12]. Events related to the lifecycle of a microservice can be exploited as well. A viable approach to train a classifier for spotting security risks or unintended behaviors leverages operations such as traversing part of the filesystem hierarchy (*e.g.*, the /etc) or accepting an incoming TCP connection [28].

Indeed, various AI-capable frameworks have been proposed to mitigate attack campaigns against microservices or improve their security levels [10]. As an example, shared network resources among containers can be monitored with the goal of learning indicators that can prevent spoofing attempts [15]. Instead, [22] addressed the problem of identifying low-rate DoS attacks through various AI models. Similarly, [18] showcases the adoption of convolutional networks to detect DDoS campaigns against the application layer of microservices, whereas [3] discusses how XGBoost allows to classify many DDoS offensive techniques. Despite the used technique, being able to collect suitable datasets to train models and tune countermeasures is of paramount importance. Thus, [6] deals with a testbed for collecting information on how a large-scale set of orchestrated containers behaves when in presence of different DDoS attacks.

Despite being based on simple heuristics or on some form of AI, detecting attacks against MSAs requires to have a proper visibility over the hardware and software at runtime. In this perspective, the majority of researchers and industrial developers are agreeing on the effectiveness of the extended Berkeley Packet Filter (eBPF) [19]. In essence, the eBPF can be used to collect a vast set of information, granting visibility on network, hardware and software resources with a unique interface [33]. At the same time, the success of the eBPF is also rooted in its ability of gathering data without the need of instrumenting container images, which are often immutable [2].

3 Testbed and Datasets

TrainTicket is an open-source application, developed by FudanSELab, that implements a realistic microservices-based train ticket reservation system. The aim is to provide to researchers and practitioners a testbed for investigating key software engineering challenges with microservices-based architectures, facing with the limited availability of suitable benchmark frameworks reflective of real-world microservices environments.

It includes 41 interconnected microservices, with each microservice dedicated to specific functional responsibilities. It is implemented by using different programming languages (Java, Node.js, Python, and Go) and exploiting databases like Mongo and MySQL.

`Train Ticket` has been used by Ficco et al. [6] to generate a dataset representing various DDoS attacks to a realistic MSA. Such dataset is publicly available at[1]. The authors simulate the nominal usage with the Locust workload generator, while the DDoS attacks (including Classic DDoS, Slow DDoS, SYN Flood, and GET Flood) were executed using the MHDDoS tool. The performance metrics were collected using CAdvisor and Prometheus tools, with sampling every five seconds across 30-min scenarios under idle and loaded conditions.

The resulting dataset consists of 10 subsets two depicting normal conditions, eight representing different attack scenarios. The dataset contains various features categorized into the following sets:

– *ContainerUsage*: Number of bytes consumed by the container on this filesystem;
– *CPUThrottling*: Total time duration the container has been throttled;
– *CPUUsage*: CPU quota of the container;
– *MemoryUsage*: Current memory usage, including all memory regardless of when it was accessed;
– *NetworkIO*: Cumulative count of bytes received/transmitted;
– *PacketsDropped*: Cumulative count of packets dropped while receiving;
– *PodReady*: Describes whether the pod is ready to serve requests;
– *ResourceLimits*: The number of requested limit resources by a container;
– *PodStatus (Restarts)*: The number of container restarts per container.

Each subset is labeled, distinguishing benign from malicious traffic allowing the identification of the specific performed attack.

4 Design of the AI-Based IDA

In this section, we describe the threat model and the solution approach adopted for revealing incoming attacks. Figure 1 illustrates the reference attack scenario where the AI-based IDA is deployed to safeguard a microservice-based application from DDoS attacks.

In more detail, an MSA is targeted by a DDoS attack, which may take various forms such as Standard DDoS, SYN floods, GET floods, or slow-rate attacks. These attacks aim to exhaust the computational or networking resources of the

---

[1] https://github.com/iotresearchunisa/MicroservicesDDoS.

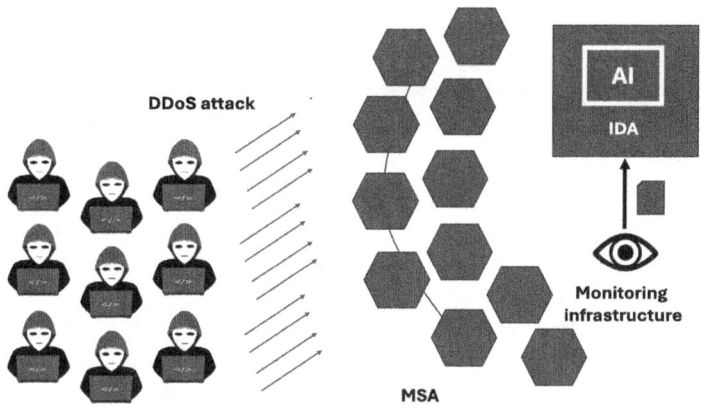

Fig. 1. AI-based IDA application scenario.

microservices, potentially degrading the system's performance or causing service outages.

To counteract these threats, an IDA is deployed alongside the application environment. It acts as the core detection component and is integrated with a monitoring infrastructure (based on tools like Prometheus, CAdvisor, and so on) that continuously collects runtime data. The monitoring layer gathers metrics such network flows, resource utilization, or other low-level indicators relevant for intrusion detection.

These data are processed and converted into a propositional view, which is used to feed the AI module responsible for real-time analysis. In our solution, we adopted a supervised approach, which means that the AI-based detector is trained on both benign and malicious traffic patterns. Leveraging the input data, it identifies anomalies and classifies ongoing events to detect potential DDoS attacks. When malicious activity is recognized, the system can raise alerts or take mitigation actions, depending on the deployment context.

Our IDA embeds four different supervised machine learning algorithms, each with distinct characteristics and offering trade-offs in terms of accuracy, interpretability, and computational cost. Specifically, we integrated four widely adopted classification models in cybersecurity literature [5, 24, 30], *i.e.*, K-Nearest Neighbors (KNN), Decision Tree (DT), Random Forest (RF), and Gradient Boosting (GB). In the following, we offer a brief overview of the functioning of each algorithm.

K-Nearest Neighbours. It is a non-parametric, instance-based classification method that assigns a label to a test sample by analyzing the labels of its nearest neighbors in the training set [23]. Specifically, given an instance a, the algorithm identifies the k training samples closest to a according to a predefined distance metric (*e.g.*, Euclidean distance, Manhattan distance). Once the top k neighbors have been identified, the class label of a is predicted as the most frequent class among those neighbors. This majority voting mechanism makes KNN suitable in scenarios where class boundaries are irregular or nonlinear. Although KNN is a relatively simple model compared to more sophisticated ones, it was chosen for its suitability in data stream processing scenarios, where real-time monitoring and attack alerting are essential. Its instance-based nature allows it to adapt to incoming data without the computational overhead of retraining, making it a practical choice for dynamic and evolving environments.

Decision Tree. It is a supervised learning algorithm whose classification process occurs through a hierarchical tree structure [14]. The tree is built starting from a labeled training dataset, recursively partitioning the data based on feature values to maximize the class purity within each resulting subset. In this structure, internal (non-leaf) nodes represent decision points where the data are partitioned based on specific feature thresholds, while leaf nodes correspond to class labels. Given a test instance a, the algorithm traverses the tree from the root to a leaf node following the decision rules at each node, determined by the feature values of a. The final prediction corresponds to the class label of the reached leaf node. Although they exhibit lower performance than other approaches, we also included DT, as they are interpretable and can assist operators in decision-making.

Random Forest. An ensemble-based machine learning algorithm integrates bagging with random feature selection to improve predictive performance and robustness [17]. It works by building a set of decision trees, each trained on a random subset of the training set obtained by sampling with repetition. To further increase the model diversity and reduce the correlation between trees, only a randomly selected subset of features is considered at each split. This strategy mitigates overfitting and improves generalization. The final prediction is obtained by either majority voting in the case of classification problems or by averaging the predictions in the case of regression problems. Aggregating the results of many trees reduces the variance of the overall model, improving the ability to generalize to unseen data. Combining different weak models, RF allows for achieving more effective performances than a single model, hence, in our scenario, it can be used when a limited number of attack examples are available.

Gradient Boosting. An ensemble learning technique builds a predictive model by sequentially combining multiple weak models, typically decision trees [8]. The idea of gradient boosting is to train each new model to correct the residual errors made by the previous one. At each iteration, the algorithm fits a new tree to the negative gradient of the loss function with respect to the predictions of the current model. The final prediction is obtained by summing the weighted outputs of all individual models. It was selected in this study because it tends to be more resistant to overfitting than individual decision trees, especially when regularization techniques are applied (*e.g.*, subsampling or limiting tree depth).

5 Experimental Setup

This section describes the experimental setup employed in this paper. Section 5.1 describes the pipeline used to prepare data for the model learning phase. Section 5.2 presents the metrics used for the evaluation of our approach.

Regarding the classification task of attacks, we built the machine learning algorithms by relying on the implementations provided by the scikit-learn library [20]. Since the dataset has missing values, we applied a mean imputation strategy using the *SimpleImputer* of scikit-learn to handle them. This step was integrated into a pipeline to impute missing values before using the classifiers. Furthermore, KNN was configured with 5 neighbors, while the DT, RF, and GB models were used with the default number of estimators.

5.1 Data Preparation

For the experimentation, we consider the dataset described in Sect. 3 and the four models introduced in the Sect. 4. In detail, to feed the model during the learning phase, we aggregated features contained in the dataset described in Sect. 3. Then, we removed columns with constant values since they are not representative for the learning phase. We removed features from monitoring services – *i.e.*, *grafana*, *prometheus*, and *nacos*. We filtered columns with less than 80% of values different from NaN, and for the remaining columns we filled NaN values with the mean value computed on the column's values. Finally, we normalized all the values using *Min-Max* according to Eq. 1:

$$x' = \frac{x - x_{\min}}{x_{\max} - x_{\min}}, \qquad (1)$$

where x represents the original value, x_{min} and x_{max} are the minimum and maximum value of the considered column, respectively.

5.2 Experimental Metrics

To evaluate the performance of the machine learning models, we consider standard classification metrics derived from the confusion matrix: Accuracy (Acc), Precision (Prec), Recall (Rec), and F1-score. These are defined as follows:

- *Acc* measures the proportion of correctly classified instances:

$$Acc = \frac{TP + TN}{TP + TN + FP + FN}; \qquad (2)$$

- *Prec* measures the proportion of true positive predictions among all positive predictions:

$$Prec = \frac{TP}{TP + FP}; \qquad (3)$$

- *Rec* measures the proportion of actual positives that were correctly predicted:

$$Rec = \frac{TP}{TP + FN}; \quad (4)$$

- *F1* is the harmonic mean of Precision and Recall:

$$F1 = 2 \cdot \frac{Prec \cdot Rec}{Prec + Rec}. \quad (5)$$

Here, *TP*, *TN*, *FP*, and *FN* represent the number of true positives, true negatives, false positives, and false negatives, respectively. A positive corresponds to a sample classified as a DDoS attack, while a negative is a sample classified as normal behavior.

6 Numerical Results

Our results demonstrate that the AI-based IDA efficiently detects and classifies DDoS attacks in microservice environments. Among the evaluated models, Gradient Boosting consistently outperforms other algorithms across varying sample sizes, achieving an accuracy of 1.000 and F1-score of 1.000 with only 2–4% of the original dataset. Random Forest also achieves perfect performance at these sample levels. Even with only 0.25% of the sample, Gradient Boosting reaches an 83% accuracy, significantly outperforming K-Nearest Neighbors (KNN), which yields only 46.2% accuracy and an F1-score of 0.330.

Table 1 outlines the evolution of model performance as a function of the data sample size. The Decision Tree model crosses 90% accuracy with just 1% of data, while Random Forest and Gradient Boosting exceed 99% accuracy at the same threshold. KNN, while simpler and more computationally efficient, shows limited performance, requiring at least 2% of the data to exceed 95% accuracy.

To understand the internal decision-making process of the models, especially for explainability, we conducted a feature correlation analysis using Random Forest as the reference. Figure 2 illustrates the top 15 features correlated with each of the four DDoS attack types:

- *Standard DDoS Attacks:* Figure 2a shows the most influential features are memory usage metrics, particularly for core services such as `kube-apiserver`, `tsdb-mysql`, and `ts-train-service`, with correlation values ranging from 0.47 to 0.85. This suggests that memory exhaustion is a distinguishing indicator of standard DDoS behavior.
- *Slow DDoS Attacks:* These are primarily characterized by consistent and high correlation in both transmitted and received network I/O across key system containers (*e.g.*, `kube-*` and `etcd`), all showing correlation values between 0.84 and 0.85 (see, Fig. 2b). This uniformity reflects the subtle but sustained pressure slow attacks place on network interfaces.
- *GET Flood Attacks:* These attacks show high correlation with container usage and CPU usage in database-intensive and user-facing services, such as `ts-basic-service`, `tsdb-mysql`, and `ts-seat-service`. Correlation values are typically around 0.77 to 0.85 (see, Fig. 2c).

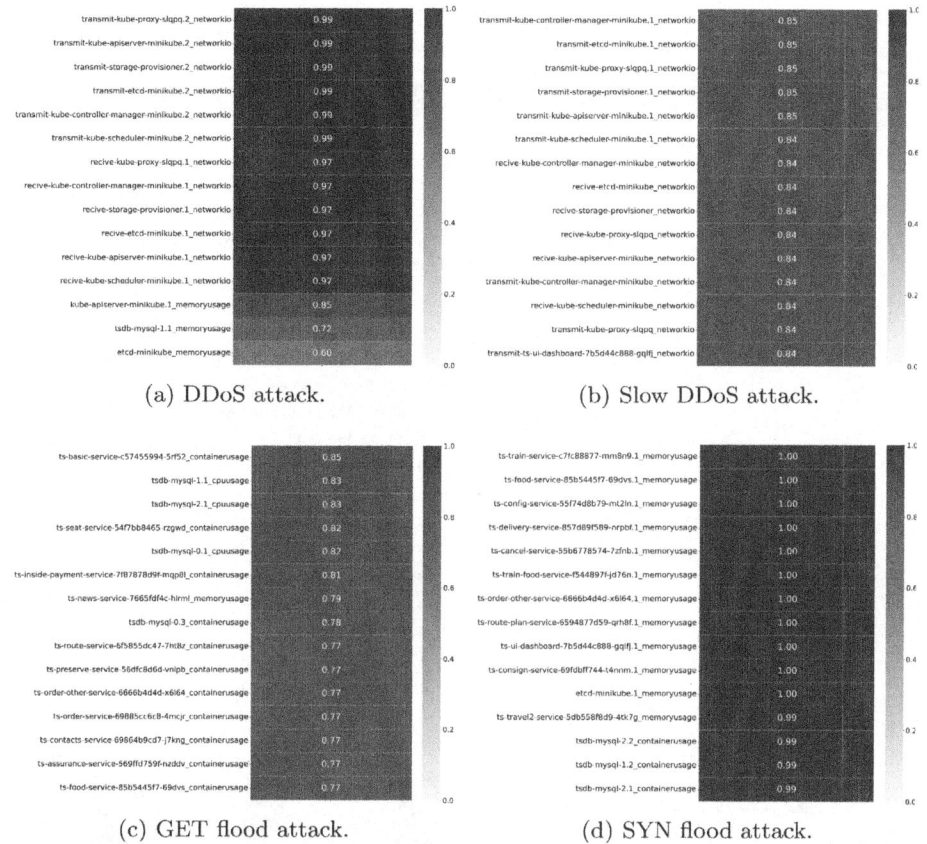

Fig. 2. Top-15 correlated features for the four attacks considered. Each feature name is fully reported.

- *SYN Flood Attacks:* The most correlated features – up to 1.00 – are memory usage metrics for frontend and service-routing components, including ts-ui-dashboard, ts-delivery-service, and ts-route-plan-service. Container and pod readiness metrics (*e.g.*, rabbitmq_podready) also contribute significantly, indicating the impact of SYN floods on service availability and startup (see, Fig. 2d).

This correlation analysis supports the effectiveness of feature selection and model design by revealing how different types of DDoS attacks affect system behavior differently. Notably, the IDA maintains robustness even under severe data scarcity, making it suitable for real-world deployments with a constrained monitoring infrastructure.

Figure 3 further confirms these findings by comparing F1-scores across algorithms and sample sizes. The steep performance improvement, especially between

Table 1. Performance metrics of different machine learning algorithms across varying sample percentages.

Sample pcg	Algorithm	Performance metrics			
		Acc	Prec	Rec	F1
0.25%	K-Nearest Neighbors	0.462	0.283	0.462	0.330
	Decision Tree	0.699	0.746	0.699	0.704
	Random Forest	0.769	0.828	0.769	0.742
	Gradient Boosting	**0.829**	**0.858**	**0.829**	**0.826**
0.5%	K-Nearest Neighbors	0.610	0.714	0.610	0.569
	Decision Tree	0.790	0.870	0.790	0.803
	Random Forest	0.903	0.915	0.903	0.902
	Gradient Boosting	**0.988**	**0.989**	**0.988**	**0.988**
1%	K-Nearest Neighbors	0.850	0.862	0.850	0.852
	Decision Tree	0.923	0.945	0.923	0.925
	Random Forest	0.996	0.996	0.996	0.996
	Gradient Boosting	**0.999**	**0.999**	**0.999**	**0.999**
2%	K-Nearest Neighbors	0.951	0.955	0.951	0.950
	Decision Tree	0.929	0.942	0.929	0.929
	Random Forest	**1.000**	**1.000**	**1.000**	**1.000**
	Gradient Boosting	0.999	0.999	0.999	0.999
4%	K-Nearest Neighbors	0.976	0.976	0.976	0.976
	Decision Tree	0.991	0.991	0.991	0.991
	Random Forest	**1.000**	**1.000**	**1.000**	**1.000**
	Gradient Boosting	**1.000**	**1.000**	**1.000**	**1.000**

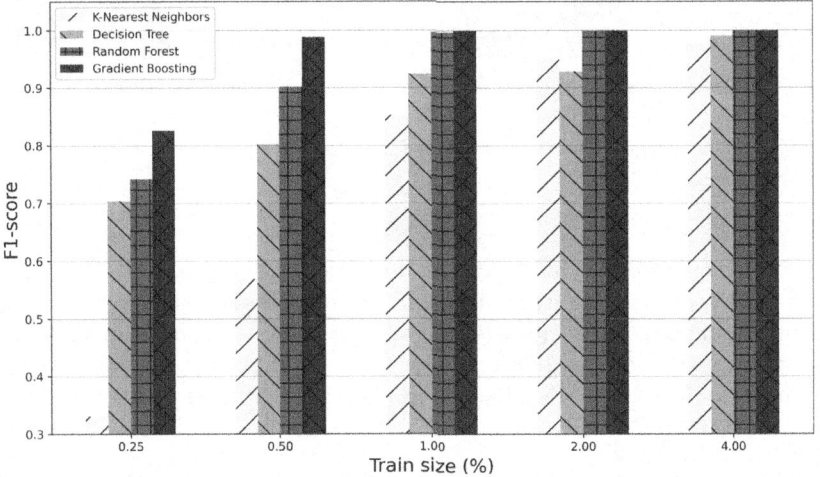

Fig. 3. A comparison of the F1-scores for the machine learning algorithms across different training dimensions. Each bar in the chart represents the performance of a specific algorithm within each training dimension.

0.5% and 1% of the training data, highlights a practical threshold for efficient model training in constrained environments.

7 Conclusions

In this paper, we presented an IDA mechanism based on AI for improving the security posture of modern MSAs. Specifically, we used four different supervised approaches to classify various DDoS attacks, *i.e.*, Standard DDoS, Slow DDoS, GET floods, and SYN floods. As shown, results obtained in a realistic testbed built on top the Train Ticker platform demonstrated the effectiveness of our approach. As an example, with an IDA leveraging a decision tree, we achieve an accuracy of ∼0.991 by considering only 4% of measurements capturing the evolution of containers.

Future work aims at refining the approach. For instance, a relevant part of our ongoing research is devoted to investigate mechanisms based on transfer learning, especially to "port" our approach to other similar scenarios. Furthermore, we are also working towards the development of a small prototype for conducting measurements. Specifically, we are interested in quantifying the resources needed to run the IA-capable IDA and the overheads caused to the monitoring infrastructure for allowing the detection.

Acknowledgments. This work was partially supported by Project SERICS (PE00000014) under the NRRP MUR program funded by the EU - NGEU.

References

1. Bremler-Barr, A., Czeizler, M., Levy, H., Tavori, J.: Exploiting miscoordination of microservices in tandem for effective DDoS attacks. In: IEEE INFOCOM 2024-IEEE Conference on Computer Communications, pp. 231–240. IEEE (2024)
2. Cassagnes, C., Trestioreanu, L., Joly, C., State, R.: The rise of eBPF for non-intrusive performance monitoring. In: NOMS 2020-2020 IEEE/IFIP Network Operations and Management Symposium, pp. 1–7. IEEE (2020)
3. Castro, J., Laranjeiro, N., Vieira, M.: Detecting dos attacks in microservice applications: approach and case study. In: Proceedings of the 11th Latin-American Symposium on Dependable Computing, pp. 73–78 (2022)
4. De Lauretis, L.: From monolithic architecture to microservices architecture. In: 2019 IEEE International Symposium on Software Reliability Engineering Workshops (ISSREW), pp. 93–96. IEEE (2019)
5. Douiba, M., Benkirane, S., Guezzaz, A., Azrour, M.: An improved anomaly detection model for IoT security using decision tree and gradient boosting. J. Supercomput. **79**(3), 3392–3411 (2023)
6. Ficco, M., et al.: A benchmark for DDoS attacks detection in microservice architectures. In: ICNC 2025 (2025)
7. Flora, J., Antunes, N.: Evaluating intrusion detection for microservice applications: benchmark, dataset, and case studies. J. Syst. Softw. **216**, 112142 (2024)
8. Friedman, J.H.: Stochastic gradient boosting. Comput. Stat. Data Anal. **38**(4), 367–378 (2002)
9. Giamattei, L., et al.: Monitoring tools for DevOps and microservices: a systematic grey literature review. J. Syst. Softw. **208**, 111906 (2024)

10. Haq, M.S., Nguyen, T.D., Tosun, A.Ş., Vollmer, F., Korkmaz, T., Sadeghi, A.R.: SoK: a comprehensive analysis and evaluation of docker container attack and defense mechanisms. In: 2024 IEEE Symposium on Security and Privacy (SP), pp. 4573–4590. IEEE (2024)
11. Jayalath, R.K., Ahmad, H., Goel, D., Syed, M.S., Ullah, F.: Microservice vulnerability analysis: a literature review with empirical insights. IEEE Access (2024)
12. Karn, R.R., Kudva, P., Huang, H., Suneja, S., Elfadel, I.M.: Cryptomining detection in container clouds using system calls and explainable machine learning. IEEE Trans. Parallel Distrib. Syst. **32**(3), 674–691 (2020)
13. Kim, Y., Park, C., Hong, D.: A robust framework for comprehensive container image vulnerability assessment. IEEE Access (2025)
14. Kingsford, C., Salzberg, S.L.: What are decision trees? Nat. Biotechnol. **26**(9), 1011–1013 (2008)
15. Kommula, A., Hu, Y.H.F., Hoppa, M.A., Olatunbosun, S.: Machine learning techniques to enhance container network security. In: 2020 International Conference on Computational Science and Computational Intelligence (CSCI), pp. 622–627. IEEE (2020)
16. Leppänen, T., Honkaranta, A., Costin, A.: Trends for the DevOps security. A systematic literature review. In: International Symposium on Business Modeling and Software Design, pp. 200–217. Springer (2022)
17. Liu, Y., Wang, Y., Zhang, J.: New machine learning algorithm: random forest. In: Liu, B., Ma, M., Chang, J. (eds.) ICICA 2012. LNCS, vol. 7473, pp. 246–252. Springer, Heidelberg (2012). https://doi.org/10.1007/978-3-642-34062-8_32
18. Marimuthu, S.: Detecting application layer DDoS attacks among microservices using spatio-temporal graph convolution networks. Ph.D. thesis, California State University, Northridge (2023)
19. Miano, S., Risso, F., Bernal, M.V., Bertrone, M., Lu, Y.: A framework for eBPF-based network functions in an era of microservices. IEEE Trans. Netw. Serv. Manage. **18**(1), 133–151 (2021)
20. Pedregosa, F., et al.: Scikit-learn: machine learning in Python. J. Mach. Learn. Res. **12**, 2825–2830 (2011)
21. Pereira-Vale, A., Fernandez, E.B., Monge, R., Astudillo, H., Márquez, G.: Security in microservice-based systems: a multivocal literature review. Comput. Secur. **103**, 102200 (2021)
22. Perez-Diaz, J.A., Valdovinos, I.A., Choo, K., Zhu, D.: A flexible SDN-based architecture for identifying and mitigating low-rate DDoS attacks using machine learning. IEEE Access **8**, 155859–155872 (2020)
23. Peterson, L.E.: K-nearest neighbor. Scholarpedia **4**(2), 1883 (2009)
24. Primartha, R., Tama, B.A.: Anomaly detection using random forest: a performance revisited. In: 2017 International Conference on Data and Software Engineering (ICoDSE), pp. 1–6 (2017). https://doi.org/10.1109/ICODSE.2017.8285847
25. Saenger, J., Mazurczyk, W., Keller, J., Caviglione, L.: VoIP network covert channels to enhance privacy and information sharing. Futur. Gener. Comput. Syst. **111**, 96–106 (2020)
26. Singleton, A.: The economics of microservices. IEEE Cloud Comput. **3**(5), 16–20 (2016)
27. Steidl, M., Leitner, M., Urbanke, P., Gattringer, M., Felderer, M., Ristov, S.: Understanding microservice runtime monitoring data for anomaly detection with structural equation modeling. In: International Conference on Product-Focused Software Process Improvement, pp. 404–413. Springer (2024)

28. Tien, C.W., Huang, T.Y., Tien, C.W., Huang, T.C., Kuo, S.Y.: KubAnomaly: anomaly detection for the docker orchestration platform with neural network approaches. Eng. Rep. **1**(5), e12080 (2019)
29. VS, D.P., Sethuraman, S.C., Khan, M.K.: Container security: precaution levels, mitigation strategies, and research perspectives. Comput. Secur. **135**, 103490 (2023)
30. Ying, S., et al.: An improved KNN-based efficient log anomaly detection method with automatically labeled samples. ACM Trans. Knowl. Discov. Data **15**(3) (2021). https://doi.org/10.1145/3441448
31. Zhou, X., et al.: Benchmarking microservice systems for software engineering research. In: Proceedings of the 40th International Conference on Software Engineering: Companion Proceedings, pp. 323–324 (2018)
32. Zuppelli, M., Guarascio, M., Caviglione, L., Liguori, A.: No country for leaking containers: detecting exfiltration of secrets through AI and Syscalls. In: Proceedings of the 19th International Conference on Availability, Reliability and Security, pp. 1–8 (2024)
33. Zuppelli, M., Repetto, M., Schaffhauser, A., Mazurczyk, W., Caviglione, L.: Code layering for the detection of network covert channels in agentless systems. IEEE Trans. Netw. Serv. Manage. **19**(3), 2282–2294 (2022)

Coastal Cities Versus Inland Areas. Hypotheses for Sustainable Regeneration Through Ecosystem Services of 'Hooking' and Rehabilitation of Brownfield Sites (CoastalCities_VS_InlandAreas 2025)

Disused Industrial Areas on the Waterfront. Between Sicily and Calabria

Celestina Fazia[1], Kh Md Nahiduzzaman[2], Cristina Natoli[3], Federica Sortino[1(✉)], and Clarastella Vicari Aversa[4]

[1] Department of Engineering and Architecture, University of Enna "Kore", 94100 Enna, Italy
`celestina.fazia@unikore.it, federica.sortino@unikorestudent.it`
[2] Citinnov SA for Integrated Territorial Planning and Smart Cities, Mohammed VI Polytechnic University (UM6P), Ben Guerir, Morocco
`khmd.nahiduzzaman@um6p.ma`
[3] Ministero dell'Ambiente e della Sicurezza Energetica (MASE), Rome, Italy
[4] Department of Architecture and Design – dAeD, University "Mediterranea" of Reggio Calabria - UNIRC, 89124 Reggio Calabria, Italy
`clarastella.vicariaversa@unirc.it`

Abstract. The relocation of industrial activities, which began as early as the last century in Europe and has accelerated in recent decades in the Mezzogiorno, has led to the gradual divestment of substantial portions of industrial assets in many rural and peripheral areas and urban centers. Because of this, even important and strategic industrial areas by the sea, such as the industrial zone of Termini Imerese, the former Puleo Brick Factory in Palermo, Sicily, and Saline Joniche in Calabria, have found themselves threatened by the progressive loss or decline of economic activities, investments, infrastructure and related services. The case studies analysed in the essay are Termini Imerese, which represents a depowered plant, the former Puleo Brick Factory in Palermo, which is a disused industrial site with considerable potential, and Saline Joniche in the province of Reggio Calabria, which is abandoned but never used. Three different case studies of industrial plants in port areas. Three cases, on the sea but different in history and design approach. Three possible and different design strategies for regeneration, preservation and enhancement of the industrial heritage, capable of involving the resources and actors of the area by returning the industrial heritage of the places to the collective cultural heritage as well.

Keywords: brownfield areas · architectonical and urban regeneration · disused industrial areas · Sicily · Calabria

1 Introduction

The delocalisation of industrial activities, which began in Europe in the last century and has accelerated in recent decades, has led to the gradual dismantling of large portions of industrial assets in the Mezzogiorno, with significant repercussions on urban, rural and peripheral areas. In particular, in the Strait of Messina area, the decline of production sites once considered strategic has led to the loss of investments, infrastructure and services, compromising territorial competitiveness. Disused industrial sites are material testimonies of historical and social relevance, but their preservation is complex due to economic and structural factors and the effects of climate change, a global phenomenon that affects various contexts transversally. The presence of industrial settlements close to urban centres raises questions about the correlation between production activities, environmental degradation and climate vulnerability, with direct repercussions on the quality of life of local communities.

The paper invites reflection on the consequences that the presence of these sites has on people and human activities, in the knowledge that not only active plants, but also partially or totally abandoned sites have negative influences on the quality of the environment and urban life.

The paper intercepts "strategies and methods for the maintenance and continuity of those meanings that traces of the past take on in relation to the needs of the present" [1] and proposes an in-depth analysis of the sites, tracing their historical evolution and evaluating the numerous attempts at redevelopment.

The paper analyses industrial delocalisation in Europe and its impact in the Mezzogiorno, introducing the concept of the "industrial cemetery" and its cultural, economic and social value. The aim is to identify sustainable regeneration strategies that integrate physical, social and economic interventions, avoiding the risk of an "elusive exchange", in which the redevelopment of degraded areas can reduce the focus on other priorities, such as housing needs and public investment.

The methodology adopted for the analysis of the case studies is based on an integrated reading of environmental, landscape, historical and urban planning data. For each site, the following were identified: the degree of environmental vulnerability, the type of territorial context, the functions envisaged or proposed in the redevelopment projects, the status of the redevelopment initiatives (completed, planned or interrupted) and the critical issues that have slowed down or prevented their implementation. The data were organised in a comparative matrix that allows us to capture similarities and differences in the transformation pro-cesses.

The three selected case studies - the former Puleo factory in the municipality of Palermo, the industrial site of Saline Joniche in the municipality of Montebello Jonico (RC) and and the depowered industrial area of Termini Imerese in the municipality of the same name located in the metropolitan city of Palermo - were chosen on the basis of strategic, landscape and methodological criteria. Geographically, the sites are located in contiguous areas of Southern Italy, allowing the phenomenon to be observed in a coherent area from a socio-economic and infrastructural point of view. The selection also reflects the desire to represent a significant range of situations typical of deindustrialisation in southern Italy: from the risk of degradation of the historical-landscape heritage (Palermo), to the environmental impact and the effects of the failure of large energy projects (Saline Joniche), to cases of partial decommissioning with reconversion difficulties (Termini Imerese). This variety makes it possible to compare different approaches to redevelopment, offering useful hints for the construction of adaptive strategies capable of responding to the specificities of places.

2 Abandoned or Depleted Industrial Areas: Differences and Opportunities

In the context of the reflection on disused industrial heritage that has taken place in recent decades, urban and territorial regeneration represents a crucial challenge and an extraordinary opportunity for the recovery and valorisation of architectural complexes otherwise destined to oblivion. The industrial heritage, with its load of history and identity, constitutes a fundamental element in the transformation process of contemporary cities, favouring the dialogue between historical memory and innovation.

The main challenge lies in finding a balance between the preservation of historical-architectural value and the need for functional adaptation to new uses. This contribution, examining three emblematic cases in Sicily and Calabria, explores the theme of urban and territorial regeneration through the reuse of disused industrial complexes, highlighting the role of architecture in favouring processes of sustainable transformation and cultural valorisation.

One of the central aspects in the debate on the regeneration of industrial heritage concerns the duality between conservation and demolition. Disused industrial sites represent material historical documents of social relevance, but their integral preservation is often difficult due to economic and structural factors. In order to mediate between the two antithetical positions, an approach based on reinterpretation and adaptive reuse has emerged in Europe and beyond, which allows the preservation of historical memory without preventing functional transformations.

Architecture plays a fundamental role in this process: the recovery of industrial spaces through cultural and creative projects, for example, has proven to be an effective strategy to revitalise the urban fabric, making these places catalysts for social and economic innovation. The inclusion of new cultural and creative functions not only allows existing structures to be safeguarded, but also makes them usable again, contributing to the revitalisation of entire city areas.

Moreover, the recovery of industrial heritage offers the opportunity to rethink the relationship between city and landscape, fostering dialogue between pre-existing structures and new urban needs. This aspect is crucial in contexts characterised by high population density, where the reuse of existing spaces represents a valid alternative to uncontrolled urban sprawl.

In Italy, the case of Milan is emblematic for understanding the variety and quality of industrial regeneration interventions in recent decades. Projects such as the MUDEC in the former Ansaldo, the Fondazione Prada in the former Distilleria Società Italiana Spiriti, and the Hangar Bicocca in the former Pirelli factories, the Armani headquarter in the former Nestlé silos, testify to how the reuse of industrial spaces can be integrated into the urban fabric, generating new poles of cultural attraction [2]. These interventions not only preserve the memory of the place but reinterpret it, creating spaces that respond to contemporary needs for sustainability and innovation [3, 4].

Internationally, numerous examples demonstrate how the adaptive reuse of industrial buildings can transform abandoned areas into new poles of cultural and economic attraction. A significant case in point is the Carriageworks Arts Centre in Sydney, born from the conversion of a former railway workshop into a centre dedicated to the performing arts [5, 6]. Here, the recovery of industrial memory has been accompanied by the introduction of flexible spaces for cultural events, in a perfect balance between past and present. Another emblematic example is the Schindler Factory in Krakow, transformed into a museum of contemporary art and historical memory. This project managed to integrate the preservation of the building with new facilities, offering a cultural experience that combines history and innovation.

Among the most famous models of urban regeneration, one cannot fail to mention the Tate Modern in London, built inside the former Bankside Power Station. This intervention has turned a former power station into one of the most important cultural hubs globally, thanks to an architectural project that has maintained the building's original shell while reinterpreting its interior spaces [7]. The success of this operation demonstrates how industrial reconversion can have a strong impact in defining new urban centralities and contributing to the enhancement of the city.

In the Netherlands, the Westergasfabriek in Amsterdam is another virtuous example of public-private collaboration in transforming a disused industrial plant into a multifunctional cultural district. The site, originally dedicated to gas production, now houses art galleries, shops, restaurants and event spaces, demonstrating the potential of industrial reuse in fostering local development.

The international approach to the theme of reusing disused industrial spaces offers further food for thought. From the United States, with pioneering examples such as the Quincy Market in Boston, to Europe, where former factories and warehouses have been converted into multifunctional cultural centres [8]. The Farnham Maltings in England, for example, became a cultural incubator through a participatory project that involved the local community from the earliest stages [9]. This regenerative development model, which blends ongoing cultural activities with the temporary use of spaces, represents a virtuous practice of how regeneration can support social cohesion and the local creative economy.

Traditionally, in Italy, industrial heritage has received sporadic and fragmented attention. The inclusion of industrial sites in the category of cultural heritage is relatively recent and still meets with resistance, due to the difficulty of recognising the historical and cultural value of architectures born for functional needs. However, a broader vision of protection has gradually become established, which considers these artefacts not only as testimonies of the past, but also as potential engines of development for the future.

The recognition of the importance of industrial heritage has led to an expansion of the regulatory and operational tools for its protection. The Cultural Heritage and Landscape Code, Legislative Decree 42/2004, updated by Legislative Decree 62/2008, introduced the concept of cultural interest for industrial sites, but much remains to be done to ensure effective protection and integrated valorisation with local communities [10]. The most successful experiences of reuse and urban regeneration show how historical memory can be a powerful catalyst for innovation. Examples of how industrial architecture, reinterpreted through new cultural uses, can become a symbol of the rebirth of entire pieces of city or territory. These projects share a holistic approach that integrates preservation of the material document with functional reinterpretation, incorporating new activities that respond to contemporary needs for sustainable development and social regeneration.

To stimulate discussion on these issues, it seems necessary to consider regeneration not only as an architectural or urban planning practice, but as a multidimensional process involving public policies, local communities, creative economy and environmental sustainability. Only through an integrated approach, which considers the specificities of each context and encourages dialogue between public and private actors, will it be possible to activate those virtuous processes capable of transforming urban voids into new engines of development.

The approach to the reinterpretation of the industrial heritage has evolved over time: from demolition and replacement interventions we have moved on to sustainable reuse strategies that recognise the testimonial value of industrial archaeology. European policies incentivise the recovery of these sites through funding programmes and guidelines for their valorisation, emphasising the need to integrate the needs of conservation with those of local development.

In the context of coastal areas, industrial heritage is of particular value. Many historic harbours, shipyards, refineries and fish processing plants are in an obsolete condition today, but offer enormous potential for conversion into multifunctional spaces. The recovery of these places can contribute not only to the preservation of industrial memory, but also to the creation of new attractive poles, capable of stimulating local economies linked to tourism, culture and environmental sustainability.

The rehabilitation of industrial heritage by the sea follows different approaches depending on the characteristics of the site and the needs of the urban and environmental context. Among the most effective strategies is the functional reuse and hybridisation of spaces modalities that lead to the transformation of disused industrial buildings into cultural centres, innovation poles or creative hubs. An emblematic example is the Tabakalera in San Sebastián, Spain, a former tobacco factory now converted into an international centre for contemporary culture, which has contributed to the regeneration of the city's waterfront [11]. Another method pursued is environmental regeneration linked to sustainability. The recovery of former coastal industrial sites often involves environmental reclamation and landscape redevelopment. In Marseilles [12], another interesting example, the vast 19th-century complex of the Docks port area has been reconverted into a multifunctional centre dedicated to art, commerce and culture. Alfonso Femia's project has reinterpreted the industrial identity of the place, creating a new gathering space for the city by including the creation of green spaces and pedestrian paths, integrating the industrial heritage with new tourist and cultural functions.

Industrial tourism and the enhancement of memory represent a strategic lever for the valorisation of disused manufacturing heritage. In Italy, a significant example is the redevelopment of the former Tonnara di Favignana, transformed into an interactive museum that tells the story of tuna fishing and Sicily's maritime traditions.

The circular economy and new production models can also be the driving force for reinterpreting urban fabrics that have lost their functions. This is the case in Rotterdam, where the M4H (Merwe-Vierhavens), a former port area in transformation, old warehouses and factories have been converted into spaces for start-ups, green companies and innovative residences [13, 14].

The recovery of industrial heritage can foster the creation of new public spaces on the waterfront, improving the quality of urban life. The case of Hamburg Hafen-City shows how the regeneration of a disused port area can generate a new sustainable neighbourhood with a strong focus on functional mixity and architectural quality [15]. In conclusion, the reuse and regeneration of disused industrial heritage is a crucial challenge for the future of contemporary cities. The preservation of historical and architectural value, combined with the integration of new cultural and creative functions, makes it possible to transform abandoned areas into vital resources for society. International examples show that the success of these interventions depends on the ability to balance preservation, innovation and sustainability, ensuring an integrated approach that valorises the past without foregoing the opportunities of the future.

In this context, it is crucial that urban and territorial policies promote effective governance models capable of combining conservation and planning in a long-term perspective. Only through a shared and interdisciplinary approach will it be possible to ensure that industrial heritage continues to be a strategic resource for urban and cultural development.

3 Case Studies

3.1 Case Study 1: The Case of Ex Puleo Brick Factory, Palermo

The former Puleo brick factory located in Palermo, the capital of the Sicilian Region and metropolitan city of the same name, is an emblematic case of the city's industrial archaeology, as it bears witness to the city's urban evolution and production dynamics in the 19th century. The factory was founded in 1878 by the knight Giuseppe Puleo in the seaside village of Acqua dei Corsari. The factory exploited the availability of local clay for the production of bricks and terracotta artefacts, constituting a strategic production pole for the city's building expansion. The industrial settlement developed along the sea coast, in an area that, although peripheral to the urban centre, was strategically located along the main routes. The original structure extended over about 2500 square metres and included not only the buildings used for production, but also structures built in later phases to fulfil social and religious purposes [16].

The products of the Puleo furnace were used by illustrious architects of the time for the construction of prestigious buildings. Among them, Giovan Battista Filippo Basile selected bricks from the Palermo factory for the completion of specific parts of the Teatro Massimo, a symbol of the city's monumental architecture [17].

The factory's decline, which began in the early 20th century, is part of a broader phenomenon of industrial disuse that affected Palermo and other Italian cities during the same century. Economic and social transformations, the increasing competitiveness of markets and the need for technological upgrades made production plants progressively obsolete [18]. The crisis caused by the First World War led to the closure of the factory, which remained inactive from 30 November 1915 to 5 May 1921, when, after the death of Cavaliere Puleo (1918), the factory was sold by his sons to the Fazio brothers. The new purchasers resumed full operations, but the depletion of locally available raw materials slowed down production and caused a huge increase in costs. The clay quarry at Villa Amanda, used for on-site supply, was exhausted, and the increased cost of transporting the material from other locations contributed to the closure of the factory. Together, these factors led to the definitive cessation of operations in 1975 [19]. The abandonment of the area generated a process of progressive degradation, turning the site into an industrial ruin with no current function.

From an urbanistic point of view, the Acqua dei Corsari area today presents a highly compromised layout. Despite its strategic location and proximity to the sea, the area suffers from serious environmental problems, aggravated by the presence of an oil products depot and an incomplete and inefficient sewage treatment plant. The site is also characterised by infrastructural marginalisation that hinders its integration with the surrounding urban fabric. Poor accessibility to services, combined with environmental pollution, has contributed to a general impoverishment of the area's social and economic fabric.

The inclusion of the Puleo factory among the assets protected by the Regional Territorial Landscape Plan [20] is a first step towards the definition of recovery and valorisation strategies. Despite the fact that the project launched by the Regional Province of Palermo in 2004 to redevelop the Oreto-Ficarazzi shoreline aimed to restore dignity to the historic bathing area, many of the planned works have never been completed. The original plan envisaged the creation of new green areas to connect the symbolic places of the southern coast, including the Sant'Erasmo railway depot, the Solarium, the Florio Stand, the Colonnella dell'Immacolata, the Bandita hamlet, the Brick Kilns and the Torre dei Corsari [21], but the failure to complete some works still leaves the area's problems of degradation and neglect unresolved (Fig. 1 and Table 1).

3.2 Case Study 2: Saline Joniche, Reggio Calabria

The industrial area of Saline Joniche, located in the municipality of Montebello Ionico, about 20 km from Reggio Calabria, is an emblematic case of environmental degradation and failure of industrialisation policies in southern Italy. The site houses the remains of Liquichimica Biosintesi, an industrial pole built in the 1970s with the aim of starting the production of bioproteins for animal feed. The infrastructure also included an industrial-commercial port, which never came into operation. However, the factory ceased operations a few days after its inauguration due to the discovery of the toxicity of the products produced, and has been abandoned ever since.

Today, the area is in an advanced state of disrepair: the metal structures are corroded and unsafe, the harbour is silted up and unusable, and the former industrial areas and groundwater are in need of urgent reclamation and safety work. Paradoxically, this context of abandonment develops in the vicinity of an environment of high ecological value: an artificial lake, a remnant of the ancient salt pans, which has been recognised as a Special Protection Area (SPA) for the presence of important bird species [21].

The Saline Joniche affair is part of a broader picture of failed attempts to industrialise Calabria. In an area historically characterised by the cultivation of bergamot and jasmine, the construction of the Liquichimica plant entailed the obliteration of entire agricultural areas and the transformation of about 2,000 m of coastline. After the closure of the plant, further industrial development projects proved ineffective: just two kilometres away, in 1989, the Officine Grandi Riparazioni delle Ferrovie dello Stato were inaugurated, also decommissioned in 2001. The result is a landscape marked by vast abandoned spaces, the symbol of an ineffective and unsustainable model of economic development.

Coastal erosion and the total lack of maintenance have aggravated the degradation of the area. Sea storms have progressively eroded the foundations of the industrial

Table 1. Descriptive-analytical table site 1 Former Mattoneria Puleo. Methodology: Celestina Fazia; Processing and Compilation: Federica Sortino

Site number:	Site number 1
Region:	Sicily
City:	Palermo
Name:	Ex Mattoneria a vapore Puleo
Expected functions:	Production of bricks, artistic vases and building artefacts
Age of construction:	1878
Dimensions (range):	area of approximately 2500 sqm
Relationship with the urbanized context:	exterior near urban areas: borough of Acqua dei Corsari along the coast road
Relationship with port area:	Existing. Proximity to Palermo's Cala for product trade
Current state of use:	abandoned, but previously used: permanently closed in 1975 and abandoned
Conversion implemented or in progress:	studies and proposals (restoration projects never implemented)
Environmental constraints present:	-
Environmental criticalities and vulnerabilities of the study area and context:	serious environmental problems amplified by the presence of a petroleum products depot and an incomplete and inefficient sewage treatment plant
Contaminated site:	Present (need for remediation indicated)
Widespread urban decay:	Present (advanced state of decay of the structure)
Lack of services and social hardship:	Present (abandoned and degraded area)
Recovery difficulties attributable to:	significant costs; contaminated site; bureaucratic and administrative criticalities

structures, leading to the collapse of entire sections of the complex. In particular, the progressive subsidence of the foundation plinths triggered a chain effect, leading to the structural collapse of some portions of the plant [22]. Today, Saline Joniche is an area poised between environmental criticalities and recovery potential. The presence of the SPA and the Pantano wetlands suggests possible reconversion strategies oriented towards the protection and enhancement of the natural heritage, in contrast with a past marked by failed industrial choices. However, any redevelopment intervention must necessarily go through careful planning, which considers environmental reclamation as an essential prerequisite for a new sustainable development of the territory (Fig. 2 and Table 2).

AREA OF INFLUENCE OF THE FORMER INDUSTRIAL AREAS OF PALERMO

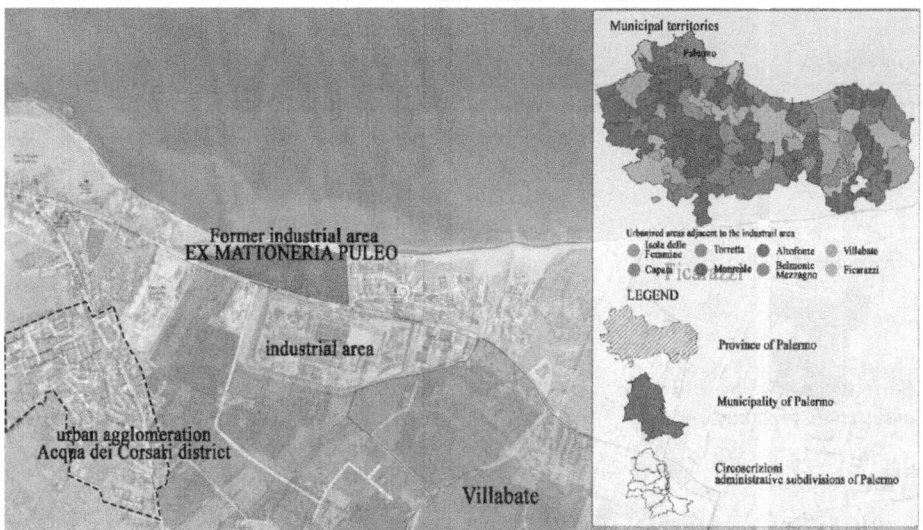

Fig. 1. Former industrial area Puleo brick factory (sites number 1), Sicily. Source: graphic design by Federica Sortino

Table 2. Descriptive-analytical table Site 2 Industrial area of Saline Joniche. Methodology: Celestina Fazia; processing and compilation: Federica Sortino

Site number:	Site number 2
Region:	Calabria
City:	Montebello Jonico
Name:	Industrial area of Saline Joniche
Expected functions:	Industrial production of bioproteins and citric acid (never fully realised); Subsequent proposal for coal-fired power plant (never realised)
Age of construction:	1970s
Dimensions (range):	area of 700.000 sqm
Relationship with the urbanized context:	Exterior near urban areas: located in the coastal hamlet of Saline Joniche
Relationship with port area:	Existing. Port built to support industry, currently unused and obstructed by sand)
Current state of use:	Abandoned, but previously used: industry closed in the 1980s, area unused since then

(*continued*)

Table 2. (*continued*)

Site number:	Site number 2
Conversion implemented or in progress:	Studies and proposals: Agapì project for an innovation district; attempts at revitalisation as a university campus and technology centre with institutional partners
Environmental constraints present:	Constraints on 18 areas, including 5 Sites of Community Importance (SCI) Environmental impacts related to unrealised projects (e.g. coal plant)
Environmental criticalities and vulnerabilities of the study area and context:	Environmental and infrastructural degradation (abandoned industrial plants, blocked harbour) Past influence of organised crime in construction and management
Contaminated site:	Potential pollution of soil and industrial infrastructure
Widespread urban decay:	deterioration of industrial facilities and surrounding area
Lack of services and social hardship:	abandonment of the area exacerbated emigration
Recovery difficulties attributable to:	Significant costs; presence of environmental constraints; bureaucratic and administrative criticalities; low attractiveness of the site

3.3 Case Study 3: Termini Imerese Industrial Area

Termini Imerese is an Italian municipality in the metropolitan city of Palermo in Sicily, 40 km from the capital, and is an important railway and maritime hub due to the presence of a well-connected railway station and a profitable commercial port. The industrial area, where the Enel Ettore Majorana power plant is located, is known for the former FIAT plant and is located in the backwater plain between the city and the archaeological area of Himera. The plant, which opened in 1970 and was characterised by a high degree of production specialisation in the automotive sector (FIAT and later also Lancia brands), was definitively decommissioned by FIAT spa in 2011. Following the closure of the FIAT plant (now Stellantis Group), a path for the re-industrialisation of the area was identified, with the signing of a Programme Agreement for the reconversion and redevelopment of the industrial pole between the Ministry of Economic Development, the Ministry of Labour, the Sicily Region and the Municipality of Termini Imerese. The area is one of the 'Complex Industrial Crisis Areas' and the Sicilian Region has recently approved the reprogramming of an agreement for the implementation of strategic works in the port and its industrial zone for a total of approximately EUR 120 million [23]. Among the planned interventions is the construction of a road connection between the port and

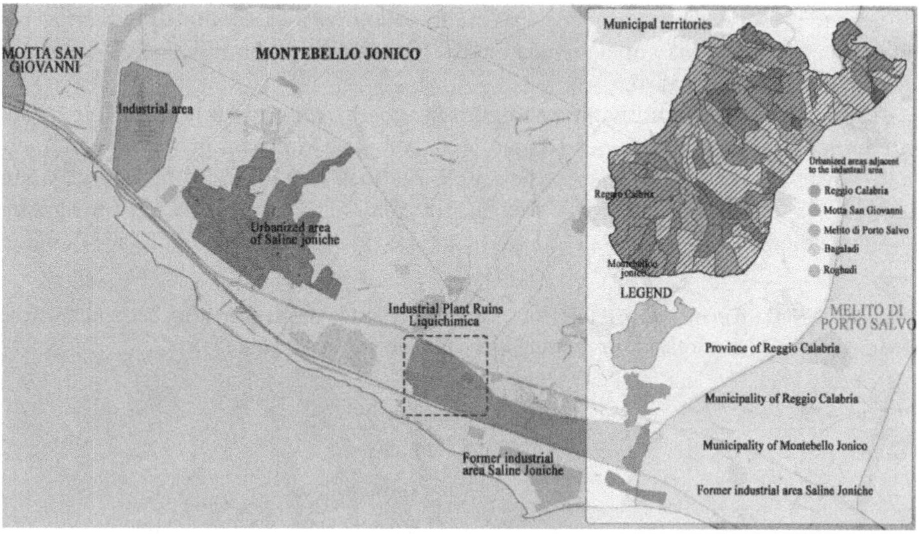

AREA OF INFLUENCE OF THE INDUSTRIAL AREA OF REGGIO CALABRIA

Fig. 2. Saline Joniche Industrial Area (Site number 3), Calabria. Source: graphic project by Federica Sortino.

State Road 113. Among the rescheduled interventions are also road connections, the completion of the wharf, and the construction of a fibre optic system.

The current need for port infrastructure renewal is part of a broader programme of territorial regeneration, outlined in the Strategic Planning Document of the Western Sicily Sea Port System (DPSS), approved by the Services Conference in 2022. This document constitutes the strategic framework for the enhancement and adaptation of the port systems of Palermo, Termini Imerese, Trapani and Porto Empedocle, with the aim of promoting integrated development in the commercial, infrastructural, tourist and urban sectors of Central-Western Sicily. A pivotal element of the DPSS is the redevelopment of the land-sea interface, no longer conceived exclusively as a transit point for goods and passengers, but as a strategic lever for economic growth and urban regeneration. In this perspective, the port of Termini Imerese is the subject of a transformation process aimed at integrating commercial functions with a new tourist vocation, favouring a mixed infrastructural set-up capable of combining economic needs with the enhancement of the territory [24]. The evolution of the port system is set in an urban context marked by an industrial crisis that began with the closure of the FIAT plant in the second decade of the year two thousand. The industrialisation that began in the 1970s initially produced economic growth, but this was followed by a progressive decline due to the ineffective management of the industrial decommissioning process.

The problem lies not so much in the establishment of a production pole, but in the manner of its realisation and subsequent decommissioning, which generated negative effects on the urban and social fabric. The transition to a tourist destination raises significant questions regarding the adjacent industrial areas. The increase in tourist traffic could stimulate investments aimed at redeveloping disused spaces, encouraging the reconversion of areas into accommodation, commercial and cultural facilities. However, the need to preserve the attractiveness of the area requires the adoption of more rigorous environmental policies, with actions aimed at reclamation and mitigation of impacts in areas that are still degraded.

The area is also culturally interesting for the nearby ruins of Himera and the related antiquarium, for the presence of Roman archaeological sites and prehistoric artefacts. In the lower part of the town is the thermal spa of the Grand Hotel delle Terme, where fine volcanic-derived waters flow. In its territory, and in the nearby towns of Sciara and Caccamo, there is the Mount San Calogero Oriented Nature Reserve (Fig. 3 and Table 3).

Table 3. Descriptive-analytical table site 3 depotenziated industrial area of Termini Imerese. Methodology: Celestina Fazia; processing and compilation: Federica Sortino.

Site number:	Site number 3
Region:	Sicily
City:	Termini Imerese
Name:	Industrial Area of Termini Imerese
Expected functions:	Industrial production, specialisation in the automotive and chemical sectors
Age of construction:	First plants in the 1950s
Dimensions (range):	> 10,000 sqm (large industrial area)
Relationship with the urbanized context:	Exterior near urban areas: area between Termini and Himera
Relationship with port area:	Existing connection to the local port
Current state of use:	Used, but downsized/ partially decommissioned: numerous warehouses abandoned for decades
Conversion implemented or in progress:	Recovery projects in progress: redevelopment planned and in progress with the Pelligra Group
Environmental constraints present:	-
Environmental criticalities and vulnerabilities of the study area and context:	Significant structural and urban decay of the area
Contaminated site:	Potentially present (former industrial area with chemical activities)
Widespread urban decay:	Present (visible decay in warehouses)
Lack of services and social hardship:	Present (economic decline and loss of employment)
Recovery difficulties attributable to:	significant costs; contaminated site; bureaucratic and administrative criticalities

AREA OF INFLUENCE OF THE INDUSTRIAL AREA OF TERMINI IMERESE

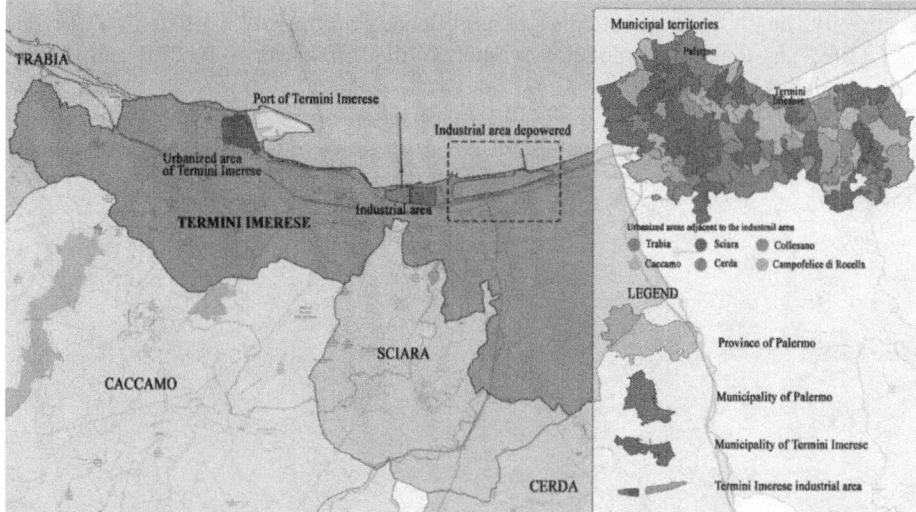

Fig. 3. Industrial area of Termini Imerese (site number 4), Sicily. Source: graphic project by Federica Sortino.

4 Strategic Solutions and Future Perspectives

The current degradation of the case studies analysed raises questions about recovery and regeneration through a project that enhances the traces of the past. These signs, instead of being erased, can become identity elements and seeds of new possibilities, reinterpreted as a memory to be preserved and a resource for the future.

A small example could be the chimney of Saline Joniche, of the former Liquichimica Biosintesi, which towers slender in the surroundings with its 174 m in height. For some, it is seen merely as a monument to the neglect and failure of a state industrialisation project that never really got off the ground and exposed the local population to serious environmental risks, bringing devastation to the area and deeply marking its recent history. And in line with this vision, again in Calabria, in the last months of 2024 the demolition of the chimneys of the Enel power station in Rossano began, seen as the last symbol to be hit of the industrialisation of the Sibaritide that never took place.

Yet it is precisely that slender concrete chimney stretching skywards that could itself become, within a broader project of architectural, urban, social and economic regeneration, an important and representative emblem of hope. Naturally framed within a wide-ranging intervention, envisaging recovery and regeneration actions for the entire area with new and different cultural, recreational, economic and social functions.

We need only think of exemplary industrial archaeology projects, barely mentioned in the previous paragraph, such as the iconic tower of the Tate Modern in London (Fig. 4), which stands inside a disused power station, designed by the Swiss firm Herzog & de Meuron, and has been one of the world's most popular museums of modern and contemporary art for several years now. "Tate Modern has changed London since 2000.

The impact it has had on urban design and the development of the South Bank and Southwark, has been as substantial as its influence on the city's artistic, cultural and social life," say the Swiss architects, winners of the Pritzker Prize in 2001 and students of the Italian Aldo Rossi.

Fig. 4. Tate Gallery of Modern Art with the tower of the former Bankside Power Station towering over the Thames and the City of London, 2019. Source: Photo by Clara Stella Vicari Aversa, 2019.

The two designers achieved fame precisely with this project to convert the former power station on the south bank of the Thames and, as further confirmation that this is the right approach, not only has the project become one of the most iconic museums in all of Europe but the same method has been taken up by the same designers and followed by many other designers, also for many other contexts in more recently regenerated former industrial areas. One thinks of Hamburg's HafenCity district, the protagonist of a vast urban and social redevelopment plan, where the Elbphilharmonie is also located, of which Herzog & de Meuron themselves chose to safeguard the existing volume, albeit internally emptied to house the new functions once used as a warehouse, with a trapezoidal plan and solid load-bearing structure - so as to support the weight of the thousands of sacks of cocoa it housed - further enhancing its image of solidity and compactness, to reuse it architecturally as the base of the new complex that stands, even more elevated and evident, on the tip of the new regenerated port. A graft to be looked to for possible recovery projects for the Puleo steam brickworks.

An emblematic example of architectural regeneration is London's Battersea Power Station on the Thames (Fig. 5), a historic coal-fired power station closed in 1986 and becoming a national monument thanks to its iconic four white smokestacks, long a part of the London skyline and a cultural symbol featured in films, video clips and on the famous cover of Pink Floyd's Animals. The ambitious restoration project, by Wilkinson Eyre [25], has transformed the power station into a multifunctional hub with 250 shops, restaurants, the 46,000 m2 Apple campus, leisure spaces, London's first Art'otel, over 250 residences and a panoramic glass lift inside one of the chimneys [26]. The latter take on a new landscape and symbolic value, dominating the view from the rooftop gardens designed by Foster + Partners and the Rooftop Pool Overlooking Battersea Power Station

Fig. 5. Battersea Power Station; London, 2023. Source: wilkinsoneyre.com/projects/battersea-power-station

[27]. The project is based on principles of integrated sustainability - environmental, economic and social - and aims to create a zero-energy neighbourhood. As stated by the architects: "we provide innovative, efficient and beautiful design solutions that strike a balance between ethical, environmental, social and economic sustainability" [28].

Like the chimneys of London, the soaring chimneys of Saline Joniche and the former Puleo steam brick factory, finally stripped of their shame and charged with a new pride, could become a highly iconic and emblematic element of the broader process of architectural regeneration of the entire area. Why then is there still talk of erasing traces of the past and demolishing what is still considered the shame of a time gone by? We need to know the past, not to deny it, but to look to the future with strength and awareness.

However, the example of London's Battersea Power Station, while representing one of the most fascinating contemporary reuse operations, also demonstrates the risks of a certain kind of regeneration: gentrification phenomena, loss of authenticity, limited accessibility for local communities and commodification of heritage have turned a site of collective memory into a luxury neighbourhood. For this reason, Battersea may be an excellent example to observe, but it is also a warning: the side effects of such transformations need to be governed and mitigated so that regeneration is truly inclusive, sustainable and respectful of the context.

It is essential that signs of the past remain legible in reuse projects, in order to give a new conscious meaning to disused industrial areas. Intervention must enhance the existing character and fit into contemporary spatial strategies, promoting an active memory and new opportunities for future reuse. It is no longer the time for the tabula rasa, but rather the time for the project of reusing the "masterless warehouses" or the "recycled ruins", which after all also belong to the "specific universe of Italian architecture, from the monuments of ancient Rome a hundred times recycled" [29]. Regenerating industrial heritage requires integrated strategies, targeted funding and participatory approaches that enhance the traces of the past in a sustainable way by proposing approaches that are as inclusive as possible and avoid marginalising vulnerable groups. It is necessary to intervene with measured and respectful projects, capable of transforming the existing without erasing its identity and cultural value. Interventions must have a naturally regenerative character not only for the areas themselves, but also for their immediate and nearby surroundings.

Also in this context, the words written 25 years ago by the two Swiss architects mentioned above, regarding the guiding architectural strategies of the project, resound prophetic and enlightening, words that were used for the competition in London but that can and should resonate every time we approach new and different regeneration interventions: "Working on the existing and its constraints requires a different creative energy. In the near future this will be an increasingly important issue in cities all over Europe. Because you cannot always start from scratch" [30].

5 Conclusions

Industrial tourism and the valorisation of historical, architectural and landscape heritage represent a possible lever for the valorisation of disused manufacturing assets. The preservation of historical and architectural value, combined with the integration of new cultural and creative functions, makes it possible to transform abandoned areas into vital resources for society. The national and international examples cited in the paper show that the success of these interventions depends on the ability to balance protection, innovation and sustainability. The limitations that have emerged, and the restraining factors, can be attributed to the particular size of the sites (Saline joniche, for example), the complexity of the environmental issues (all three case studies) and the administrative procedures, linked to the protection regime. From the analyses of the case studies, thanks to the proposed reading methods, it emerged the need to implement projects for the regeneration of industrial areas that are synergic and in a sustainable and innovative key, also by developing, for example, risk assessment and risk management approaches.

More and more frequently today, in fact, we are faced with climatic events of extraordinary magnitude, which, for example, could jeopardise not only homes, but also production and plants, or compromise the functionality of infrastructures serving the same companies, such as sewerage and drainage systems. Here, a series of preventive actions and operational solutions for climate risk management can increase the resilience of businesses and the chances of success of planned regeneration projects. All this is also intertwined with the natural choice and awareness towards the integration of new uses and functions, compatible with the new redeveloped places but above all capable of activating new ways of regeneration. It is necessary that these problematic abandoned areas become a "resource for transformation" [31] and that new spaces flourish that are capable of restoring a collective and shared dimension, activating a strategic role in the construction of the rediscovered identity of the places themselves.

Contribution Authors. Although the research is the result of the work carried out jointly by all the authors, which Celestina Fazia and Clara Stella Vicari Aversa are the supervisor, the drafting of the essay is to be attributed differently to each of them: § Abstract, by Celestina Fazia, Kh Md Nahiduzzaman, Federica Sortino; § 1. Introduction by Celestina Fazia, Kh Md Nahiduzzaman, Clara Stella Vicari Aversa, Federica Sortino; § 2. Abandoned or depleted industrial areas: differences and opportunities by Cristina Natoli; § 3. Case studies by Celestina Fazia, Federica Sortino, Clara Stella Vicari Aversa; § 4. Strategic solutions and future perspectives by Clara Stella Vicari Aversa; § 4. Conclusions, by Celestina Fazia, Clara Stella Vicari Aversa, Kh Md Nahiduzzaman, Cristina Natoli. The contributions are outcomes of some research carried out by the authors in their respective laboratories and in a joint convention related to "A.Ma.Te sponde", Agreement between Department of Architecture and Territory of the Mediterranean University of Reggio Calabria and Department of Engineering and Architecture of Kore University of Enna.

References

1. Russo, M.: Aree dismesse. Forma e risorsa della «città esistente». Ed. Scientifiche Italiane, Napoli (1998)
2. Negri, M., Politini, S.: Metamorfosi Urbane. Milano dall'archeologia industriale agli stili di vita del XXI secolo. Milano, Urban Center (2018). https://www.artribune.com/mostre-evento-arte/metamorfosi-urbane/
3. Natoli, C., Ramello, M.F.: Strategie di rigenerazione del patrimonio industriale. Creative factory, heritage telling, temporary use, business model. Edifir, Firenze (2017)
4. Preite, M., Maciocco, G.: Fabbriche ritrovate. Patrimonio industriale e progetto di architettura in Italia. Effigi, Roma (2021)
5. Tonkin Zulaikha Greer: Carriageworks Arts Centre. https://tzg.com.au/project/carriageworks-arts-centre/. Accessed 12 Feb 2025
6. De Manincor, J.: Carriageworks. Architecture Australia (2007). https://architectureau.com/articles/carriageworks/. Accessed 12 Feb 2025
7. Rogic, T.: Transformation of the Bankside Power Station into the Tate Modern in London: subversiveness of The Old. In: Overolland **4**, pp. 101–114 (2016)
8. Robiglio, M.: Re-USA: 20 American Stories of Adaptive Reuse. A Toolkit for Post-Industrial Cities. Jovis, Berlin (2017). https://www.artribune.com/professioni-e-professionisti/who-is-who/2018/05/intervista-matteo-robiglio/
9. Farnham Maltings. https://farnhammaltings.com/. Accessed 12 Feb 2025
10. Gazzetta Ufficiale: Serie Generale, n.110 del 13–05–2011, D.L. 70/2011 Decreto Sviluppo; Serie Generale, n.166 del 16–07–1941, Legge 22 aprile 1941, n. 633 Protezione diritto d'autore
11. Fernández Jubín, S.: De la antigua Fábrica de Tabacos de San Sebastián a la nueva Tabakalera: un estudio integral. In: E-RPH Revista electrónica de Patrimonio Histórico **34**, pp. 86–126 (2024). https://doi.org/10.30827/erph.34.2024.28431
12. Pietrangeli, M.: Atelier(s) Alfonso Femia *AF517 tra recupero e innovazione: i Docks di Marsiglia. In: Metamorfosi – Quaderni di architettura **4**, 116–121 (2018)
13. Jansen, M., Brandellero, A., van Houwelingen, R.: Port-city transition: past and emerging socio-spatial imaginaries and uses in rotterdam's makers district. In: Urban Planning **6**(3), 166–180 (2021). https://doi.org/10.17645/up.v6i3.4253
14. Caridà, F.: Rotterdam e la controversia delle trasformazioni di una città in movimento. Analisi del quartiere di Merwe-Vierhavens attraverso attori e contesto e formulazione di scenari progettuali per sua riqualificazione. Master's thesis, Politecnico di Torino (2022)

15. Frediani, G.: HafenCity Hamburg. In: Paesaggio Urbano. Urban Design **1**, pp. 57–79 (2011)
16. Pileri, M.A.: Quando a Palermo si facevano i mattoni (2024). https://www.palermoviva.it/quando-a-palermo-si-facevano-i-mattoni/. Accessed 17 Feb 2025
17. Fatta, G.: Architettura e tecnica nella costruzione del teatro Massimo VE di Palermo. In: Meccanica dei Materiali e delle Strutture 1 (2012)
18. Agnello, F.: Il disegno dei luoghi della produzione: tecniche/tecnologie. Tre esempi siciliani fra XVIII e XIX secolo. PhD thesis, Università di Palermo (1995)
19. Mauro, P., Pileri, M.A.: Palermo, La costa e la "mattoneria a vapore Puleo", riuso e riqualificazione: un istituto di biologia marina. Master's thesis, Università degli Studi di Palermo (2004)
20. Regione Siciliana: Piano territoriale paesistico regionale. Palermo (1999)
21. Assemblea Regionale Siciliana: Resoconto stenografico della 229ª seduta della XIII legislatura (2004)
22. Martino, G., Tralongo, S.: L'Avifauna della ZSC IT9350143 Saline Joniche e zone umide limitrofe: check-list commentata. In: Gli Uccelli d'Italia **46**, 162–180 (2021)
23. Barrilea, V., et al.: Realtà aumentata e tecniche di geomatica per la valorizzazione del patrimonio sottomarino. In: LaborEst **21**, 5–9 (2020)
24. Regione Siciliana: Termini Imerese, Accordo Irsap-Comune. https://www.regione.sicilia.it/la-regione-informa/termini-imerese-accordo-irsap-comune. Accessed 17 February 2025
25. Autorità di Sistema Portuale del Mare della Sicilia Occidentale: Documento di Programmazione Strategica del Sistema Portuale del Mare di Sicilia Occidentale. https://adsppalermo.portaletrasparenza.net/it/trasparenza/pianificazione-e-governo-del-territorio.html. Accessed 13 February 2025
26. Battersea Power Station, UK. https://batterseapowerstation.co.uk/
27. Editorial team: Two Foster + Partners buildings near Battersea Power Station completed. In: Domusweb (2024). www.domusweb.it/en/news/gallery/2024/06/16/battersea-roof-gardens-and-50-electric-boulevard-in-london-completed.html
28. Wilkinson Eyre: Battersea Power Station, UK. https://www.wilkinsoneyre.com/projects/battersea-power-station last accessed 13 February 2025
29. Ciorra, P.: Per un'architettura non edificante. In: Ciorra, P., Marini, S. (eds.) Recycle, Electa, Milano, p. 22 (2011)
30. Herzog, J., De Meuron, P.: The Tate Modern Project, Competition 2005, Project 2005–2012, Realization 2010–2016, London, UK. https://www.herzogdemeuron.com/projects/263-the-tate-modern-project/. Accessed 13 February 2025
31. Secchi, B.: Le condizioni sono cambiate. In: Casabella 498, Italy (1984)

Cities, Technologies and Planning 2025 (CTP 2025)

Communal Level Cybersecurity Incidents in the Slovak Republic

Miroslav Fečko, Ondrej Mitaľ(✉), and Silvia Ručinská

Department of Public Policy and Theory of Public Administration, Faculty of Public Administration, Pavol Jozef Šafárik University in Košice, 04011 Košice, Slovak Republic
{miroslav.fecko,ondrej.mital,silvia.rucinska}@upjs.sk

Abstract. The study investigates issues surrounding cybersecurity, one of the crucial topics connected with digital transformation of society. Municipalities and cities help to shape digital transformation at local level, mainly thanks to growing use of digital solutions. This tendency also leads to higher vulnerability of municipalities and cities. The study uses a literature review and multiple case study method to examine the relevance of bottom-up approach of municipalities and cities in building cybersecurity and responding to cyberattacks. Regarding the conditions of the Slovak Republic and increasing occurrence of cyberattacks targeting municipalities and cities, 5 cases of cyberattacks were analysed, focusing on mainly on type of the attacks and caused impact. The main benefit of the study is contribution to existing empirical findings that confirm the importance of bottom-up approaches in cybersecurity agenda at local level. Municipalities and cities have become relevant actors that utilize outcomes of digital transformation on local communities, but also important actors that can formulate locally specific cybersecurity policies and face cyberattacks.

Keywords: Cybersecurity · cyberattacks · cyberincidents · municipalities and cities · bottom-up approaches · local public policies · Slovak Republic

1 Introduction

The digital transformation of society increases the use of digital technologies and new innovative solutions in almost every aspect of social life. This trend is notably identified at various levels of governance, including municipalities and cities nearest to the citizens. The implementation of new technologies facilitates the rationalisation of competencies´ execution and the provision of public services, leading to an improvement in the quality of life among local communities. This shift not only optimises the execution of competencies but also improves the responsiveness of local governments to the needs and preferences of their communities, ensuring more effective service delivery [26, 73].

At the same time, public sector organisations that use digital technologies daily are becoming more vulnerable. Cyberattacks are increasingly targeting cities and municipalities, which often have very limited resources for cybersecurity, thus, cyberattacks pose active threats to the security of public life and citizens at the local level [20, 46, 64]. The increase in cyberattacks has led to a stronger focus on the importance of cybersecurity at all levels of governance, including municipalities and cities.

This study aims to realize preliminary research on the bottom-up responses of local governments in the face of cyberattacks. Using a multiple case study methodology, the study examines examples of cyberattacks on municipalities and cities within the Slovak Republic from 2018 to 2025. The selection of case studies on municipalities and cities helped us to identify important patterns and demonstrate the variety of cyberattacks suffered.

2 Local Government and Cybersecurity – Understanding and Challenges

2.1 Importance of Cities and Municipalities in Contemporary Democracies

Local government's current role and importance reflect decentralisation tendencies in a democratic state governed by the rule of law [62, 78]. Municipalities and cities have a natural tendency to face modern trends and challenges, thanks to which they can enrich their own functioning but mainly improve the provision of services to citizens and entrepreneurs living and residing in the given territory [71].

Many municipalities and cities, therefore, develop individual governance approaches and policies as they try to respond to different challenges and meet local stakeholders' needs [7, 81]. Local level of government is directly involved in exploring what can be achieved together with other local stakeholders, what problems can be solved, and how [8, 17]. Municipalities and cities concentrate their power and resources on providing various types of public services, mainly to increase the quality of life in a particular territory.

Municipalities and cities can be perceived as actors with a natural tendency to face modern trends and challenges, thanks to which they can enrich their functioning and execution of original and transferred competencies, but mainly improve the provision of public goods and quality of life. As irreplaceable actor in the policy process, municipalities and cities can participate in national public policies and create their own specific local public policies. Sometimes, the voice of the lowest level of public administration is the only one that can affect the outcome of higher levels of public policies in current states. Put differently, central governments are often unable to register and solve all public issues at the municipal level of governance. In other cases, municipalities and cities must react quickly because central governments need time to formulate and implement local public policy. This tendency is also underlined by the fact that municipalities and cities represent the level of governance, which can be considered as the nearest to citizens´ everyday life needs [66, 70].

2.2 Municipalities and Cities in the Centre of Digital Transition

Municipalities and cities play a central role in their rapid and sustainable development, which helps them address a wide range of contemporary challenges [25]. Cities face more significant pollution, more traffic congestion, and higher demand for energy and sanitation services due to urban growth, thus, to resolve the problems associated with urbanisation, the cities should incorporate smart solutions [2, 75]. From the practical point of view, the important role of municipalities and cities as policy actors are irreplaceable, as was proven many times in various local public issues, such as sustainable development [9, 50], health and wellbeing [55, 68], climate change adaptation and mitigation [11, 16], as well as digital transformation [31, 57]. Mainly, digital transformation is mostly outlined as a crosscutting trend that affects many other challenges and issues in municipalities and cities [26, 35].

The complexity of managing life in municipalities and cities requires new methods and smart, innovative ways to deal with urbanisation and foster more efficient, sustainable, and habitable urban areas [10, 15]. Cities use ICT and digital solutions to improve residents' living conditions, mainly through their interconnection with other aspects of the territory [4, 49].

Municipalities and cities are increasingly dependent on digital technologies that help them rationalise their roles and competencies, making them vulnerable [6, 21, 80]. Vulnerability is higher, especially in cities that aim to be digital or technological leaders [28, 38]. The rapid growth of hyperconnectivity and digitalisation in cities accelerated interest in cybersecurity issues worldwide [14, 39, 63, 65].

2.3 Cybersecurity as a Complex Agenda for Municipalities and Cities

Cybersecurity can be defined as the adoption of real-time monitoring, detection, and identification technology to protect systems, networks, and programs from potential threats, attacks, and data leakage [40]. At the local level, especially in municipalities and cities, an integrated cybersecurity framework must be seen through a holistic approach, which includes mainly a digital trust platform, cyber response and resilience, privacy by design, cyber competencies and awareness program, cyber threat intelligence and analysis platform [63].

Cybersecurity can also be explored as a strategy for organisations to protect networks, computers, programs, and data from attacks, damage, or unauthorised access [39]. Cybersecurity encompasses a broad range of practices, tools and concepts related closely to those of information and operational technology security [30]. Summing it up, cybersecurity has emerged as a critical part of modern urban governance at the local level, as municipalities and cities should reflect their responsibilities beyond traditional physical infrastructure and in cyberspace [37].

Cybersecurity solutions are a result of the intensive use of digital transformation and cyberattacks [33, 44]. Considering the responsibility of local governments to protect their assets, cybersecurity has become among other important functions important function because governments are under constant or nearly constant cyberattacks [3, 60]. Cyberthreats are increasing and local governments are often under-resourced and underprepared for them [27]. The increasing number of researchers demonstrates that cyberattacks at the local level are ubiquitous and can happen at any time without any indication [40, 52]. The nature of cyberattacks and threats can vary, which in turn affects the character and impact of cyber incidents affecting the functioning of IT systems and public services [5, 53]. A cyber incident occurs when a cyberattack affects the confidentiality, integrity, or availability of an IT system [18, 58]. In other words, a cyberattack is the event that leads to the declaration of a cyberincident.

Cities should deal with different types of cyberattacks that may influence the proper execution of their functions, such as device hijacking, data theft, distributed denial of services (DDoS), man-in-the-middle attacks, and permanent denial of services (PDoS) [42]. This typology of cyberattacks can be widened, and based on the CyberPeace Institute analysis, the public sector and public administration face various cyber incidents, mainly DDoS attacks, wiper attacks, malware attacks, hack and leak, defacement, cyber-enabled information operations, cyber espionage, and ransomware [19]. To be more concrete, cyberattacks in the public sector can include following malicious actions, botnet, email compromise, denial of service (DOD) or distributed denial of service (DDOS), hack or leak, phishing, malware, malvertising, man in the middle, ransomware, spear-phishing, supply chain attack or zero-day [43]. The European Agency for Cybersecurity defines the content of cyberattacks mainly as ransomware, malware, social engineering threats, threats against data, threats against the availability of services, threats against the availability of the internet, disinformation or misinformation, and supply chain threats [24]. The main cyberattacks which may occur at the communal level's smart applications are denial of service, malware, eavesdropping, identity spoofing, false information, message modification, and traffic analysis [1, 54].

The local level of governance can be extremely vulnerable to cyberattacks for different reasons. The most common reasons for the vulnerability of municipalities and cities to cyberattacks include mainly, the sensitivity of data, the hundreds of different-sized entities that make it challenging to handle, budgetary and personal limits of local governance, confidential document sharing with other parts of public administration, as well as the popularity of digital solutions among the local stakeholders [37].

The rising occurrence of cyberattacks at the communal level forces cities and municipalities to reconsider cybersecurity policies and cybersecurity plans significantly [28, 34, 51, 60]. The legal norms' amendments must also reflect conceptual changes and the reflection of cyberattacks in strategies and plans [41]. Put differently, technological and legal aspects cannot be separated in planning and implementing cybersecurity measures [45]. In this regard, responses to cyberattacks should be primarily observed at the organisational level of municipalities and cities. However, cybersecurity issues can also be pushed to the level of personal behaviour to utilise the personal aspect of cybersecurity [79]. Thus, cybersecurity in municipalities and cities is also the issue of individuals' awareness and preparedness. The cybersecurity topics discussed can be seen as essential for the future development of the field and can also be explored as standalone questions.

Growing attention is cybersecurity at the local level, gaining not only in practice but also in research. Cybersecurity issues and cyberattacks were precisely analysed in Sweden [3], United States of America [59], Poland [23, 41], Italy [14], England and Wales [13], and Ukraine [29]. In this regard, there is an urgent and significant need for deeper research on local cybersecurity in order to make cybersecurity in local government more effective and resilient [67].

3 Methodology

This study aims to realize preliminary research on the bottom-up responses of local governments in the face of cyberattacks. Using a multiple case study methodology, the study examines examples of cyberattacks on municipalities and cities within the Slovak Republic from 2018 to 2025. The research question aims to analyse whether cybersecurity can be assumed as a significant priority and policy agenda at the local level. Through this analysis, the study intends to provide valuable insights into how local governments can strengthen their cybersecurity practices and effectively tackle the challenges presented by cyber threats.

This study conducts a theoretical examination of cybersecurity issues, with particular emphasis on the impact of cyber threats and cyberattacks on municipalities and cities. Furthermore, the theoretical framework presents an analysis of the significance of local government and verifies the motivation for using a bottom-up approach to address these challenges. Through this exploration, the study aims to emphasise the essential role that municipalities and cities have in strengthening their cybersecurity practices and effectively responding to emerging digital threats.

A literature review was used to integrate findings and perspectives from empirical findings. Previous research was investigated to demonstrate the contemporary state of knowledge and relationship between bottom-up responses of local government and cybersecurity issues. Theoretical analysis was used to analyze the contemporary state of research focusing on the phenomenon of cybersecurity and cyberattacks in the conditions of cities and municipalities.

In this study, we will therefore pay attention to cyberattacks cases on municipalities and cities in the conditions of the Slovak Republic. The multiple case study method was selected. The multiple case study method helps to analyse and compare conducted data to understand the similarities and differences between the cases [32, 82]. Case studies focus the attention on a description of the subject who was the target of the cyberattack, a description of the attacker and possible motives, an analysis of the cyber incident and its impacts, a description of providing information on cyberattack to the public, and also the context of the cyberattacks and created impacts. Although the attacker's identity and the cyberattack's character are important, this study primarily focuses on the significant impact of these incidents on municipalities and cities.

The analysed case studies were selected to demonstrate similarities and differences between different types of cyberattacks. In this regard, the study does not offer a comprehensive analysis of all cyberattacks on public institutions in the Slovak Republic. The selection of case studies on municipalities and cities helped us to identify important patterns and demonstrate the variety of cyberattacks suffered. The multiple case studies method leads to stronger knowledge and lessons learned from cyberattacks.

4 Results

The following case studies analyse cyberattacks on municipalities and cities in the Slovak Republic. Each of the five case studies includes a description of the subject who was the target of the cyberattack, a description of the attacker and possible motives, an analysis of the cyber incident and its impacts, a description of providing information on cyberattack to the public, and also the context of the cyberattacks and created impacts. The identity of the attacker and the character of the cyberattack are indeed important components of the overall analysis. However, this study primarily concentrates on the impact of such incidents on municipalities and cities. Understanding these consequences is essential for examining the responses of local governments to cyber threats.

4.1 Case 1 - Attack Motivated by a Global Event

The capital city of Slovakia, Bratislava, suffered a cyberattack on Wednesday, May 31, 2023. An unnamed hacker group claimed responsibility for the realisation of this cyberattack. The group mentioned that one of the reasons for their activity is that the city was hosting an international conference with global impact focused on global security issues, GLOBSEC, organised by a think-tank established in Bratislava.

As a consequence of the cyberattack, the services of the PAAS-regulated parking system, the services of the city's public transport company, the city's website and other city services were denied and declared inoperable [12, 22]. At the same time, the city´s management guaranteed that the datasets were not lost or endangered. Most IT systems affected by the cyberattack, as well as the city's website, were restored the next day [12]. Information about the cyberattack was published on the city's website, official social media pages, as well as regional and national media. The information provided to the public was consistently updated and made readily available, ensuring timely and relevant access to necessary insights.

Cyberattack occurred during a global event has an ambition to spread fear and uncertainty among citizens, but also participants of the conference from all over the world. In this regard, the potential intention of the attackers was to create an impression that the city´s management cannot handle this kind of global event, and also that such kind of events may lead to discomfort of citizens caused by the denial of important public services. Nevertheless, the unnamed hacker group accomplished their goal and disrupted the functioning of digital solutions adopted by the city. However, the approach of the city in this situation can be perceived as appropriate.

4.2 Case 2 - Attack on IT Systems

On October 26, 2021, the city office in the city of Malacky suffered a cyberattack. No specific entity claimed responsibility for the attack, but indications pointed to the attack being carried out from abroad [56]. In this case, the attacker and the attacker's motive for the cyberattack are unknown.

The cyberattack targeted the city's IT systems. The cyberattack caused delays in processing public complaints and proposals, and at the same time, limited and slowed down communication between the public and the city office [56, 76]. In this case, the public was informed about the cyberattack via the city's website and regional media. The information provided to the public was consistently updated and made readily available, ensuring timely and relevant access to necessary insights.

In this case, a cyberattack leads to the immediate disruption of the city´s office functioning. Even when the extent of harm from the cyberattack had not been verified at the time of the cyberattack, the city office correctly informed its citizens.

4.3 Case 3 - Attack on Critical Infrastructure

On January 24, 2025, the city of Trenčín suffered a cyberattack, targeting a part of critical infrastructure, the Trenčín Waterworks and Sewerage. While the identity of the attackers remains uncertain, the incident aimed to threaten the delivery of one of the essential public services. The attacker´s anonymity also makes it impossible to identify the motive that led to the cyberattack.

In this case, the cyberattack was successfully stopped before causing a negative impact. The Trenčín Waterworks and Sewerage organisation´s cyber protection was very well secured, so the attackers did not infiltrate the IT system, and no data was lost or compromised [69].

The city´s management informed the public of the cyber incident afterwards. The public was assured that the critical infrastructure object and its functionality were not compromised.

Analysed cyberattack on the critical infrastructure was successfully stopped thanks to the existing cyber protection framework. City´s decision not to inform immediately can be perceived as very rational, thus, the public was informed after a precise check status of waterworks and sewerage systems. Informing the public without checking the operability could cause the spread of panic and fear. In this regard, the intention of the attackers to cause the mentioned negative impacts was not achieved.

4.4 Case 4 - Stolen Public Funds

In January 2024, the municipality of Kojšov became the target of a cyberattack. This incident was targeted towards the acquisition of public funds from the municipal office bank account. The identities of the attacker and the basic motives for their actions remain unverified and cannot be objectively confirmed.

As a direct financial impact of the cyberattack, public funds of up to 10,000 € were stolen from the bank account of the municipality of Kojšov [61]. In this case, the cyberattack was proven as a phishing attack, which was confirmed by law enforcement entities and also the bank in which the municipality has its bank account [48].

Information about the cyberattack was immediately published on the city website, as well as regional and national media. Information, including the results of the investigation, was published with the use of the same communication channels.

The character of this cyberattack is in its comparison to previous ones, different in that the harm caused by the attackers cannot be restored to the original state. In this regard, attackers have achieved their goal and have received the mentioned amount of public funds.

4.5 Case 5 - Attack from the Internal Environment

The city district of Košice, particularly the Sídlisko KVP, was the target of a cyberattack in November 2019. The cyberattack was carried out by an anonymous attacker, thus, the motives of the cyberattacks also remain unknown.

The attackers caused failures of the IT systems on the server and damaged the information and data stored on the server, while the virus on the server caused partial data loss, inoperability of email communication, and data on invoices and financial statements has been compromised [47]. The attack was carried out from within the city district itself, directly in the city office building, by intentionally attacking the server [77].

Information about the attack was provided after the attack, via the website, and regional and national media. The official statement of the city district summarises all known details on the cyberattack.

This case is very specific because it is the only case where a cyberattack was realised during the physical presence of the attacker in the building of the city office. Besides, only in this case was the permanent loss of data achieved by the attackers.

5 Discussion

Municipalities and cities as actors of digital transformation must reflect cybersecurity issues and cyber threats. Due to the rise in cyberattacks in the public sector from intensive digitalisation, we would expect the central government to address this challenge.

As municipalities and cities increasingly engage in digital transformation, it is inevitable that they will become potential targets for cyberattacks. Both theory and practice have confirmed that municipalities and cities are the target of cyberattacks due to the intensive digitalisation of the execution of competencies and the provision of public services. Table 1 includes a comprehensive summarisation of analysed cases focusing on the analysed aspects of cyberattacks.

Municipalities and cities can be perceived as targets of cyberattacks, regardless of their size and territorial location. The abovementioned cases demonstrated that cyberattacks might occur in the capital city with almost 500,000 citizens, but also in a city with almost 20,000 citizens (Malacky) or less than 700 citizens (Kojšov).

Identification of attackers can be very difficult in cyberattack cases. Claiming responsibility for the attack by a specific attacker or a group of attackers is usually the only opinion that can help during this process. Such identification with cyberattacks is usually associated with the need to gain attention and grow the attackers' reputation.

In four out of five cases, the attackers focused their attention on the operability or functioning of IT systems, servers or the provision of public services. Case 3 also demonstrated that critical infrastructure at the local level is a target of cyberattacks. At the same time, Case 4 demonstrated that even a relatively small amount of finances is still attractive for attackers.

Providing information on cyberattacks to the public can be crucial when cyberattacks cause the denial of public services. In this regard, when citizens cannot get benefits from the use of common public services, they should be informed about this discomfort. As was demonstrated by Case 3, even delaying information can be acceptable in some cases.

Table 1. Comprehensive summarisation of cyberattacks

	Size of municipality/city	Attacker	Type of incident	Impact	Information of the public
Case 1 Attack motivated by a global event	478 040	hacker group	DDoS	denial of public services, website	immediate
Case 2 Attack on IT systems	18 804	anonymous (external)	DDoS	delays in communication, processing	immediate
Case 3 Attack on critical infrastructure	55 416	anonymous (external)	infiltration to IT system	none	subsequent
Case 4 Stolen public funds	698	anonymous (external)	phishing	public funds stolen	immediate
Case 5 Attack from the internal environment	21 675	anonymous (internal)	internal intentional	IT system and server, data loss	immediate

Source: authors

The issues surrounding cybersecurity, including cyber threats and cyberattacks, are relevant to all levels of public administration, encompassing municipalities and cities. The extensive range of competencies held by municipalities and cities, along with the public services they deliver, indicates that cybersecurity may present significant challenges for local self-governing entities. The main reasons for the cybersecurity issues faced by local governments are primarily their limited human resources, a lack of skilled personnel, and financial constraints that restrict their ability to create effective cybersecurity infrastructure.

Based on the presented theories and case studies, it has been demonstrated that municipalities and cities are exposed to cyber threats and cyberattacks. Consequently, despite their restrictions and limitations, they need to prioritise the cybersecurity topic as a significant part of their agenda. In this regard, creating cybersecurity systems is not mandatory, but it is necessary to devote time and resources to it. However, the capacities for creating cybersecurity systems, evaluating cyber threats and preventing cyberattacks must be allocated at the expense of other activities, especially development and innovation.

Cybersecurity cannot be perceived as the original competence of municipalities and cities mentioned in legal acts. The significant role that municipalities and cities play in the digital transformation process necessitates that they develop their own cybersecurity systems. There are no viable alternatives for these local entities in ensuring the security and integrity of their digital infrastructure.

The significant role that municipalities and cities play in the digital transformation process pushes them to develop their cybersecurity systems. There are no viable alternatives for local entities in ensuring the security and integrity of their digital infrastructure. In this regard, the intention of municipalities and cities to solve cybersecurity issues confirms the municipalities' bottom-up strategy for addressing trends, challenges, and problems that the central government does not systematically tackle.

6 Conclusion

Challenges and issues surrounding cybersecurity and cyberattacks have evolved into a crucial topic of digital transformation, including municipalities and cities. Based on previous research, building cybersecurity systems at a local level of self-government is the result of intensive digital transformation, higher vulnerability of municipalities and cities and a trend of increasing occurrence of cyberattacks.

The results revealed that cybersecurity has evolved into an important local policy agenda, because cyberattacks target not only central state administration, but also municipalities and cities. According to the analysed case studies and negative impacts of cyberattacks, cybersecurity was identified as a local policy agenda that municipalities and cities must deal with. The analysed cyber incidents highlight the urgent need to strengthen the resilience and robustness of municipalities and cities, as they increasingly face a mixture of challenges, issues, crises and situations that require effective emergency and crisis management.

The study contributes to cybersecurity discussions at all levels of government, focusing mainly on the position of municipalities and cities. The importance of research is underlined by the increasing rate of cyberattacks targeting municipalities and cities and their digital solutions, enhancing the quality of local communities´ lives. At the same time, there are still numerous unanswered questions connected to cybersecurity at the local level. Realized research can be further extended from the following perspectives, mainly broadening empirical evidence, international comparison, analysis of cyberattacks in the context of different sophistication of cybersecurity infrastructures and solutions adopted by the municipalities and cities.

Acknowledgments. The article is created as a result of a project Cybersecurity Competence Center at Pavol Jozef Šafárik University in Košice supported by the Ministry of Investments, Regional Development and Informatisation of the Slovak Republic, Grant no: 17R05–04-V01–00007.

References

1. Al-Turjman, F., Zahmatkesh, H., Shahroze, R.: An overview of security and privacy in smart cities' IoT communications. Transactions on Emerging Telecommunications Technologies **33**(3), e3677 (2022). https://doi.org/10.1002/ett.3677
2. Andrade, R.O., Yoo, S.G., Tello-Oquendo, L., Ortiz-Garcés, I.: A comprehensive study of the iot cybersecurity in smart cities. IEEE Access **8**, 228922–228941 (2020). https://doi.org/10.1109/ACCESS.2020.3046442

3. Andreasson, A., Artman, H., Brynielsson, J., et al.: Cybersecurity work at Swedish administrative authorities: taking action or waiting for approval. Cogn. Technol. Work **26**, 709–731 (2024). https://doi.org/10.1007/s10111-024-00779-1
4. Anthony Jnr, B.: A case-based reasoning recommender system for sustainable smart city development. AI & Society: Knowledge, Culture and Communication **36**, 159–183 (2021). https://doi.org/10.1007/s00146-020-00984-2
5. Australian Government.: Information security manual. https://www.cyber.gov.au/sites/default/files/2025-03/04.%20ISM%20-%20Guidelines%20for%20cybersecurity%20incidents%20%28March%202025%29.pdf. Accessed 27 April 2025
6. Baig, Z.A., Szewczyk, P., Valli, C., Rabadia, P., et al.: Future challenges for smart cities: cyber-security and digital forensics. Digit. Investig. **22**, 3–13 (2017). https://doi.org/10.1016/j.diin.2017.06.015
7. Beck, D., Ferasso, M., Storopoli, J., Vigoda-Gadot, E.: Achieving the sustainable development goals through stakeholder value creation: Building up smart sustainable cities and communities. Journal of Cleaner Production **399**, article ID 136501 (2023) https://doi.org/10.1016/j.jclepro.2023.136501
8. Bjørgen, A., Fossheim, K., Macharis, C.: How to build stakeholder participation in collaborative urban freight planning. Cities **112**, article ID 103149 (2021) https://www.sciencedirect.com/science/article/pii/S0264275121000470
9. Blasi, S., Ganzaroli, A., De Noni, I.: Smartening sustainable development in cities: Strengthening the theoretical linkage between smart cities and SDGs. Sustainable Cities and Society **80**, article ID 103793 (2022) https://doi.org/10.1016/j.scs.2022.103793
10. Braga, I.F.B., Ferreira, F.A.F., Ferreira, J.J.M., Correia, R.J.C., Pereira, L.F., Falcão, P.F.: A DEMATEL analysis of smart city determinants. Technology in Society **66**, article ID 101687 (2021) https://doi.org/10.1016/j.techsoc.2021.101687
11. Brand, C., Götschi, T., Dons, E., Gerike, R., et al.: The climate change mitigation impacts of active travel: Evidence from a longitudinal panel study in seven European cities. Global Environmental Change **67**, article ID 102224 (2021) https://doi.org/10.1016/j.gloenvcha.2021.102224
12. BratislavaDEŇ.: Bratislava is under attack by hackers, several services are out of order. https://bratislavaden.sk/bratislava-je-pod-utokmi-hackerov-viacero-sluzieb-nefunguje/. Accessed 27 Mar 2025
13. Brett, M.: An overview of current issues and practice relating to local government cyber security in England and Wales. Cyber Security: A Peer-Reviewed Journal **4**(4), 330–344 (2021)
14. Busetti, S. Scani, F.M.: Evaluating incident reporting in cybersecurity. From threat detection to policy learning. Government Information Quarterly **42**(1), article ID 102000 (2025) https://doi.org/10.1016/j.giq.2024.102000
15. Carrasco-Farré, C., Snihur, Y., Berrone, P., Ricart, J.E.: The stakeholder value proposition of digital platforms in an urban ecosystem. Research Policy **51**(4), article ID 104488 (2022) https://doi.org/10.1016/j.respol.2022.104488
16. Ceci, M., Caselli, B., Zazzi, M.: Soil de-sealing for cities' adaptation to climate change. TeMA - Journal of Land Use, Mobility and Environment **16**(1), 121–145 (2023). https://doi.org/10.6093/1970-9870/9395
17. Clement, J., Manjon, M., Crutzen, N.: Factors for collaboration amongst smart city stakeholders: A local government perspective. Government Information Quarterly **39**(4), article ID 101746 (2022) https://doi.org/10.1016/j.giq.2022.101746
18. Cremer, F., et al.: Cyber risk and cybersecurity: a systematic review of data availability. The Geneva Papers on Risk and Insurance - Issues and Practice **47**, 698–736 (2022). https://doi.org/10.1057/s41288-022-00266-6

19. CyberPeace Institute.: Public administration: Public administration and defence; compulsory social security. https://cyberconflicts.cyberpeaceinstitute.org/impact/sectors/public-administration. Accessed 27 Mar 2025
20. CYBERSEC.: The Rise of Cyber Resilience in European Smart Cities. https://www.cybersec-365.com/articles/the-rise-of-cyber-resilience-in-european-smart-cities. Accessed 27 Mar 2025
21. de Souza, K.E., Ferrari, F.C., de Camargo, V.V., Ribeiro, M. Offutt, J.: A systematic review of fault tolerance techniques for smart city applications. Journal of Systems and Software **219**, article ID 112249 (2025) https://doi.org/10.1016/j.jss.2024.112249
22. Dopravný podnik Bratislava.: Hacker Attack Also Cranked the DPB Website. https://www.facebook.com/DPBratislava/posts/hackerský-útok-ochromil-aj-web-dpbod-dnešného-rána-čelí-bratislava-hlavné-mesto-/630368655794810/. Accessed 27 Mar 2025
23. Dudziak-Gajowiak, D., Szleszyński, A.: Resilience of public administration bodies to cyberattacks. Scientific Journal of the Military University of Land Forces **55**(3), 182–205 (2023). https://doi.org/10.5604/01.3001.0053.8961
24. European Union Agency for Cybersecurity.: ENISA Threat Landscape 2022. https://www.enisa.europa.eu/sites/default/files/publications/ENISA%20Threat%20Landscape%202022.pdf. Accessed 27 Mar 2025
25. Evans, J., Vácha, T., Kok, H., Watson, K.: How cities learn: from experimentation to transformation. Urban Planning **6**(1), 171–182 (2021). https://doi.org/10.17645/up.v6i1.3545
26. Fečko, M., Ručinská, S., Mitaľ. O.: Trends and challenges of the communal digital and green transition. In: Ručinská, S., Bernhart, J., Cecon, F., Dumitrescu, G.C. (eds.) Exploring digital and green concepts: Knowledge base for cities and municipalities. Wolters Kluwer: Praha, pp. 32–37 (2024)
27. Frandell, A., Feeney, M.: Cybersecurity threats in local government: a sociotechnical perspective. The American Review of Public Administration **52**(8), 558–572 (2022). https://doi.org/10.1177/02750740221125432
28. Fusi, F., Jung, H., Welch, E.: Technological vulnerability and knowledge of cyber-incidents: threats to innovativeness in local governments? Public Manag. Rev. **27**(3), 545–571 (2025). https://doi.org/10.1080/14719037.2023.2250362
29. Fyshchuk, I., Noesgaard, M.S., Nielsen, J.A.: Managing cyberattacks in wartime: the case of Ukraine. Public Administration Review, pp. 1–9. (2024) https://doi.org/10.1111/puar.13895
30. Galinec, D., Steingartner, W.: Combining cybersecurity and cyber defense to achieve cyber resilience. In: 2017 IEEE 14th International Scientific Conference on Informatics, Poprad, Slovakia, pp. 87–93 (2017). https://doi.org/10.1109/INFORMATICS.2017.8327227
31. Gasco-Hernandez, M., Nasi, G., Cucciniello, M., Hiedemann, A.M.: The role of organizational capacity to foster digital transformation in local governments: the case of three European smart cities. Urban Governance **2**(2), 236–246 (2022). https://doi.org/10.1016/j.ugj.2022.09.005
32. Gustafsson, J.: Single case studies vs. multiple case studies: a comparative study. https://hh.diva-portal.org/smash/get/diva2:1064378/FULLTEXT01.pdf. Accessed 27 Mar 2025
33. Hamid, B., Jhanjhi, N., Humayun, M., Khan, A., Alsayat, A.: Cyber security issues and challenges for smart cities: a survey. In: 2019 13th International Conference on Mathematics, Actuarial Science, Computer Science and Statistics (MACS), Karachi, Pakistan, pp. 1–7. (2019) https://doi.org/10.1109/MACS48846.2019.9024768
34. Hatcher, W., Meares, W.L., Heslen, J.: The cybersecurity of municipalities in the United States: an exploratory survey of policies and practices. J. Cyber Policy **5**(2), 302–325 (2020). https://doi.org/10.1080/23738871.2020.1792956
35. Holzinger, A., Weippl, E., Tjoa, A.M., Kieseberg, P.: Digital transformation for sustainable development goals (SDGs) - a security, safety and privacy perspective on AI. In: Holzinger,

36. A., Kieseberg, P., Tjoa, A.M., Weippl, E. (eds.) Machine Learning and Knowledge Extraction, vol 12844, pp. 1–20. Springer, Cham (2021) https://doi.org/10.1007/978-3-030-84060-0_1
37. Hospodárske Noviny, Bratislava was hit by a cyberattack, the city's network was overloaded. Most systems have already been restored. https://hnonline.sk/slovensko/96086311-bratislavu-postihol-kyberneticky-utok-mestska-siet-bola-pretazena-vaecsinu-systemov-uz-obnovili. Accessed 27 Mar 2025
38. Hossain, T.S., Yigitcanlar, T., Nguyen, K., Xu, Y.: Cybersecurity in local governments: a systematic review and framework of key challenges. Urban Governance (2025). https://doi.org/10.1016/j.ugj.2024.12.010
39. Houichi, M., Jaidi, F., Bouhoula, A.: Cyber security within smart cities: a comprehensive study and a novel intrusion detection-based approach. Computers, Materials & Continua **81**(1), 393–441 (2024) https://doi.org/10.32604/cmc.2024.054007
40. Chaudhuri, A., Bozkus Kahyaoglu, S.: Cybersecurity assurance in smart cities: a risk management perspective. EDP Audit, Control, and Security Newsletter **67**(4), 1–22 (2023). https://doi.org/10.1080/07366981.2023.2165293
41. Chen, D., Wawrzynski, P., Lv, Z.: Cyber security in smart cities: a review of deep learning-based applications and case studies. Sustainable Cities and Society **66**, article ID 102655 (2021) https://doi.org/10.1016/j.scs.2020.102655
42. Chodakowska, A., Kańduła, S., Przybylska, J.: Cybersecurity in the local government sector in poland: more work needs to be done: more work needs to be done. Lex Localis: Journal of Local Self-Government **20**(1), 161–192 (2022). https://doi.org/10.4335/20.1.161-192
43. Institute for Defense & Business, What Are the Cybersecurity Risks for Smart Cities?. https://www.idb.org/what-are-the-cybersecurity-risks-for-smart-cities/. Accessed 27 Mar 2025
44. Jaikaran, C.: Cybersecurity: Selected Cyberattacks. https://www.congress.gov/crs-product/R46974. Accessed 27 Mar 2025
45. Javed, R. et al.: Future smart cities: requirements, emerging technologies, applications, challenges, and future aspects. Cities **129**, article ID 103794 (2022) https://doi.org/10.1016/j.cities.2022.103794
46. Johnstone, M.N., Crowley, M., Murray, G.: Actor behaviour, notable incidents in critical infrastructures, and risks to the health sector. In: Mohiuddin, A. (eds.) Ransomware Evolution, pp. 33–49. CRC Press, Boca Raton (2025) https://doi.org/10.1201/9781003469506
47. Jones, E., Lake, M., Chaudhuri, A., Sehic, M., Rijnders, D., Coleman, Y.: For the public sector, cyber resilience has never been more important. https://www.weforum.org/stories/2022/07/how-do-you-safeguard-a-city-from-cyber-attacks/. Accessed 27 Mar 2025
48. Korzár Košice.: Hacker attack paralyzes KVP, information about old invoices is gone. https://kosice.korzar.sme.sk/c/20971804/hackersky-utok-paralyzoval-kvp-prec-su-informacie-o-starych-fakturach.html. Accessed 27 Mar 2025
49. Korzár Spiš.: Thousands of Euros Withdrawn from Municipal Account. Bank Talks About Phishing, Mayor Talks About Russian Hackers. https://spis.korzar.sme.sk/c/23436729/z-uctu-obce-vytiahli-tisice-eur-banka-hovori-o-phishingu-starostka-o-ruskych-hackeroch.html. Accessed 27 Mar 2025
50. Leclercq, E.M., Rijshouwer, E.A.: Enabling citizens' right to the smart city through the co-creation of digital platforms. Urban Transform **4**(2), 1–19 (2022). https://doi.org/10.1186/s42854-022-00030-y
51. Lee, C., He, Z., Yuan, Z.: A pathway to sustainable development: Digitization and green productivity. Energy Economics **124**, article ID 106772 (2023) https://doi.org/10.1016/j.eneco.2023.106772
52. Lewallen, J.: Emerging technologies and problem definition uncertainty: the case of cybersecurity. Regulation & Governance **15**, 1035–1052 (2021). https://doi.org/10.1111/rego.12341

52. Li, F., Yan, X., Xie, Y., Sang, Z., Yuan, X.: A review of cyber-attack methods in cyber-physical power system. In: 2019 IEEE 8th International Conference on Advanced Power System Automation and Protection (APAP), Xi'an, China, pp. 1335–1339 (2019) https://doi.org/10.1109/APAP47170.2019.9225126
53. Li, Y., Liu, Q.: A comprehensive review study of cyber-attacks and cyber security; emerging trends and recent developments. Energy Rep. **7**, 8176–8186 (2021). https://doi.org/10.1016/j.egyr.2021.08.126
54. Logota, E., Mantas, G., Rodriguez, J., Marques, H.: Analysis of the impact of denial of service attacks on centralized control in smart cities. In: Mumtaz, S., Rodriguez, J., Katz, M., Wang, C., Nascimento, A. (eds.) Wireless Internet. WICON 2014, pp. 91–96. Springer, Cham (2015) https://doi.org/10.1007/978-3-319-18802-7_13
55. Lowe, M., et al.: City planning policies to support health and sustainability: an international comparison of policy indicators for 25 cities. Lancet Glob. Health **10**(6), e882–e894 (2022). https://doi.org/10.1016/S2214-109X(22)00069-9
56. Malacky.: Cyber attack on city hall. https://malacky.sk/archiv/index803e.html?page=clanok_cely&id=11075. Accessed 27 Mar 2025
57. Millard, J.: Impact of digital transformation on public governance - New forms of policy-making and the provision of innovative, peoplecentric and inclusive public services. Publications Office of the European Union, Luxembourg (2023). https://doi.org/10.2760/204686, JRC133975
58. Nette, A.: What's the Difference Between a Cyber Incident and Data Breach?. https://www.hivesystems.com/blog/whats-the-difference-between-a-cyber-incident-and-data-breach. Accessed 27 Apr 2025
59. Norris, D.F., Mateczun, L.K.: Cyberattacks on local governments 2020: findings from a key informant survey. Journal of Cyber Policy **7**(3), 294–317 (2022). https://doi.org/10.1080/23738871.2023.2178319
60. Norris, D.F., Mateczun, L., Joshi, A., Finin, T.: Managing cybersecurity at the grassroots: evidence from the first nationwide survey of local government cybersecurity. J. Urban Aff. **43**(8), 1173–1195 (2022). https://doi.org/10.1080/07352166.2020.1727295
61. Noviny.: Thousands of euros have been stolen from the municipal account. The mayor talks about a hacker attack. https://www.noviny.sk/krimi/874437-z-obecneho-uctu-odisli-tisice-eur-starostka-hovori-o-hackerskom-utoku. Accessed 27 Mar 2025
62. OECD.: Making Decentralisation Work: A Handbook for Policy-Makers, OECD Multi-level Governance Studies. OECD Publishing, Paris (2019). https://doi.org/10.1787/g2g9faa7-en
63. Pandey, P., Golden, D., Peasley, S., Kelkar, M.: Making smart cities cybersecure: Ways to address distinct risks in an increasingly connected urban future. https://www2.deloitte.com/us/en/insights/focus/smart-city/making-smart-cities-cyber-secure.html. Accessed 27 Mar 2025
64. Pichlmayr, J.: Cyber Security for Our Communities. https://www.kdz.eu/en/news/blog/cyber-security-our-communities. Accessed 27 Mar 2025
65. Pinto, G., Wang, Z., Roy, A., Hong, T., Capozzoli, A.: Transfer learning for smart buildings: A critical review of algorithms, applications, and future perspectives. Advances in Applied Energy **5**, article ID 100084 (2022). https://doi.org/10.1016/j.adapen.2022.100084
66. Prebilič, V., Kukovič, S.: Cooperation between local communities and the civil protection in overcoming the COVID-19 Crisis: Ad Omnia Parati Sumus. Annals for Istrian and Mediterranean Sudies: Series Historia et Sociologia **31**(3), 535–544 (2021)
67. Preis, B., Susskind, L.: Municipal cybersecurity: more work needs to be done. Urban Affairs Review **58**(2), 614–629 (2022). https://doi.org/10.1177/1078087420973760
68. Rebecchi, A., Capolongo, S.: Healthy Design and Urban Planning Strategies framing the SDG 11 Sustainable Cities and Communities. European Journal of Public Health **31**, ckab164.733 (2021). https://doi.org/10.1093/eurpub/ckab164.733

69. Regióny Trenčín.: Another CYBER ATTACK! Hackers attacked a critical infrastructure facility: It is believed to be the same group as the cadastre. https://trencin.zoznam.sk/dalsi-kyberneticky-utok-hackeri-napadli-objekt-kritickej-infrastruktury-ma-ist-o-tu-istu-skupinu-ako-pri-katastri/. Accessed 27 Mar 2025
70. Ručinská, S., Fečko, M., Mitaľ, O., Jesenko, M.: Bottom-up response: the role of municipalities and citie in compensating and supporting central government's role. Journal of Comparative Politics **16**(1), 25–42 (2023)
71. Ručinská, S., Fečko, M.: eServices as a challenge for small municipalities: slovak republic experiences. In: Hemker, T., Müller-Török, R., Prosser, A., Scola, D., Szádeczky, T., Urs, N. (eds.) Central and Eastern European eDem and eGov Days 2020: Conference Proceeding. Facultas Verlags: Wien, pp. 383–392 (2020). https://doi.org/10.24989/ocg.338.30
72. Ručinská, S., Mitaľ, O., Fečko, M.: Dobré spravovanie a odolnosť obcí a miest v dobe digitálnej transformácie. Leges: Praha (2024)
73. Ručinská, S., Fečko, M., Mitaľ, O.: Municipalities and cities in the center of the digital and green transition. In: Lisowski, R., Scholz, L., Trüe, Ch. (eds.). Academia, Administration, Digitalization and Sustainability. Nomos: Baden-Baden, pp. 19–38 (2025). doi.org/https://doi.org/10.5771/9783957104434-19
74. Schlegel, T.: Cyber Attacks on Municipalities. https://abouttrust.tuvsud.com/en/digitization/cyber-attacks-on-municipalities. Accessed 27 Mar 2025
75. Szymoniak, S., Kubanek, M., Kesar, S.: AI-based enhancing of the smart city residents' safety. In: Marcinkowski, B., Przybylek, A., Jarzębowicz, A., Iivari, N., Insfran, E., Lang, M., Linger, H., Schneider, C. (eds.) Harnessing Opportunities: Reshaping ISD in the post-COVID-19 and Generative AI Era, Gdańsk, Poland, pp. 1–4. University of Gdańsk, Gdansk (2024) https://doi.org/10.62036/ISD.2024.10
76. Teraz.sk.: Malacky City Hall restores systems after hacker attack. https://www.teraz.sk/regiony/malacky-mestsky-urad-obnovuje-chod-sy/586905-clanok.html. Accessed 27 Mar 2025
77. TVNoviny.sk.: Hacker paralyzes local office in Košice: Experts now investigating whether sensitive information was leaked. https://tvnoviny.sk/domace/clanok/95866-hacker-paralyzoval-miestny-urad-v-kosiciach-experti-teraz-skumaju-ci-neunikli-citlive-informacie?__tuu7ntqxozayndugcxfzydhlntyyxndhzhe=dnywatdn&__tuu7ntqxozkzmj0gcxfzydhlntyyxndhzhe=-a1-v3&__tuu7ntqxozy0nzagcxfzydhlntyyxndhzhe=-a1-v3&__tuu7ntqxpda%20mjagcxfzydhlntyyxndhzhe=-a1-v3&__tuu7ntqxpda2pd0gcxfzydhlntyyxndhzhe=-a1-v3&__tuu7ntqxpdu3mtqgcxfzydhlntyyxndhzhe=-a1-v3. Accessed 27 Mar 2025
78. Vasyltsiv, T., Biletska, I., Mulska, O.: Organizational and financial instruments of decentralizaton and development of united territorial communities in Ukraine: Poland´s experience. Management Theory and Studies for Rural Business and Infrastructure Development, **43**(2), 276–287 (2021). https://doi.org/10.15544/mts.2021.24
79. Verhulsdonck, G., Weible, J.L., Helser, S., Hajduk, N.: Smart cities, playable cities, and cybersecurity: a systematic review. International Journal of Human-Computer Interaction **39**(2), 378–390 (2021). https://doi.org/10.1080/10447318.2021.2012381
80. Vitunskaite, M., He, Y., Brandstetter, T., Janicke, H.: Smart cities and cyber security: are we there yet? A comparative study on the role of standards, third party risk management and security ownership. Comput. Secur.Secur. **83**, 313–331 (2019). https://doi.org/10.1016/j.cose.2019.02.009
81. Voytenko Palgan, Y., Mont, O., Sulkakoski, S.: Governing the sharing economy: Towards a comprehensive analytical framework of municipal governance. Cities **108**, article ID 102994. https://doi.org/10.1016/j.cities.2020.102994
82. Yin, R.K.: Case Study Research Design and Methods. SAGE Publications, Thousand Oaks (2013)

Decision Support System for Urban Road Safety: A Comparison Between Two Different City Size

Michele Pinna[1(✉)], Gianfranco Fancello[1], Patrizia Serra[1], Sergio Useche[2], and Francisco Alonso[2]

[1] Cagliari University, Piazza D'Armi 1, 09127 Cagliari, Italy
michele.pinna@unica.it
[2] INTRAS, Valencia University, C/ Serpis 29, 3° Floor (TT), 46022 Valencia, Spain

Abstract. Among the objectives of the European Union in the field of road safety there is "Vision Zero", which aims to halve the number of deaths in road accidents by 2030 and reach zero deaths by 2050. The present contribution proposes a methodology for investigating and identifying preliminary indicators of road safety in urban networks for the development of a Decision Support System to assist road safety managers. The proposed approach for data research and urban road safety analysis is applied on two different urban scales: a metropolis and a city with fewer than 30,000 inhabitants. The identification of urban routes and their overlap, along with the integration of various urban traffic elements such as incidents, traffic flows, and urban attractors within a GIS environment, can enable the correlation of multiple layers related to infrastructure, safety, and accessibility, involving different actors in the decision-making process. At a practical level, this paper presents potential survey choices for identifying safety-related indicators according to the observation area. It is also highlighted how research in metropolitan cities like Madrid can benefit from a high availability of data, while smaller cities require alternative methods and data to build thematic databases. Future studies will focus on selecting the definitive KPIs (Key Performance Indicators) to be used in the creation of a DSS for Urban Road Safety.

Keywords: Road Safety · Cities · GIS · Urban Traffic Index · Exemplified Comparison

1 Introduzione

In recent years, progress has been made in the management of road safety, yet much remains to be done to further reduce crashes, particularly fatalities. Urban road safety holds a central position for municipal administrations and public agencies. Research of this kind supports the European objective known as "Vision Zero", which aims to halve road deaths by 2030 and eliminate them entirely by 2050 [1]. Most safety analyses have traditionally focused on non-urban areas, where fatality rates tend to be higher; however, urban environments though generally involving less severe outcomes–record a high frequency of incidents [2]. The significant number of crashes, injuries of varying severity, and deaths highlights the need to examine urban settings more closely, in order to identify ways to reduce risks. Various factors contribute to road safety, both in quantitative and qualitative terms, including the number of accidents and traffic flow levels [3]. Beyond identifying roads with higher crash rates, it is important to examine the issue from multiple urban traffic perspectives such as incident patterns, infra-structure attractiveness, traffic flow intensity, and pavement conditions. Geographic Information Systems (GIS) are useful for analyzing the spatial distribution of crashes [4] and for locating critical points within the infrastructure. In this study, we propose a method for collecting spatial data and overlapping it with the road network to derive traffic-related indicators relevant to urban safety.

Another aim of this contribution is to illustrate how data analysis methods can vary depending on the size and structure of the urban area. In large metropolitan contexts, data availability is often extensive, while in smaller municipalities, information needs to be gathered through different channels fieldwork, conventional databases, or more recent sources such as TomTom Traffic (TTT). At a practical level, identifying multidimensional urban traffic indicators can help lay the groundwork for the development of a Decision Support System (DSS) that can assist in setting priorities for road safety improvements [4]. Establishing such priorities helps decision-makers allocate available resources more effectively and supports public authorities in identifying which road segments require the most immediate attention [5]. To investigate this topic, it is necessary to define either aggregated or disaggregated safety indicators, depending on quantitative and/or qualitative criteria that reflect different aspects of the issue. Overlaying the road network with layers related to crash records, traffic flows, pavement conditions, and attractors–such as hospitals, schools, supermarkets, restaurants, and retail areas can help detect overlaps and potential conflict zones [6]. The Central Urban District (CDB), particularly during daytime hours, is subject to high traffic volumes and population density, and hosts commercial facilities, schools, and government offices [7]. Accordingly, it is expected that structuring the road network into routes made up of multiple urban streets may help providing a more realistic reflection of how decision-makers tend to address traffic management in practice [8]. In the following sections, we describe how urban elements were identified, how they were linked to the network, and how these associations were used to define the indicators.

2 Literature Review

In previous studies, a number of authors have moved beyond single variable analyses of crashes [9, 10], focusing instead on the development of indices aimed at identifying hotspots associated with urban attractors such as accessibility and the spatial distribution of trip generators o prioritize roads or routes that may have greater relevance for intervention and broader effects on communities [11]. Some studies have relied on different indicators relating to crash frequency, accessibility, and population density.

The relationship between urban road crashes and various factors such as infrastructure design, environmental conditions, and traffic volumes has been widely examined [5]. Traffic flow volumes have a measurable influence on crash risk, and several investigations have assessed their role in shaping safety outcomes [12].

Pavement conditions have been objectively assessed using the Pavement Condition Index (PCI), which provides a structured approach for evaluating road surface quality and preservation status [13]. For these reasons, we considered it relevant to explore the issue through an integrated and interdisciplinary approach, considering three main thematic areas and their related traffic elements. Previous research underscores the value of addressing safety from multiple perspectives and considering a range of contributing factors [14]. Some studies also point out the limitations of conventional crash prediction models, while others [15] identify segments with higher priority for action, helping decision-makers manage prevention resources through structured assessment criteria.

3 Methodology

The selected methodology outlines two different approaches for identifying itineraries and preliminary indicators, with the goal of developing a DSS in the context of urban road safety. For this study, we selected two case studies: a large city Madrid and a small municipality Iglesias, located in southwestern Sardinia, Italy. The first was chosen for the wide availability of public data, downloadable from online geoportals [16] and [17], useful for obtaining a detailed analysis with respect to the various elements of urban traffic. The other city, under 30,000 inhabitants, was taken as a second case study to highlight the fact that in small realities the detailed analysis relating to road safety can be underestimated or limited to some available traffic elements. Iglesias does not have a municipal geoportal, so data collection required more elaborate research methods and alternative sources, including the use of up-to-date traffic information provided by the TomTom Traffic database. For both cases, we also relied on open-source databases such as OpenStreetMap (OSM) and Google Earth, which were used to integrate additional data for example, identifying accommodation facilities, places of worship, various commercial activities, and infrastructure elements such as traffic lights, pedestrian crossings, and so on.

3.1 Itinerary

By itineraries, we refer to segments of the urban road network made up of multiple links (arcs) that belong to the same service level. Rather than analyzing single links or points, we opted for a route-based approach, as this better reflects the way policymakers usually plan and invest in road safety improvements. In urban contexts, interventions such as road resurfacing, replacement of traffic signs, or analysis of hazardous locations are typically carried out on stretches of road composed of multiple streets.

The selection of itineraries was based on a classification system that organizes roads by their level of service. By grouping links under street names, we identified those that belonged to the same route. What most clearly differentiates the two analyses is the network complexity: Madrid's network is extensive, with itineraries spanning several kilometers and clearly defined service levels, while Iglesias has a more compact network, with shorter routes about one kilometer each despite also having a service hierarchy, though with more overlap in road functions.

In Iglesias, given that the most recent available traffic data dated back to 2017, we decided to use the TTT network to define itineraries and obtain updated traffic flow data, as well as other information. TTT data are particularly useful, as they provide various types of flow reports real-time, by hour of the day, and across the entire yearwith a penetration rate of about 3%, which can be used as a conversion factor for estimating vehicles per hour on the network. These data are based on vehicles equipped with Tom-Tom navigation systems and smartphones (e.g., iPhone and Huawei devices). Although the system does not capture the entire volume of traffic, it does offer valuable indicators such as average travel speeds and delay times across different times of the day. These indicators provide insight into traffic flow patterns in terms of travel times and delays.

In the following sections, we present the data obtained based on the observation layers, their sources, and the methods used to integrate them into the GIS project particularly focusing on how the itineraries were linked to the road network. One of the innovative aspects of this study lies in the integrated comparison of itineraries with different urban traffic elements, using geoprocessing tools within the GIS environment.

3.2 Fields of Analysis

Safety. The safety category primarily includes accident data and related indica-tors. The main difference between the two case studies is the size of their databases. In Madrid, about 4,000 injury causing crashes occur each year, whereas Iglesias has an average of around 40 per year, with a total dataset of about 400 recorded incidents from 2011 to 2022. The distribution of these incidents is illustrated in the figure.

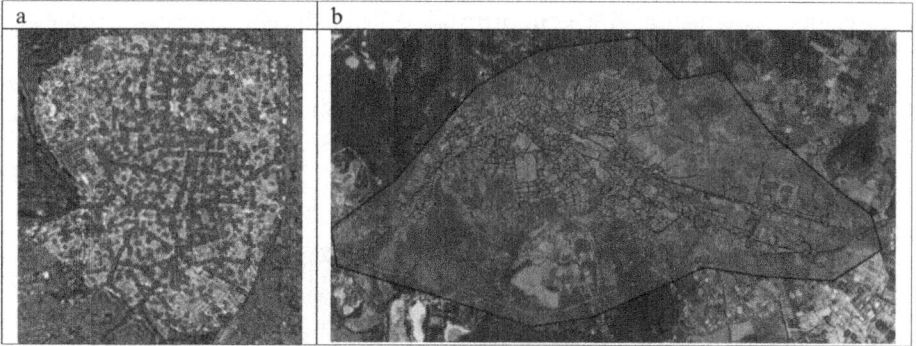

Fig. 1. Madrid's urban crashes 2024 (a) left, Iglesias's urban crashes 2014 - 2022(b) right.

Accessibility. The Accessibility Group contains data on population density and urban attractors. An attractor is a point in the urban network that attracts people and vehicles at certain times of the day such as schools, public offices, supermarkets, shops, etc. [6]. In addition to the latter, bus stops have been identified, which expose vulnerable users, such as pedestrians, to conflicts with vehicles. The data relating to traffic attractors were handled differently between the two cases, as will be described later.

Infrastructure. The infrastructure group includes elements related to pavement, the presence of intersections with or without traffic lights, pedestrian crossings, sidewalk surfaces, the percentage of cycle paths per route and the number of LED street lamps. The indicators proposed for these elements vary in the two case studies according to the databases generated and the usefulness or otherwise with respect to the context of analysis.

4 Application Results

4.1 Madrid Case Study

The analysis focused on a delimited area of approximately 6 by 6 kms within the broader urban development. This area was defined using the shapefile named "area_madrid.shp," within which the relevant urban data were observed. The urban area is characterized by centres with a high residential concentration, located in different areas of the city, a Central Business District (CDB) in general a historic centre of the city with businesses such as shops, supermarkets, university, banks, offices, hotels, cinemas and theatres [18], while hospitals are widespread in the northern area (Fig. 5a). The CBD has high traffic intensity and a high population density [7]. The primary network analysed makes all these areas well connected. Once the area was established, the street network was identified in order to de-fine urban itineraries and integrate the various urban and infrastructure related elements linked to Safety, Accessibility, and Infrastructure.

Identification of Madrid Routes

The network has been organized into hierarchical urban itineraries using OSM data, which for the moment has been preferred over the geoportal data for a better organization and wealth of information. The OSM network is hierarchical into primary, secondary, tertiary, residential and service. We focused on the primary network (Fig. 2b) identified through the selection of the arcs with the "highway" field. To define the Madrid Routes, the arches with the same name as the street were joined to form paths (Fig. 2a). As a final result, 18 itineraries of average length of 5 km each were identified.

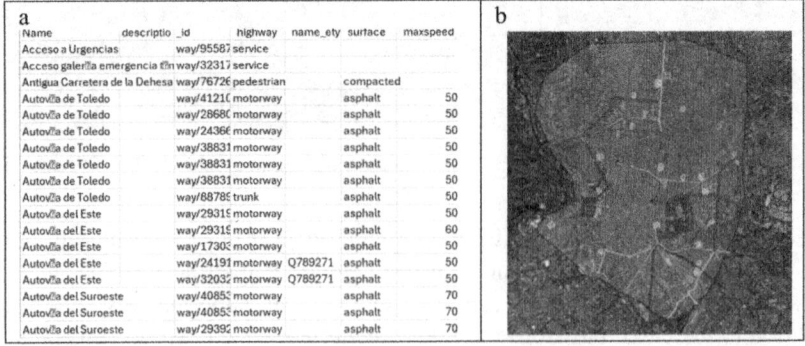

Fig. 2. Attribute table of OSM (a), Madrid Street and Routes choosing (b).

Gruppo Safety of Madrid

Crashes. The crash database was obtained from the municipal geoportal [16], from which we downloaded data on road crashes occurring in 2024 within the urban center (Fig. 1). For this study, we only considered crashes involving injuries. These data, formatted as CSV files, were easily geolocated thanks to the presence of X and Y coordinates. A total of 4,163 crashes were recorded within the area of analysis, with approximately 1,000 of them located along the identified itineraries (Fig. 3).

The crash attribute table includes various variables such as location and address, type of circumstance, sex, injury severity, road user type, age, and more. Among the derived indicators, we estimated severity levels by classifying injury outcomes as Minor, Serious, or Fatal, aggregated from the "lesività" field in Table 1.

For the case of Madrid, the Safety group includes three indicators:

- Accident Index of Itinerary j (I_Accj), calculated as the ratio between the sum of the accidents (Acci) characterizing each of the n arcs that make up itinerary j and the length Dj of the itinerary itself (Eq. 1);
- Average severity index of the accident in Route j (I_Sevj), calculated as the ratio between the sum of the degrees of injury (dlz) associated with each of the m accidents z occurred along route j and the total number of accidents (Accj) occurred along the same route (2);
- Pedestrian Accident Index (I_PedAccj), calculated as the ratio between the sum of accidents involving pedestrians (PedAcc) that occurred along the n arches that make up itinerary j and the total number of accidents falling within itinerary j itself (3)

$$I\_Acc_j = \frac{\sum_{i=1}^{n} Acc_i}{D_j} \quad (1)$$

$$I\_Sev_j = \frac{\sum_{z=1}^{m} Acc_i dl_z}{Accj} \quad (2)$$

$$I\_PedAcc_j = \frac{\sum_{i=1}^{n} PedAcc_i}{\sum_{i=1}^{n} Acc_i} \quad (3)$$

where

Acc_i is the number of accidents characterizing each of the n arcs that make up itinerary J

dl_z is the level of severity associated with each of the m incidents z falling within route j
Accj is the total number of accidents characterizing the route j
$PedAcc_i$ is the number of accidents involving pedestrians that occurred along the n arches that make up the route j
D_j is the length of the route j

Accessibility Group Madrid. For the Accessibility group in Madrid, we defined six indicators based on traffic flow, population density, and the location of key urban traffic attractors, namely schools, hospitals, supermarkets, and bus stops.

Table 1. Damage type and level.

Code	Damage type	Damage level
01	Emergency care without subsequent admission	Low
02	Income less than or equal to 24 h	Low
03	Admission of more than 24 h	High
04	Died 24 h	Dead
05	Outpatient healthcare thereafter	Low
06	Immediate health care in a health centre or mutual insurance company	Low
07	Health care only at the scene of the accident	Low
14	No healthcare	x
77	Unknown, No health care	x

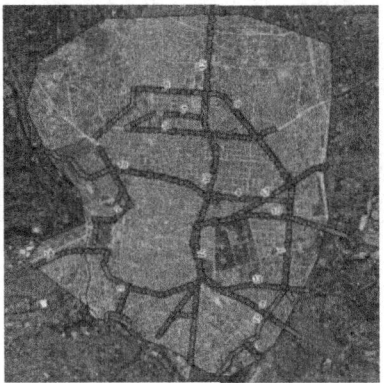

Fig. 3. Madrid Routes Crashes.

Flow Intensity. Madrid. I Traffic flow data were obtained from the municipal geoportal and were linked to the road network by merging–through the common "Id" field the CSV tables containing the geographic coordinates of traffic monitoring stations with the corresponding traffic flow data recorded during the observation period (November 2024) (Fig. 4a). The dataset included several variables, such as flow intensity (expressed in vehicles/hour), occupancy time, load, and average speed.

Using a "spatial join" between traffic monitoring stations and the urban itineraries, we assigned traffic intensity values to each itinerary. Traffic flow intensity was considered a suitable indicator to capture differences in vehicular volumes across itineraries in absolute terms (Fig. 4b).

To obtain a single intensity index for each itinerary j, which might intersect segments with different traffic intensities, we assigned the maximum intensity value recorded along the itinerary. This approach was chosen as a conservative estimate, assuming the worst case traffic conditions across the entire segment.

$$\text{Flow Intensity}_j = MaxIi \tag{4}$$

where:

$MaxI_i$ is the maximum intensity recorded along one of the arcs i that make up itinerary j

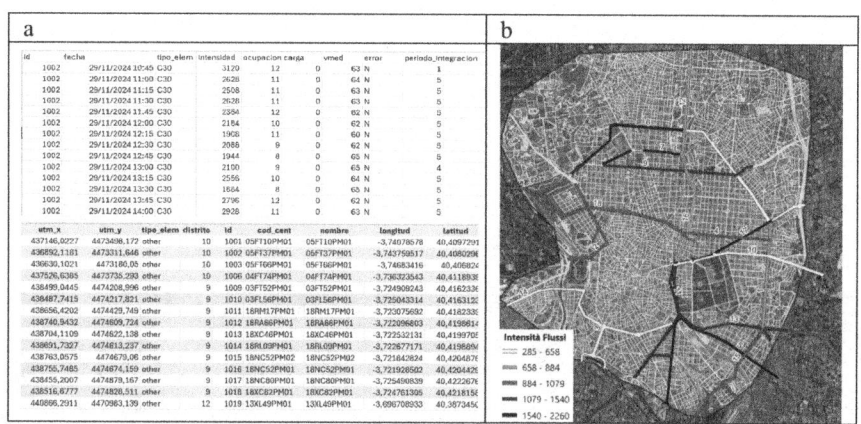

Fig. 4. Flows Table (a), Route Intensity Flows(b).

Traffic Attractors. The processing of the traffic attractors database required more time because, although several elements such as markets, hospitals, and schools were widely available on the geoportal, they needed to be reorganized into unique fields and further integrated with external databases like OSM. For this reason, the OSM database was ultimately preferred due to its homogeneity and data richness.

After gathering numerous elements of various typologies and levels of attractivity, we decided to focus only on indicators related to the number of hospitals, schools, and supermarkets. These were considered priorities due to their potential to generate intense traffic flows, thereby increasing users' exposure to crash risks particularly for vulnerable users, such as in the case of schools. These indicators were associated with the primary road network using a 1-km buffer, based on the assumption that the primary network exerts a wider spatial influence, connecting with attractors that are not necessarily adjacent. By counting, for each itinerary, the number of hospitals, schools, and supermarkets within this 1 km buffer, we estimated an attractiveness index of the itinerary (I_Attractivenessj) as the ratio between the total number of attractors (TotAttractorsj) and the length Dj of the itinerary itself (5).

$$I\_Attractiveness_j = \frac{TotAttractorsj}{D_j} \tag{5}$$

where:

$TotAttractors_j$ is the total of the Attractiveness elements belongs to itinerary j.

Bus stop. Bus stops are directly connected to the flow of pedestrians and therefore to their accessibility to the attractors, but they also represent a parameter relating to exposure to the risk of being run over by vehicles in transit near the stops. To associate the bus stops (Fig. 5b) a buffer of 30 m of the stops was considered in order to intersect the adjacent routes and count the number of stops per route. The index is calculated as the ratio between the number of stops and the length of the route (6).

$$I\_Bus_j = \frac{TotBus_j}{D_j} \qquad (6)$$

where:

$TotBus_j$ is the total of the bus stop belongs to itinerary j

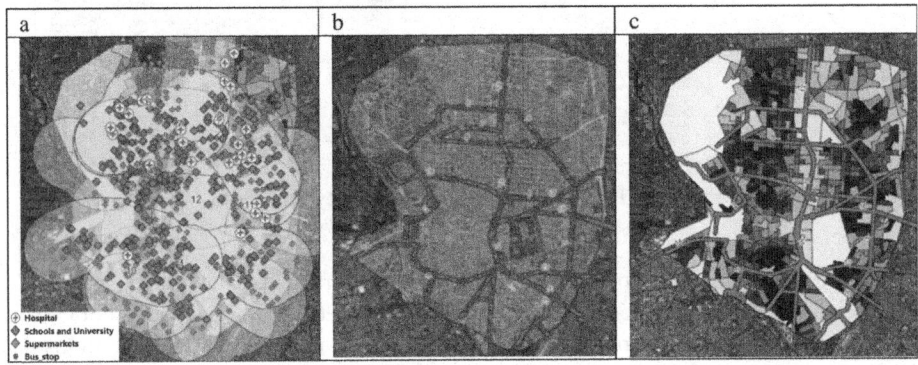

Fig. 5. Route buffer in attractors (a), Route's bus stop (b) Population density (c).

Population density. To estimate an index of population density, the shape of the routes was superimposed on the shape of the density (Fig. 5c), downloaded from the geoportal. The figure represents the population per square kilometer within the neighborhood section under 10,000 inhabitants. The intersection generates an array that for each row shows the route j and the intersecting density value. To obtain a unit density index for the route, an average value per kilometre is derived by dividing the sum of the intersecting densities and the length of the route (7).

$$Index\,Density_j = \frac{Tot\,Density_j}{D_j} \qquad (7)$$

where:

$Density_j$ is the density belongs to itinerary j

Infrastructure Madrid Group. As far as the infrastructure group is concerned, the main element falls on the condition of the pavement, subsequently the number of traffic lights, intersections without traffic lights, the surfaces of the sidewalks, the number of LED Lampposts, the pedestrian crossings and the lengths of the cycle paths were estimated.

Pavement. As far as asphalt is concerned, its status has been defined according to the shape file relating to the asphalting interventions carried out, attributing a PCI value of 100 to the sections of the route intersected with it, for the sections not intersected, we have assumed a PCI equal to 70. In fact, this choice derives from sample observations of the roads made through Street View (SW), it was found that most of the asphalt was of sufficient quality. In order to estimate the lengths of the two types of asphalt, for each itinerary, an intersection procedure was first performed between asphalt shapes, with PCI 100 and shapes itineraries, then with the "Symmetrical difference" function the sections for which PCI 70 is assumed were extracted, copying the latter in the first intersection we can a table of the Itineraries with PCI 100 and 70 (Fig. 6a). In order to provide a unit value of PCI, for each Itinerary, the weighted average of the lengths of the sections has been made by their value of PCI (8).

Numbers of Traffic Light. For the identification and localization of the traffic lights, the data of the geoportal were integrated with those of OSM obtaining a shape file of the traffic lights present in the study area. In order to be able to associate the traffic lights to the network and therefore to each route, we intersected the points with the network after creating a buffer of 5 m, and then counted them for each route, the index is given by the ratio with the length of the intercepted route (Fig. 6b).

Intersections without traffic lights. To identify the intersections without traffic holes, we first located them, through the intersection of the lines of the total network of Madrid with the lines of the identified routes. By intersecting the traffic light buffer with the identified intersections, the intersections without difference traffic lights were obtained (Fig. 6c).

Sidewalk Surfaces. To identify the sidewalk surfaces of each Route, we buffered 30 m of the Routes to overlap them with the polygon of the adjacent sidewalks. To count the surfaces, we intersected the sidewalks with the route buffer and then added up the areas identified for each one. The index is given by the ratio between the sum of the areas of the j-th Route and the length of the j-th Route (Fig. 7a).

Bike Lines. Madrid's bike lane network was downloaded from the geoportal and intersected with the itineraries. This allowed us to calculate the percentage of bike lane length relative to the total length of each itinerary (Fig. 7b).

Pedestrian Crossings. Pedestrian crossings were identified exclusively using OSM. Their integration with the itineraries followed the same method used for bus stops (Fig. 8a).

LED Lampposts. We considered the number of LED lampposts along the itineraries relevant. The dataset includes lampposts with LED lights, mixed lighting, and traditional lighting types. The indicator represents the number of LED lampposts out of the total number of lampposts in each itinerary (Fig. 8b).

Below, we present the main infrastructure-related indices considered. The indices for traffic lights, unsignalized intersections, bike lanes, and lampposts (8) were all calculated as the ratio of the number of elements within itinerary j to the length of itinerary j (6):

$$Index\_PCI_j = \frac{\sum_{r=1}^{n} PCI_{rj} * length_{rj}}{D_j} \qquad (8)$$

The various indices relating to the different traffic elements such as the number of traffic lights, intersections without traffic lights, pedestrian crossings, cycle paths and street lamps, have all been calculated as the ratio of the sum of the elements falling within route j divided by the length of route j (9):

$$Index\ E_j = \frac{TotElementsj}{D_j} \qquad (9)$$

where:

$PCI_{rj} * length_{rj}$ is the product of the PCI r times the length r belonging to route j
D_j is the length of the route j
E_j is the element of the estimated index that belongs to route j

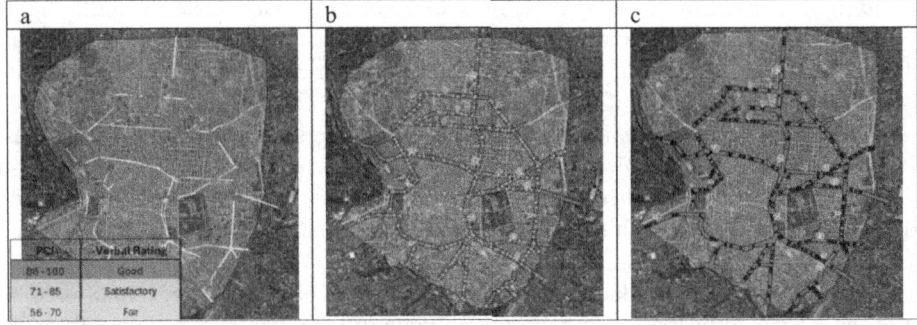

Fig. 6. PCI Pavement (a), Traffic lights(b), Intersections without Traffic lights (c).

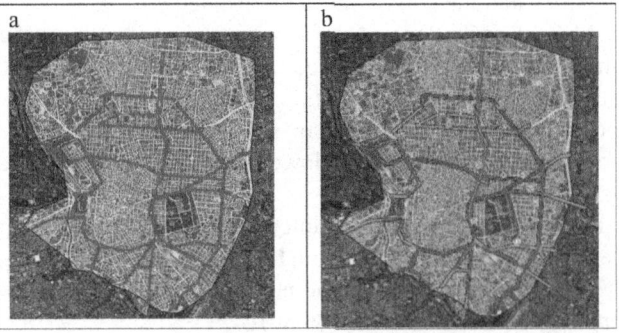

Fig. 7. Sidewalk (a), Cicle line(b).

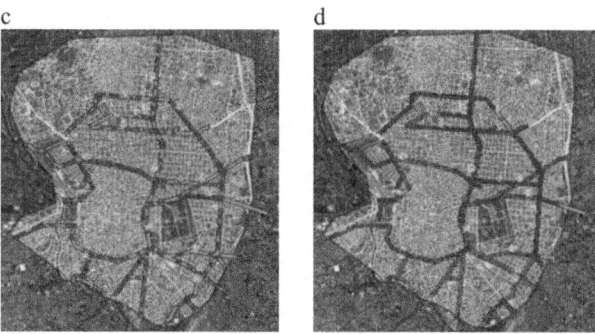

Fig. 8. Crossway (a), Led Illumination in green (b).

Case Study Iglesias. The town of Iglesias, located in the south of Sardinia (Italy), is an example of a small town with less than 30,000 inhabitants consisting of a central urban core, with a historic center characterized by the presence of a CDB with various commercial activities, schools, hospital and public offices, residential nuclei located in various areas of the city and peripheral areas with larger commercial activities such as supermarkets, cinemas and sports facilities.Also in this case we have divided the research into two parts, identification of the itineraries and elements of the three destination areas (Infrastructure, Safety and Accessibility) highlighting the similarities and differences compared to the case of Madrid in terms of databases and survey methodologies. For the elements of safety, we used the accident database, obtained through authorization at the Contact Center of the Institute of Statistics (Istat), for the years 2011 and 2021, while in 2022 for the moment we entered the partial data provided by the local police. For this case study, we considered all the urban attributes present, both high and low, with respect to the generation of traffic flows. This choice is due to the fact that in a small urban center, the main network allows you to reach almost all urban attractions. In particular, in the case of Iglesias, the main network passing adjacent to the historic urban center, takes charge of flows due to the presence of different commercial activities and city meeting places. The methodology we describe has been applied to the entire urban and sub-urban area of about 6 x 2 km.

Definition of Iglesias Itineraries. For the road network of Iglesias we could count on several alternatives, the road network of the regional geoportal, the network developed by our research department and the network obtained from the purchase of the TTT database. We used the latter as it had all the information necessary for identifying the itineraries, i.e. the hierarchy with the name of the streets and the values of traffic flows updated to the last two years (Fig. 2). Another advantage of this database is that it divides the network into two directions of travel. The TTT network hierarchizes the network through the "FRC" field, an acronym for Functional Road Class, a field used to merge partial arcs together with the street name field. We have carried out a further hierarchization, defining it as "primary" by introducing a network of Itineraries obtained as the sum of partial arcs characterized by FRC values ranging from 2 to 5. As a final result, 16 itineraries of average length of 1 km each were identified, two of which of about 2.5 km, as we can see in Fig. 9.

Fig. 9. Iglesias's Routes.

Safety Group Iglesias. The safety group includes indicators derived from the accident database, built using data obtained from ISTAT. As with the ISTAT data for Madrid, we have access to detailed information regarding the type of event, its severity, and details about the users involved. To simplify data interpretation, we organized the database so that each accident record includes the total number of injuries, pedestrian victims, and fatalities involved in each incident. This approach allows for indices comparable to those used for Madrid, with the difference that the Severity Index in this case lacks a parameter differentiating the se-verity levels of the injuries.

Accessibility Group Iglesias. For the accessibility group, we propose different indices due to both the lower availability and variety of data, and the lesser necessity for such detailed indicators.

Traffic flows. Using TTT databases, we estimated a traffic intensity value expressed in vehicles per hour, based on the Hits field corresponding to the morning peak hour (8 a.m.). To obtain these values, we generated a 54-day report from the TomTom Move platform, aiming to compute average values that best represent network behavior over a three-month work period.

The Hits field indicates the number of cars detected in the ith segment of the j-th itinerary. This number does not reflect the actual volume of vehicles using the network per hour, since, as stated by TomTom, it represents approximately 3% of the total. To estimate the actual number of circulating vehicles, we adjusted the data using a 3% penetration rate and divided it by the 54 days of observation. We also validated these values through on-site field measurements. From an operational standpoint, by merging the values from the CSV file with the itinerary network using the "Id" field, we obtained a representation of the maximum average intensity values for each itinerary (Fig. 10).

Traffic attractors. Unlike in Madrid, urban attractors were considered in their entirety and are often located adjacent to the primary network, which shows no major differences

Fig. 10. Flow intensity.

in levels of attractiveness. The itineraries reach various attractors directly, particularly as the primary road network runs alongside the historic city center, where there are many commercial activities such as shops, private offices, and more, which we assigned lower attractiveness values.

The attractiveness index refers to the overall attractiveness of each itinerary, calculated as the sum of all attractors located nearby. The work involved geolocating these activities within the GIS project and assigning different weights based on activity type [19], with maximum values (10) for schools, hospitals, and supermarkets, and lower values (1–2) for small businesses and shops. To obtain the data, we used multiple databases including Google Earth, OpenStreetMap (OSM), and a highly useful list provided by the Municipality of Iglesias used for the waste tax (TARI). This list includes a key parameter surface area which we used to estimate differentiated weights based on the size of each establishment.

To spatially distribute point-based attractiveness values across the urban network, we applied a Kernel Density analysis (Fig. 11a) using a dedicated plugin, defining each element's attractiveness value based on the Val1 parameter [19]. The density map was generated using a 100-m search radius weighted by Val1.

This parameter was calculated as follows: $Val1 = \sqrt{(P \times T \times S)}$, where: P is the weight of the activity type, T is the exposure or operating time (ranging from 3 to 8), and S is a sensitivity value (ranging from 10 to 1), introduced to reflect the risk to vulnerable users in the case of an accident–particularly near schools and bus stops.

The Val1 parameter was then used to generate the Kernel Density map, which was subsequently vectorized. By intersecting the itineraries with this vector layer, we produced a matrix with rows representing each itinerary and its corresponding attractiveness. The unique attractiveness value for each itinerary was derived from the sum of all intersected values (Fig. 11b).

Population density. Population density data was obtained from the ISTAT web site and integrated into the Itinerary network using the same calculation methodology as for Madrid.

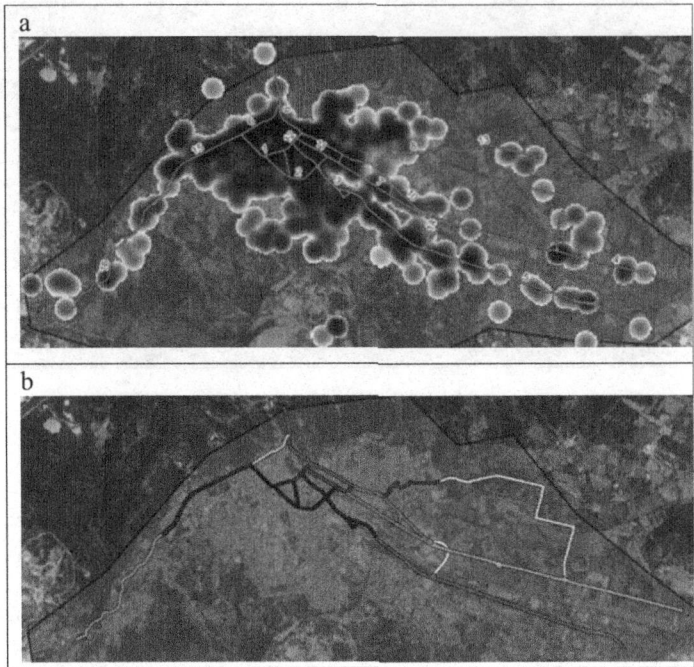

Fig. 11. Kernel density of attractiveness(a), Route's attractiveness(b).

Bus stops. Bus stop locations for this case study were identified using Google Earth and verified using Google Maps. Integration into the itineraries and calculation of the related indices followed the same method used for Madrid.

Infrastructure Group Iglesias

Pavement conditions. Unlike Madrid, due to the lack of a dedicated asphalt data base, we opted for an objective assessment of pavement conditions. Condition ratings were assigned using PCI (Pavement Condition Index) values derived from visual inspection by Street View and attributed to each road segment (Fig. 12) To assign a single PCI value to each itinerary, we computed a weighted average based on segment lengths, divided by the total length of the itinerary as described in Eq. 9.

Pedestrian crossings. The list of pedestrian crossings was compiled through OSM data and supplemented with manual additions identified by satellite imagery (2022) provided by the Sardinia Geoportal. This analysis allowed us to distinguish between flat crossings and raised ones. The proposed index is the percentage of crossings per itinerary length, weighted by the proportion of raised crossings.

Number of intersections. In this regard, we calculated the number of intersections for each itinerary by intersecting the identified itinerary network with the overall road network.

Bicycle Lanes and Traffic Lights. Indices for bicycle lanes and traffic lights were not included in the analysis, as they were not considered relevant. Only one signalized intersection and one improperly constructed bicycle lane were identified.

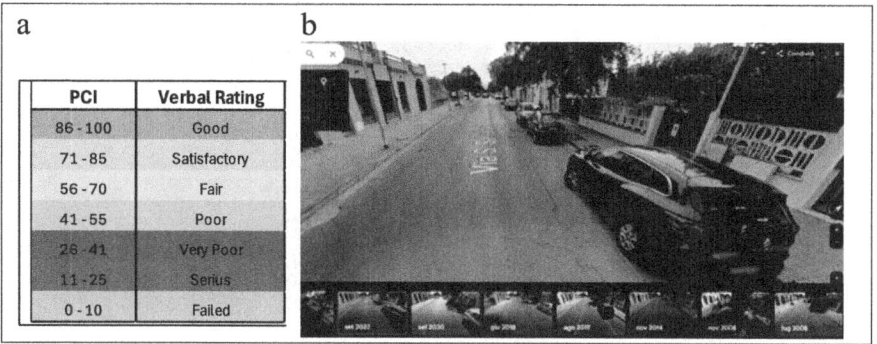

Fig. 12. Street View osservation(a), PCI values (b).

5 Comparison and Differences

Looking at the two figures below, we see a summary of the identified indicators for the two case studies, along with the main data sources. For the Safety and Accessibility groups, we used the same types of indicators, while for the Infra-structure group there are differences due to the lack of available data and the negligible relevance of certain indicators to the context of the study.

Regarding Accessibility, the main difference in the case of Iglesias lies in the approach used to calculate the attractiveness index. In this case, all attractors were considered, not just those with high attractiveness, as was done for Madrid. The infrastructure group includes fewer indicators because the number of traffic lights and the length of bicycle lanes were not deemed numerically relevant. Other indicators, such as the number of LED Lampposts and sidewalks, were not included due to the unavailability of georeferenced datasets and the inability to assess their numerical relevance.

The lack of available data highlights how analyzing road safety can be more time-consuming in areas albeit not large in size that lack georeferenced data, compared to metropolises or large cities with well-structured geoportals. Moreover, for cities without a geoportal, data collection times increase with the size of the city and the number of inhabitants (Fig. 13).

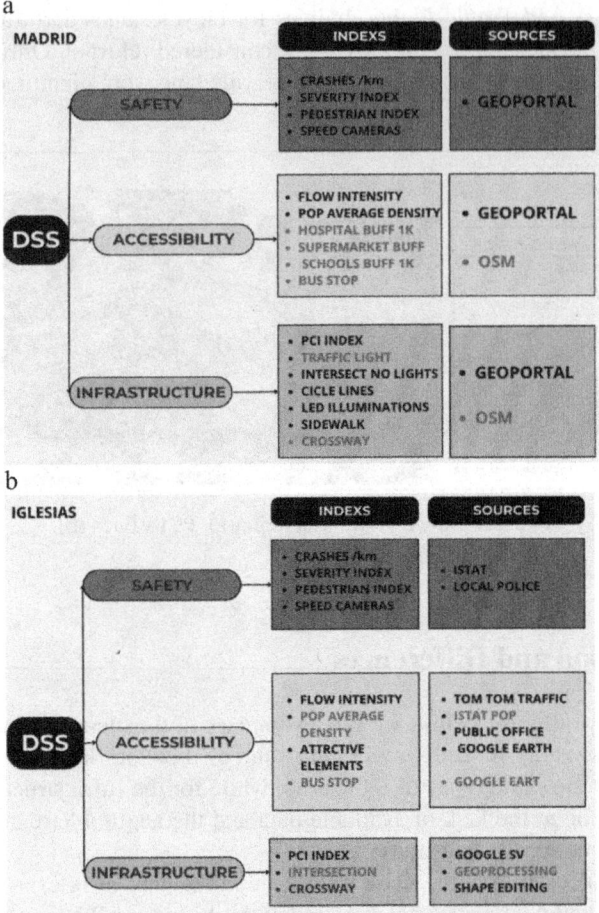

Fig. 13. DSS Flow Chart Madrid (a), DSS Flow Chart Iglesias (b).

Acknowledgements. This study was carried out within the MOST Sustainable Mobility National Research Center and received funding from the European Union Next-Generation EU (PIANO NAZIONALE DI RIPRESA E RESILIENZA (PNRR) MISSIONE 4 COMPONENTE 2, INVESTIMENTO 1.4 D.D. 1033 17/06/2022, CN00000023). This manuscript reflects only the authors' views and opinions, neither the EU nor the EC can be considered responsible for them.

References

1. European Commission, Directorate-General for Mobility and Transport,: Next steps towards 'Vision Zero' EU road safety policy framework 2021–2030, Publications Office (2020). https://data.europa.eu/doi/10.2832/
2. Cabrera-Arnau, C., Prieto Curiel, R., Bishop, S.: Uncovering the behaviour of road accidents in urban areas, Royal Society Open Science (2020)

3. Moyo, T., Mbatha, S., Aderibigbe, O.-O., Gumbo, T., Musonda, , I.: Assessing Spatial Variations of Traffic Congestion Using Traffic Index Data in a Developing City: Lessons from Johannesburg, South Africa (2022)
4. Fancello, G., Carta, M., Fadda, P.: A decision support system for road safety analysis. Transportation Research Procedia **5**, 201–210 (2015)
5. Çepni, M.S., Arslan, O.: A GIS approach to evaluate infrastructure variables influencing the occurrence of traffic accidents in Urban Roads. International Journal of Environment and Geoinformatics **4**(1), 17–24 (2017)
6. Pinna, M., Fancello, G., Serra, P., Porcu, E., Ponti, M.: An Integrated Approach for Urban Road Safety Analysis, DICAAR - Department of CIVIL and Environmental Engineering and Architecture. University of Cagliari, Italy. (2024)
7. Borruso, G.: The role of cartography in the definition of the central business district. First notes for a methodological approach, A.I.C. Bulletin nr. 126–127–128/2006
8. Fancello, G., Carta, M., Fadda, P.: Road intersections ranking for road safety improvement: comparative analysis of multi-criteria decision making methods. Transp. Policy **80**, 188–196 (2019)
9. Li, K., Cai, L., Jiang, F., Zhou, W.: Design and application of an attractiveness index for urban hotspots based on GPS trajectory data. IEEE Access **6**, 55976–55985 (2018). Stato della arte
10. Loret, E., Gullotta, G., Fea, M., Sarti, F.: Traffic fluxes and urban congestion: a simple approach with the attractors' method. J. Geogr. Inf. Syst. **4**, 494–502 (2012)
11. Stević, Ž., Das, D.K., Kopić, M.: A novel multiphase model for traffic safety evaluation: a case study of South Africa. Mathematical Problems in Engineering, 5584599 (2021)
12. Theofilatos, A., Ziakopoulos, A.: Traffic flow volume and safety. In: International Encyclopedia of Transportation; Vickerman, R., Ed.; Elsevier: Oxford, pp. 692–698 (2021)
13. Pinatt, J., Chicati L.: Evaluation of pavement condition index by different methods: case study of Maringá, Brazil, Technology Center, Civil Engineering Department, Colombo Avenue 5790, University Garden, Maringá 87020–900, Brazil (2020)
14. Montella, A.: An integrated approach to improving road safety: scenarios, lines of action and research proposals. National Research Council-Transport Finalized Project (1999)
15. Martins, M.A., Garcez, T.V.: A multidimensional and multi-period analysis of safety on roads. Accid. Anal. Prev. **162**, 106401 (2021)
16. https://geoportal.madrid.es/
17. https://datos.madrid.es
18. Gullotta, G., Loret, E., Stewart, C., Sarti, F.: Traffic attractors and congestion in the urban context, the case of the city of Rome. J. Geogr. Inf. Syst. **12**, 545–559 (2020)
19. Intini, P., Berloco, N., Fonzone, A., Fountas, G., Ranieri, V.: The influence of traffic, geometric and context variables on urban crash types: a grouped random parameter multinomial logit approach. Analytic Methods in Accident Research **28**, 100141 (2020)

A Phygital Space-Related Storytelling of a Cultural Intangible and Social Experience. The *Telve Humanscape / Mappe del sentire* Application

Letizia Bollini(✉) [iD] and Giulia Faccin

Free University of Bozen-Bolzano, Piazza Università 1, 39100 Bolzano, Italy
letizia.bollini@unibz.it

Abstract. The paper aims to address the transformation of the relationship between the *physical* and *digital* experience of urban space in the field of Cultural Intangible Landscape Heritage. In order to do that, it introduces the concept of the *phygital* and discusses its potential application in the field of CILH storytelling thanks to a pilot case study. *Telve Humanscape / Mappe del sentire*, has been conceptualised and designed to map, explore and narrate the transformation of the Talvera River area in Bolzano, thanks to the memories, stories and experiences of local people.

Keywords: Phygital story-telling · Cultural Intangible and landscape Heritage · site-specific experience design

1 *Phygital*: Converging Spaces and New Human-Interactions Paradigma

The way we know and relate to the physical environment and people far and near us has been profoundly transformed in the face of technological change.

The Internet in the 1990s [1], the mobile revolution inaugurated in 2007 and the continuous return of devices and environments of virtual and cross-reality, from Sutherland's *Sword of Damocles* [2] to the hype of meta-verses (from MUDs to MMOs, from Second Life to the Meta-Metaverse), our experience is no longer even *mediated* by the digital, but even *post*-digital [3, 4]. The level of integration or interference of digital devices and technology has now become an organic part of our seamless living, but the spectrum covered or mediated by devices or supported by smart domains is broad and ranges from interaction limited to our smartphone or personal devices as a source of information in a situated context, being present in a place and at a time, to the more fluid and transparent ones where our moving around in space generates, even without us being aware of it (or because of surveillance), interactions and data. Furthermore, the paradigm of our very being is leaping of discontinuity [5], thanks to the convergence with artificial intelligences (such as the generative ones). Such a transformation that has completely eroded certain ontological statutes has yet to find its own epistemology capable of redefining and conceptualising the collision between the different planes, the *physical* and the *digital*, the *real* and the *virtual*, understood in their multiple and ambiguous definitions.

In its disarming banality, perhaps, the term *phygital* seems to be able to encompass and render the complexity of the collapse of the two planes, opening up a multitude of possible interpretations, but above all restricting it to the necessary co-efficiency of the dual condition of being/existing or being able to experience in the two reals, that is, in a continuum of the *physical* and the *digital*. "Obviously, it is a mixture of the words physical and digital. It was coined in 2007 by Chris Weil of the [Australian] advertising agency Momentum Worldwide. In its original context of marketing communications, it refers to building relationships with customers in both the physical and digital worlds. From this communicative origin, it has spread to many other disciplines. In each field, phygital is used with a different meaning." [6].

The professional world has created and appropriated this umbrella term, which nevertheless coexists with several other terms and definitions, most of which are oriented towards the technology – Augmented Reality (AR), Virtual Reality (VR), Cross Reality (XR), to name just a few of the most common—rather than the human experience. The potential that remains to be explored, however, lies precisely on this side of the question. That is, how the fusion of the real, embodied, situated experience and the digital, broadly speaking, mediated, enabled, enhanced or augmented by technology, generates new possible modes of experience and knowledge. Or, interpreting the phenomenon, from the point of view of design possibilities, as the hybridisation between the two realms, can be explored, designed and understood. Possible developments are also promising in areas very different from corporate marketing and omnichannel retailing; indeed, it is in the cultural, intangible and historical realms that this blended form of experience seems to be fulfilling its potential to provide people with a meaningful, rich and articulate experience of knowledge.

In fact, digital media is increasingly used to enrich and contextualize physical spaces, like museums or historical sites, giving visitors a more immersive and participatory experience. The technologies mentioned create a new dynamic between the physical and the digital, enhancing traditional ways to explore an exhibit or, more generally "displayed" information. In fact, by focusing on digital technologies as a means for a deeper and multilayered narration of cultural heritage, they open the possibility of keeping the significance of the existing space while being able to connect information directly to the location. Emplacement [7, 8] reframes information or digital content as not just something that exists in digital space but is specifically "placed" within physical spaces and is intended to interact with people in the context of those spaces. It connects the physical environment and the digital one in a way that both influence people's perceptions. This is pivotal in sites where infrastructural intervention would alter the physical spaces (such as heritage sites), weakening the relationship between the person and endangering the authenticity of the place itself. Emplacement allows the individual to be immersed in the significance of the material space, while they are given the chance to digitally access context-aware information, enhancing or altering the user's understanding. Furthermore, embodied cognition suggests that digital elements in physical environments support and enhance cognitive engagement, making interactions with physical objects more intuitive and meaningful [9].

Not only does emplacement grant visceral, emotional and cognitive engagement to physical spaces without jeopardising (heritage) sites [10], but most importantly, it allows them to develop according to the necessities of time and society, preventing their *museification*. In the digital realm, layering is potentially limitless and offers infinite chances to re-frame, compare, and add information and details [11].

2 The Cultural Heritage Dilemma

This paper will frame heritage as a social construct where its meanings are negotiated through past-present and power relations, with an active role in meaning and identity-making. Consequently, it becomes evident that while heritage has always been a part of human history, what has evolved is rather how it is defined, framed, and valued within (Western) society. Institutionalisation has played a crucial role in the preservation of heritage, facilitating both international interest and cooperation. This process has resulted in the safeguarding of remarkable cultural sites and practices across the globe, allowing us to experience and witness the richness of diverse cultural traditions. However, like any institutional framework, heritage preservation is inherently centralized, following top-down directives [12]. Consequently, cultural heritage underwent a process of categorisation that, while enabling the development of modern preservation practices, also embedded values and models of heritage rooted in the context from which these categories originated (the West). Laurajane Smith [12] introduced the concept of *Authorised Heritage Discourse* (AHD), which highlights the elite, nation-state-driven nature of institutionalized heritage practices. This does not suggest that institutions (such as ICOMOS *the International Council on Monuments and Sites*, ICOM the *International Council of Museums*, and UNESCO) have nation-state-driven agendas. Nevertheless, they are inherently bound to values and views which resonate in the society (Western) and time (post-WW2) they were founded. This inevitably influences the policies, structure and approaches to heritage, inevitably "overlooking some communal, intangible cultural practices that are other from the Western conception of heritage." [13]. In other words, the AHD promotes a Western vision of cultural construction and conservation, privileging elite values and their own cultural traditions assuming them as the parameters of heritage. The AHD is facilitated by one double-edged founding principle: *universal value* which undoubtedly originates and operates as a way to foster international cooperation and cohesion. However, as Cleere [14] points out, the notion of universality has been subject to criticism, as it is deeply rooted in the European cultural tradition, and shaped by historical and aesthetic parameters derived from classical philosophy. He argues that such a concept can only truly apply to the earliest phases of human cultural development or to the global culture of the late twentieth century. Moreover, the cultural diversity of human experience means that different societies perceive significance in different ways, and not all cultures share the same understanding of heritage and its values, sometimes to the extent that these differences become insurmountable. This highlights the tensions inherent in the application of universal value as it may unintentionally impose a Eurocentric framework on diverse heritage expressions. If we accept heritage as a process of meaning-making, we must also seek out the spaces and practices through which meaning is actively mediated in contemporary life. Heritage is not merely a static testimony of the past [15]. Rather, it exists in the continuous and dynamic negotiation between past and present. This perspective urges us to move beyond a fixed institutionalised notion of heritage and recognise it as an evolving social construct, shaped by ongoing cultural interactions, reinterpretations and reimagining. Heritage is as much about the past as it is of the present and recognising it as such qualifies preservation. This shift towards an often-standardised notion of heritage, facilitated by a disconnect between the general public and the intangible, is also a consequence of the rise of heritage experts. These experts, as spokespeople for institutionalised notions of heritage, play a crucial role in shaping the dominant narrative. It is, then vital to understand what heritage means today and whether trends of institutionalisation prevent us from protecting and valuing the meaning-making processes of contemporary collective identity. To do so, it is paramount to focus on the concepts of space and place. Laurajane Smith noted in her fieldwork that many communities cherished heritage sites as much as the intangible cultural practice that took place there. In her view, these sites may not always be architecturally impressive, but their significance stems from the participatory collective value that local people and communities attach to them [16] The "sense of place" that residents identify as heritage is site-specific to the practices, experiences, and histories. By stressing the importance of place and action as a unified whole, we agree that heritage cannot be fully relished if these elements are disconnected. One notable example highlighted by Smith [17] is the Wanyi Aboriginal Australian community, where "it became obvious that it was important for the women to recite and record these histories, not at home over a table, but in their cultural territory or 'country' and, where relevant, at the appropriate cultural site" [12] There is, in fact, an abyss between "space" (an abstract, undefined concept) and "place" (a space that is given meaning through human experience and interaction) [18].

Soja's *thirdspace* theory [19] transcends the traditional dualism of physical and imagined spaces by merging the two into a unified realm where both the real and the perceived coexist. In this sense, heritage can be seen as a "third space" where the past and present continually interact and reshape one another. This aligns with the idea that heritage is not static but actively created through the lived experiences and interpretations of individuals and communities, thus allowing for a more inclusive, fluid understanding of cultural practices and places. By applying Soja's thirdspace to heritage, we can better appreciate how spaces of memory, identity, and cultural practice evolve and how these meanings are constantly renegotiated through collective experience and social interaction.

A difference was investigated with different yet related perspectives by both Yi-Fu Tuan [18] as well as John Brinckerhoff Jackson [20]. The former focused on the social construction of the concept of places that become meaningful through the emotions, memories, and identities that people attach to them, while the vernacular landscape, theorised by Jackson are "those everyday landscapes shaped by ordinary people, rather than designed by architects or urban planners."

In this context, therefore, exploring the concept of cultural heritage connected to an inhabited and lived space implies a reflection on its holistic transformation that persists beyond the moment in which its symbolic meaning is fixed in cultural-historical terms.

Two opposing forces must be grasped, a centripetal one that would like the space crystallised in its *meaningful* representation at a given moment, as the only one possible. On the other hand, a centrifugal and vital force that invests it and continues its transformative flow. To them also corresponds a sort of dual statute, that of the external and cultural gaze that looks at a specific place as a *museum-object* and expropriates it of its experience by virtue of the higher value of its preservation and transmission to the future as a memory of present/past. On the other hand, there is the internal, grassroots one of those who have shaped that place over time, loading it with their own personal and collective values, rituals and experiences, the very ones to whom it owes its value in cultural, social and intangible terms. The paradox, therefore, is to disconnect these two elements, the *place* and the *community* that produce its *meaning* through its own human fabric and daily experience.

However, the Talvera River, together with the Isarco and the Adige, which flow just outside the city, constitute a significant orographic basin both in environmental terms and in terms of urban structure. The two most recently built parts of the city concerning the original historic core, in fact, are respectively beyond Talvera - the Italian area later conurbated with Gries, an originally autonomous German-speaking urban core, and then towards the increasingly newer districts in the different waves of urbanisation of the area up to the urabian limits represented by the Novacella area, Don Bosco and the autonomous and eco-sustainable Casanova neighbourhoods. On the other side, beyond Isarco, the city is also characterised by the trade fair, the industrial area and the technological pole constituted by the NOI Tech park and the new seat of the faculty of engineering, noncjé by the shopping centres and the airport is configured as an almost autonomous structure for the rest of the urban territory (Fig. 1).

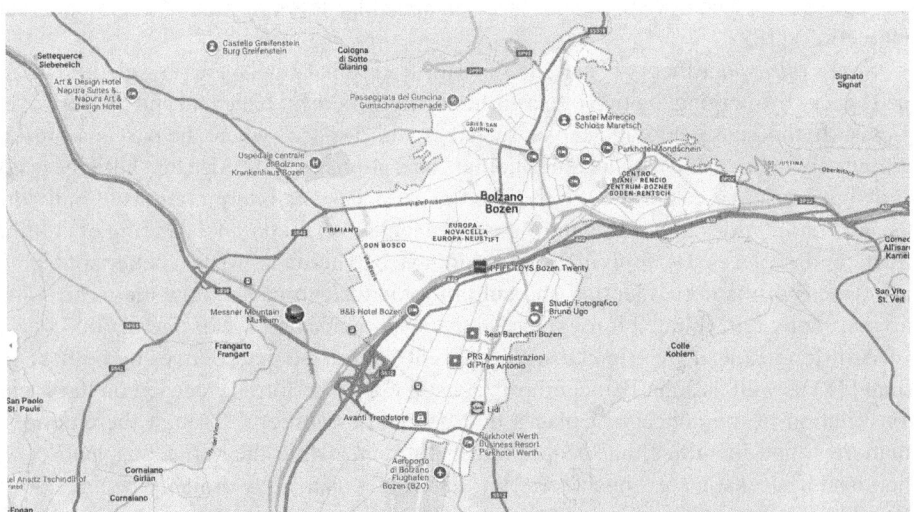

Fig. 1. Map of the city of Bolzano, showing the Talvera flowing into the Isarco/Eisack and, outside the urban area, the Adige river.

3 Landmarks and the Social Construction of a Place

The project ALICE *A-maz(e)-ing: phygitaL storytelling in desIgn for Cultural landscapes & hEritage* – funded by the Free University of Bozen-Bolzano as a Start-up project between 2021 and 2024 – explores the evolution of interaction design and digital communication, with a focus on multimodal narratives, the perception of phygital space, and the people and social experience, both from the theoretical as well as a methodological point of view in strong relation with the landscape and intangible heritage context. In its initial phase, the study explores how to apply the concept of generous interfaces – proposed by Whitelaw [21] – in space-based [22] and multimodal interactions [23] in the blended/phygital scenario. The research also investigates the shifting of the historical idea of cultural heritage (GLAMS, monuments, collections and so on) to more grassroots phenomena of the intangible heritage, including the immaterial social expressions and traditions aimed to preserve cultural and knowledge diversity.

In cities like Bolzano, where urban spaces continually evolve, the project addresses the complexities of representing tangible and intangible heritage in its contemporaneity. Through the application of multimodal narratives, augmented reality, and geolocation tools, the project seeks to move beyond traditional forms of heritage representation. It aims to transcend static depictions of heritage by incorporating more dynamic, participatory approaches rooted in the local context and social experience. This is particularly relevant in exploring how digital tools can interact with and preserve the vernacular landscape together in everyday, lived environments that are often overshadowed by official narratives.

Starting from the exploration of the local area, certain elements, both spatial and social, emerge clearly. But precisely because of its historical-cultural, ethnographic and linguistic complexity, the city and the territory of the province make the discovery, analysis, understanding and study of this urban and human space particularly complex, especially for those who are not organically part of one of the local communities. However, in the course of the exploration and discovery of the city, certain symbolic elements emerge overbearingly as belonging to one of the communities and/or historical stratifications, see, in this regard, the research such as the one conducted and presented at the ICCSA 2023 [24] on the *Laubengasse,* or the in-depth studies on the Fascist era and the "Italian" city, and the new urbanisation and the musealisation of certain neighbourhoods as in the Bolzanism experience [25].

However, the Talvera River, together with the Isarco and the Adige, which flow just outside the city, constitute a significant orographic basin both in environmental terms and in terms of urban structure. The two most recently built parts of the city for the original historic core, in fact, are respectively *Oltre Talvera* (Beyond Talvera) – the Italian area later conurbated with Gries, an originally autonomous German-speaking urban core, and then towards the increasingly newer districts in the different waves of urbanisation of the area up to the urban limits represented by the Novacella area, Don Bosco and the autonomous and eco-sustainable Casanova neighbourhoods. On the other side, *Olte Isarco* (Beyond Isarco), the city also characterised by the trade fair, the industrial area and the technological pole constituted by the NOI Tech park and the new headquarters of the faculty of engineering, as well as by the shopping centres and the airport, is configured as an almost autonomous structure with respect to the rest of the urban territory (Figs. 2 and 3).

Fig. 2. The newly built Talvera bridge connects the municipalities of Gries, Dodiciville and Bolzano, 1900–02. (Source: Collection of historical postcards, 52. https://opencity.comune.bolzano.it/. CC BY-NC-ND 4.0)

The Talvera seems to be a natural and urban *limens* in this area, a watershed in a literal sense, concerning the zoning of the city, but on the contrary a social catalyst. A sort of free zone designed to become the promenade and urban park capable of bringing nature back into the centre of an urbanised and anthropic territory that contrasts with the city's mountainous surroundings. In addition, the very history of the city's relationship with the river turns out to be paradigmatic for social relations and the processes of symbolic construction of certain underlying values. The research therefore took this privileged relationship as a starting point and explored the post-modalities offered as a local case study, as well as a paradigm of other modes of relationship between urban spaces and river courses. Starting from these considerations, the research, therefore, analysed a series of case studies in which the relationship between city and river – one of the most common conditions in the processes of settlement in a territory and the development of urban structures in human history – developed according to different paradigms and recognisable, archetypal patterns. Among the possible ones, some recurring constructs have been identified. While not representing an exhaustive mapping, those identified propose significant patterns in terms of urban planning and the relationship or social experience of the territory. Among these, it is worth highlighting a few significant typologies, of which the Talvera represents one of the possible models for the subsequent development of the communication project of the case study. a) a

Fig. 3. The former town hall at Ponte Talvera (Source: Public Works Photographic Fund, 638. https://opencity.comune.bolzano.it/. CC BY-NC-ND 4.0)

negation relationship. This is the model adopted, for example in Italy by cities such as Genoa, Milan or Bologna and many others. Watercourses, whether torrential or with a stable course, have often been buried, covered or made to flow under buildings and transport infrastructures, denying their natural presence and forcing them into artificial beds. The adoption of this model often corresponds to episodes, sometimes dramatic, of overflowing and flooding. Especially under the transformations due to climate change, this solution increasingly shows its inadequacy in the construction of a homeostatic relationship between the city and its territory; b) A *dialogical* relationship in which the city and the river coexist. The former welcomes the river's course into its space while containing it and controlling it within routes and embankments that can also capture its seasonal variability and extreme events. Whether it is Paris or Rome, the course of the river also becomes an opportunity for the use of natural space within the urbanised territory; c) a relationship of *coexistence* in which the natural space of the river finds its freedom within the urban structure with ample room for flooding or variations in the course of natural cycles and extreme events; d) and finally a relationship of *cancellation*, as in the case of the city of Valencia, where the river was even diverted from its natural course, precisely because of the catastrophic nature of its floods, and the urban void left behind became an opportunity to rethink space in a social and shared dimension. Recent events (the torrential rains and the flooding in the winter of 2024 with dramatic consequences in terms of deaths) deeply question this model that seemed to be winning in its artificial balances.

The Talvera, in this sense. Represents a compromise in terms of the reorganisation of its space within the urban structure, but is unique in terms of how its "reorganisation" was conceived and realised.

4 The *Telve Humanscape / Mappe del sentire* App: A Case Study

Drawing from Herzfeld's [26] concept of cultural intimacy, which posits that national identity often relies on informal, local practices, the project focuses on the heritage that emerges from the everyday spaces and social memories of local communities. In the context of Bolzano, the Talvera River area serves as a relevant case study in demonstrating that although this area may not be celebrated in traditional forms of heritage, it holds considerable contemporary socio-cultural and meaning-making significance that underwent 4 major phases. The Talvera-Talfer River and its Promenade (also known as the Wassermauer Promenade) have undergone numerous transformations over the years, mirroring the city's development, and its relation to nature and between communities. In its early days, the river was primarily a functional element for the city, providing water for industry, particularly for mills, the slaughterhouse in Macello and the numerous vineyards. However, it also posed risks due to frequent flooding, making the area surrounding it dangerous and unpredictable. This instability discouraged the formation of a cohesive public space where people could meet and engage, limiting the river's potential to become a recognized meaning-making site. In 1934, during the Fascist regime, the architect Marcello Piacentini was commissioned to draft the expansion plan for the city of Bolzano. Piacentini's project envisioned the creation of a district with a distinctly Italian character, with the Victory Monument at its core. This project was part of a broader strategy by the Fascist regime to Italianise South Tyrol, which had been annexed to the Kingdom of Italy in 1919 (Figs. 4 and 5).

Fig. 4. View from the Talversa Bridge towards the Victory Monument (Courtesy of the authors).

While most of its projects have been realised, the rectification of the Talvera-Talfer has not been implemented and the riverbed together with its margins remained significantly unchanged. It was with Michele Lettieri [27] that, for the first time, the Talvera

Fig. 5. The actual town hall at Ponte Talvera (Courtesy of the authors).

River was truly reimagined as a space for the people. Between 1970 and 1977, Lettieri worked to transform this space into the Prati del Talvera, Bolzano's most important public park. His project was unique because it was not only a municipal effort but also involved students from the Istituto Tecnico per Geometri "Andrea e Pietro Delai", the Italian Army's IV Alpine Army Corps, and the municipal gardening department. This collaborative approach helped turn what was once an underutilized and unstable landscape into a vital green lung for the city. In the present day, the river is undergoing a further transformation. The Bacini Montani, a provincial agency responsible for water management, is working on the re-naturalisation of the river's flow. This project aims to restore a more natural and ecological balance, improving the river's environmental health and ensuring its continued role as a central and sustainable part of the city's fabric.

The Talvera River area presents a rich repository of historical traceability, archival materials, and both tangible and intangible elements of local cultural heritage. While it may initially appear devoid of immediately recognizable, visually triggered stereotypical narratives, this very quality offers an opportunity to explore urban development and its socio-environmental and political implications. The site provides a seemingly neutral ground through which the complexities and historical responsibilities embedded in the city's biography can be critically examined (Fig. 6).

In this initial phase of the research, emphasis has been placed on historical-archival investigation, prioritising the direct analysis of a diverse range of documentary sources. These include photographic, audiovisual, iconographic, and cartographic

Fig. 6. Images of the Michele Lettieri's autobiography: *Un torrente di ricordi. Racconti conviviali della vecchia Bolzano* [A torrent of memories. Convivial tales of old Bolzano] published in 2015.

materials, alongside institutional paperwork, correspondence, and urban planning proposals. Engaging with these resources has also allowed for an intersection with pre-existing studies and projects, conducted by both institutional and non-institutional entities, such as *Lungomare, Platform Cultural Heritage Cultural Production*, the *Historical Archive*, Fondo Lettieri, Fondo Rasmo, *Bacini Montani, Giardinerie Pubbliche, Stadtarchiv Bozen*. This allowed us to historically and visually map valuable facts and testimonies and put them into relation with the present state of the area and the lived experience. These materials helped us understand the complex relationship between urban development, social cohesion and the natural environment, offering insights into historical trends, present desires and future possibilities. The outcome provided a comprehensive database of visual and written material about the development of the Talvera area, reinforcing our thesis that, while visually discreet, it is a site rich in socio-cultural and historical significance. From this evidence, it was clear that the river and its surroundings have undergone continuous change and evolution, shaped by and reflecting the mutual relationship between the socio-ecological and political contexts (Fig. 7).

Doreen Massey argued that space is a social product, shaped by social, economic, and political relations rather than being a static, pre-existing container. She emphasizes that space is dynamic, always in the process of being made. In *For Space* (2005), she writes: "Space is the product of interrelations; as constituted through interactions, from the immensity of the global to the intimately tiny" [28]. To align with this perspective, methods of one-to-one and participatory qualitative research have been applied in this study. These approaches allow us to gather and analyse non-numerical and personal perspectives on how the Talvera area is, was, and will be lived. Additionally, they have enabled us to access individuals' social realities beyond pre-existing networks. To align with the project objectives and the chosen methodology, the following operations were outlined: one-to-one interviews with individuals who frequent the Talvera area, voice message chains, open calls for contributors in local newspapers, and open-call contributions in local Facebook groups. These operations are currently in the early stages and progressing. Therefore, results and conclusions will be available at the end of the assignment. So far, 26 participants, without age limitations, have shared audio memories, which have been categorised as follows: Italian (local linguistic group), Italian (non-local), Expats, and German (local linguistic group).

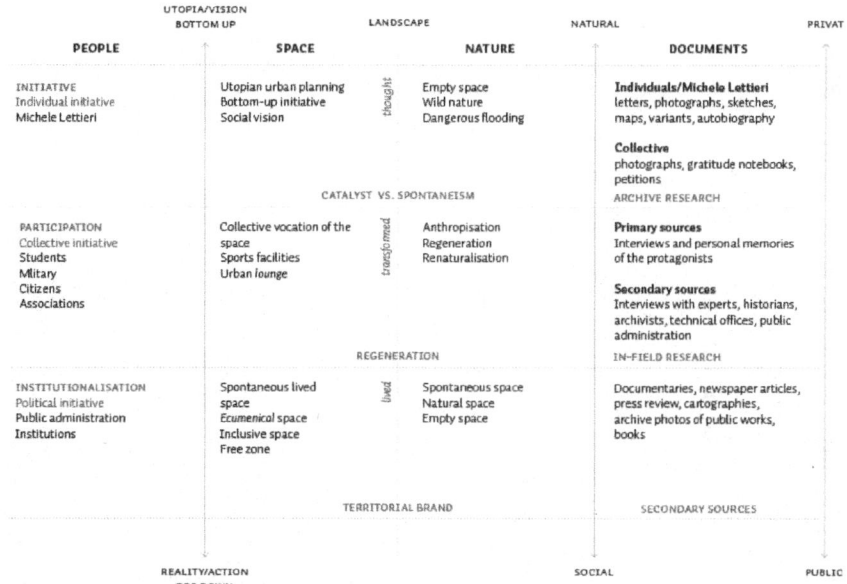

Fig. 7. The diagram shows the analysis made on the 4 project research tracks, 1) people, 2) space, 3) nature, 4) documents and the different levels of interpretation: a) individual, b) collective and c) institutional (Courtesy of the authors).

This project explores the blending of physical space and digital technology in the context of intangible heritage and collective experiences. It moves beyond traditional digital transpositions (like guided tours) by leveraging augmented reality (AR) to enhance the experience of *heritage* while preserving the real-world environment. The emphasis on perceiving ourselves as being in *space*, and the prosthetic potential of digital tools shape the project's focus on spatially embedded, responsive experiences. Drawing on Doreen Massey's insight that "there is no other place than the place we empathise with or perceive with", this project reinforces the notion that heritage is intimately tied to the lived experience of space. Massey's concept challenges us to rethink how places are not simply geographical locations but are understood and experienced through emotional and cultural engagement. This idea is central to the project, which uses geolocation and user proximity as triggers to create a digital experience that is both spatially embedded and responsive to the physical world around it (Figs. 8 and 9).

The use of augmented reality (AR) as a tool offers a way to connect digital interactions with physical environments without overwhelming or distorting the actual context. Rather than creating a virtual space separate from the real world, as is often the case in fully digital experiences, the AR experience interacts with and depends on the user's physical presence in the space. The digital environment integrates into the tangible one as a continuum. They enhance one another, not replace or substitute. We asked casual park regulars to share visual and/or audio memories and hopes. We then recorded, archived and geolocated where these memories belong to form a tapestry of significance. As the user navigates Prrati del Talvera, these recollections fade in and out between historical

Fig. 8. The *Telve Humanscape / Map*pe del sentire prototype: situated interactions with historical documentation (Courtesy of the authors).

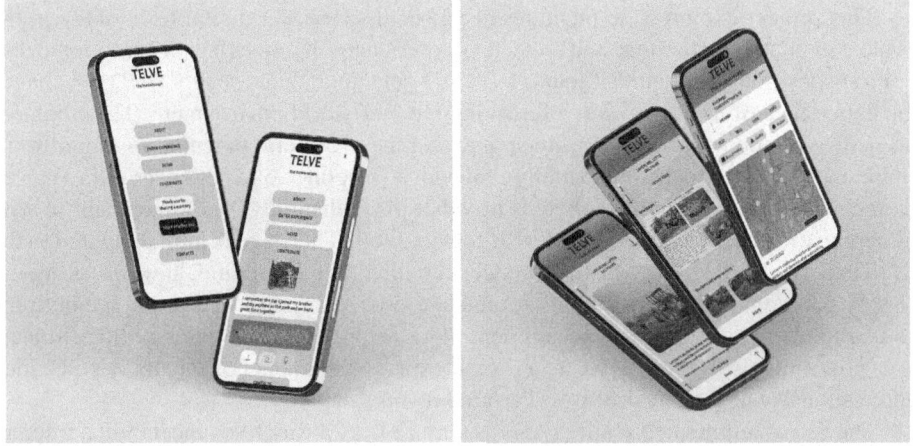

Fig. 9. The *Telve Humanscape / Mappe del se*ntire prototype: a) login and acoustic interactions; b) geobased interactions (Courtesy of the authors).

materials. In this manner, users are afforded the ability to navigate freely within the "real space", allowing them to spontaneously gravitate towards points of interest or receive notifications upon nearing one. This dynamic not only ensures that the materials remain spatially unobtrusive and readily accessible but also underscores the project's commitment to preserving the eco-systemic integrity of analogue environments. Consequently, in certain instances, users may be alerted to the presence of a significant point; however, access to its content will be contingent upon a requisite number of individuals occupying the same area. This density-dependent activation is particularly pertinent in cases where the materials pertain to collective experiences. By employing this approach, the project seeks to safeguard the communal nature of a blended environment while mitigating the isolating tendencies frequently associated with digital realms. Furthermore, it ensures that the experience remains congruent with the collective identity of the place it seeks to augment and narrate. Simultaneously, the project aligns with the sociological concept of *boundary objects,* as introduced by Davide Spallazzo [29], wherein users, as well as analogue and digital environments, engage in interaction at liminal thresholds.

This mirrors the concept of *heterotopia,* as described by Michel Foucault [8], where spaces can be understood as historical situations, sites of layered meaning, and cultural narratives that unfold in relation to their surroundings. This approach allows the project to preserve the historical context of the place while enhancing it with digital overlays that add depth and interactivity, rather than replacing the physical environment. The project's dynamic, where content is triggered only when a sufficient number of users are present in a given area, highlights its commitment to preserving the collective, shared experience of space, which is a key feature of intangible heritage. The use of density-based access introduces an important aspect: material content related to shared experiences becomes accessible only when the social conditions, in this case, the gathering of a certain number of users in proximity, are met. This preserves the ecological nature of heritage, where the experience is not simply about individual consumption but about the social interaction that often defines how heritage is shared, passed down, and experienced in real-world contexts. This strategy of keeping the digital experience inherently social and contextual resonates with Henri Lefebvre's notion that space is not just an empty container, but a socially produced entity that reflects the relationships, identities, and interactions of people within it. Lefebvre's model of space [30], perceived, conceived, and lived space, can be seen in this approach. By avoiding the isolation that digital technologies often impose, this project uses AR not to replace the physical, collective experience of place, but to enhance it by aligning digital interventions with the spatial dynamics of the real world. The boundary object of the AR experience lies at the intersection of digital technology and the physical world, enabling a collaborative, context-aware experience of heritage that is not only more inclusive but also more dynamic and socially embedded.

Through this approach, the project respects the ecological nature of heritage, fostering a collective, immersive experience that reinforces the idea that heritage is not simply a static object to be viewed, but a shared, lived experience that connects individuals.

5 Conclusions

In conclusion, this project seeks to further the development of an ethnographic map that captures the evolving and living heritage of the Talvera, weaving together archival materials and contemporary testimonies. By documenting and mapping these narratives, we aim to preserve the dynamic and collective memory of the place, ensuring that its intangible cultural heritage remains accessible and resonant. Rather than imposing a rigid digital framework, the project prioritises an approach that enhances, rather than overrides, the organic social experience of the site. This ensures that interactions remain fluid and spontaneous, preserving the organic process of meaning-making and significance negotiation, which qualifies the Talvera as a living heritage site and its social dimension. The next phase will focus on developing a functional prototype and user testing to refine its responsiveness and inclusivity. Additionally, multilingual integration will be a key priority, fostering accessibility and engagement across diverse communities, ultimately reinforcing the project's role as a participatory and socially embedded storytelling medium.

Acknowledgments. Although the paper is the joint work of both authors, Letizia Bollini is the author of paragraphs 1 and 3 and Giulia Faccin of paragraphs 2, 4 and 5.

References

1. Turkle, S.: Life on the Screen: Identity in the Age of the Internet. Simon & Schuster, New York (1997)
2. Sutherland, I.E.: The ultimate display. In: Proceedings of IFIP 65, **2**, pp. 506–508 (1965). http://www.universelle-automation.de/1965_Boston.pdf. Accessed 27 Mar 2025
3. Wiser, M.: The Computer for the 21. Century (1991). https://web.archive.org/web/20111116133741/http://wiki.daimi.au.dk/pca/_files/weiser-orig.pdf. Accessed 27 Mar 2025
4. Negroponte, N.: Beyond Digital Wired, 12 (1998). https://www.wired.com/1998/12/negroponte-55/. Accessed 27 Mar 2025
5. Accoto, C.: Il mondo in sintesi. Cinque brevi lezioni di filosofia della simulazione. Egea, Milano (2022)
6. Ilius, L.: A Definition of 'Phygital': The space where real and virtual dimensions meet, Talent Transformation (2023). https://insights.talentformation.com/a-definition-of-phygital-the-space-where-real-and-virtual-dimensions-meet/. Accessed 27 Mar 2025
7. Resmini, A.: The Spatial Turn in Information Architecture. In Bollini, L. (ed.) Per-forming Spaces. On Designing Phygital Narratives within the Cultural Heritage Ecosystem. Biblion Edition, Milano (2025)
8. Vidler, A., Foucault, M., Johnston, P.: Heterotopias. *AA files* **69** (2014): 18–22. https://www.jstor.org/stable/pdf/43202545.pdf?casa_token=UKOLhVAdVLgAAAAA:xHeqvwA-TfcEA4Bs-990L6KxdQBruJ2cnZHoKlzbgjniPcW-jkhuUkaWhUNkYzMSCn3ArD7_31Tm_k2TWPhQP2oR1kpjGP8nqe2XtmvHc9yVPinEwys. Visited 27 Mar 2025
9. Kirsh, D.: Embodied cognition and the magical future of interaction design. ACM Transactions on Computer-Human Interaction (TOCHI) **20**(1), 1–30 (2013). https://avant.edu.pl/wp-content/uploads/Avant-David-Kirsh-Embodied-Cognition-and-the-Magical-Future.pdf. Visited 27 Mar 2025
10. Morville, P.: Ambient Findability: What We Find Changes Who We Become. O'Reilly Media Inc, San Francisco (2005)
11. Bollini, L.: Dall'ipertesto alla performance multimodale: Forme di rappresentazione digitale dell'allestimento. In: Borsotti M.& Sartori, G. (Eds.): Il progetto di allestimento e la sua officina. Luogo, memoria ed evento: Mostre alle Fruttiere di Palazzo te, Mantova, pp. 33–35. Skirà, Milano (2009)
12. Smith, L.: Uses of heritage. Routledge, Abingdon-on-Thames (Uk) (2006)

13. ([15] Faccin 2025). In: Bollini, L. (ed.) Per-forming Spaces. On Designing Phygital Narratives within the Cultural Heritage Ecosystem. Biblion Edition, Milano (2025)
14. Cleere, H.: Designating World Heritage Industrial Sites. In: International Engineering History and Heritage: Improving Bridges to ASCE's 150th Anniversary, pp. 171–174 (2001)
15. Urry, J.: Sociology of time and space. The Blackwell companion to social theory (1996)
16. Bollini, L.: Territories of digital communities. Representing the social landscape of web relationships. In: Computational Science and Its Applications-ICCSA 2011, Santander, Spain, June 20–23, 2011. Proceedings, Part I 11, pp. 501–511. Springer, Berlin Heidelberg (2011)
17. Smith, L., Akagawa, N.: Intangible Heritage. Routledge, London (2009)
18. Tuan, Y.-F.: Space and Place: The Perspective of Experience. University of Minnesota Press, Minneapolis (1977)
19. Soja, E.W.: Thirdspace: Toward a new consciousness of space and spatiality. In: Communicating in the Third Space, pp. 63–75. Routledge, Abingdon-on-Thames (Uk) (2008)
20. Jackson, J.B.: The future of the vernacular. Understanding ordinary landscapes, pp. 145–156 (1997)
21. Whitelaw, M.: Generous interfaces for digital cultural collections. Digital humanities quarterly **9**(1), 1–16 (2015)
22. Bollini, L.: Per-forming Spaces. Interaction, experience, and interface design at the phygital turn. In: Bollini, L. (ed.) Per-forming Spaces. On Designing Phygital Narratives within the Cultural Heritage Ecosystem. Biblion Edition, Milano (2025)
23. Bollini, L.: Registica multimodale. Il design dei new media. Maggioli Editore, Rimini (2008)
24. Bollini, L., Mastroianni, M.L.: Typographic topology/topographic typography. reading the urban identity through the historical typescape: hypothesis for an AR situated mobile app. In: O. Gervasi et al. (eds.): Computational Science and Its Applications – ICCSA 2023, LNCS, vol 14105, pp. 613–629. Springer, Cham (2023)
25. Bolzanism Museum. https://www.bolzanism.com/. Visited 27 Mar 2025
26. Herzfeld, M.: Spatial cleansing: Monumental vacuity and the idea of the West. J. Mater. Cult. **11**(1–2), 127–149 (2006)
27. Lettieri, M.: Un torrente di ricordi. Racconti conviviali della vecchia Bolzano, Edition Raetia, Bolzano (2015)
28. Massey, D.: For space. SAGE Publications, Thousand Oaks (CA) (2005)
29. Spallazzo, D.: Exploring the role of boundary objects in mobile experiences for the cultural heritage field. In: Bollini, L. (Ed.): Per-forming Spaces. On Designing Phygital Narratives within the Cultural Heritage Ecosystem. Biblion Edition, Milano (2025)
30. Lefebrve, H.: The Production of Space. Basil Backwell (1991)

Methodologies for Wildland-Urban Interface (WUI) Fire Risk Assessment – Case Study North-Eastern Attica Region

Angeliki Papazoglou[1](✉) , Apostolos Lagarias[2] , and Anastasia Stratigea[1]

[1] Department of Geography and Regional Planning, School of Rural, Surveying and Geoinformatics Engineering, National Technical University of Athens, Athens, Greece
angeliki.papazoglou@hotmail.com, stratige@central.ntua.gr
[2] Department of Regional Planning and Development, School of Engineering, University of Thessaly, Volos, Greece
lagarias@uth.gr

Abstract. In the light of the Climate Change era, wildfires in forest areas appear to be intensified, placing at risk the urban fabric being in close proximity to wildland fire prone areas. Such a risk causes severe socio-economic and environmental consequences, calling for proactive policy action and rendering Disaster Management planning an urgent need. In support of this urgency, this study aims at assessing fire risk in Wildland-Urban Interfaces (WUIs), i.e. urban and peri-urban areas that are settled in the forests' neighborhood or in close proximity to them. Towards this end, it aims at: establishing a pool of factors/criteria and a pool of methodologies related to WUIs Fire Risk Assessment; and testing/comparing results produced by two methodologies, selected from the above set, namely the Analytical Hierarchy Process (AHP) and the Random Forest algorithm through the Forest-Based Classification tool. Results obtained by the two methodologies demonstrate a rather diversified spatial pattern of forest fire risk, which is further validated by the inspection of the impacts (burned area) of recurrent wildfire incidents, occurring in the study area in the time span 2000-2023; while fire risks in WUIs are sketched in the study area, calling for proactive policy action for ensuring resilience to future forest fire incidents in this quite vulnerable area of Attica Region.

Keywords: Climate Change · Wildland-Urban Interface · Fire Risk Assessment

1 Introduction

In recent decades, wildfires are increasing in frequency and severity, both at the global and the European level, a fact that is tightly associated with Climate Change (CC) repercussions. In addition, climatic models' projections indicate a rising frequency of droughts, hot extrsemes and extended heat waves as well as a declining trend in precipitation rates. That said, climatic conditions that favor fire incidents are expected to be amplified, leading to the culmination of both the number and intensity of fire incidents as well as the extension of the fire season. This holds even truer for the Mediterranean territory, namely one of the most vulnerable to CC regions of the world [1], marked by extensive heat waves and droughts [2]. CC implications in the Mediterranean are thus leading to an increasing fire risk and incalculable consequences for both the natural and human ecosystems, a fact that is further exacerbated due to the intense urbanization and urban sprawl occurring in this region [1–4]. Rising of fire risk has, in turn, led to the upgrading of firefighting resources, intense production of fire risk-related information and efforts for awareness raising in Southern European countries, like Portugal, Spain, Italy and Greece. In addition, frequency and intensity of fire incidents advocate the need for more proactive action in order for the recurring wildfire events to be prevented and/or managed; and their adverse impacts to be mitigated [5].

In the Mediterranean region, *Wildland-Urban Interfaces* (WUIs) are nowadays gaining scientific attention with respect to fire risk assessment. Such interfaces are defined as the zones, within which the urban fabric comes into close contact with fire prone vegetation areas. This continuously expanding urban sprawl trend near forested areas is mainly the outcome of population growth; and is remarkably noticeable along the Mediterranean urban coast due to the flourishing of the tourism activity and the poorly planned urban growth. Such an urbanization pattern further exaggerates the consequences of fire incidents of respective urban settlements [3], provided that WUI are considerably vulnerable to fire risk due to their proximity to flammable wildland areas, with fire incidents threatening people's life and property, urban infrastructure and integrity of the natural ecosystems [6, 7].

In recent years, many wildfires are related to WUIs fire risk. In the Mediterranean Region in particular, there are several worth mentioning examples, like the one of Portugal in June 2017, where an extreme fire disaster resulted in very high losses in terms of human lives, structures and forest areas [6]; or that of Sardinia, Italy, where severe and quite extended losses of natural ecosystems occurred in the time span 2005-2019 due to a huge number of fire outbreaks, the majority of which were due to human negligence [7]. The scale of losses in WUIs in the Mediterranean due to forest fire incidents is enormous at all levels, being both environmental (loss of biodiversity and natural ecosystems) and socioeconomic (human live loss, destruction of urban infrastructure, economic losses, etc.). In addition, the proportion of human-caused wildfires due to either negligence or intention in WUIs is quite high in the Mediterranean Region, compared to the rest regions of the world.

Greece has also suffered significant impacts from major fire incidents during the recent past. These have caused remarkable damages to extensive forest areas, but also to urban settlements lying in their vicinity. The most recent and disastrous ones were in 2021 and 2023. In 2021, Evia Island had suffered a devastating wildfire that was perceived as the largest forest fire in the history of Greece. This fire burned more than 400 km^2 forest areas and caused severe damages to the surrounding settlements [8]. In July 2023, another wildfire broke out on the island of Rhodes – Dodecanese Region in Southeastern Greece – resulting in extensive forest damages and evacuations of residents and tourists from the neighboring urban constellations [9]. In August 2023, the megafire in the Evros region – north-eastern part of Greece – destroyed 58% of the National Forest Park of Dadia-Lefkimmi-Soufli, i.e. a forest area protected since 1980 due to its exceptional biodiversity and the endangered species inhabiting in this forest; while placing at fire risk the adjacent to the burned forest area settlements and also burning most periurban land around the city of Alexandroupolis [9]. Specifically in the Region of Attica, where the study area of the present work belongs, forest fires occurring since 2017 have, according to the European Forest Fire Information System (EFFIS), burned 37% of the region's forest areas, resulting in a huge environmental disaster, noticed not only in terms of forests and vegetation loss, but also in terms of deterioration of the quality of life of local population and the integrity of built infrastructure [10]. Among them falls the deadly wildfire in Mati in July 2018 – a distinct example of forest fire in a WUI – marked as the deadliest disaster event in the recent history of Greece [3].

Taking into consideration the severity and frequency of forest fire events, recent studies indicate the urgent need for integrating proactive strategies alongside with early warning systems into Disaster Management Plans. Preparedness, mitigation and adaptation strategies are principal parts in Disaster Management, highlighting the importance of wildfire risk assessment in *urban and peri-urban areas* [5]. Furthermore, the realization of the factors that influence the ignition and spread of a fire as well as the exploration of methodologies through which fire risk can be assessed is a crucial part of disaster management [11].

That said, the *goal* of this work is to assess the risk of a wildfire in forest areas in close proximity to urban ones (i.e. WUIs). For that purpose, it aims at establishing a pool of factors (or otherwise criteria) and methodologies that can support *fire risk assessment* in *Wildland-Urban Interfaces*. This is accomplished by an extensive literature review, investigating: i) the abundance of factors that are associated with wildfire incidents; and ii) the methodologies that are implemented in different areas, with a specific focus on cases in the Mediterranean region. This knowledge is used for conducting fire risk assessment in a specific study area, by properly selecting the most relevant case-specific factors/criteria. These are used as input to two selected methodologies, namely the Analytical Hierarchy Process (AHP) and the Random Forest algorithm through the Forest-Based Classification tool in order for: forest fire risk assessment, provided by the two methodologies, to be assessed, mapped and compared as to the outcomes produced, user-friendliness and usability; and the WUIs that are at fire risk to be sketched. GIS technologies also form an integral part in the applied part of this work.

The structure of the paper has as follows: Section 2 presents the steps of the methodological framework and elaborates on literature-driven fire-related factors and methodologies used for fire risk assessment. Section 3 presents the study area and its attributes; and attempts to assess and map the risk to fire of this area, based on the use of two methodological approaches and relevant factors out of the literature-based pool established. Finally, in Sect. 4 critical discussion and conclusions on the results obtained by the two methodologies are provided, commenting on the specific attributes of each one and their outcomes in relation to fire risk assessment in the study area in general and the WUIs in particular.

2 Materials and Methods

2.1 The Methodological Approach

The methodological approach of this study consists of the following three stages (Fig. 1):

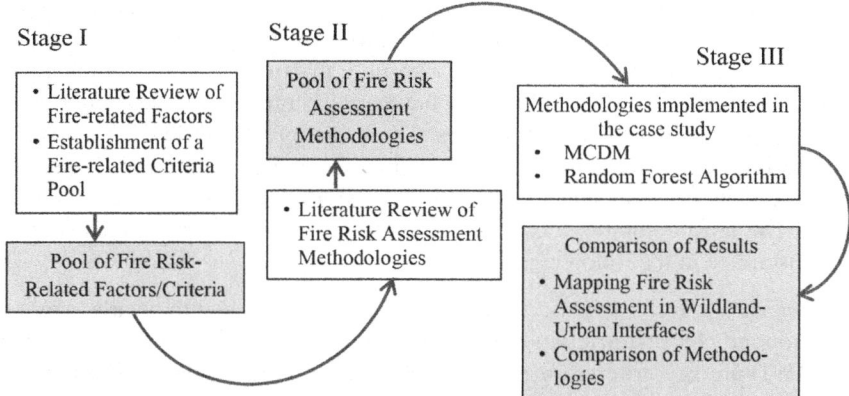

Fig. 1. Stages of the Methodological Framework.

- Stage I: Compilation of relevant literature on the factors/criteria directly related to fire phenomena and the area characteristics, such as topography, environment, etc.; and establishment of a fire risk-related *factors/criteria pool* that is adapted to both the study area at hand and the specific attributes of countries in the Mediterranean Region.
- Stage II: Compilation of literature on fire risk assessment methodologies and mapping of their attributes. This search gathered a plethora of methodologies, some of which are rather conventional, while others make extensive use of state-of-the-art technologies.
- Stage III: Use of two of the above-mentioned methodologies for implementation in the study area of this work, using properly selected factors/criteria from the established pool. The purpose of this implementation is to comparatively analyze results produced by the two methodologies and make inferences as to their performance, user-friendliness and effectiveness in Fire Risk Assessment and mapping, as a proactive action for feeding disaster management strategies in WUIs.

2.2 Establishing a Pool of Fire Risk Assessment Criteria

The identification of fire risk-related factors or criteria is a critical task of the relative assessment process and is strongly depended on the specific attributes of the area at hand (e.g., wind, humidity). In addition, the study of the interrelationships among the factors influencing fire occurrence is an intricate issue and demarcates fire ignition conditions [11].That said, the identification of the contributing factors and the appropriate choice of relevant criteria is expected to make a great contribution to fire risk assessment, not only by improving results of the fire risk assessment methodology, but also by ensuring a successful outcome [12].

In their fire risk assessment research work, Aksoy et al. [13] have analyzed a large number of studies related to this research topic and have created an extensive list of factors/criteria that can be used in fire risk assessment and can be categorized according to their field of relevance. As such can be mentioned elevation and slope, falling into the topographic attributes of the area at hand; temperature and wind speed, introducing climatic characteristics; factors related to spatial structure, like distance from settlements; network configuration, e.g. road network; agricultural activities; and water resources. In addition, the work of Aksoy et al. [13] contains criteria relating to vegetation and soil moisture as well as fire-fighting resources. The diversity of criteria demonstrates that, depending on the study area and its particularities, scientists are prompted to select the appropriate ones for assessing fire-related dimensions, such as risk and vulnerability [12, 13]. The most common, literature-based factors/criteria in fire-related studies are shortly discussed in the following.

Topographical Factor/Criterion. Topography is a factor related to an area's morphology and topographic characteristics. Elevation, Slope, Aspect and Topographic Wetness Index (TWI) are key criteria for reflecting the topographic dimension, with each one of them being directly related to and influencing the general behavior of a forest fire. The progress of a forest fire affects directly the disaster management process and the conditions of fire suppression [12, 14]. Elevation is an important criterion since it relates to the prevailing climatic conditions, such as temperature, humidity and wind speed; and can directly influence the ignition and behavior of the fire. Similarly, slope is related to the spread pattern of fire, with steep slopes impeding firefighting efforts and favoring the speed of fire spreading. Aspect is related to the percentage of sunlight received by an area, making south-southwest aspects more prone to fire events. Finally, TWI is related to the soil moisture, being an important criterion for fire ignition and spread [14–16].

Environmental Factor/Criterion. Forest fire risk research has demonstrated that the type of forest and vegetation are significantly influencing fire ignition and progression. While vegetation is generally flammable, criteria related to Vegetation Density and Moisture levels are greatly impacting the way fires behave [13]. Additionally, the type of leaves plays a crucial role in determining how vegetation responds to fire, so criteria like Forest Type, Dominant Leaf Type and Plant Type are important dimensions in fire risk assessment. Specifically, coniferous trees are more susceptible to fire due to their leaf structure and the presence of highly flammable pine needles. These pine needles form a litter layer around the tree base, which provides another criterion, referred to as Stand crown closure. In contrast, broad-leaved trees, with their moisture-rich foliage, have a different ignition rate and are less prone to fire risk [13–15]. The Normalized Difference Vegetation Index (NDVI), as a means for assessing the criterion directly related to vegetation and fuel, provides quite important information on the vegetation conditions. NDVI indicates the state of vegetation's health, where high values of NDVI indicate healthy vegetation, low values indicate dry vegetation with higher fire risk rates, values near zero indicate the absence of vegetation, while negative values indicate water areas [16, 17].

Climate Factor/Criterion. The decisive influence of weather conditions on the occurrence of a fire has drawn the attention of scientists to the study of fire weather circumstances and the way these contribute to fire risk [4]. Long heat waves and high temperatures affect the moisture content of vegetation, rendering it dry and more flammable, thus leaving forests more vulnerable and prone to fire [16]. As far as precipitation is concerned, this is directly related to the soil moisture and relative humidity of an area. A decrease in the frequency and amount of precipitation, combined with high temperatures, causes a decrease in the relative humidity of an area, thus increasing the risk of fire and creating conducive conditions for its progression [14]. High wind speeds also affect the conditions of fire spread and the speed at which it progresses, impeding its suppression from fire services. Therefore, climatic criteria, such as temperature, humidity and wind speed are critical in fire risk assessment, demarcating the conditions for fire ignition and expansion [14, 15, 17].

Human Factor/Criterion. Literature review witnesses that the majority of forest fires are caused by human negligence. Thus, criteria related to population, activities and attributes of the urban environment are of particular importance. Areas with increased population density and settlements near forested areas (WUIs) increase the risk of ignition due to the intensity of population activities, rendering criteria of population density and forests' distance from settlements very important. Thus, the criteria of distance from road network as well as agricultural and tourist activities respectively delineate areas with an increased likelihood of fire ignition, as they appear to be in proximity with human activities. Similarly, the proximity to water resources, e.g. a lake or a river neighboring forest places, where recreation activities take place, are more vulnerable to fire events [14, 17].

2.3 Exploring Methodologies for Fire Risk Assessment

Methodologies for forest fire risk assessment are rapidly developing due to the imperative need of fire occurrence estimation [5]. In fact, fire risk assessment has recently raised to a topic of great concern in the research and policy community. These methodologies can be classified into three general categories, namely those based on the experience of researchers, those using statistical methods and those using machine learning tools [11, 18].

In the field of Geosciences and Geospatial Data, Machine Learning and Deep Learning are gaining momentum and are rapidly growing due to their prediction potential and promising results [11, 19]. Machine learning, as part of the Artificial Intelligence, offers today several algorithms for relevant use, taking advantage of the variety of data and the extensive use of human-centric parameters. The choice of a specific algorithm depends on the research question and the desired outcome [13]. Their efficiency is directly related to the quantity and quality of the data used [19]. A great advantage of methodologies, using machine learning methods, is the automation of respective processes, thanks to the evolution of technology and computing power [11, 20], thus eliminating the human factor and the possible bias as to the studied object [18].

According to an extensive literature review on the application of machine learning methodologies in studies related to fire occurrence and management [19, 21], respective methodologies can be classified into four main categories, namely: Supervised Learning, Unsupervised Learning, Semi-supervised Learning, and Reinforcement Learning [19, 21]. In Jain's et al. [19] review, methodologies are demonstrated in a very informative diagram, depicting the most commonly used algorithms and their potential fields of application [19]. In general, Supervised Learning algorithms are used for classification and regression; Unsupervised Learning algorithms are primarily used for clustering, density estimation and association; while Semi-supervised Learning is a combination of the above [21].

The detailed presentation of the methodologies goes beyond the scope of the present study. However, it should be noted that the combination of Machine learning algorithms with Geographic Information Systems (GIS) is an interesting field of evolving methodologies and interaction among technologies, taking advantage of the capabilities of each tool in order for the best possible outcome to be achieved [13, 20]. Among the most commonly used methods are Decision Trees, namely machine learning algorithms used for both classification and regression analysis purposes. The most commonly used algorithm is the *'Random Forest'*, which consists of multiple Decision Trees and its basic idea is that at each node of each tree a random selection of features is made [19]. Table 1 provides a synoptic review of the methodologies used for Fire Risk Assessment in descending order of user-friendliness.

Furthermore, the majority of studies appearing in the literature uses Geographic Information Systems (GIS) and Remote Sensing for fire risk assessment. The implementation of methodologies varies. Some cases use geostatistical analyses to calculate risk, taking into consideration the relationships among criteria and the contribution of criteria to the fire occurrence assessment; while others digitize, analyze and categorize data through satellite imagery [18].

The use of spatial information technologies, tools and software is extended for risk assessment and mapping. Thus, in conjunction with GIS tools, the use of Multi-Decision-Making Methods (MCDM) for risk assessment and mapping is noticeable. An example is the Analytic Hierarchy Process (AHP) [14, 15, 22, 23], which uses a variety of criteria and subcriteria and assigns weights to them according to their importance to a potential fire event [13, 15, 18]. Statistical methods, such as linear and logistic regression analysis, are also used to analyze the relationships among fire occurrence factors.

Based on the literature review as to the factors/criteria as well as the currently available methodologies for fire risk assessment/mapping, two methodologies are selected and applied in order for fire risk assessment to be conducted in the study area; and results obtained by each methodology to be compared. The first choice is *Analytic Hierarchy Process* (AHP), namely a Multi-Decision-Making Method (MCDM) for analyzing scenarios using GIS technologies [14]. The second is the *Random Forest Algorithm*, implemented by use of the Forest-Based Classification and Regression tool in ArcGIS Pro software [24]. Selection criteria of the two methodologies are the level of their user-friendliness and the moderate level of specialization required for their application, both providing the chance of being used by less-experienced staff at the community level for articulating local disaster management plans. The scope of their practical implementation is to assess effectiveness of results obtained by the distinct philosophies for fire risk assessment these reflect, with the AHP being based on the researcher's experience and the evaluation problem at hand; and the Forest-Based Classification Tool on automated procedures for deriving assessment outcomes.

Table 1. Classification of methodologies for Fire Risk Assessment, Source: Own Elaboration.

Category	Methodology Examples	Examples of Tools/Techniques	Advantages	User-Friendliness
Experience-based	Expert's Judgment and Evaluation	Based on the researcher's expertise	Flexible and adaptable Comparison of a variety of criteria and subcriteria	Most user-friendly for non-experts No need of technical tools or software
MultiCriteria Decision Making (MCDM)	Analytic Hierarchy Process (AHP)	GIS Comparison of a variety of criteria and subcriteria	Systematic approach combining qualitative and quantitative data	User-friendly for non-experts Use of expert's judgment and systematic methods
Statistical Methods	Linear and Logistic Regression	Regression models Statistical software (e.g., R, SPSS)	Quantitative measures	Moderately user-friendly Requires basic statistical background, familiarity with statistical software and model interpretation
Machine Learning Methods	Supervised Learning, Unsupervised Learning, Semi-supervised Learning, Reinforcement Learning	Decision Trees, Random Forest (Supervised) Clustering, Density Estimation (Unsupervised), Various ML algorithms	Reduction of human bias and subjectivity Automation and capability of handling complex, high-dimensional data	Least user-friendly for non-experts Requires expertise in data science, programming, and algorithm selection It demands technical skills to train, evaluate, and interpret models

(*continued*)

Table 1. (*continued*)

Category	Methodology Examples	Examples of Tools/Techniques	Advantages	User-Friendliness
Geospatial Analysis	GIS and Remote Sensing	GIS Remote Sensing data	Spatial interpretation Visual representation at various scales	Challenging for non-experts Need of technical expertise, GIS software and spatial analysis techniques
Hybrid Methods	GIS + Machine Learning Integration	GIS tools and spatial data ML algorithms	Combination of spatial data with ML models Accuracy and predictive power Large-scale projects	Challenging for non-experts Integrating GIS and ML requires expertise User-friendly interfaces

3 Implementation of the Methodological Framework - Results

3.1 The Study Area

The study area (Fig. 2) comprises six Municipalities (Municipality of Oropos, Marathonas, Rafina-Pikermi, Pallini, Penteli and Dionisos), all closely related to the recurrent wildfires occurring in Northeastern and Eastern Attica Region in the time span 2000-2023. Three of these municipalities are located in the eastern seaside area of the Attica Region, while the study area borders the Mountains of Penteli and Parnitha that prevail in the Region's scenery. All six municipalities cover an area of 712.82 km^2; while their population, according to the 2021 Census, amounts to 222,914 inhabitants [25]. The climate of the region is generally characterized as maritime, with dry, very warm and extensive summer [26].

Given that the eastern part of the study area is located in the coastal part of the Attica Region, much of the area under consideration hosts tourism activities, with seasonal population being increased during the summer time (May-August), a period that coincides with the main fire season. Additionally, agricultural activities are taking place in the area, being the main occupation of the permanent population. Studying recent forest fire incidents, occurring in 2017, 2018 and 2024, as well as historical fire events, occurring in 2005 and 2009, it is inferred that the study region is plagued by recurrent wildfire events, with extensive repercussions on both the natural and the socioeconomic environment. These imply that both population and the area at hand are exposed to extensive fire risk during the fire season. The municipalities located in the inner part of the study region are directly related to Penteli Mountain and represent peri-urban areas close to forests, a fact that fully exposes urban settlements to fire events. A characteristic example of this state is the Varnavas area, a part of the Municipality of Marathonas. The wildfire incident on August 2024, which reached the outskirts of the urban space of metropolitan

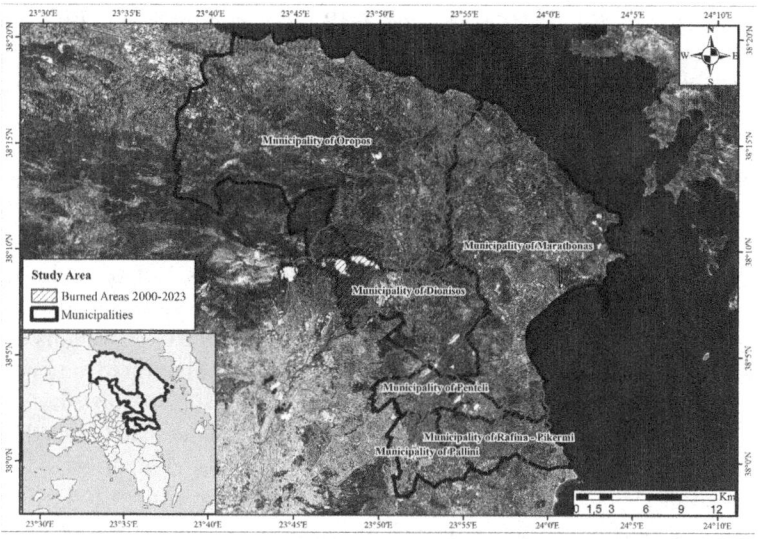

Fig. 2. Location of the study region, boundaries of municipalities (black line) and burned area through recurrent fire incidents (shaded area in red lines). Source: Own elaboration.

Athens, placed Varnavas area in a highly risky position [27]. The recurrence of fire events stresses the vulnerability of this area, while rendering fire risk assessment an essential task that, in addition, needs to be directly embedded in both the general (at the Region's level) and the local disaster management plans (at the municipalities' level).

3.2 Assessing Risk of Fire in the Study Area

The selection of data sets for fire risk assessment is driven by the need for a holistic approach. Thus, it takes into consideration all fire-related criteria/subcriteria and all dimensions of the study area. Topography-related subcriteria (Elevation, Slope, Aspect) are extracted using the Digital Surface Model (DSM), obtained from the Copernicus program. Vegetation and Land Cover subcriteria [Dominant Leaf Type (DLT), Tree Cover Density (TCD), NDVI index and Urban Atlas] were obtained from Copernicus program as well, along with Sentinel-2 Satellite Images for the extraction of NDVI index. DLT, TCD and Urban Atlas data refer to 2018, since this is the most recent data in the program. Meteorological Data (Temperature, Wind Speed, Humidity and Precipitation) were downloaded from E-OBS, Copernicus program, collecting daily gridded meteorological data, referred to the time period 2000-2023. The same holds for the Burned Areas for the time period 2000-2023 [27]. Data related to 2021 Population-Housing Census were acquired from the Hellenic Statistical Authority, along with Settlements and Greek Municipalities' Shapefiles [25]. Road and Hydrographic Network are downloaded from Geofabrik's website [28]. The implementation of the selected methodologies and the creation of the fire risk maps are based on the ArcGIS software, specifically on ArcGIS 10.8.2 and ArcGIS Pro 3.3.

Analytical Hierarchy Process (AHP). The AHP, pioneered by Saaty [29], is one of the most renowned Multi-Decision-Making Methods (MCDM) and serves as a systematic framework for structuring and analyzing complex decision-making scenarios. AHP is extensively utilized across various disciplines and topics; and is capable of effectively incorporating both qualitative and quantitative data. The process simplifies decision-making by breaking down a problem into a hierarchy that leads to a better understanding and evaluation of potential alternatives, using multiple criteria and subcriteria that facilitate a more comprehensive and nuanced analysis [14, 23, 30]. On the first stage, the problem is analyzed and relevant criteria and subcriteria are selected. Each subcriterion is scored on a unified scale (1 to 5 or 1 to 10) [14, 15, 22, 31]. Secondly, a Pairwise Comparison of criteria and subcriteria is taking place [30]. Next, the weights of each criterion and subcriterion are calculated in order for their contribution to the final decision to be determined [32]. Finally, the consistency of comparisons is carried out by use of the Consistency Ratio (CR). The CR value should be no greater than 0.10, otherwise the demanded consistency is not met, leading to the revision of comparisons. Calculation of CR (Equation 1) presupposes estimation of the Consistency Index (CI) (Equation 2), where λmax is defined as the maximum eigenvalue, n is the number of criteria/subcriteria used in the analysis and RI is the Random Consistency Index [32].

$$CR = \frac{CI}{RI} < 0.1 \sim 10\% \tag{1}$$

$$CI = \frac{\lambda max - n}{n - 1} \tag{2}$$

Table 2. Selected criteria for assessing risk to fire in the study region.

	Low Risk									High Risk
	1	2	3	4	5	6	7	8	9	10
Elevation (m)	0-100		100-200		200-400		400-800			>800
Slope (%)	0-5			5-15		15-25		25-35		>35
Aspect	N	NE, NW	E		Flat	SE, W		S		SW
Temperature (°C)	25.5-26	26-26.5	26.5-27	27-27.5	27.5-28	28-28.5	28.5-29	29-29.5	29.5-30	>30
Wind Speed (m/s)	<2.5	2.5-3	3-3.5	3.5-4	4-4.5	4.5-5	5-5.5	5.5-6	6-6.5	>6.5
Humidity (%)	>80	75-80	70-75	65-70	60-65	55-60	50-55	45-50	40-45	<40
Precipitation (mm/y)	>200	120-200		80-120		30-80		10-30		<10
DLT	No Tree				Broad Leaved					Coniferous
TCD	0-10	11-20	21-30	31-40	41-50	51-60	61-70	71-80	81-90	91-100
NDVI	<0.1		0.1-0.3		0.3-0.5		0.5-0.7		0.7-0.9	>0.9
Population Density (Nr)	0-1000		1000-5000			5000-10000		10000-15000		>15000
Distance from Settlements (m)	>3000		2000-3000			1000-2000		500-1000		<500
Distance from Road Network (m)	>2000		1000-2000			500-1000		250-500		<250
Distance from Recreational Waters (m)	>2000		1000-2000			500-1000		250-500		<250
Land Use		Water Wetlands Open Spaces		Urban Fabric			Agricultural Areas			Forests and Vegetation Areas

The particular criteria and subcriteria for the AHP that are used as fire risk variables reflect the peculiarities of the study area and are shown in Table 2. The calibrated scores in Table 2 show the rating of the fire risk for the selected criteria and subcriteria. Furthermore, in Table 3 the values of Consistency Ratio (CR) are indicated as well as the weights of the criteria and subcriteria.

Forest-based classification. Forest-Based Classification and Regression tool is included in the Modeling Spatial Relationships toolset in ArcGIS PRO software and uses the Random Forest algorithm, developed by Leo Breiman and Adele Cutler [33]. Through model creation and training using a training dataset, it aims at predicting unknown values in a dataset using the same explanatory variables as the training dataset. The model creates a forest, which consists of a number of decision trees, each of which is generated from a random subset of the training dataset and provides a prediction for the research subject. Each prediction contributes to the final one, which is derived from all the decision trees created, i.e. the entire forest. The possibility of using the tool with a smaller variety of variables, as well as its intuitive nature are important advantages in selecting this tool [24]. Table 4 indicates the Importance Values of the Subcriteria, as these occurred from Forest-Based Classification tool and are used for Fire Risk assessment.

Table 3. AHP's criteria/subcriteria weights

Factor/Criterion	CR	Weight	Subcriterion	CR	Weight
Topography	0.0515247	0.068	Elevation	0.0477254	0.106
			Slope		0.633
			Aspect		0.261
Climate		0.152	Temperature	0.0650317	0.272
			Wind Speed		0.540
			Humidity		0.131
			Precipitation		0.057
Environment		0.456	DLT	0.0201833	0.123
			TCD		0.557
			NDVI		0.320
Urban Space		0.324	Population Density	0.0812568	0.289
			Distance From Settlements		0.110
			Distance From Road Network		0.287
			Distance From Recreational Waters		0.047
			Land Use		0.267

Table 4. Importance values (weights) of the subcriteria according Forest-Based Classification

Subcriterion	Importance Value	Subcriterion	Importance Value
NDVI	0.0867	Distance from Road Network	0.0775
Precipitation	0.0865	Distance from Settlements	0.0771
Elevation	0.0841	Temperature	0.0742
Distance from recreational waters	0,0828	Humidity	0.0716
Population density	0.0811	TCD	0.0371
Slope	0.0795	Land Use	0.0039
Wind Speed	0.0777	DLT	0.0027
Aspect	0.0775		

3.3 Empirical Results

After the appropriate data preparation, the two methodologies were implemented in order for the final Forest Fire Risk Assessment maps to be derived. Following the calibration of the subcriteria in a unified scale [fire risk scores 1 to 10 as shown in Table 2], the subcriteria maps were generated (Fig. 3). The final maps were produced using the associated weights assigned to the Criteria/Subcriteria, which are shown in Table 3 for AHP and Table 4 for Forest-Based Classification respectively. Final Forest Fire Risk Assessment maps are demonstrated in Figures 4 and 5, in association with Burned Areas and Settlements; and depict the pattern of Fire Risk in the study area.

Regarding the Fire Risk map derived from AHP (Fig. 4a), the fire risk values range from 1.76 to 7.64. Most high fire risk values (brown color) appear in the Western – North-Western part of the study area (Municipalities of Oropos and Dionisos), with intermediate risk values (yellow color) occurring in the Southern part (Municipalities of Penteli and Pallini). In contrast, the coastal part of the study area (Municipality of Marathonas and Rafina-Pikermi) shows moderately low risk values (green color). Very low values display limited occurrences within the study area (blue color).

As for the fire risk map derived from Forest-Based Classification (Fig. 4b), the fire risk values range from 2.65 to 6.56. The different fire risk pattern is apparent between the two maps. In Fig. 4b, the presence of increased values (brown color) is more extensive throughout the study area, with a more pronounced occurrence in the Southern part of the area (Municipalities of Penteli and Pallini). Intermediate fire risk values (yellow color) appear as a continuation of the higher values, with moderately low fire risk values (green color) being relatively limited in the study area. A distinct difference with Fig. 4a is the appearance of several points with low fire risk values (blue color). Results, estimated by the two methodologies, display a small difference in the range of fire risk values, with the Forest-Based Classification tool estimating values slightly lower than AHP.

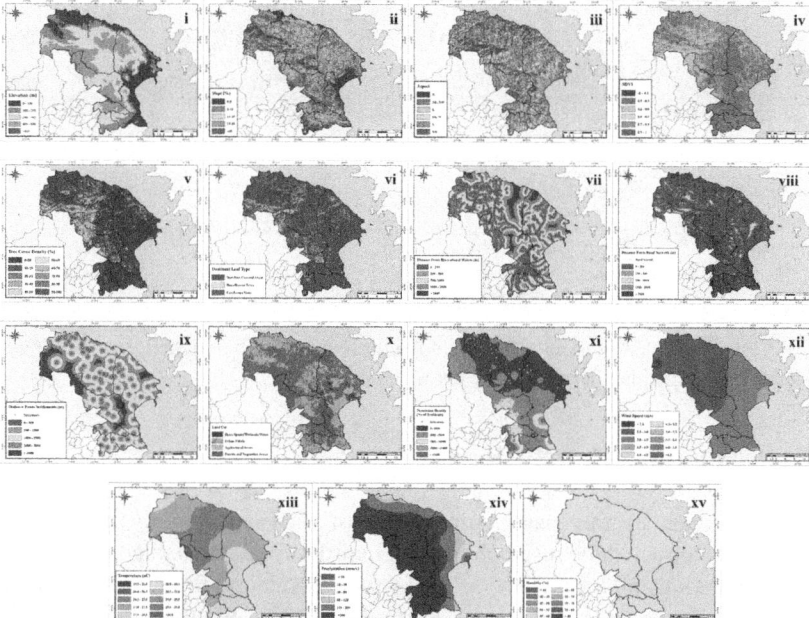

Fig. 3. Maps of the criteria used for the two methodologies. i) Elevation, ii) Slope, iii) Aspect, iv) NDVI, v) TCD, vi) DLT, vii) Distance from Recreational Waters, viii) Distance from Roads, ix) Distance from Settlements, x) Land Use, xi) Population Density, xii) Wind Speed, xiii) Temperature, xiv) Precipitation and xv) Humidity.

However, the difference in the fire risk pattern assessed by them in the study area is rather noticeable.

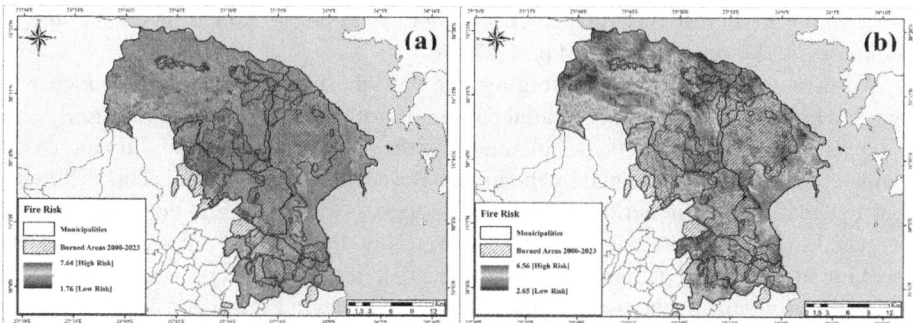

Fig. 4. Forest Fire Risk Assessment Maps and Burned Areas 2000-2023 – a) AHP methodology and b) Forest-Based Classification Tool, Source: Own elaboration.

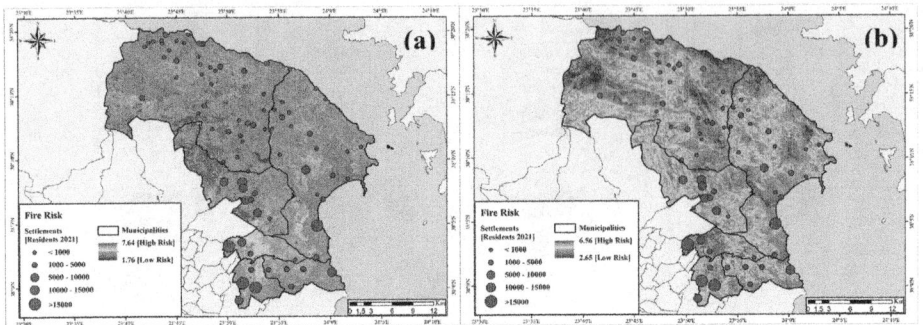

Fig. 5. Forest Fire Risk Assessment Maps and Settlements at risk – a) AHP methodology and b) Forest-Based Classification Tool, Source: Own elaboration.

4 Discussion and Conclusions

In the last few years, the increasing vulnerability of WUIs, affected by the rising number of wildfires has attracted the research interest in order for data-enabled policy response, targeting mitigation and adaptation of WUIs to the escalating fire incidents that are due to climate change, to be articulated [2, 3]. In this respect, the focus of this work is on highlighting the factors that affect wildfire occurrences in WUIs and are considered in fire risk assessment studies; and the methodologies utilized for this purpose. That said, a range of placed-specific factors/criteria (see Table 2) and two methodologies, namely the AHP and the Random Forest algorithm through the Forest-Based Classification tool are selected for implementation in a specific case study. The scope of this study is to assess the risk to fire in the study region in general and WUIs in particular; and compare the results produced by each methodology. Both methodologies are quite user-friendly. However, certain expertise in the subject is definitely needed for their best implementation. More precisely, AHP relies mainly on the researcher's experience and literature-enabled decisions; while the Forest-Based Classification tool is rather grounded in state-of-the-art technology and more automatized procedures.

Worth noticing is also the diverging outcome these methodologies produce with regard to both the values and the spatial pattern of forest fire risk in the study area. As far as the values are concerned, those calculated by the AHP appear to be slightly increased, compared to the ones calculated by the Forest-Based Classification tool. This difference is attributed to the researcher's estimation, who appears to give slightly higher risk values, compared to an automated procedure. However, this difference is not a significant one. Speaking of the spatial pattern of the forest fire risk, a notable divergence is observed in the results produced by the two methodologies, as shown in Fig. 4a and 4b. Comparison of the spatial pattern of forest fire risk produced by the two methodologies and the one of the burned areas due to the recurrent fire incidents of the last years raises some noticeable points. More specifically, AHP results (Fig. 4a) indicate a lower forest fire risk in the coastal or the near to the coast part of the study area, compared to the one produced by the Forest-Based Classification (Fig. 4b). The latter seems to better fit to the repeatedly burned coastal parts of the study area in the past years in contrast to the AHP results that seem to underestimate fire risk in this part. Regarding the fire risk assessment in

WUIs, the Forest-Based model (Fig. 5b) also shows a better matching between higher fire risk values and WUI areas, as it is shown for example in the southern part of the study area, compared to the AHP (Fig. 5a), in which the coastal side displays a lower fire risk despite the increased population and the number of settlements.

In terms of the accuracy and consistency of the tested methodologies, CR value in AHP (less than 0.10) demonstrates that the pairwise comparison among the subcriteria/criteria is valid and the procedure displays the consistency needed in order to proceed and create the final map. In the Forest-Based Classification model, the values of F1-score (0.90 on the training data and 0.83 on the validation dataset) indicate that the model is capable of identifying fire prone and non-fire prone areas in an effective way. The small difference between the validation accuracy and the training set suggests a possible over-fitting. However, the model appears to be robust and performs successfully.

The comparison of the two methodologies unveils that the Forest-Based Classification model provides the opportunity to optimize the model through the output indexes that accompany the final results; whereas in AHP it is in the researcher's convenience and decision to modify the subcriteria/criteria or the weights in case that the outcome is not satisfactory. Finally, it should be noted that data quality and data availability at different time scales are quite important in further improving the outcome of this research. This could allow for the: implementation of the methodologies both prior to and after major wildfire events; investigation of the accuracy of the outcomes with respect to future events and areas at risk; and capturing of particularities within WUIs. Apart from data issues, testing the aforementioned methodologies in a further expanded forest area in the neighboring of the studied one or in other case studies could enhance knowledge as to their performance. This holds true especially for the Forest-Based Classification model. Moreover, enriching the criteria pool could support replicability of these methodologies in other regions as well and comparability of produced results. Lastly, as technology is an integral part of current research on these topics and is advancing at a rapid pace, it may be beneficial to test and compare state-of-the-art methodologies using AI with more conventional ones in order for the AI advantages and the efficiency of their results to be investigated.

5 Disclosure of Interests.

The authors have no competing interests to declare that are relevant to the content of this article.

References

1. IPCC, 2023: Climate Change 2023: Synthesis Report. Contribution of Working Groups I, II and III to the Sixth Assessment Report of the Intergovernmental Panel on Climate Change [Core Writing Team, H. Lee and J. Romero (eds.)]. IPCC, Geneva, Switzerland.', Intergovernmental Panel on Climate Change (IPCC) (2023). https://doi.org/10.59327/IPCC/AR6-9789291691647
2. Trucchia, A., Meschi, G., Fiorucci, P., Provenzale, A., Tonini, M., Pernice, U.: Wildfire hazard mapping in the eastern Mediterranean landscape. Int. J. Wildland Fire **32**(3), 417–434 (2023). https://doi.org/10.1071/WF22138

3. Ganteaume, A., Barbero, R., Jappiot, M., Maillé, E.: Understanding future changes to fires in southern Europe and their impacts on the Wildland-Urban Interface. J. Safety Sci. Res. **2**(1), 20–29 (2021). https://doi.org/10.1016/j.jnlssr.2021.01.001
4. Papavasileiou, G., Giannaros, T.M.: Synoptic-scale drivers of fire weather in Greece. Sci. Total Environ. **925**, 171715 (2024). https://doi.org/10.1016/j.scitotenv.2024.171715
5. Jones, M.W., Kelley, D.I., Burton, C.A., Di Giuseppe, F., Barbosa, M.L.F., Brambleby, E., et al.: State of wildfires 2023–2024. Earth Syst. Sci. Data **16**(8), 3601–3685 (2024). https://doi.org/10.5194/essd-16-3601-2024
6. Nunes, A.N., Figueiredo, A., Pinto, C., Lourenço, L.: Assessing wildfire hazard in the Wildland-Urban Interfaces (WUIs) of central Portugal. Forests **14**(6), 1106 (2023). https://doi.org/10.3390/f14061106
7. Scarpa C., Elia M., D'Este M., Salis M., Rodrigues M., Arca B., et al.: Modelling wildfire activity in Wildland–Urban Interface (WUI) areas of Sardinia, Italy. Int. J. Wildland Fire **33**(12) (2024). https://doi.org/10.1071/WF24109
8. Gemitzi, A., Koutsias, N.: A Google Earth Engine code to estimate properties of vegetation phenology in fire affected areas – a case study in North Evia wildfire event on August 2021. Remote Sens. Appl. Soc. Environ. **26**, 100720 (2022). https://doi.org/10.1016/j.rsase.2022.100720
9. Dosiou, A., Athinelis, I., Katris, E., Vassalou, M., Kyrkos, A., Krassakis, P., et al.: Employing copernicus land service and sentinel-2 satellite mission data to assess the spatial dynamics and distribution of the extreme forest fires of 2023 in Greece. Fire **7**(1) (2024). https://doi.org/10.3390/fire7010020
10. Meteo, https://www.meteo.gr/article_view.cfm?entryID=3355. Accessed 25 April 2025. [In Greek]
11. Zhang, G., Wang, M., Liu, K.: Deep neural networks for global wildfire susceptibility modelling. Ecolog. Ind. **127**, 107735 (2021). https://doi.org/10.1016/j.ecolind.2021.107735
12. Borisova, B., Todorova, E., Ihtimanski, I., Glushkova, M., Zhiyanski, M., Georgieva, M., et al.: Wildfire risk assessment and mapping – an approach for Natura 2000 forest sites. Trees Forests People **16**, 100532 (2024). https://doi.org/10.1016/j.tfp.2024.100532
13. Aksoy, E., Kocer, A., Yilmaz, İ., Akçal, A.N., Akpinar, K.: Assessing fire risk in Wildland–Urban Interface regions using a machine learning method and GIS data: the example of Istanbul's European side. Fire **6**(10) (2023). https://doi.org/10.3390/fire6100408
14. Sivrikaya, F., Küçük, Ö.: Modeling forest fire risk based on GIS-based analytical hierarchy process and statistical analysis in Mediterranean region. Ecolog. Info. **68**, 101537 (2022). https://doi.org/10.1016/j.ecoinf.2021.101537
15. Sari, F.: Forest fire susceptibility mapping via multi-criteria decision analysis techniques for Mugla, Turkey: a comparative analysis of VIKOR and TOPSIS. Forest Ecolog. Manag. **480**, 118644 (2021). https://doi.org/10.1016/j.foreco.2020.118644
16. Jiang, W., Qiao, Y., Zheng, X., Zhou, J., Jiang, J., Meng, Q., et al.: Wildfire risk assessment using deep learning in Guangdong Province, China. Int. J. Appl. Earth Observ. Geoinf. **128**, 103750 (2024). https://doi.org/10.1016/j.jag.2024.103750
17. Parvar, Z., Saeidi, S., Mirkarimi, S.: Integrating meteorological and geospatial data for forest fire risk assessment. J. Environ. Manag. **358**, 120925 (2024). https://doi.org/10.1016/j.jenvman.2024.120925
18. Sevinç, V.: Mapping the forest fire risk zones using artificial intelligence with risk factors data. Environ. Sci. Pollution Res. **30**, 4721–4732 (2023). https://doi.org/10.1007/s11356-022-22515-w
19. Jain, P., Coogan, S.C.P., Subramanian, S.G., Crowley, M., Taylor, S., Flannigan, M.D.: A review of machine learning applications in wildfire science and management. Environ. Rev. **28**(4), 478–505 (2020). https://doi.org/10.1139/er-2020-0019

20. Purnama, M.I., Jaya, I.N.S., Syaufina, L., Çoban, H.O., Raihan, M.: Predicting forest fire vulnerability using machine learning approaches in the Mediterranean region: a case study of Türkiye. IOP Conf. Ser. Earth Environ. Sci. **1315**(1), 012056 (2024). https://doi.org/10.1088/1755-1315/1315/1/012056
21. Sarker, I.H.: Machine Learning: algorithms, real-world applications and research directions. SN Comput. Sci. **2**(3), 160 (2021). https://doi.org/10.1007/s42979-021-00592-x
22. Maniatis, Y., Doganis, A., Chatzigeorgiadis, M.: Fire risk probability mapping using machine learning tools and multi-criteria decision analysis in the GIS environment: a case study in the national park forest Dadia-Lefkimi-Soufli, Greece. Appl. Sci. **12**(6) (2022). https://doi.org/10.3390/app12062938
23. El Mazi, M., Boutallaka, M., Saber, E., Chanyour, Y., Bouhlal, A.: Forest fire risk modeling in Mediterranean forests using GIS and AHP method: case of the high Rif forest massif (Morocco). Euro-Med. J. Environ. Integ. **9**(3), 1109–1123 (2024). https://doi.org/10.1007/s41207-024-00591-3
24. ESRI, https://pro.arcgis.com/en/pro-app/latest/tool-reference/spatial-statistics/an-overview-of-the-spatial-statistics-toolbox.htm. Accessed 10 Feb 2025
25. ELSTAT, https://www.statistics.gr/en/home/. Accessed 01 Mar 2025
26. Krina, A., Koutsias, N., Pleniou, M., Xystrakis, F.: Climatic classification of Greece: update–future estimation–relation with forest vegetation. In: Proceedings of the 18th Panhellenic Forestry Conference & International Workshop, pp. 1088–1095. Edessa, Greece (2017). [In Greek]
27. Copernicus, https://www.copernicus.eu/en. Accessed 05 Feb 2025
28. Geofabrik, https://download.geofabrik.de/europe/greece.html. Accessed 05 Jan 2025
29. Saaty, T.L.: The analytic hierarchy process. Agric. Econ. Rev. **70**, Mcgraw Hill, New York (1980)
30. Saaty, T.L.: Highlights and critical points in the theory and application of the analytic hierarchy process. Europ. J. Oper. Res. **74**(3), 426–447 (1994). https://doi.org/10.1016/0377-2217(94)90222-4
31. Papazoglou, A., Pigaki, M.: comparative study for the investigation of safe movement with the method of space syntax: the case of Mati, Eastern Attica. In: Gervasi, O., et al. (eds.) Computational Science and Its Applications – ICCSA 2023 Workshops. ICCSA 2023. Lecture Notes in Computer Science, Vol 14105, pp. 579–597. Springer, Cham (2023). https://doi.org/10.1007/978-3-031-37108-0_37
32. Vargas, R.V., Pmp I.-B.: Using the analytic hierarchy process (AHP) to select and prioritize projects in a portfolio. In: PMI Global Congress (2010). https://ricardo-vargas.com/downloads/download-file/6888/12430
33. Breiman, L.: Random Forests. Mach. Learn. **45**(1), 5–32 (2001). https://doi.org/10.1023/A:1010933404324

Real-Time IoT with Edge Computing: Efficiency, Security, and Future Trends

Teresa Guarda[1,2,3](✉) [iD] and Washington Torres[1,2]

[1] Universidad Estatal Península de Santa Elena, La Libertad, Ecuador
tguarda@gmail.com
[2] Facultad de Sistemas y Telecomunicaciones, La Libertad, Ecuador
[3] Algoritmi Centre, University of Minho, Guimarães, Portugal

Abstract. The growth of the Internet of Things (IoT) has increased the need for fast data processing, efficient bandwidth use, and stronger privacy protection. Traditional cloud systems often fall short in these areas, especially for applications that rely on immediate responses. Edge computing helps solve these problems by processing data close to where it is created. This makes systems faster, reduces the load on networks, and keeps sensitive data more secure. This work is a review paper about how edge computing is being used in IoT systems and how it supports real-time actions in areas like healthcare, smart cities, and industrial automation. It also looks at how edge computing works with 5G networks and Artificial Intelligence (AI) to allow devices to make quick decisions on their own. Several case studies show how these technologies improve daily operations and protect personal data. The paper also talks about current challenges such as the cost of setting up edge systems, keeping devices secure, and making sure different devices can work together. Even with these issues, the findings show that edge computing is becoming essential for building smarter and more reliable IoT systems.

Keywords: Edge computing · Internet of Things (IoT) · Real-time Data Processing · Artificial Intelligence · 5G Networks

1 Introduction

The Internet of Things brings together devices and sensors into connected systems that produce large amounts of data throughout the day. In many practical cases, like monitoring equipment, responding to health alerts, or managing traffic, this data needs to be processed right away to support rapid decision-making. Although cloud computing can handle and store massive datasets, it often falls short when immediate action is needed, especially in settings where even a slight delay can cause problems. Sending data back and forth to remote servers can cause delays, which can limit the performance of IoT applications [1].

Edge computing takes a different approach by handling data closer to where it produced, often directly on the device or nearby. This technique shortens the time needed to process information, lowers the strain on network traffic, and reduces how much sensitive data must leave the local environment. This helps reduce wait times, skips over data that isn't needed, and protects sensitive information. It also keeps delays down, uses bandwidth more wisely, and cuts back on how much private data gets sent to the cloud [2].

As more IoT systems are built and used in different areas, edge computing is becoming more important in how these systems are planned. It helps them run faster, stay more secure, and work more efficiently [1].

This paper looks at how edge computing is growing in IoT. It focuses on how it allows data to be processed right where it's needed, keeps personal data more private, and deals with important technical limits. The paper also describes how edge computing connects with tools like artificial intelligence (AI) and 5G networks. Real-world cases from healthcare, smart cities, and industry are included to show how it works in practice.

2 Background

This section establishes the basis for comprehending how edge computing facilitates IoT systems. It explains how processing data closer to where it is generated helps reduce delays, limits the exposure of sensitive information, and increases the dependability of connected devices. These points are important for grasping why edge computing is becoming a practical solution as IoT networks continue to grow (Fig. 1).

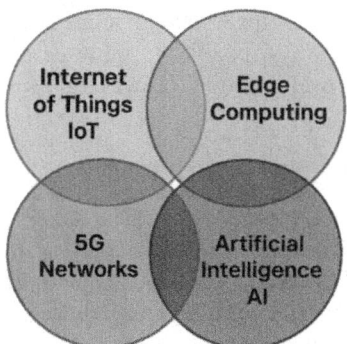

Fig. 1. Figure illustrates the interconnection between the key technologies that enable efficient and real-time IoT systems: Edge Computing enhances the responsiveness of IoT devices, while 5G Networks enable low-latency communication, AI provides intelligent data processing capabilities at the edge, and IoT connects various devices, forming the foundation for seamless and efficient data flow in modern applications.

2.1 Internet of Things (IoT)

The Internet of Things refers to the interconnection of commonplace things, devices, and equipment via networks that facilitate data transmission and reception. Devices within an IoT system may range from a basic temperature sensor to intricate systems such as autonomous vehicles or industrial robots. While working, they gather data that can be utilized to maintain operational alignment, identify concerns promptly, and facilitate rapid decision-making.

A persistent difficulty in IoT is the necessity for immediate data processing. A delay, even a little one, might restrict the system's responsiveness and may impact safety, cost, or efficiency in some instances. Conventional cloud computing, despite its capabilities, frequently falters in scenarios demanding rapid responses [3].

2.2 Edge Computing

Edge computing is a type of distributed system that processes data close to where it is generated, rather than sending everything to distant cloud servers [4]. By bringing computation to the edge of the network, this approach reduces delays, uses bandwidth more efficiently, and makes systems more responsive—an advantage for tasks that depend on quick data handling [1, 5]. It has proven especially useful in settings that require real-time processing, like autonomous driving, smart infrastructure, and industrial control. These systems depend on up-to-the-second analysis of sensor data to support fast, accurate decisions [2]. Processing information locally also allows these systems to react quickly without needing constant access to the cloud [6].

In IoT settings, edge computing handles raw data directly at the source. It filters out unnecessary details and forwards only relevant or summarized information to the cloud [1]. This reduces traffic on communication networks and lowers the demand for cloud storage [7]. This approach also helps in remote areas or places with poor connectivity, where cloud access is not always reliable. In these cases, being able to process data locally provides a clear and useful advantage over traditional cloud-based models [8].

2.3 5G Networks and the Internet of Things

5G is especially useful in edge computing because it cuts the time needed to move data between devices. In places where time is critical, such as hospitals or industrial systems, this makes a real difference. Processing data locally, without sending it to distant servers, lets equipment respond right away to changing conditions. This avoids delays that could stop workflows or put safety at risk [2].

In urban areas, 5G connects sensor networks built into roads and public infrastructure. These sensors give up-to-date information that helps city systems act quickly. For example, they can change traffic signals or send maintenance crews when needed. Having timely and reliable data helps cities control traffic better, save energy, and respond faster when public safety is at risk [9].

A key feature that makes 5G stand out is how quickly it moves information. This low delay is especially important when edge computing runs systems that need immediate responses. Low latency is critical for edge computing in situations where a quick reaction is essential. In healthcare or industrial automation, even a short delay can affect how the system works or put safety at risk. Processing data locally helps keep systems stable and able to react fast in these high-pressure settings [2].

2.4 Artificial Intelligence and Edge Computing

Artificial Intelligence (AI) is increasingly being used in edge computing to expand what IoT devices can do. Tools like machine learning (ML) allow data to be processed directly on the device, without needing to send it to the cloud. This makes it possible for IoT systems to react quickly to real-time data and make decisions on the spot [4].

This setup is especially useful in settings where fast responses are essential for example, spotting unusual patterns in patient data, predicting equipment failures before they happen, or helping autonomous vehicles respond to changing road conditions [10]. When AI processes data directly on the device, it reduces the need to send large volumes to the cloud. This not only eases network traffic but also keeps personal information stored locally, where it is less likely to be exposed [4].

In healthcare, edge-based AI can evaluate patient data from wearable devices in real time [11]. It can detect warning signs, such as changes in heart rate or irregular glucose patterns, and send alerts right away, without sharing personal health data beyond the device. By combining AI with edge computing, it is also possible to create systems that adjust while they work. These self-learning systems improve how IoT applications respond over time, making them more efficient and able to handle more complex tasks [12].

3 The Importance of Edge Computing in Internet of Things

As the number of IoT devices grows, so does the volume of data they produce. In cloud-based systems, this data is usually sent to distant servers for processing—a process that can lead to delays and strain network capacity. For applications that rely on immediate feedback, such as autonomous driving, medical monitoring, or industrial control, even small delays can create serious problems. In time-sensitive systems, even a delay of a few milliseconds can lead to missed responses or system errors [2].

Edge computing addresses the problem by enabling data to be processed close to where it is collected, either on the device itself or on a nearby server (Table 1). This reduces transmission time, lowers latency, and allows systems to respond in real time when fast decisions are needed [8].

Edge computing improves bandwidth efficiency by performing local filtering and processing of data before sending only relevant or aggregated information to the cloud [5, 13]. This is critical in environments where connectivity is intermittent or costly, including remote locations or large-scale sensor networks. In agriculture, sensors equipped with IoT technology can track environmental variables like soil moisture, temperature, and humidity [14]. With edge computing, the system can act on that data right away by activating irrigation or issuing alerts without relying on continuous communication with cloud servers.

The combination of Artificial Intelligence (AI) and Machine Learning (ML) with edge computing marks a meaningful step forward in the development of these technologies. Running AI models directly on the device allows IoT systems to make decisions based on real-time data [15]. In smart cities, systems are expected to respond to constant shifts in traffic flow, energy usage, and public safety demands. Applying AI at the edge

Table 1. Comparative Overview of Edge Computing Benefits Across IoT Sectors.

Sector	Application Area	Key Benefits	Challenges
Healthcare	Remote monitoring, wearables	Real-time alerts, data privacy, reduced latency	Device security, cost of deployment
Smart Cities	Traffic control, surveillance	Fast response, reduced network load, local insights	Integration across systems
Industrial Automation	Predictive maintenance	Faster diagnostics, low downtime, cost reduction	Interoperability, infrastructure costs
Agriculture	Smart irrigation	Real-time response to sensor data	Rural connectivity, device resilience
Autonomous Vehicles	Real-time navigation	Low latency, on-board decision-making	Data overload, safety certification

gives these systems the ability to adjust based on what is happening locally, improving their performance as they operate over time.

4 Enhancing Privacy and Security with Edge Computing

IoT systems frequently handle personal or sensitive information, and transmitting this data over networks can expose it to unauthorized access [16]. When large volumes of data are stored in one central location, as in most cloud-based systems, they become more attractive and vulnerable to cyberattacks. Even before it reaches the cloud, transmitting personal information across the internet exposes it to interception, which may compromise privacy or security [1].

Edge computing reduces that risk by processing sensitive data locally. Only selected or anonymized information is sent to the cloud, lowering the chance of exposure [2]. For example, in healthcare, wearable devices like smartwatches or ECG monitors can analyses data directly on the device. If they detect signs of concern, such as an irregular heartbeat, alerts can be sent immediately to healthcare staff. Because the system shares only the data that is strictly necessary, it helps protect patient confidentiality and reduces the risk of a [7].

Edge computing also improves system security by embedding protective measures into the devices themselves [16], as summarized in Table 2. These may include secure boot mechanisms, hardware-level authentication, and encryption designed to keep data safe while it is being processed or sent. In the energy sector, for example, smart meters and industrial sensors that handle data locally reduce the risk of intrusion by limiting how much sensitive information leaves the device [1].

Table 2. Key differences between traditional cloud-based and edge computing-based IoT systems in terms of data privacy and security.

Traditional Cloud-Based IoT	Edge Computing-Based IoT
Data collected by IoT devices is transmitted to the cloud for processing	Data is processed locally on the device or nearby edge server
Entire data payload, often including sensitive information, is transferred	Only selected, anonymized, or aggregated data is sent to the cloud
Centralized storage creates a single point of failure	Distributed processing reduces attack surface
High risk of interception during transmission	Local analysis limits exposure and improves response time
Security added at the cloud level	Security mechanisms built into edge devices (e.g., encryption, secure boot)
Slower feedback in time-sensitive cases	Real-time alerts and adaptive system behavior

This approach also supports techniques like differential privacy and data anonymisation. These methods ensure the data sent to the cloud cannot be linked to individual users [8]. These strategies are especially important in fields like finance, where devices handle confidential records and must follow strict data protection rules [2].

5 The Future of Edge Computing in Internet of Things

The growth of edge computing in the Internet of Things (IoT) is closely connected to recent advances in 5G and artificial intelligence. 5G networks, known for their high speed and low delay, are expected to support edge computing by allowing data to be transferred and processed almost instantly.

As illustrated in Fig. 2, edge computing plays a key role between IoT devices and the cloud. Edge nodes equipped with AI and ML tools receive data from local devices, analyses it on-site to support real-time decisions, and send only selected information to the cloud. 5G enables this structure by providing fast, secure, low-latency communication across all layers.

The growing integration of 5G and edge computing is shifting how real-time systems are designed. These technologies are particularly valuable in contexts where delayed decisions carry consequences—including autonomous mobility, remote healthcare procedures, and automated industrial processes [5] (Table 3).

In the case of autonomous vehicles, much of the required processing can now be done on board. By analyzing sensor data directly within the vehicle, edge computing removes the need to consult remote servers before reacting. At the same time, 5G allows continuous, low-latency communication with nearby infrastructure from traffic lights to other cars ensuring that critical information flows fast enough to support safe navigation [1].

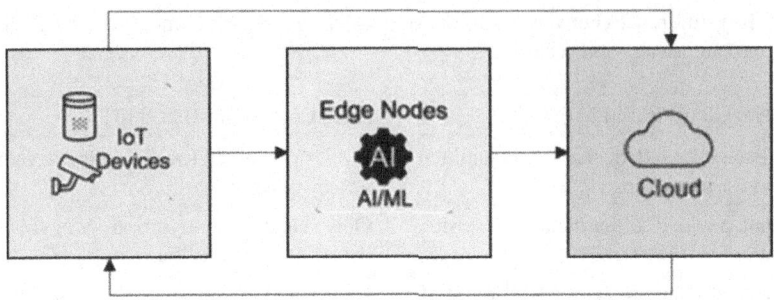

Fig. 2. Integration of Edge Computing, AI, and 5G in IoT Systems.

Table 3. Synergies of Edge Computing with Emerging Technologies

Technology	Role in Edge-IoT Integration	Impact on System Performance
5G	Enables ultra-low latency and high-speed communication	Real-time processing, faster response
Artificial Intelligence	Local data analysis and decision-making at the edge	Autonomous systems, privacy improvements
Cloud Computing	Long-term storage and deeper analytics	Offloads non-urgent processing
ML Ops	Model deployment and maintenance at the edge	Continuous learning, model optimization

Urban systems benefit in similar ways. When edge nodes analyses sensor data locally and 5G handles communication, cities can respond to traffic conditions and service needs almost as they happen. This improves both coordination and public safety, especially in densely monitored areas.

Artificial intelligence, when deployed at the edge, allows systems to respond with more flexibility and independence. Instead of sending all information to the cloud, these systems can analyses patterns locally, adapt to their environment, and act based on what is happening in real time. In industrial settings, this kind of edge-based intelligence makes it possible to spot irregularities before they turn into failures, allowing teams to intervene early and avoid unexpected downtime [17].

Rather than simply speeding up data processing, edge computing is becoming part of the foundation for building smarter, more autonomous systems. It supports real-time adaptation, helps maintain system stability, and reduces reliance on external infrastructure all of which are essential for responsive and resilient IoT operations.

6 Challenges and Trade-Offs

Despite its advantages, edge computing comes with several practical difficulties. One of the core challenges lies in managing devices that are spread across many locations. In contrast to centralized cloud systems, edge environments depend on infrastructure that can coordinate thousands or even millions of nodes in different places [18]. This distributed nature not only complicates management but also introduces significant heterogeneity in device capabilities and protocols [19, 20] (Table 4).

One of the ongoing difficulties in deploying edge-based IoT systems is getting devices from different manufacturers to function properly within the same environment. In practice, these components are rarely built with interoperability in mind [21]. Many follow their own communication rules, data formats, or hardware configurations [22, 23]. As a result, getting devices from different vendors to operate together often takes more time than initially planned. Integrating these devices frequently encounters setbacks, largely because many of them do not adhere to the same technical standards or communication protocols [24]. In many situations, technical teams end up spending considerable time making manual adjustments to ensure that devices can communicate effectively. This process can involve reconfiguring system parameters, rewriting certain settings, or adding middleware layers to bridge compatibility gaps between components [25]. When the system includes a large number of devices, these interventions tend to escalate quickly, introducing unexpected delays that were not factored into the original project timeline [26].

Even after the system is fully operational, technical mismatches might still cause unexpected behavior, especially under real usage conditions where inconsistencies are more likely to appear than during controlled testing [4].

Security risks also increase when edge devices are placed in locations where it is hard to control physical access. Unlike centralized data centers, these devices may be exposed to theft, tampering, or other types of physical interference. In these situations, security must begin at the device level. Systems need to include strong hardware protections, verified identity credentials, and tools that can detect unexpected behavior in real time. Without this foundation, edge infrastructure becomes easier to breach, both physically and remotely [2].

This exposure raises the risk of tampering, theft, or direct manipulation. Addressing this risk requires more than software-based solutions. It calls for secure hardware, authenticated access, and mechanisms that can detect unauthorized changes in how devices behave. Without these measures, attackers may use these weaknesses, both physically and remotely, to access sensitive data or disrupt system stability [2].

Without these protections, edge nodes can become simple entry points for both physical interference and cyberattacks [2].

Cost is another challenge, especially at the infrastructure level. While edge computing reduces the need for centralized cloud services, it requires investment in local hardware and reliable networks [7]. This can be a major problem for smaller organizations or those in less developed regions, where it is harder to cover the initial costs.

Table 4. Main challenges and trade-offs in edge computing environments, including technical, operational, and economic barriers affecting deployment and maintenance.

Challenge Area	Description	Consequences
Distributed Device Management	Managing a large number of geographically dispersed nodes with heterogeneous capabilities and protocols	Complex infrastructure coordination and increased maintenance effort
Interoperability Issues	Difficulty in integrating devices from different vendors due to non-standard communication protocols and data formats	Delays in deployment due to manual configuration and middleware requirements
Post-Deployment Issues	Unexpected behavior may occur under real-world usage, despite successful testing	Operational instability and performance degradation in live environments
Physical Security Risks	Edge nodes in remote or unsecured locations are vulnerable to theft and tampering	Greater risk of unauthorized physical access and damage
Cybersecurity Vulnerabilities	Lack of secure hardware, identity credentials, and real-time monitoring increases vulnerability to cyberattacks	Potential data breaches and system compromise
Infrastructure Costs	High initial investment in local infrastructure poses a challenge for small or under-resourced organizations	Limited adoption in budget constrained or developing regions

7 Conclusions

Edge computing is becoming a core part of how the Internet of Things (IoT) is growing. It allows devices to handle data close to where it's collected, which helps systems act in real time, lowers delays, and adds better protection for sensitive information. With this local processing, IoT devices can react quickly to events, run more efficiently, and keep user data safer. When combined with new technologies like 5G and Artificial Intelligence (AI), edge computing gives IoT systems even greater potential. This technology can be applied in real ways across several areas, including autonomous vehicles, health monitoring, city infrastructure, and industrial operations. But there are still important issues to work through. These include managing a large number of devices spread across different locations, protecting those devices from security threats, and handling the high costs involved in setting up the required systems. As these challenges are gradually addressed, edge computing is expected to keep playing a strong role in helping IoT systems become more reliable, quicker to respond, and better at keeping data safe in many different settings.

One area that still needs more attention is how to make edge-based IoT systems easier to integrate when the devices involved don't follow the same standards. This remains a practical challenge in many real deployments. At the same time, there's a need for simpler, more adaptable security solutions especially for devices with limited computing resources, where traditional models often don't apply. We still don't fully understand how these systems behave once they're placed in environments where conditions can't be controlled. What works in testing doesn't always hold in real-world use. Watching how they respond over time to stress, faults, or changing inputs could help uncover the kinds of problems that don't show up in short-term trials. These challenges go beyond technical engineering. Addressing them will likely require input from other fields as well, especially if we expect edge computing to support systems that people can rely on systems that remain clear, secure, and manageable, even as they grow more complex.

References

1. Zhang, J., Fan, B.: Edge computing in information technology: enhancing real-time data processing for IoT applications. Artif. Intell. Digit. Technol. **1**(1), 1–19 (2024). https://doi.org/10.70088/3852aq53
2. Anarbayevich, A.: Harnessing edge computing for enhanced security and efficiency in IoT networks. Am. J. Appl. Sci. Technol. **4**(3), 18–23 (2024). https://doi.org/10.37547/ajast/volume04issue03-04
3. Jha, D.N., et al.: IoTSim-edge: a simulation for modeling the behavior of Internet of Things and edge computing environments. Softw. Pract. Exp. **50**(6), 844–867 (2020). https://doi.org/10.1002/spe.2787
4. Bhanage, S., Patil, S.: Edge computing technology: revolutionizing daily existence. Int. Res. J. Mod. Eng. Technol. Sci. **6**(6), 1–3 (2024). https://doi.org/10.56726/irjmets52305
5. Jaddoa, A., Sakellari, G., Panaousis, E., Loukas, G., Sarigiannidis, P.G.: Dynamic decision support for resource offloading in heterogeneous Internet of Things environments. Simul. Model. Pract. Theory **101**, 1–13 (2020). https://doi.org/10.1016/j.simpat.2019.102019
6. Patel, U.: Edge computing and its role in IoT: analyze how edge computing is transforming IoT by processing data at the edge of the network, reducing latency and enhancing data security. Int. J. Innov. Sci. Res. Technol. **9**, 1751–1756 (2024). https://doi.org/10.38124/ijisrt/ijisrt24may791
7. Nalayini, P., Sudha, M., Egamberdieva, S., K.S., V.S., Rajkumar, R.: Edge computing in the era of IoT: enhancing data processing and reducing latency for smart applications. Nanotechnol. Percept. **20**(6), 145–154 (2024). https://nano-ntp.com/index.php/nano/article/view/2497/1874
8. Mohsin, M., Shahrouzi, S., Perera: Composing efficient computational models for real-time processing on next-generation edge-computing platforms. IEEE Access **12**, 24905–24932 (2024). https://doi.org/10.1109/access.2024.3365652
9. Mohit, M.: The role of edge computing in IOT: enhancing real time data processing capabilities. Int. J. Adv. Res. Electr. Electron. Instrum. Eng. **6**(12), 8811–8819 (2017). https://doi.org/10.15662/ijareeie.2017.0612002
10. Dec, G., et al.: Role of academics in transferring knowledge and skills on artificial intelligence, Internet of Things and edge computing. Sensors **22**(7), 1–34 (2022). https://doi.org/10.3390/s22072496
11. Subramanian, S.: IoT and edge computing for smart manufacturing: architecture and future trends. Int. J. Eng. Comput. Sci. **13**(10), 26504–26522 (2024). https://doi.org/10.18535/ijecs/v13i10.4922
12. Pasupuleti, M.: AI-enabled edge computing: revolutionizing IoT with real-time optimization. Int. J. Acad. Ind. Res. Innov. **4**(11), 29–64 (2024). https://doi.org/10.62311/nesx/46687

13. Shi, W., Cao, J., Zhang, Q., Li, Y., Xu, L.: Edge computing: vision and challenges. IEEE Internet Things J. **3**(5), 637–646 (2016). https://doi.org/10.1109/JIOT.2016.2579198
14. Wolfert, S., Ge, L., Verdouw, C., Bogaardt, M.J.: Big data in smart farming–a review. Agric. Syst. **153**, 69–80 (2017). https://doi.org/10.1016/j.agsy.2017.01.023
15. Algarni, S., El-Samie, F.E.: Energy-efficient distributed edge computing to assist dense Internet of Things. Future Internet **17**(1), 1–23 (2025). https://doi.org/10.3390/fi17010037
16. Gudnavar, A., Naregal, K.: Edge computing in Internet of Things (IoT): enhancing IoT ecosystems through distributed intelligence. AIBTIA **2**(3), 1–7 (2023). https://doi.org/10.46610/aibtia.2023.v02i03.001
17. Gambheer, R., Bhat, M.S.: Optimized compressed sensing for IoT: advanced algorithms for efficient sparse signal reconstruction in edge devices. IEEE Access **12**, 63610–63617 (2024). https://doi.org/10.1109/access.2024.3396494
18. Ren, J., Zhang, D., He, S.Z., Li, T.: A survey on end-edge-cloud orchestrated network computing paradigms. ACM Comput. Surv. **52**(6), 1–36 (2019). https://doi.org/10.1145/3362031
19. AlQerm, I., Wang, J., Pan, J., Liu, Y.: BEHAVE: behavior-aware, intelligent and fair resource management for heterogeneous edge-IoT systems. EEE Trans. Mob. Comput. **21**(11), 3852–3865 (2021). https://doi.org/10.48550/arxiv.2103.11043
20. Contreras, L., Bernardos, C.: Overview of architectural alternatives for the integration of ETSI MEC environments from different administrative domains. Electronics **9**(9), 1–20 (2020). https://doi.org/10.3390/electronics9091392
21. Niu, X., et al.: Workload allocation mechanism for minimum service delay in edge computing-based power Internet of Things. IEEE Access **7**, 83771–83784 (2019). https://doi.org/10.1109/access.2019.2920325
22. Ali, M., Anjum, A., Rana, O., Zamani, A.R., Balouek-Thomert, D., Parashar, M.: RES: real-time video stream analytics using edge enhanced clouds. IEEE Trans. Cloud Comput. **10**, 792–804 (2020). https://doi.org/10.1109/tcc.2020.2991748
23. Mukhtar, N., Mehrabi, A., Kong, Y., Anjum, A.: Edge enhanced deep learning system for IoT edge device security analytics. Concurr. Comput. Pract. Exp. **35**(13), e6764 (2021). https://doi.org/10.1002/cpe.6764
24. Das, A., Wazid, M., Yannam, A., Rodrigues, J., Park, Y.: Provably secure ECC-based device access control and key agreement protocol for IoT environment. IEEE Access **7**, 55382–55397 (20219). https://doi.org/10.1109/access.2019.2912998
25. Liu, L., Kang, L., Li, X., Zhou, Z.: Service reliability based on fault prediction and container migration in edge computing. Appl. Sci. **13**(23) (2023). https://doi.org/10.3390/app132312865
26. Peng, K., Liu, P., Peng, T., Huang, Q.: Security-aware computation offloading for mobile edge computing-enabled smart city. J. Cloud Comput. Adv. Syst. Appl., 1–13 (2021). https://doi.org/10.1186/s13677-021-00262-6

NET4SAFE: Network for Emergency and Safety Management. A Platform for Emergency Management and Accessibility

Annamaria Felli, Cristina Montaldi(✉), Vanessa Tomei, Emilio Marziali, and Francesco Zullo

Department of Civil, Construction-Architectural and Environmental Engineering, University of L'Aquila, Piazzale E. Pontieri 1, Monteluco di Roio, 67100 L'Aquila, Italy
cristina.montaldi@univaq.it

Abstract. The constant increase in the frequency and intensity of impactful climate events, combined with the Italian territory's complex morphology and extreme urban fragmentation, underscores the urgent need for tools that support more resilient and effective planning. This study introduces an innovative and scalable methodology for analyzing territorial accessibility. The model is based on an initial application of network theory, which, through geospatial data, represents urban settlements and their infrastructural connections. The aim is to identify areas most vulnerable due to limited accessibility to both services and key infrastructure networks. The study sets the foundation for the development of an operational tool to support emergency planning and response management. The proposed system serves as an efficient Decision Support System (DSS) for public authorities, adaptable to various territorial scales and integrable with demographic, building, and risk-related indicators. This approach addresses a gap in territorial knowledge and aims to provide an accurate representation of the infrastructural fabric. Such representation enables the definition of intervention priorities and risk mitigation strategies, ultimately promoting sustainable urban development.

Keywords: Network Planning · Emergency Management · Decision Support System

1 Introduction

The fragmentation of settlements currently observed across the Italian territory has made settlement systems highly energy-consuming and increasingly costly to manage for public administrations. This configuration lacks resilience and contributes to various environmental issues, as evidenced by the growing frequency of climate-related emergencies. These events increasingly expose the inherent vulnerabilities of a territory already heavily affected by multiple types of risk. Such dysfunctions concern the energy footprint of settlements, the fragmentation of natural habitats, access to social services, resilience to environmental hazards, and the decline of ecosystem functions. In Western industrialized countries, there has been an uncontrolled expansion of urbanized land, often unjustified by significant demographic changes. In Italy, this phenomenon—commonly referred to in the scientific literature as 'sprawl'—has long been regarded as a sign of effective governance, with regulations that have favored the development of new areas over the regeneration of existing ones. A scattered pattern of growth which, due to the specific characteristics of the national context, makes land recovery and management more complex. To describe the Italian case, the term 'sprinkling' has been proposed, as it more accurately captures the fragmented distribution of settlements across the territory—an aspect typical not only of Italy but also of other regions in Southern Europe [1]. Italy's high degree of administrative fragmentation—7,893 municipalities as of 2025—represents an emblematic case that highlights, about territory, environment, and social communities, the issues and dysfunctions that arise in the absence of spatial planning and a strategic interpretation of development goals. For these reasons, urban planning in Italy has been described as 'molecular', with serious consequences including excessive urbanization, the loss of coordinated planning, difficulties in infrastructure management, and poor efficiency in the rational organization of public services—ultimately resulting in unstructured growth and high energy consumption [2–5]. Moreover, in recent years, the urbanization process has accelerated on a global scale, transforming cities into the main hubs of human life, with both beneficial and problematic implications. The United Nations (UN) and the European Union (EU) urge the protection of soil, the environment, and the landscape—factors recognized as valuable components of natural capital—and promote the achievement of net-zero land take by 2050. This goal should be aligned with demographic growth and pursued without increasing the current rate of land degradation by 2030. It is in response to these objectives that new techniques and tools for spatial planning must be adopted, capable of providing timely and appropriate responses to territorial transformations. These should support the sustainable management of land and its proper uses through effective response actions embedded in urban policies [6–9].

In this context, the first essential aspect to address concerns the understanding of the geography of the country's settled areas, their demographic structure, their level of accessibility, and the risks to which they—together with the connecting infrastructures—are exposed. Such knowledge becomes a fundamental prerequisite both in the early stages of emergency management and for the implementation of appropriate actions aimed at mitigating vulnerability to various types of risk. In particular, the role of road connections will be analyzed, focusing on their distribution and typology, as well as their implications for urban and rural resilience.

The methodology is grounded in the principles of network theory, identifying nodes while simultaneously analyzing the systems of connections. Numerous scientific studies [10–17] have addressed the concept of 'node theory' in the field of urban planning. The presence of nodes necessitates connectivity, which can be supported by various modes of transport and by the broader system of relationships between nodes and their connections. Road and transit connections are typically local in scope and often take the form of a grid, which characterizes the layout of many cities. In contrast, rail, maritime, and air links integrate the city into a broader context of distribution and trade, often on a global scale [18]. In this way, the analysis enables the identification of areas that are more vulnerable in terms of accessibility and isolation, where the quality of connections plays a key role. It considers not only the number of connections but also their specific weight, thereby contributing to a more accurate representation of the infrastructural resilience of a municipality or individual settlement areas. The work presented outlines a methodology currently under development, aimed at identifying and assessing the degree of accessibility of territories at both municipal and urban/peri-urban scales. Areas with better connectivity are generally more integrated into economic and social networks, facilitating access to public services, promoting sustainable mobility, and ensuring their reachability in emergencies.

Conversely, poorly connected areas tend to remain isolated and vulnerable, with the risk of being excluded from timely interventions in the event of catastrophic events. This vulnerability is further exacerbated by an urban structure which, although diverse and historically stratified, presents significant weaknesses in terms of emergency resilience. In a context where physical spaces are constantly intertwined with their social constructions, the idea of place as a fixed, material entity is surpassed. Place instead becomes a 'space of flows', making the adoption of advanced technological tools crucial to support risk and emergency management. In this way, the concept of the city shifts from a spatially bounded, human-centered phenomenon to a dynamic and complex urban system, which, in its incompleteness and indeterminacy, becomes the stage where urban elements take shape and adapt. The city emerges as an evolving organism, where past, present, and future merge, reflecting social dynamics and the ongoing attempts to regulate their interactions and spatial organization, that is, the urban development process in terms of conservation, transformation, or change concerning its original state [19].

2 Material

The data comes from institutional and open-source sources, such as ISTAT [20] for municipal boundaries and census sections and OpenStreetMap (OSM) for the road network [21]. The geographic data about census sections are available in shape file format from the website of Istituto Nazionale di Statistica (Istat). The scale of data representation is not uniform across the national territory, varying from a scale of 1:5 000 (typically in urban areas) to a scale of 1:25 000 (primarily in low or very low population density areas). Different attributes are associated with this census section. The one that has been used to identify the urban areas is the typology of the location (TIPO_LOC).

The field can take the following values:

1. *Inhabited centre*: an aggregate of contiguous or neighbouring houses with interposed streets, squares and the like, or in any case brief solutions of continuity characterized by the existence of public services or establishments (school, public office, pharmacy, shop or similar) that constitute an autonomous form of social life and, generally, also a gathering place for the inhabitants of the neighbouring areas to manifest the existence of a form of social life coordinated by the centre itself. Tourist meeting places, groups of villas, hotels, and the like intended for holidays, inhabited seasonally, must be considered as temporary inhabited centers, provided that during the period of seasonal activity they present the requirements of the centre.
2. *Inhabited nucleus*: inhabited locality, without the gathering place that characterizes the inhabited centre, consisting of a group of at least fifteen contiguous and neighbouring buildings, with at least fifteen families, with interposed roads, paths, squares,

farmyards, small vegetable gardens, small uncultivated areas and the like, provided that the interval between house and house does not exceed thirty meters and is in any case less than that between the nucleus itself and the nearest of the manifestly scattered houses.
3. *Production location*: an area in an extra-urban area not included in inhabited centres or nuclei in which there are more than 10 local units, or whose total number of employees is greater than 200, contiguous or close with interposed streets, squares and the like, or in any case brief solutions of continuity not exceeding 200 m; the minimum area must correspond to 5 hectares.
4. *Scattered houses*: houses scattered in the municipal area at such a distance that they cannot even constitute an inhabited nucleus.

In our case, urban areas are defined as the whole of inhabited center and nucleus (the sum of class 1, 2 and 3).

For the structural aggregate, it was referred to the Department of Civil Protection [22] created a dataset of structural aggregates across Italy to support post-earthquake damage assessment activities. This dataset, developed with the contribution of Regions, Autonomous Provinces, and the Revenue Agency, integrates data from regional geotopographic databases, cadastral maps, and Istat administrative boundaries (updated to 2021). The project harmonized heterogeneous data, ensuring uniformity at the national level. Released under an Open CC-BY 4.0 license, the dataset can be integrated with locally produced maps and has multiple applications. The cartographic data, divided by macro-regions, along with the related metadata, are available for free reuse through the GitHub platform, along with general information about the entire project. The data is available in shapefile format and requires specific software (GIS) for consultation. The polygonal layer of the built-up area is derived from the analysis of ortho-rectified images through the combined use of "feature extraction" techniques via deep learning methodologies and supervision for the control and correction of the algorithms [22–24].

Data on road infrastructure and points of interest come from OpenStreetMap. Data can be downloaded via the https://download.geofabrik.de/ portal. The OpenStreetMap Project based at OpenStreetMap.org, is a worldwide mapping effort that includes more than a million volunteers around the globe (https://osmfoundation.org/wiki/About) who contribute and maintain data on roads, trails, cafes, train stations and much more. OpenStreetMap emphasizes local knowledge. Contributors use aerial imagery, GPS devices, and low-tech field maps to verify that OSM is accurate and up-to-date. The data in question can be downloaded in.shp geographical format and, depending on the type of information to which they refer, can be point, linear or polygonal files.

Specifically, downloadable data, which are geographical data in.shp format, provide on different layers data relating to buildings, land uses, natural elements, places, points of interests, railways, and transportation lines. Table 1 shows the categories of OSM roads used in this study. The nomenclature and symbology adopted in methodological treatment are also reported.

Table 1. Classification of considered road network

OSM class	Istat classification	Adopted symbology
Motorway	Motorway	▬▬▬
Trunk		
Primary	State, Regional, and Provincial roads	▬▬▬
Secondary	Extra-Urban roads	———
Tertiary	Urban roads	———
Residential		
Unclassified		

3 Methodology

The proposed work aims to define a schematic methodology for characterizing urban areas based on accessibility. In this context, accessibility is understood as the number of connections between different urban areas and the type of infrastructure linking them. The underlying principle is as follows: the higher the number of connections a territorial entity has with others, the greater its level of accessibility. High accessibility is particularly crucial in emergency contexts. The principles underlying the methodology are based on network theory, identifying and characterizing nodes while simultaneously analyzing the systems of connection [25–28].

This methodology aims to provide a support tool for emergency management in two distinct contexts: ordinary conditions and emergencies. In the former, the goal is to identify the most underserved areas to improve accessibility by addressing infrastructural weaknesses. In emergencies, the use of this methodology makes it possible to provide essential geographical information, such as the location of the event triggering the emergency, the affected population, and the condition of the infrastructure.

The model is based on a graphical representation of the network of connections between major urban centres and smaller settlements, organized according to an infrastructural hierarchy.

Specifically, Figs. 1 and 2 illustrate two different territorial configurations, utilizing the same system of symbols to ensure consistency and comparability between the representations. In particular, the legend accompanying the figures distinguishes two primary groups of symbols: one pertaining to the road network and the other to the urbanized areas.

The road network is depicted through the use of lines, with the thickness of each line varying proportionally to the vehicular flow capacity that the corresponding infrastructure is able to support. More precisely, motorways are represented by the thickest lines, symbolizing their ability to accommodate the highest volume of vehicular traffic. Conversely, urban streets are illustrated with the thinnest lines, reflecting their function as routes characterized by a significantly lower traffic capacity and reduced vehicular flow. This differentiation in line thickness offers an immediate visual cue regarding the hierarchical importance of the various road types in the territorial framework. Regarding urban centers, these are represented using squares whose dimensions and shades of grey vary according to the density of urbanization they exhibit. The differences in both size and coloration serve to convey the relative importance and functional role of each settlement within the overall territorial system. Larger squares shaded in dark grey correspond to densely urbanized centers, indicating areas with a high concentration of buildings and activities. In contrast, smaller squares with lighter grey tones are used to represent production sites or smaller inhabited nuclei, which are characterized by a lower degree of urbanization. This symbolic approach allows for a nuanced visualization of both the infrastructural and urban structure of the territory, enabling a more comprehensive understanding of the relationships between different nodes and the transport routes that connect them. By integrating variations in line thickness and square attributes, the graphical representation effectively communicates the complex interplay between urban density and infrastructural connectivity.

As previously mentioned, Fig. 1 and Fig. 2 show two different territorial configurations. Each configuration has significant implications not only for everyday mobility patterns and the efficiency of movement across the territory but also, and perhaps even more critically, for the management of emergency situations. The spatial organization of settlements and the structure of the road network profoundly influence how evacuate areas can be evacuated, how quickly emergency services can intervene, and how resilient a territory can be when subjected to natural disasters, accidents, or other crises.

In particular, the configuration of the territory affects factors such as the redundancy of routes, the accessibility of peripheral areas, and the potential isolation of certain settlements under emergency conditions. A fragmented or poorly interconnected territory may exacerbate response times and limit the effectiveness of rescue operations, while a more structured and hierarchical network can facilitate faster and more reliable interventions. Thus, analyzing and understanding these two territorial models is crucial for both the planning of mobility systems in ordinary circumstances and the preparation of effective emergency response strategies.

Figure 1 shows a territorial configuration characterized by a polycentric and scattered distribution of settlements, accompanied by a complex yet fragmented infrastructural network. The presence of main urban centers, minor settlements, and productive areas, distributed heterogeneously across the territory and connected through a multi-level road hierarchy (including highways, national/regional/provincial roads, and urban and extraurban roads), suggests a reticular settlement model lacking a dominant central structure. However, the spatial distribution of settlements appears dispersed, and the road network is rather discontinuous, relying heavily on numerous secondary roads that are often inadequately structured. In such a context, functional connections between the different poles are fragile and vulnerable, particularly in emergencies (e.g., extreme weather events, natural disasters), where access to services and the timeliness of emergency response may be seriously compromised.

Figure 2, on the other hand, presents a more orderly and hierarchical configuration, with three main poles connected by a clear infrastructural axis. In this context, the management of connections becomes more efficient, with a denser road network that offers more effective alternative routes, reducing the risk of isolation of some areas and improving accessibility to essential services.

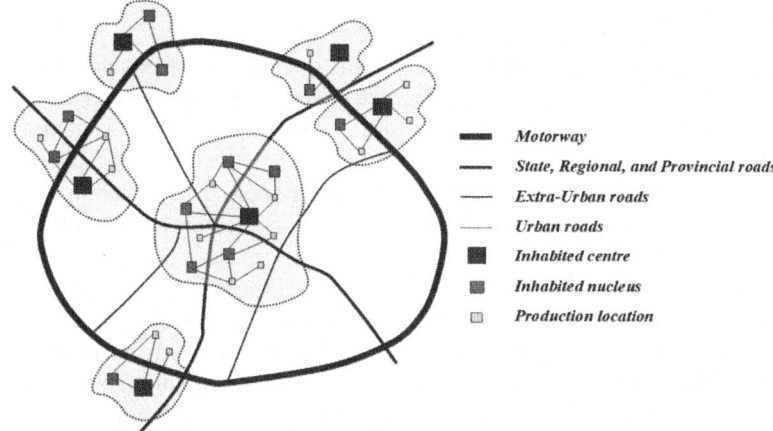

Fig. 1. Territorial configuration with fragmented connections (Authors' elaboration)

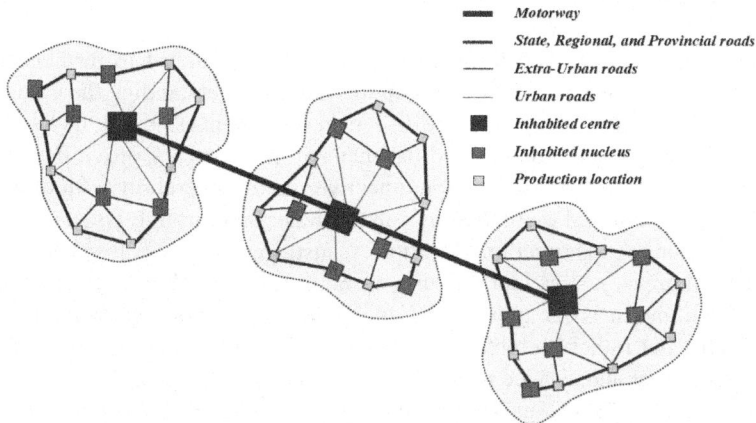

Fig. 2. Territorial configuration with more structured connections (Authors' elaboration)

Within this framework, three main nodes are identified, representing the primary urban centres, which are interconnected by a hierarchically structured transport network. This network includes motorways—as the primary axis of connection between urban centres—national, regional, and provincial roads that link the urban centres to the surrounding territory, and extra-urban and urban roads that provide local connectivity between smaller settlements. This organization makes it possible to assess the degree of accessibility of the various settlements and the role of urban centres in the distribution of territorial functions.

Settlements have been classified into three categories based on their size and level of connectivity, as previously outlined in the materials section:

- Inhabited centre
- Inhabited nucleus

- Production location.

This classification enables the analysis of the distribution of population and infrastructure, highlighting the degree of dependence of smaller settlements on the main urban centres. To make these dynamics more intuitive, the graphical representation employs varying sizes and line thicknesses to indicate the relative weight of each node, while connections are differentiated according to their function. This visual approach highlights the urban hierarchy and the relationships between different sectors, offering a clear overview of territorial organization and its underlying functional logic.

The developed model provides an immediate interpretation of the urban network, highlighting how nodes are distributed and interconnected. Each node assumes a specific role within the system, depending on the number of buildings, the extent of built-up areas, and its functional use—whether residential, commercial, administrative, or industrial. This distinction allows for an understanding not only of the network structure but also of the weight and significance of each node within the urban fabric.

4 Discussion and Conclusions

The methodology, although still under development and subject to further validation, represents a preliminary yet significant step forward in understanding the vulnerabilities and resilience of areas characterized by dispersed settlements [29, 30]. Its flexible structure allows the model to be adapted to different territorial contexts, providing an effective tool for analyzing road infrastructure connectivity and vulnerability. An effective representation of the applied methodology can be illustrated through an analogy with the human body: main roads function like arteries, ensuring the connection between central and peripheral areas, just as blood nourishes bodily tissues. However, in the territorial context, the situation is far more complex. There are no homogeneous tissues composed of cells, but rather a collection of scattered housing units which, although they have infrastructural and service needs, are not organized uniformly. This configuration results in high costs for ordinary management and, above all, for emergency response. Settlement dispersion thus represents a critical challenge for territorial planning, raising questions about its long-term sustainability and the system's capacity to cope with catastrophic events.

The real territorial system is not as rigidly structured as the model; in fact, the real-world scenario often features a high degree of settlement dispersion, resulting in very high emergency management costs. Figure 3 illustrates a typical configuration found in Italy, where a strong tendency towards dispersed urbanization can be observed. For this purpose, structural aggregates produced by the Civil Protection Department are also included.

One of the most critical aspects to consider is the impact of the loss of an infrastructural node following an emergency event (such as a landslide, flood, or earthquake). If the node is highly connected, its disruption can trigger cascading effects throughout the network, compromising the system's capacity for intervention, and emergency response is therefore essential to assess how the territorial system can reorganize itself in the event of an emergency to ensure a rapid and effective response. This requires advanced tools capable of simulating crisis scenarios and optimizing the management

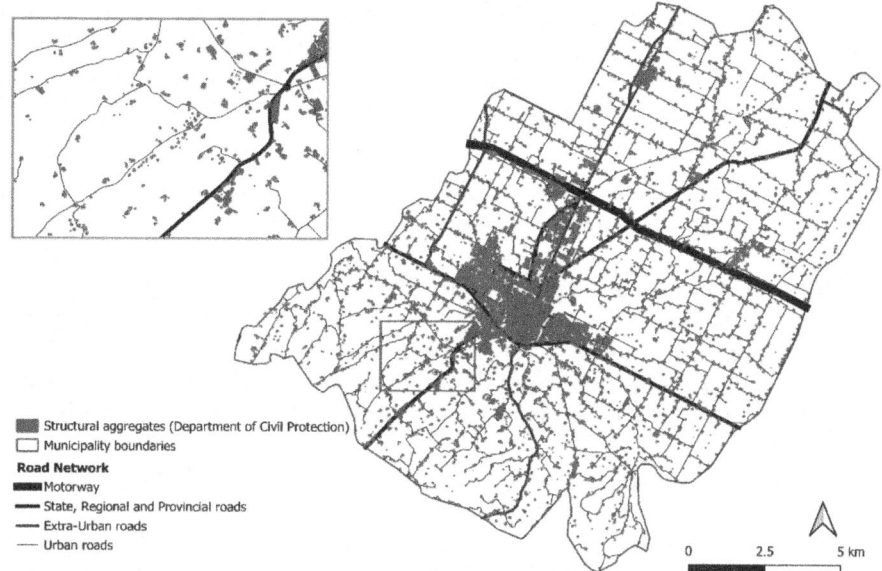

Fig. 3. Typical urban configuration in Italy with road network and structural aggregates (Authors' elaboration)

of available resources. The analysis is based on data from the Italian National Institute of Statistics (ISTAT), relating to census sections, which provide the number of inhabitants for each area. However, in zones characterized by dispersed settlements, such data are poorly representative as they are not directly associated with individual urban clusters. To improve the accuracy of the model, it would be beneficial to integrate data from the Civil Protection Department on structural aggregates, allowing for the estimation of the average number of inhabitants per dwelling and enabling a more realistic representation of population distribution. To provide a representative analysis, it is important to select a heterogeneous sample of Italian municipalities characterized by different levels of settlement dispersion, connectivity, and vulnerability to environmental risks. The selection of municipalities must consider the geographical and infrastructural diversity of the country, from poorly connected mountainous areas to medium-sized urban centres that serve as key nodes within the national road network [1, 31].

Further development of the research could involve the creation of an interactive platform that not only represents population distribution and the location of urban nodes but also highlights the main risks associated with each node. Such a platform could support the updating of emergency management plans and serve as a valuable tool for risk mitigation and territorial planning. A more detailed analysis should include:

- The classification of connections between nodes (national roads, motorways, secondary roads) to assess access capacity and vulnerabilities within the road network.
- The identification of open areas within nodes, including an analysis of the coverage ratio, the percentage of impervious surface relative to the total area—which affects the territory's resilience in the event of extreme weather events.

- The building and population density to better characterize the function of the nodes and to understand their weight within the settlement network.
- The identification of points of interest (POIs), such as essential services and strategic infrastructures, to estimate population flows and their concentration across different areas.

The use of data from OpenStreetMap could enhance the understanding of mobility dynamics, as areas with a high concentration of services tend to attract more people, increasing their criticality in emergencies.

Further development could involve the integration of artificial intelligence algorithms or optimization models to define the most efficient routes to reach affected areas, avoiding random interventions based solely on calls received by operational centres. Once the damaged and compromised infrastructures have been identified, the system could estimate the number of people affected, enabling more targeted and informed interventions.

A key point to highlight is that building density alone is not sufficient to characterize the urban fabric. For instance, an area with skyscrapers and one with low-rise buildings may have the same building density but differ entirely in terms of habitability and population accommodation capacity. For this reason, it is essential to integrate demographic data with information on the distribution of buildings. In abandoned historic centres, for example, there may be high building density but very few actual residents.

A more effective approach could involve the introduction of an index that relates building density to the resident population, such as the residential density at the census section level. Residential density provides information on the number of inhabitants per unit of area, while the average number of inhabitants per building helps estimate the actual human presence in each context. ISTAT data on vacant housing represent crucial information for understanding the real resident population.

An additional level of analysis could include mobility flow data, providing information on the centrality and relative importance of the nodes. Finally, to enhance the readability and interpretation of the results, the schematic representation could be enriched with satellite imagery and other geospatial data. "Since the research is based on the application of a specific methodology, the schematic representation becomes a key element for visualizing the structure of the analyzed urban system, enabling an immediate understanding of territorial and functional dynamics. This approach, by integrating both quantitative and qualitative data, provides more effective tools for territorial planning and management, intending to improve urban resilience and the capacity to respond to environmental risks.

Acknowledgments. This work is part of the project "Paride *"Piattaforma per la prevenzione delle emergenze ed il supporto alla sicurezza del territorio"*.

Disclosure of Interests. The authors have no competing interests to declare that are relevant to the content of this article.

References

1. Felli, A., Di Pietro, G., Marziali, E., Zullo, F.: Il disperso italiano: un'emergenza nell'emergenza. Progettare Nel Disordine-Progettare IL Disordine (2024)
2. Calafati, A.G.: Economia della città dispersa, Università degli studi di Ancona, Dipartimento di economia (2003)
3. Romano, B., Ciabò, S.: Il futuro del paesaggio: tra urban sprawling e sviluppo sostenibile, Riconquistare il paesaggio. La Convenzione Europea del Paesaggio e la Conservazione della Biodiversità in Italia, pp. 257–267 (2008)
4. Romano, B., Zullo, F., Fiorini, L., Ciabò, S., Marucci, A.: Sprinkling: an approach to describe urbanization dynamics in Italy. Sustainability **9**, 97 (2017)
5. Romano, B., et al.: Sostenibilità, resilienza, adattamento per la tutela degli ecosistemi e la ricostruzione fisica in Italia Centrale (2020–2022). Rapporto tecnico finale – Progetto Sost.EN.&Re. Università degli Studi dell'Aquila (2022). ISBN 978-88-946095-1-614:41
6. Romano, B., Fiorini, L., Zullo, F., Marucci, A.: Una valutazione delle dinamiche di consumo di suolo in Italia: Gli esiti della ricerca DICEAA. In: Caring fo Our Soil: Aver Cura Della Natura dei Territori; WWF Italia Onlus, Rome, Italy, pp. 19–28 (2017)
7. Felli, A., Zullo, F.: Legislative foundations: exploring land take laws and urban regeneration policies in Italy and Europe. Land **13**(713) (2024)
8. Montaldi, C.: Consumo di suolo: Un complesso quadro di politiche, definizioni e soglie. Territorio **2023**(103), 147–156 (2024)
9. Tomei, V., Romano, B., Zullo, F.: Advanced planning tool mosaic (A-PTM) decision support tool towards the sustainable development goals. In: Marucci, A., Zullo, F., Fiorini, L., Saganeiti, L. (eds.) INPUT 2023. LNCE, vol. 463, pp. 717–727. Springer, Cham (2024). https://doi.org/10.1007/978-3-031-54096-7_62
10. Facchinetti, M.: Intorno al nodo: processi di densificazione urbana e territoriale nelle aree ad alta accessibilità infrastrutturale, Editore Pitagora (2007)
11. Claramunt, C., Winter, S.: Structural salience of elements of the city. Environ. Plan. B. Plan. Des. **34**(6), 1030–1050 (2007)
12. Cheng, J., Bertolini, L., le Clercq, F., Kapoen, L.: Understanding urban networks: comparing a node-, a density-and an accessibility-based view. Cities **31**, 165–176 (2013)
13. Schaub, M.T., Lehmann, J., Yaliraki, S.N., Barahona, M.: Structure of complex networks: quantifying edge-to-edge relations by failure-induced flow redistribution. Netw. Sci. **2**(1), 66–89 (2014)
14. Natapov, A., Czamanski, D., Fisher-Gewirtzman, D.: A network approach to link visibility and urban activity location. Netw. Spat. Econ. **18**, 555–575 (2018)
15. Ma, J., Shen, Z., Xie, Y., Liang, P., Yu, B., Chen, L.: Node-place model extended by system support: evaluation and classification of metro station areas in Tianfu new area of Chengdu. Front. Environ. Sci. **10**, 990416 (2022)
16. Antropia. https://www.antropia.it/la-teoria-dei-grafi-nella-citta-di-konigsberg/. Accessed 25 Jan 2025
17. The Geography of Transport Systems. https://transportgeography.org/contents/chapter8/transportation-urban-form/cities-connectivity/. Accessed 25 Jan 2025
18. Cvetinovic, M., Nedovic-Budic, Z., Bolay, J.C.: Decoding urban development dynamics through actor-network methodological approach. Geoforum **82**, 141–157 (2017)
19. Ewing, R., Pendall, R., Chen, D.: Measuring sprawl and its transportation impacts. In: Hanson, G.S. (ed.) Urban Sprawl: Causes, Consequences, and Policy Responses. Urban Land Institute, pp. 55–77 (2002)
20. Istituto Nazionale di Statistica (Istat). https://www.istat.it/. Accessed 13 Feb 2025
21. Open Street Map (OSM). https://www.openstreetmap.org/. Accessed 07 Feb 2025

22. Dipartimento della Protezione Civile. https://rischi.protezionecivile.gov.it/it/approfondimento/dataset-nazionale-degli-aggregati-strutturali-italiani/. Accessed 15 Feb 2025
23. Regione Emilia-Romagna – Geoportale: Edificato 2018 ottenuto con tecniche di feature extraction tramite machine learning (2018). https://geoportale.regione.emilia-romagna.it/notizie/servizi-e-applicazioni/edificato2018-ottenuto-con-tecniche-di-feature-extraction-tramitemachine-learning
24. Olivucci, S., Nerieri, M., Ruggieri, G., Romani, M., Ceresini, S., Gentili, G.: Il nuovo strato edificato da tecniche "deep learning" come fonte per l'aggiornamento del database topografico e per il monitoraggio del consumo di suolo. In: Atti della Conferenza ASITA 2019, Trieste, Italia, 2019, pp. 811–818 (2019). ISBN: 978-88-941232-5-8
25. Ding, R., et al.: Application of complex networks theory in urban traffic network researches. Netw. Spat. Econ. **19**, 1281–1317 (2019)
26. Milanović, J.V., Zhu, W.: Modeling of interconnected critical infrastructure systems using complex network theory. IEEE Trans. Smart Grid **9**(5), 4637–4648 (2017)
27. Faramondi, L., Setola, R., Panzieri, S., Pascucci, F., Oliva, G.: Finding critical nodes in infrastructure networks. Int. J. Crit. Infrastruct. Prot. **20**, 3–15 (2018)
28. LaRocca, S., Guikema, S.: A survey of network theoretic approaches for risk analysis of complex infrastructure systems. In: Vulnerability, Uncertainty, and Risk: Analysis, Modeling, and Management, pp. 155–162 (2011)
29. Khan, M.T.I., Anwar, S., Sarkodie, S.A., et al.: Natural disasters, resilience-building, and risk: achieving sustainable cities and human settlements. Nat. Hazards **118**, 611–640 (2023)
30. Baffoe, G., Zhou, X., Moinuddin, M., et al.: Urban–rural linkages: effective solutions for achieving sustainable development in Ghana from an SDG interlinkage perspective. Sustain. Sci. **16**, 1341–1362 (2021)
31. La Rosa, D.: Metodologie per le sintesi del piano. In: Mancuso, C., Martinico, F., Nigrelli, F.C. (eds.) I Piani Territoriali Paesaggistici nella Provincia di Enna. INU (2008)

Digital Transition: Effects on Housing Mobility, Market, Land Governance (DIGITRANS 2025)

The Subjective Dimension in Settlement Choices: Approaches and Tools for Detecting Preferences

Fabrizio Battisti(✉) [iD] and Melania Perdonò

Department of Architecture, University of Florence, 50121 Florence, Italy
{fabrizio.battisti,melania.perdono}@unifi.it

Abstract. The ongoing digital transition profoundly affects people's habits and customs, their lifestyles and also the choice related to the place to live. The choice related to the place to live is strongly conditioned by the incidence of the cost of housing (buying or renting), which is dependent on the market and income capacity. It should be noted, however, that the growing interest in the concept of well-being understood as a paradigm of quality of life may lead to new interests in residential demand effectively untying the digital transition - at least potentially - workers in the tertiary sector from the physical place of work. Based on the above, this paper aims to illustrate some results of a Project of Significant National Interest under the Ministry of Universities and Research (MUR)'s approved call No. 1409 of 14-9-2022 (PRIN 2022 PNRR) entitled "Housing mobility and digital transition. Evaluation tools and technologies for understanding current and future people's living needs, supporting territorial governance and regeneration processes." This Research project is configured as a prodromal study and investigation activity for understanding, among demographic phenomena, housing mobility, which significantly affects urbanization phenomena on which land use and protection, urban regeneration, and the protection and enhancement of agricultural activity, issues of interest to the PNRR, depend. In detail, the present work returns the results of a survey, conducted through the tool of the questionnaire, widely used in social research, aimed at investigating, with reference to the Tuscan regional territory, the subjective dimension in settlement choices, in order to identify the territorial areas that, without considering the market and objective qualification characters and therefore without objective feedback, are nevertheless more attractive.

Keywords: Land Government · Social Research · Questionnaires · Well-being · Digital Transition

1 Introduction

The ongoing digital transition profoundly affects people's habits and customs and may affect their lifestyles. With particular reference to the consideration concerning the place to live, although this choice is strongly conditioned by the incidence of the cost of housing (buying or renting), which is dependent on the market and income capacity, it should be noted, however, that the growing interest in the concept of well-being understood as a paradigm of quality of life can determine new interests of residential demand, effectively freeing the digital transition - at least potentially - workers in the tertiary sector, which in Italy weighs about 2/3 of total employment, from the physical place of work. Such possibilities occur for the first time in the history of modern man; those traditional "home-to-work" distance constraints that have profoundly influenced people's choice of living place since at least the 18th century onward are overcome, not having been effectively overcome even by the technological advancement of means of transportation.

However, the choice of where to live is strongly influenced by the amount of money available for housing compared to income, typically focused on rent or mortgage payments and potential borrowing for an upfront purchase. Considering this, it is believed that the digital transition may nonetheless create significant effects on the choice of living location, where, in addition to the mortgage-to-rental-income ratio and the characteristics that objectively define a place, personal expectations, ambitions, and preferences play a role, suggesting a subjective dimension that this work explores.

Based on the above, this contribution aims to illustrate some results related to the Project of Significant National Interest referred to in the Call for Proposals no. 1409 of 14-9-2022 (PRIN 2022 PNRR) approved by the Ministry of University and Research (MUR) with D.D. no. 1235 of August 1, 2023 and admitted for funding with D.D. no. 1378 of September 1, 2023, ERC SH - Social Sciences and Humanities, main ERC subfield SH7_7 Cities; urban, regional and rural studies entitled "Housing mobility and digital transition. Evaluation tools and technologies for understanding current and future people's living needs, supporting territorial governance and regeneration processes," and which therefore results among the Research projects funded by the European Union under the Next Generation EU. This research project is configured as a study and investigation activity, preliminary to understanding the demographic phenomena of housing mobility, which significantly affects urbanization and should therefore be duly considered in territorial governance activities.

In detail, this contribution returns the results of a survey, conducted through the questionnaire instrument, widely used in social research, aimed at investigating, concerning the Tuscan regional territory, the subjective dimension in settlement choices, to identify the territorial areas that, without considering the market and objective qualification characters and therefore without objective feedback, are nevertheless more attractive.

2 Preference Capture Techniques Used in Social Research: Focus on Interviews and Questionnaires

It is well established in science that one can acquire even scientific knowledge of social facts [1]. In social research, particular importance is placed on studying methods and techniques for constructing the "empirical base" of data and information to support the research activities.

Within the framework of preference detection processes associated with land governance, the use of interviews and questionnaires is predominantly observed. These instruments exhibit strong correlations, to the extent that, over time, the questionnaire in social research has evolved into an implementation tool for structured interviews, thereby transcending the early classifications [2] that differentiated the two instruments based on the distinct outputs they offered (qualitative for interviews and quantitative for questionnaires). Currently, within the domain of social research, the questionnaire is recognized as a variant of structured interview [1, 3–7]. Below is a literature review concerning interviews and the questionnaire as conceptualized in social research.

2.1 The Interviews

Interviews serve as a fundamental survey technique for qualitative social research. Since the early developments in sociology and anthropology, they have been used to gather information. This technique facilitates direct, verbal, and rich subjective data, focusing on the interviewee's personal experiences, perceptions, and social dynamics. [7, 8] Moreover, the advent of technology has dismantled the spatial barrier, enabling interviews to be conducted not only live but also via telephone, video call, or online platforms (e.g., online, asynchronous interviews). This advancement has expanded research contexts and comparisons across different populations, even those that are very distant. Although the interview technique may appear straightforward, it necessitates specific caveats: i) it must be based on a dyadic interviewer-interviewee relationship, in which the former plays the role of asking questions and the latter of providing answers while adhering to the rules established by the researcher [9]; ii) it assumes that the interviewer possesses exceptional skills in reprocessing the data obtained.

According to a rather popular sociological approach, interviews can be classified according to different criteria:

1. The presence or absence of eye contact;
2. The distribution of power among actors;
3. The degree of freedom granted to the respondent.

The selection of the classification criterion is contingent upon the initial objectives, the nature of the research to be undertaken, and, most importantly, the specific context in which the interview is administered. Of particular significance, for ensuring the validity and authenticity of the interview results, is the level of freedom afforded to the interviewees. In this regard, interviews can be categorized as: i) unstructured; ii) semi-structured; iii) structured. The subsequent descriptions elaborate on these types of interviews, with a particular emphasis on the structured interviews that can be conducted utilizing a questionnaire.

Unstructured and Semi-structured Interviews
The unstructured interview, also known as the free interview, involves a more open and conversational format. The questions are not predetermined, and the researcher only sets the topic to be addressed. The goal of this type of interview is to explore the interviewee's point of view in depth, which is a significant advantage. The unstructured interview aims to stimulate a free narrative, which is why it develops over a fairly long time horizon (limitation), a factor that strongly influences the choice of sample size to be analyzed [9, 10]. It is mainly used in preliminary surveys, when, once the research problems have been identified, the next step is to formulate hypotheses. The difficulties of analysis are high, as there is a total lack of a basic structure, making data processing challenging.

Semi-structured interviews combine elements of structured and unstructured interviews. Again, the researcher prepares a set of questions that he or she wishes to receive answers to from the interviewee. However, criteria for flexibility are also maintained: the researcher can indeed use additional questions beyond those planned, enhancing the quantity and quality of the material produced by the interviewee [11]. Typically, this type of interview is utilized in social research where there are complex areas to analyze. In fact, rigor in the topics covered is combined with flexibility in the exchange of responses. The goal is to collect opinions and comments that may not have been captured in the preparation stages and that will significantly impact the continuation of the project [10, 12].

Advantages include flexibility in responding, interpreting, and exploring a specific theme; adaptability and responsiveness in addressing emerging issues and initiating new lines of inquiry; and greater preparation for the interviewer (alternative formulations, explanations, suggested answers to help the respondent). Disadvantages relate to the subsequent processing of the data, which can take a long time, and to possible inconsistency in responses, leading to their misinterpretation.

Structured Interviews: Implementation Through Questionnaires
Structured interviews, also referred to as standardized, have a rigid form, leaving little room for interpretation by the interviewee. The interview is characterized by the use of a standardized instrument, the same for all respondents, with very few (or no) parts that allow the respondent to freely express his or her position [13]. The respondent is required to answer a questionnaire, consisting of a set of fixed questions and predetermined answers from which to choose one, and almost no open-ended questions, i.e., questions to which he or she can answer freely, without adhering to a range of possible answers provided by the researcher/interviewer [9]. This type of interview is therefore used in social research contexts where there is a need to collect standardized and easily comparable data; moreover, it can be somewhat traced back to a quantitative interview. The advantages of this approach lie in certain factors such as standardization, efficiency, and collection of specific data linked to specific variables. Limitations include limited depth regarding the topics covered and less flexibility in respondents' answers.

The questionnaire represents perhaps the most widely used survey instrument in social research: it serves as a formal (more or less structured) stimulus. Although it is sometimes noted in the scientific literature that face-to-face interviews and surveys (including those conducted by telephone or in a computerized manner) are also considered forms of questionnaires, in this case, we will refer to an instrument of information gathering, primarily in written form, containing multiple questions to be answered by the subject to whom it is administered. In this sense, the questionnaire is understood to differ from the survey in the amount of information required. This social research instrument is therefore linked to self-completion [14, 15]. This raises two issues to address: constructing questionnaires suitable for self-completion and establishing a connection between the questionnaire and the subject to whom it is administered. Regarding the specific characteristics of a questionnaire suitable for self-completion, it should be noted that, in the absence of an interviewer who asks the questions and records the answers, there may be a lack of support for guidance and explanations on the correct interpretation of the task to be performed. Therefore, the questionnaire, along with an essential accompanying explanation sheet, needs to be self-sufficient and should not result in difficulties of interpretation or ambiguity in cases of self-completion. As a general rule, it is preferable not to demand excessive effort from respondents and to avoid lengthy and complex questionnaires that could result in non-cooperation or loss of attention when formulating reasoned responses. Open-ended questions should also be minimized because they require expressing one's thoughts-a far more challenging task than choosing from a list of prepackaged answers. It may be useful to adequately motivate the respondent by accompanying the questionnaire with a cover letter that explains the purpose of the survey and appeals to a sense of responsibility, the social relevance of the issue addressed, or the importance of obtaining certain information. Conversely, the task becomes easier if the questionnaire is aimed at a specific target audience, as in this case, it is sometimes possible to invoke, through proper illustration, concrete "category interests" of which the respondent may be aware and therefore find credible.

2.2 Considerations on the Choice of Technique

After carefully analyzing the survey instruments, it is considered beneficial for achieving the objectives of this paper to utilize structured interviews conducted through the questionnaire (survey).

Unstructured or semi-structured interviews have certain limitations when used for the intended survey, such as the reliability of responses and the time required for implementation. Social research has always focused on the interaction between the interviewer and interviewee; this relationship can pose a risk of reducing "subjectivity" in the interviewee's response if not managed properly. Therefore, the data may not be entirely reliable, compromising the study's results. Additionally, conducting interviews with large samples of individuals presents practical limitations related to monetary and time resources: the data requiring reprocessing is time-consuming and necessitates specialized subjects.

The survey technique, on the other hand, serves as a solid analytical tool for the research project's topic on housing mobility issues. Studies detect a close correlation between residential satisfaction and economic, social, and psychological factors [16], and in this contribution, we aim to investigate it precisely. The use of the survey enables the collection of representative data, validated through statistical techniques that ensure the analysis's robustness. For collecting data, surveys are employed—a systematic method useful for gathering information from a sample of individuals to construct quantitative descriptors of the attributes of the larger population of which these entities are members [5]. Surveys allow for the gathering of both quantitative and qualitative data and are particularly useful for understanding complex phenomena such as housing mobility, a central theme of PRIN research.

3 The Construction of the Questionnaire

The structure of the questionnaire follows the methodological guidelines for constructing reliable and validated survey instruments [4]. It is divided into four sections, and in particular it is oriented to more general questions in the first part and moves to more specific questions in the subsequent parts, in order not to influence the respondent's answers [6]. Specifically, the sections are:

1. Introduction and instructions
2. Sociodemographic framework
3. Well-being and general satisfaction
4. Future Perspectives

The following is a brief description of the structure of the questionnaire.

3.1 Introduction and Instructions

The questionnaire must be completed in the absence of a supervisor since it is administered to respondents through an electronic form; therefore, an initial part introducing the research topic and providing solid instructions for completion is necessary [6]. Clarity of instructions and the purpose of the research are essential to ensure reliable and comparable responses, reducing free interpretation by respondents.

3.2 Sociodemographic Framework

This section collects demographic information and consists of multiple-choice, closed-ended questions that define clusters of respondents, providing a more complete understanding of the sample [17]. The questions include: i) age, classified into six bands (<18 to >60); ii) current place of residence; iii) length of residence in current dwelling (less than one year, 1–5 years, 6–10 years, more than 10 years, forever); iv) housing situation (home owned with or without mortgage, renting, host, other); v) household composition (family of origin, with partner, alone, with roommates, other); vi) occupation (primary sector, secondary sector, tertiary sector, student, not employed).

3.3 Well-Being and General Satisfaction

This section explores participants' opinions about the quality of life in their current place of residence. The questions include both open-ended and closed-ended responses on a Likert scale (1 to 10) [18], a widely used measurement in social research that defines the directionality of respondents' answers. To ensure clarity in the compilation, the meaning assigned to the numbers from 1 to 10 is explicitly stated, where $1 =$ Not at all satisfied and $10 =$ Completely satisfied. Furthermore, several questions are formulated in open form, requiring short answers, which allows for deeper qualitative information, although they are more complex to rework. The questions in this section are: i) How satisfied are you with your current life? (from 1 to 10); ii) How satisfied are you with your current city of residence? (1 to 10); iii) What aspects do you appreciate most about your current city? (open answer, keywords); iv) What aspects do you like least about your current city? (open answer, keywords);

The Subjective Dimension in Settlement Choices 137

3.4 Future Perspectives

The last section of the questionnaire investigates future life expectations, specifically asking respondents to answer questions regarding: (i) the frequency with which they have thought about relocating (frequently, sometimes, rarely, never); (ii) the possibility of relocating to another city or country (yes, no); (iii) preferred destinations for possible relocation (open-ended response); (iv) the motivations that would prompt relocation (career opportunities, cost of living, climate conditions, family motivations, study); (v) the factors that might deter relocation (economic difficulties, family ties, job uncertainty, difficulty in adapting); and (vi) the ideal place to live without restrictions (open answer). For the purposes of the research and concerning the topic discussed, this part focuses more on potential future developments regarding housing mobility. This section allows for the mapping of hypothetical movements of individuals. Therefore, a tool such as surveys, when appropriately combined with further studies, can be an invaluable resource for administrations, urban planners, policymakers, and others. Furthermore, this section is crucial for understanding the subjective determinants of housing mobility and for identifying recurring patterns in respondents' residential behavior [19].

4 Results

The survey questionnaire was submitted to a significant sample of 130 individuals from diverse social groups representing a range of urban and rural backgrounds. Most respondents came from large urban centers, such as Florence (24%) and Pisa (12%), while the remainder were evenly distributed among medium-sized cities and suburbs (Fig. 1).

Socio-demographically, the surveyed sample is divided by age into six groups (Fig. 2). Individuals in the <18 (8%) and >60 (9%) categories represent a smaller percentage of the sample than the other age groups. Regarding family composition (Fig. 2), the sample analysis shows that 29% live with their family of origin, 38% with their partner(s), 21% alone, and the remaining 12% live with roommates or in other housing situations, indicating that more living situations with two or more cohabitants are present. Employment status indicates that about 40% of respondents are employed in the tertiary sector, followed by 21% in the secondary sector. The unemployed—both those in education and those not working—account for 13% of the sample. On the other hand, concerning housing situation, the distribution appears to be balanced among homeowners (with and without a mortgage) and renters, who account for 31%, 34%, and 31% of respondents, respectively. In fact, the data align with Italian averages.

In the second section, in agreement with the expected results, it is confirmed that individuals are not fully satisfied with the place where they live. When asked to assign a score from 1 to 10 regarding general living well-being, about 45 percent of respondents consider themselves fully satisfied; however, this percentage drops when referring to their place of residence, where most respondents agreed on a score between 5 and 6. Interweaving the data, it is possible to note that individuals with lower satisfaction scores predominantly reside in urban centers (Florence, Pisa, Prato), suggesting a negative impact on quality of life and housing conditions. In contrast, smaller towns and rural areas report higher levels of place satisfaction. In the following questions, focusing on

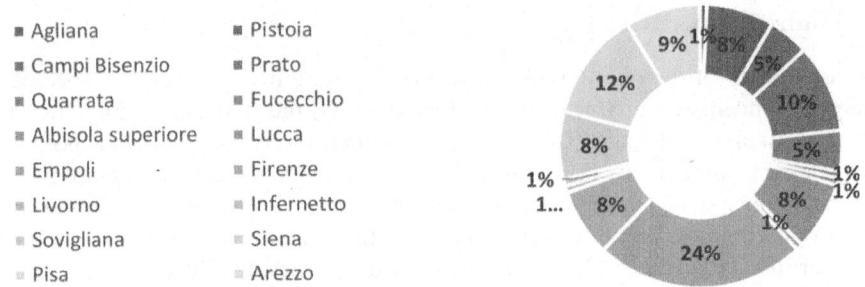

Fig. 1. Origin of the sample of respondents

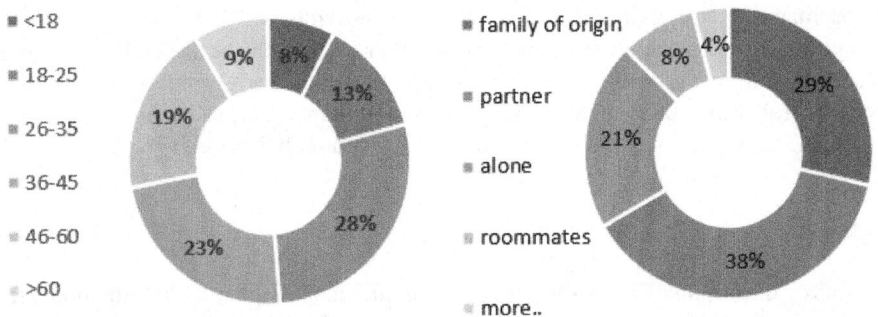

Fig. 2. Percentages by age of respondent sample, Percentages by household composition (from left to right)

the motivations for living place satisfaction/satisfaction (open-ended question), recurring keywords are found, presented in the following graphs (Fig. 3 and Fig. 4).

Fig. 3. Positive impacting factors

The most impactful factors for well-being (Fig. 3) include: environment (10%), history/culture (13%), and neighborhood services (17%). Conversely, negative factors (Fig. 4) pertain to issues related to poor infrastructure management (14%)—many expressed discomfort due to inadequate road maintenance or water services—compared to traffic and general confusion (10%) and the cost of living (15%). The data indicates a

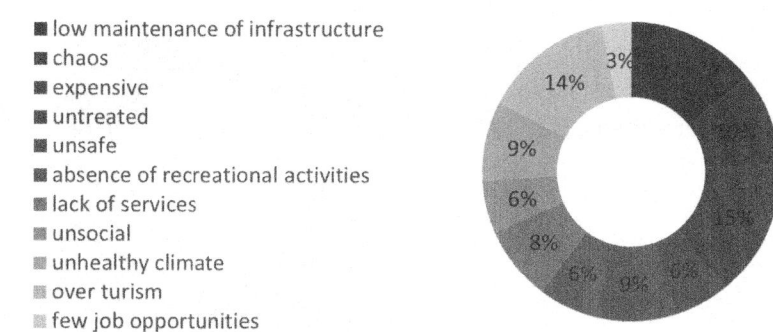

Fig. 4. Negative impacting factors

trend of growing dissatisfaction in large urban centers, primarily due to increasing economic pressures, with high housing costs exacerbated by the tourism market. In contrast, rural areas appear generally more livable regarding environmental quality; however, they lack services and infrastructure maintenance. This overarching dissatisfaction is reflected in the data from the third section, where more than 50% of respondents indicated a desire to relocate. Consequently, the possibilities of relocation, any limitations, and the directions of potential moves were explored more thoroughly in this final section. Our data reveals that although a significant percentage of individuals are willing to relocate, as many as 54% lack the feasibility to do so. The reasons are illustrated in the graph (Fig. 5).

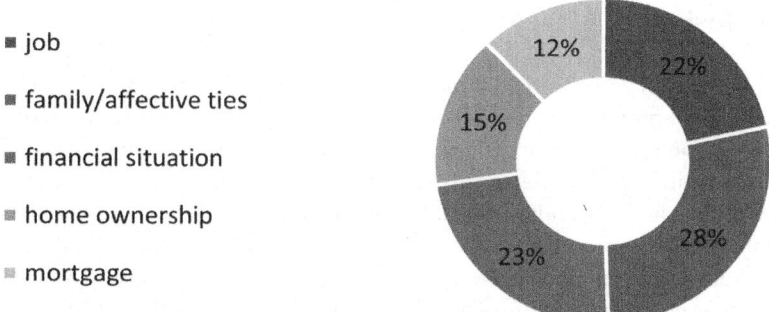

Fig. 5. Limiting factors for transfer

The sphere of affections and financial situations, in addition to work, particularly affects this limitation, suggesting additional factors related to housing mobility. Next, to define a mapping of hypothetical moves, respondents are asked what type of place they would like to move to and whether there is a willingness to relocate. In this case, the majority of the sample of respondents expressed interest in moving to small towns and villages (31%) or to a rural/natural area (24 percent). Few expressed an intention to move to large cities (9%). Generally speaking, relocations would take place within the Tuscan region, with only a small percentage moving abroad (12%) (Fig. 6).

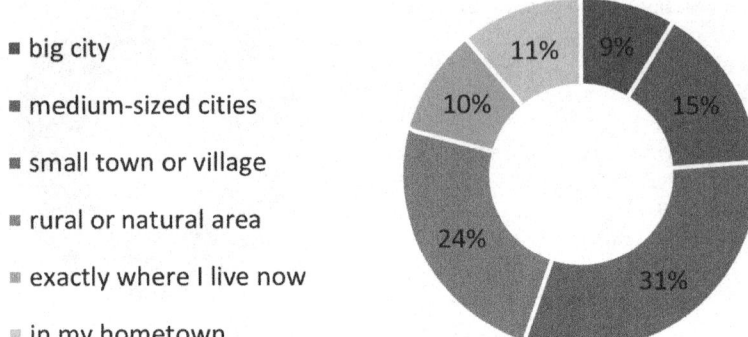

- big city
- medium-sized cities
- small town or village
- rural or natural area
- exactly where I live now
- in my hometown

Fig. 6. Direction of transfers

The survey conducted revealed that the tendency of the surveyed sample is to relocate to other cities, mostly within the same regional or national area and in small or rural towns (Fig. 6). This willingness increases among residents of large cities, where the cost of living and unhealthy environments negatively impact quality of life. In contrast, the tendency to relocate decreases or is nullified for most individuals who have always lived in the same place since birth, particularly in small to medium-sized towns. This happens due to a sense of attachment to the area and social bonds formed over the years, which continue to be crucial in determining where to live.

5 Conclusions

The examination of social research methodologies, tools, and techniques aimed at capturing individual preferences, desires, and attitudes serves as a precursor to developing technologies and assessment tools tailored to understanding the settlement needs of the current and future digital society. This knowledge can facilitate spatial governance processes by clarifying, particularly in Italy, the guidelines for appropriately sizing plans and planning initiatives related to urban and territorial regeneration and the housing policies needed, leading to necessary legislative and regulatory adjustments.

This research reveals that urban areas, such as large cities like Florence and Pisa, experience lower satisfaction levels due to high living costs and environmental pressures. In contrast, smaller towns and rural areas are viewed more positively regarding ecological quality, notwithstanding their infrastructure and service limitations. Notably, a considerable proportion of respondents expressed a desire to relocate; however, financial limitations and social connections emerged as significant barriers to mobility, especially for individuals residing in extensive urban settings.

However, the study has several limitations that should be addressed in future research. The sample size, while significant, could be expanded to include a more diverse and representative group of respondents, particularly those from smaller communities or more remote areas, to ensure more accurate and comprehensive results. Additionally, future studies could explore the potential impact of other variables, such as employment status or digital connectivity, on relocation intentions and housing satisfaction.

Despite these limitations, the study highlights significant trends that can inform urban and territorial planning, especially in light of the digital transition. The study suggests that understanding new settlement preferences influenced by the digital transition can guide spatial governance and urban regeneration efforts, including establishing equitable housing policies that address the evolving trends of population movement, urbanization, and environmental factors.

Future research could delve deeper into regional differences in housing satisfaction and intentions to relocate, emphasizing how digital technologies could influence future settlement trends. Additionally, exploring how local and national policies can evolve to promote more sustainable and inclusive living conditions in urban and rural settings is essential.

Awareness of the digital transition's new settlement requirements is a crucial resource for spatial governance efforts. This understanding can lead to urban and territorial regeneration processes that effectively respond to new housing demand patterns and pave the way for fair housing policies. Thus, it is vital to be well-versed in the techniques that social research has developed over time.

References

1. Marradi, A. (cur.): Costruire il dato. Sulle tecniche di raccolta delle informazioni nelle scienze sociali, FrancoAngeli, Milano ((1988))
2. Ricolfi, L.: La ricerca empirica nelle scienze sociali. Una tassonomia, «Rassegna italiana di sociologia» (3), 389–418 (1995)
3. Dillman, D.A., Smyth, J.D., Christian, L.M.: Internet, Phone, Mail, and Mixed-Mode Surveys: The Tailored Design Method. Wiley, Hoboken (2014)
4. Fowler, F.J.: Survey Research Methods. Sage Publications, Thousand Oaks (2013)
5. Groves, R.M., Fowler Jr., F.J., Couper, M.P., Lepkowski, J.M., Singer, E., Tourangeau, R.: Survey Methodology. Wiley, Hoboken (2009)
6. Brace, I.: Questionnaire Design, How to Plan, Structure and Write Survey Material for Effective Market Research, 4th edn. MRS (2018)
7. Knott, E., Rao, A.H., Summers, K., Teeger, C.: Interviews in the social sciences. Nat. Rev. Methods Primers **2**(73) (2022)
8. Summers, K., Teeger, C.: Introduction: making the case for qualitative interviews. Int. J. Soc. Res. Methodol. **23**(6), 1–6 (2020)
9. Corrao, S.: L'intervista nella ricerca sociale. Quaderni di Sociologia **38**, 147–171 (2005)
10. Kvale, S., Brinkmann, S.: InterViews: Learning the Craft of Qualitative Research Interviewing, 2nd edn. Sage Publications, Thousand Oaks (2009)
11. Semeraro, R.: The qualitative analysis of research data in education. Giornale Italiano della ricerca educativa **IV**(7), 7–106 (2011)
12. Fontana, A., Frey, J.H.: The Interview: from neutral stance to political involvement. In: Silverman, D.D. (ed.) Qualitative Research: Theory, Method, and Practice, pp. 47–71. Sage Publications, Thousand Oaks (2005)
13. Mann, P.H.: Methods of Sociological Enquiry. Basil Blackwell, Oxford (1968)
14. Guarini, M.R., Battisti, F., Buccarini, C.: Rome: re-qualification program for the street markets in public-private partnership. A further proposal for the Flaminio II street market. Adv. Mater. Res. **838–841**, 2928–2933 (2014). ISBN 978-303785926-1, ISSN 10226680. https://doi.org/10.4028/www.scientific.net/AMR.838-841.2928

15. Guarini, M.R., Battisti, F.: Benchmarking multi-criteria evaluation: a proposed method for the definition of benchmarks in negotiation public-private partnerships. In: Murgante, B., et al. (eds.) ICCSA 2014. LNCS, vol. 8581, pp. 208–223. Springer, Cham (2014). https://doi.org/10.1007/978-3-319-09150-1_16
16. Van Ham, M., Hedman, L., Manley, D., Coulter, R., Östh, J.: Neighbourhood Effects Research: New Perspectives. Springer, Dordrecht (2018)
17. Sox, C.H., Stewart, M., Hoy, D.: Comparison of open and closed questionnaire formats in obtaining demographic information from Canadian general internists. J. Clin. Epidemiol. **52**(10), 997–1005 (1999)
18. Likert, R.: A technique for the measurement of attitudes. Arch. Psychol. **140**, 1–55 (1932)
19. Clark, W.A., Huang, Y.: The life course and residential mobility in British housing markets. Environ Plan A **35**(2), 323–339 (2003)

Evaluating Inner Areas Potentials
(EIAP 2025)

The Cultural Value of the *Tratturi* in Molise (Italy)

Maddalena Chimisso[✉][iD]

University of Molise, Campobasso, Italy
maddalena.chimisso@unimol.it

Abstract. This article deals with the subject of the tratturi (sheep-tracks) in Molise, and in particular Tratturo Castel di Sangro-Lucera, with a detailed focus on the Campobasso-Torella del Sannio territorial system.

Starting from the reconstruction of the historical framework of the tratturi that crossed Molise, the article presents a mapping of the officially recognised cultural heritage located in the area between Campobasso and Torella del Sannio. This mapping has been carried out by means of archival research in open access digital archives, such as the database of the Central Institute for Cataloguing and Documentation, with a particular focus on the General Catalogue of the Cultural Heritage. This archival research reveals a rich cultural heritage that is often little known and undervalued, even by the local communities themselves.

The aim of this paper is therefore to highlight this heritage in order to raise awareness of it as a first step towards its future valorisation.

Keywords: Tratturi (sheep-tracks) · Cultural Heritage · Open Access Digital Archives

1 *Tratturi*: an Historical Introduction

In the first tome of *Il Molise dalle origini ai nostri giorni*, Giambattista Masciotta reflected on the Roman and medieval road network in the Province of Molise, enumerating sheep tracks (henceforth *tratturi*) among the primary communication pathways. Masciotta highlighted that these "majestic routes" were preserved due to beneficial laws that accorded them "a sacred character of intangibility", and that they facilitated communication between people during the periods in which they were established. Masciotta also emphasized the undoubted economic advantage that the sheep tracks represented for Molise, whose singular fortune was that of being located between "the wild Abruzzo and fertile Apulia", since for this reason it was the obligatory zone of transit between the two regions [1]. Indeed, the *tratturi* functioned as the routes for the seasonal movement of animals from the pastures of the plain to the mountain pastures and vice-versa, and from the beginning they were privileged places for trade, creating a complementary interdependence between the economies of the traversed territories [2].

This distinctive road system, closely connected to the practice of transhumant sheep farming [3], involved not only Italy but also Spain, southern France, the Balkans and

Greece [4] and can be read as a common economic denominator that, over a long period of time, interested the Mediterranean Europe [5]. In fact, this dense network of sheep tracks is still a tangible sign of the landscape of transhumant work, that the practice of sheep farming has fixed in the territory over the centuries [6] (Fig. 1).

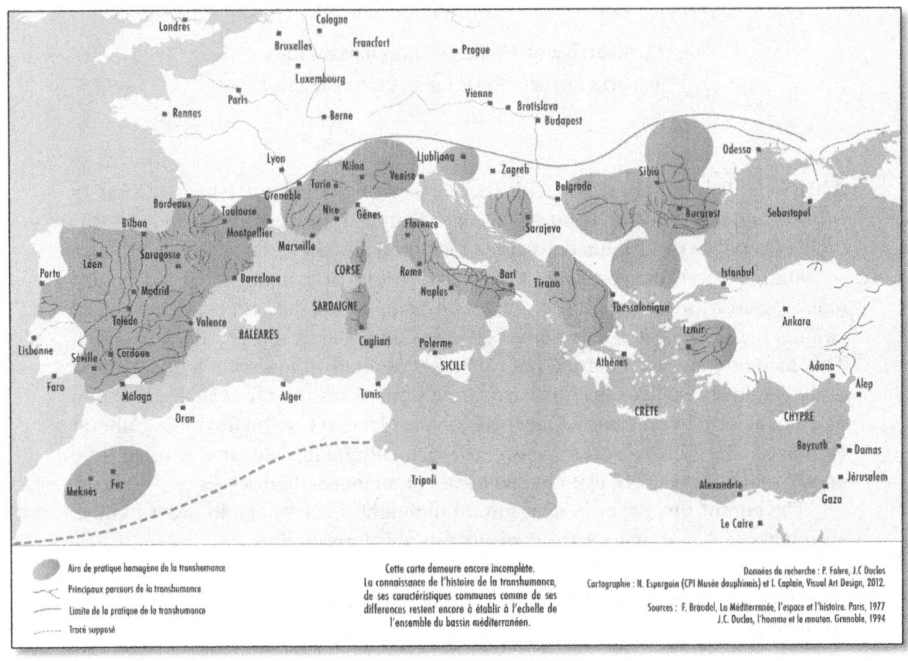

Fig. 1. Ancient transhumance routes in the Mediterranean region of Europe. In: LA ROUTO Homepage https://larouto.eu/cartes-des-itineraires-de-transhumance/, last accessed 2025/03/28.

The regular migration of men and herd provided fiscal resources that no State could neglect, so the organisation and protection of the transhumance system became a public priority [7]. Among the systems of protection and regulation of transhumant sheepfarming, the Spanish *Mesta* is unquestionably one of the first of these institutions: the labour union of Spanish breeders, protected directly by the Crown, was born in 1273 with the clear aim of protecting and developing the national wool industry and managing the important economic flows deriving from the taxes paid for the passage of flocks over certain pastures [8–10]. The Spanish model was evidently adopted as a paradigm by Alfonso d'Aragona when, through the *Prammatica* of 1 August 1447 [11], he established a dedicated office to manage this business: the *Dogana della mena delle pecore di Puglia* [12–14], initially based in the village of Lucera and subsequently in the city of Foggia [15]. The initiative made transhumance compulsory for owners of at least twenty Gentile breed sheep [16–18]. This decision was motivated by the objective of revitalising the economy of numerous Apulian territories that had been paralysed by the war between the *Angioini* and the *Aragonesi* [19], as well as by the Abruzzi shepherds' need for areas with a temperate climate where they could breed and graze their flocks.

The fiscal and territorial structure of the pastoral system adopted by Alfonso d'Aragona, while allocating the majority of the land of the Apulian Tavoliere to grazing, deviated from the slavish imitation of the Spanish model by recognising the need to reserve a portion of the state-owned land for agricultural use.

The routes traversed by the herds exhibited a hierarchical organisation. The most important routes were the four *Regi Tratturi* that facilitated the movement of the herds from Abruzzo to the Tavoliere via Molise: L'Aquila-Foggia, Celano-Foggia, Pescasseroli-Candela, Castel di Sangro-Lucera [20–22]. The *tratturi* were also connected to the so-called *tratturelli*, tracks of lesser. The function of this road network extended beyond mere transportation, providing essential resting points for transhumant livestock during their nomadic movements, as well as offering designated grazing areas where herds could repose and await distribution of leased grazing grounds [23].

While the efficacy of the *Dogana* system established for the fiscal control and management of state-owned territory is indisputable, the inherent limits of this administrative structure soon became evident.

The forty-nine chapters of the *Prammatica* confirmed the primacy of "pastoral reason" [24] over agricultural reason, thus contributing to the aggravation of the different interests between agricultural and pastoral practices, especially with regard to the availability of land to be used. In fact, agricultural production activities were subordinate to pastoral ones: part of the land used for agricultural purposes had to be reserved periodically for grazing, and this, due to the need to cultivate larger areas and the difficulty of maintaining constant control over such vast territories, often led farmers to occupy illegally portions of *tratturo*, taking it away from grazing [25].

Therefore, the necessity to periodically verify the accuracy of the sheep-track system became increasingly apparent. Consequently, the so-called *reintegre*, precise measurement and thorough control operations, were initiated by specialized technicians known as the *regi compassatori* [26, 27]. These operations were undertaken with the objective of verifying the usurped portions of *tratturo* and re-assigning it to its original destination. Indeed, the relationships between farmers and stockbreeders were not at all idyllic. As has previously been indicated, the engraving that appears at the cover of the second volume of Stefano Di Stefano's *Ragion Pastorale*, depicting a shepherd playing the flute in the shade of a tree while watching over his grazing flock and a farmer ploughing the fields nearby, must be read more as an omen than as a true description of the relationships that existed between shepherds and farmers.

The numerous *reintegre* that took place in the more than three centuries of activity of the *Dogana* attest the continuous siege to which the Tavoliere state territory was subjected and the constant need for the government to intervene to restored the *status quo* [28–30]. This dynamic has contributed to fuelling a persistent state of perplexity regarding the validity of this particular system of fiscal management, which was regarded by somebody as obsolete, particularly from the latter half of the eighteenth century onwards. Nevertheless, the conflict between breeders and farmers did not subside with the suppression of the *Dogana*, which was formally abolished by Law No. 75 of 21 May 1806 [31]. The responsibility for the administration of state-owned land was passed to a newly constituted body, the Tavoliere Administration, which continued both the work of mediation between the various users of the land and the action of surveillance of the sheep track network: the *reintegre* thus continued throughout the 19th century [32] (Fig. 2).

Fig. 2. Maps of *Tratturi* in Italy in 1959, Commissariato per la reintegra dei tratturi. In: Atti dei seminari di studi e catalogo della mostra itinerante, Fondazione Architetti Chieti Pescara (eds), Un Paesaggio senza confini: il tratturo. Edizioni Menabò, Ortona, p. 21 (2020).

2 Tools and Methods

The research was conducted as part of a detailed archival excavation, with the primary objective being to bring to light the rich documentary heritage of geo-historical sources (cartographic sources, documentary sources) that directly concern the *tratturi* as well as the *corpus* of documents useful for mapping the cultural heritage of the territorial area that was chosen for investigation. The methodology employed in this study comprised archival excavation and research in Open Access Digital Archives, in addition to an initial analysis of the reference literature.

The initial archival survey conducted for the *Tratturo Castel di Sangro-Lucera* revealed significant insights into the historical development of this region. The survey encompassed a range of historical archives, including the Campobasso State Archives, the Foggia State Archives, the archive of the Central Institute for Cataloguing and Documentation (*Istituto Centrale per il Catalogo e la Documentazione*, henceforth ICCD). In particular for the *Tratturo Castel di Sangro-Lucera reintegre* were carried out in June 1844 and between September 1881 and July 1883. The results of these operations, which were produced in 1844 and 1881–1883 respectively, consist of 51 maps and 40 plates from the 1844 reintegration [33], and 90 maps and 74 planimetric plans from the 1881–1883 reintegration [33].

The research aims to gather data and knowledge on the historical landscapes of transhumance, with particular attention to their role as elements for understanding the relational and performative aspects of landscape. The project will entail an evaluation of various geo-historical sources (cartographic sources, documentary sources) for the purpose of mapping the cultural heritage associated with transhumance and *tratturi*, and the establishment of collaborative pathways for the valorization of geo-historical transhumance landscapes.

The geographical area studied is the territory of the Molise municipalities that have signed the Institutional Development Contract - Tourism Development along the Sheep Tracks (*Contratto Istituzionale di Sviluppo - Sviluppo turistico lungo i tratturi,* henceforth CIS), an agreement for tourism development along the sheep trails. The present research, in particular, concerns the Campobasso-Torella del Sannio territorial system of the *Tratturo Castel di Sangro-Lucera*, with a detailed focus on the events related to the municipalities of Campobasso, Campodipietra, Castropignano, Civitanova del Sannio, Duronia, Froso-lone, Oratino, Ripalimosani, Torella del Sannio (Fig. 3).

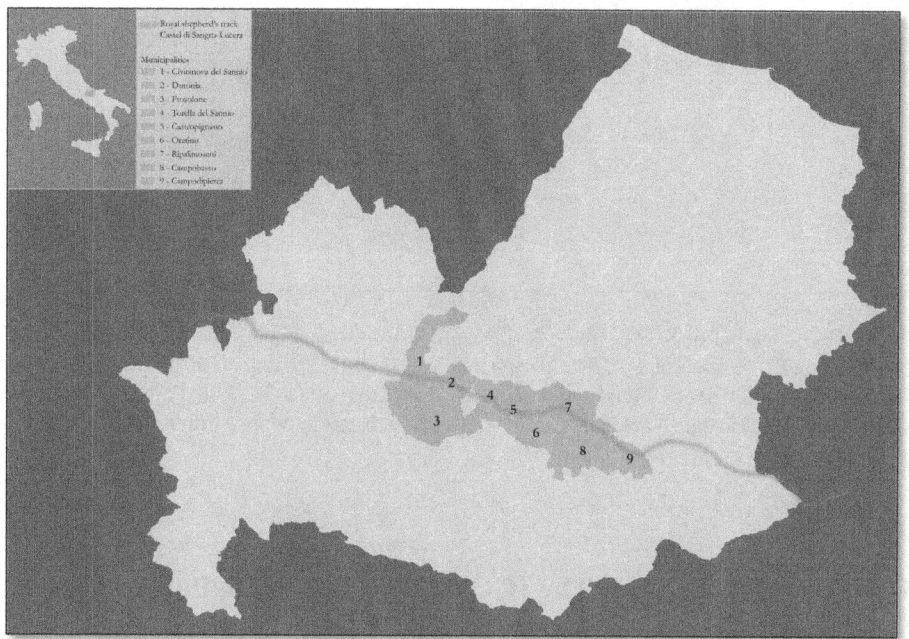

Fig. 3. Location of study area. The Campobasso-Torella del Sannio territorial system of the *Tratturo Castel di Sangro-Lucera* with a detailed focus on the municipalities of Campobasso, Campodipietra, Castropignano, Civitanova del Sannio, Duronia, Frosolone, Oratino, Ripalimosani, Torella del Sannio. Authors' elaboration with dr. Giuseppe Di Felice, March 2025.

It is important to note that some of the municipalities in the study area «find their main reference in the Strategia Nazionale per le Aree Interne (SNAI; in English, Inner Areas National Strategy)» [34–38].

In particular, the municipalities of Civitanova del Sannio, Duronia, Frosolone and Torella del Sannio are part of the Molise SNAI area designated as Alto Medio Sannio [39]: it is evident that this aspect constitutes a significant benefit for the implementation of a revitalization strategy for the area, with a particular emphasis on cultural heritage (Fig. 4) [40–43].

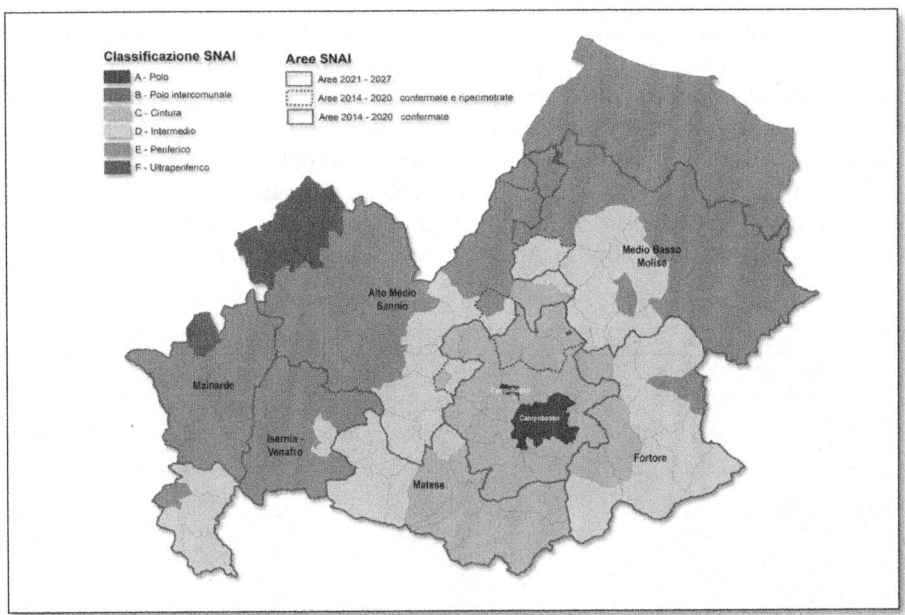

Fig. 4. Classification of SNAI Areas: A – Pole, B – Inter-municipal pole, C – Urban belt, D – Intermediate, E – Peripheral, F – Ultra-peripheral. Specifically, SNAI areas 2014–2020 confirmed, SNAI areas 2014–2020 confirmed and replanned, SNAI areas 2021–2027. In: FomezPA Segreteria Aree Interne: La Strategia Nazionale per le Aree Interne. Regione Molise Programmazione 2021–2027, Dossier regionale, May 2022, p. 5.

3 Knowing to Protect: The ICCD Open Access Digital Archive

There are many studies that provide important information on the possible perspectives for recovery and reuse actions of the sheep track heritage [44, 45]. If recovery and reuse can be understood as the final stages of the heritage conservation process, it is only by recourse to the databases of the institutions officially responsible for census and cataloguing that one can get an idea of the "volume" of the officially recognised heritage and the actual patrimonialization process that has affected it over time.

In terms of cultural heritage, the web accelerates access to several digital OA platforms: authentic open digital archives that can be referenced for research.

The ease of access to and open dissemination of scientific research, the availability of open data and metadata to be consulted and referenced for studies and insights are an integral part of what the *UNESCO Recommendation on Open Science* (2021) [46] defines as Open Science Infrastructures; these are the shared research infrastructures (virtual or physical) of which, together with open access publication platforms, the archives and databases of the different scientific domains are an integral part.

This UNESCO Recommendation is the expression of a process formally initiated in 2002 by the *Budapest Open Access Initiative* (BOAI 2002) [47], one of the milestones for open access to scientific resources and the dissemination of knowledge. The Budapest Declaration emphasises the great potential of the web in providing the definition of Open Access, i.e. the possibility of free and open access to scientific studies and research available in electronic format. Twenty years later, while the above concepts are well established, the *BOAI20 Recommendations*, published in 2022, reaffirm some of the principles already expressed, stating that «open access is not an end in itself, but a means to further ends. Above all, it is a means to the equity, quality, usability, and sustainability of research» [48].

The *Berlin Declaration on Open Access to Knowledge in the Sciences and Humanities* (2003) also recognises that «the Internet has fundamentally changed the practical and economic realities of the dissemination of scientific knowledge and cultural heritage». It sets out a number of actions to be taken to support the transition to the electronic open access paradigm, by encouraging scholars to publish research and scientific works in an Open Access environment, and by encouraging cultural heritage holders to support Open Access by making their resources available online [49].

The promotion of open data policies stimulates the distribution of scientific research, the encouragement of multidisciplinary collaboration, the initiation of virtuous mechanisms of collective growth. These policies are capable of activating and implementing actions for the protection and enhancement of the cultural heritage. The knowledge of this cultural heritage is undoubtedly instrumental in its design.

Considering the cultural heritage linked to the *tratturi* in Molise, we have chosen to conduct a first quantitative and qualitative exploration starting from the database of the Central Institute for Cataloguing and Documentation, specifically searching the General Catalogue of Cultural Heritage. The open data available in this digital archive of cultural heritage provides at different levels of detail directly proportional to the degrees of depth of the catalogue sheets that make accessible information concerning the geographical-administrative location of the catalogued cultural properties, the historical information concerning it (architectural modifications, uses and/or changes of intended use), the legal status and the protection restrictions.

The decree of the President of the Republic no. 805 of 3 December 1975 about the organisation of the Ministry of Cultural and Environmental Heritage, formally established the Central Institute for Cataloguing and Documentation (art. 12). Article 13 of the regulatory provision clarifies its functions in the field of cataloguing and documentation of cultural heritage of archaeological, historical-artistic and environmental interest [50]. The ICCD was entrusted with a number of tasks, including the formulation of general cataloguing programmes for cultural heritage, the establishment of the methodological guidelines to be followed, the establishment and management of the General Catalogue of Cultural Heritage, and the promotion and coordination of the executive activity of cataloguing.

The ICCD web portal offers open access to a very rich documentary heritage. The Historical Archive of Catalogue sheets which preserves the records from the first cataloguing campaigns conducted between 1889 and 1969 (the year the Central Office for the Catalogue was established), contains 21.914 sheets [51]. Meanwhile, the database of the General Catalogue of Cultural Heritage makes accessible 3.044.862 sheets [52].

It is precisely the ICCD sheets that allow an initial evaluation of the cultural potential of this inner area connected to the *tratturi* under examination. Specifically, the data collected concern three categories of cultural heritage: movable properties, immovable properties, intangible heritage. Movable properties are objects and artefacts which can be moved, including those currently immobilised by installation. By this we mean that they are currently incorporated in a given context, but could theoretically be dismounted and moved. Examples are frescoes, lapidary works, or inscriptions inserted in structural walls. Immovable properties are sizeable properties, attached to or incorporated in the earth's surface. Examples are buildings, monumental complexes, and territorial areas. Intangible heritage is cultural heritage in the form of traditional events, techniques, and knowledge, in examples are village festivals, choral, instrumental and theatre performances, artisanal techniques and oral literature [54]. However, particular attention has been paid to the immovable heritage in the areas of architectural, landscape and archaeological heritage, which are undoubtedly the most immediately tangible cultural features and which can be experienced first-hand by travelling along these areas crossed by the *tratturi*.

For the Campobasso-Torella del Sannio segment of the *Tratturo Castel di SangroLucera*, which we have chosen to study, the data achieved revealed the abundant presence of cultural heritage: the sheets compiled over the years by the ICCD attest an undoubted historical value. Specifically, out of a total of 27.482 cataloguing records in the ICCD's Open Access Digital Archives relating to the municipalities that have joined the CIS 22.657 relate to movable properties, 17 to intangible heritage and 2404 to immovable properties; furthermore, in the latter category, 2.301 sheets relate to the sector of architectural and landscape properties, 103 records to that of archaeological properties [53].

With regard to enhancing the *tratturi*, which also involves cultural heritage more or less known, cultural assets present in the territories and along the track itself, it seems interesting a comparison between the ICCD sheets concerning the whole of Molise, those relating to the municipalities belonging to the CIS and those relating to the municipalities crossed by the section of the *tratturi* chosen as a case study (Fig. 5, Table 1). In addition, the specific details of the type of properties identified by the ICCD for each municipality are also interesting in order to reflect on possible actions for their protection and valorization from a touristic perspective.

There is no doubt that the area under investigation also has a conspicuous cultural heritage that has already been surveyed and that represents a first performative aspect of the landscape, as well as a starting point for the inhabitants to become more aware

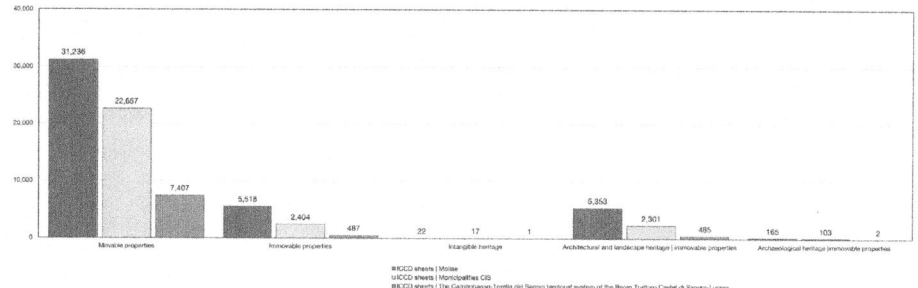

Fig. 5. ICCD sheets | comparison between Molise, municipalities CIS, Campobasso - Torella del Sannio territorial system. Author's elaboration, May 2025.

Table 1. Comparison between the ICCD sheets concerning the whole of Molise, those relating to the municipalities belonging to the CIS and those relating to the municipalities crossed by the section of the *tratturi* chosen as a case study. Author's elaboration, January 2025.

Properties	ICCD sheets	Molise	ICCD sheets	Municipalities CIS	ICCD sheets |The Campobasso-Torella del Sannio territorial system of the *Tratturo Castel di Sangro-Lucera*
Movable properties	31.236	22.657	7.407
Immovable properties	5.518	2.404	487
Intangible heritage	22	17	1
Architectural and landscape heritage	immovable properties	5.353	2.301	485
Archaeological heritage	immovable properties	165	103	2

of the cultural value of their territory, which can trigger practices of protection and enhancement (Fig. 6, Table 2).

From the typological plurality of the cataloguing forms of the census, it is immediately clear that, for the territorial area under consideration, we are encountering a complex heritage corpus, in relation to which the interdisciplinary perspective is essential and the variety of cataloguing forms used and to be used according to the specific cases to be studied appears immediately understandable and explainable.

A careful analysis of this rich documentary heritage, integrated with the multiplicity and typological variety of sources that are emerging and will emerge from the subsequent phases of research, will make it possible to provide a detailed picture of the cultural heritage linked to the *tratturi* that crosses these municipalities, to examine the economic

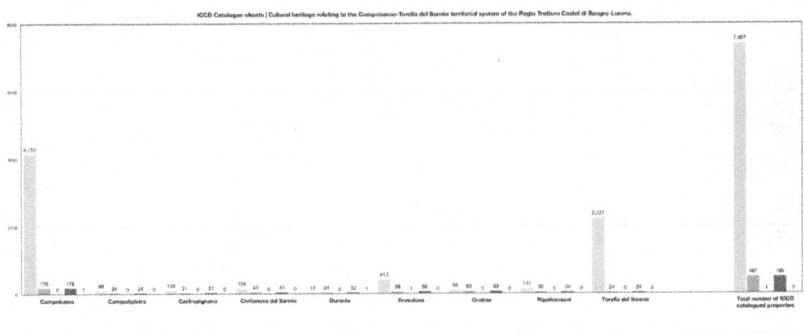

Fig. 6. Bar chart titled "ICCD Catalogue sheets | Cultural heritage relating to the Campobasso-Torella del Sannio territorial system of the Regio Tratturo Castel di Sangro-Lucera." It displays data on cultural heritage properties across various locations. Key data points include Campobasso with 4,155 properties, Torella del Sannio with 2,227, and a total of 7,407 ICCD catalogued properties. Categories are color-coded: movable properties, immovable properties, intangible heritage, architectural and landscape heritage, and archaeological heritage. Author's elaboration, March 2025.

and social transformations that have affected this area in the long term, and to understand how the landscape is used today. Furthermore, adopting a historical perspective will facilitate a reflection on the long-term role of these territories, which are neither nor fragile. This will enable the laying of the knowledge base for implementing appropriate strategies for cultural and economic revitalisation.

4 Towards the Complete Patrimonialization Process of the *Tratturi*

The recurrent measurements and controls carried out over a long period of time, from the 15th to the 19th century, testify the great attention paid to the entire system of *tratturi* in southern Italy and to the public land that the government protected as a source of considerable economic income. The importance of protecting this fiscal heritage is underlined by the body of legislation that, from the 19th century and for most of the 20th century, concerned the *tratturi*. The concepts of preservation and conservation are present both in Decree no. 1057 of 5 September 1811, concerning the decree containing provisions for the preservation of sheep routes in the Tavoliere of Apulia [54], and in Royal Decree no. 196 of 5 January 1911 that approves the regulations for the preservation, management and custody of *tratturi* [55]. In both cases, the articles that regulate the activities of conservation and protection refer to the safeguarding of the *tratturi*, which are considered as assets that are part of the financial activity of the State in terms of taxation and the collection of fees for the use of public land.

The same perspective can also be found in Royal Decree no. 2801 of 29 December 1927 [56] whose Chapter III, on the implementation of plans for the maintenance of sheepfolds, provides for their possible preservation, but only with a view to the economic protection of State property. However, in a regulatory provision dating back a few years before that mentioned above, we can already read about one of the first measures taken

Table 2. Central Institute for Cataloguing and Documentation | ICCD Catalogue sheets | Cultural heritage relating to the Campobasso-Torella del Sannio territorial system of the *Tratturo Castel di Sangro-Lucera*. Author's elaboration, January 2025.

Municipalities	ICCD sheets | Movable properties	ICCD sheets | Immovable properties	ICCD sheets | Intangible heritage	ICCD sheets| Architectural and landscape heritage| Immovable properties	ICCD sheets | Archaeological heritage | Immovable properties
Campobasso	4.155	176	0	175	1
Campodipietra	99	24	0	24	0
Castropignano	104	31	0	31	0
Civitanova del Sannio	158	43	0	43	0
Duronia	17	33	0	32	1
Frosolone	413	55	1	55	0
Oratino	93	63	0	63	0
Ripalimosani	141	38	0	38	0
Torella del Sannio	2.227	24	0	24	0
Total number of ICCD catalogued properties	**7.407**	**487**	**1**	**485**	**2**

to protect the historical value of the heritage associated with *tratturi*. Article 12 of Royal Decree no. 3244 of 30 December 1923 applied to the archive of the *Dogana* all the organic regulations governing the archival service in the State Archives, underlining that this included all the ancient and modern documents relating to the technical, economic and legal aspects of the *tratturi* [57]: this was the formal recognition of the historical value of the documentary heritage, made up of iconographic and catographic sources, accounting records, annual accounts and civil proceedings, that the archive preserved. However, the process of transforming the heritage of the *tratturi* into a heritage site was far from immediate: it was only in 1976, with the decree of the Ministry of Cultural Heritage and the Environment of 15 June, that the historical, testimonial and cultural value of this heritage was officially recognised [58, 59], whose considerable interest was recognised from a composite point of view for its archaeological, political, military, economic, social and cultural history. Molise, a land crossed by numerous *tratturi*, was the first to have its heritage linked to the *tratturi* protected; this protection was extended to the *tratturi* of Abruzzo, Puglia and Basilicata through the decree of 22 December 1983 [60].

The fiscal perspective has certainly played a very important role in the protection and conservation of what is now recognised in all respects as a cultural heritage, as well as the undeniable importance of the ministerial decree of 15 June 1976, which represents an essential turning point in the affirmation of "the patrimonial-cultural value" [61] of traditional agricultural assets. However, much remains to be done in terms of both protection and valorisation. We need to start again from the historical research which, by deepening the exploration and the analysis of the rich documentary heritage available, would allow us to actively recover the paths of men and animals, and perhaps even overcome "the paradox of the *tratturi* heritage" [61]: a heritage that too often oscillates between protection and oblivion, or that is divided between immaterial practices (transhumance), whose value is universally recognised, thanks also to its inclusion in the *Liste représentative du patrimoine culturel immatériel de l'humanité* (December 2019), and the territorial infrastructures (*tratturi*) which are still (and since 2006) included in the UNESCO Tentative Lists [62], that is the list in which States indicate the cultural heritage properties that they wish to propose for inclusion in the World Heritage List.

5 Conclusions

It is evident that, over an extended period, the network of *tratturi* has played a pivotal role in connecting the entire southern region of Italy. This network has not only facilitated the establishment of urban centres along the routes frequented by shepherds but also fostered the development of commercial hubs for the marketing of sheep farming products. Furthermore, it has also led to the emergence of various structures and infrastructure essential for the management of flocks and the facilitation of shepherds' mobility, including taverns and mills. The significance of these transhumant spaces in terms of history and culture is evident. The mapping of these areas is a crucial step in understanding, valuing and promoting the inner sections of the territory traversed by this infrastructure [59].

However, despite the formal precautionary measures implemented by the property, the protection regulations issued by local authorities are often perceived as a restriction on action rather than an effective tool for valorisation. Consequently, the preservation methodologies employed are deemed to be neither comprehensive nor proactive, thereby engendering a state of limbo for cultural heritage, which persists in a state of flux between the realm of memory and the threat of oblivion [64].

The value of historical research is not to provide "recipes" on what to do, but to provide adequate tools and knowledge so that choices can be made on what to actually preserve and recover. These choices should be made on the basis of studies and research to support cultural planning appropriate to specific territorial areas considered fragile.

Acknowledgments. This research *Paesaggi relazionali della transumanza. La fonte geostorica come strumento per un approccio performativo del paesaggio*, overseen by scientific tutor Prof. Marco Petrella, is being carried out by the Department of Biosciences and Territory of the University of Molise. The study is financed by the project *Sviluppo turistico lungo i tratturi – recupero e valorizzazione del percorso tratturale; incentivazione e potenziamento dell'offerta turistica,*, CUP: D78C20000210006 (Tourist development along the t*ratturi* recovery and enhancement of the t*ratturi*; incentives and enhancement of the tourist offer) according the agreement between the Municipality of Campodipietra and the Research Centre for Biocultural Resources and Local Development of the University of Molise (scientific director: Prof. Letizia Bindi).

References

1. Masciotta, G.: Il Molise dalle origini ai nostri giorni, La Provincia di Molise, vol. I, pp. 69–70. Palladino Editore, Campobasso (2006)
2. Petrocelli, E.: Il divenire del paesaggio molisano. Dall'accampamento dell'homo erectus alle proposte dei beni ambientali e storico-culturali, Edizioni Enne, Campobasso (1984)
3. Parisi, R.: Il patrimonio industriale del Molise. Architetture, infrastrutture e paesaggi. Proposte e ricerche. Economia e società nella storia dell'Italia Centrale, **66**(XXXIV), 86–105 (2011)
4. Paone, N.: Molise in Europa: tratturi, cañadas, drailles, drumurile oierilos, Cosmo Iannone, Isernia (2006)
5. La transhumance dans les pays méditerranéens du XVe au XIX siècle. Mélanges de l'Ecole française de Rome. Moyen-Age, Temps modernes, **2**(100), (1988). https://www.persee.fr/issue/mefr_0223-5110_1988_num_100_2
6. Fabre, P.: La Routo. Sur les pas de la transhumance. In: Russo, S., Bourdin, S. (eds.), I tratturi fra tutela e valorizzazione, pp. 73–91, Claudio Grenzi Editore, Foggia
7. Braudel, F.: Civiltà e imperi del Mediterraneo nell'età di Filippo II, volume primo, Piccola Biblioteca Einaudi, Torino (1949, edition 2002)
8. García Martín, P.: El patrimonio cultural de las cañadas reales, Junta de Castilla y León, Valladolid (1990)
9. Rodríguez Pascual, M.: La trashumancia. Cultura, cañadas y viajes, Edilesa, Léon (2001)
10. Vidal-González, P.: Les drailles espagnoles. Patrimoine culturel. Nouvelles propositionsde développement durable. In: Pastoralisme méditerranéen: patrimoine culturel et paysager et développement durable, Lerin F. (eds.), Actes de la deuxième réunion thématique d'experts sur le pastoralisme méditerranéen, pp. 59–69, Options Méditerranéenne Série A: Séminaire Méditerranéens, 93, Centre International de Hautes Études Agronomiques Méditerranéennes, (2010)
11. Coda, M.: Breve Discorso del principio, privilegi et istruttioni della Regia Dohana della mena delle pecore di Puglia, Napoli (1666)
12. Di Cicco, P.: La dogana delle pecore di Foggia: elementi per una pianta generale del Tavoliere. Grafiche Ciampoli, Foggia (1971)
13. Marino, J.A.: Wheat and Wool in the Dogana of Foggia. An Equilibrium Model for Early Modern European Economic History. Mélanges de l'Ecole française de Rome. Moyen-Age, Temps modernes, **2**(100), 871–892 (1988)
14. Di Cicco, P.: Fonti per la storia della Dogana delle pecore nell'Archivio di Stato di Foggia. Mélanges de l'Ecole française de Rome.Moyen-Age, Temps modernes, **2**(100), 937–946 (1988)
15. Musto, D.: La Regia Dogana della Mena delle pecore di Puglia, Quaderni della rassegna degli Archivi di Stato, Tipografia La Galluzza, Roma (1964)
16. Del Treppo, M.: Agricoltura e transumanza in Puglia nei secoli XIII-XVI: conflitto o integrazione? In: Guarducci, A. (ed.) Agricoltura e trasformazione dell'ambiente. Secoli XIII-XVII, pp. 455–460. Atti della XI Settimana di studi dell'Istituto internazionale di storia economica Francesco Datini, Firenze (1984)
17. Marino, J.A.: Pastoral Economics in the Kingdom of Naples. John Hopkins University Press, Baltimora-Londra (1988)

18. Russo, S.: Il conflitto tra agricoltura e pastorizia transumante nella Dogana di Foggia in età moderna. Mélanges de l'École française de Rome. Antiquité, **128**(2) (2016). https://journals.openedition.org/mefra/3451
19. Galasso, G.: Il Regno di Napoli. Il Mezzogiorno angioino e aragonese, I, UTET, Torino, (1992)
20. Di Marzo, D.: I tratturi, Tipografia Nazionale G. Bertero, Roma (1905)
21. D'Amelio, M. (eds.): Nuovo digesto italiano, pp. 419–446, *sub vocem*, UTET, Torino, (1940)
22. Paone, N.: La transumanza. Immagini di una civiltà, Cosmo Iannone Editore, Isernia (1987)
23. Cialdea, D. (eds.): Il Molise come terra di transito. I tratturi come modello di sviluppo del territorio, p. 27, Arti Grafiche La Regione, Ripalimosani, (2007)
24. Di Stefano, S.: La Ragion Pastorale over comento sul la Pramatica. LXXIX. De Officio Procuratoris Caesaris, Stamperia Domenico Roselli, Napoli (1731)
25. Iazzetti, V.: Le alterne misurazioni, le usurpazioni e gli atlanti delle reintegre, pp. 130–142. In: La Civiltà della transumanza, Petrocelli, E. (eds), (1999)
26. Di Cicco, P.: I compassatori della Regia Dogana delle pecore: la cartografia doganale nel cinquecento. Bollettino storico della Basilicata **6**, 274–295 (1990)
27. Petrella, M.: Geometrie e topografie del territorio. I Regi Compassatori della Dogana di Foggia tra misurazione, rappresentazione e gestione. Bollettino dell'Associazione Italiana di Cartografia, **161**, pp. 72–82 (2017)
28. Di Cicco, P.: La cartografia tratturale. La Capitanata. Rassegna di vita e di studi della Provincia di Foggia, **24**, 51–57 (1987)
29. Di Salvia, B.: L'Atlante delle reintegre di Nicola Conte e Vincenzo Magnacca del 1778 sul tratturo della valle del Miscano. In: Ivone, D. (ed.) La Transumanza nell'Economia dell'Irpinia in Età Mo- derna, pp. 179–200. Editoriale Scientifica, Napoli (2002)
30. Chimisso, M.: Sul paesaggio contemporaneo dei tratturi. In: Atti dei seminari di studi e catalogo della mostra itinerante, Fondazione Architetti Chieti Pescara (eds), Un Paesaggio senza confini: il tratturo. pp. 52–59, Edizioni Menabò, Ortona, (2020)
31. Apulian Table Law no. 75 of 21 May 1806 (*Legge sul tavoliere di Puglia n. 75 del 21 maggio 1806*). In: Collezione degli editti, Collezione degli editti, determinazioni, decreti e leggi di S.M. da' 15 febbraio a' 31 dicembre 1806, Stamperia Simoniana, Napoli [1807]
32. Nardella, M.C.: La salvaguardia dei tratturi: dalla Dogana delle pecore al Commissariato per la reintegra. In: La Civiltà della transumanza. Storia, cultura e valorizzazione dei tratturi e del mondo pastorale in Abruzzo, Molise, Puglia, Campania e Basilicata, Petrocelli, E. (eds.), pp. 479–492, Cosmo Iannone Editore, Isernia (1999)
33. State Archive of Campobasso: Tratturi, tratturelli e riposi reintegrate in forza del Real Decreto de' 9 ottobre 1826. La parte in Molise del Tratturo di Motta (1844)
34. State Archive of Campobasso: Tratturo Lucera-Casteldisangro nella provincial di Campobasso che attraversa I tenimenti di Gambatesa, Pietracatella, Toro, Campodipietra, Campobasso, Ripalimosani, S. Stefano, Oratino, Castropignano, Torella, Molise, Duronia, Civitanova, Chiauci, Pescolanciano, Carovilli, Roccasicura, Forlì, Rionero, verificato dal 16 settembre 1881 al 16 luglio 1883 giusta il Decreto ministeriale del 17 marzo 1875, (1881–1883)
35. Mastronardi, L., Giannelli, A., Romagnoli, L.: Detecting the land use of ancient transhumance routes (Tratturi) and their potential for Italian inner areas' growth. In Land Use Policy **109**(2), 1 (2021). https://doi.org/10.1016/j.landusepol.2021.105695
36. Barca, F., McCann, P., Rodríguez-Pose, A.: The case for regional development intervention: place-based versus place-neutral approaches. J. Reg. Sci. **52**(1), 134–152 (2012). https://doi.org/10.1111/j.1467-9787.2011.00756.x
37. Barca, F., Casavola, P., Lucatelli, S. (eds.): Strategia nazionale per le aree interne: definizione, obiettivi, strumenti e governance, Ministero dello Sviluppo Economico, Dipar- timento per lo Sviluppo e la Coesione Economica, Unità di Valutazione degli Investimenti Pubblici, Roma (2014)

38. Parisi, R.: Sui borghi dell'osso. "Centri minori" e "aree interne" in prospettiva storica. In: La Città Palinsesto. Tracce, sguardi e narrazioni sulla complessità dei contesti urbani storici, Capano, F., Visone, M. (eds.), pp. 437–444, I, FedOA - Federico II University Press, Napoli, (2020)
39. Barca, F.: An agenda for a reformed cohesion policy. A place-based approach to meeting European Union challenges and expectations Independent Report prepared at the request of Danuta Hübner, Commissioner for Regional Policy (2009). https://www.europarl.europa.eu/meetdocs/2009_2014/documents/regi/dv/barca_report_/barca_report_en.pdf
40. FomezPA Segreteria Aree Interne: La Strategia Nazionale per le Aree Interne. Regione Molise Programmazione 2021–2027, Dossier regionale (2022). https://politichecoesione.governo.it/media/3174/snai-dossier-regionale-molise.pdf
41. Oteri, A., M.: Strategie e politiche per il rilancio dei piccoli centri nelle aree interne. Una prospettiva a misura d'uomo. ArchHistor EXTRA, **7**, 41–59 (2020)
42. Cerquetti, M., Ferrara, C., Romagnoli, A., Vagnarelli, G.: Enhancing intangible cultural heritage for sustainable tourism development in rural areas: the case of the "marche food and wine memories" project (Italy). Sustainability **14**, 16893 (2022). https://doi.org/10.3390/su142416893
43. Rossitti, M., Torrieri, F.: The THEMA tool to support heritage-based development strategies for marginal areas: evidence from an Italian inner area in Campania Region. Region **9**(2), 109–129 (2022). https://openjournals.wu.ac.at/ojs/index.php/region/article/view/394
44. Battisti, A., Valese, M., Calvano, A., Natta, H.: Architectural heritage and digital transition: intangible components as regeneration infrastructure for inner rural areas. In: Battisti, A., Baiani, S. (eds.) ETHICS: Endorse Technologies for Heritage Innovation. Designing Environments, pp. 21–43, Springer (2024)
45. Buccomino, V.: Per una bibliografia sui tratturi. Università degli Studi del Molise, Campobasso (2001)
46. Meini, M., Petrella, M.: Lo spazio reazionale della transumanza: usi, valori, visioni. Documenti geografici **3**, 1–15 (2023)
47. UNESCO: Recommendation on Open Science. UNESCO, Paris (2021)
48. Budapest Open Access Declaration (2002). https://www.budapestopenaccessinitiative.org/read/
49. Budapest Open Access Declaration 20 (2022). https://www.budapestopenac-cessinitiative.org/boai20/
50. Berlin Declaration on Open Access to Knowledge in the Sciences and Humanities (2003). https://openaccess.mpg.de/Berlin-Declaration
51. Decree of the President of the Republic no. 805 of 3 December 1975. In: Gazzetta Ufficiale, Serie Generale no. 23 of 27.01.1976 - Ordinary supplement, GAZZETTA UFFICIALE Homepage (1975). https://www.gazzettaufficiale.it/eli/id/1976/01/27/075U0805/sg
52. ICCD Homepage. https://dati.beniculturali.it/applicazioni_/applicazione-schede/. Accessed 28 March 2025
53. ICCD Homepage. https://catalogo.beniculturali.it. Accessed 28 March 2025
54. ICCD Homepage. http://www.iccd.beniculturali.it/it/documenti. Accessed 28 March 2025
55. State Archive of Campobasso, Demanio II, envelope 1, Tratturi
56. Royal Decree no. 196 of 5 January 1911. In: Gazzetta Ufficiale on 2 May 1911, no. 193, pp. 2441–2448. GAZZETTA UFFICIALE Homepage. https://www.normattiva.it/urires/N2Ls?urn:nir:stato:regio.decreto:1911-01-05;196. Accessed 28 March 2025
57. Royal Decree no. 2801 of 29 December 1927: In: Gazzetta Ufficiale of 28 February 1928, no. 49. GAZZETTA UFFICIALE Homepage. https://www.normattiva.it/urires/N2Ls?urn:nir:stato:regio.decreto:1927-12-29;2801~art61. Accessed 28 March 2025

58. Royal Decree no. 3244 of 30 December 1923. In: Gazzetta Ufficiale of 12 March 1924, no. 61. GAZZETTA UFFICIALE Homepage. https://www.normattiva.it/urires/N2Ls?urn:nir:stato:regio.decreto:1923-12-30;3244. Accessed 28 March 2025
59. Parisi, R.: La pecora e l'architettura. L'immaginario dell'Arcadia nelle pratiche di tutela dei percorsi tratturali. In: Ballacchino, K., Bindi, L. (eds.) Cammini di uomini, cammini di animali. Transumanze, pastoralismi e patrimoni bio-culturali, pp. 185–197, Edizioni il Bene Comune, Campobasso (2017)
60. Parisi, R.: Il paesaggio come patrimonio storico e come progetto culturale. Edilio Petrocelli e il Molise (1984–2011). In: Lombardi, N., Palmieri, G., Zilli, I. (eds.) Il Molise di Edilio Petrocelli, pp. 97–118, Edizioni il Bene Comune, Campobasso (2017)
61. Chimisso, M.: Sul paesaggio contemporaneo dei tratturi. In: Atti dei seminari di studi e catalogo della mostra itinerante, In: Fondazione Architetti Chieti Pescara (eds.) Un Paesaggio senza confini: il tratturo. Edizioni Menabò, Ortona, pp. 52–59 (2020)
62. UNESCO INTANGIBLE CULTURAL HERITAGE Homepage. https://ich.unesco.org/fr/procedure-d-inscriptions-00809. Accessed 28 March 2025
63. UNESCO TENTATIVE LISTS Homepage. https://whc.unesco.org/en/tentativelists/5005/. Accessed 28 March 2025
64. Chimisso, M., Ciuffetti, A. (eds.): Il Lavoro tra passato e future. Fragilità e opportunità di un patrimonio nei territorio dell'Italia contemporanea, Soveria Mannelli, Rubbettino (2024)

The Role of Cultural and Natural Heritage in a Place-Based Strategy for Inner Peripheries

Priscilla Sofia Dastoli(✉) and Francesco Scorza

School of Engineering, Laboratory of Urban and Regional Systems Engineering, University of Basilicata, 10, Viale dell'Ateneo Lucano, 85100 Potenza, Italy
{priscillasofia.dastoli,francesco.scorza}@unibas.it

Abstract. There is an increasing tendency to promote a locality as a tourist destination, focusing on the widespread wealth of cultural and natural heritage, without considering local development integrated with priority aspects such as essential services. The study illustrates how the Objective of enhancing the cultural and natural heritage of the medio Agri area (Basilicata region-Italy) has been articulated within a sustainable development strategy. The area belongs to the inner peripheries according to the classification carried out at European level by the ESPON PROFECY project [1, 2] and is made up of six municipalities classified as ultra-peripheral by the National Strategy for Inner Areas (SNAI). In the preliminary stages of implementing the place-based strategy, the main weaknesses of the area were identified, as well as the priority objectives to address them. Having promoted advanced forms of governance in the area and improved the network of essential services for residents, the focus can now turn to enhancing the considerable heritage that has been identified. This has been done by designing a tourist itinerary that is set up to promote the natural, scenic and architectural attractions of the area. The itinerary links the municipalities in the area and those nearby, focusing on slow mobility, eco-sustainable tourism, the gastronomic and wine sectors, and social and economic development projects. The aim is to increase the attractiveness of the area through a widespread network of hubs and services that can jointly meet the needs of residents and tourists.

Keywords: Inner peripheries · Natural and cultural heritage · Place-based sustainable strategy

1 Introduction

In recent years, the enhancement of cultural and natural heritage and its link with tourism has been widely seen as a solution for development, especially at the local level. Following some successful experiences, many development policies have focused exclusively on tourist attractions, with the aim of turning them into launch pads for local growth [3–5].

In the case of the inner peripheries [1], i.e. areas far from the main centres that provide essential services (education, health and mobility), this trend is taken to extremes and becomes a simplistic solution to complex problems, usually caused by demographic decline.

In Italy, inner peripheries have important environmental resources (water resources, agricultural systems, forests, natural and human landscapes) and cultural resources (archaeological heritage, monuments, historical settlements, abbeys, small museums). In 2013, the Italian government promoted the National Strategy for Inner Areas (SNAI) [6–10]. It is an economic development strategy for inner areas based on the currently unexploited 'territorial capital' available in these areas, including natural, cultural and cognitive capital, the social energy of the local population and potential residents [11].

In Italy, the term *'inner areas'* is currently widely used and, as stated in the Partnership Agreement of the National Strategy for Inner Areas, it refers to *'those areas that are significantly distant from centres providing essential services (education, health and mobility), rich in important environmental and cultural resources, highly diversified as a result of centuries of anthropisation and by nature'*. About a quarter of Italy's population lives in these areas, which cover more than sixty per cent of the country's territory and are organised into more than four thousand municipalities' [11].

In the European panorama, numerous expressions used in the scientific debate on the subject emerge which, even if with different meanings, refer to the concept of Italian inner areas: *inner peripheries* [12–15]; *peripheral area* [16, 17]; *marginal area* [18, 19]; *inner areas* [10, 14, 20, 21]; *internal areas* [19, 22–24]; *inland area* [25–28]; *low dynamic area* [12]; *sparsely populated area* [29–32]; *rural areas* [33]; *lagging regions* [34, 35].

The ESPON PROFECY project (update 2022) has led to the unification of the term "inner peripheries" with the themes of "inner areas" as understood in the Italian context; however, there is still some confusion about the most correct terminology to use in order to unambiguously identify these areas beyond national borders. The question of the definition and classification of inner areas is a topic that is still being debated today. Therefore, in this research the term inner peripheries will be used to refer to the issues of inner areas in the European panorama; instead, the term inner areas [7, 20, 36, 37] will be used to refer to the specific Italian inner areas, using a similar literal translation used in the definition of the National Strategy for Inner Areas (SNAI) [38].

With regard to the develop of the SNAI, according to the 2020 report of the Italian Agency for Territorial Cohesion, a total amount of 1.14 million euros has been allocated to the inner areas. Looking at the distribution of these funds between the different areas of SNAI intervention, two main categories were considered: services and local development (Table 1). Within these, the two sectors most covered are mobility/transport, with 22% of the total, and cultural and environmental heritage, with 18% (Fig. 1).

The multi-level character of SNAI has been implemented at a local level, involving the community in the specific and unique definition of economic development strategies in 72 project areas. Local communities have developed integrated strategies based on their territorial capital, including cultural and landscape assets in an ecosystem linked to other territorial resources. The present study has been carried out in the same way, defining a sustainable and resilient development strategy for the medio Agri, in the Basilicata region. This study was conducted as part of the Italian project RI.P.R.O.VA.RE (Re-inhabiting Countries. Operational Strategies for the Enhancement and Resilience of

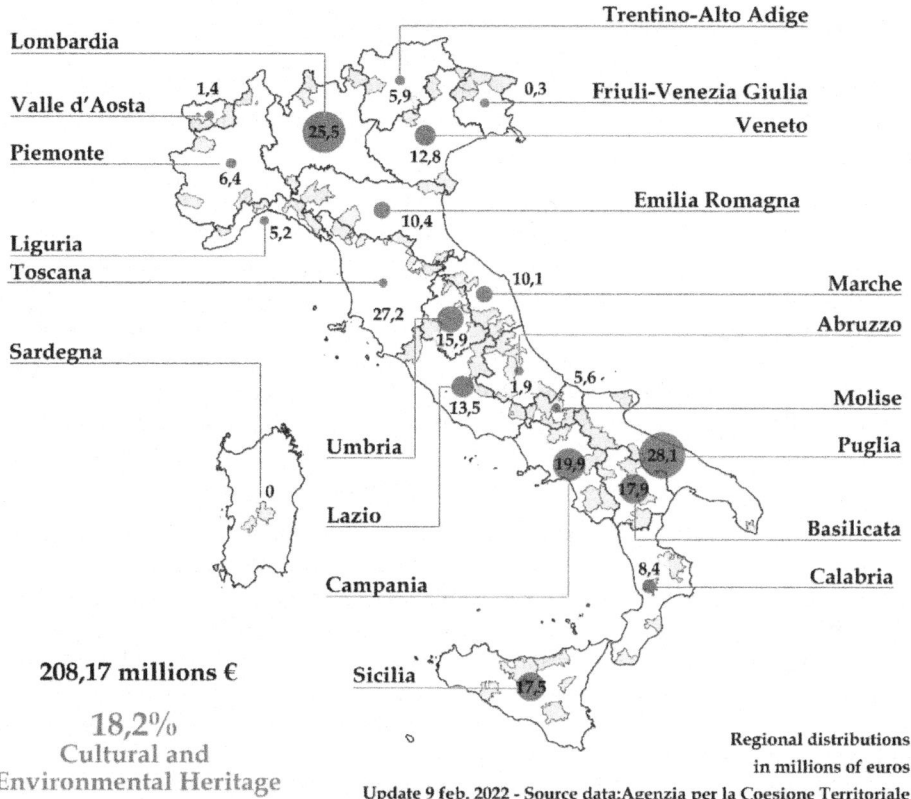

Fig. 1. Cultural and Environmental Heritage sector funding of the SNAI. Regional distributions in millions of euros for the 2014–2020 programming cycle

Table 1. Funds sector of the National Strategy for Inner Areas (2014–2020 programming cycle).

Sector	Euro (million)
Health	137 (12%)
Education	116 (10%)
Mobility/Transport	255 (22%)
Cultural and environmental heritage	208 (18%)
Agriculture	106 (9%)
Energy	88 (8%)
Digital services and infrastructures	62 (5%)
Other	190 (16%)

Inner Areas) [10, 39], which has seen experimentation in two southern regions, Campania and Basilicata. A particular emphasis has been placed on the active involvement of decision makers and local communities in the project.

The integrated sustainable development strategy of medio Agri pursues five General Objectives, composed of one or more strategic lines, to which policies and actions correspond:

1. To promote advanced forms of governance and widespread and stable participation of citizens in decision-making processes;
2. To set up a network organisation of the most important essential services for the population and businesses, to be provided also through the new information technologies;
3. The enhancement of the natural and cultural heritage, the promotion of the tourism development and the support of urban regeneration projects;
4. Strengthening the economic system through interventions in the key sectors of agriculture and handicrafts;
5. Improve safety and practicality of existing infrastructure.

Objective III, entitled 'Enhancing the Natural and Cultural Heritage', constitutes an element of an integrated strategy within which the promotion of advanced forms of governance and the reorganisation of essential services are prioritised. The definition of Objective III has been influenced by initiatives to promote cycle tourism in Italy and abroad, which has a strong cultural and economic impact [40–44]. The enhancement of inner areas through sustainable tourism opportunities requires the planning of innovative services, which must be organised in such a way as to improve the sustainable mobility of the area's inhabitants [45].

A significant effort to promote sustainable tourism and slow mobility has been made in the nearby region of Calabria with the development of the 'Ciclovia dei Parchi' (Park Cycle Route), which has been awarded the Italian Oscar for Cycle Tourism 2021. In a similar vein, Basilicata is making slow progress, with two major projects that involve the region and reconnect it with Apulia, Campania and Calabria. The first of these is the 'Ciclovia dell'Acquedotto Pugliese' (Apulian Aqueduct Cycle Route), which connects Apulia and Campania, crossing the territory of Basilicata. The second is the 'Ciclovia della Magna Grecia' (Magna Graecia Cycle Route), which is approximately 1,130 kms in length and crosses Basilicata, Calabria and Sicily. Another noteworthy initiative is the route entitled 'the Sacred Woods Cycle Route from Pescopagano to Castrovillari', which crosses the western part of the Potenza province from the border with Campania to the border with Calabria. This final itinerary also crosses the Val d'Agri with the Calvello-Sarconi and Sarconi-Castelsaraceno sections (through Spinoso, San Martino d'Agri and San Chirico Raparo).

In light of the considerations outlined above, the proposal for the medio Agri is to link up with initiatives already underway and to promote the development of sustainable tourism and slow mobility in an even more significant way. In order to achieve this, a reconfiguration of the slow mobility system is proposed; said reconfiguration will be implemented through a widespread network of nodes and services which will jointly respond to the needs of the local population and visitors to the area.

2 A Methodological Approach Based on Three Pillars: Context Analysis, Participation (Living Lab) and Territorial Strategy (Place-Based Design)

The methodology adopted for strategy implementation in the medio Agri pilot area (Fig. 2) stems from the Logical Framework Approach (LFA). This is a logical ordering procedure, which is part of Project Cycle Management (PCM). The LFA refers to the cyclical nature of planning. It is divided into an analysis phase and a synthesis phase [46–48]. The Logical Framework is presented as a tool for implementing and controlling the design process and for evaluating decisions.

The first activity is to organise and plan all activities. Each context is different and requires a specific strategic plan. Through an internal and external diagnosis, a second activity focuses on the evaluation of the context. In particular, a context analysis was carried out through desk research (information in open access databases, public reports, websites, publications, scientific publications. Participatory activities and interaction with stakeholders also deepened our knowledge of the medio Agri pilot area.

In the third part, the strategic objectives are defined as strong ideas to be used to found the intervention plan and to derive the corresponding strategic lines to be adopted. This stage uses problem and objective tree techniques to organise problems from causes to effects and objectives from means to ends. The focus of the participatory process, in particular the Living Lab [49–51], was concentrated on this phase of the LFA, applying the Analytic Hierarchy Process (AHP) to the selection of priority objectives for the study area.

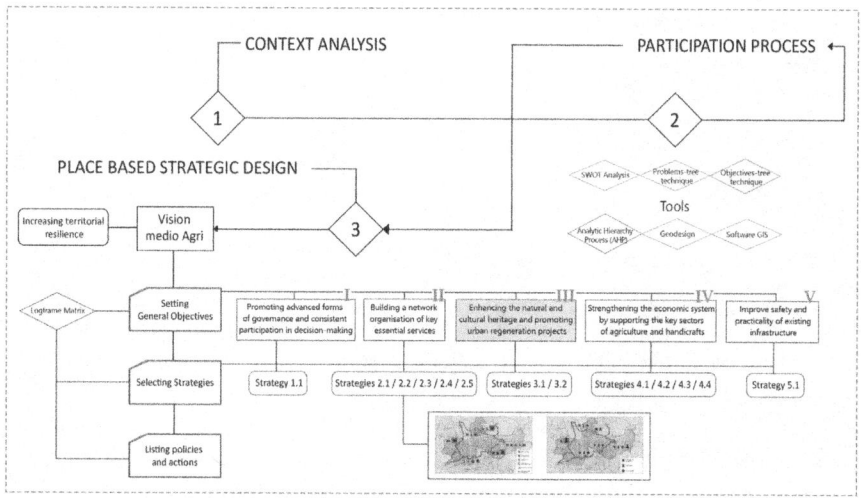

Fig. 2. Flow-chart of the methodology adopted in developing the medio Agri area strategy.

The final activity, which belongs to the Synthesis phase, is to define the objectives for each strategic theme and identify the actions to be developed [27]. In particular, this coincided with the development of the medio Agri area strategy.

The logframe matrix is usually used for the synthesis phase of the LFA, which is concerned with breaking down the project idea into operational details and ensuring the feasibility and sustainability of the project. This is a method for presenting the overall picture of an operation. It includes the following elements:

- the general objective: this includes the long-term benefits for society, the ultimate aim of the project and its purpose;
- the specific objective (or strategy): this defines the basic stages of the project;
- the Target Results: which coincide with the services made available to the project's target audience;
- the Actions (or activities): which represent the means to pursue the specific objectives and obtain the target results.

A number of well-known tools, particularly in the participatory process, are used in such a methodological approach: SWOT Analysis, Heritage walk, Problems tree and Objectives tree techniques, Geodesign tool [52–56].

3 The Val d'Agri Area Context

The medio Agri area covers the central sector of the Agri river basin (Fig. 3), one of the five rivers that cross Basilicata and flow into the Ionian Sea. The area is predominantly mountainous in its western part, with the Monte Raparo Site of Community Interest (SCI); most of the remaining area is hilly, with sandy and conglomeratic hills, which characterise it for its high hydrogeological risk.

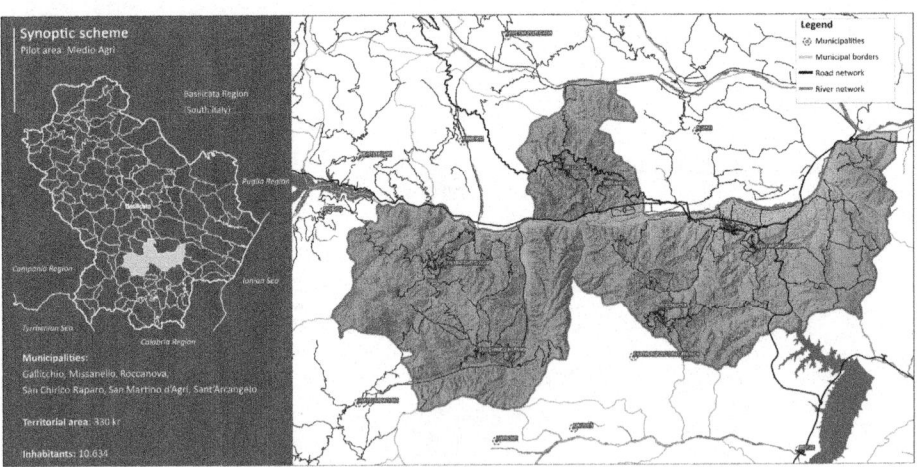

Fig. 3. Location of the medio Agri pilot area in Basilicata Region.

Moreover, the Val d'Agri's largest territorial unit is specialised in oil extraction activities due to the presence of Europe's largest onshore oil field [57, 58]. This generates major conflicts between oil resource industrial exploitation and environmental protection issues.

According to the SNAI classification, the six municipalities that are part of the survey group (Gallicchio, Missanello, Roccanova, San Chirico Raparo, San Martino d'Agri and Sant'Arcangelo) fall within class F - ultra-peripheral, i.e. those municipalities in the inland areas that are more than 70 min away from a pole that simultaneously has a complete upper secondary school offer, at least one hospital with a level I d.e.a. and at least one silver railway station. An evident migration phenomenon in the sample area leads to progressive depopulation. In the last decade, almost a thousand people have left the area; approximately 8% of the population currently stands at 10,634.

Mainly to overcome the lack of services, which compounds the marginal character of the area, the medio Agri municipalities Union (Missanello, Roccanova, San Chirico Raparo, and Sant'Arcangelo) was established in 2017, recently expanded with the inclusion of the municipalities of Gallicchio and Armento. This Union aims to face up jointly to the difficulties affecting the area, starting with accessibility to essential services (education, health, transport). The setting up of the Union of municipalities affected the choice of the area to be researched because it is believed that the smaller centers should join institutional forms of association between municipalities, both to ensure sustainable management of services and functions and to guarantee more opportunities for citizens.

The medio Agri area has significant potential, especially in cultural and natural heritage, with a high ecological value of the ecosystems [59–61]. In particular, the area is affected by the perimeter of the 'Appennino Lucano Val d'Agri-Lagonegrese National Park', by a ZSC 'Murge di S. Oronzo', by a ZPS 'Lucano Apennines, Agri Valley, Monte Sirino, Monte Raparo' and by two SIC 'Lago Pertusillo' and 'Monte Raparo' [49].

The objects subject to landscape protection are those covered by a specific protection decree and those 'ope legis' according to Legislative Decree 42/2004 'Code of Cultural Heritage and Landscape'. This information has been obtained from the Basilicata Region portal dedicated to the Regional Landscape Plan (PPR).

There are 22 sites protected under art. 10 of the Code in the medio Agri area (Table 2). The municipality with the highest number of assets is Sant'Arcangelo, followed by Gallicchio.

The medio Agri area is also rich in archaeological heritage in the form of ancient tracks, of which a total of twelve have been identified (Table 3).

4 Objective III: Enhancing Natural and Cultural Heritage

The medio Agri strategy has been carried out through a number of activities that follow the methodology stages. Here special attention is given to the way in which Objective III "Enhance the natural and cultural heritage and promote urban regenerations projects" of the overall strategy was formulated.

Encouraging the use of the natural and cultural heritage is of great value both to the inhabitants, for whom the quality of life is improved by the provision of more services, and to tourists, due to the presence of natural and cultural resources scattered throughout the medio Agri area. In particular, in order to promote the enjoyment of the natural, scenic and architectural beauty of the area, the development of a tourist itinerary is planned (Fig. 4) [47, 62].

This route can be accessed in different ways, either via the existing road network or by creating safer cycle and footpaths to link the municipalities in the medio Agri

Table 2. Monumental heritage under protection (art. 10 Legislative Decree 42/2004)

Municipality	PPR Code	Monumental heritage
Aliano	BCM_010d	Palazzo Caporale
San Martino d'Agri	BCM_383d - BCM_384d	Palazzo Sifola - Palazzo Manzone
Sant' Arcangelo	BCM_397d - BCM_398d - BCM_402d - BCM_403d - BCM_404d - BCM_399d - BCM_400d - BCM_401d	Palazzo Molfese - Masseria Molfese - Ruderi della Cavallerizza - Masseria Difesa Monte Scardaccione - Torre Molfese e Cappella S. Croce - Palazzo Scardaccione - Palazzo di Gese - Chiesa e Convento di S. Maria d'Orsoleo
Gallicchio	BCM_110d - BCM_109d	Ex Palazzo Baronale - Cappella Madonna del Carmine
Missanello	BCM_239d - BCM_240d	Palazzo Castiglione - Chiesa e Convento S. Maria delle Grazie
Roccanova	BCM_365d - BCM_366d	Palazzo Fortunato - Palazzo Mendaia
San Chirico Raparo	BCM_375d - BCM_376d	Palazzo Barletta - Abbazia S. Angelo
Armento	BCM_011d	Monastero di Santa Maria

area. In addition to the six municipalities specifically involved in the experimentation and research, the municipalities of Armento, Castelsaraceno and Aliano have also been considered, as they represent significant strengths and attractions for the promotion of strategies for the development of tourism in the area. The neighbouring municipalities are characterised by the presence of important tourist attractions, as in the case of Aliano and Castelsaraceno.

The idea is to reorganise the mobility around intermodal hubs equipped and supplied with a minimum (but variable) number of low-emission vehicles (cars and bicycles, including electric ones) for the transport of residents and visitors, depending on the population and services present. These vehicles can be used on a shared basis and interact with an on-demand transport and carpooling system.

Linked to the proposal to create a new tourist route in the area is the recent promotion of the "Raparello MTB" route, about 30 kms long, which crosses the municipalities of San Chirico Raparo, San Martino d'Agri and Castelsaraceno.

The management of the service and the supply of equipment to the municipalities will be the responsibility of the Municipalities Union and will be determined by the seasons, customs and needs that may arise. The equipment will be organised in intermodal areas (16) located in residential areas, near rest areas and supra-local connection infrastructures. In this respect, it is planned to provide safe crossings of the Fondovalle dell'Agri near the Armento, Gallicchio-Missanello and Roccanova-San Brancato junctions.

Starting from the main tourist itinerary, it is planned to adapt the signposting, reorganise the network of paths and existing itineraries according to a network of cultural and

Table 3. Archaeologically assets under protection (art. 10 Legislative Decree 42/2004)

Municipality	PPR Code	Archeologically assets
Sant' Arcangelo	BCT_332	nr 336 -PZ Tratturo Comunale di Rosano
Aliano	BCT_043/BCT_044/	nr 074 -MT Tratturo Comunale di Aliano-Montalbano/nr 075 -MT Tratturo Aliano-Montalbano
Armento	BCT_053	nr 325bis -PZ Tratturo Comunale S. Biagio
Castelsaraceno	BCT_123/BCT_159/BCT_160	nr 332 -PZ Tratturo Comunale della Serra/nr 331 -PZ Tratturo Comunale San Lorenzo/nr 333 -PZ Tratturo Comunale Favino
San Chirico Raparo, Calvera	BCT_124/BCT_328	nr 330 -PZ Tratturo Comunale della serra/nr 328 -PZ Tratturo Comunale Le Mattine
Roccanova	BCT_313/BCT_314	nr 335 -PZ Strada Comunale detta Regio Tratturo di Roccanova/nr 334 -PZ Strada Comunale detta Regio Tratturo di Roccanova

naturalistic destinations that can be enjoyed (in different ways). In this sense, it is necessary to promote and coordinate existing projects, such as the itineraries linked to the network of nature trails (e.g. Parco dei Calanchi, Murgia di Sant'Oronzo, Tibetan Bridge), food and wine production (see the section on strengthening the relationship between agriculture and tourism), archaeological heritage, historical-religious and historical-artistic itineraries (routes and monasteries of the Byzantine monks).

Special rest areas have been identified at strategic points along the routes (at the beginning, end or in between) in order to better organise the use of the routes, arrival by public transport and car parking in suitably equipped and signposted areas, which may be subject to surveillance.

Within the framework of this line of action, different methods of intervention in the natural heritage are possible, with the aim of creating, adapting and improving structures and infrastructures in order to promote better exploitation and use of resources and the spread of environmentally sustainable tourism. In particular, in order to promote the protection and development of areas of particular environmental value (e.g. Natura 2000 sites and other areas of natural interest), provision can be made for:

– specific works to recover the physical and natural environment for social and economic development projects;
– works to adapt, create and improve infrastructures connected to their usability (paths, visitor centres, etc.);

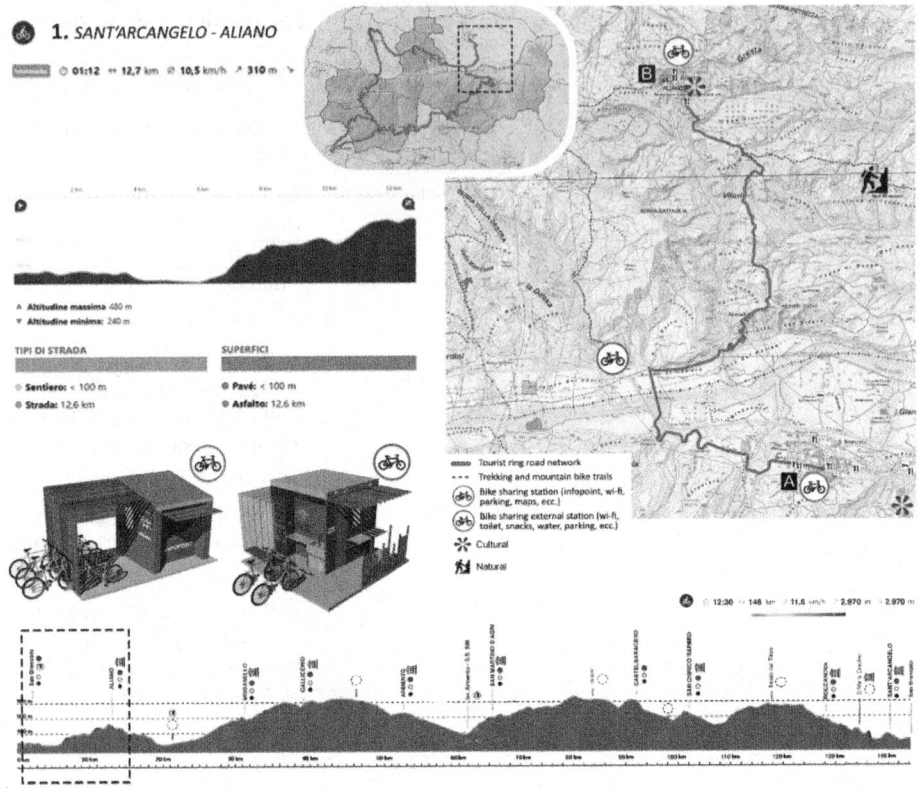

Fig. 4. The first stage of the tourist enhancement itinerary to reach the area's cultural and naturalistic attractions, with an intermodal system of sustainable mobility.

– thematic installations, also with the aim of developing innovative forms of eco-sustainable tourism.

With regard to cultural heritage, on the other hand, the interventions are aimed at its protection and enhancement. In particular, the following may be envisaged: interventions aimed at the recovery, adaptation and enhancement of cultural heritage in its various forms (tangible and intangible), including:

– making the sites safe;
– setting up service facilities;
– placing signs and posters;
– creating specific websites;
– creating a 'local museum system.

These interventions aim at the creation and enhancement of thematic itineraries aimed at promoting the knowledge and tourist use of sites of cultural identity and historical-artistic interest, in order to create a "territorial network" that favours economic development. In this sense, it is necessary to use the available resources and a renewed planning capacity of the local authorities to trigger virtuous processes of enhancement.

It is necessary to take as a starting point the 'good project practices' already existing in the territory, with the aim of generating replicable models in relation to the individual specificities that the territory offers, and of promoting strong synergetic initiatives at supra-municipal level. Aliano and Castelsaraceno, with their different offers, already represent a very attractive context for tourists, also from other regions and foreign countries. Armento, the third municipality considered in the context of a broad territory classification, is an area with great potential for the enhancement of natural and cultural resources. In particular, projects such as the recovery and re-use of the historic village of Casale and the development of a cycle path are important opportunities for the enhancement of the medio Agri area.

The three municipalities surrounding the area in which the six municipalities specifically considered are located play a strategic role in the promotion of the innermost area of the medio Agri; these municipalities are, in fact, the outpost connecting the area of Lagonegrese (Castelsaraceno), the Matera mountains (Aliano) and the inner area of Camastra-Alto Sauro (Armento). The proposal for a tourist itinerary linking and networking the nine territorial realities of the participating municipalities is a development of a proposal put forward by the Gallicchio participants in the Living Lab and concerns the "Tourist Project" promoted by the Municipal Administration.

5 Conclusions

The scientific literature, the proposed methodology and the results of the experiments carried out in the Medio Agri region confirm that it is not necessary to impose ready-made solutions from above, but rather to design the planning process on the basis of the unexploited territorial capital of the inner peripheries. The National Strategy for Inner Areas (SNAI) has tried to follow this path, considering it to be the only valid one, but not without difficulties. In fact, place-based local development strategies require a set of tailor-made approaches, models and tools capable of transforming local characteristics into engines of sustainable development. In activating an area with the characteristics of the medio Agri, the participatory process is the most demanding phase, both in terms of the preliminary activities designed to obtain a specific result from the participatory process, and in terms of the meetings with stakeholders [63].

The proposed integrated strategy is based primarily on strengthening territorial governance and raising awareness of sustainable development issues. Specific strategies are related to a significant improvement in the quality of life in the area concerned (in particular, the reorganisation of basic services) and to the economic development of the sectors that best interpret the potential and identity values available in the area (in particular, agriculture and tourism). If achieved, these objectives would increase the overall resilience of the communities and territories concerned.

Objective III of the strategy aims to promote the territory and its cultural and natural resources through a series of measures (both tangible and intangible) intended to develop a well-equipped tourist itinerary. This includes: exploiting natural resources by reactivating tourist routes and trails; creating an integrated system of sustainable mobility and car-pooling; using old buildings in the historic centre to offer hospitality to visitors; setting up special information points. In this case, too, the initiative must be integrated with other interventions and placed in a cycle of territorial development. The general objective is to promote the management, protection and enhancement of the natural heritage in order to support socio-economic development and sustainable tourism [64]. With regard to the cultural heritage, the interventions are aimed at the protection, recovery, adaptation and valorisation of the monumental heritage. The itinerary, which crosses the area's most valued cultivations (olive groves and vineyards) and places of transformation (cellars, oil mills, etc.), allows for the marketing of local quality products [65].

The definition of the objective is not exhaustive, as there are many actions to be carried out, but the strategy has provided an initial reference on which to integrate effective and innovative actions.

References

1. ESPON: PROFECY (Inner Peripheries in Europe) - Final Report (2017). https://archive.espon.eu/sites/default/files/attachments/D5FinalReportPROFECY.pdf
2. PROFECY. https://archive.espon.eu/inner-peripheries. Accessed 30 May 2023
3. Blair, H., Bosak, K., Gale, T.: Protected areas, tourism, and rural transition in Aysén, Chile. Sustainability **11**(24), 1–22 (2019). https://doi.org/10.3390/su11247087
4. Azevedo, P.: The ways of Saint James in Trás -os-montes and Alto Douro as an example of soft tourism in rural areas. Countrys. Eur. **13**(2), 314–329 (2021). https://doi.org/10.2478/euco-2021-0020
5. Kouřilová, J., Pělucha, M.: Economic and social impacts of promoting cultural heritage protection by the Czech rural development programme 2007–2013. Eur. Countrys. **9**(3), 486–503 (2017). https://doi.org/10.1515/euco-2017-0029
6. Barca, F.: Disuguaglianze territoriali e bisogno sociale. La sfida delle 'Aree Interne'. In: Lettura annuale Ermanno Gorrieri, Modena: Stampa Grafiche TEM, pp. 31–33 (2016). http://www.irpais.it/disuguaglianze-territoriali-bisogno-sociale/
7. Punziano, G.: Health, mobility, education: strategies for inner areas. Sci. Reg. **18**(1), 65–92 (2019). https://doi.org/10.14650/92353
8. Moscarelli, R., Fera, A.: National strategy for inner areas 10 years later: a proposal of comparative analysis between the phases 2014–2020 and 2021–2027. Contemporanea **24**(1), 101–120 (2024). https://doi.org/10.14650/108247
9. Di Giusy, P., Laura, S.: Toward an Italian national strategy for inner areas 2.0, as an opportunity of institutional learning. Lessons from an action-research process. Archivio di Studi Urbani e Regionali (129), 47–70 (2020). https://doi.org/10.3280/ASUR2020-129003
10. Galderisi, A., Fiore, P., Pontrandolfi, P.: Strategie Operative per la valorizzazione e la resilienza delle Aree Interne: il progetto RI.P.R.O.VA.RE. BDC. Boll. Del Cent. Calza Bini **20**(2), 297–316 (2020). https://doi.org/10.6092/2284-4732/7557
11. Accordo di Partenariato 2014–2020: Strategia nazionale per le Aree interne: definizione, obiettivi, strumenti e governance. Aedon, Riv. di arti e Dirit. line (3/2018), 1–69 (2018). https://doi.org/10.7390/92260
12. ESPON GEOSPECS: Inner Peripheries : a socio-economic territorial specificity (2013). https://archive.espon.eu/sites/default/files/attachments/GEOSPECS_Final_Report_inner_peripheries_v14.pdf
13. ESPON: PROFECY – Processes , Features and Cycles of Inner Peripheries in Europe - Handbook, December 2017. https://archive.espon.eu/sites/default/files/attachments/D5HandbookPROFECY_0.pdf

14. Servillo, L., Russo, A., Barbara, F., Carrosio, G.: Inner peripheries: towards an EU place-based agenda on territorial peripherality. Ital. J. Plan. Pract. **VI**(1), 42–75 (2016)
15. Copus, A., Noguera, J.: Inner peripheries: what are they? What policies do they need? Agriregionieuropa **12**(45), 1–6 (2016)
16. Pezzi, M.G., Urso, G.: Peripheral areas: conceptualizations and policies. Introduction and editorial note. Ital. J. Plan. Pract. **6**(1), 1–19 (2016)
17. Pileček, J., Jančák, V.: Theoretical and methodological aspects of the identification and delimitation of peripheral areas. Acta Univ. Carolinae, Geogr. **46**(1), 43–52 (2011) https://doi.org/10.14712/23361980.2015.41
18. Cialdea, D., Cervelli, E., Pindozzi, S.: Land development support in marginal areas: an opportunity of environmental quality implementation, April 2019 (2018)
19. Cervelli, E., di Perta, E.S., Pindozzi, S.: Identification of marginal landscapes as support for sustainable development: GIS-based analysis and landscape metrics assessment in Southern Italy areas. Sustainability **12**(13) (2020). https://doi.org/10.3390/su12135400
20. Blečić, I., Saiu, V., Cecchini, A., Trunfio, G.: Decision-support tools for territorial regeneration: a GIS-based multi-criteria evaluation utilizing the territorial capital framework (2024). https://doi.org/10.1007/978-3-031-54096-7_32.
21. Dastoli, P.S., Scorza, F., Murgante, B.: Impact evaluation: an experiment on development policies in Agri Valley (Basilicata, Italy) compared with new urban agenda themes. In: Gervasi, O., et al. (eds.) ICCSA 2021. LNCS, vol. 12957, pp. 621–633. Springer, Cham (2021). https://doi.org/10.1007/978-3-030-87013-3_48
22. Gola, M., Fior, M., Arruzzoli, S., Galuzzi, P., Capolongo, S., Buffoli, M.: A research method for locating community healthcare facilities in Italy: how to guarantee healthcare for all. J. Integr. Care (2023). https://doi.org/10.1108/JICA-05-2023-0034
23. Bovis, C.: The role and function of structural and cohesion funds and the interaction of the EU regional policy with the internal market policies - chapter 4. In: The Role of the Regions in EU Governance, pp. 81–108 (2011). https://doi.org/10.1007/978-3-642-11903-3_4
24. Pilogallo, A., Saganeiti, L., Scorza, F., Murgante, B.: Assessing the impact of land use changes on ecosystem services value. In: Gervasi, O., et al. (eds.) ICCSA 2020. LNCS, vol. 12253, pp. 606–616. Springer, Cham (2020). https://doi.org/10.1007/978-3-030-58814-4_47
25. Ruiz-Martínez, I., Esparcia, J.: Internet access in rural areas: brake or stimulus as post-covid-19 opportunity? Sustainability **12**(22), 1–17 (2020). https://doi.org/10.3390/su122 29619
26. González, J.J.C., Herrero, J.A.R., Aboitiz, R.J.: Residential aspirations and perception of rural youth of the opportunities offered by their environment: the case of a Spanish inland rural area. Eur. Countrys. **13**(4), 785–805 (2021). https://doi.org/10.2478/euco-2021-0042
27. Dastoli, P.S., Pontrandolfi, P.: Strategic guidelines to increase the resilience of inland areas: the case of the Alta Val d'Agri (Basilicata-Italy). In: Gervasi, O., et al. (eds.) ICCSA 2021. LNCS, vol. 12958, pp. 119–130. Springer, Cham (2021). https://doi.org/10.1007/978-3-030-87016-4_9
28. Scrofani, L., Novembre, C.: The inland areas of Sicily. From rural development to territorial reorganization. Semest. di Stud. e Ric. di Geogr., 113–121 (2015). http://semestrale-geografia.org/index.php/sdg/article/view/72
29. Karacsonyi, D., Taylor, A.: Understanding demographic and economic patterns in sparsely populated areas–a global typology approach. Geogr. Ann. Ser. B Hum. Geogr. **105**(3), 228–247 (2023). https://doi.org/10.1080/04353684.2022.2103445
30. Muilu, T.: Rural policies for sparsely populated areas in Finland - old problems, new challenges and future opportunities. Eur. Countrys. **13**(2), 479–491 (2021). https://doi.org/10.2478/euco-2021-0028

31. Carson, D.A., Carson, D.B., Argent, N.: Cities, hinterlands and disconnected urban-rural development: perspectives from sparsely populated areas. J. Rural. Stud. **93**, 104–111 (2022). https://doi.org/10.1016/j.jrurstud.2022.05.012
32. Lehtonen, O.: Population grid-based assessment of the impact of broadband expansion on population development in rural areas. Telecomm. Policy **44**(10), 102028 (2020). https://doi.org/10.1016/j.telpol.2020.102028
33. Ciommi, M., Egidi, G., Salvia, R., Cividino, S., Rontos, K., Salvati, L.: Population dynamics and agglomeration factors: a non-linear threshold estimation of density effects. Sustainability **12**(6) (2020). https://doi.org/10.3390/su12062257
34. Hansmeier, H., Koschatzky, K.: Lagging regions between economic restructuring and addressing societal challenges (2025). https://doi.org/10.1007/s10037-025-00222-6
35. S. Republic and C. Republic: Development and causes of migration in lagging regions in the years 2017 – 2021: a case study of the Slovak republic, pp. 53–64 (2024)
36. Bertolini, P., Pagliacci, F.: Quality of life and territorial imbalances. A focus on Italian inner and rural areas. Bio-Based Appl. Econ. **6**(2), 183–208 (2017). https://doi.org/10.13128/BAE-18518
37. Rizzo, A.: Disaster management in the inner areas: a window of opportunity for national strategy (SNAI). In: Calabrò, F., Della Spina, L., Bevilacqua, C. (eds.) ISHT 2018. SIST, vol. 101, pp. 13–21. Springer, Cham (2019). https://doi.org/10.1007/978-3-319-92102-0_2
38. Agenzia per la Coesione Territoriale. https://www.agenziacoesione.gov.it/?lang=en
39. D'Andria, E., Fiore, P.: The RI.P.R.O.VA.RE. project for the regeneration of inland areas: a focus on the Ufita area in the Campania region (Italy). Buildings **13**(2) (2023). https://doi.org/10.3390/buildings13020336
40. Fortunato, G., Scorza, F., Murgante, B., Dastoli, P.S.: The Lagonegro-Rotonda cycle path, a community-based management model: ECO-CICLE perspectives. LaborEst **24**, 45–49 (2022). https://doi.org/10.19254/LaborEst.24.07
41. Fortunato, G., Scorza, F., Murgante, B.: Hybrid oriented sustainable urban development: a pattern of low-carbon access to schools in the City of Potenza. In: Gervasi, O., et al. (eds.) ICCSA 2020. LNCS, vol. 12255, pp. 193–205. Springer, Cham. https://doi.org/10.1007/978-3-030-58820-5_15
42. Carbone, R., et al.: Using open data and open tools in defining strategies for the enhancement of Basilicata region. In: Gervasi, O., et al. (eds.) ICCSA 2018. LNCS, vol. 10964, pp. 725–733. Springer, Cham (2018). https://doi.org/10.1007/978-3-319-95174-4_55
43. Scorza, F., Fortunato, G.: Cyclable cities: building feasible scenario through urban space-morphology assessment. J. Urban Plan. Dev. (2021). https://doi.org/10.1061/(ASCE)UP.1943-5444.0000713
44. Fortunato, G., Scorza, F., Murgante, B.: Cyclable city: a territorial assessment procedure for disruptive policy-making on urban mobility. In: Misra, S., et al. (eds.) ICCSA 2019. LNCS, vol. 11624, pp. 291–307. Springer, Cham (2019). https://doi.org/10.1007/978-3-030-24311-1_21
45. Murgante, B., Scorza, F., Fortunato, G., Dastoli, P.S.: A place syntax approach to fifteen minutes cities. In: Proceedings 13th International Space Syntax Symposium, SSS 2022, University of Basilicata, School of Engineering, Potenza, Italy (2022). https://www.scopus.com/inward/record.uri?eid=2-s2.0-85145612362&partnerID=40&md5=e9f3cde33d94ccb9c2b4f6f1add2aaec
46. Las Casas, G., Sansone, A.: Un approccio rinnovato alla razionalità nel piano. In: Politiche e strumenti per il recupero urbano, Monfalcone (GO): Edicomedizioni (2004)
47. Scorza, F., Pilogallo, A., Las Casas, G.: Investigating tourism attractiveness in inland areas: ecosystem services, open data and smart specializations. In: Calabrò, F., Della Spina, L., Bevilacqua, C. (eds.) ISHT 2018. SIST, vol. 100, pp. 30–38. Springer, Cham (2019). https://doi.org/10.1007/978-3-319-92099-3_4

48. Scorza, F., Casas, G.L., Murgante, B.: Overcoming interoperability weaknesses in e-government processes: organizing and sharing knowledge in regional development programs using ontologies. In: Lytras, M.D., Ordonez de Pablos, P., Ziderman, A., Roulstone, A., Maurer, H., Imber, J.B. (eds.) WSKS 2010. CCIS, vol. 112, pp. 243–253. Springer Heidelberg (2010). https://doi.org/10.1007/978-3-642-16324-1_26
49. Dastoli, P.S., Pontrandolfi, P.: Methods and tools for a participatory local development strategy. In: Calabrò, F., Della Spina, L., Piñeira Mantiñán, M.J. (eds.) NMP 2022. LNNS, vol. 482, pp. 2112–2121. Springer, Cham (2022). https://doi.org/10.1007/978-3-031-06825-6_203
50. Scorza, F., Casas, G.B.L., Murgante, B.: That's ReDO: ontologies and regional development planning. In: Murgante, B., et al. (eds.) ICCSA 2012. LNCS, vol. 7334, pp. 640–652. Springer, Heidelberg (2012). https://doi.org/10.1007/978-3-642-31075-1_48
51. Soligno, R., Scorza, F., Amato, F., Casas, G.L., Murgante, B.: Citizens participation in improving rural communities quality of life. In: Gervasi, O., et al. (eds.) ICCSA 2015. LNCS, vol. 9156, pp. 731–746. Springer, Cham (2015). https://doi.org/10.1007/978-3-319-21407-8_52
52. Dastoli, P.S., Pontrandolfi, P., Scorza, F., Corrado, S., Azzato, A.: Applying geodesign towards an integrated local development strategy: the Val d'Agri case (Italy). In: Gervasi, O., Murgante, B., Misra, S., Rocha, A.M.A.C., Garau, C. (eds.) ICCSA 2022. LNCS, vol. 13379, pp. 253–262. Springer, Cham (2022). https://doi.org/10.1007/978-3-031-10545-6_18
53. Scorza, F.: Training decision-makers: GEODESIGN workshop paving the way for new urban agenda. In: Gervasi, O., et al. (eds.) ICCSA 2020. LNCS, vol. 12252, pp. 310–316. Springer, Cham (2020). https://doi.org/10.1007/978-3-030-58811-3_22
54. Steinitz, C., Orland, B., Fisher, T., Campagna, M.: Geodesign to address global change (2022). https://doi.org/10.1016/B978-0-12-820247-0.00016-3
55. Campagna, M.: Geodesign: (a personal) retrospective, and perspectives. In: Marucci, A., Zullo, F., Fiorini, L., Saganeiti, L. (eds.) INPUT 2023. LNCE, vol. 467, pp. 114–121. Springer, Cham (2024). https://doi.org/10.1007/978-3-031-54118-6_11
56. Steinitz, C.: On change and geodesign. Landsc. Urban Plan. **156**, 23–25 (2016). https://doi.org/10.1016/j.landurbplan.2016.09.023
57. Las Casas, G., Scorza, F., Murgante, B.: Conflicts and sustainable planning: peculiar instances coming from Val D'agri structural inter-municipal plan. In: Papa, R., Fistola, R., Gargiulo, C. (eds.) Smart Planning: Sustainability and Mobility in the Age of Change. GET, pp. 163–177. Springer, Cham (2018). https://doi.org/10.1007/978-3-319-77682-8_10
58. Scorza, F.: Towards self energy-management and sustainable citizens' engagement in local energy efficiency agenda. Int. J. Agric. Environ. Inf. Syst. **7**(1), 44–53 (2016). https://doi.org/10.4018/ijaeis.2016010103
59. Saganeiti, L., Pilogallo, A., Faruolo, G., Scorza, F., Murgante, B.: Territorial fragmentation and renewable energy source plants: which relationship? Sustainability **12**(5), 1828 (2020). https://doi.org/10.3390/SU12051828
60. Las Casas, G., Murgante, B., Scorza, F.: Regional local development strategies benefiting from open data and open tools and an outlook on the renewable energy sources contribution. Green Energy Technol., 275–290 (2016). https://doi.org/10.1007/978-3-319-31157-9_14
61. Pilogallo, A., Scorza, F.: Mapping regulation ecosystem services (ReMES) specialization in Italy. J. Urban Plan. Dev. (2021)
62. Dastoli, P.S., Scorza, F.: Geodesign in the strategic planning track: a participatory itinerary. J. Digit. Landsc. Archit. **2023**(8), 400–408 (2023). https://doi.org/10.14627/537740043
63. Pontrandolfi, P., Scorza, F.: Making urban regeneration feasible: tools and procedures to integrate urban agenda and UE cohesion regional programs. In: Gervasi, O., et al. (eds.) ICCSA 2017. LNCS, vol. 10409. Springer, Cham(2017). https://doi.org/10.1007/978-3-319-62407-5_40

64. Gatto, R.V., Corrado, S., Scorza, F.: Towards a definition of tourism ecosystem. In: 18th International Forum on Knowledge Asset Dynamics (IFKAD) - Managing Knowledge for Sustainability (2023)
65. Saganeiti, L., Pilogallo, A., Izzo, C., Piro, R., Scorza, F., Murgante, B.: Development strategies of agro-food sector in Basilicata region (Italy): evidence from INNOVAGRO project. In: Misra, S., et al. (eds.) ICCSA 2019. LNCS, vol. 11624, pp. 347–356. Springer, Cham. https://doi.org/10.1007/978-3-030-24311-1_25

Data-Driven AI Approach to Address Territorial Strategies. Why Investing in Agri-Food Sector to Enhance the Valsesia Inner Area

Diana Rolando[1], Alice Barreca[1], Giorgia Malavasi[1], and Manuela Rebaudengo[2](✉)

[1] Architecture and Design Department, Politecnico di Torino, Viale Mattioli 39, 10125 Turin, Italy
{diana.rolando,alice.barreca,giorgia.malavasi}@polito.it
[2] Interuniversity Department of Regional and Urban Studies and Planning, Politecnico di Torino, Viale Mattioli 39, 10125 Turin, Italy
manuela.rebaudengo@polito.it

Abstract. In recent years, data-driven artificial intelligence (AI) approaches have gained prominence in territorial planning and economic development, enabling policymakers to analyse large datasets and formulate evidence-based strategies. This study aims to develop and apply a data-driven AI approach to analyse past funded projects to support decision-making processes and the development of strategic actions in Italy's inner territories, focusing on the Valsesia SNAI Inner Area and the enhancement of the Agri-food chains and rural development sector. The study employs data mining techniques such as Latent Dirichlet Allocation (LDA) topic modeling and clustering to analyse thematic and financial data from the "OpenCoesione projects" dataset. Findings highlight that while infrastructure investments are substantial, funding for research, innovation, and business competitiveness in the agri-food sector remains underdeveloped. The study underscores the importance of private-public financing mechanisms and strategic investment to enhance regional development. Conducted within the Branding4Resilience (B4R) project by the Politecnico di Torino Research Unit, this research can contribute to optimizing SNAI strategy implementation and broader territorial policies, fostering the competitiveness of agri-food SMEs and supporting sustainable socio-economic growth in Valsesia.

Keywords: Inner Areas · Data-driven AI approach · SNAI strategy

1 Introduction

In recent years, the use of data-driven artificial intelligence (AI) approaches has gained increasing attention in the field of territorial planning and economic development [9, 15]. These methodologies enable policymakers and local authorities to analyse large datasets, extract meaningful insights, and formulate evidence-based strategies. The integration of AI-driven analyses with participatory governance models is particularly relevant in the context of inner territories, where economic and social challenges require tailored interventions. Inner territories across Italy face significant socio-economic challenges [24], including demographic decline, limited access to essential services, and economic stagnation [1, 7]. Traditional development policies often fail to address these issues effectively due to fragmented data, limited stakeholder engagement, and suboptimal allocation of financial resources. A key problem lies in the lack of systematic, data-driven evaluation mechanisms that can guide funding decisions and policy interventions [2]. Without a structured approach to assessing past projects and their impacts, there is a risk of inefficient resource allocation and missed opportunities for sustainable growth.

While previous studies have explored regional development policies in rural economies [10–12, 14], few have integrated AI-based methodologies to systematically evaluate the effectiveness of past interventions. The research aims to bridge this gap by leveraging AI-driven analyses to support informed decision-making and optimize territorial development strategies. In this scenario, thematic and financial analyses on funded projects can highlight (good) lessons learnt and represent effective drivers for local development of inner territories; therefore, the availability of open data and accessible national databases plays a crucial role in supporting data-driven analyses able to address territorial strategies.

This study focuses on the Valsesia Inner Area, recently recognized as part of the Italian National Strategy for Inner Areas (SNAI), which represents a valuable case study for assessing the potential of data-driven approaches in guiding territorial strategies. This research was conducted by the Politecnico di Torino Research Unit (RU) in the context of the Branding4Resilience (B4R) research project of national interest (PRIN 2017— Young Line), which was funded by the Italian Ministry of University and Research (MUR) for a four-year duration (2020–2024) [7]. In accordance with the goals of the B4R project, the Polito RU triggered a collaboration-based approach between Academia and the Valsesia Mountain Union, which has been constantly involved and consulted during the first phases of the B4R project focused on understanding and analyzing local territorial challenges, as well as on developing co-design activities [13, 18, 19, 21, 22]. In 2023 the Polito RU participated to six thematic Focus Groups organized by the Valsesia Mountain Unions in the context of the SNAI strategy definition process, finalized to identify priority actions and interventions around which the SNAI strategy can be oriented. The Focus Group on the Agri-food chains and rural development sector stimulated a very effective dialogue with stakeholders and highlighted the high potential and crucial role of SMEs in fostering local development, as they could contribute to employment, innovation, and the sustainable use of natural resources. In this context, quantitative and qualitative data were collected, and data-driven analyses were performed in order to support Valsesia Mountain Union in this important decision-making process. Particular attention was focused on the "OpenCoesione projects" dataset, which allowed interesting thematic and financial analyses on funded projects at national and regional levels, which highlighted the "Competitiveness of companies" and "Research and Innovation") as the less considered thematic scopes in Piedmont Region in the past [25, 26].

This research aims to develop and apply a data-driven AI approach to analyse past funded projects to support decision-making processes and the development of strategic actions in the context of the Valsesia SNAI Inner Area, with a specific focus on the Agri-food chains and rural development sector. The main objectives are to analyse categories, typologies, costs, and funding of past funded projects, as well as the detailed descriptions of each project, identifying the Key Strategic Actions (KSA) used to develop and/or enhance the Agri-food chains and rural development sector, along with the related public and private funding.

Through data mining techniques such as Latent Dirichlet Allocation (LDA) topic modelling and clustering [6, 17], the research identifies key investment patterns and funding gaps. The findings reveal that while significant resources have been allocated to infrastructure, investments in research, innovation, and business competitiveness in the agri-food sector remain limited. The study also highlights the role of private-public financing mechanisms in shaping regional development trajectories. By drawing insights from past experiences and ongoing strategic planning, the study seeks to provide recommendations for optimizing not only the SNAI strategy implementation but also other territorial development policies able to enhance the competitiveness of agri-food SMEs and contribute to the socio-economic growth of Valsesia.

The paper is structured as follows: Sect. 2 presents the methodological approach adopted, while Sect. 3 introduces the case study and explains the data sampling process. Section 4 discusses the results achieved by analysing 2 subsamples ("Competitiveness of companies" and "Research and Innovation") and Sect. 5 provides concluding remarks.

2 Methodological Approach

The Politecnico di Torino B4R Research Unit developed a data-driven AI approach to analyse past funded projects and support Local Authorities in addressing territorial strategies in the Valsesia Inner Area. The methodological approach is developed in 5 phases (Fig. 1).

A. Goal Definition

Once a specific territorial context is selected as case study, data-driven analyses are performed to identify gaps and opportunities to be assumed as objectives. This approach builds on lessons learned from strategies implemented in the past that can contribute to identifying strategic gaps in the lacking thematic scopes allocate resources effectively and designing development. This phase also combines data-driven analysis with listening and debate with stakeholder who can contribute to identify the lacking thematic scopes and to define strategic priorities for the formulation of new action proposals.

B. Data Collection and Dataset Import

After the identification of lacking thematic scopes, it is fundamental to collect data on the projects previously financed in the areas of interest identified in line with the set objectives and validated by the competent institution. Open data and national databases can represent great support to perform thematic and financial analyses on funded projects, to be used as (good) lessons learnt.

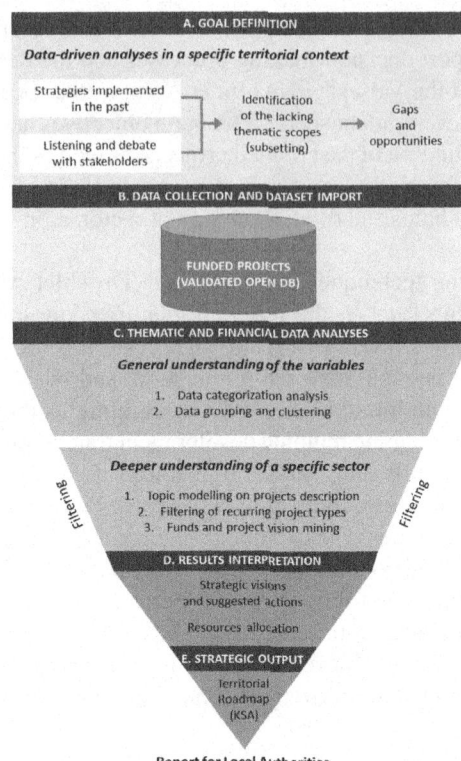

Fig. 1. Methodological approach developed and applied by the Polito RU to analyse past funded projects alongside the Valsesia SNAI Strategy definition process (Source: Authors' elaboration)

C. Thematic and Financial Data Analyses

The analyses conducted starting from the selected database are based on the integration of existing technologies in the field of project management, data analysis and artificial intelligence, that can be further developed as a Project Intelligence System [23]. In particular, the insights derived from Pivot Table data analyses are further enhanced by specific analyses performed with AI support.

First, a general understanding of the funding distribution of projects and actions is pursued through:

1. Data categorization analysis: analysis of the number of funded projects and the related invested amount of public funds;
2. Data grouping and clustering: aggregation of data through thematic grouping, reducing redundancy and improving clarity, focusing on specific development actions.

Secondly, 3 subsequent analyses contribute to a deeper understanding of the funding distribution and strategic focus of the funded projects, particularly filtering data on a specific sector, resulting from the data-driven analyses performed in the selected territorial context:

1. Topic modeling on project descriptions: Latent Dirichlet Allocation (LDA) [6, 17] a statistical model that discovers hidden thematic structures in large text collections by treating documents as mixtures of topics and topics as distributions of words, is applied to identify latent topics within project descriptions. This approach helps uncover thematic patterns and categorize projects based on their textual content;
2. Filtering of recurring project types: the most frequently occurring project types are identified by analysing textual descriptions, allowing for the grouping of projects into meaningful categories that reflect common investment themes.
3. Funds and project vision mining: the main strategies employed in the selected specific sector are examined, determining their prevalence and significance within the dataset. Identified strategies are linked to their respective funding amounts, enabling a quantitative assessment of financial allocation per strategy. The distribution of public and private funding across different strategies is then calculated, providing a clear comparative view of investment patterns.

D. Results Interpretation
The analysis of results provides strategic visions and suggested actions to drive decision-making. Key insights help optimize resource allocation, ensuring socio-economic growth and territorial enhancement of the selected geographic area, guiding decisions on infrastructure, economy and sustainability.

E. Strategic Output
Through this framework, Local Authorities and their consultants are equipped with the tools and insights needed to enhance decision-making and drive impactful development initiatives. The achieved results can be shared with stakeholders through a report containing a Territorial Roadmap, outlining Key Strategic Actions (KSA), goals, and public and private funding allocation.

3 Case Study and Data Sample

In June 2022, the Valsesia and the Biellese Orientale Mountain Unions achieved the important goal of being identified as "Valsesia Inner Area", funded in the context of the second SNAI programming cycle. Since December 2022, the two Mountain Unions organized six thematic Focus Groups to engage in dialogue with local actors and stakeholders, aiming to identify and share key challenges and opportunities related to the Valsesia territory. Due to the close collaboration between Academia and local actors during B4R project, the Valsesia Mountain Union involved the Polito RU as a technical expert in both field activities and in the meetings organized by the Control Room which coordinates policy implementation across institutional levels and ensures alignment among actors. This collaboration aimed to consolidate dispersed knowledge (internal RU team meetings), share insights from the B4R project and contribute to discussions with stakeholders, to support Local Authorities in addressing territorial strategies in the Agri-food sector which, based on the findings of the thematic Focus Groups, represents a strategic sector for the enhancement of the Valsesia SNAI area.

Starting from the lessons learnt from the past, a national open-source database containing all the information related to projects funded at the national level since the programming cycle 2000–2006 was selected. It was downloaded from the OpenCoesione portal (www.opencoesione.gov.it), that is an open government initiative on cohesion policies in Italy and promotes a widespread civic participation by monitoring the effectiveness of interventions with the publication of data on funded projects. This dataset (accessed in December 2024) contains around 1,049M funded projects described by 199 variables; The variables selected for this research are illustrated in Table 1.

4 Results

The proposed data-driven AI approach for analysing funded projects and supporting Local Authorities in addressing territorial strategies was applied in the context of the Valsesia SNAI strategy definition process by analysing the strategies implemented in the past SNAI programming cycle and participating to the six thematic Focus Groups organized by the two Mountain Unions since December 2022. The data-driven analyses and the dialogue with local actors and stakeholders highlighted key challenges and opportunities related to two thematic scopes, which in the past have been less considered in Piedmont Region.

The first thematic scope ("Competitiveness of companies") includes financial engineering instruments such as guarantee funds, loan funds, credit access mechanisms, co-guarantees, and counter-guarantees. It also includes more traditional business support measures, such as fostering new business creation (e.g., under Legislative Decree No. 185/2000), establishing new production plants, expanding and modernising existing facilities, and improving the functionality of production areas. Other measures within this theme include program contracts to support investments by large enterprises and Integrated Facilitation Packages (PIA), which can cover productive investments, business support services, and corporate training.

The second thematic scope ("Research and Innovation") encompasses support for the demand for research and innovation by businesses, including financial engineering tools, through funding for companies engaged in industrial research and experimental development projects, often in collaboration with universities and public research centres. Additionally, funding is provided to support research supply by universities and research centres, including the enhancement of research infrastructure and laboratories, technology transfer to businesses (such as technology districts and innovation hubs), and advanced business services for research and innovation.

According to these selected thematic scopes, two datasets were extracted from the "OpenCoesione projects" dataset and thematic and financial data analyses were performed. The first analysis (Sect. 4.1) critically examines and cross-references some variables (categories, typologies, costs, and funding), while the second analysis (Sect. 4.2) focuses on the detailed descriptions of each project, identifying the Key Strategic Actions (KSA) used to develop and/or enhance the Agri-food chains and rural development sector, along with the related public and private funding.

Table. 1. Data sample main variables (Source: Authors' elaboration)

Data structure		Data content	Data value	
Field acronym	Field name		Vocabulary	Field type
OC_SINTESI_PROGETTO	Project summary	Detailed description of the project	Open	Text
OC_DESCR_CICLO	Programming Cycle	Description of the programming cycle	Closed: 2000–2006; 2007–2013; 2014–2020; 2021–2027)	Text
OC_TEMA_SINTETICO	Thematic scope	Summary description of the thematic scope (Aggregation of EU priority topics into summary scopes)	Closed: Environment, Administrative capacity, Competitiveness of companies, Culture and Tourism, Energy, Social Inclusion and health, Education and training, Employment and work, Digital networks and services, Research and innovation, Transport and mobility	Text
OC_DESCR_CATEGORIA_SPESA	Expenditure category	Description of the expenditure category	Closed: 27 different categories of expenditure (ref. metadati_progetti_tracciato_esteso.xls)	Text
CUP_DESCR_TIPOLOGIA	Project typology	Description of the type of project according to the CUP (Italian Unique Project Code)	Closed: 45 different typologies of project (ref. metadati_progetti_tracciato_esteso.xls)	Text
CUP_DESCR_CATEGORIA	Project category	Description of the category of project according to the CUP	Closed: 139 different categories of project (ref. metadati_progetti_tracciato_esteso.xls)	Text
FINANZ_PRIVATO	Private funds	Amount of financing from private source	Open	Number in Euros
FINANZ_TOTALE_PUBBLICO	Total public funds	Total public funding sources	Open	Number in Euros
COSTO_REALIZZATO	Implemented cost	Value of the works and project activities carried out	Open	Number in Euros

4.1 Data Categorization, Grouping and Clustering

Competitiveness of Companies (Dataset 1)

The analysis started with the identification of the first subset, consisting in 31.976 records related to a total amount of public funds of about 7.500M€. The chart (Fig. 2) shows the distribution of the number of interventions by type (CUP_DESCR_TIPOLOGIA) and their related average values. Four main typologies account for 44% (*new construction*), 26% (*other typology*) 8% (*modernization*) and 7% (*expansion*) of total programmed interventions; the remaining part (about 15% of the total) is divided into 24 typologies. The overall average amount is about €235.000 with the highest values recorded for 'work incentives' (10 interventions funded at €30 million each), 'Applications and web platforms' (2 interventions, each funded at €19 million), and 'Liquidity shortage' (2 interventions, each receiving €15 million). Conversely, the lowest values are associated with expenditure categories related to supply/purchase (average values between 0,01 and 0,08M€. In terms of total public funding (Fig. 3), three categories (*other*, *new construction*, *expansion*) account for approximately 75% of the total allocation, leaving 25% for the remaining typologies. Interestingly, although physical interventions on buildings or new construction account for the majority of projects, they represent only a third of the total funded amount.

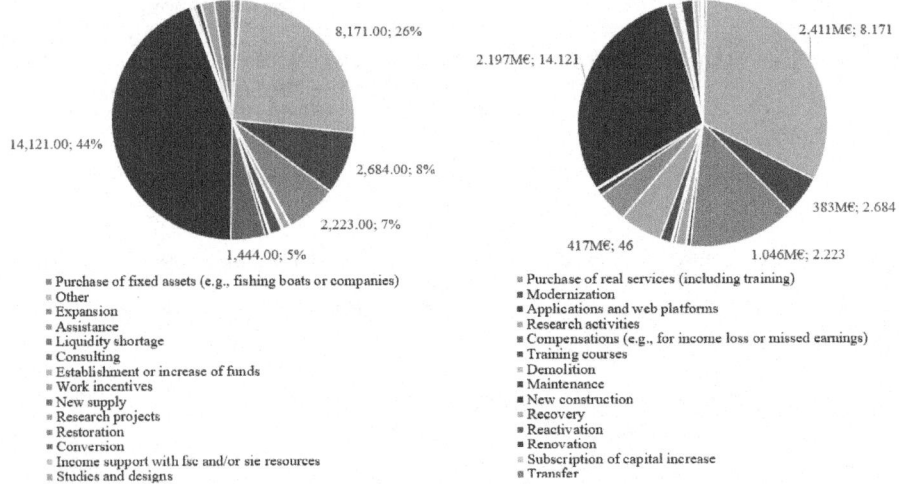

Fig. 2. DATASET 1 - Number of intervention (and related average values) per intervention's typology (Source: authors' elaboration)

Fig. 3. DATASET 1 - Total public funding and number of interventions per typology (Source: authors' elaboration)

As shown in the financing mix (Appendix, Fig. 8), since 2000, public resources have consistently dominated, covering about 75% of total funding, with 12 expenditure types relying entirely on public support. Private contributions were most significant in 'New supply' (70%) and 'Conversion' (55%), with over one-third of total private investment—amounting to €7.5 billion—dedicated to new constructions. To better support the development of the Valsesia strategy, the analysis shifted focus toward local economic enhancement. Standard Excel tools proved inadequate for this purpose, leading to the use of artificial intelligence to regroup funding categories. This reclassification improves data readability and clarifies the allocation of resources across infrastructure, activities, and technology transfer (Appendix, Tables 2 and 3).

Research and Innovation (Dataset 2)

Starting with the identification of the second subset, we selected 10.442 records related to a total amount of public funds of about 6.150M€. The chart (Fig. 4) shows the distribution of the number of interventions by type (CUP_DESCR_TIPOLOGIA) and their related average values. Three main typologies account for 40% (*research activities*), 32% (*research projects*) and 22% (*other typology*) of total programmed interventions; the remaining part (1/3 of the total) is divided into 14 typologies, with less than 100 interventions each. The overall average amount is just under €590,000 with the highest values recorded for 'establishing or increasing a loan fund' (a single intervention funded at €270 million), 'new supply' (26 interventions, each funded at €6.3 million), and 'technical assistance' (5 interventions, each receiving €5 million). Conversely, the lowest values are associated with expenditure categories more linked to intangible actions, such as 'conversion' (24 interventions with an average value of approximately €70,000), 'expansion' (87 interventions averaging €115,000 each), and 'work incentives' (2 interventions, each funded at €150,000). In terms of total public funding (Fig. 5), the same three categories account for approximately 88% of the total allocation, leaving just over 10% for the remaining typologies. Interestingly, physical buildings intervention (e.g., renovation and expansion) do not dominate either in terms of funding or the number of interventions. Instead, the funds have been primarily directed towards research projects and the purchase of equipment.

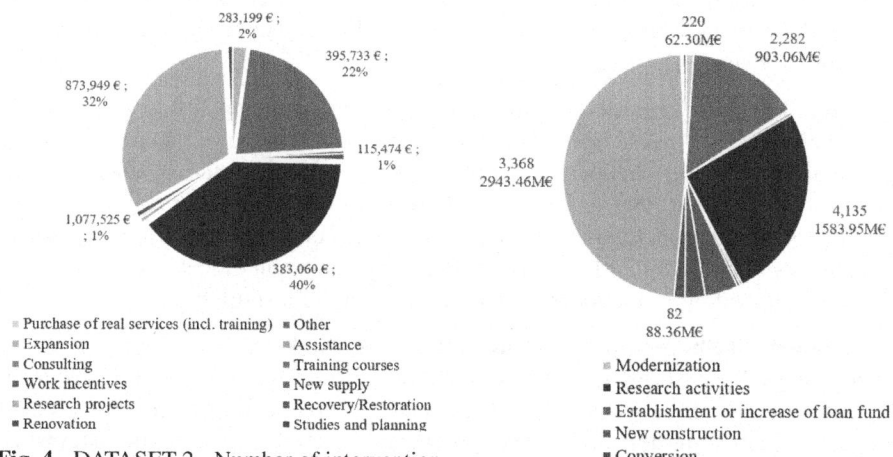

Fig. 4. DATASET 2 - Number of intervention (and related average values) per intervention's typology (Source: authors' elaboration)

Fig. 5. DATASET 2 - Total public funding and number of interventions per typology (Source: authors' elaboration)

In terms of the financing mix (Appendix, Fig. 9), it can be seen that analyzing all the programming cycles since 2000 without distinction, private and public resources were activated in relationship 30%–70%; in some typologies of expenditure the funding was only public. The typologies most financed by private money were Expansion and Conversion (68% of the amount of their interventions), followed by 'Research activities' (48% of the amount was financed by private capitals).

'Research projects', on the other hand, were financed by private funds for less than a quarter of the entire amount, 23%. However, if we look at the total private funding, which amounts to almost 2,700M€, about 54% has been invested specifically in research activities. For this subset too, it was decided to use artificial intelligence to group similar elements (categories); in this case, the new classification allows for the distinction between infrastructural and/or productive investments for SMEs and, for example, the development and promotion of the tourism and cultural sector (see Appendix, Tables 4 and 5).

4.2 Topic Modelling, Filtering and Data Mining

Competitiveness of Companies (Dataset 1)
Based on the themes identified through Topic Modeling with LDA, five main KSA have emerged for the enhancement and development of the agri-food chains and rural development sector:

Technological Innovation and Digitalization of the Agri-Food Sector. This strategy focuses on integrating advanced technologies into the agri-food sector. It includes the use of artificial intelligence, IoT (Internet of Things), blockchain, and smart sensors to improve agricultural production, optimize resources, and ensure product traceability. Additionally, blockchain technology enables full transparency in the agri-food supply chain, ensuring product quality and origin. Companies investing in this strategy aim to reduce operational costs, increase sustainability, and enhance competitiveness in international markets.

Sustainability and Organic Farming. The growing focus on sustainability has led many companies to invest in organic and regenerative farming practices. This strategy involves reducing chemical inputs, implementing crop rotation, and promoting agricultural techniques that preserve soil fertility. Businesses adopt organic certifications to enhance product value and appeal to environmentally conscious consumers. Organic production is often linked to short supply chains and local markets, reducing the environmental impact associated with logistics and transportation.

Development of Short Supply Chains and Local Markets. Short supply chains are a key strategy for ensuring fair income for farmers and promoting a more sustainable consumption model. This approach encourages direct sales of agricultural products, eliminating intermediaries and allowing producers to achieve higher profit margins. Key tools include farmers' markets, solidarity purchasing groups (GAS), and digital platforms for direct sales. Consumers are increasingly favoring local products to minimize environmental impact while ensuring freshness and quality.

Promotion of Typical Products and Made in Italy. Italy's rich food and wine heritage represents a distinctive economic and cultural asset. This strategy focuses on promoting PDO (Protected Designation of Origin), PGI (Protected Geographical Indication), and

Slow Food Presidium products, with the goal of enhancing the international recognition of Made in Italy. Participation in trade fairs, events, and marketing campaigns is encouraged to increase the perceived value of these products. Agri-food companies are also investing in food and wine tourism, offering immersive experiences linked to the production and tasting of local specialties.

Circular Economy and Food Waste Reduction. The circular economy applied to the agri-food sector aims to reduce waste throughout the supply chain. Strategies may include the reuse of agricultural by-products, the transformation of surplus food into new products, and the adoption of biodegradable and compostable packaging. Innovative resource management models are being developed to minimize environmental impact and maximize efficiency. Leading companies are investing in biotechnologies to recover nutrients from waste, transforming them into natural fertilizers or biofuels. These strategies represent the main development pathways for the agri-food sector, with a strong focus on innovation, sustainability, and the promotion of Italy's agri-food heritage.

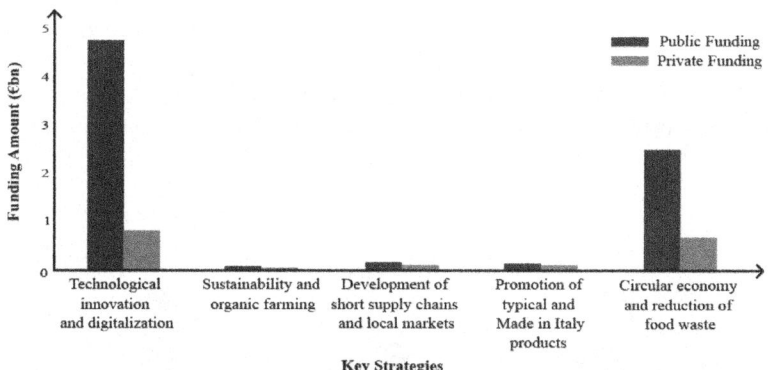

Fig. 6. "Competitiveness of companies" thematic scope: key strategies and related funding (Source: Authors' elaboration on OpenCoesione data consulted on February 2025, processed using AI)

Analyzing the aggregated public and private funding for each key strategy reveals (Fig. 6) that the majority of funds have been concentrated in Technological Innovation and Digitalization and Circular Economy and Food Waste Reduction, with a predominant share coming from public funding. In contrast, the funding allocated to the other key strategies (Sustainability and Organic Farming, Development of Short Supply Chains and Local Markets, and Promotion of Typical Products and Made in Italy) appears to be significantly more limited.

Research and Innovation (Dataset 2)
Based on the themes identified through Topic Modeling with LDA, three main KSA have emerged for the enhancement and development of the agri-food chains and rural development sector:

Production Optimization and Sustainability. This strategy focuses on enhancing agricultural efficiency while reducing environmental impact through precision farming, circular production models, and renewable energy. Techniques such as crop rotation, organic farming, and IoT-based monitoring optimize resource use and improve sustainability. Digital tools like blockchain ensure supply chain transparency, while public and private investments accelerate the adoption of eco-friendly solutions. Public and private support for these projects is essential to accelerate the adoption of sustainable solutions and enhance the resilience of the agri-food sector.

Product Development and Market Expansion. Innovation in new food products and market expansion is driven by functional, organic, and plant-based foods, responding to changing consumer preferences. Companies may invest in alternative proteins, sustainable packaging, and AI-driven personalized nutrition. In addition, strategies like digital marketing, e-commerce, and international certifications support global competitiveness, with funding helping businesses enter emerging markets and scale innovative solutions. Thanks to public and private funding, agri-food businesses can test new solutions, enter emerging markets, and enhance sector competitiveness, addressing sustainability and global food security challenges.

Technology Integration and Food Safety. Advanced technologies like blockchain, AI, and IoT enhance food safety and quality, ensuring traceability and fraud prevention. Public and private funding enables large-scale adoption, reinforcing global food security. With public and private funding, these innovations can be implemented on a large scale, improving food quality and safety worldwide.

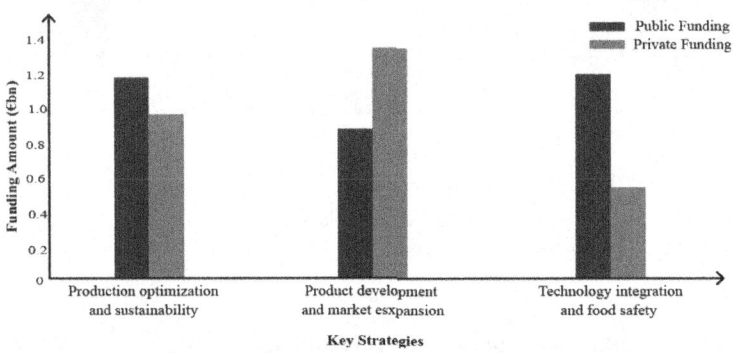

Fig. 7. "Research and Innovation" thematic scope: key strategies and related funding (Source: Authors' elaboration on OpenCoesione data consulted on February 2025, processed using AI)

Analyzing the aggregated public and private funding for each key strategy reveals (Fig. 7) that the most significant investments are directed toward Production Optimization & Sustainability and Product Development & Market Expansion. Notably, private funding plays a dominant role in Product Development & Market Expansion, highlighting strong market-driven interest in this field.

5 Conclusion

Assuming the challenge of shaping a stronger strategy for territorial enhancement—beyond the financing of projects—inner areas can greatly benefit from the support of Academia in multiple ways [2–4, 24]. Previous research [5, 8, 16, 20] demonstrated how academic institutions can effectively help these territories by: (i) addressing the lack of data and information at the municipal level; (ii) identifying opportunities and threats within the territorial context; (iii) developing and sharing coherent design concepts; and (iv) supporting local actors in making strategic decisions within complex frameworks. This study further explores how Academia can contribute to the Strategy-shaping process, especially during the participatory planning, helping local actors articulate actions, priorities and align strategic actions.

Within the "B4R research project", the Polito RU adopted a collaboration-based approach [20]: this not only enabled meaningful knowledge exchange with local actors in Alta Valsesia [13] but also provided a valuable contribution during the territorial engagement formulation of the Valsesia SNAI strategy. While in many cases, strategies and interventions are defined primarily at the political level, the collaborative method used in this context proved particularly effective in the initial stages of local actors' engagement. However, the process fell short of its potential: early drafts of strategic actions and related impacts (including economic effects) showed limited coherence between proposed initiatives, identified vulnerabilities, and actual territorial potential.

This paper focuses on the ongoing process of defining the Valsesia SNAI strategy. It highlights how, starting from lacking thematic scopes identified in Piedmont's 2014–2020 SNAI programmes, past national funding experiences can be analysed to identify relevant typology of interventions and potential financial allocations—thus informing and guiding Local Authorities in enhancing the competitiveness of SMEs in the Agri-food chains and rural development sector.

Despite the wide amount of available national-level data (more than one million records and about 200 variables), the analysis of funded projects cannot rely on open data. A cross-analysis with the underlying strategies is needed, particularly to examine the detailed content within individual project records.

Furthermore, the ministerial classifications used for reporting purposes are not effective in analysing the replicability of actions. Designed primarily for transparency and statistical reporting, they lack the depth needed for strategic insights.

In the two analysed thematic scopes (*Competitiveness of companies* and *Research and innovation*), key variables that would be crucial for scaling up actions—such as company size, industry sector, or level of internationalization—are not directly accessible through the existing database. This limitation was addressed using AI, which provided valuable strategic insights (KSA) from the two subsamples, that can effectively inform actions aimed at revitalizing local economies.

By providing a roadmap for evidence-based decision-making, the research demonstrates how AI-driven approaches can enhance policy effectiveness, ensuring that future funding programs align with local development needs. The insights generated from the case study offer valuable lessons for other inner areas facing similar challenges, ultimately contributing to a more strategic and impact-oriented approach to regional policy design.

Future research directions include:

- in the short term: further project-specific studies, particularly final degree projects emerging from the summer school initiative named "Socio-Economic Challenges for Inner Areas and Fragile Territories: a Bridge between Italy and Virginia";
- in the long term: a critical review of the final Valsesia SNAI strategy, followed by authors' methodological structuring of the entire process. This new structuring should move beyond reliance on individual consultants' expertise and instead draw on lessons learned from data, capitalizing on successful experiences already identified as strategic in other fragile areas.

Appendix

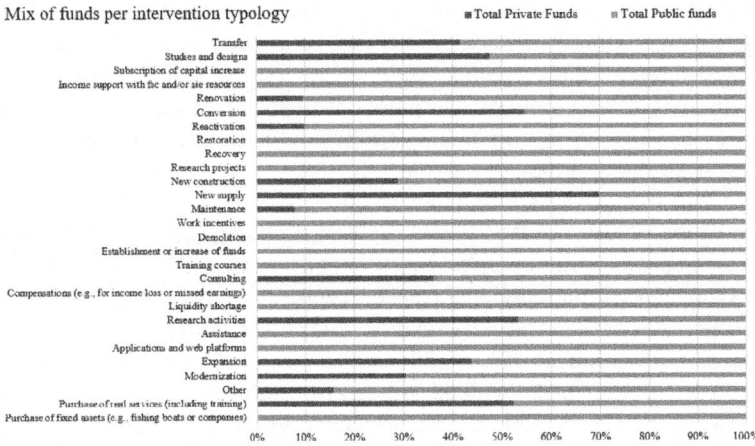

Fig. 8. Dataset 1 - Total public funding and number of interventions per typology (Source: authors' elaboration)

Table 2. Dataset 1 - Interventions and funds split by harmonized category (Source: Authors' elaboration using AI)

CUP_DESCR_CATEGORIA[a]	Total Private funding (M€)	Total Public funding (M€)	Total implemented costs (M€)	Average Funded Amount (€)
Other structures, works, and infrastructures	545 €	1.519 €	908 €	422.143,50 €
Other services for businesses and the community	113 €	679 €	444 €	310.368,90 €
Technologies and innovation (ICT, new materials, energy, good practices, transfer, etc.)	209 €	1.117 €	485 €	264.671 €
Cultural, tourism and recreational services/infrastructures	93 €	525 €	393 €	349.494 €
Agricultural and forestry investments (production, energy, aquaculture, irrigation, etc.)	236 €	952 €	597 €	281.134 €
Health, social, and education services/infrastructure	39 €	168 €	142 €	217.489 €
Training and employment support	24 €	94 €	70 €	178.171 €
Administrative support, governance, technical assistance	6 €	29 €	26 €	141.588 €
University and research	- €	30 €	30 €	30.544.882 €
Environmental protection and energy transition	41 €	217 €	120 €	224.985 €

(*continued*)

Table 2. (*continued*)

CUP_DESCR_CATEGORIA[a]	Total Private funding (M€)	Total Public funding (M€)	Total implemented costs (M€)	Average Funded Amount (€)
Transport and logistics	38 €	453 €	399 €	1.799.569 €
Commerce and industrial support structures	407 €	953 €	1.038 €	166.719 €
Total	**2.574 €**	**7.506 €**	**5.650 €**	**234.740 €**

[a]The following list identifies the new classification, which is more effective than the ministerial one, and specifies which associations have been made to reduce the range of the field CUP_DESCR_CATEGORIA:

Other structures, works, and infrastructures: includes miscellaneous infrastructures, urban furniture, non-specific public works | *Other services for businesses and the community*: groups various support services to SMEs, local authorities, and the public; | *Technologies and innovation*: includes ICT, energy, new materials, transfer of best practices, smart systems; |*Cultural, tourism and recreational services/infrastructures*: combines investments in tourism, culture, leisure, and related infrastructure; | *Agricultural and forestry investments*: covers aquaculture, irrigation, protected crops, forestry, etc.; | *Health, social, and education services/infrastructure*: includes schools, hospitals, social housing, and public health;| *Training and employment support*: all measures for education, training, lifelong learning, and labor market access; | *Administrative support and technical assistance*: includes public administration, evaluations, and institutional transparency; | *University and research*: kept distinct as a strategic sector; | *Environmental protection and energy transition*: includes green infrastructure, renewable energy, environmental protection;

Transport and logistics: roads, ports, rail, logistics and connected infrastructure; | *Commerce and industrial support structures*: investments supporting commerce, industrial areas, business equipment.

Table 3. Datatset 1 - Interventions and funds split by harmonized expenditure category (Source: Authors' elaboration using AI)

OC_DESCR_CATEGORIA_SPESA[a]	Total Public funding (€)	Number of interventions	Average Funded Amount (€)
Other (miscellaneous expenditures and unspecified investments)	2.521 M€	6.555	384.608,30 €
Infrastructure and development for SMEs (including commercial infrastructure, social infrastructure, and urban regeneration projects)	236 M€	82	2.882.386,06 €
Productive investments in SMEs (including energy efficiency, research, and business support services)	1.107 M€	1.421	779.371,41 €

(*continued*)

Table 3. (*continued*)

OC_DESCR_CATEGORIA_SPESA[a]	Total Public funding (€)	Number of interventions	Average Funded Amount (€)
Research, innovation, and entrepreneurship support for SMEs	1.626 M€	1.037	1.568.415,13 €
Investments in enterprises directly connected to research and innovation	497 M€	32	15.539.726,40 €
Cluster and business network support (mainly for SMEs)	73 M€	200	364.146,81 €
Support for environmentally sustainable production processes in SMEs	1 M€	4	365.284,72 €
Self-employment and entrepreneurship support	104 M€	1.316	78.824,55 €
Development and promotion of tourism, cultural, and creative industries	203 M€	1.945	104.318,05 €
Total	**7.506 M€**	**31.976**	**234.739,64 €**

[a]The following list identifies the new classification, which is more effective than the ministerial one, and specifies which associations have been made to reduce the range of the field OC_DESCR_CATEGORIA_SPESA:

Support for research, innovation, and SMEs: included incentives, support measures, and innovation-related assistance; | *Research and innovation activities*: combined R&D activities from public and private research centers, including networking; | *Research and innovation infrastructures*: merged public and private research infrastructures, including science parks and healthcare facilities; | *Investments in research infrastructure and equipment*: unified investments in research-related infrastructure for SMEs and large enterprises; | *Productive investments and technology transfer*: combined investments in productive activities and technology transfer initiatives; | *Research and innovation processes*: merged innovation activities in SMEs and large enterprises, including technology transfer and cooperation; | *Support for clusters and business networks*: consolidated all measures related to business clusters and networks; | *Higher education and skills development*: grouped all initiatives aimed at improving education and workforce skills; | *Urban and rural regeneration*: kept as a distinct category.

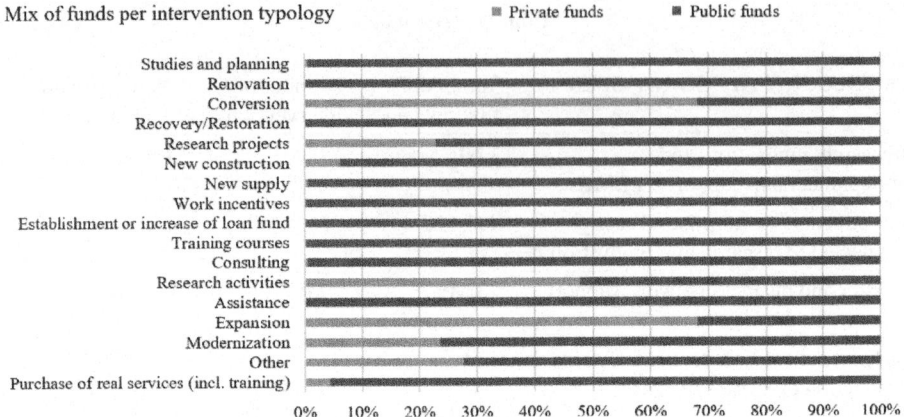

Fig. 9 - Dataset 2 - Percentage of private and public funds per intervention's typology (Source: authors' elaboration)

Table 4. Dataset 2 - Interventions and funds split by harmonized categories (Source: Authors' elaboration using AI)

CUP_DESCR_CATEGORIA[a]	Total Private funding (M€)	Total Public funding (M€)	Total implemented costs (M€)	Average Funded Amount (€)
Other research and technologies (chemical, mechanical, general)	1.950 €	3.983 €	2.946 €	534.929 €
Biotechnologies and health (human health, medical research, healthcare innovation)	134 €	435 €	90 €	647.057 €
Environment and territory (protection, exploration, planning)	93 €	282 €	62 €	881.136 €
Innovation, production, and technology transfer	254 €	864 €	474 €	351.023 €
Industrial, agricultural, and energy production technologies	154 €	665 €	288 €	1.080.764 €

(*continued*)

Table 4. (*continued*)

CUP_DESCR_CATEGORIA[a]	Total Private funding (M€)	Total Public funding (M€)	Total implemented costs (M€)	Average Funded Amount (€)
Experimentation, diversification, and product validation	30 €	72 €	19 €	507.455 €
Advanced technologies (aerospace, materials, telecommunications, IT)	222 €	562 €	104 €	703.396 €
Total	**2.697 €**	**6.150 €**	**3.722 €**	**588.948 €**

[a]The following list identifies the new classification, which is more effective than the ministerial one, and specifies which associations have been made to reduce the range of the field CUP_DESCR_CATEGORIA:
Other research and technologies: grouped chemical, mechanical, and general research technologies; | *Biotechnologies and health*: merged biotechnology, general health, and healthcare innovation; | *Environment and territory*: combined protection, exploration, and environmental planning.; | *Innovation, production, and technology transfer*: unified innovation processes and technology transfer activities; | *Industrial, agricultural, and energy production technologies*: consolidated production technologies related to industry, agriculture, and energy; | *Experimentation, diversification, and product validation*: grouped activities related to product experimentation and development; | *Advanced technologies*: integrated aerospace, materials, telecommunications, and IT technologies.

Table 5. Dataset 2 - Interventions and funds split by harmonized expenditure category (Source: Authors' elaboration using AI)

OC_DESCR_CATEGORIA_SPESA[a]	Total Public funding (€)	Number of interventions	Average Funded Amount (€)
Support for research, innovation, and SMEs	438.341.284 €	1.063	412.362 €
Research and innovation activities in public and private centers (including networking)	3.026.802.632 €	3.838	788.641 €
Research and innovation infrastructures (public and private, including science parks and healthcare)	388.878.991 €	161	2.415.397 €
Investments in research-related infrastructure and equipment (SMEs and large enterprises)	436.627.900 €	1.015	430.175 €

(*continued*)

Table 5. (*continued*)

OC_DESCR_CATEGORIA_SPESA[a]	Total Public funding (€)	Number of interventions	Average Funded Amount (€)
Productive investments and technology transfer for SMEs and enterprises	435.807.277 €	902	483.157 €
Research and innovation processes in SMEs and large enterprises	879.855.964 €	2.242	392.442 €
Support for clusters and business networks (mainly benefiting SMEs)	591.233.222 €	803	736.280 €
Improving higher education to increase participation and education levels	38.698.818 €	111	348.638 €
Urban and rural regeneration	915.049 €	2	457.525 €
Total	**6.149.796.392 €**	**10.442**	**588.948 €**

[a]The following list identifies the new classification, which is more effective than the ministerial one, and specifies which associations have been made to reduce the range of the field OC_DESCR_CATEGORIA_SPESA:

Support for research, innovation, and SMEs: included incentives, support measures, and innovation-related assistance; | *Research and innovation activities*: combined R&D activities from public and private research centers, including networking; | *Research and innovation infrastructures*: merged public and private research infrastructures, including science parks and healthcare facilities; | *Investments in research infrastructure and equipment*: unified investments in research-related infrastructure for SMEs and large enterprises; | *Productive investments and technology transfer*: combined investments in productive activities and technology transfer initiatives; | *Research and innovation processes*: merged innovation activities in SMEs and large enterprises, including technology transfer and cooperation; | *Support for clusters and business networks*: consolidated all measures related to business clusters and networks; | *Higher education and skills development*: grouped all initiatives aimed at improving education and workforce skills; | *Urban and rural regeneration*: kept as a distinct category.

References

1. Bacci, E., et al.: La sfida dell'accessibilità nelle aree interne: riflessioni a partire dalla Valle Arroscia. TERRITORIO **96** (2021). https://doi.org/10.3280/tr2021-096007
2. Calabrò, F., Cassalia, G., Lorè, I.: A project of enhancement and integrated management: the cultural heritage agency of Locride. In: Calabrò, F., Della Spina, L., Piñeira Mantiñán, M.J. (eds.) NMP 2022. LNNS, vol. 482, pp. 278–288. Springer, Cham (2022). https://doi.org/10.1007/978-3-031-06825-6_27
3. Calabrò, F., Mafrici, F., Meduri, T.: The valuation of unused public buildings in support of policies for the inner areas. the application of SostEc model in a case study in Condofuri (Reggio Calabria, Italy). In: Bevilacqua, C., Calabrò, F., Della Spina, L. (eds.) NMP 2020. SIST, vol. 178, pp. 566–579. Springer, Cham (2021). https://doi.org/10.1007/978-3-030-48279-4_54
4. Campolo, D., et al.: A cultural route on the trail of Greek monasticism in Calabria. Smart Innov. Syst. Technol. **101**, 475–483 (2019). https://doi.org/10.1007/978-3-319-92102-0_50/FIGURES/4

5. Curto, R., et al.: A multicriteria decision aid perspective that guides an incremental development of knowledge and fosters relationships and decisions. EURO J. Decis. Processes **10**, 100023 (2022). https://doi.org/10.1016/j.ejdp.2022.100023
6. Falush, D., et al.: Inference of population structure using multilocus genotype data: linked loci and correlated allele frequencies. Genetics **164**(4), 1567 (2003). https://doi.org/10.1093/GENETICS/164.4.1567
7. Ferretti, M., et al.: Atlante – BRANDING4RESILIENCE. Ritratto di quattro territori interni italiani (2024)
8. Ferretti, M., et al.: Branding4Resilience: explorative and collaborative approaches for inner territories. Sustainability **14**(18) (2022). https://doi.org/10.3390/su141811235
9. Grieco, B., Somma, M., Raiola, M.L., Sacco, S., Zizzania, P., Cerreta, M.: A decision support system for cultural and territorial infrastructures: a place-based and community-driven strategy in Inner Italy. In: Gervasi, O., Murgante, B., Garau, C., Taniar, D., C. Rocha, A.M.A., Faginas Lago, M.N. (eds.) ICCSA 2024. LNCS, vol. 14820, pp. 373–387. Springer, Cham (2024). https://doi.org/10.1007/978-3-031-65285-1_24
10. Hadjou, L., Duquenne, M.N.: A theoretical and methodological approach of fragile areas: the cases of Greek regions crossed by the Egnatia road. Reg. Sci. Inq. **5**, 2 (2013)
11. Han, H., Laiô, S.K.: Decision network: a planning tool for making multiple, linked decisions. Environ. Plan. B. Plan. Des. **38**, 1 (2011). https://doi.org/10.1068/b35153
12. Li, H., et al.: Analytical framework for integrating resources, morphology, and function of rural system resilience—an empirical study of 386 villages. J. Clean. Prod. **365** (2022). https://doi.org/10.1016/j.jclepro.2022.132738
13. Malavasi, G., Barreca, A., Rebaudengo, M., Rolando, D.: A stakeholder analysis to support resilient strategies in the Alta Valsesia inner area. In: Gervasi, O., et al. (eds.) ICCSA 2023. LNCS, vol. 14106, pp. 262–276. Springer, Cham (2023). https://doi.org/10.1007/978-3-031-37111-0_19
14. Marucci, A., et al.: Marginality assessment: computational applications on Italian municipalities. Sustainability **12**(8) (2020). https://doi.org/10.3390/SU12083250
15. Montoyo, A., et al.: Geo.IA: artificial geo-intelligence platform to Solve Citizens problems and facilitate strategic decision making in the public administration. In: CEUR Workshop Proceedings, vol. 3729, pp. 1–5 (2024)
16. Norese, M.F., et al.: DIKEDOC: a multicriteria methodology to organise and communicate knowledge. Ann. Oper. Res. **325**, 2 (2023). https://doi.org/10.1007/s10479-022-04711-6
17. Pritchard, J.K., et al.: Inference of population structure using multilocus genotype data. Genetics **155**(2), 945–959 (2000). https://doi.org/10.1093/GENETICS/155.2.945
18. Rolando, D., et al.: Managing knowledge to enhance fragile territories: resilient strategies for the Alta Valsesia area in Italy. In: International Forum on Knowledge Asset Dynamics: Knowledge Drivers for Resilience and Transformation, pp. 1421–1440 (2023)
19. Rolando, D., et al.: The enhancement of the Alta Valsesia territorial potential: a collaboration-based approach between academia and local actors. In: Computational Science and Its Applications – ICCSA 2024 Workshops, Hanoi, Vietnam (2024)
20. Rolando, D., Barreca, A., Rebaudengo, M.: The SAVV+P method: integrating qualitative and quantitative analyses to evaluate the territorial potential. In: Gervasi, O., et al. (eds.) ICCSA 2023. LNCS, vol. 14106, pp. 249–261. Springer, Cham (2023). https://doi.org/10.1007/978-3-031-37111-0_18
21. Rolando, D., Rebaudengo, M., Barreca, A., et al.: La valutazione delle potenzialità territoriali attraverso un approccio multidimensionale per le aree interne. LaborEst **25**, 24–29 (2022)
22. Shakhsi-Niaei, M., Iranmanesh, S.H.: Intelligent systems in project planning. Intell. Syst. Ref. Libr. **87** (2015). https://doi.org/10.1007/978-3-319-17906-3_21

23. Spatari, G., Lorè, I., Viglianisi, A., Calabrò, F.: Economic feasibility of an integrated program for the enhancement of the Byzantine heritage in the Aspromonte National Park. the case of Staiti. In: Calabrò, F., Della Spina, L., Piñeira Mantiñán, M.J. (eds.) NMP 2022. LNNS, vol. 482, pp. 313–323. Springer, Cham (2022). https://doi.org/10.1007/978-3-031-06825-6_30
24. Torriani, C., et al.: Exploratory Data analysis to support the second SNAI programming cycle. Submitted to Aestimum (2025)
25. Torriani, C., Barreca, A., Rebaudengo, M., Rolando, D.: Projects and funding in Italian inner areas: learning from the 2014–2020 programming of the SNAI national strategy. In: Gervasi, O., et al. (eds.) ICCSA 2023. LNCS, vol. 14106, pp. 233–248. Springer, Cham (2023). https://doi.org/10.1007/978-3-031-37111-0_17
26. Trovato, M.R., Nasca, L.: An axiology of weak areas: the estimation of an index of abandonment for the definition of a cognitive tool to support the enhancement of inland areas in Sicily. Land **11**(12) (2022). https://doi.org/10.3390/land11122268

Renewable Energy Communities as a Tool for a Just Green Transition in Inner Areas: A Pilot Project in Sardinia (Italy)

Ivan Blečić, Alessandro Sebastiano Carrus, Eleonora Congiu, Giuseppe Desogus, and Valeria Saiu[✉]

University of Cagliari, Via Santa Croce 67, Cagliari, Italy
{ivanblecic,alessandros.carrus,eleonora.congiu,gdesogus,
v.saiu}@unica.it

Abstract. Access to energy is a crucial global challenge that influences economic development, environmental sustainability, and social equity. Renewable Energy Communities (RECs) have emerged as a transformative model to promote local engagement in renewable energy initiatives, particularly in rural and marginalized areas. This study examines the role of RECs in Inner Areas, with a specific focus on Sardinia, Italy, highlighting their potential to enhance local energy security, reduce costs, and foster economic revitalization. While European and national policies, such as the Green Deal and the Italian National Recovery and Resilience Plan (PNRR), have allocated funds to support RECs, their implementation in Inner Areas remains limited due to regulatory complexities, administrative hurdles, and financial constraints. By presenting the REC design process in this context, the study explores both the opportunities and critical challenges that persist. To assess the feasibility of RECs, we propose a multi-scenario simulator designed to support decision-making by performing hourly calculations of energy flows, financial cash flows, and environmental benefits. This tool enables a preliminary evaluation of REC profitability by simulating different community configurations and considering key variables such as energy production, self-consumption, storage dynamics, and surplus energy management in compliance with Italian regulations. The study highlights the importance of strengthening institutional support, enhancing community education, and developing policy frameworks that facilitate the creation of collaborative territorial networks.

Keywords: Inner Areas · Renewable Energy Communities · multi-scenario simulations

1 Introduction

Ensuring access to clean and affordable energy is a crucial challenge that intersects with broader goals of sustainability, equity, and economic resilience. Current global and European strategies, such as the UN 2030 Agenda [1] and the European Green Deal [2], emphasize that the transition from fossil fuels to renewable sources must be inclusive and territorially balanced. This shift requires not only technological innovation but also strong engagement of local communities and institutions to ensure a just and participatory green transition [3–5].

In this context, Renewable Energy Communities (RECs), introduced by the EU Renewable Energy Directive (RED II) [41], offer a transformative model of decentralized energy production. These communities empower local actors through democratic participation, encouraging energy autonomy, reducing vulnerability to energy poverty, and stimulating economic regeneration, particularly in rural and marginal territories.

Peripheral regions, especially Europe's so-called Inner Areas – characterized by demographic decline, limited services, and economic marginalization – have a strategic role to play. Here, RECs can counteract spatial inequalities by mobilizing local resources and fostering community-led energy planning. However, meaningful implementation requires not only infrastructure, but also sustained institutional support, education, and inclusive governance to build public trust and participation.

In Italy, several recent policies—such as the National Recovery and Resilience Plan (PNRR) and Regional Operational Programmes—are starting to recognize and support the potential of RECs in Inner Areas. Nevertheless, further research is needed to evaluate their actual impact and to identify remaining obstacles. Understanding how these measures contribute to a more just and inclusive energy system is essential for promoting a truly equitable green transition.

This study focuses on the practical application of a simulation tool designed to support the development of Renewable Energy Communities (RECs) in marginal areas, with a specific case study in the municipality of Simala, located in the Inner Areas of Sardinia, Italy. The objective is to evaluate the feasibility and potential benefits of REC initiatives in territories that are often underserved, highlighting the specific challenges faced by peripheral regions—such as regulatory barriers, lack of technical expertise, and limited financial resources.

The proposed tool aims to assist local stakeholders—including small municipalities, policymakers, and technical partners—in estimating shared energy flows, cost savings, and revenue distributions within RECs. In doing so, it supports the planning and expansion of energy communities in nearby villages, promoting a more equitable distribution of renewable energy opportunities.

By addressing the gap between national REC policy and on-the-ground implementation in disadvantaged areas, this study contributes to the broader goal of a just green transition, a concept that underlines the importance of leaving no community behind in the energy transition process.

The paper is structured as follows: Sect. 2 outlines the research design; Sect. 3 presents the materials and methods, including Inner Areas and REC regulatory context; Sect. 4 describes the multi-scenario simulation tool; Sect. 4 introduces the case study of Simala; Sect. 5 present the results; and Sect. 6 discuss the implications of case study application and concludes with final remarks.

2 Research Design

This contribution aims at presenting the preliminary outcomes of the valuable support that a research team of the University of Cagliari is providing to the Municipality of a small rural village called Simala, sited in an inner area of the Sardinia Region, to establish a new renewable energy community. The process herein described may be summarized through the following crucial steps:

1. **Citizen engagement through public meetings:** this stage of the process turned out to be crucial to explain the main operating principles of RECs to common unskilled citizens and, at the same time, involve them in the project
2. **Data collection:** Directly during public meetings and also indirectly through subsequent contacts with interested people, useful data related to potential consumption and production profiles of the potential REC members are collected
3. **Multi-scenario simulations:** Based on collected data from the involved citizens and on a specific set of input data, multi-scenario simulations are performed through an excel-based simulator (implemented for this specific purpose) to assess both the energy and the economic balance of various REC configurations.

All steps mentioned above are fundamental to support the REC promoter to make informed decisions and enable the success of the REC project.

3 Materials and Methods

3.1 Renewable Energy Communities and Inner Areas

Access to energy is both a critical challenge and a major opportunity in today's world, shaping economic development, environmental sustainability, and social equity. Global and European policies emphasize that the shift from fossil fuels to renewable energy is not just a technological transformation but a multidimensional process that must integrate social, economic, and environmental considerations. In this context, international frameworks such as the UN 2030 Agenda – particularly Sustainable Development Goal 7 (SDG 7) [6] – and European initiatives like the Green Deal [2] highlight the importance of a balanced territorial development [7] and the need for collaborative action among governments, businesses, and civil society.

To ensure a more resilient and inclusive energy system, it is essential to develop decentralized and local and community-driven renewable energy solutions [8]. These measures not only strengthen local resilience and reduce dependence on external energy providers but also drive economic growth, combat energy poverty and ensure that vulnerable communities are not left behind in the transition process.

Within this framework, Renewable Energy Communities (RECs), formally introduced in Europe by the Renewable Energy Directive 2018/2001 (RED II) [9], emerge as a transformative model. RECs promote local engagement in renewable energy initiatives through social innovation and democratic participation, empowering communities to take an active role in a sustainable and inclusive energy future [10]. By decentralizing energy production and distribution, these communities enhance local energy security, lower energy costs, combat energy poverty, and stimulate economic revitalization.

In this context, rural and marginal territories – often overlooked in traditional energy planning – play a crucial role in the development and expansion of RECs initiatives [11]. In particular, areas identified by the European Union as "Inner Peripheries" which face challenges such as demographic decline, inadequate infrastructure, and economic marginalization, are increasingly recognized for their untapped potential in this transition [12, 13]. In these contexts, RECs can offer a solution to de-territorialization process, which has led to the concentration of services and activities in metropolitan areas and the resulting impoverishment of peripheral territories [14, 15]. Small municipalities, which characterize the settlement type in Inner Areas, can directly manage renewable energy infrastructure and facilitate partnerships between local stakeholders. Furthermore, REC initiatives can create new employment opportunities in the renewable energy sector, fostering local economic diversification and enhancing energy autonomy.

The successful implementation of energy communities in Inner Areas requires more than just technological infrastructure. It necessitates strengthened community education, long-term institutional support, and policies that empower local actors to take ownership of energy transitions. The protests against large-scale renewable energy projects, which were implemented without adequate local involvement, have sparked significant resistance and low public acceptance [16, 17].

These events highlight the importance of ensuring local engagement and participation in energy planning, as ignoring community concerns can lead to opposition and undermine the success of renewable energy initiatives. In contrast, bottom-up energy initiatives ensure local engagement and participation in energy planning, leveraging territorial resources, and fostering energy literacy, as an essential element encompassing awareness, attitude, and behavior toward sustainable energy consumption [18].

In Italy, the Inner Areas, a specific category of Inner Peripheries [19–21], play a crucial role in the development of RECs. Although the 2014–2020 National Strategy for Inner Areas (SNAI) adopted in 2012 to revitalize these areas, does not explicitly consider this potential [22–26], the Italian National Recovery and Resilience Plan (PNRR), through Mission 2 "Green Revolution and Ecological Transition" (Investment 1.2), allocates 2.2 billion euros to establish renewable energy systems with a capacity of at least 200 kW in municipalities with populations under 5,000 inhabitants [27], many of which are located in the Inner Areas. These interventions enable an alternative approach to traditional renewable energy production, which often depends on large-scale systems that occupy vast agricultural land, compromising both its productivity and landscape value [28–30].

Other recent policy developments in Italy have demonstrated a growing institutional commitment to expanding Renewable Energy Communities (RECs) in Inner Areas. Notably, during the 2021–2027 planning cycle, several Regional Operational Plans (POR) have included the establishment of RECs as a specific objective, allocating funds to promote them. For instance, regions such as Lombardy, Emilia-Romagna, Lazio, Campania, Sicily, and Sardinia have launched initiatives to support the development of RECs, with resources partially provided by EU structural funds [31].

However, further research is indeed necessary to evaluate the effectiveness of these measures in overcoming existing challenges. While the transposition of the enabling framework for RECs has progressed, and specific measures have been introduced in the national support scheme for renewables, an assessment of barriers and potential for the development of energy communities is still missing. These efforts can foster a more inclusive and diversified energy landscape, ensuring sustainable development while empowering Inner Areas.

While the transposition of the enabling framework for RECs has progressed, and specific measures have been introduced in the national support scheme for renewables, an assessment of barriers and potential for the development of energy communities is still missing. An analysis conducted by the authors using data from "Ricerca sul Sistema Energetico - RSE" (Research on the Energy System), the research company of "Gestore Servizi Energetici - GSE" (Energy System Operator), updated as of March 2025, shows that only a small number of municipalities in these regions, classified by SNAI as peripheral or ultra-peripheral areas, have an active REC, 16 out of the 70 RECS nationwide [32].

In this context, Sardinia has 13 RECs, four of which are active, while nine are in the planning or implementation phase. However, only three are located within peripheral areas, highlighting the challenges these regions face. Regulatory complexities, administrative hurdles, limited technical expertise, and financial constraints continue to hinder the feasibility of such initiatives [33]. Efforts in this direction can foster a more inclusive and diversified energy landscape, ensuring sustainable development while empowering Inner Areas. RECs general operating principles.

Renewable Energy Communities (RECs) are citizen-driven energy actions aimed at contributing concretely to the clean energy transition, by increasing public acceptance of renewable energy projects and fighting energy poverty conditions [34].

A REC is a true community of people, which not only may include common households but also small-medium enterprises (SMEs), local or territorial authorities (including local administrations, research and training bodies), religious and third sector bodies which voluntarily become partners to constitute a non-profit legal subject, with the sole aim of producing and sharing energy from renewable sources, obtaining economic, environmental and social benefits for the community.

REC members may assume the following roles in the community:

- *Producers,* which own renewable energy production systems, and they wholly make the produced energy available for the REC
- *Prosumers,* which own renewable energy systems, directly self-consume a quote of the produced energy and feed the surplus energy into the power grid
- *Consumers,* which virtually consume the clean energy supplied by *Producers* and *Prosumers* of the REC.

RECs are yearly rewarded with public economic incentives based on the energy which is virtually consumed by all members (i.e. the so-called *shared energy*). As a matter of fact, the shared energy corresponds to the quote of the surplus energy fed into the grid which is virtually and simultaneously withdrawn from the grid by the REC members. Additionally, *Producers* and *Prosumers* may sell the surplus produced energy to the Energy Services Manager (called GSE). Besides the economic benefits, RECs also generate environmental benefits in terms of avoided CO_2 emissions enabled by the increased production of clean energy. Moreover, ensuring greater accessibility to clean energy also to vulnerable people, RECs may provide a true contribution to the energy poverty fight, thus potentially generating also social collective benefits. Inner areas, due to their specific vulnerabilities, may therefore take strong advantage of RECs economic, environmental and social benefits being involved with a key role in the green transition.

4 Simala's REC: A Case Study

The REC project described in this paper is located in the municipality of Simala, a small town in the central-western part of the Sardinian Region, within the province of Oristano (see Fig. 1). As of 2024, the population has declined to 293 inhabitants from 467 in 1991 [30], reflecting an average annual decrease of 1.2% over the past 32 years. This demographic shift underscores a predominance of elderly residents, primarily retirees, who face a heightened risk of energy poverty.

According to the 2011 ISTAT census, the aging index (the ratio of the over-65 population to the 0–14 age group, multiplied by 100) stands at 383. Additionally, only 2.8% of the population is under the age of six, compared to a regional average of 4.8% and a national figure of 5.6%. Household sizes are shrinking, averaging 2.3 members in 2011, while nearly 30% of elderly residents live alone. Moreover, 43% of households lack a nuclear family structure, consisting of either single-person households or individuals without direct family ties.

The local housing stock is characterized by relatively large units, averaging approximately 126 m^2 per dwelling, with nearly 90% owner-occupied. However, the overall state of conservation is far from optimal. Only 48% of buildings are in good condition – a decline from pre-2011 levels – while nearly 10% are in a state of severe disrepair. Despite a rising potential for use, approaching 30%, the underutilization index exceeds 50%, and due to depopulation, new development is virtually non-existent. In essence, the local housing stock is substantial in relation to the population yet increasingly obsolete and underutilized, with figures well below the Sardinian regional average.

This analysis highlights the urgent need for measures to counteract both depopulation and population aging, as well as the consequent progressive abandonment of residential buildings.

The project of the REC could play a crucial role in addressing these challenges. Reducing energy costs would provide much-needed relief to the predominantly elderly population, which is particularly vulnerable. Furthermore, although the elderly population is generally less familiar with new technologies and tends to resist change [35], they can still play an active role in the efficient operation of an energy community. Their constant presence at home enables more effective management of energy consumption. With proper guidance, they could adopt energy-efficient behaviors that maximize self-consumption of the electricity generated by the REC's systems.

Additionally, establishing an associative entity could help counteract the deterioration of the housing stock. The REC could initiate maintenance programs, serving as a technical support hub for its members and pooling multiple users to reduce renovation costs. This collective approach could foster both economic sustainability and community resilience.

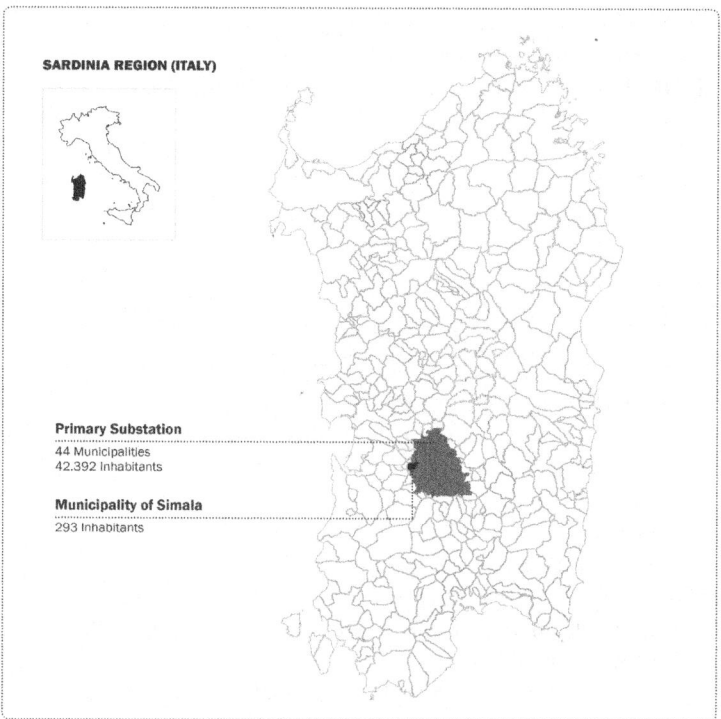

Fig. 1. The Municipality of Simala and its Primary Substation, which serves 44 municipalities.

4.1 Multi-scenario Simulator

Performing technical, economic and environmental analysis is a fundamental step in the establishment pathway of a new REC to preliminarily assess the profitability of a REC project based on an accurate evaluation of the expected economic and environmental benefits for the community, by also considering direct and indirect social impacts. In this regard, it is worth remarking that energy communities are not static entities, as they may go through relevant transformations in their original configuration during their lifecycle. In accordance with the latest Italian regulations [36], new renewable energy communities are entitled to receive from the Italian Energy Services Manager (*i.e.* the so-called GSE) a cash back yearly incentive proportional to the so-called "shared energy" for the next 20 years, and additionally, producers and prosumers may sell the surplus produced energy to the GSE.

All this considered, an accurate simulator may provide a powerful decision support tool to enable an hourly calculation of the REC energy flows, of the related cash flows and of the REC-generated environmental benefits. In this perspective, an Excel-based simulator has been developed to allow multiple-scenario simulations considering different potential REC configurations.

The proposed simulator requires the following input data:

- Number of potential members of the energy community, distinguished by category (producers, prosumers, consumers).
- Energy demand of potential members of the REC (estimated or user-provided).
- Technical data concerning new photovoltaic (PV) systems to be installed (e.g. peak power, Balance Of System - BOS, location and related solar irradiance, tilt, azimuth and number of solar panels).
- Technical data concerning battery energy storage systems (BESS) to be installed (e.g. storage capacity, battery efficiency, depth of discharge, hourly charging and discharging rates).

Based on input data mentioned above, the presented simulator returns the hourly-calculated values of the following energy flows:

- The clean energy produced by the PV systems owned by producers and prosumers of the REC. The energy directly self-consumed by prosumers when the related PV systems are actively operating.
- The energy consumed by consumers and prosumers (when PV system is not fully supplying prosumers loads).
- The energy stored in BESS.
- The surplus produced energy to be sold to the GSE by producers and prosumers.
- The total amount of energy hourly is withdrawn from the electricity distribution network by all REC members.
- The so-called shared energy (*i.e.* the energy virtually shared between REC members, which is hourly calculated as the minimum value between the surplus produced energy injected into the power grid by producers and prosumers, and the energy simultaneously withdrawn from the electricity distribution network by the energy community).

The proposed simulator hourly estimates the produced energy based on the peak power of PV systems, the PV panels efficiency and the solar global irradiance. The solar global irradiance on the tilted and oriented surfaces of PV panels is analytically calculated in compliance with the Italian standard concerning climatic data related to cooling and heating of buildings [37], by taking advantage of PVGIS [38] hourly data concerning the global and the diffuse solar irradiance on the horizontal plane of a typical meteorological year (TMY) dataset selected from a 2005–2020 period.

As far as the estimation of the energy consumed is concerned, the proposed simulator allows to use both user-provided real consumption data and standard consumption profiles, obtained from average consumption values of real consumption data. However, since electricity bills generally present data aggregated by months and time slots, to make energy flows calculation more accurate, hourly coefficients have been first extracted from 12 residential load curves (i.e. three per season, one for working days, the second for days before holidays and the third one for non-working days, made available by Gallanti et al. [39] and then applied to hourly values of residential consumptions. For non-residential users, simulations were based on real monthly electricity consumption data provided by users, broken down by time slot and then evenly distributed hourly.

Hourly values of production and consumption provide in turn an accurate basis for an hourly estimation of the remaining energy flows of the REC (the surplus energy fed into the power grid, the energy withdrawn from the grid and the shared energy). This accurate hourly calculation of expected energy flows allows for an equally precise estimation of expected cash flows. The economic feasibility of potential REC scenarios can thus be assessed based on detailed estimates of the following costs and revenues:

- The initial investment costs (CAPEX) for the installation of new PV systems.
- The operation and maintenance costs (OPEX).
- The money saved in electricity bills deriving from the directly self-consumed energy by *prosumers*.
- The revenues from the surplus produced energy, sold by *producers* and *prosumers*
- The revenues from incentives granted for the *shared energy*.

The proposed simulator assumes a reasonable market electricity price of 0.25 €/kWh to estimate savings in electricity bills. Regarding revenues from the sale of surplus energy, the energy produced by prosumers and producers and injected into the power grid is valued according to the hourly energy zonal price (ZP_h) made available by the Italian Energy Services Operator (GSE). Specifically, the proposed simulator estimates the yearly revenues from the sold energy by using hourly values of the zonal price (ZP_h) for the Sardinia region (*i.e.* the so-called SARD) referred to the 2024 and made publicly available on the GSE portal.

In accordance with the Italian regulations concerning RECs [36], the energy virtually shared between energy community members is subject to a reward tariff ($SE_{rt,h}$) defined by the following formulas:

$$SE_{rt,h} = 60 \frac{€}{MWh} + \left(\min(\max(0; 180 - ZP_h); 40)\right) \frac{€}{MWh} \quad (1)$$

$$SE_{rt,h} = 70 \frac{€}{MWh} + \left(\min(\max(0; 180 - ZP_h); 40)\right) \frac{€}{MWh} \quad (2)$$

$$SE_{rt,h} = 80 \frac{€}{MWh} + \left(\min(\max(0; 180 - ZP_h); 40)\right) \frac{€}{MWh} \quad (3)$$

where the Eq. (1) is used for PV systems with a peak power greater than 600 kW, while the formula (2) applies to systems with a peak power between 200 kW and 600 kW. Expression (3) is adopted for PV systems with a total power lower than or equal to 200 kW. Moreover, the shared energy is also rewarded through an additional tariff of €10.57/MWh (2024 value) to repay the reduction in the use of grid infrastructures. Furthermore, the proposed simulator includes a basic estimation of the potential environmental benefits generated by RECs. Specifically, it calculates the potentially avoided CO_2 emissions by multiplying the total amount of the produced clean energy by a conversion coefficient of 0.702 tCO2/MWh [40].

5 Results

After the engagement activities carried out by the research team, different potential members have been identified and involved in the project. The Municipality may be considered the main promoter of the REC project. Additionally, the Municipality decided to become an active member of the REC, assuming two different roles:

- a *consumer* through its headquarters.
- a *producer*, providing a PV system of about 25 kWp to be installed on the roof of a temporary unused building.

Even though 23 citizens have expressed interest in being involved in the REC project during engagement activities, only three commercial activities and ten families have been identified as potential members as they provided real consumption data from electricity bills. The related annual consumptions are summarized in Table 1.

Table 1. Annual electricity consumption of potential REC members.

Activity	Member type	Consumptions (kWh/year)
Municipality headquarter	Consumer	24740
Cultural center	Consumer	1133
Farm	Consumer	2177
Shop	Consumer	7627
Residential	Consumer	2664
Residential	Consumer	3028
Residential	Consumer	2349
Residential	Consumer	1897
Residential	Consumer	2242
Residential	Consumer	3574
Residential	Consumer	2741
Residential	Consumer	3951
Residential	Consumer	1524
Residential	Consumer	7094

The public and commercial activities have generally an hourly distribution that concentrates electrical loads during the daily hours. The same cannot be observed usually in residential consumers. However, in the specific case of a rural village, a different pattern can be observed. Figure 2 shows the distribution of the annual electrical consumption (2498 kWh/year) of the average residential member of the Simala REC per time slot. It is evident that in Simala residential electrical loads are mainly concentrated during daily hours. This peculiar condition is due to the high percentage of retired old people living in the village of Simala, that occupy houses during the day. This aspect brings a certain population vulnerability to light, but as far as the REC balance is concerned, it is a positive aspect since such load profiles increase the immediate consumption of PV systems production.

The simulation of REC energy balance has been carried out considering a hypothesis of 25 kWp PV, corresponding to the size of the PV system that the Municipality is going to install. The related monthly production is summarized in Fig. 3 even if all energy flows

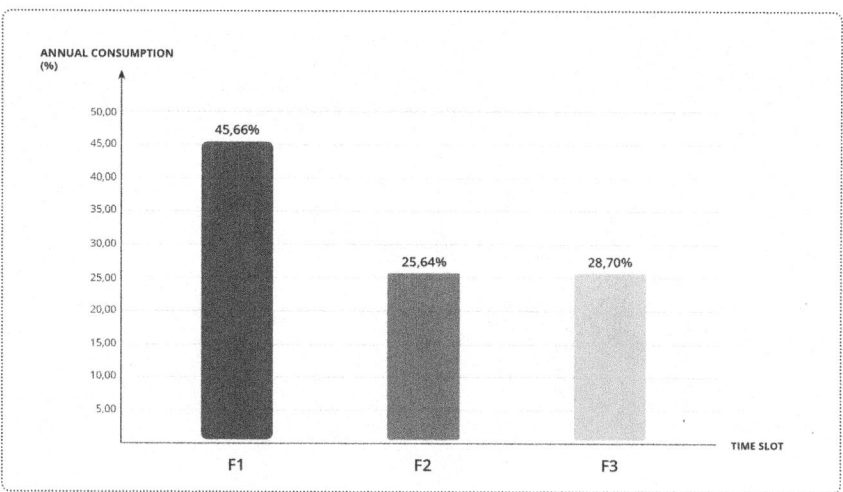

Fig. 2. Annual percentage of electrical consumption of an average residential member per time slot (F1 refers to daily hour in ferial days, F2 evening and Saturday daily hours, F3 nights and Sunday) assumed as standard residential profile in simulations.

(included the produced energy) are hourly estimated. As for the rest of the regional territory, the high insulation makes the use of PV systems for REC quite profitable.

A well-designed and well-balanced energy community should pursue the objective of maximizing the percentage of the energy produced, which is virtually self-consuming by the REC members (i.e. the shared to produced energy ratio). For this aim, three different scenarios have been simulated. The first (Scenario 0) refers to a realistic number of 25 potential members; the second (Scenario 1) foresees an increment of residential members up to 35; the third (Scenario 2) up to 55. For the three scenarios the ratio between shared energy and produced energy is: 84.7%; 92.3%; 98.4%. Considering that the maximum REC potential in terms of virtually sharable energy turned out to be already almost reached with a percentage of 84.7% of the produced energy which resulted to be shared for the first (Scenario 0), the hypothetical number of REC members required to be only slightly increased to finally maximize the shared energy with the third scenario (Scenario 2).

In Fig. 4 the monthly energy flows for the most performing scenario are presented. The balance of REC is optimal since all energy production is simultaneously virtually consumed by REC members within a one-hour time interval. Note that in this peculiar configuration there are no prosumers, so the self-consumed energy is zero.

The next step of simulation has been to check if the optimal energy configuration provides also the best economic outcome. The PV systems installation costs have been neglected since the Municipality is providing for it and it is not charged to the REC. The yearly costs directly attributable to the community are the following: costs for the management and administration of the CER (including maintenance costs of the monitoring platform) assumed equal to 3000 €; rent of the metering devices (50 € per

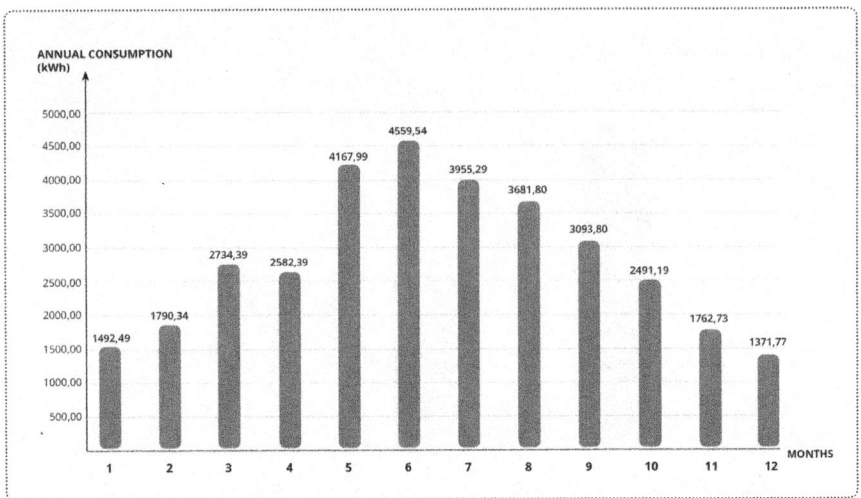

Fig. 3. Monthly energy production of a 25 kWp PV systems in Simala.

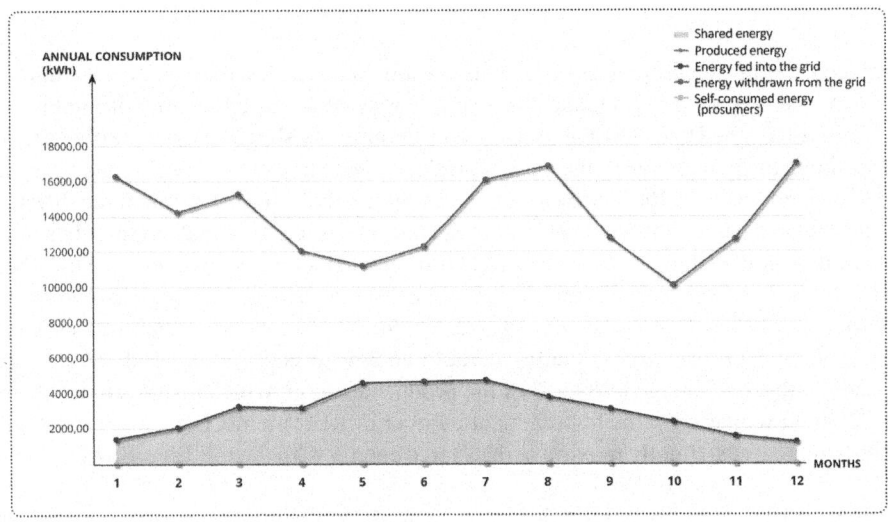

Fig. 4. Monthly energy flows for the most performing scenario (2). The energy produced is fully consumed by the REC.

device). While the platform cost is fixed, the metering devices' increases by the number of members.

According to Italian legislation RECs can have the following sources of revenue: reduction of supply bills (only for prosumer members that in this configuration are absent); incentives for energy fed into the grid and sold to the GSE based on the energy market price in Sardinia (the simulator is able to calculate hourly values and multiply them for hourly production); premium tariff incentives (TIP) calculated on the basis of shared energy. For PV systems with a power ≤200 kWp such as those foreseen for Simala REC, it is 120.0 €/MWh [31]. It is evident that there are fixed costs and costs that depend on the number of members, as well as revenues that depend only on the PV power (feed-in tariff) and revenues that depend on the number of members that affect the shared energy as shown above. The overall cost/revenue balance for different configurations is summarized in Table 2 and Table 3.

Table 2. REC costs analysis per scenario. * The last scenario refers to the doubling of scenario 0 to another village.

Number of residential members	Management and administrative costs (€)	Monitoring system costs (€)	Total (€)
25	3000,00	1250,00	4250,00
35	3000,00	1750,00	4750,00
55	3000,00	2750,00	5750,00
61*	3000,00	3050,00	6050,00

Table 3. REC revenue analysis per scenario. * The last scenario refers to the doubling of scenario 0 to another village.

Number of residential members	Feed-in tariff (€)	Shared energy tariffs (€)	Total (€)
25	3061,42	3932,96	6994,38
35	3061,42	4288,75	7350,17
55	3061,42	4570,61	7632,03
61*	6122,92	7856,72	13979,60

It is evident that both costs and revenues increase by the residential members number. To understand which is more affected by the expansion of REC, the total amount per member has been compared in Table 4.

The last row of the previous tables refers to a scenario where the REC is doubled in another village doubling also the PV power, the public, commercial and residential consumers. While from a mere energy point of view scenario 2 seems to be the most sustainable, an economic analysis shows that expanding the REC within the same context without expanding production is not profitable.

6 Discussion and Concluding Remarks

The advancement of Renewable Energy Communities (RECs) offers a strategic pathway toward a just and inclusive green transition, particularly in Inner Areas that face long-standing economic and infrastructural disadvantages. By promoting community-led, decentralized energy systems, RECs contribute not only to environmental goals but also

Table 4. REC cost/revenue analysis per scenario and member. * The last scenario refers to the doubling of scenario 0 to another village.

Number of residential members	Total costs per member (€)	Total revenues per member (€)	Difference (€)
25	170,00	279,78	109,78
35	135,71	210,01	74,29
55	104,55	138,76	34,22
61*	99,18	229,17	129,99

to social equity and territorial cohesion, key pillars of a sustainable energy transition. RECs can enhance local energy security, reduce dependence on external providers, and generate socio-economic benefits for marginalized territories.

This study has explored the specific challenges and opportunities associated with implementing RECs in marginal territories such as Inner Areas, focusing on the case of Sardinia, Italy. The findings underline that while RECs hold significant transformative potential, their widespread diffusion is still constrained by regulatory complexity, limited administrative capacity, and funding barriers. Small municipalities, in particular, require targeted support to initiate and sustain such initiatives.

The proposed multi-scenario simulation tool represents a concrete step toward addressing these gaps. By enabling local actors to assess the economic, technical, and social dimensions of REC implementation, the tool supports informed decision-making and facilitates tailored energy planning at the local level. Nonetheless, achieving a truly just green transition in Inner Areas will require more than technological solutions. Coordinated policies, long-term institutional commitment, and active community involvement are essential to ensure that no territory is left behind. Future research should deepen the analysis of REC impacts over time, refine participatory governance models, and develop integrated planning approaches that align local energy resilience with broader sustainability objectives. In this perspective, RECs are not just an energy innovation, they are a lever for systemic change, capable of empowering communities and bridging territorial divides within the European green transition.

Acknowledgments. Authors wish to thank the Municipality of Simala, that promoted and financed the study.

Disclosure of Interests. The authors have no competing interests to declare that are relevant to the content of this article.

References

1. United Nations: Resolution A/RES/70/1. Transforming our World: The 2030 Agenda for Sustainable Development. United Nations, New York, NY, USA (2015)
2. European Commission: A European Green Deal (2019). https://ec.europa.eu/info/strategy/priorities-2019-2024/european-green-deal_en. Accessed 25 June 2022

3. Baute, S.: The distributive politics of the green transition: a conjoint experiment on EU climate change mitigation policy. J. Eur. Publ. Policy, 1–29 (2024). https://doi.org/10.1080/13501763.2024.2304609
4. Hussain, S.A., Razi, F., Hewage, K., Sadiq, R.: The perspective of energy poverty and 1st energy crisis of green transition. Energy **275**, 127487 (2023). https://doi.org/10.1016/j.energy.2023.127487
5. Axon, S., Morrissey, J.: Just energy transitions? Social inequities, vulnerabilities and unintended consequences. Build. Cities **1**, 393–411 (2020). https://doi.org/10.5334/bc.14
6. UN Department of Economic and Social Affairs Goal 7: Ensure access to affordable, reliable, sustainable and modern energy for all. https://sdgs.un.org/goals/goal7. Accessed 20 Mar 2025
7. European Commission: Territorial Agenda 2030 "A future for all places". Adopted at Informal meeting of Ministers responsible for Spatial Planning and Territorial Development and/or Territorial Cohesion 1 December 2020, Germany (2020). https://territorialagenda.eu:443/ta2030/. Accessed 7 May 2022
8. United Nations Department of Economic and Social Affairs: Accelerating SDG 7 achievement. Policy Brief 24 Energy Sector Transformation: Decentralized Renewable Energy for Universal Energy Access. United Nations (2025)
9. European Parliament and Council of the European Union: Directive (EU) 2018/2001 of the European Parliament and of the Council of 11 December 2018 on the promotion of the use of energy from renewable sources (2018). https://eur-lex.europa.eu/legal-content/EN/TXT/?uri=uriserv:OJ.L_.2018.328.01.0082.01.ENG&toc=OJ:L:2018:328:TOC. Accessed 27 Sept 2024
10. Chodkowska-Miszczuk, J., Kola-Bezka, M., Lewandowska, A., Martinát, S.: Local communities' energy literacy as a way to rural resilience. An insight from inner peripheries. Energies **14**, 2575 (2021). https://doi.org/10.3390/en14092575
11. Gaman, F., Iacoboaea, C., Aldea, M., Luca, O., Stănescu, A.A., Boteanu, C.M.: Energy transition in marginalized urban areas: the case of Romania. Sustainability **14**, 6855 (2022). https://doi.org/10.3390/su14116855
12. De Toni, A., Vizzarri, M., Lasserre, B., Carrosio, G., Sallustio, L., Di Martino, P.: Inner peripheries: dealing with peripherality and marginality issues within the European policy framework. TERRA **24** (2020). https://doi.org/10.7203/terra.7.17239
13. Noguera, J., Copus, A.: Inner peripheries: what are they? What policies do they need? Agriregionieuropa **45** (2016)
14. Bolognesi, M., Magnaghi, A.: Verso le comunità energetiche. Scienze del Territorio, 142–150 (2020). https://doi.org/10.13128/sdt-12330
15. Kitchen, L., Marsden, T.: Creating sustainable rural development through stimulating the eco-economy: beyond the eco-economic paradox? Sociol. Rural. **49**, 273–294 (2009). https://doi.org/10.1111/j.1467-9523.2009.00489.x
16. Lombardi, M., Prosperi, M., Fascia, G.: Social innovation for energy transition: activation of community entrepreneurship in inner areas of Southern Italy. In: Constable, E. (ed.) Transitioning to Affordable and Clean Energy. MDPI (2022)
17. Sankaran, S., Clegg, S., Müller, R., Drouin, N.: Energy justice issues in renewable energy megaprojects: implications for a socioeconomic evaluation of megaprojects. Int. J. Manag. Proj. Bus. **15**, 701–718 (2022). https://doi.org/10.1108/IJMPB-06-2021-0147
18. Lino, B., Contato, A., Ferrante, M., Frazzica, G., Macaluso, L., Sabatini, F.: Re-inhabiting inner areas triggering new regeneration trajectories: the case study of Sicani in Sicily. Sustainability **14**, 976 (2022). https://doi.org/10.3390/su14020976
19. Kercuku, A., Curci, F., Lanzani, A., Zanfi, F.: Italia di mezzo: the emerging marginality of intermediate territories between metropolises and inner areas. REGION **10**, 89–112 (2023). https://doi.org/10.18335/region.v10i1.397

20. Rossi, A.D.: Riabitare l'Italia: Le aree interne tra abbandoni e riconquiste. Donzelli Editore (2019)
21. Italian Agency for Territorial Cohesion: OpenCoesione - Strategia Nazionale Aree Interne (2021). https://opencoesione.gov.it/en/strategie/AI/. Accessed 3 Dec 2022
22. Carrosio, G.: A place-based perspective for welfare recalibration in the Italian inner peripheries: the case of the Italian strategy for inner areas. In: Osti, G., Bock, B. (eds.) FrancoAngeli, Milano, pp. 50–64 (2016)
23. De Toni, A., Vizzarri, M., Di Febbraro, M., Lasserre, B., Noguera, J., Di Martino, P.: Aligning inner peripheries with rural development in Italy: territorial evidence to support policy contextualization. Land Use Policy **100**, 104899 (2021). https://doi.org/10.1016/j.landusepol. 2020.104899
24. Romagnoli, L., Di Renzo, P., Mastronardi, L.: Modelling income drivers in peripheral municipalities: the case of Italian Inner Areas. Sustainability **14**, 14754 (2022). https://doi.org/10. 3390/su142214754
25. Rossitti, M., Torrieri, F.: Circular economy as 'catalyst' for resilience in inner areas. Sustain. Mediterr. Constr., 64–67 (2021)
26. Blečić, I., Cecchini, A., Muroni, E., Saiu, V., Scanu, S., Trunfio, G.A.: Addressing peripherality in Italy: a critical comparison between inner areas and territorial capital-based evaluations. Land **12**, 312 (2023). https://doi.org/10.3390/land12020312
27. Italian Government: Le missioni e le componenti del PNRR (2021). www.governo.it. https:// www.governo.it/it/approfondimento/le-missioni-e-le-componenti-del-pnrr/16700. Accessed 4 Oct 2024
28. Montaldi, C., Zullo, F., Giannobile, L.: Renewable energy communities in 'inland' areas: challenges and opportunities. Scienze del Territorio **12**, 53–64 (2024). https://doi.org/10. 36253/sdt-15741
29. Dino, G.E., Raimondi, C., Gracceva, F., Sanseverino, E.R., Piacentino, A.: The renewable energy communities: an innovative application to a small mountain Italian municipality. In: 2024 International Conference on Renewable Energies and Smart Technologies (REST), pp. 1–5 (2024)
30. Mangano, G.: Renewable energy communities: enabling technologies and regenerative models for the green and digital transition in the inner areas. In: Bevilacqua, C., Balland, P.A., Kakderi, C., Provenzano, V. (eds.) NMP 2022. LNNS, vol. 639, pp. 309–331. Springer, Cham (2023). https://doi.org/10.1007/978-3-031-34211-0_15
31. REScoop.EU Italy: Cohesion & Regional Development Funds. https://www.rescoop.eu/pol icy/financing-tracker/cohesion-regional-development-funds/italy-cohesion-regional-develo pment-funds. Accessed 21 Mar 2025
32. Ricerca sul Sistema Energetico - RSE. RSE. https://www.rse-web.it/en/. Accessed 21 Mar 2025
33. Carrosio, G., Presti, V.L.: Politiche di inclusione nelle aree fragili: i migranti e l'approccio territoriale della Strategia Nazionale per le Aree Interne: Inclusion Policies in Fragile Areas: Migrants and the Territorial Approach of the National Strategy for Internal Areas. Culture e Studi del Sociale **3**, 87–95 (2018)
34. European Commission Energy communities. https://energy.ec.europa.eu/topics/markets-and-consumers/energy-consumers-and-prosumers/energy-communities_en. Accessed 24 July 2024
35. Trevisan, R., Ghiani, E., Pilo, F.: Renewable energy communities in positive energy districts: a governance and realisation framework in compliance with the Italian regulation. Smart Cities **6**, 563–585 (2023). https://doi.org/10.3390/smartcities6010026
36. MASE: D.M. 414/2023 (CACER decree). Ministero dell'Ambiente e della Sicurezza Energetica (MASE), Italy (2023)

37. UNI: UNI 10349-1:2016 Riscaldamento e raffrescamento degli edifici - Dati climatici - Parte 1: Medie mensili per la valutazione della prestazione termo-energetica dell'edificio e metodi per ripartire l'irradianza solare nella frazione diretta e diffusa e per calcolare l'irradianza solare su di una superficie inclinata, Italy (2016)
38. European Commission: Photovoltaic Geographical Information System (PVGIS) (2022). https://re.jrc.ec.europa.eu/pvg_tools/en/. Accessed 17 Oct 2024
39. Gallanti, M., Grattieri, W., Maggiore, S., Marino, A.: Analisi ed evoluzione negli anni delle curve di carico dei clienti domestici. L'Energia Elettrica 1. L'Energia Elettrica 1 (2012)
40. Naitana, A., et al.: Piano energetico Ambientale Regionale della Sardegna 2015–2030. Terzo rapporto di Monitoraggio (2023)
41. European Parliament and Council of the European Union:018. Directive (EU) 2018/2001 of the European Parliament and of the Council of 11 December 2018 on the promotion of the use of energy from renewable sources (2018). https://eur-lex.europa.eu/legal-content/EN/TXT/?uri=uriserv:OJ.L_.2018.328.01.0082.01.ENG&toc=OJ:L:2018:328:TOC. Accessed 27 Sept 2024

Territorial Inequalities in Adaptive Reuse Opportunities: Evidence from Lombardy Region (Italy)

Marco Rossitti(✉) and Francesca Torrieri

Politecnico di Milano, Via Ponzio 31, 20133 Milan, Italy
marco.rossitti@polimi.it

Abstract. In recent years, the official and academic debate has focused on heritage adaptive reuse as a strategic driver to promote sustainable territorial development by fostering local communities' sense of belonging, creating economic opportunities, and embracing the circular economy paradigm in territorial transformations. Despite the focus, many marginal areas still struggle to capture benefits from reusing built heritage assets, thus highlighting the need for new knowledge bases and decision-support tools for the policy realm. In this context, the paper aims to answer this need by proposing a methodological tool, inspired by a mass appraisal logic, to assess economic opportunities related to reusing abandoned heritage properties at large administrative scales. Such a tool can help analyze and quantify imbalances between urban and marginal areas, providing preliminary information that supports effective funding allocation and heritage-based policy design for spatial justice. The tool's preliminary application to a subset of abandoned heritage properties in the Lombardy Region (Italy) demonstrates its potential for heritage-based territorial cohesion policies, together with the limits and future research challenges toward its spreading and effective implementation as a decision-making tool.

Keywords: Territorial inequalities · Abandoned Heritage · Adaptive Reuse · Mass Appraisal · Evaluation

1 Introduction

Cultural heritage is widely recognized as a key and multifaceted resource in promoting sustainable territorial development [1, 2]. Its benefits range from fostering local communities' sense of belonging and responsibility toward their 'places', thus enhancing well-being, to creating new economic opportunities [3–5]. Concerning its 'built' dimension, heritage reuse contributes to the global challenge of making the 'circular' paradigm effective by reducing environmental impacts through the reduction of resource consumption and waste generation [6, 7].

For these reasons, the official and academic debate has focused on reusing and enhancing heritage resources as drivers to promote development in marginal territorial contexts [8–12].

However, despite this focus and awareness [13], many marginal regions at the international level are still unable to capture any benefit from built heritage assets or approach them as a means for social justice [14]. The "negative spiral" affecting these territorial contexts, stemming from the interplay of several factors and historical processes (deindustrialization, depopulation, marginalization, etc.), has exacerbated the spatial imbalance and inequalities between urban areas and marginal territorial contexts [14]. Understanding the extent of such inequalities represents a crucial knowledge task to orient policy efforts toward their reduction by assisting marginal territories in their development challenge and effectively deploying heritage's potential and contribution.

Based on these premises, the paper proposes a methodological tool, inspired by a mass appraisal approach [15], to expeditiously assess the economic opportunities related to reusing abandoned heritage properties at large administrative territorial scales, thus highlighting and quantifying the existing imbalances between urban and marginal areas. Its implementation offers a preliminary information layer which, if properly integrated with the necessary cultural and social considerations about heritage reuse, can provide valuable support to effective funding allocation and orient policy design in the heritage field toward achieving spatial justice. In this sense, it aligns with the Council of Europe's recommendation for local and regional authorities to «take measures to acquire information and improve their knowledge base» and «to produce new tools and instruments» for a more effective policy implementation [14].

After providing an overview of the challenges and territorial inequalities related to abandoned heritage reuse in Sect. 2, Sect. 3 describes the proposed methodological tool.

The tool, inspired by a mass appraisal logic, addresses the expression of a 'specifically valid' judgment about the economic opportunity of reuse through the lens of the transformation value appraisal criterion [16]. Section 4 describes its preliminary application to a subset of abandoned heritage properties in the Lombardy Region (Italy), included in the Italian Ministry of Culture's dataset, and its results [17]. These results are then assumed, in Sect. 5, as the basis to discuss the opportunities, limits, and future research efforts related to implementing and spreading the proposed methodology as a decision-support tool for heritage and territorial cohesion policies.

2 The Adaptive Reuse of Abandoned Heritage Properties: Challenges and Territorial Inequalities

The adaptive reuse of heritage properties, intended as the process of providing a building or structure with a new function to give it new life [18] and recognized as an established practice in contemporary placemaking, entails a high level of complexity stemming from multiple and co-occurring challenges.

First, the willingness to include heritage properties in contemporary life schemes requires balancing the preservation of their tangible and intangible values with modern requirements concerning safety, usability, and energy efficiency [19–21]. Together with it, the high costs associated with restoration and maintenance interventions and the need to deal with legal constraints act as deterrents to the private sector's engagement in heritage reuse affairs [22, 23], thus imposing most of the technical and financial burden of addressing heritage abandonment on public administrations. The inability to manage such a burden, also depending on the scarcity of adequate resources, has often led to overlooking another crucial challenge for the success of adaptive reuse interventions: engaging the social fabric, managing conflicting interests, and aligning priorities and decisions with local needs and demands [24, 25].

These challenges, related to the 'intrinsic' nature and specificities of heritage assets, become even more pronounced in marginal areas. Indeed, these territorial contexts often experience a weak administrative capacity in terms of financial and human resources, clashing with the complexity required by approaching heritage assets [26]. Compared to urban contexts, the lack of a vibrant economic environment and the related demand for vacant spaces further reduce private sector involvement, which is discouraged by the investment risk and the high uncertainty in yielding any return [27]. Both these factors limit the reuse possibilities to accessing funding channels with the related risk of prioritizing the requirement of funding calls over the characteristics of the assets and the actual local needs in the design of the intervention.

Within the complex 'marginalization' vortex affecting these territorial realities, the ongoing demographic shrinking dynamics, more pronounced among the population's younger segment [28], pose another relevant challenge to the prospects of reusing abandoned properties in marginal areas. The demographic loss in the younger population, inevitably attracted by the educational, employment, and social opportunities offered by urban contexts, indeed, while reducing the demand for new activities or spaces, deprives these areas of their social innovation capital [29].

The co-occurrence of all these hurdles outlines a critical situation that the most recent policy efforts at different scales have only partially mitigated. To further push these efforts toward effectiveness, thus creating a policy and funding environment able to counter spatial inequalities, new knowledge bases and decision-support tools are required. From this perspective, identifying and understanding the extent of territorial inequalities in heritage adaptive reuse opportunities between urban contexts and marginal areas can provide valuable and necessary, even if not sufficient, information to answer this need.

3 A Methodological Tool to Assess the Economic Opportunities of the Adaptive Reuse of Abandoned Heritage Properties

The willingness to orient policy efforts toward reducing territorial inequalities in marginal areas by leveraging the potential from the adaptive reuse of abandoned heritage properties calls for a sound knowledge base and appropriate methodological support to build it.

From this perspective, the paper proposes a methodological tool to assess the economic opportunities from reusing abandoned heritage properties at large administrative territorial scales, thus highlighting and quantifying the existing imbalances between urban and marginal areas.

The applicability, practicality, and speed of use attributes required for a tool to be effectively applied at large territorial scales and to many assets hint at adopting a mass appraisal logic for its structuring.

Mass appraisal is a systematic approach to expressing a value judgment for many properties at a specific point in time using standardized procedures [30]. It is a cost-effective approach to valuing multiple properties simultaneously while ensuring consistency and fairness [31]. However, the unique features of heritage properties, which clash with the standardization requirements behind mass appraisal approaches, have hindered their implementation in heritage valuation issues.

To deal with this aspect, the proposed methodological tool addresses the expression of a 'specifically valid' value judgment about the economic opportunities of adaptive reuse through the lens of the transformation value appraisal criterion [32]. The adoption of this 'lens' enables expressing a convenient judgment as the difference between the 'gross development value' of the property under the provided reuse hypotheses and all the incurred costs [33]. In this sense, it allows balancing the need for standardization with considering the specific conditions of the asset and the compatibility of the reuse scenario, which both represent essential factors when dealing with heritage resources.

The proposed methodological tool is structured into three steps. The first step, *Knowledge frame structuring*, involves collecting all the basic and relevant information about the heritage properties under analysis as the input for the value judgement expression. This information includes: the location; the construction period; the typology of the property, expressed in terms of its original use; the conservation state (on a five-point qualitative scale: from very poor to optimum); the ownership status (public, private, or mixed); and the legal protection status (*ope legis* or by a specific legal act). Together with collecting this information, the first step also requires defining the 'compatible' reuse scenarios in terms of new uses for the considered property.

The second phase, *Transformation Value appraisal*, requires elaborating the information gathered in the previous step into cost and revenue parameters, which serve as inputs for estimating the transformation value related to the defined reuse scenarios, according to the formal Eq. (1):

$$TV_i = \frac{V_{mi} - K_t}{q^n} \quad (1)$$

where:

- V_{mi} is the most probable market value of the abandoned heritage property after its transformation related to the reuse hypothesis i. It can be assessed through one of the internationally recognized direct or indirect market value appraisal methodologies [33].
- K_t is the transformation cost related to the considered property. This cost can be appraised through a synthetic direct procedure based on the property's conservation state and typology.
- $q^n = (1+r)^n$ is the discount factor, based on the definition of the discount rate r [34].

After the transformation value appraisal, the phase requires identifying the reuse hypothesis, ensuring the best economic performance and, thus, the "highest and best" reuse of the property from a financial perspective [33].

The third and last step, *Judgment about the economic opportunities of adaptive reuse*, feeding on the result of the appraisal step, deals with grouping the abandoned heritage assets, according to their reuse opportunities into two clusters: the 'financial sustainable' cluster, including properties for which the 'high and best' reuse hypothesis leads to a positive performance in terms of estimated transformation value; the 'financial unsustainable' cluster, including the other properties, for which the 'high and best' reuse is not able to generate a positive financial result. Together with it, within each cluster, it is possible to further categorize the properties under analysis based on the magnitude of the result.

The output of the three-step methodological tool (Fig. 1), thus, can provide a useful knowledge basis to orient public decision-making and funding allocation, as well as private investments, in the heritage field toward effectiveness and, by highlighting territorial differences in the adaptive reuse economic opportunities, toward spatial justice.

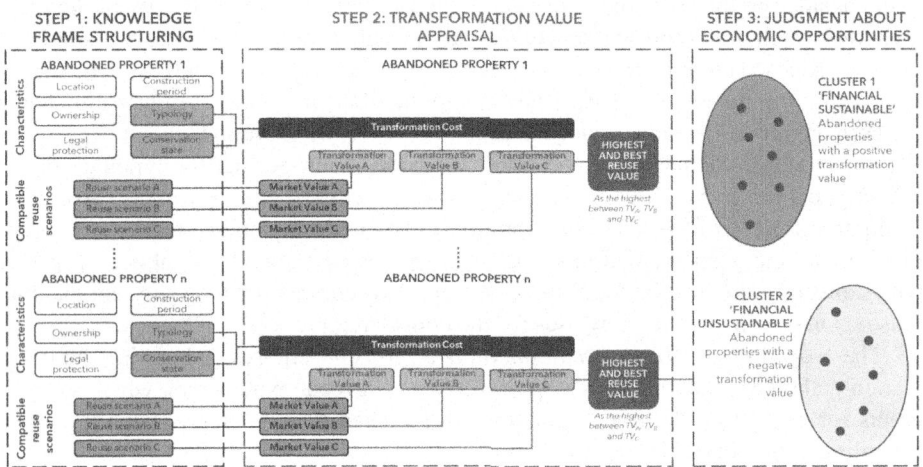

Fig. 1. Proposed three-step methodological approach inspired by a mass appraisal logic (Authors' elaboration)

4 Investigating the Economic Opportunities from the Adaptive Reuse of Heritage Properties: Evidence from Lombardy Region

4.1 Introduction to the Case Study

The proposed methodological tool's opportunities in supporting decision-making about adaptive reuse of abandoned heritage properties while properly managing territorial inequalities require testing it on a case study. Italy, the country with the highest number of UNESCO sites and more than 200,000.00 protected heritage assets [35], represents a relevant territorial context for this purpose.

The widespread presence of heritage assets across the country, many of which are managed by public administrations lacking the financial resources for proper conservation and management, has made protecting abandoned properties a key concern in territorial planning. To address this concern, in 2019, the Italian Ministry of Culture launched a project to map abandoned heritage properties across the national territory [17].

To date, this project has documented about 3,000 abandoned heritage properties widespread across the national territory (Fig. 2): most of the mapped assets are in the Lombardy Region (515 assets) in the North, followed by the Marche Region (290 assets) in the Center, and Sardegna island (280 assets).

Concerning the Lombardy Region, as the territorial context with the highest number of records included in the Ministry of Culture's census, 11 out of the 12 provinces host abandoned properties with the highest concentration in Milan (118), Mantova (110), and Cremona (95) (Fig. 3).

Fig. 2. Number of mapped abandoned heritage properties per Italian Region (Authors' elaboration on the Italian Ministry of Culture's Mapping of abandoned heritage properties)

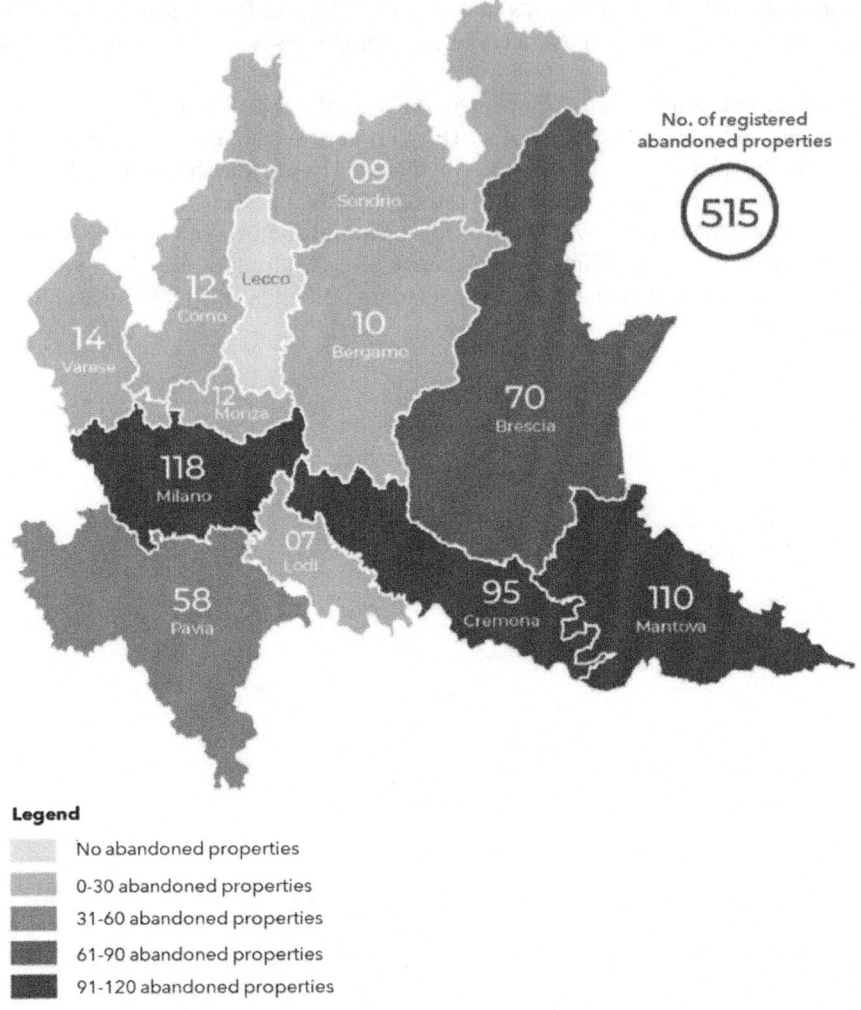

Fig. 3. Number of abandoned heritage properties for Lombardy Region's province (Authors' elaboration on the Italian Ministry of Culture's Mapping of abandoned heritage properties)

Regarding these assets' typology, expressed in terms of original use, it is possible to identify 12 typologies: industrial, leisure, military, hospital, administrative, religious; residential, hospitality, rural, school, museum, and railway station. The residential typology is the most frequent (107 assets, corresponding to the 20.8% of the whole sample of mapped properties), followed by the industrial typology (70 assets, equal to the 13,6% of the sample) (Fig. 4).

The focus on the property's conservation state, instead, reveals their critical condition and the related risk of losing some cultural witnesses of the past. Instead, in all the Lombardy Region's provinces at least 50% of the assets are in a poor or very poor conservation state (Fig. 5): the most critical situation can be observed in Bergamo,

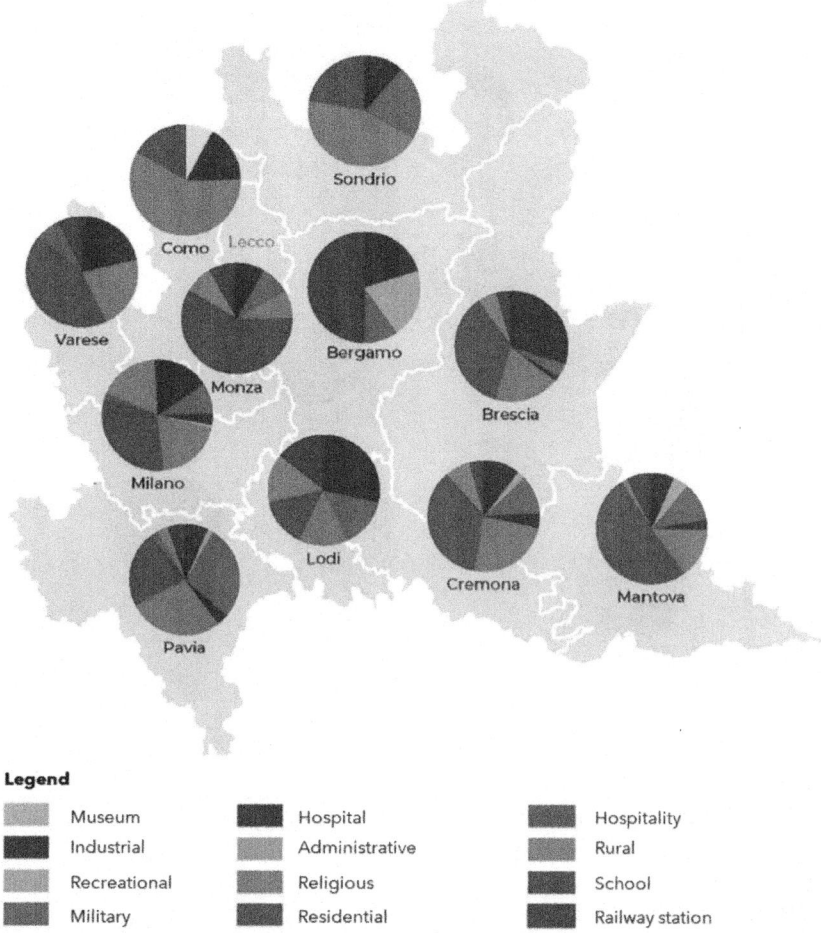

Fig. 4. Distribution of the identified typologies of heritage properties per Lombardy Region's province (Authors' elaboration on the Italian Ministry of Culture's Mapping of abandoned heritage properties)

Sondrio, Pavia and Lodi provinces, where the percentage of properties in a poor or very poor conservation state range from 80% to 90% of the total.

Given the variety of typologies, location, and conditions, the set of abandoned heritage properties mapped by the Ministry of Culture's census in Lombardy Region is an interesting sample for testing the proposed methodological tool.

However, in its first application as a 'pilot' case study, the tool's implementation focuses on a subset of the sample of abandoned properties. This subset is identified according to two criteria:

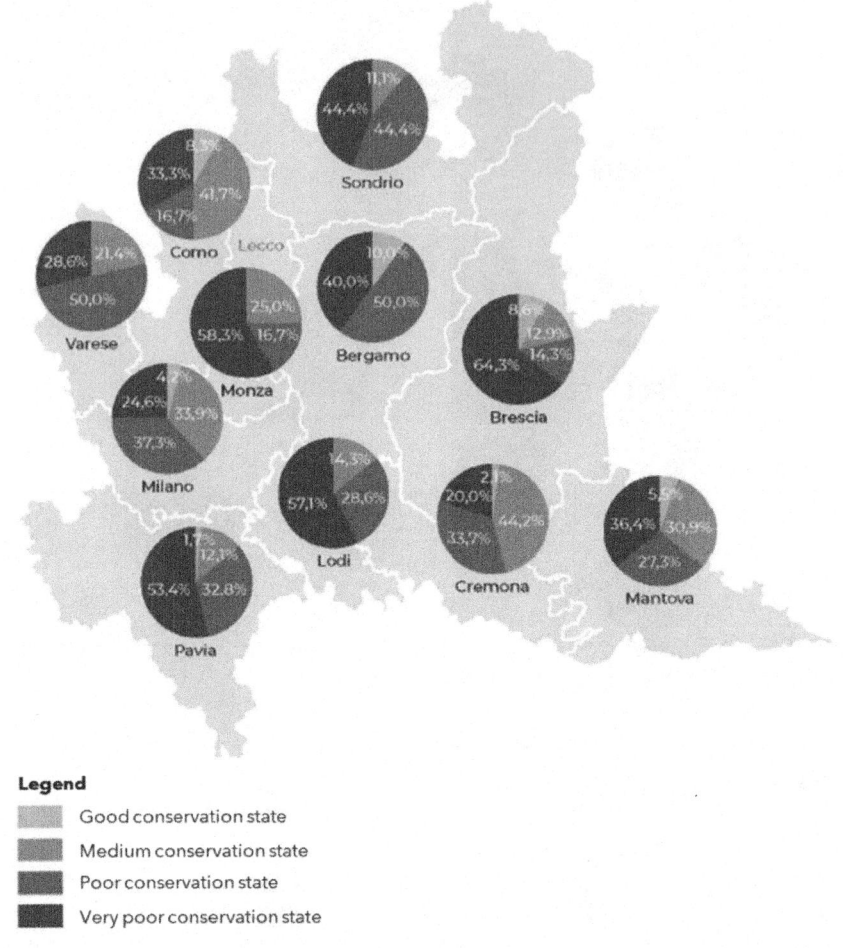

Fig. 5. Conservation state of abandoned properties per Lombardy Region's province (Authors' elaboration on the Italian Ministry of Culture's Mapping of abandoned heritage properties)

- A 'typological' criterion. This criterion leads to focusing on military and industrial properties that, given their less rigid functional layout, are more prone to undergo adaptive reuse processes under different scenarios.
- A 'territorial distribution' criterion. Based on this criterion, one province is selected since it allows for evaluating and comparing the economic opportunities of adaptive reuse between contexts characterized by different marginality conditions: Brescia province. This criterion, thus, enables highlighting the existence and the extent of territorial inequalities in the reuse opportunities for abandoned properties.

For these reasons, the proposed methodological tool is applied to military and industrial properties in Brescia province.

4.2 The Methodological Tool Implementation

The proposed methodological tool (Fig. 1) implementation to the selected subset of abandoned heritage properties in Lombardy Region first requires structuring the reference knowledge frame (Step 1) about their characteristics and reuse opportunities. To this aim, an information sheet is built for each property based on the data provided by the Ministry of Culture's census. Together with it, as a first application, for each property, three general reuse scenarios are defined: reuse as a residential asset, reuse as a commercial asset, and reuse as a tertiary asset.

Based on this information and hypotheses, it is possible to move to the second step in the methodological tool implementation: the Transformation Value appraisal. This step requires turning the information about the properties and the defined reuse scenarios into cost and revenue data, as input for applying the formal Eq. (1).

Concerning the transformation cost, it is appraised through a syntethic direct procedure based on parametric construction costs (€/sqm), which are identified, for each conservation state, through the analysis of different Estimate Metric Computations (EMC) related to projects for properties like the ones under analysis in terms of characteristics and location. This parametric construction cost is, then, turned into a whole transformation cost through a parametric estimation of the other cost items (professional fees, urbanization fees, when necessary, overheads) (Table 1).

Table 1. Parametric construction cost for each conservation state (Authors' elaboration)

Property's conservation state	Typology of intervention	Transformation cost
Medium conservation state	Minor intervention	**1,354 €/sqm**
Poor conservation state	Medium intervention	**1.924 €/sqm**
Very poor conservation state	Major intervention	**2.495 €/sqm**

The market value appraisal, instead, is performed for each reuse scenario through a direct mono-parametric procedure by referring to the value provided by the Official Real Estate Observatory in Italy (OMI), for the property's zone, related to: residential properties in an optimum conservation state for the residential scenario; commercial properties in an optimum conservation state for the tertiary scenario; office properties in an optimum conservation state for the tertiary scenario [36]. Once the input parameter for the formal Eq. (1) is provided, it is possible to appraise a transformation value for each of the three defined reuse scenarios and, by comparing them, identify the 'high and best' reuse scenario as the one ensuring the best financial performance. This performance, thus, can be assumed as the basis for the last step in the proposed methodological tool's implementation: the *Judgement about the economic opportunities of adaptive reuse*.

4.3 Results

The proposed methodological tool's implementation to the industrial and military abandoned heritage properties in Brescia Province, as of today included in the Italian Ministry of Culture's census, provides preliminary insight about the territorial dimension of the challenges of reusing these assets (Table 2).

Table 2. Results from the implementation of the methodological tool to the mapped abandoned properties in Brescia province (Authors' elaboration)

Id	Property	Municipality	Classification	Typology	Conserv. state	Residential TV [€/sqm]	Commercial TV [€/sqm]	Tertiary TV [€/sqm]
1	Ex Cavallerizza di Brescia	Brescia	Center	Industrial	Medium	1845.8	1745.8	1145.8
2	Ex Mulino di Brescia	Brescia	Center	Industrial	Very poor	-295	-1095	-995
3	Ex Segheria Vallaro	Vione	Peripheral	Industrial	Very poor	-345	-1195	-995
4	Ex Mulino della Lama	Trenzano	Peri-urban	Industrial	Very poor	-1245	-1595	-1585
5	Strada delle Cartiere	Toscolano Maderno	Intermediate	Industrial	Medium	2245.8	-54.2	395.8
6	Cartiera di Garde	Toscolano Maderno	Intermediate	Industrial	Very poor	1105	-1195	-745
7	Complesso produttivo Maina di Mezzo	Toscolano Maderno	Intermediate	Industrial	Very poor	1105	-1195	-745
8	Complesso produttivo Maina Superiore	Toscolano Maderno	Intermediate	Industrial	Very poor	1105	-1195	-745
9	Complesso produttivo Vago	Toscolano Maderno	Intermediate	Industrial	Very poor	1105	-1195	-745
10	Complesso produttivo Contrada	Toscolano Maderno	Intermediate	Industrial	Very poor	1105	-1195	-745
11	Complesso produttivo Luseti	Toscolano Maderno	Intermediate	Industrial	Very poor	1105	-1195	-745
12	Insediamento produttivo Covoli	Toscolano Maderno	Intermediate	Industrial	Very poor	1105	-1195	-745
13	Complesso produttivo Quattro Ruote	Toscolano Maderno	Intermediate	Industrial	Very poor	1105	-1195	-745
14	Ex Filanda di Palazzo Bargnani Dandolo	Adro	Peri-urban	Industrial	Poor	-595	-1195	-1095
15	Ex Serre di Villa Mazzotti	Chiari	Peri-urban	Industrial	Very poor	-795	-1045	-995
16	Ex Mulino Pilù	Palazzolo sull'Oglio	Peri-urban	Industrial	Very poor	-695	-1295	-1245
17	Fabbricati Casere - Ex Magazzini Generali	Brescia	Center	Industrial	Poor	-245	-1195	-745
18	Ex Mulino della Borgognina	Brescia	Center	Industrial	Poor	-45	-695	-495
19	Fornaci da calce di Ponte Crotte	Brescia	Center	Industrial	Very poor	-45	-945	-795
20	Centro nautico del Garda	Toscolano Maderno	Intermediate	Industrial	Very poor	1105	-1195	-745
21	Ex Officina del gas	Salò	Intermediate	Industrial	Poor	2305	1105	605
22	Ex Caserma maggiore Giovanni Randaccio	Brescia	Center	Industrial	Poor	205	-845	-695
23	Ex Caserma Achille Papa	Brescia	Center	Industrial	Very poor	-395	-1195	-945
24	Ex Caserma dei Bersaglieri Goito	Brescia	Center	Industrial	Poor	2005	2205	1305

Classifying the municipalities in which the properties are located according to zones defined by the main territorial cohesion policy in Italy – the National Strategy for Inner Areas (NSIA)[1] [37] – reveals the territorial disparities in the economic opportunities from the reusing abandoned properties. Indeed, the effect of the municipalities' accessibility on their local real estate market's dynamics [38] becomes evident from comparing the economic opportunities related to the different reuse scenarios in terms of appraised transformation value. Indeed, properties belonging to the 'Financial sustainable' cluster are mainly located in the only municipality classified as a 'center' (Brescia) and in "intermediate" municipalities, which are attractive from a touristic point of view due to their location on the Garda Lake (Toscolano Maderno and Salò). On the contrary, the other 'peri-urban' and 'peripheral' municipalities show negative results in terms of transformation value for all the defined reuse scenarios, thus confirming the existence of a territorial disparity issue in the economic opportunities of adaptive reuse.

Together with the centrality of the 'location' aspect, the results from the tool's pilot application also reveal the crucial role of the conservation state in the reuse opportunities of abandoned properties: also in Brescia, as the main center in the province, the poor or very poor conservation state of an asset leads to a negative result in terms of transformation value. Finally, it is worth mentioning that for all the analyzed properties the 'high and best' reuse option, ensuring the best performance in terms of transformation value, is related to the residential function. Furthermore, in several cases - as the abandoned properties in Toscolano Maderno – the residential reuse option is the only one ensuring a positive financial result. Such evidence adds another point to the already complex challenge of tackling the abandonment of heritage properties through their adaptive reuse and further highlights the extent of territorial inequalities. Indeed, even if industrial or military heritage properties are more flexible than other heritage assets in terms of transformation potential, the need to preserve their tangible and intangible system of values can clash with the interventions required to host a residential function.

5 Discussion and Conclusions

The paper aims to contribute to the challenge of orienting policy efforts in the heritage field toward effectiveness and spatial justice by providing a sound knowledge basis to leverage abandoned heritage properties' potential in reducing territorial inequalities and promoting marginal territories' development. From this perspective, it proposes a three-step methodological tool, inspired by a mass appraisal approach [15], to expeditiously assess the economic opportunities of reusing abandoned heritage properties at large administrative territorial scales, thus highlighting and quantifying the existing imbalances between urban and marginal territorial contexts.

---

[1] The National Strategy for Inner Areas (NSIA) divides the national territory into five zones (centers, peri-urban areas, intermediate areas, peripheral areas, and ultra-peripheral areas) according to an accessibility indicator, that is measured in minutes needed to reach the closest center. According to this classification, inner areas, as the focus of this territorial cohesion policy, include all the municipalities resulting in intermediate (20–40 min to reach the closest center), peripheral (40–75 min required), and ultraperipheral (more then 75 min required).

The 'pilot' test on the case study, represented by the abandoned heritage properties in Brescia Province as mapped by the Italian Ministry of Culture's mapping, allows for reflection on its possible contribution to the challenge against heritage abandonment. It provides a preliminary information layer about the economic opportunities of reuse which, if properly integrated with the necessary cultural and social considerations about the properties' characteristics and values and their potential role within their territorial contexts and planning processes, can offer valuable support to public and private interventions in the adaptive reuse field. From a public perspective, it can guide the definition of effective and tailored funding allocation mechanisms to reuse processes, based on the specific features of the assets and their location, thus orienting policy design in the heritage field toward achieving spatial justice. From a private perspective, instead, it can provide an information ground to orient and promote investments in the adaptive reuse, thus triggering public-private collaboration mechanisms in addressing the abandonment challenge [39].

The willingness to fully deploy the proposed methodology's potential as a decision-support tool, thanks to its implementation in different territorial contexts, requires dealing with its current limits. They can be identified in the narrow perspective toward the defined reuse scenarios – currently limited to the residential, commercial, and tertiary functions – and the lack of accurate data for their scalability and replicability to other heritage typologies and territorial contexts. For this reason, future research perspectives will be mainly devoted to building a comprehensive dataset of cost input data, related to the different heritage typologies and conservation states, and revenue data, related to a broader array of reuse hypotheses, that must be necessarily defined by considering their reference contexts' vocations and directly interacting with their reference communities. Such an effort can help reconcile the standardization required for the tool's large-scale implementation by adopting the necessary context-based and heritage-sensitive perspective toward the adaptive reuse theme.

Acknowledgments. Sofia Cattai, a graduate student in Architectural Design at Politecnico di Milano, developed part of the methodological approach implementation within her thesis (supervisor: Francesca Torrieri; co-supervisor: Marco Rossitti).

Disclosure of Interests. The authors have no competing interests to declare that are relevant to the content of this article.

References

1. United Nations: Transforming Our World: The 2030 Agenda for Sustainable Development (2015). https://sdgs.un.org/2030agenda. Accessed 24 Mar 2025
2. Assumma, V., Datola, G., Mondini, G.: New cohesion policy 2021–2027: the role of indicators in the assessment of the SDGs targets performance. In: Gervasi, O., et al. (eds.) ICCSA 2021. LNCS, vol. 12955, pp. 614–625. Springer, Cham (2021). https://doi.org/10.1007/978-3-030-87007-2_44
3. Oppio, A., Dell'Ovo, M.: Cultural heritage preservation and territorial attractiveness: a spatial multidimensional evaluation approach. In: Pileri, P., Moscarelli, R. (eds.) Cycling & Walking for Regional Development. Research for Development, pp. 105–125. Springer, Cham (2021). https://doi.org/10.1007/978-3-030-44003-9_9

4. Imperiale, A., Vanclay, F.: Using social impact assessment to strengthen community resilience in sustainable rural development in mountain areas. Mt. Res. Dev. **36**(4), 431–442. https://doi.org/10.1659/MRD-JOURNAL-D-16-00027.1
5. Assumma, V., Barbieri, S., Bottero, M., Caprioli, C.: Supporting the planning management of UNESCO sites: a literature review between urban showcase and gentrification. In: Gervasi, O., Murgante, B., Garau, C., Taniar, D., Rocha, A.M.A.C., Faginas Lago, M.N. (eds.) ICCSA 2024. LNCS, vol. 14821, pp. 147–162. Springer, Cham (2024). https://doi.org/10.1007/978-3-031-65308-7_11
6. Rudan, E.: Circular economy of cultural heritage—possibility to create a new tourism product through adaptive reuse. J. Risk Financ. Manag. **16**(3), 196 (2023). https://doi.org/10.3390/jrfm16030196
7. Della Spina, L., Assumma, V.: Development strategies for the Mediterranean coastal landscape: adaptive decision-making processes for implementing the circular economy in the redevelopment of the Reggio Calabria waterfront. Land **14**(2), 301 (2025). https://doi.org/10.3390/land14020301
8. Verardi, F., Angrisano, M., Fusco Girard, L.: New development policies for the internal areas of Southern Italy. General principles for the valorization of rural areas in Calabria Region: Valori e Valutazioni **33**, 105–116 (2023). https://doi.org/10.48264/VVSIEV-20233308
9. Angrisano, M., Nocca, F., Scotto di Santolo, A.: Multidimensional evaluation framework for assessing cultural heritage adaptive reuse projects: the case of the seminary in Sant'Agata de' Goti (Italy). Urban Sci. **8**(2), 50 (2024). https://doi.org/10.3390/urbansci8020050
10. Rossitti, M., Torrieri, F.: Circular economy as 'catalyst' for resilience in inner areas. Sustain. Mediterr. Constr. Spec. Issue **5**, 64–67 (2021). https://www.sustainablemediterraneanconstruction.eu/en/edizioni-speciali/si-2021-05/si-2021-05-064/
11. Dell'Ovo, M., Dezio, C., Mottadelli, M., Oppio, A.: How to support cultural heritage-led development in Italian inner areas: a multi-methodological evaluation approach. Eur. Plan. Stud. **31**(9), 1799–1822 (2023). https://doi.org/10.1080/09654313.2022.2135367
12. Rossitti, M., Oppio, A., Torrieri, F., Dell'Ovo, M.: Tactical urbanism interventions for the urban environment: which economic impacts. Land **12**(7), 1457 (2023). https://doi.org/10.3390/land12071457
13. European Union, From Social Inclusion to Social Cohesion – The Role of Culture Policy (2019). https://www.europeanheritagehub.eu/wp-content/uploads/2024/02/from-social-inclusion-to-social-cohesion-NC0219637ENN-1.pdf. Accessed 25 Mar 2025
14. Council of Europe: Culture without borders: Cultural heritage management for local and regional development (2021). https://rm.coe.int/culture-without-borders-cultural-heritage-management-for-local-and-reg/1680a28883. Accessed 24 Mar 2025
15. Sdino, L., Rosasco, P., Torrieri, F., Oppio, A.: A mass appraisal model based on multi-criteria evaluation: an application to the property portfolio of the bank of Italy. In: Calabrò, F., Della Spina, L., Bevilacqua, C. (eds.) ISHT 2018. SIST, vol. 100, pp. 507–516. Springer, Cham (2019). https://doi.org/10.1007/978-3-319-92099-3_57
16. Manganelli, B.: Una proposta di sintesi tra tradizione estimative italiana e standard internazionali di valutazione. Valori e Valutazioni **18**, 9–16 (2017). https://siev.org/wp-content/uploads/2020/02/04_Manganelli.pdf
17. Ministero della Cultura: Direzione Generale Archeologia Belle Arti e Paesaggio. Beni Culturali Abbandonati. Ricognizione territoriale. https://beniabbandonati.cultura.gov.it/. Accessed 24 Mar 2025
18. Vafaie, F., Remøy, H., Gruis, V.: Adaptive reuse of heritage buildings; a systematic literature review of success factors. Habitat Int. **142**, 102926 (2023). https://doi.org/10.1016/j.habitatint.2023.102926

19. Bottero, M., Dell'Anna, F., Nappo, M.: Evaluating tangible and intangible aspects of cultural heritage: an application of the PROMETHEE method for the reuse project of the Ceva–Ormea railway. In: Mondini, G., Fattinnanzi, E., Oppio, A., Bottero, M., Stanghellini, S. (eds.) SIEV 2016. GET, pp. 285–295. Springer, Cham (2018). https://doi.org/10.1007/978-3-319-78271-3_23
20. Conejos, S., Langston, C., Chan, E.H.W., Chew, M.Y.L.: Governance of heritage buildings: Australian regulatory barriers to adaptive reuse. Build. Res. Inf. **44**(5–6), 507–519 (2016). https://doi.org/10.1080/09613218.2016.1156951
21. Colucci, E., et al.: Documenting cultural heritage in an INSPIRE-based 3D GIS for risk and vulnerability analysis. J. Cult. Herit. Manag. Sustain. Dev. **14**(2), 205–234. https://doi.org/10.1108/jchmsd-04-2021-0068
22. Koo, H.J., Kelly, D., Deman, D.: Risk assessment of the challenges in the adaptive reuse of historic buildings. J. Constr. Eng. Manag. **150**(9), 04024119 (2024). https://doi.org/10.1061/JCEMD4.COENG-14569
23. Zedeat, Z.F.: Adaptive reuse challenges of Jordan's heritage buildings: a critical review. Int. J. Urban Sustain. Dev. **16**(1), 95–107 (2024). https://doi.org/10.1080/19463138.2024.2329661
24. Pintossi, N., Ikiz Kaya, D., van Wesemael, P., Pereira Roders, A.: Challenges of cultural heritage adaptive reuse: a stakeholders-based comparative study in three European cities. Habitat Int. **136**, 102807 (2023). https://doi.org/10.1016/j.habitatint.2023.102807
25. Pintossi, N., Ikiz Kaya, D., Pereira Roders, A.: Identifying challenges and solutions in cultural heritage adaptive reuse through the historic urban landscape approach in Amsterdam. Sustainability **13**(10), 5547 (2021). https://doi.org/10.3390/su13105547
26. Lynch, N.: Remaking the obsolete: critical geographies of contemporary adaptive reuse. Geogr. Compass **16**(1), e12605 (2022). https://doi.org/10.1111/gec3.12605
27. Vardopoulos, I.: Adaptive reuse for sustainable development and land use: a multivariate linear regression analysis estimating key determinants of public perceptions. Heritage **6**(2), 809–828 (2023). https://doi.org/10.3390/heritage6020045
28. Rossitti, M., Oteri, A.M., Torrieri, F.: Understanding geographies of architectural heritage abandonment in inner areas: a multi-dimensional investigation. In: Gervasi, O., Murgante, B., Garau, C., Taniar, D., Rocha, A.M.A.C., Faginas Lago, M.N. (eds.) ICCSA 2024. LNCS, vol. 14819, pp. 3–16. Springer, Cham (2024). https://doi.org/10.1007/978-3-031-65282-0_1
29. Fava, F.: Commoning adaptive heritage reuse as a driver of social innovation. Naples and the scugnizzo liberato case study. Sustainability **14**(1), 191 (2022). https://doi.org/10.1007/978-3-031-65282-0_1
30. Kontrimas, V., Verikas, A.: The mass appraisal of the real estate by computational intelligence. Appl. Soft Comput. J. **11**(1), 443–448 (2011). https://doi.org/10.1016/j.asoc.2009.12.003
31. Dimopoulos, T., Ioakim, V.: A discussion on mass appraisals: case study on land plots, views of local appraisers and the future in property valuations. J. Prop. Tax Assess. Adm. **21**(1), 5–20 (2024)
32. Rossitti, M., Datola, G., Oppio, A., Torrieri, F.: Assessing the market value of heritage properties: theoretical and methodological issues. In: Calabrò, F., Madureira, L., Morabito, F.C., Piñeira Mantiñán, M.J. (eds.) NMP 2024. LNNS, vol. 1183, pp. 204–213. Springer, Cham (2024). https://doi.org/10.1007/978-3-031-74501-0_22
33. International Valuation Standards Council: International Valuation Standards. Effective 31 January 2025 (2024). https://viewpoint.pwc.com/dt/gx/en/ivsc/international_valuat/assets/IVS_effective_31_January_2025.pdf. Accessed 26 Mar 2025
34. Del Giudice, V., Passeri, A., Torrieri, F., De Paola, P.: Risk analysis within feasibility studies: an application to cost-benefit analysis for the construction of a new road. In: Liu, H.W., Wang, G., Zhang, G.W. (eds.) ICAEMAS 2014. AMM, vol. 651–653, pp. 1249–1254. Scientific.Net, Baech (2014). https://doi.org/10.4028/www.scientific.net/AMM.651-653.1249

35. Ministero della Cultura: Vincoli in rete. https://vincoliinrete.beniculturali.it/VincoliInRete/vir/utente/login. Accessed 28 Mar 2025
36. Agenzia delle Entrate. Osservatorio del mercato immobiliare. https://www.agenziaentrate.gov.it/portale/aree-tematiche/osservatorio-del-mercato-immobiliare-omi. Accessed 28 Mar 2025
37. Rossitti, M., Torrieri, F.: The THEMA tool to support heritage-based development strategies for marginal areas: evidence from an Italian inner area in Campania Region. Region **9**(2), 109–129 (2022). https://doi.org/10.18335/region.v9i2.394
38. Yang, J., Lee, S., Im, J., Cho, K., Park, H.: Perceptual disparities in transportation accessibility, neighborhood quality, and satisfaction across metro, urban, and rural areas. Sensors Mater. **36**(9), 3899–3916 (2024). https://doi.org/10.18335/10.18494/SAM5174
39. Torrieri, F., Crisopulli, A., Rossitti, M.: Assessing the feasibility of PPPs for cultural heritage enhancement in UNESCO sites: the case of Matera (Italy). Land **14**(4), 898 (2025). https://doi.org/10.3390/land14040898

Convergences Versus Gaps. Capital Axiology as a Cognitive Pattern of Territorial Fragility

Maria Rosa Trovato[1](✉) , Ludovica Nasca[1] , Salvatore Giuffrida[2] , and Vittoria Ventura[1]

[1] Department of Civil Engineering and Architecture, University of Catania, 95124 Catania, Italy
`mrtrovato@dica.unict.it, ludovica.nasca@phd.unict.it, vittoria.ventura@unict.it`
[2] Department of Architecture, University of Palermo, 90128 Palermo, Italy
`salvatore.giuffrida@unipa.it`

Abstract. The Italian territory is characterised by significant and persistent disparities. South of Italy is the most backward region in the euro area, having suffered severely from the Great Crisis of 2008 and more recently from the Covid-19 crisis and the ongoing Russian-Ukrainian and Israeli-Palestinian conflicts. Although it is characterised by strong inter-regional disparities, coastal areas and rural or inland areas, it has great potential. It is populated by a third of Italy's population and characterised by a productive fabric that could generate positive effects for the country. The backwardness problem of the Southern Italy has been a national priority, as evidenced by the policies adopted to support the development of these depressed areas. The implementation of a cohesion policy aimed at territorial rebalancing should be based on a systemic vision of the problem, at least at the regional level. A systemic view of the problem can be developed on the basis of appropriate knowledge support. To this end, the study proposes a cognitive model on a regional scale, based on fuzzy clustering, applied to the case study of the region of Sicily, developed in the axiological perspective of the forms of territorial capital, with the aim of identifying gaps and convergences on a regional and infra-regional scale. The region of Sicily is considered in this study as representative of South of Italy. At the regional level, the cognitive model showed less significant gaps for human, economic, natural and environmental capital than for urban capital and, as expected, deep gaps for infrastructural capital.

Keywords: Intra-regional gaps · Territorial rebalancing · Fuzzy clustering

1 Introduction

The Italian territory is characterised by significant and persistent disparities. The South of Italy (called Mezzogiorno) is the largest backward territory in the European area, which suffered severely from the great crisis of 2008 [1] and, most recently, that related to the Covid-19 crisis and the ongoing Russian-Ukrainian, Israeli-Palestinian conflicts [2]. Although characterised by strong interregional differentiations, coastal areas and rural or inland areas, has great potential. In fact, they are populated by over twenty million inhabitants (one third of the Italian population), and is characterised by a productive system that - although weak and incomplete - could generate positive effects for the country. The issue of the late development of southern Italy has been a national priority, as evidenced by the policies adopted to support the development of these depressed areas, the identification [3] and amount of funding, under the impulse of the cohesion policies and the European Regional Development Fund (ERDF), Cohesion Fund (CF), European Social Fund Plus (ESF+), and the Just Transition Fund (JTF). In Italy, the National Recovery and Resilience Plan, Decree-Law No. 13 was adopted on February 24, 2023, which contains urgent provisions for the implementation of the PNRR and the National Plan of Complementary Investments (PNC), as well as for the implementation of cohesion policies and the common agricultural policy [4–6]. It stipulates that at least 40 per cent of the territorially allocable resources are to be allocated to southern regions [7, 8]. The establishment of a fund to combat deindustrialisation- DPCM November 30, 2021 [9] aimed at contrasting the phenomena of deindustrialisation and impoverishment of the productive and industrial system of various territorial areas. The fund provides for the granting of economic incentives to manufacturing companies that carry out investments to upgrade or redevelop existing production facilities or to install new production activities. The establishment of a Support Fund for Marginalised Municipalities Law No. 178 of December 39, 2020 [10] and DPCM September 30, 2021 [11], the first one established the Fund, the second one provided for the increase of the relative provision, amounting to 90 million euros (30 mln for each year from 2021 to 2023, ex paragraph 65 sexies of the same Law No. 205/2017), for an additional 90 million euros, allocated at the rate of 30 mln for each of the years 2021-2022-2023, for 'disadvantaged municipalities' exposed to the risk of depopulation, suffering from social deprivation, whose population has low income levels (below the first quartile of the distribution of Italian municipalities). The institution of a fund to support the development of municipalities in inland areas [12]. The establishment of a Special Economic Zone for the South - 'ZES unica' covering the territories of the regions of Abruzzo, Basilicata, Calabria, Campania, Molise, Apulia, Sicily, Sardinia [13] is aimed at boosting employment in the South by offering financial and administrative benefits to businesses. The establishment of an SEZ Mission Structure in charge of monitoring and updating the SEZ Strategic Plan, and of managing the resources allocated to the interventions instrumental to the implementation of Mission 5 Component 3 (M5C3) - 'Special Interventions for Territorial Cohesion' of the National Recovery and Resilience Plan (PNRR), intended to support special interventions for territorial cohesion, including investments to combat educational poverty and the strengthening of Special Economic Zones. Cohesion policies and related funds have started to produce their first positive effects even in a difficult context characterised by pandemics, conflicts and strong macroeconomic fluctuations. While there is a slight trend in the narrowing of gaps in the national territory, this trend takes a long time to manifest itself in the infra-regional context. The differences between municipalities on a regional scale are still significant, perhaps as a consequence of the capacity of the strongest and most hegemonic cities to attract capital flows, people and technologies compared to small towns or villages, or because the former start from very different conditions than the latter [14]. Dobrescu et al. 2014 [15] point out that growth poles can better fulfil their vocation by integrating and implementing innovative collaborative networks in a polycentric territory. Weak territories risk being further weakened even by ad hoc policies and funding, exposing themselves to a gradual and ineluctable loss of their values [16]. The implementation of policies aimed at supporting cohesion and aimed at territorial rebalancing should be based on a systemic view of the issue at least on a regional scale [17]. Camagni et al. 2012 and Capello et al. 2013 [18, 19], in this regard, proposed an overview of the main theories of regional development and formalised economic models. They provide the basis to support the development of a coordinated territorial model. With appropriate cognitive support, a systemic view of the problem can be developed. In this regard, the study proposes a knowledge model at regional scale based on fuzzy clustering applied on the Sicily region case study, as a representative region of the southern issue, developed in the axiological perspective of the forms of territorial capital, aimed at detecting divergences and convergences at infra-regional scale. The identification of clusters on a regional scale and infra-regional of convergence areas and gaps could support the identification of the most effective and efficient territorial rebalancing strategies, aimed at enhancing the former and reducing the latter.

2 Approaches to the Territorial Gaps

According to economic theories of neoclassical inspiration, territorial inequalities are interpreted following the principles of rationality and market equilibrium, whereby peripheral areas correspond to those areas far from the development centres. In the second half of the 20th century, Francois Perroux developed the theory on industrial polarisation, giving strong support to territorial rebalancing interventions, which were criticised by free market supporters, fuelling a heated debate between supporters of state intervention and supporters of the market as the solver of any dysfunction [20]. Immanuel Wallerstein developed the system-world approach and classified world countries into central, semi-peripheral and peripheral countries, highlighting how this classification to the distribution of power and capitalist-type processes of exploitation. According to this approach, peripheral countries are functional to the economic development of the centre [21]. This structuralist approach provides a justification for corrective interventions aimed at reducing imbalances. An analysis carried out by the World Bank (2009) [22] aimed at surveying the different levels of development on a planetary level, identified the centres of at least 50,000 inhabitants that offer services, host activities and perform important functions, to define all the other localities that are distant from them and cannot access the preconditions of development. Further studies such as those by Czapiewski and Janc 2009 [23] and Franklin 2019 [24] show how the concentration of advanced industrial and tertiary activities in certain locations can significantly increase spatial disparities. The OECD distinguishes between rural and urban areas [25]. Capello et al. 2011 [26], dealing with the issue of peripheral areas have shown that local communities are much more exposed to international events, increasing inequalities and territorial imbalances. Herrschel identified rural areas as areas far from power [27]. Dematteis showed the greater role played by central areas compared to peripheral areas, which in many cases are even lacking [28]. Medeiros [29] taking up the European Spatial

Policy in 2006 [30], proposed to mitigate the imbalances induced by urban polarisation, using a polycentric urban system. Pezzi a Urso [31], have demonstrated how many non-metropolitan areas can become suburbs. Copus et al. in 2017 [32] gave a functionalist interpretation of peripheral areas proposed in the classification developed in the ESPON-funded Profecy project. This interpretation of peripherality associates the concept of spatial peripherality with socio-economic marginality and the distance of an area from the centres offering important services, which to some extent echoes Bock's definition of peripherality, which does not depend on distance but on the lack of connection of political and socio-economic relations [33]. Therefore, even spatially non-peripheral areas could be classified as such, because they do not interact with global economic networks. Some studies on gaps including, those of Chieffallo et al. 2022 highlight the dichotomy between urban (centre) and rural (peripheral) areas [34, 35]. Bignante et al. 2022, pointed out the triggering of imbalances related to the relocation of companies, particularly when they affect areas of less developed countries and neglect peripheral areas of more advanced countries [36]. Bignante et al. 2022 highlight the risk of triggering the brain-drain phenomenon for distant/peripheral centres compared to developed ones and thus suggest corrective interventions [36].

3 The Case Study. South of Italy Territorial Gap

There are deep territorial gaps between the South and the Centre-North. These are result of a progressive settling of disadvantageous conditions linked to an asymmetry in the values of the initial configuration and development dynamics. In these weak contexts, the dynamics are often characterised by low or no development of some areas. By a low or absent level of implementation of national policies. In some cases, they are the result of policies that have led to a reduction in services for reasons related to cuts in public spending, or by an unequal distribution of funding for efficient infrastructure provision. And still, from a low level of local governance, cultural backwardness and socio-economic vulnerabilities. A local geography of the gaps shows in some contexts strong differences even on an infra-regional scale. In many regions of Southern Italy, there are differences between coastal territories and peripheral territories, between cities and inland/rural areas; these differences are even more serious if we consider that the strongest local territories are in any case weak territories from the national point of view. ISTAT noted in its report of 25 January 2023 entitled 'The territorial gaps in the PNRR: ten objectives for the South [37] strong regional and infra-regional differences, showing critical contexts, which confirm the classification of areas according to the criteria of geographical peripherality (distance from the Centre-North), and territorial marginality (the so-called 'internal areas'). The report highlighted a low sustainability of gaps, due to the impact on the demographic structure of the south, which in the future prospects appears increasingly fragile. The 'per capita GDP' has been around 55–58% of that of the Centre-North for more than two decades in the South. The level of education in the South confirms a serious backwardness: in 2020, one third (32.8%) of South Italians aged 25–49 had completed at most the third grade of secondary school compared to 24.5% in the Centre-North; 22.6% had a tertiary degree compared to 27.6% in the Centre-North. The entire South has youth employment rates well below the average.

This condition has led to a worrying resurgence of mass emigration. In 2020, the South and the Islands lost as many as 42 young residents (25–34 years old) out of every 100 population movements in extra-regional internal flows (+22 in the Centre-North) and 56 out of every 100 in foreign flows (49 in the Centre-North). This phenomenon is more pronounced in the provinces with low employment and in the 'internal areas'. While the digitisation process has been very rapid in the Centre-North over the last two decades, the South has not yet caught up with the starting gap, as about 60 per cent of residents have limited opportunities to access ultra-wideband.The water network in the South registers losses for about half of the water for civil use, an issue that has become even more critical due to the drought risk to which the entire Italian territory and particularly that of the South is exposed. The endowment of transport infrastructure in the South is lower than in the rest of the country. The density of the railway network, especially the high-speed network, is much lower (0.15 km per 100 km2 of surface area in the South; 0.8 in the North; 0.56 in the Centre). Education outcomes in the South are significantly worse than in the rest of Italy. In the 2021–2022 period, 42.7% of Southern upper V students have 'very weak' competences in mathematics compared to 28.3% in the rest of Italy; and only 6.7% are at a 'very good' level compared to 14.9% in Italy. The supply of childcare services is growing throughout the country, but the gaps are still significant; in fact, for two-thirds of children (0–3 years) in the South the level of supply is below national standards and for the rest the level of supply is very low or null. In the South of Italy - especially in some regions affected by the redirection plans (6 out of 7 in this breakdown) - the contraction of public spending has negatively affected the Essential Levels of Care (LEA), which has led to widespread 'health emigration' to the facilities of the Centre-North. The delays in the South are increasing the risks of an excessive and non-reversible demographic impoverishment. Between 2011 and 2020, the first population decline in the recent history of the South was recorded ($-642,000$ inhabitants; $+335,000$ in the Centre-North). With unchanged trends, in 2030 residents will fall below the critical threshold of 20 million for the first time, with a reduction on a ten-year basis of about four times that of the Centre-North (-5.7% and 1.5%). The population loss affects young people. National Institute of Statics has predicted for 2035, an increase in the average age of the population of the South compared to that of the Centre-North. The significance of these phenomena, if not managed, exposes the South to a process of involution, putting its social structure at risk. Sicily is a region in southern Italy where all these issues are detectable. Sicily is the largest region in Italy with an area of 25,832 square kilometres. The population density of Sicily is 194 inhabitants per square kilometre. The resident population, based on the census of 31 December 2022, amounts to 4,814,016 inhabitants, a decrease compared to 2021 ($-19,313$ persons; -0.4%). This decrease is due to the negative values of the natural balance and internal migration. Sicily has 391 municipalities. More than a quarter of the population (26.3%) lives in the four municipalities with more than 100,000 inhabitants (Palermo, Catania, Messina and Syracuse) and just under a quarter in those with between 20,001 and 50,000 inhabitants (24.3%). The average age will increase from 44.9 to 45.2 years in 2021. Ragusa and Catania are the youngest provinces (44.1 and 44.2 years respectively), while Messina and Enna are the oldest (46.7 and 46.5 years respectively). In Sicily, a new record for the birth rate was reached in 2022, with a decrease of 425 units. The death rate rose from 12.2 per thousand in 2021 to 12.3 per thousand in 2022 [38]. An analysis of the gaps on an infra-regional scale for Sicily is not available in the literature. One of the objectives of this study is to detect gaps and convergences on an infra-regional scale for Sicily.

4 Method

The methodological approach supporting the cognitive model of convergences and gaps for the Region of Sicily is based on the following phases:

- Identification of the forms of territorial capital;
- Construction of a geo-database of indicators characterising the forms of territorial capital;
- Analysis of the territorial clusters based on a fuzzy clustering of the indicators characterising the forms of territorial capital, with the aim of highlighting intra-regional convergences and gaps. Fuzzy clustering is a technique that is part of soft clustering. It allows data to be allocated to clusters in such a way that elements in the same cluster are as similar as possible, while elements in different clusters are as dissimilar as possible. It is an effective tool for identifying the underlying structures of a dataset based on similarity measures. In the context of the proposed research, fuzzy clustering makes it possible to identify indicator clusters for different forms of capital, taking into account the specific characteristics of the data. These are characterised by different degrees of similarity to the clusters, so that hard clustering would reduce the information content of the data, which is best captured by soft clustering.
- Spatial cluster analysis using QGIS to identify convergences and gaps of territorial capital forms at the regional scale, based on clusters number generated (high cluster size corresponds to high divergence at the regional scale, low cluster size corresponds to low divergence or convergence at the regional scale).
- Analysis of the minimum and maximum values and standard deviations of the indicators of territorial Capital forms in order to identify convergences and gaps at the infra-regional level.

4.1 The Territorial Capital Forms

Based on the categories introduced by Camagni [39] to classify, six territorial capital forms were identified, namely: human capital (HC), urban capital (UC), natural capital (NC), economic capital (EC), environmental capital ($ENVC$) and infrastructure capital (IC). For the six territorial capital forms, 13 indicators were identified for human capital, 26 indicators for urban capital, 5 indicators for natural capital, 30 indicators for economic capital and 67 indicators for infrastructure capital. These indicators were selected with reference to the dataset of the Agency for Territorial Cohesion [40] and that of the Council of Ministers [41], based on the territorial capital forms introduced by Camagni [39]. Figure 1 highlights the indicators characterising the different territorial capital forms. The 127 indicators selected to characterise the six forms of territorial capital have been georeferenced. Together they constitute the basic geodatabase to support spatial analyses, instrumental in identifying gaps and convergences.

Human capital
HC1-Residential population
HC2-Population density
HC3-Average annual rate of change of resident population
HC4-Old-age index
HC5-Percentage of foreign population
HC6-Incidence of young single-parent families
HC7-Incidence of young couples with children
HC8-Early exit from the education and training system
HC9-Incidence of lone elderly persons
HC10-Incidence of mixed couples
HC11-Share of pupils at risk of dropping out of secondary school
HC12-Share of pupils at risk of dropping out of lower secondary schools
HC13-Italian/foreigner school attendance ratio

Urban capital
UC1-Variation in the building under-utilisation rate
UC2-Variation in the under-utilisation index of dwellings
UC3-Variation in the under-utilisation rate of dwellings in built-up areas
UC4-Index of dwelling dispersion
UC5-Index of concentration of building use types
UC6-Index of compactness of urban areas
UC7-Urban landscape fragmentation index
UC8-Under-use of dwellings index
UC9-Fixed-site retail trade density
UC10-Index of building expansion in urban centres and settlements
UC11-Residential attractiveness index
UC12-Residential mobility
UC13-Population incidence in crowded conditions
UC14-Housing crowding index
UC15-Rate of building vacancy
UC16-Drop-out rate of dwellings in built-up areas
UC17-Housing exclusion index
UC18-Incidence of residential buildings in a poor state of repair
UC19-Index of availability of services in the dwelling
UC20-Average age of recent housing stock
UC21-Percentage of cars with low environmental impact
UC22-Net human density
UC23-Incidence of population living in cores and scattered dwellings
UC24-Average real estate rent
UC25-Average real estate value
UC26-Urban (non-agricultural) green area per capita

Economic capital
EC1-Total Employment in Local Units in the Municipality
EC2-Manufacturing employment at Local Units in the municipality
EC3-Tourism employment in the local units of the municipality
EC4-Manufacturing Sector Employment in Local Units
EC5-Employment in tourism sector in local units
EC6-Population employed in agriculture in 2001
EC7-Utilised agricultural area by location of the enterprise centre
EC8-Share of manufacturing employment in local units in the municipality
EC9-Share of tourism employment in the local units of the commune
EC10-% change in manufacturing employment between 1971 and 2001
EC11-% change in employment in the service sector between 1971 and 2001
EC12-% change in population employed in agriculture between 1971 and 2001
EC13-% change in utilised agricultural area by location of farm centre
EC14-Herfindahl-Hirschman concentration index
EC15-Change in economic dynamism index
EC16-Employment rate
EC17-Employment turnover index
EC18-Change in unemployment rate
EC19-Unemployment Rate
EC20-Youth unemployment rate
EC21-Incidence of young people out of the labour market and training
EC22-Incidence of households with potential economic hardship
EC23-Average income
EC24-Gini index
EC25-Italian/Foreign Employment Ratio
EC26-Male/Female employment ratio
EC27-Utilised Agricultural Area (UAA) as a percentage of total agricultural area
EC28-Percentage of persons employed in ODA and KIBS enterprises
EC29-Percentage of APS and KIBS enterprises
EC30-Index of Economic Dynamism

Natural capital
NC1-Area covered by forest
NC2-Percentage of forest area
NC3-Percentage of municipal protected area
NC4-Presence or absence of Natura 2000 network (Sic/ZPS/ZSC)
NC5-Average agricultural value

Infrastructural capital
IC1-Population mobility by private car
IC2-Daily mobility for study or work
IC3-Commuting index for work
IC4-Commuting index within the city
IC5-Index of road accessibility to commercial centres
IC6-Rail Accessibility Index
IC7-Index of accessibility to railway stations
IC8-Index of Mobility by Public Transport
IC9-Slow Mobility
IC10-University presence index
IC11-Composite accommodation function rate
IC12-Number of State Places of Culture
IC13-Number of stadiums
IC14-Number of amusement and entertainment hubs
IC15-Number of commercial hubs
IC16-Number of ordinary hospital beds per 10,000 inhabitants
IC17-Index of dynamism of public institutions
IC18-Ordinary pharmacies per 10,000 inhabitants
IC19-Libraries per 10,000 inhabitants
IC20-Drinking water supplied to the municipal network per capita
IC21-Percentage of separate waste collection
IC22-Density of installed photovoltaic systems
IC23-Number of CNR institutes
IC24-Number of CNR sites
IC25-Number of locations of non-NRC research bodies and institutes
IC26-Number of science parks, technological districts and centres of excellence
IC27-Number of beds in hospital facilities
IC28-Number of hospitals
IC29-Number of hospitals with DEA
IC30-Number of elderly people enrolled in ASL of the municipality
IC31-Number of beds in residential facilities for the elderly
IC32-Number of kindergartens
IC33-Number of primary school
IC34-Number of secondary school
IC35-Number of secondary school
IC36-Number comprehensive school
IC37-Number Permanent Territorial Centre
IC38-Number of vocational colleges
IC39-Number of technical colleges
IC40-Number of higher education institutions
IC41-Number of educational establishments
IC42-Number of teacher training institutes
IC43-Number of Artistic Institutes
IC44-Number Classical High School
IC45-Number Scientific High School
IC46-Number Artistic High School
IC47-Number of Academies and Conservatories
IC48-Number of boarding schools and teacher training colleges
IC49-Number of Territorial Centres Pupils
IC50-Number of Vocational Colleges Pupils
IC51-Number of Technical Colleges Pupil
IC52-Number of pupils at scientific high schools
IC53-Number of Primary School Pupils
IC54-Number of Secondary School Pupils
IC55-Number of pupils master school
IC56-Number of pupils art school
IC57-Number of pupils secondary school
IC58-Number of pupils artistic high school
IC59-Number of students in classical high school
IC60-Number of stations per municipality
IC61-Number of Platinum Type Station
IC62-Number of stations of type Gold
IC63-Number of stations of type Silver
IC64-Number of stations of type Bronze
IC65-Share of population without fixed network broadband
IC66-Share of population without fixed-line and/or mobile broadband
IC67-Precence of a railway station of type at least Silver

Environmental capital
ENVC1-Seismic risk indicator
ENVC2-Class of population exposed to landslide phenomena
ENVC3-Standard deviation of altitudes
ENVC4-Surface area of land consumed in areas of high and very high seismic hazard
ENVC5-Percentage of municipal area at high and very high PAI landslide hazard
ENVC6-Resident population at risk in areas of high and very high landslide hazard
ENVC7-Surface area of soil consumed in areas with high and very high landslide hazard
ENVC8-Percentage of municipal surface area at high hydraulic hazard
ENVC9-Resident population at risk in areas of high hydraulic hazard
ENVC10-Surface area of soil consumed in high hydraulic hazard areas
ENVC11-Total number of establishments with Major Accident Hazard
ENVC12-Soil consumed per capita
ENVC13-Municipal waste production per capita

Fig. 1. Indicators of forms of territorial capital: *HC*, *UC*, *EC*, *NC*, *IC* and *ENVC*

5 Results

The indicators for each of the six capital forms were analysed with fuzzy clustering, using NCSS Statistical software [42]. The Kaufman and Rousseeuw algorithm was used for fuzzy clustering. This is a medoid algorithm, which call PAM (Partition Around Medoids). With reference to this approach, the cluster centroid is defined as an element of a cluster whose average dissimilarity with respect to all objects in the cluster is minimal, so that it will be the most central point of a given set of points. The clusters number was selected for each form of capital on the basis of two goodness-of-fit statistics, namely Dunn's normalised partition coefficient and Kaufman's normalised partition coefficient. The criterion used for the selection of the solution, i.e. the number of clusters, is the one that maximises Dunn's normalised partition coefficient and minimises Kaufman's normalised partition coefficient.

Fuzzy clustering for human capital revealed two clusters. In the first cluster fall municipalities with a lower level of human capital endowment and in the second those with a higher endowment. C_1 cluster has its centroid in the municipality San Michele di Ganzaria, in the Messina province. C_2 cluster has its centroid in the municipality of Comiso, in the Ragusa province. Figure 2 shows the map of C_1 and C_2 regarding Human Capital.

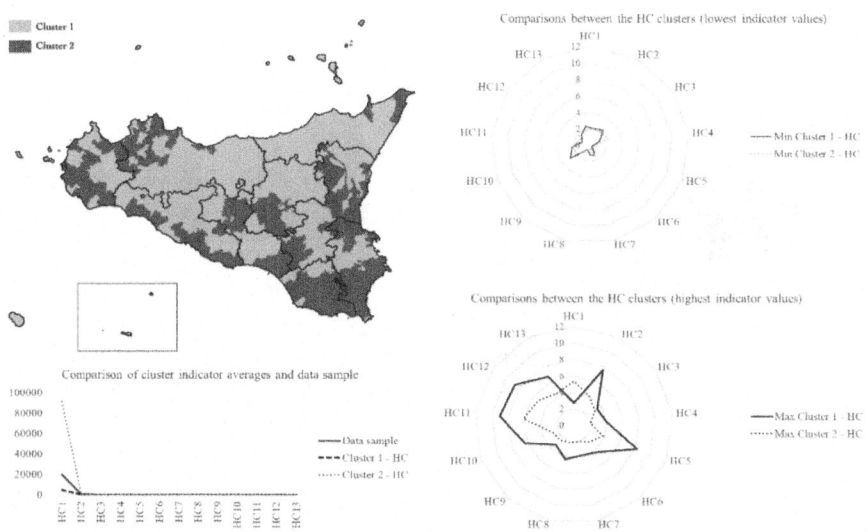

Fig. 2. Human Capital distribution in C_1 and C_2 clusters

C_1 includes 81.40% of the municipalities in the Agrigento province, 81.82% in the Caltanissetta province, 63.79% in the Catania province, 90.00% in the Enna province, 97.22% in the Messina province, 90.24% in the Palermo province, 41.67% in the Ragusa province, 74.14% in the Siracusa province, and 70.83% in the Trapani province. C_2 includes 18.60% of the municipalities in the Agrigento province, 18.18% in the Caltanissetta province, 36.21% in the Catania province, 10.00% in the Enna province, 2.78% in the Messina province, 9.76% in the Palermo province, 58.33% in the Ragusa province, 42.86% in the Syracuse province, and 29.17% in the Trapani province. In terms of the minimum and maximum standardised values for the thirteen indicators, municipalities with a higher level of human capital endowment fall into the first cluster rather than the second, as shown in Fig. 3. Indicators average values comparison shows that the values for HC1 - *residential population* and HC2 - *population density* for C_2 are higher than the corresponding values for C_1, , due to the presence in this cluster of the provincial capitals (Agrigento, Caltanissetta, Catania, Enna, Messina, Palermo, Ragusa, Siracusa and Trapani). C_2 is characterised by a higher value of the standard deviation of the indicators, highlighting a greater variability of the human capital endowment within the cluster, and therefore a greater divergence than that of cluster C_1, which is characterised by a greater convergence.

Fuzzy clustering for urban capital showed three clusters: C_1, C_2 and C_3.

C_1 has its centroid in Mazzarrà Sant'Andrea municipality, in the Messina province. C_2 has the centroid in Malvagna municipality, in the Messina province. C_3 has its centroid in Paceco municipality, in the Trapani province. Figure 3 shows the map of C_1, C_2 and C_3 regarding Urban Capital. C_1 includes 20.93% of the municipalities in the Agrigento province, 59.09% in the Caltanissetta province, 22.41% in the Catania province, 70.00% in the Enna province, 17.59% in the Messina province, 47.56% in the Palermo province, 30.33% in the Ragusa province, 52.33% in the Siracusa province, and 0.00% in the Trapani province.

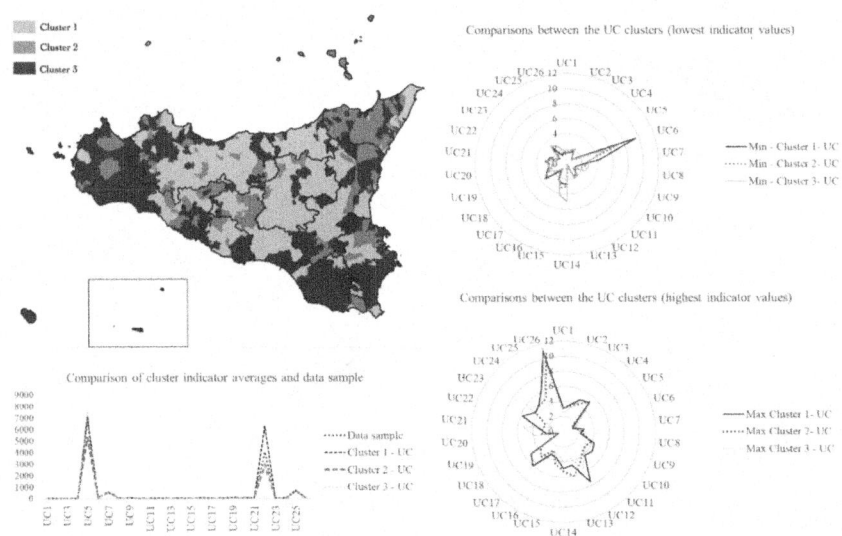

Fig. 3. Urban Capital distribution in C_1, C_2 and C_3 clusters

C_2 includes 32.56% of the municipalities in the Agrigento province, 13.64% in the Caltanissetta province, 20.69% in the Catania province, 15.00% in the Enna province, 50.00% in the Messina province, 19.51% in the Palermo province, 8.33% in the Ragusa province, 19.05% in the Siracusa province, and 20.83% in the Trapani province. C_3

includes 46.51% of the municipalities in the Agrigento province, 27.27% in the Caltanisetta province, 56.90% in the Catania province, 15.00% in the Enna province, 32.41% in the Messina province, 32.93% in the Palermo province, 58.33% in the Ragusa province, 28.57% in the Siracusa province, and 79.17% in the Trapani province. Indicators average values comparison shows higher values for the UC5- *index of concentration of building use types* for C_1 compared to C_2 and C_3, and higher values for the UC22- *net human density* for C_1 compared to C_2 and comparable to C_3. C_1 includes the provincial capitals of Catania, Enna, Messina and Palermo, while C_3 includes the provincial capitals of Agrigento, Ragusa, Siracusa and Trapani, with Caltanissetta instead in C_2. C_1 is characterised by a higher value of the standard deviation of the indicators, highlighting a greater variability of the urban capital endowment within the cluster, and therefore a greater divergence, although not as marked as in C_2, and more marked than in C_3. The latter cluster is characterised by greater convergence.

Fuzzy clustering for Infrastructure Capital determined five clusters C_1, C_2, C_3, C_4 and C_5. Figure 4 shows the map of C_1, C_2, C_3, C_4 and C_5 regarding Infrastructural Capital. C_1 has its centroid in the municipality Collesano, in the Palermo province. C_2 has its centroid in the municipality of Oliveri, in the Messina province. C_3 has its centroid in the municipality of Realmonte, in the Agrigento province. C_4 has its centroid in the municipality of Butera, in the Caltanissetta province. C_5 has its centroid in the municipality of Mascali, in the Catania province. C_1 includes 2.23% of the municipalities in the Agrigento province and 100.00% in the Palermo province. C_2 includes 97.67% of the municipalities in the Messina province. C_3 includes 100.00% of the municipalities in the Siracusa province and 100.00% in the Trapani province. C_4 includes 2.27% of the municipalities in the Agrigento province, 100.00% in the Caltanissetta province, 100.00% in the Enna province, 0.93% in Messina province, and 100.00% in the Ragusa province. C_5 includes 100% of the municipalities in the Catania province. In this case, the fuzzy clustering showed five clusters, indicating a significant variation in infrastructure capital endowment at the regional level. This classification coincides with the administrative boundaries of the Sicilian provinces. This instance, C_1 includes only municipalities in the Palermo province, including the municipality of Palermo; C_2 includes only municipalities in the Messina province; C_3 includes municipalities in the Agrigento, Trapani and Siracusa province; C_4 includes municipalities in the Caltanisetta, Enna and Ragusa province; C_5 includes municipalities in the Catania province (Fig. 4). At infra-regional level, based on the maximum standardised values of the sixty-seven indicators, the municipalities with the highest level of infrastructure capital endowment are highlighted in C_2 (Fig. 4), followed by C_1, C_5, C_3 and C_4. In terms of the minimum standardised values for the sixty-seven indicators, the municipalities with the lowest level of infrastructure capital endowment fall into C_1, followed by C_4, C_3, C_5 and C_2, as shown in Fig. 4. This shows a more pronounced divergence of the values of this endowment in C_1, less pronounced in C_3, C_4 and C_5, and a convergence in C_2. The comparison of the average values of the indicators shows higher values of IC31 - *number of beds in residential facilities for the elderly* for C_1 compared to C_5, C_2, C_3, C_4. C_4 is characterised by a higher value of the standard deviation of the indicators, which indicates a greater variability of the infrastructure capital endowment within the cluster, i.e. a greater divergence. The divergences become progressively less marked, again with reference to the values of the highest standard deviation of the indicators in C_3, C_1, C_5 and less divergence in C_2. The latter cluster is characterised by greater convergence.

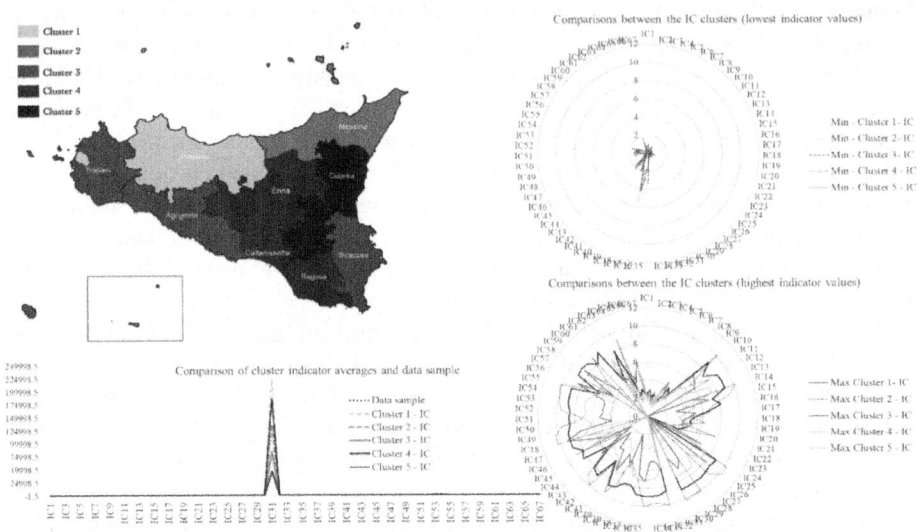

Fig. 4. Infrastructure Capital distribution in C_1, C_2, C_3, C_4 and C_5 clusters

Fuzzy clustering for Economic Capital identified two clusters C_1 and C_2. C_1 has its centroid in the Villafrati municipality, in the Palermo province. C_2 has its centroid in the Troina municipality, in the Enna province. C_1 includes 74.42% of the municipalities in the Agrigento province, 77.22% in the Caltanissetta province, 75.59% in the Catania province, 35.00% in the Enna province, 93.52% in the Messina province, 76.83% in the Palermo province, 50.00% in the Ragusa province, 61.50% in the Siracusa province, and 62.50% in the Trapani province. C_2 includes 25.58% of the municipalities in the Agrigento province, 22.738% in the Caltanissetta province, 22.41% in the Catania province, 65.00% in the Enna province, 6.48% in the Messina province, 23.17% in the Palermo province, 50.00% in the Ragusa province, 38.10% in the Siracusa province, and 37.50% in the Trapani province. Figure 5 shows the map of C_1 and C_2 regarding Economic Capital. In this case, the fuzzy clustering revealed two clusters, indicating a less significant divergence in economic capital endowment level at regional level. At infra-regional level, the minimum and maximum values of the standardised values of the thirty indicators highlight the municipalities with a higher level of economic capital endowment in C_1 than in C_2 (Fig. 5). Indicators average values comparison of shows that C_2 has higher values for EC1-*Total employment in local units in the municipality*, EC5-*Employment in the tourism sector in local units*, EC7-*Utilised agricultural area by location of the enterprise centre*, compared to C_1. C_2 is characterised by a higher value of the standard deviation of the indicators, which indicates a greater variability of the economic capital endowment within the cluster, i.e. a greater divergence. The divergences are less pronounced, again with respect to the values of the maximum standard deviation of the economic capital indicators in C_1.

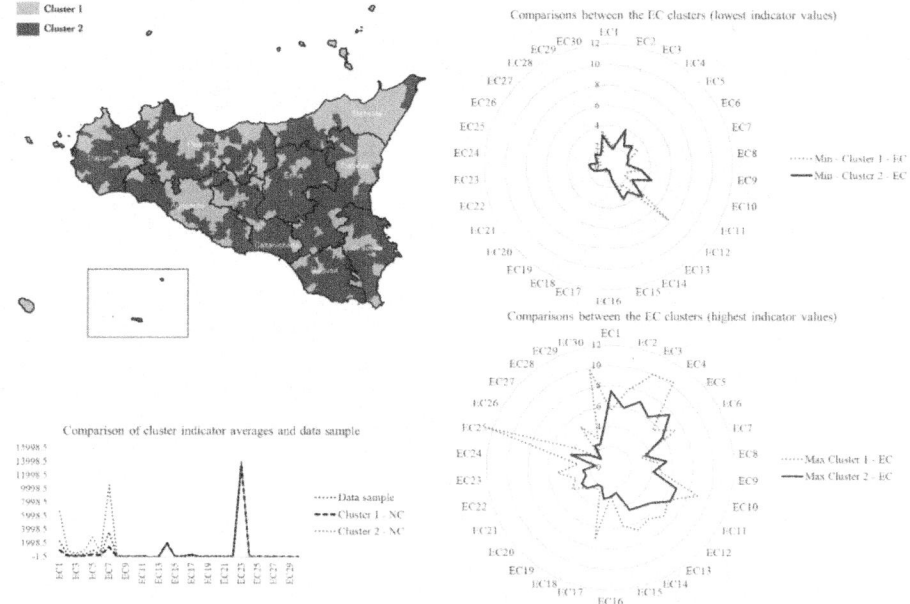

Fig. 5. Economic Capital distribution in C_1 and C_2 clusters

Fuzzy clustering for Natural Capital identified two clusters C_1 and C_2. C_1 has its centroid in Partinico municipality, in the Palermo province. C_2 has its centroid in Serradifalco, in the Caltanissetta province. C_1 includes 13.95% of municipalities in the Agrigento province, 0.00% in the Caltanissetta and Enna provinces, 67.24% in the Catania province, 67.59% in the Messina province, 36.59% in the Palermo province, 75.00% in the Ragusa province, 76.19% in the Siracusa province and 95.83% in the Trapani province. C_2 includes 86.05% of municipalities in the Agrigento province, 100.00% in the Caltanissetta province, 32.76% in the Catania province, 100.00% in the Enna province, 32.41% in the Messina province, 63.41% in the Palermo province, 25.00% in the Ragusa province, 23.81% in the Siracusa province and 4.71% in the Trapani province. Figure 6 shows the map of C_1 and C_2 regarding Natural Capital.

In this case, the fuzzy clustering revealed two clusters, indicating a less significant variation in natural capital endowment at regional scale. At infra-regional scale, the minimum and maximum values of the standardised values of the five indicators highlight the municipalities with a higher level of natural capital endowment in C_1 than in C_2 (Fig. 6). Indicators average values comparison of the shows higher values of the indicator NC5-*Average agricultural value* in C_1 and higher values of the indicator NC2-*Forest area* in C_2. C_2 is characterised by a higher value of the standard deviation of the indicators, indicating a higher variability of the natural capital endowment within the cluster, i.e. a greater divergence. Less pronounced divergences, again in relation to the values of the maximum standard deviation of the natural capital indicators in C_1.

Fuzzy clustering for Environmental Capital identified two clusters C_1 and C_2. C_1 has its centroid in Raccuja municipality, in the Messina province. C_2 has its centroid

244 M. R. Trovato et al.

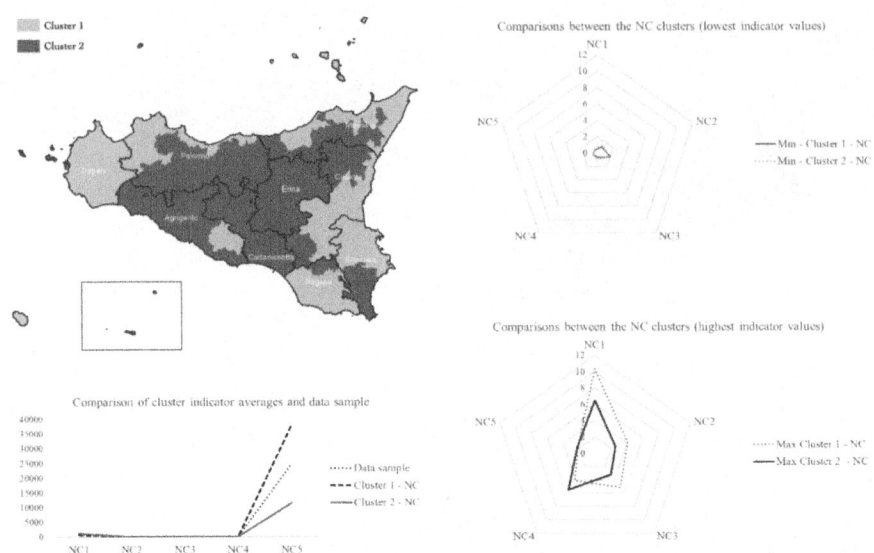

Fig. 6. Natural Capital distribution in C_1 and C_2 clusters

in Camporotondo Etneo municipality, in the Catania province. C_1 includes 32.56% of municipalities in the Agrigento province, 27.27% in the Caltanissetta province, 24.14% in the Catania province, 50.0.0% in the Enna province, 38.89% in the Messina province, 36.59% in the Palermo province, 91.67% in the Ragusa province, 57.14% in the Siracusa province and 50.00% in the Trapani province. C_2 includes 67.44% of municipalities in the Agrigento province, 68.18% in the Caltanissetta province, 75.86% in the Catania province, 50.00% in the Enna province, 61.11% in the Messina province, 63.41% in the Palermo province, 8.330% in the Ragusa province, 42.86% in the Siracusa province and 50.00% in the Trapani province. Figure 7 shows the map of C_1 and C_2 regarding Environmental Capital.

In this case, fuzzy clustering showed two clusters, indicating less significant variation in environmental capital endowment at the regional level. The environmental capital indicators provide information on the exposure of municipalities to different environmental risks. At infra-regional scale, the minimum and maximum values of the standardised values for the thirteen indicators highlight the municipalities with a higher level of environmental risk in C_1 than in C_2 (Fig. 7). Indicators average values comparison shows that C_1 has higher values for the indicators ENV4-*Surface area used in areas of high and very high seismic hazard*, ENV6-*Population at risk in areas of high and very high landslide hazard*, ENV9-*Population at risk in areas of high hydraulic hazard*, ENV12-*Soil consumption per capita*, ENV13-*Municipal waste production per capita*. C_1 is characterised by a higher value of the standard deviation of the indicators, indicating a greater variability of environmental risk within the cluster, and therefore a greater divergence. The divergence is less marked, again with respect to the values of the highest standard deviation of the environmental capital indicators in C_2, i.e. less variability of environmental risk within the cluster.

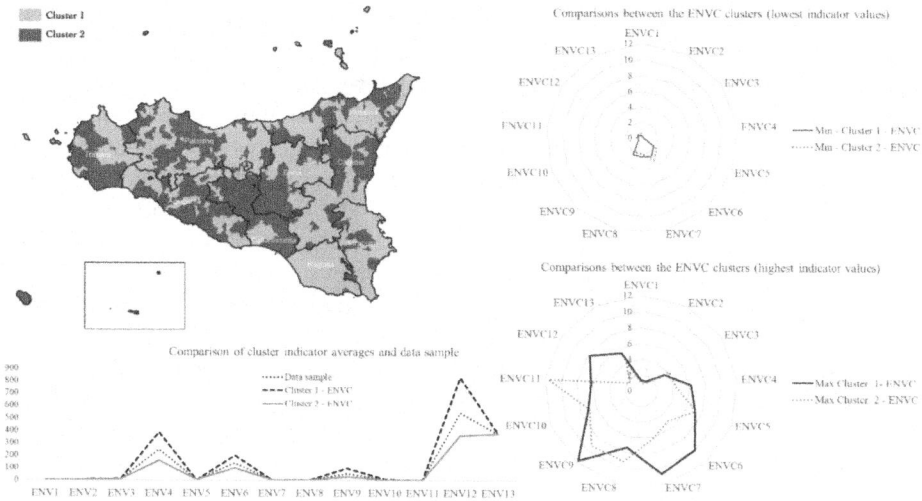

Fig. 7. Environmental Capital distribution in C_1 and C_2 clusters

6 Conclusion and Discussion

The cognitive model proposed, developed in the axiological perspective of the forms of territorial capital, aimed at highlighting divergences and convergences at the regional and infra-regional scale, applied to the region of Sicily, representative of the Southern Italy or weak areas with respect to the national territory, has highlighted:

- Less marked divergence at regional scale for human, economic, natural and environmental capital.
- More marked divergences at regional scale for urban capital.
- Strong divergences at regional scale for infrastructure capital.
- Divergences in human capital values for the two clusters identified, and significant divergences within cluster C_2 on the infra-regional scale.
- Divergences in urban capital values for the three clusters identified and divergences are significant within cluster C_1, which includes the provincial capitals of Catania, Enna, Messina and Palermo, and less marked for cluster C_2, which includes the provincial capitals of Agrigento, Ragusa and Siracusa, and greater convergence for C_3, even though it includes the provincial capitals of Trapani and Caltanissetta, as regards the infra-regional scale.
- Divergences in infrastructure capital values for the five clusters identified, which in most cases coincide with the administrative boundaries of the nine Sicilian provinces. Intra-regional divergences are more pronounced with different values of the level of infrastructural capital endowment, the variability being accentuated for cluster C_1 and less accentuated for clusters C_3, C_4 and C_5. There is a low convergence in cluster C_2. The divergences observed in terms of infrastructure endowment highlight a strong criticality, not only in terms of distribution, but also in terms of the general level of endowment at regional level, which is already low compared to the national level. In fact, the areas characterised by higher values of territorial capital endowment

in the estimated classification, with reference to the regional scale, have a lower level of infrastructure capital endowment than the areas in the centre-north. Thus, in this classification, the areas characterised by lower values of infrastructure capital endowment show very marked disparities compared with those in the Centre-North; divergences with regard to the infra-regional scale in the economic capital values for the two clusters identified. With regard to the infra-regional scale, there are more significant divergences for cluster C_2, which includes both coastal and inland areas. This is mainly due to the fact that the nine provincial capitals of Sicily are included in cluster C_2. Less significant divergences in economic capital values for cluster C_1.

- Divergences in natural capital infra-regional scale values for the two clusters identified are due to their different distribution in the territory of Sicily. With regard to the infra-regional scale, there are more significant divergences for cluster C_2, due to a greater variability of natural capital endowment, and less for cluster C_1. Cluster C_1 is characterised by the higher value of the indicator NC5-*Average agricultural value* in cluster C_1, while cluster C_2 is characterised by the higher value of the indicator NC2-*Percentage of forest area* in cluster C_2.
- Divergences with regard environmental capital values in infra-regional scale, in this case representative of the exposure of municipalities to different environmental risks for the two clusters identified. The municipalities with the highest risk of environmental damage are those belonging to cluster C_1, which is characterised by the highest values of the indicators ENV4-*Surface area of land consumed in areas of high and very high seismic hazard*, ENV6-*Resident population at risk in areas of high and very high landslide hazard*, ENV9-*Resident population at risk in areas of high hydraulic hazard*, ENV12-*Soil consumed per capita*, ENV13-*Municipal waste production per capita*. This cluster is characterised by a greater variability in the environmental risk of the municipalities in it than cluster C_2. This cluster is characterised by greater variability in the environmental risk of the municipalities within it than cluster C_2.

The cognitive model proposed, which aims to highlight convergences and gaps territorial capital endowment at regional and infra-regional levels, might be helpful for decision-makers to identify policies, measures and ad hoc funding to support the development of these areas effectively and efficiently. In particular, analyses of human, urban, infrastructural and economic capital, by highlighting the weakest and strongest areas, might be supportive for policies aimed at territorial rebalancing and the development of measures to reduce gaps and strengthen areas with higher levels of these forms of capital [43, 44]. Natural capital analyses, by highlighting convergences and gaps, might be supportive for the identification of appropriate measures to protect, conserve and enhance the natural heritage. Environmental capital analyses might be supportive for policies development to mitigate environmental risks, which are becoming increasingly severe and recurrent, including those related to climate change. Future developments of this research are aimed at providing a general overview of convergences and gaps for the regions of southern Italy, but it could also be extended to the regions of central and northern Italy. Such a process could provide a complete cognitive picture of convergences and gaps in the Italian territory, on the basis of which targeted and integrated actions could be planned, in compliance with the principle of territorial equity. Future developments will concern identifying more robust measures about convergences and gaps at regional and infra-regional scales.

Disclosure of Interests. The authors have no competing interests to declare that are relevant to the content of this article.

References

1. SVIMEZ: Rapporto 2011 sull'economia del mezzogiorno (2011)
2. AA. VV: "L'Italia dei divari", Rivista Il Mulino, LXXI, 4; Banca d'Italia (aprile 2022), "La crescita dell'economia italiana e il divario nord-sud", Questioni di economia e finanza, n. 683 (2022)
3. European Union: Consolidated version of the Treaty on the Functioning of the European Union Part three- Union policies and internationa actions tole XVIII- Economic, social and territorial cohesion. Official Journal of the European Union, C 326/1, 26.10.2012
4. Presidente della Repubblica: Disposizioni urgenti per l'attuazione del Piano nazionale di ripresa e resilienza (PNRR) e del Piano nazionale degli investimenti complementari al PNRR (PNC), nonche' per l'attuazione delle politiche di coesione e della politica agricola comune. (23G00022) (GU Serie Generale n.47 del 24-02-2023)
5. Presidente della Repubblica: Decreto Legge 6 agosto 2021, n. 111. Misure urgenti per l'esercizio in sicurezza delle attivita' scolastiche, universitarie, sociali e in materia di trasporti. (21G00125) (GU Serie Generale n.187 del 06-08-2021)
6. Presidente della Repubblica: Decreto Legge 1 luglio 2021, n. 101. Conversione in legge, con modificazioni, del decreto-legge 6 maggio 2021, n. 59, recante misure urgenti relative al Fondo complementare al Piano nazionale di ripresa e resilienza e altre misure urgenti per gli investimenti. (21G00111)
7. Presidente della Repubblica: Decreto Legge 31 maggio 2021, n. 177 Governance del Piano nazionale di ripresa e resilienza e prime misure di rafforzamento delle strutture amministrative e di accelerazione e snellimento delle procedure. (21G00087)
8. Presidente della Repubblica: Legge 29 luglio 2021. N. 108. Conversione in legge, con modificazioni, del decreto-legge 31 maggio 2021, n. 77, recante governance del Piano nazionale di ripresa e resilienza e prime misure di rafforzamento delle strutture amministrative e di accelerazione e snellimento delle procedure. (21G00118)
9. Decreto del Presidente del Consiglio di Ministri 30 novembre 2021: Ripartizione, termini, modalita' di accesso e rendicontazione dei contributi per la realizzazione di interventi di sostegno alle attivita' economiche finalizzati a contrastare fenomeni di deindustrializzazione per ciascuno degli anni dal 2021 al 2023. (22A00106)
10. Legge 30 dicembre 2020, n. 178. Bilancio di previsione dello Stato per l'anno finanziario 2021 e bilancio pluriennale per il triennio 2021–2023. (20G00202)
11. Decreto del Presidente del Consiglio di Ministri 30 settembre 2021: Modalita' di ripartizione, termini, modalita' di accesso e rendicontazione dei contributi a valere sul Fondo comuni marginali, al fine di realizzare interventi di sostegno alle popolazioni residenti nei comuni svantaggiati, per ciascuno degli anni dal 2021 al 2023. (21A07265)
12. Decreto del Presidente del Consiglio dei Ministri 24 settembre 2020: Ripartizione, termini, modalita' di accesso e rendicontazione dei contributi ai comuni delle aree interne, a valere sul Fondo di sostegno alle attivita' economiche, artigianali e commerciali per ciascuno degli anni dal 2020 al 2022. (20A06526)

13. Italian Government. decree-law no. 124/2023. https://www.gazzettaufficiale.it/eli/id/2023/11/16/23A06374/SG - Text of decree-law no. 124 of September 19, 2023 (in Gazzetta Ufficiale - Serie generale - no. 219 of September 19, 2023), coordinated with conversion law no. 162 of November 13, 2023 (in the same Gazzetta Ufficiale on page 1). 124 (in Official Gazette - General Series - no. 219 of 19 September 2023), coordinated with Conversion Law no. 162 of 13 November 2023 (in this same Official Gazette, p. 1), on: 'Urgent provisions on cohesion policies, for the relaunch of the economy in the areas of Southern Italy, as well as on immigration'. (23A06374)
14. Trovato, M.R., Nasca, L.: An axiology of weak areas: the estimation of an index of abandonment for the definition of a cognitive tool to support the enhancement of inland areas in Sicily. Land **11**(12), 2268 (2022). https://doi.org/10.3390/land11122268
15. Dobrescu, E.M., Edith Mihaela Dobre, E.M.: Theories regarding the role of the growth poles in the economic integration. Procedia Econ. Finance **8**, 262–267 (2014)
16. Nasca, L., Giuffrida, S., Trovato, M.R.: Value and quality in the dialectics between human and urban capital of the city networks on the land district scale. Land **11**, 34 (2022). https://doi.org/10.3390/land11010034
17. Giuffrida, S., Trovato, M.R., Ventura, V., Cappello, C., Nasca, L.: Concepts and tools for the emergence of the axiological subject in the prospect of territorial rebalancing. In: Calabrò, F., Madureira, L., Morabito, F.C., Piñeira Mantiñán, M.J. (eds.) NMP 2024. LNNS, vol. 1186, pp. 208–217. Springer, Cham (2024). https://doi.org/10.1007/978-3-031-74679-6_20
18. Capello, R., Lenzi, C.: Territorial Patterns of Innovation. An Inquiry on the Knowledge Economy in European Regions. Routledge Advances in Regional Economics, Science and Policy (2013)
19. Camagni, R., Capello, R.: Regional competitiveness and territorial capital: a conceptual approach and empirical evidence from the European union. Reg. Stud. **47**(9), 1383–1402 (2012). https://doi.org/10.1080/00343404.2012.681640
20. Scrofani, L., Accordino, F.: Divari territorialie criteri SNAI ripensare la classificazione delle aree interne e periferiche
21. Wallerstein, I.: The Modern World System. Academic Press, New York (1974)
22. The World Bank: World development indicators (2009). https://ocuments1.worldbank.org/curated/en/886211468340850838/pdf/541680WDI0200910Box345641B01PUBLIC1.pdf
23. Czapiewski, K.L., Janc, K.: Internal peripheries of socio-economic development in Poland. In: Kovacs, A.D. (ed.) Old and New Bor-derlines/Frontiers/Margins, Pécs, Centre for Regional Studies of Hungarian Academy of Sciences, pp. 109–122 (2009)
24. Franklin, R.: The demographic burden of population loss in US cities, 2000–2010. J. Geogr. Syst. **23**, 209–230 (2019)
25. OECD: Regional Tipology, Directorate for Public Governance and Territorial Development (2011)
26. Capello, R., Fratesi, U., Resmini, L.: Globalizzazione e crescita regionale in Europa: tendenze passate e scenari futuri. Springer, Berlino (2011)
27. Herrschel, T.: Regional development, peripheralisation and marginali-sation and the role of governance. In: Herrschel, T., Tallberg, P. (eds.) The Role of Regions? Networks, Scale, Territory, Kristianstad, Kri-stianstad Boktryckeri, pp. 85–102 (2011)
28. Dematteis, G.: Di quali territori parliamo: una mappa delle Aree Interne, Intervento al convegno "Le Aree Interne: nuove strategie per la programmazione 2014–2020 della politica di coesione territoriale", Roma, Palazzo Rospigliosi, 15 dicembre 2012
29. Medeiros, E.: Territorial cohesion: an EU concept. Eur. J. Spat. Dev. **60**, 1–30 (2016)
30. Faludi, A.: The European spatial development perspective. Eur. J. Spat. Dev. **4**(3) (2006)
31. Pezzi, M.G., Urso, G.: Peripheral areas: conceptualizations and policies. Introduction and editorial note. Ital. J. Plan. Pract. **6**(1), 1–19 (2016)

32. Copus, A., Mantino, F., Noguera, J.: Inner peripheries: an oxymoron or a real challenge for territorial cohesion? IJPP Ital. J. Plan. Pract. **VII**(1), 24–49 (2017)
33. Bock, B.: Rural marginalisation and the role of social innovation: a turn towards nexogenous development and rural reconnection. Sociol. Rural. **56**(4), 552–573 (2016). 36
34. Chieffallo, L., Palermo, A., Viapiana, M.F.: Tecniche geo-statistiche per la mappatura territoriale di divari multipli: la 'geografia' della Regione Calabria. Archivio di studi urbani e regionali **133**(1), 104–129 (2022). 37
35. Trovato, M.R., Nasca, L., Giuffrida, S., Ventura, V.: Centre versus periphery. Territorial imbalance from perspectives of the multiple capital dimensions. In: Calabrò, F., Madureira, L., Morabito, F.C., Piñeira Mantiñán, M.J. (eds.) NMP 2024. LNNS, vol. 1186, pp. 237–246. Springer, Cham (2024). https://doi.org/10.1007/978-3-031-74679-6_23
36. Bignante, E., Celata, F., Vanolo, A.: Geografie dello sviluppo. Una prospet-tiva critica e globale, Torino, Utet (2022)
37. ISTAT: I divari territoriali nel PNRR: dieci obiettivi per il mezzogiorno. Statistiche FOCUS (2023)
38. ISTAT: Il Censimento permanente della popolazione in Sicilia (2024). https://www.istat.it/wp-content/uploads/2024/05/Focus-CENSIMENTO-2022-SICILIA.pdf
39. Camagni, R.: Territorial cohesion: a theoretical and operational definition, in the European union. Scienze Regionali Ital. J. Reg. Sci. **9**(1), 115–118 (2010)
40. Agency for Territorial Cohesion: National Strategy for Inner Areas. https://www.agenziacoesione.gov.it/strategia-nazionale-aree-interne/la-selezione-delle-aree/
41. Governo italiano, presidenza del Consiglio del Consiglio dei Ministri: Urban index. Indicatori per le politiche urbane. https://www.urbanindex.it/indicatori/
42. NCSS Statistical software. https://www.ncss.com
43. Trovato, M.R.: Human capital approach in the economic assessment of interventions for the reduction of seismic vulnerability in historic centres. Sustainability **12**(19), 8059 (2020). https://doi.org/10.3390/su12198059
44. Minioto, C., Martinico, F., Trovato, M.R., Giuffrida, S.: Data and values: axiological interpretations of building sprawl landscape risk in the rural territory of Noto (Italy). Land **12**(6), 1258 (2023). https://doi.org/10.3390/land12061258

Decision-Making CIA Process (DeMaCIA) to Support SNAI Strategies: The Case of Castelluccio Inferiore in Basilicata, Italy

Cristina Coscia[1](✉) [iD], Silvia Gron[1] [iD], and Enrico Vercellino[2]

[1] Architecture and Design Department, Politecnico di Torino, Viale Mattioli 39, 10125 Turin, Italy
{cristina.coscia,silvia.gron}@polito.it
[2] Chorus srl, Via Angelo Brofferio 3, 10121 Turin, Italy
e.vercellino@chorusdesign.it

Abstract. The debate on Inner Areas has produced the SNAI strategy (since 2014). It involves public and private actors, aiming to reverse the dynamics of small towns' depopulation and the citizenry's inaccessibility to primary services. We configured an intervention project for the Lucanian territory with an interdisciplinary approach and evaluated it through scenario simulation (DeMaCIA). The study is realized within an Agreement between the Municipality of Castelluccio Inferiore (PZ) and the Polytechnic University of Turin (2020–2025). Analyzing the use of resources deployed over the past 10 years (SNAI and PNRR) reveals a lack of population involvement. While identifying possible strategies to trigger active resident participation, we hypothesized the configuration of a Renewable Energy Community (REC) embedded in the site of the Old Mills, as a way to enable the collective sharing of the environmental and cultural resources of their area. The paper focuses on the methodology adopted by building a process to be applied in other fragile contexts.

Keywords: SNAI · Community Impact Analysis (CIA) · REC · Basilicata Region

1 Introduction

As is well known, areas referred to as "Inner Areas" (IA) in the Italian context cover 60% of the peninsula's land area and are home to 22% of the population. IAs are closely related to the morphological characteristics of mostly mountainous terrains, where poor accessibility comes with an absence of economic development. Most of these areas are organized into smaller centers, which fail to provide residents with adequate essential services, such as health, education, and mobility. The activation in 2014 of the National Strategy of Inner Areas (SNAI) [1] has triggered policies for territorial development to improve these services and the economic system in territories at risk of marginalization, especially as they are affected by depopulation [2]. The SNAI mainly uses European Funds to implement this process: after the first round of funding (2014–2020), a second one (2021–2027) has started. The policies of the Basilicata Region have been examined to check SNAI's effects on the national territory. The case study of the community of Castelluccio Inferiore (PZ) has been chosen to reflect on a methodological proposal to support Public Administrations' (PAs) planning process and the community's effective participation as an inclusive action embodying SNAI in its principles and effectiveness. The manufacturing sector can play a new role in achieving the goals proposed by the SNAI for IAs and in consciously developing practices for adapting to contemporary needs while working in parallel on countering the climate crisis and reconstituting fragile communities. In Castelluccio Inferiore the sequence of events has distorted its identity.

1.1 Background: The SNAI for the Basilicata Region

The SNAI 2014–2020 cycle for the Basilicata Region involved 4 IAs: Alto Bradano, Montagna Materana, Marmo Platano, and Mercure-Alto Sinni-Val Sarmento, formed by the aggregation of 42 Municipalities. The Partnership Agreement (PA) 2014–2020 [3] indicates two priorities: the first concerns "the adjustment of the quality/quantity of the supply of essential services," such as education, health and mobility, as well as the network of services required to ensure their maximum accessibility; the second is directed toward the activation of "Local Development Projects" [4]. The financial resources are distributed to the zones through the programs of the European Regional Development Fund (FESR), European Social Fund (FSE), European Agricultural Fund for Rural Development (FEASR), and Complementary Operational Program (POC). These are compounded by other funding, such as the contributions of the Stability Law (147/2013), for a total of about 138 M€ (DR Basilicata 53/2017).

In the distribution of funds, most interest is placed on roads (44.4% of investments), followed by Energy, Social Inclusion, and Tourism (11–15% of funds), and finally, Education and Business Aid (8%).

From 2019 to 2022, the subscriptions to the Framework Programme Agreement (FPA) by the 4 areas occurred at different times, especially hindered by the years of the pandemic. This delay did not allow for achieving effective results by the end of the period and carrying out ex post evaluations useful for planning the new cycle.

After the abolition of the Agency for Territorial Cohesion (DPCM of Nov. 10, 2023), the SNAI has been reappointed by the Department for Cohesion Policies and the South also in the 2021–2027 period, as established by the Partnership Agreement (PA) 2021–2027 [3, 5]. The new configuration introduces some changes for the new cycle, in addition to the identification of new areas and the redefinition of the perimeters of some of them: among them, the adoption of sectoral measures to support shared projects between Municipalities is deemed relevant [6]. The implementations follow the drafting of Cohesion Agreements, indicating the objectives and the coordinating entity of the funding. The interest in enhancing IAs originates from their geomorphologically defined and recognizable geomorphologically "compact" system, representing "an identifiable socio-historical unity that has been consolidated over time through socio-economic relationships" [7]. While recognizing the need to find a common denominator for defining territorial areas, it is clear that the SNAI has limitations in taking into account territorial complexity and specificities. For Basilicata, the same objective compactness represented by both a "physical-geomorphological" unity and a "historical-social identity" unity has been left aside, choosing instead the municipal administrative borders as a reference.

Within the AP, Basilicata proposes new IAs for the SNAI program: a new re-mapping of the IAs 2014–2020 is planned, with the inclusion of 3 areas in particular: Medio Agri; Basento; Vulture with 23 municipalities and 2 Urban Areas that circumscribe the cities of Potenza and Matera with 12 municipalities, thus doubling the total number of municipalities involved by the SNAI. At the same time, a new classification of IAs is applied by changing the allocation of some municipalities from Peripheral to Ultra-peripheral.

This territorial layout is aimed at fulfilling the goals of the regional FESR and FSE-PLUS program, Basilicata 2021–2027. It follows the principle of the configuration of a "network of integrated territories", avoiding too many fragmentations, urging actions and objectives that solidify complementarity between municipalities in the provision of services (DR Basilicata 581/2023). The amount for the new cycle decreases by 6%; this is made more onerous by the increase of the involved area, penalizing the municipalities included in the first cycle of IAs in favor of newly established ones. The new SNAI program is concurrent with the National Recovery and Resilience Plan (PNRR) 2021–2026, which also directs its resources to the policy of strengthening IAs. The common goals involve balanced and sustainable spatial development through the redistribution of new economic opportunities to strengthen local communities, supported by extensive infrastructure (transportation and technology). PNRR funds thus integrate with FESR and FSE funds. The PNRR allocates 1.8 B€ to the Basilicata Region, funding a total of 3528 projects. The data for the 1st half of 2024 show that, in the distribution of investments by mission, there is a prevailing 50.8% budget for Mission 3 "Infrastructures for Sustainable Mobility" (M3) and a 20% for Mission 2 "Green Revolution and Ecological Transition" (M2) [8]. PNRR funds mostly benefit the SNAI regarding the improvement of essential services (health, education, and mobility), while little is directed to supporting economic development and job creation, without materializing the SNAI's ultimate goal of providing these areas with new growth opportunities that enable people to stay, work, and invest in their home areas.

In examining how ongoing projects have considered the possibility of triggering development based on local specificities, generating economic activity and involving communities in a participatory manner [2], a varied presence of small, non-institutionalized initiatives emerges. Unfortunately, these are neither cataloged nor easily comparable in terms of size and outcomes.

The involvement of residents mainly concerns the sectors of sustainable tourism (nature-based or agritourism), agriculture (enhancing local products), culture (historical heritage), and education (outdoor education), as is also the case in other IA in Italy [9].

1.2 Background: The MASV IA

The Mercure-Alto Sinni-Val Sarmento (MASV) area is characterized by more inhabitants and a higher extension than the other areas identified for the Basilicata Region, in addition to the presence of the Pollino National Park.

In the 2014–2020 SNAI, it consisted of 19 municipalities, 14 of which were included in the Ultra-peripheral category: with the new 2021–2027 cycle, the MASV area has been

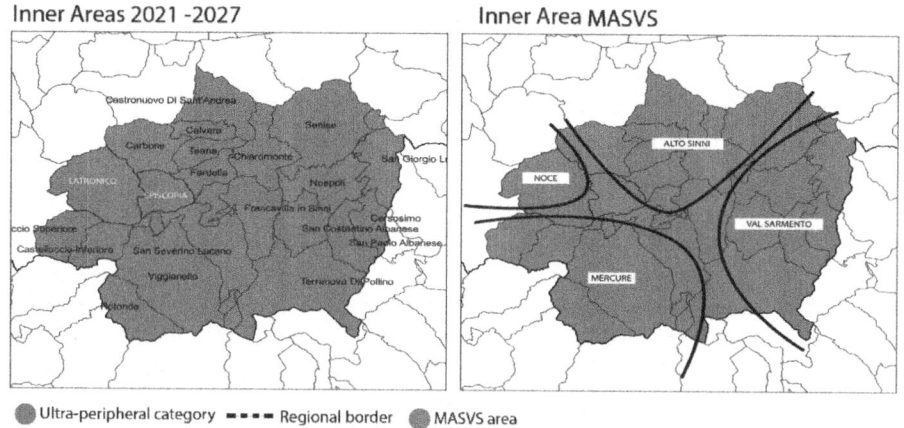

Fig. 1. Left side: MASVS perimeter, classification, 2021–2027 cycles. Right side: Mercure's valley. (Source: Authors' elaboration)

re-perimetered by including two new municipalities (Episconia and Latronico). Moreover, it is fully considered Ultra-peripheral (Fig. 1). The development of the Apennine ridge is closely linked to the dynamics of the IAs in this area. Moreover, the territory is characterized by an impervious orography, which prevents agile connections between even close territories. A notable element is the presence of the A2 Salerno-Reggio Calabria highway section, which allows for faster travel, in contrast with the total absence of the railway system. In the 2014–2020 cycle, MASV signed the Framework Agreement on November 11, 2020, managing funds amounting to 59 M€ to implement 136 projects. This consists of 34 M€ from the FESR, 21 M€ from the Basilicata COP, and 4 M€ from the SNAI for Basilicata. In the 2021–2027 cycle, the MASV IA has acquired 15 M€ for Priority 11 OS 5.2 and 3 M€ for Priority 5 OS 3.2, compounded by 300,000 € from CIPESS 41/2022, for a total of 18.4 M€ [10]. Fund distribution is coordinated by the lead municipality, Francavilla in Sinni. Each project often turns out to be a stand-alone entity. The use of funds reveals that the greatest critical issues arise from the absence of synergic territorial programs involving multiple centers in building a network defined by local identities that do not always correspond to administrative boundaries.

2 Strategies and Research Questions

The complex framework depicted in §1 clearly shows the need to outline a *problem-solving* approach and identify a methodological proposal to support operational intervention methods through a control room, synergistically cooperating with citizens according to participatory, consultative, and co-design methods. The methodological approach outlined in §3 starts with the following research questions:

Is it possible to configure processes that are strongly anchored with territorial identities? Can PAs be supported in identifying innovation-triggering processes, able to produce new opportunities for land preservation? In Basilicata, and in particular in the

MASV IA, which themes and resources could build a relationship between population, institutions, and territory?

3 Research Methodology: The Decision-Making CIA Process (DeMaCIA) Method

The goal of the research is to design new forms of IA development that enhance the specificity of places and encourage the involvement of all stakeholders within an area. This paper fine-tunes the methodological framework for Castelluccio Inferiore to evaluate whether it can be extended to other contexts. Starting from the analysis of the specific phenomena of MASV (and energy production for the Castelluccio case study), we intend to highlight the research methodology to support the *decision-making* of PAs, which has focused on three pillars: 1. The SNAI, 2. Renewable Energy Communities (RECs) model, 3. Generative Economy principles. These three elements, when considered together, represent an integrated and innovative response to territorial challenges for revitalizing local communities and fostering sustainable and participatory development. Specifically, RECs are groups of private individuals, Small and Medium Enterprises, territorial entities, or local authorities that decide to establish a legal form to produce and share energy collectively, deriving collective benefits of social, environmental, and economic nature. These decentralized energy production and management models contribute to fostering energy autonomy through a social innovation process that can overcome the concept of the citizen as a mere consumer, transforming him or her into a co-producer and fostering a culture of participatory and sustainable management of territorial energy resources.

Communities that invest in renewable energy can also access public funding and tax incentives, making this model a real opportunity for local economic development. The PNRR plans to take action by accelerating the development of small-scale energy communities and distributed systems through tariff incentives, grants, and financing for the construction of plants up to a total of 5 GWatts (by 2027). This approach aligns with the SNAI and REC initiatives, where the redistribution of economic benefits from incentives can be a powerful tool for building an economic system that respects local resources and communities' rhythms and vocations. Energy becomes a common good, accessible for all, with care for the most vulnerable citizens and the most marginalized groups, socially and/or geographically.

The synergy between the SNAI, RECs, and generative economy principles can be a paradigm shift for the development of Italian IAs by helping to transform the local development model, making it more sustainable. In light of the three pillars mentioned, the research group of the Polytechnic of Turin[1] has developed a methodological proposal for a multi-phase process to support the *decision-making* of the PAs involved in the SNAI and responsible for financing, which must act and generate multidimensional impacts on the "fragile" areas that are the object of such strategies. The methodological approach is based on the CIA Decision-Making Approach (DeMaCIA) [11], which has

---

[1] Programma di Riposizionamento Competitivo e Strategico: Convenzione Comune di Castelluccio Inferiore (PZ) e DAD Politecnico di Torino, Torino 16.03.2021.

developed from the original Community Impact Analysis (CIA) Method but includes a step-based parallel process of stakeholder consultation (structured by interest groups in the Lichfield style) (following phases 0, 2, and 3 in Fig. 2) and a collegial assembly presentation of the final scenario. The adopted methodology is proposed with some new activities (Fig. 2, multi-phase process) to assess the role of each stakeholder based on their multi-dimensional impact on the scenario within the development of the SNAI.

Four phases are proposed, aimed at allowing a flexible application of this classical methodology in different study areas through amendments and adaptions to better represent the field of expertise and the role of specific actors.

As it is well-known, in literature the CIA method and its development into the CIE are included among Cost-Benefit Analysis (CBA) techniques [11] but classified as a variant that overcomes some of the limits of the CBA itself [12–14], since it allows the simulation of scenarios, the precise definition of areas of investigation, the identification of subjects, the introduction of the temporal variable for the evaluation of the consequences, and the application of qualitative evaluations on the outcomes. European legislation, particularly the Next Generation Bauhaus [14], emphasizes the importance of community involvement and dictates that processes must include policies to support active citizenship activities. Against this backdrop, DeMaCIA proves to be a robust and effective method in facilitating such processes and in transparently highlighting the positive and/or negative impacts (in both qualitative and quantitative and qualitative-quantitative terms) for each stakeholder group that certain IA development alternatives may generate at specific points in the process. The DeMaCIA facilitates the engagement and co-design community process and supports it in the stages of defining strategic elements within the construction of alternative scenarios, analyzing their temporally (short-medium and long-term) and dimensionally (on-site and off-site) heterogeneous spillovers. DeMaCIA's methodological proposal has 4 steps: it represents an "evolved" version of the CIA method, obtained by strengthening its processual logic, collaborative-consultative mode, and problem-solving capability [15, 16].

The strength of the traditional CIA lies in its robust structuring of strategies to support the identification of intervention scenarios always about community groups: it maintains its investigative nature concerning the subsequent phase of the CIE, in which qualitative assessments are formalized through the most suitable techniques. In DeMaCIAthese elements are maintained, but the "traditional" process is accompanied by specific moments of consultation and interaction with stakeholders that provide aspects of convergence or indicate potential and further critical issues to be taken into account in the final phase of impact assessment: in this sense, they strengthen its nature of aid to the decision-making process, making it more participatory and scalable even to small realities.

It is essential to set research objectives (Phase 0) aligned with the PAs that create development levers concerning the critical issues highlighted in §2 and impacts for the stakeholders involved. This serves as a prerequisite for outlining both the geographical boundaries and possible thematic or methodological constraints. The analysis of the competitive framework in the territorial context (Phase 1) is based on data collection and knowledge construction activities to understand the characteristics and peculiarities of the area (cultural heritage, natural resources, territorial planning, and "intangible" heritage). The outputs of this phase consist of: 1. Understanding the territory's vocation, evaluating its strengths and weaknesses (competitive framework model and SWOT Analysis); 2. Identifying a user base interested in undertaking this type of experience and choosing alternative ways of enjoying the cultural heritage of the sample area.

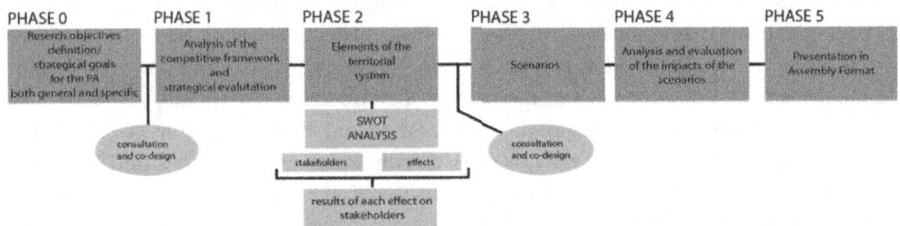

Fig. 2. The methodological approach: the Decision-Making CIA process (Source: Authors' elaboration)

The synergy between the SNAI, RECs, and generative economy principles can be a paradigm shift for the development of Italy's mountainous areas. The combination of these strategies can help transform the local development model, making it more sustainable, inclusive, and resilient **(Phase 2)**. Thus, local communities no longer serve as merely passive beneficiaries of economic policies but become active participants in the transformation of their local areas and can proactively contribute to the improvement of the proposed scenarios. In this vision, the future of IAs will shift from isolation and depopulation to rebirth, based on a participatory and regenerative approach, capable of enhancing the natural, social, and economic resources present on site according to a development model centered on people's well-being and environmental protection. In this phase, DeMaCIA was tested in the technical steps (inherited from the traditional CIA model) of structuring the elements of the System, individuating the effects (to be successively translated into impacts), and identifying and classifying the Community interest groups to be consulted. **Phase 2** and **Phase 3** represent the decisional design to support the identification of alternative development scenarios compared to the current state (zero option). Finally, support is provided to PAs in **Phase 4** through the analysis and evaluation of the preferable scenario resulting from the analysis of impacts, which can be illustrated in an assembly to the interest groups, structured according to the CIA.

4 Focus Area (FA): Castelluccio Inferiore (PZ)

The municipality of Castelluccio Inferiore (population 1911 in 2024) is one of the 21 municipalities that constitute the MASV IA (Mercure area) established in 2014. With the new classification – 2021–2027 – Castelluccio is considered Ultra-peripheral due to the continuous population decline estimated at −10.28% in the decade 2011–2020 (see ISTAT data). The territory is located within the Mercure plain, in Valle del Mercure-Lao, a valley that develops between the Basilicata and Calabria Regions and constitutes a system of close relations between the municipalities of the two regions (see Fig. 1). The pivotal elements around which the anthropogenic development of the valley revolves are hydrography and orography. Hydrography drives the development of routes, connections, and residential, manufacturing, and production settlements. The orography provides an interesting demarcation between the Lucanian territory, characterized by the soft reliefs of the Mercure plain, and the Calabrian territory of the Lao gorges, the valley floor, and the coast.

An initial observation of the centers shows that most of those located on the river stretches have a large productive fabric characterized by the presence of now-disused factories. It is not difficult to imagine that the characteristics of the area, combined with the mountainous landscape's richness of materials, favored the development of manufactures, which used water power and represented the region's main economy until the first two decades of the 20th century. The presence of water was the basis for the operation of most of the facilities, as it favored processes in mills, spinning mills, oil mills, sawmills, and tanneries in the area. The interesting aspect of this phenomenon lies in the development of the technologies for the construction of the plants. Indeed, they adapted to the singularities of the river landscape with integrated systems between water networks of locks, reservoirs, aqueducts, dams, and canals. The role of these constructions is fundamental because they allowed for proper management of the flow of water, which, once used, was conveyed to the manufacturing building located further downstream, resulting in a serial pattern that produced control over the river course. This aspect laid the foundation for a reinterpretation of the role of manufacturing in marginal areas. Through a more specific analysis of the succession of production dynamics, it has been possible to investigate the phenomena that have defined its recent historical development, helping to slow down and subsequently accelerate the marginalization process. We refer to the events that led to the construction of the large Enel Mercure Power Plant. Starting with the discovery of lignite deposits, used as a fuel for electricity production, from the 1920s onward, the dynamics of the valley changed abruptly. Inhabitants were employed in tunnel mining and transportation to the Campania centers where the process of combustion and transformation into energy took place. This system completely changes the socio-economic fabric of the valley by attracting a large flow of labor. In the post-war period, the construction of the Power Plant, positioned at lignite mining sites to enable a reduction of time in processing the raw material directly on site, was a turning point. Much of the population was employed at the Power Plant in the early years, and the urban fabric of the municipality was altered to accommodate previously nonexistent functions such as cinemas, theaters, sports fields, after-work spaces, and workers' housing. Castelluccio became the center of a significantly larger manufacturing system, attracting population, new technologies, and new functions and changing the social fabric. The process came to an abrupt halt with the closure of the power plant, which was considered obsolete as early as the 1980s, with major consequences for the Valley's municipalities and population employment, affecting population decline. The extraordinary development helped to reflect on the positive aspects that both manufacturing and industrial production had had on the center of Castelluccio. The manufacturing businesses had successfully exploited the specificities of the area through skillful management of the resources of the individual communities owning the plants, which became collectors of social activities and hubs of aggregation for the inhabitants.

4.1 Projects and Funding

The current condition of the municipality of Castelluccio Inferiore is typical of a municipality that is experiencing depopulation dynamics. Most residents live near the historic center, where mainly tertiary activities are concentrated. Within the historic center, however, many buildings are in a state of disrepair, particularly in the Rizzano and St. Anna districts: the Enel district suffers from depopulation, with several unoccupied dwellings in an obviously advanced state of deterioration.

The Municipality of Castelluccio adopted a program (2024–2029 mandate) to reknit together intentions already made explicit in part from 2020 with the "Tourism, Culture, Major Events Enhancement Project. "The initial goal was to build opportunities fueled by the enhancement of historic sites. Six projects were launched, among them: "revisiting mining sites" for the localization of tunnel portals, "conversion of the former municipal headquarters into a Museum Hub" to narrate the manufacturing history by documenting the features of local industrial archaeology, "the recovery and enhancement of Borgo dei Mulini" including the environmental restoration of the banks of the S. Giovanni river, the conversion of buildings such as the Spinning Mill (which had just been renovated at the time) to house the Interactive Museum on Pollino Geosites, and the inclusion, along Mill Street, of a new building for a Research Center. In the new program (C.C. Resolution 29.6.2024), "Productive Activities & Opportunities for Development and Technological Innovation" also include future intentions related to the former manufacturing areas, and thus the "completion of the existing facilities of the former Spinning Mill and the acquisition of the existing Mill with educational and tourist purposes" and the "reopening of the Lignite Mine" located in Pietrasasso – Fiumara del Pegno, formerly ex SME (Enel) for educational-tourist purposes". The enhancement program is supported by the "realization in the former Municipal House of the Civic Museum where to allocate community artifacts and historical traces" Within the SNAI 2014–2020, the Municipality of Castelluccio Inferiore directly managed 6 projects totaling 656,000 €. The budget was mainly allocated to the Energy theme (62%, 3 projects) with interventions regarding optimization of public lighting, energy efficiency, and electricity production from renewable sources for a school and the municipal house. 30% (1 project for 198,000 €) was earmarked for the redevelopment of Borgo dei Mulini (culture and tourism theme) – FESR Basilicata 2014–2020, while the remaining funds go to the purchase of equipment for carrying out innovative teaching in the middle school (networks and digital services theme) and for fire prevention and firefighting (environment theme). These projects are known to be 90% completed. The Castelluccio center is also involved in inter-municipal and regional projects, such as upgrading the water network to reduce aqueduct network losses, distribution of a defibrillator for each municipality (managed by Francavilla in Sinni), upgrading of SP46 (managed by the provincial administration); hydrogeological works, the renovation of the Outpatient Clinics (managed by ASL PZ), and the installation of the broadband telecommunications network. Regarding manufacturing sites, the Borgo dei Mulini, near the historic center, is where the old manufacturing buildings are located. Considered one of the best-preserved mills and factories in the Lucanian Apennines, the enhancement of the complex involved the architectural recovery of the old Spinning Mill. Unfortunately, upon completion of the works, the building, without a specific purpose, soon became isolated from its context. Hence, the need arose for PA to define an effective enhancement strategy. From the analysis, the theme of manufacturing is avowedly an identity fact (interest in the village of mills and lignite quarries), and the process of valorization is underway, as proven by the approved programs. Unfortunately, to make this process effective, we lack two elements: the population's effective involvement and coordination throughout project phases. This requires a control room carrying out the process (knowing its stages and objectives) and can build connections on even heterogeneous but synergistic areas to expand diffusion and benefits. Against this backdrop of potential and critical issues, we suggested and proposed to the Castelluccio PA the experimentation of the DeMaCIA and initiated it (§5), to structure the preliminary decision-making phase and support the identification of a final scenario shared by the community and characterized by the ambitious challenges highlighted by the SNAI.

5 Results

The PoliTo research team applied the aforementioned 4-phase methodological approach (DeMaCIA process Method, §3) to the Castelluccio Inferiore (PZ) territory. The following were performed: the definition of the main objectives, synergic with the three SNAI pillars (§2), and the competitive framework; the identification of the elements of the system, the classification of the effects, the structuring of the stakeholders and actors to determine the main potential actors to be involved in enhancement processes to reactivate the territory, the transformation of the effects into impacts for each interest group, and the identification of alternative scenarios to the current state, supporting the phase of assessing the impacts on the development scenario recommended to the PA. Below are the application details and results of each phase:

Phase 0 *Definition of research objectives/PA strategic goals*

This is the preliminary stage where the objectives identified within the critical themes that emerged during the IA context analysis phases were interwoven with those resulting from the dialogue with PAs and citizens. The project's general objectives focused on the themes identified by the SNAI, contextualized through reinterpretation to meet the specific needs of Castelluccio. The strategic goals are: 1. Demographic trend reversal: depopulation/emigration; 2. Increased citizen services: citizenship services, restitution of disused public space, and 3. Territorial heritage enhancement. The proposals devised for the municipality interpret the historical vocation of Mercure and its manufacturing history, articulating it through new forms of energy production related to RECs. The specific project objectives are: 1. Proposal contextualization, by giving attention to the specific characteristics of the territorial context; 2. Innovative development by introducing new forms of sustainable energy production and social innovation for community value rethinking and development through RECs; 3. The enhancement of land resources by proposing functions and activities that can meet the current demand; 4. The ability to trigger an attraction mechanism for potential and future demand from a larger territorial basin through a synergistic process among the Bacino del Mercure municipalities; 5. Participation, intended as the ability to ground systems of involvement to integrate different levels of roles belonging to different types of users with particular regard toward PA, citizens, and businesses; 6. Project compatibility with the physical characteristics of the asset and with the current urban and planning constraints, aimed at preserving its environmental integrity and historical and cultural value. These goals were explained to the communities. Within this phase, expanded territorial areas were also defined, including territories excluded from the MASV area, to develop and interpret vocations and possibilities of more territories regardless of the administrative limits imposed in the SNAI. The definition of the areas was carried out by identifying the time intervals for the application of the evaluation model, also considering the time required for the preparation, establishment, and steady-state phases of the RECs.

Phase 1 *Analysis of the competitive framework and strategic evaluation*

In this phase, strategically preparatory to the CIA phases in the strict sense, thematic analyses were conducted on the territory (Population, Economy, Environment, Mobility and Accessibility, Heritage, and Processuality) according to the traditional Competitive Framework Analysis Method, synthesized into the SWOT Analysis and CIA explorations [12]. This allowed structuring the System Elements, then fine-tuned in a consolidated form in Phase 2.

Phase 2 *Elements of the territorial system*

In this phase, two complex but strategic application steps were developed, as they are pivotal to the final evaluation phase: 1. The identification of the objectives and system elements; 2. The identification of the effects for interest groups. The applied methodology considers all areas the project intends to act on, dividing subjects by interest groups. Two main categories are identified: 1. Operators-producers, i.e., entities that contribute to activating the territory; 2. Consumers, i.e., passive individuals who consume and use the goods and services produced. To strengthen the bottom-up logic and transparent decision-making, a further technical step of the DeMaCIA included the identification and classification of interest groups according to the taxonomy indicated by Lichfield [11], yet considering their close relation to the objectives defined in Phase 0, and refocused with the PA (see Fig. 3). These technical steps in the method allowed for greater transparency in discussions with interest groups and more detail to explain the strategic levers of the scenarios "under construction.

Phase 3 *Scenarios*

The results of Phases 1 and 2, highlighting strategic elements related to objectives, contexts, timing, and interest groups, have fed the construction of the alternative scenario to Option 0, namely the Bottom-up Scenario (see Fig. 4). It envisions the introduction of an energy community within Bacino del Mercure. In this context, the promotion of the REC as the result of an initiative by the citizens is simulated, providing for greater community management of resources, facilities, and related funding. The role of administrations in this context, while present, is limited to community participation and support. Since all specific contexts and possibilities for the RECs of each specific municipality cannot be studied, in the meta-design proposal, specific solutions have been simulated for the municipality of Castelluccio, and then procedures and outcomes have been extended to neighboring municipalities to study future impacts and effects. Regarding the steps related to the establishment of the REC in this scenario, "mild" solutions are

Decision-Making CIA Process 261

GOALS	
CX_	CONTEXTUALISATION
IN_	INNOVATION
VA_	VALORIZATION
AT_	ATTRACTIVENESS
PA_	PARTECIPATION
CO_	COMPATIBILITY

EXTENDED SCOPE		
LINKAGES	urban services	
	transport and accessibility	
	circuits and networks	
	communication routes	
FABRICS	economic	
	social	
	cultural	
	environmental	

SITE		
POPULATION	that lives	
	that works	
	that visits	
ARTIFACTS and PHYSICAL ELEMENTS	soil	
	structures	
	natural resources	
	cultural resources	
	services	
	transport networks	
	buildings and areas	
	open spaces	
ACTIVITIES and USES	residential	
	productive	
	tertiary	
	cultural	
	leisure	
	consumption	

Extract of the table of the assessment of the impacts on the stakeholders selected among those considered most significant for the **BOTTOM-UP SCENARIO** in the 3-10 year time

	BOTTOM_UP OPTION					
	ASSESSMENT of IMPACTS on DIFFERENT INTEREST GROUPS AND on the RELEVANT SPECIFIC OBJECTIVES on the SITE in REFERENCE to the PILOT PROJECT (3 – 10 years)					
Goals	FINANCIAL IMPACT	TAXI IMPACT	ECONOMIC IMPACT	SOCIAL IMPACT	CULTURAL IMPACT	ENVIRONMENTAL IMPACT
			OPERATORS_PRODUCERS			
			PUBLICS			
			EUROPEAN UNION			
CX_	Subsequent funding to encourage energy communities to promote Energy Transition		Choice between different projects to finance (in terms of attractiveness and competitiveness of the system, within a framework of environmental and territorial sustainability and social cohesion)			
			ITALIAN STATE			
CX_	Expenditure to support the works	Tax breaks				
IN_			Greater selection of supported projects (of innovative valorisation)			
			BASILICATA REGION			
CX_	Provision of funding for recovery and maintenance works			Strengthening social cohesion		
IN_	Provision of funding for recovery and maintenance works			Rethinking and developing community value		
			MUNICIPALITY OF CASTELLUCCIO INFERIORE			
CX_	Expenditure to support the works			Participation in the phases of dialogue with citizens as figures supporting the work. Investment in involving the entire population to make them an active protagonist of the project	Protection, improvement and enhancement of the conditions of cultural heritage	Environmental redevelopment. Reducing emissions
IN_	Expenditure to support the works		Greater selection of projects to support	Improving the way you interact with the PA		Environmental redevelopment
VA_	Expenditure to support the works		Regeneration and enhancement of existing artefacts. Profitable economic asset in the municipal territory			Environmental redevelopment
AT_	Expenditure to support the works			Better visibility of the entire Municipality	Increase in cultural offerings	Greater liveability of public spaces
			PRIVATE			
			BUILDERS			
CO_	New projects (investments and financial returns) Cost due to the construction of the systems		Economic returns	New job opportunities also in the maintenance sector		
IN_	New projects (investments and financial returns) Cost due to the construction of the systems		Economic returns	New training possibilities		
			ENERGY COMMUNITY MEMBERS			
CO_	New projects (investments and financial returns) Lowering of bills	Selling the energy produced at a higher price than the market price	Economic returns	Social cohesion, re-appropriation and direct management of one's assets, possibility of dialogue and negotiation with public bodies and companies	Direct management and renewal of its cultural heritage, recovery of former mill production spaces, recovery and transmission of the industrial past	Environmental redevelopment
			INHABITANTS			
PA_				Greater involvement of workers in the problems, opportunities and positive realities of the Energy Transition	Greater stimuli for cultural growth	
CO_				Management of your assets		Environmental redevelopment
			WORKERS			
CX_	Financial Flow Opportunities			Greater involvement of workers in the problems, opportunities and positive realities of the Energy Transition		

Fig. 3. Decision-Making CIA process-Phase 2: system elements and example of assessment of impacts on different groups of interest (Source: Authors' elaboration)

simulated involving smaller generation systems, also considering the community management mode. After the necessary pathways of study, analysis, involvement, and work with the citizenry (preliminary phase), some specific interventions are planned in specific areas of the Municipality for the realization of systems. All the generators present in the territory were mapped and considered; moreover, three main nodes were identified. These play a key role in the transition process of the Municipality of Castelluccio: they are Borgo dei Mulini, the Enel district, and the former railway station.

With reference to the regional technical map, Borgo dei Mulini – where, as already highlighted, there is a complex context of historical manufacturing buildings – in this scenario has been identified as the site of a mini-hydroelectric plant for energy production. This new innovative element aims to fit into the environmental context of Borgo dei Mulini, in continuity with the system of existing manufactures, contributing to their regeneration and the enhancement of existing artifacts. Traditional techniques are adopted, while historical infrastructures are relied on to guarantee the protection of the environmental context of the San Giovanni torrent.

In addition to being a key part of the municipality's history, the Enel district is an interesting node for integrating renewable energy generation and (virtual) self-consumption systems. The required redevelopment work on buildings has been turned into an opportunity to combine residential spaces with productive systems placed on roofs. As anticipated, the last item concerns the former Castelluccio train station. The railway track dismission left the artifact completely isolated from its context, at the center of an open space used for parking. The reconversion of the railroad track into a bicycle path also helps consolidate the image of this part of the city as a key element in the city's territorial connection. Within this scenario, the artifact and its neighboring space are rethought as elements serving the community. When the REC's development reaches maturity, the former station can become the site of a center for the logistical management of transport and connections. It will also be possible to include innovative electric public transport to serve REC member municipalities, spaces for charging electric cars, and an e-bike system to serve the population and tourist flows to Pollino Park. The community resource management of the REC is intended as an opportunity for the citizenry to rethink the role of buildings and production infrastructure. In the past, these communities' economy and survival revolved around manufacturing buildings such as mills, olive oil mills, and spinning mills. Similarly, the transformation nodes developed within this scenario are meant as possible community attractors. The aim of combining energy production and management with community spaces such as green areas, spaces for children and the elderly, and venues for associations and cultural activities is to rebuild a connection between the population and the productive artifacts to create a direct relationship between the objects and the people who own them. Indeed, a consultation step with the stakeholder groups identified in Phase 2 will take place (Fig. 4).

Phase 4 *Analysis and evaluation of the impacts of the scenarios*

The "winning" Bottom-up Option scenario, subjected to the CIA's preliminary assessment and presented to the assembly, turned out to be the one most aligned with the SNAI challenges and generates the most positive impacts for the largest number of community groups involved (see Fig. 5). Some transversal themes emerged through the development of the model, bearing particular relevance in the final evaluation. These

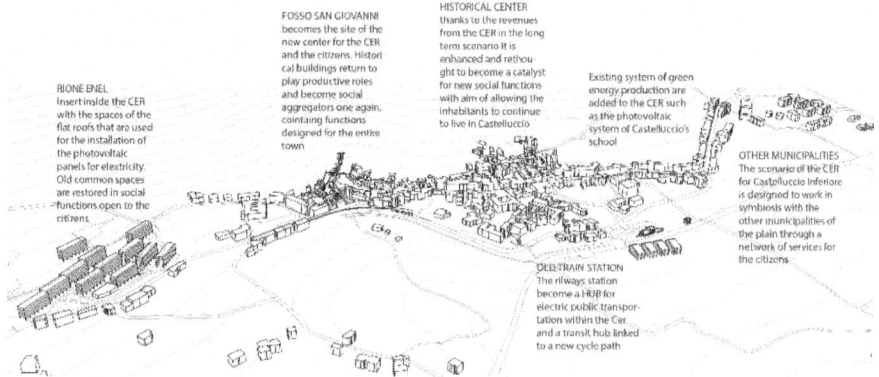

Fig. 4. View of the proposed interventions for the Bottom-up scenario of Castelluccio Inferiore (Source: Authors' elaboration)

pivotal elements can be traced to three keywords: Governance, Heritage, and People. Governance indicates the important role that PAs, at various levels, play in project development. The role of the public is considered to be of fundamental importance in each of the scenarios, as it is not possible to imagine the development of a REC without taking it into account. In the Bottom-up scenario, the relationship between the public and private sectors is horizontal; in this proposal, entities serve as involved subjects and are not directly responsible for processes, as they operate in favor of REC members by supporting their decisions and operational steps.

This approach enables the coordinated management of assets and production facilities by fostering dialogue between administrations and their citizens, sharing expenses, responsibilities, and burdens. The second point concerns heritage and the relationship of energy communities with it, both regarding the landscape and the built environment. In the Bottom-up scenario, this is favored by a Bottom-up awareness-raising process on heritage, with a focus on manufacturing heritage. The direct management of artifacts, as in the case of Castelluccio, not only fosters knowledge collection on the area and the development of a collective memory of the industrial age but also a sense of belonging for the community members toward their historical artifacts. The last theme, indicated by the keyword "people," concerns people and citizens. As already anticipated, user involvement is one of the cornerstones of the development of RECs. For this reason, the Bottom-up scenario adopts the optimal path for the establishment of the energy community.

Starting from the preparation phase, engagement is developed by raising awareness among citizens, leading them to act on their energy and resource consumption habits. It is important to see how the scenarios continuously overlap regarding their themes and expected effects and outcomes; this characteristic denotes a complexity in the theme of

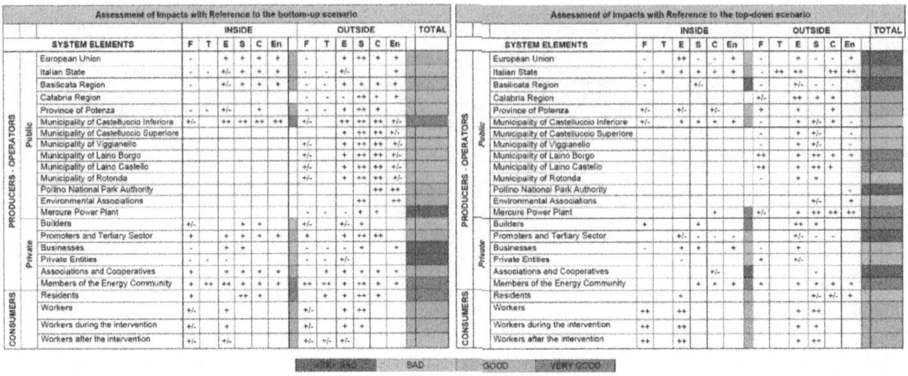

Assessment of Impacts with Reference to the bottom-up scenario

			INSIDE							OUTSIDE							TOTAL
		SYSTEM ELEMENTS	F	T	E	S	C	En		F	T	E	S	C	En		
PRODUCERS - OPERATORS	Public	European Union	-		+	+	+	+		-		+	++	+	+		
		Italian State	-	-	+/-	+	+	+		-	-	+/-			+		
		Basilicata Region	-		+/-	+	+	+		-	-	+	+	+	+		
		Calabria Region								-	-	-	++	+	+		
		Province of Potenza	-	-	+/-		+			-	-	+	++	+			
		Municipality of Castelluccio Inferiore	+/-		++	++	++	++		+/-		++	++	++	+/-		
		Municipality of Castelluccio Superiore										+	++	++	+/-		
		Municipality of Viggianello								+/-		+	++	++	+/-		
		Municipality of Laino Borgo								+/-		+	++	++	+/-		
		Municipality of Laino Castello								+/-		+	++	++	+/-		
		Municipality of Rotonda								+/-		+	++	++	+/-		
		Pollino National Park Authority												++	++		
		Environmental Associations											++		++		
		Mercure Power Plant								-	-	-	+	+			
	Private	Builders	+/-			+	+			+/-		+/-	+				
		Promoters and Tertiary Sector	+		+	+	+	+		+		+	++	++			
		Businesses	-		+	+				-	-	-	+		+		
		Private Entities	-	-	-					-	-	+/-					
		Associations and Cooperatives	+		+	+	+	+			+	+	+	+	+		
		Members of the Energy Community	+	++	++	+	+	+		++	++	+	++	+	+		
CONSUMERS		Residents	+			++	+				+	+	++	+			
		Workers	+/-		+					+/-		+	++				
		Workers during the intervention	+/-		+					+/-		+	+				
		Workers after the intervention	+/-		+/-					+/-	+/-	+/-					

Assessment of Impacts with Reference to the top-down scenario

			INSIDE							OUTSIDE							TOTAL
		SYSTEM ELEMENTS	F	T	E	S	C	En		F	T	E	S	C	En		
PRODUCERS - OPERATORS	Public	European Union	-		++	-	-	+		-		+	-	-	+		
		Italian State	-	+	+	+	+	+		-	++	++		++	++		
		Basilicata Region	-			+/-				-		+/-	-	-			
		Calabria Region								+/-		++	+	+			
		Province of Potenza	+/-		+/-		+/-			+		+		+			
		Municipality of Castelluccio Inferiore	+/-		+	+	+	+		-		+	+/-	+	-		
		Municipality of Castelluccio Superiore								-		+	+/-		-		
		Municipality of Viggianello								-		+	+/-		-		
		Municipality of Laino Borgo								++		+	++	+	+		
		Municipality of Laino Castello								++		+	++	+			
		Municipality of Rotonda								-		+	+				
		Pollino National Park Authority													-		
		Environmental Associations											+/-		+		
		Mercure Power Plant					+			+/-		+	++	++	++		
	Private	Builders	+			+						++	+				
		Promoters and Tertiary Sector			+/-	-	-	-				+/-	-	-			
		Businesses	-		+	+		+		-		+					
		Private Entities			-					+		+/-					
		Associations and Cooperatives					+/-						-				
		Members of the Energy Community				+	+	+		-		+	+	+	+		
CONSUMERS		Residents			+								+/-	+/-	+		
		Workers	++		++							+	++				
		Workers during the intervention	++		++							+	+				
		Workers after the intervention	++		++							+	++				

VERY BAD BAD GOOD VERY GOOD

Fig. 5. Decision-Making CIA Process - Phase 4: the Final Evaluation Grid Final Impact Assessment (Source: Authors' elaboration)

RECs, which this paper has attempted to address without claiming to propose definitive solutions[2]. These sporadic experiences, still lacking clear regulations and decrees, prove that such a radical process of change requires considerable time and effort. In any case, the bottom-up option turns out to be an extremely interesting alternative for the development of energy communities in IAs, because it allows for transversal work between the main themes, and because it produces more continuous and distributed effects over time, leading to cohesive development of the whole territory as visible in the simulation for Mercure and the Municipality of Castelluccio Inferiore.

Figure 5 reports the summary of the final evaluation, where the numerous effects of the bottom-up scenario (Fig. 3 – Phase 2), linked to the strategic objectives of the interventions (submitted to the moment of consultation and co-design and therefore shared in Phase 3) are traced back to a taxonomy of impacts (of a quantitative, qualitative and mixed nature) already indicated by Lichfiled: F (Financial), T (Tax), E (Economics), S (Social), C (Cultural), En (Environmental). The evaluation of the impacts is carried out about the different "community groups" (classified into active/public and public operators and passive/public and private consumers), but also taking into account the territorial variable (on-site and off-site) and the temporal variable (short-term impacts and medium/long-term impacts). DeMaCIA draws on the CIA (not the CIE), since it is an approach to be applied in the process of building strategic intervention scenarios (in

[2] Since there is no comprehensive mapping of REC experiences in municipalities within IAs, a few specific cases deemed significant by experiences and outcomes are here reported. According to GSE (Gestore Servizi Energetici) data alone, in Italy as of the end of 2022, there were 67 active configurations and a total of 501end customers connected to CSC (Collective Self-Consumption) and REC configurations. Regarding RECs active in areas involved in the SNAI, we highlight the experience of the Gubbio Energy Community, 2023. Several are projects underway: *BeCom*E project, Comuni Bandiere Arancioni, and Ciclovia dell'Appennino to concretely implement these new forms of renewable energy diffusion in 25 small Italian municipalities. The Nextappenino program presented 25 eligible projects funded by the NRP Supplementary Fund measure dedicated to the economic and social revitalization of earthquake-affected areas. Regarding European calls for proposals, we highlight the LIFE project "Encom HUB".

our case the bottom-up scenario) compared to the more conservative top-down scenario. The evaluation process takes place in a descriptive-qualitative form: the different impacts are indicated (where present) according to their positive gradient (creation of resources and/or positive externalities, light and dark green, with scores from + to ++) or according to their negative gradient (expenditure of resources and/or social costs, yellow and red, with scores from – to --) or by indicating a coexistence of positive and negative impacts. The right column (Total) of the two scenarios shown in Fig. 5 represents the final result, according to a graphic restitution that takes into account the synthesis of the impacts for each community group and highlights the scenario that generates the greatest number of positive impacts (and the containment of the greatest number of negative impacts) for the majority of the stakeholders involved.

6 Conclusions

The 3 research questions highlighted in §2 were answered (outlining a process and a decision-making methodology) in the DeMaCIA process, supporting the PA and interest groups, and producing bottom-up community engagement. The sharing-based sequence of consultation and reporting phases, which outline the strategic objectives in coherence with the SNAI objectives and the specific characteristics of the context, the elements of the IAs system, the multidimensional impacts, the interest groups involved, etc., makes the decision-making process more transparent, despite its complexity and, often, unpredictability and conflictuality, and can be traced back to the three keywords: Governance, Heritage, and People.

An initial answer is provided in the preparatory phases required for designing a knowledge acquisition process for building shared strategies through a problem-solving approach. These DeMaCIA phases have systematized and made interoperable (and sometimes geo-referenced) data and information despite the multi-layered nature of the heritage, which often makes interactions between public actors unharmonized and deficient. In addition, DeMaCIA presents some notable technical aspects: expanding the scope and the strategic analysis to a wider territory ("expanded" territorial scopes), including both the Lagonegrese area, with Lagonegro as the main node for managing territorial flows, and Valle del Mercure-Lao, suggested analyzing a crucial theme for the area under study: manufacturing. Phases 0, 1, and 2, which included the definition of the system elements and the potential development levers for the configuration of a new shared bottom-up scenario, have brought out more clearly the most strongly identity-based processes in the area: indeed, in most urban centers located on river courses, the production fabric is characterized by the presence of now-disused mills. In the reconstruction of the competitive framework and the evaluation phase of the SWOT Analysis, the focus is on the role of large-scale production in the context of Castelluccio, stressing the transformations that the production process has triggered since the early 1900s. For a certain time, Castelluccio had become the center of a significantly larger production system capable of attracting population, new technologies, and new functions, and changing its social fabric. All these elements have disappeared in the contemporary situation.

The DeMaCIA proposal updated the traditional CIA method based on some operational assumptions (particularly for the identification of community groups to interact with and the assessment of impact based on categories attributed to subjects). These seem suitable for different conditions of marginality, the gaps to identify, and the different transformation trajectories in different contexts. The integrated preparatory investigations (Phase 0, 1, 2, and 3) prior to Phase 4, aimed at the qualitative-descriptive assessment of impacts, highlight a significant potential for analysis and decision support, scalable in contexts like IAs, where information and databases are sometimes incomplete or not systematized and interoperable.

DeMaCIA's premise is to root decision-making in Bottom-up community involvement, in continuous interaction with the PA and supporting collaboration even in potential conflict situations. The theme of identity and memory is closely linked to heritage and the relationship of RECs with their heritage, both landscape and built environment: in the Bottom-up scenario, this is fostered through a bottom-up awareness-raising process on heritage, particularly manufactures. About the final results, it was decided to continue the development of this work with the bottom-up option. On the one hand, this is because it allows for intersecting; on the other hand, its effects are decidedly more widespread and distributed over time (Fig. 5). This leads to a cohesive development of the entire Mercure territory and, in particular, the Municipality of Castelluccio Inferiore. In this sense, despite not representing a final solution, the final scenario may provide the PA and communities with a new starting point and even a better focus for current funding. Concerning DeMaCIA, consultation methods (Focus Groups, PSMs, etc.) and other Evaluation methods can be identified and better fine-tuned, as a complement to the currently tested methodology to identify more accurately the demand targets in the stakeholder tables. These include the Delphi Method (expert evaluation on final scenarios) or other tools [17, 18]. The experimentation illustrated here represents an initial application that can provide elements to decision-makers for the subsequent transition, also exploiting more quantitative and monetary-based assessment tools (CIE, LCC, LCA, DCFA, Business Plan, etc.).

References

1. Dipartimento per le politiche di coesione e per il sud: SNAI. https://politichecoesione.governo.it/it/politica-di-coesione/strategie-tematiche-e-territoriali/strategie-territoriali/strategia-nazionale-aree-interne-snai/. Accessed 15 Feb 2025
2. Barca, F., Casavola, P., Lucatelli, S.: Strategia nazionale per le aree interne. definizione, obiettivi, strumenti e governance. Materiali UVAL **31** (2014)
3. Commissione Europea: Decisione di Esecuzione della Commissione del 29.10.2014. https://www.agenziacoesione.gov.it/wp-content/uploads/2019/09/decisione_commissione_2014.pdf. Accessed 15 Feb 2025
4. Agenzia per la Coesione Territoriale: Accordo di Partenariato 2014–2020 Italia Sezioni 3 e 4. https://www.agenziacoesione.gov.it/wp-content/uploads/2019/09/Accordo_di_Partenariato_SEZIONI_3_e_4.pdf. Accessed 15 Feb 2025
5. Accordo di Parternariato. https://politichecoesione.governo.it/it/politica-di-coesione/la-programmazione-2021-2027/strategie-2021-2027/accordo-di-partenariato-2021-2027/. Accessed 15 Feb 2025

6. SNAI: Criteri per la selezione delle AI da sostenere nel ciclo 2021–2027. https://politichecoesione.governo.it/media/2810/snai-criteri-per-la-selezione-delle-aree-da-sostenere-nel-ciclo-21-27.pdf. Accessed 15 Feb 2025
7. Regolamento UE 1060/2021. https://eur-lex.europa.eu. Accessed 15 Feb 2025
8. Regione Basilicata: Il PNRR in Basilicata. https://pnrr.regione.basilicata.it/. Accessed 15 Feb 2025
9. Ferretti, M., Favargiotti, S., Lino, B., Rolando, D.: Branding4Resilience: explorative and collaborative approaches for inner territories. Sustainability **14**(18) (2022)
10. Coesione Italia: AI – MASV. https://opencoesione.gov.it/it/dati/strategie/BAS_AI4/. Accessed 15 Feb 2025
11. Lichfield, N.: Community Impact Evaluation: Principles and Practice. Routledge, London (2005)
12. Elwood, S.A.: GIS use in community planning: a multidimensional analysis of empowerment. Environ Plan A **34**(5), 905–922 (2002)
13. Coscia, C., De Filippi, F.: L'uso di piattaforme digitali collaborative nella prospettiva di un'amministrazione condivisa. Il progetto Miramap a Torino. Territorio Italia **1**, 61–104 (2016)
14. Tagliareni, G.: Il centro storico di Cammarata (AG) programmazione e valutazione per la valorizzazione e lo sviluppo locale sostenibile. Politecnico di Torino, Torino (2010)
15. Rancati, A.: New European Bauhaus: A designer's retrospective. DRS DL, Boston (2024)
16. Coscia, C., Fregonara, E., Rolando, D.: Project management, briefing and territorial planning. The case of military properties disposal. Territorio **73**, 135–144 (2015)
17. Brady, S.R.: Utilizing and adapting the Delphi method for use in qualitative research. Int. J. Qual. Methods **14**(5) (2015)
18. Fregonara, E., Coscia, C.: Analisi multi criteria, approcci life cycle e Delphi method: una proposta metodologica per valutare scenari di progetto. Valori e valutazioni **23**, 107–117 (2019)

Mapping Vulnerability of Industrial Heritage for Adaptive Reuse: A Spatial Multi-criteria Analysis Approach

John Cullen Sayegh[1], Federica Cadamuro Morgante[2], Rossana Gabaglio[2], Oana Cristina Tiganea[2], and Marta Dell'Ovo[2](✉)

[1] Politecnico di Milano, Piazza Leonardo da Vinci, 32, 20133 Milan, MI, Italy
[2] Department of Architecture and Urban Studies (DAStU), Politecnico di Milano, 20133 Milan, MI, Italy
marta.dellovo@polimi.it

Abstract. Renewing unused industrial buildings and landscapes has gained attention in academia and industry. Often clustered due to agglomeration effects and zoning, industrial sites form complex spatial systems across territories. Frequently polluted and located near key infrastructure, these areas faced decline and abandonment as economies transitioned to service-based models. Adaptive reuse of this "industrial heritage" offers cost-effective, sustainable solutions that preserve cultural and historical value.

While significant projects can revitalize economically and demographically depressed regions, the lack of coherent spatial planning often leads to suboptimal outcomes when redeveloping sites individually. Despite increasing interest from both public and private sectors, decisions about site location, scale, and future use remain unclear.

To address this, the paper proposes a replicable, context-specific, multi-scalar framework to identify optimal uses for sites within their broader industrial systems. Geospatial Information Systems (GIS) and Multi-Criteria Decision Analysis (MCDA) are particularly effective, enabling the overlay and weighting of geospatial attributes to assess strengths and weaknesses. Once sites are scored, building-scale MCDA integrates technical and social analyses to determine optimal reuse strategies.

Keywords: Adaptive Reuse · Spatial Multicriteria Analysis · Industrial Heritage

1 Introduction

1.1 Background: Industrial Heritage

The rapid pace of innovation that characterized the Industrial Revolution meant that much of the built heritage related to newfound industrial production was quickly superseded, often replaced with newer nearby structures [1]. The resulting spatial pattern of these industrialized areas reflected an evolving relationship between urban development and production; usually, industrial sites clustered together to form industrial districts because of agglomeration effects, resource availability, and transportation access [2]. The advent of deindustrialization in the latter half of the 20th century in Western Europe and North America has led to the gradual abandonment of many obsolete industrial sites while at the same time throwing many urban areas into economic crisis. Occurring at the same time as deindustrialization, a burgeoning sub-discipline of cultural heritage concerned with the valorization of industrial buildings and landscapes has appeared.

At this time, the preservation and reuse of industrial heritage became a topic of serious academic and economic discourse. Since then, so-called "industrial heritage" has joined the ranks of other types of cultural heritage as worthy of valorization. These former industrial areas' tangible and intangible memories have recently received greater appreciation as a form of cultural heritage, particularly for communities closely tied to former industrial activities [3]. This recognition of inherent artistic value, coupled with the high demand for land in critical urban areas and contamination, has made them subjects of reuse by both public and private actors [4]. The problem of what to do with such abandoned properties remains a question for urban planners, developers, city governments, and nearby residents.

1.2 Adaptive Reuse

In the past, historic buildings have often hosted functions that did not represent the intended original use of the structure. This process of adaptive reuse, which can be defined as the "[introduction of] new content into an existing container (building, infrastructure, place, area), content that differs from the one for which the container was originally designed," has recently expanded to industrial heritage [5, 6]. The latter half of the 20th century witnessed the widespread clearing of historic and obsolete industrial structures, which were considered highly contaminated and incongruent with new functions. Several studies focusing on small and medium-sized towns have underscored the unique socio-economic vulnerabilities and governance challenges in these contexts, requiring tailored adaptive reuse frameworks [7–9]. The closure of these industrial areas particularly impacts communities located beyond large metropolitan centers characterized by economic diversification and a strong service sector, where the disappearance of a single industry or company can have significant negative financial consequences, demand for the redevelopment/reuse of existing buildings is low, and the properties' size is disproportionate to the existing urban context [8, 10]. Moreover, adaptive reuse efforts in such contexts must contend with environmental remediation, complex governance frameworks, and the coordination of multiple and often conflicting actors, including public authorities, private investors, and local communities [10, 11].

While adaptive reuse has many challenges, especially concerning industrial heritage, it offers several benefits. If done well, the adaptive reuse of industrial structures can develop a solution that honors the area's history and local culture, offers a much more sustainable solution than new construction, and provides an area with new economic and employment opportunities [5, 10]. Typological and locational features of industrial buildings—such as large open floor plans, generous ceiling heights, robust structural grids, and location near key infrastructure—make them well-suited for transformation [6]. Existing industrial structures benefit from several typological factors—they are located at central infrastructural nodes along regional transport systems and offer highly flexible structures with wide bays and high ceilings, modular structural systems, and extensive natural daylight [12]. Several examples of net-positive large-scale adaptive reuse projects exist; the IBA Emscher Park in the Ruhr region of Germany, the Ex-Pirelli/Bicocca area of Milan, Italy, and the HafenCity redevelopment located in Hamburg, Germany, attest to the latent possibilities of industrial heritage transformation. While many of these projects have been successful, they remain small and are all located in urban areas with high demand, expertise, and capital nexus. Lower-density areas and smaller towns do not have such advantages, and thus redevelopment of industrial heritage in these areas is significantly retarded.

The paper proposes an integrated multi-scale approach to support decision-makers in understanding the strengths and weaknesses of potential adaptive reuse scenarios for industrial heritage.

2 Literature Review

The literature review was conducted using Scopus, a database of academic papers with extensive peer-reviewed research. It allows users to easily choose keywords, authors, and topics of interest to locate the most relevant sources for their queries. The rehabilitation of abandoned and unused industrial buildings, especially those classified as industrial heritage, has become a vital area of research and practice within urban regeneration and cultural heritage conservation. Industrial heritage represents a crucial aspect of cultural and economic history, particularly in regions that have experienced significant industrialization [4]. The preservation and adaptive reuse of industrial sites have become important subjects of scholarly inquiry, especially in the context of sustainable development. An extensive literature review was conducted covering publications from 2008 to November 2024, with the search executed between July and November 2024, to explore potential methodological approaches for a comprehensive adaptive reuse plan at the regional and building scale.

From the initial Scopus search, other cited academic articles in peer-reviewed journals were examined to expand the literature review. More than thirty academic papers were selected for their relevance to specific keywords listed in Fig. 1—mainly focusing on a matrix of nine criteria, four of which dealt with methodological criteria (various multi-criteria methodologies, discourse/comparative analyses, case study approaches, and other analytical frameworks), followed by five thematic approaches (socio-cultural, environmental, governance, economic, and mixed). Figure 1 highlights the literature review process. Based on methodological approaches, case studies, and theoretical frameworks, these sources provide a comprehensive understanding of the current discourse around industrial heritage rehabilitation, decision-making processes related to cultural heritage, and planning approaches to small and medium-sized towns.

Given the complexity of the decision problem and the multiple dimensions and perspectives to be considered to assess the values elicited by the industrial heritage, after a first exploratory analysis of studies on the adaptive reuse topic [8, 13–19], the Multicriteria Decision Analysis (MCDA) has been used as a primary filter and keywords in combination with others. As shown in Fig. 1, five different combinations of keywords have been tested, and the filters applied to screen the research have been based on the coherence of the title and the abstract. At the same time, additional contributions cited in other papers have been analyzed. In the following sections, the primary findings will be discussed.

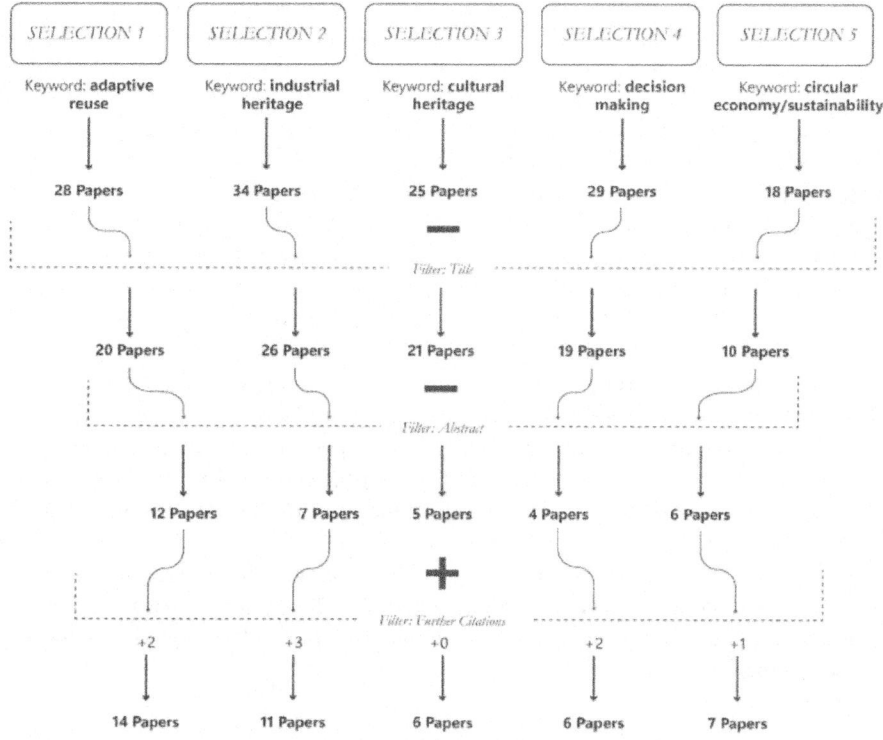

Fig. 1. Literature review process

2.1 The Value of Industrial Heritage

A recurring theme across the literature is the recognition of industrial heritage as an essential component of cultural heritage. Several authors [8, 9, 20–23] emphasize that the value of industrial heritage extends beyond its physical structure to include intangible cultural aspects such as memory, identity, and social history. [9] argue that industrial heritage should be considered a cultural asset contributing to communities' local identity and historical continuity. Their work highlights the importance of incorporating community values and memories into the decision-making process for industrial site rehabilitation. This approach is essential in preserving the physical aspects of industrial heritage and its socio-cultural significance. Similarly, [24] underscore the importance of recognizing industrial heritage as part of cultural heritage in their analysis of adaptive reuse projects in Norway. They argue that industrial sites should be rehabilitated in ways that acknowledge and preserve their historical and cultural contexts, which often involve complex relationships between the site's physical and symbolic meanings. These studies support the notion that industrial heritage is about preserving buildings, maintaining a connection to the past, and fostering a sense of place. [25] expands on this by providing a theoretical framework for understanding cultural heritage, including tangible and intangible aspects. [25] traces the evolution of cultural heritage protection from the Athens Charter to the Krakow Charter, arguing that industrial heritage must be understood within the broader context of the preservation discourse. According to [25], industrial buildings are not merely relics of the past but repositories of collective memory and symbols of industrial society's socio-economic transformations. This perspective broadens the scope of industrial heritage preservation, suggesting that efforts to rehabilitate these sites must engage with their material and symbolic dimensions.

In the case of some places, the potentialities offered by a particularly striking natural landscape or built heritage can strengthen local regeneration attempts, building on network effects between nearby localities. [20] expounds on this point by focusing on 13 castles in the Val d'Aosta region of Italy, which were analyzed using an approach conceived around the idea of "-wares" (Orgware, Civicware, Ecoware, Finware, Hardware, Software) whereby each site was evaluated using an initial SWOT analysis and an analytic network process. Experts from planning, conservation, economics, and local administrators then worked together—via focus groups and targeted interviews—to assign weights to each "-ware," generate standardized suitability maps, and identify the strongest clusters of castles that could mutually reinforce one another. This networked approach highlights which sites are most "ready" for adaptive reuse and reveals where the greatest synergies lie in forging a shared regeneration strategy. The joining of weighted criteria (aspatial) and GIS data (spatial) offers a novel, relational approach to cultural heritage strategy, using an operational principle underlying the methodology proposed in this research work.

2.2 Community Participation and Social Value

In addition to cultural significance, community participation is a critical factor in successfully rehabilitating industrial heritage. Several studies highlight the need to include local communities in the planning and decision-making processes for these projects to ensure that redevelopment efforts align with the social and cultural needs of the community. [23] use Complex Social Value (CSV) theory to demonstrate how inclusive decision-making processes can harmonize diverging interests between official development proposals and community perspectives. Their case study illustrates the value of engaging community stakeholders in the redevelopment process, as it helps to preserve social cohesion and reduce conflict over how the site should be used. The role of local communities in shaping industrial heritage rehabilitation is further explored by [26]. They argue that local NGOs and community organizations play a vital role in advocating for preserving industrial heritage, mainly when these sites are at risk of being redeveloped in ways that prioritize economic gains over cultural conservation. By fostering civic engagement, communities can rehabilitate industrial heritage sites to reflect local values and contribute to long-term social sustainability.

This participatory approach contrasts with more expert-driven methods, such as the PROMETHEE method employed by [27] to evaluate adaptive reuse strategies. While the PROMETHEE method provides a structured, expert-based framework for decision-making, it has been critiqued for its lack of community input. In their evaluation of abandoned industrial heritage sites, the authors rely heavily on quantitative indicators such as architectural quality, accessibility, and property value while also considering the social or cultural significance of the sites to the local community. The correct weight between top-down, expert-driven approaches and bottom-up, community-centered, social-value-driven models highlights an ongoing debate regarding the decision-making process in industrial heritage rehabilitation.

2.3 Methodological Approaches to Heritage Regeneration

Various methodological approaches have been developed to guide the rehabilitation of industrial heritage, with many studies emphasizing the importance of multi-criteria decision-making frameworks. [27] apply the PROMETHEE method to evaluate adaptive reuse strategies based on 15 indicators, ranging from accessibility and architectural quality to environmental sustainability and social value. This multi-criteria approach allows decision-makers to weigh various factors when considering the viability of different reuse scenarios, ensuring that economic and cultural considerations are considered. [28] propose a similar decision-support framework using Multi-Attribute Value Theory (MAVT) to assess complex cultural heritage systems. Their study highlights the need for integrating public participation into decision-making processes, especially when managing public goods like industrial heritage. By combining quantitative and qualitative data, these decision-support systems offer a holistic approach to evaluating adaptive reuse projects, helping planners and policymakers make informed decisions that balance the competing demands of heritage preservation, economic development, and social sustainability. Other studies, such as the work of [20], integrate Geographic Information Systems (GIS) with multi-criteria decision analysis to evaluate the rehabilitation potential of industrial heritage sites. These multi-criteria spatial decision-support systems (MC-SDSS) allow planners to incorporate geospatial data into the evaluation process, making it possible to consider factors like landscape features, proximity to community services, and environmental impacts when assessing potential reuse scenarios. These methodological innovations provide valuable tools for guiding the rehabilitation of industrial heritage sites in a way that is both data-driven and responsive to local contexts. [29] utilize the MCDA approach and TOPSIS (Technique for Order Preference by Similarity to Ideal Solution) to compare adaptive reuse project alternatives for a cluster of abandoned industrial buildings in Salerno, Italy. The analysis was coupled with 14 adaptive reuse proposals evaluated using the aforementioned methodology, stakeholder input, and an operational circularity process. In their study of the revitalization of modernist architectural heritage in Ivrea, Italy, [30] utilize the Delphi Method, a methodology associated with a survey of experts.

Given these premises, the field has advanced methodologically by developing multi-criteria decision-making frameworks that evaluate adaptive reuse strategies holistically. These frameworks, which combine expert-driven quantitative indicators with qualitative assessments of cultural and social value, provide a comprehensive approach to industrial heritage rehabilitation. The challenge will be to balance the often-competing demands of economic development, cultural preservation, and environmental sustainability to ensure industrial heritage's long-term viability and relevance in contemporary urban contexts.

3 Case Studies Analysis

In parallel with the literature review, adaptive reuse case studies have been analyzed and selected according to specific features to be compared. Four relevant case studies from across Europe were selected to observe how preservation and adaptive reuse of heritage assets can be applied in real-world examples. While approaches vary to preserve and reuse industrial heritage across geographic and cultural contexts, some commonalities emerge from a broad study of extant sites.

The selection of the case studies is based on an interconnected network of similar cultural, historical, economic, or geographic factors related to physical places that have undergone architectural and ecological restoration. They represent cultural landscapes with numerous examples of adaptive reuse projects where old functions are replaced with newer uses. The four selected case studies (the Hybrit Initiative in Norbotten, Sweden, the IBA Emscher Park in the Rhine-Ruhr area of Germany, the Leeds & Liverpool Canal redevelopment in the U.K., and the Mudejar Territory Routes in Zaragoza, Spain) vary significantly in geographic reach, infrastructural connections, architectural and landscape quality, and governance/economic model, but they offer examples of landscape-scale, regional planning in diverse European contexts. These case studies highlighted the real-world application of adaptive reuse processes, re-industrialization strategies, and cultural heritage preservation. They provided a valuable supplement to the literature review in developing a context-specific methodology.

Case studies have been analyzed considering the stakeholders involved in the process, the size, the year of the project, the new function, the cost of the intervention, and the architects and/or planners hired to design the new project. Table 1 below shows a comparative analysis of the four case studies. It is organized into six core criteria—Management Authority, Architect/Planner, Cost, Functions, Year, Size, Location, and Stakeholders—to ensure a coherent basis for comparison across diverse European contexts. The analysis provides a vital output related to tangible results and allows us to understand the most important factors that could influence the success or failure of a project. By systematically juxtaposing governance structures, funding scales, and functional outcomes, this comparative framework reveals underlying patterns and critical success variables that may remain obscured in narrative descriptions. Highlighting variations in management authorities and economic models demonstrates how institutional frameworks can accelerate or hinder adaptive reuse initiatives, while cost disparities underscore the impact of project scale on resource allocation and stakeholder engagement.

4 Methodology

This section outlines a proposed methodological framework rather than detailing application to a specific case study context. It draws directly on two foundations: (1) the literature review, which distilled a consistent set of thematic criteria (cultural-touristic,

Table 1. Case studies' comparative analysis

Criteria	Hybrit Initiative, Norbotten	IBA Emscher Park	Leeds & Liverpool Canal Corridor	Mudejar Territory Routes
Management Authority	Region Norrbotten, LKAB, H2 Green Steel & HYBRIT Consortium, SSAB	Planungsgesellschaft IBA Emscher Park GmbH	Canal & River Trust	Territorio Mudejar Association
Architect and Planner	N.A.	Karl Ganser (Managing Director), Christoph Zopel (NRW Minister for Urban Planning)	BDP	N.A
Cost	200billion SEK	€ 2.5 billion	£ 68–95 million	N.A
Functions	Economic-Technological, Governance-Public Services	Economic-Technological, Environmental-Ecological, Cultural-Touristic	Environmental-Ecological, Cultural-Touristic	Cultural/Touristic
Year	2022 - Present	1989–1999	2022 - Present	2018 - Present
Size	99 km^2	800 km^2 (Total Area)	37 km along Leeds & Liverpool Canal	17,274 km^2
Location	Norbotten, Sweden	North Rhine Westphalia, Germany	Lancashire, U.K.	Zaragoza, Spain
Stakeholders	Swedish Government, County Administrative Board of Norrbotten, Region Norrbotten, Local Municipalities (Luleå, Gällivare, Kiruna, Boden), LKAB, SSAB, H2 Green Steel & HYBRIT Consortium, Vattenfall, Luleå University of Technology	Emschergenossenschaft, Lippeverband, Kommunalverband Ruhrgebiet, Deutsche Bahn, RAG AG, Latz + Partner, 20 Municipalities, Federal State of North Rhein Westphalia, Landwirtschaftskammer Nordrhein-Westfalen, NABU, BUND, Deutscher Bauernverband e.V, Thyssen Krupp, University of Duisburg-Essen, TU Dortmund, FH Sudwestfalen	Canal & River Trust, SuperSlow Way Arts Programme, Historic England, Arts Council, Creative Lancashire, University of Central Lancashire, Lancashire County Council, Burroughs of Pendle, Burnley, Blackburn with Darwen, and Hyndburn, Newsground, Arts Partners in Pennine Lancashire, Incredible Edible, Lancashire BME Network	Territorio Mudejar Association, Local Munipalities, Province of Zaragoza, University of Zaragoza, College of Architects of Aragon, ICOMOS, Archibishopric of Zaragoza

governance-social, economic-technological, and environmental-ecological) and corresponding value functions; and (2) the comparative case-study analysis, which revealed empirical patterns in governance structures, cost scales, stakeholder configurations, and adaptive reuse outcomes. The literature review informs the choice and standardization of criteria. At the same time, the case studies lend insight into context-sensitive weighting, iterative phasing, and governance mechanisms that proved successful (or otherwise) in real-world settings. A methodology was targeted that could be applied to industrial-territorial spatial systems characterized by small and medium-sized cities and towns that suffer from post-industrial degradative processes, where the lack of sufficient economic resources or social capital dooms them to continued decline. This socio-economic planning model should be flexible and adaptive to regions undergoing post-industrial decline and where adaptive reuse scenarios have amorphous and undefined goals, budgets, and stakeholders.

A two-phase iterative and flexible model is proposed to consider the former industrial area's territorial characteristics and the asset's physical specificity (Fig. 2). The methodology aims to define priority areas to be renovated and select suitable adaptive reuse scenarios for the industrial heritage resulting from the spatial analysis.

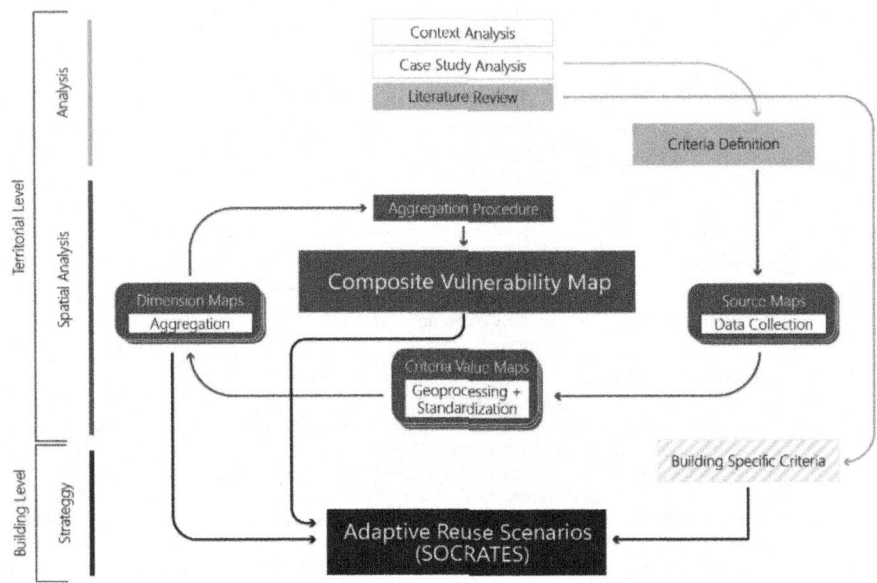

Fig. 2. Combined GIS + MCDA Adaptive Reuse Methodology

4.1 Territorial Level

Given the spatial characterization of the decision problem, a combined Geographic Information System (GIS) and Multicriteria Decision Analysis (MCDA) methodology is suggested [31] since it offers a robust framework for addressing complex decision-making processes like adaptive reuse planning [20] by integrating quantitative and qualitative data. GIS provides spatial data visualization and analysis. MCDA offers a structured decision-making process that identifies potential options regarding a decision problem and incorporates qualitative and quantitative criteria based on specified values [8]. Working together, GIS and multi-criteria decision analysis can be utilized to identify and evaluate options relating to spatial decisions. Applications of GIS and MCDA are numerous; the methodology has been used to assess drought risk [32], determine preservation strategies for cultural heritage [21], and the site location of public schools [33], among many other cases.

The strength of the GIS + MCDA approach lies in its flexibility; implementing a context-dependent component utilizing GIS ensures its adaptability across differing territories and scales, while the MCDA component introduces user-determined weighted judgments to narrow down policy and/or best-use case scenarios. Given that contextualization of the strategic planning/methodological model is a necessary step in testing the replicability of the approach in diverse post-industrial milieus, GIS was used to map and analyze context-specific geographical, environmental, and socio-economic factors to determine sites that are best suited for adaptive reuse scenarios. The multi-criteria decisional analysis (MCDA) portion is equally important; the MCDA process assigns value judgments to a standardized set of data (collected using GIS inputs), thereby uniting spatial and aspatial analyses [31, 34].

Considering Fig. 2, the preliminary analysis of the literature review, together with supporting the selection of the most coherent methodology, helps define a consistent set of criteria to understand the vulnerability and attractiveness of the site under analysis to determine the most urgent intervention to be done. Three inputs—an in-depth survey of established MCDA frameworks in the scholarly literature, examining salient contextual features from the four case studies (e.g., governance models, cost scales, stakeholder constellations), and the relevance and availability of context-specific data—first informed a detailed set of criteria and sub-criteria, which were then organized into the four overarching themes (cultural-touristic, governance-social, economic-technological, and environmental-ecological). Here, "vulnerability" refers to the degree to which the study area is exposed to various negative factors such as socio-economic decline, environmental contamination, or lack of infrastructure and educational opportunities, to name a few examples.

The value tree defined consists of criteria that could be georeferenced in space to be easily visualized. Within this context, it is possible to mention the main critical dimensions that deserve to be deeply investigated, such as: i) Cultural-Touristic: Identifying areas of historical and cultural significance and potential recreational and leisure opportunities; ii) Governance-Social Services: Assessing opportunities for community engagement and the benefits of revitalization for underserved populations; iii) Economic-Technological: Evaluating factors such as proximity to transportation infrastructure, market accessibility, and potential for job creation; iv) Environmental-Ecological: Considering contamination levels, remediation costs, and the feasibility of integrating renewable energy solutions. Once a robust set of criteria has been defined, it is possible to start collecting data, which includes raster and vector datasets from various authorities and official geoportals, as well as aggregated demographic data to obtain Source Maps. After a series of geo-operations selected carefully considering the nature of the criteria (e.g., Euclidean Distance, Density, Classification, etc.), it is possible to visualize Criterion Maps, which, after the standardization, a process that allows the making of homogenous different units of measurement, became Value Maps. According to the software selected for the elaboration, the new a-dimensional scale obtained after the standardization could be from 0 to 1 or from 0 to 10 (where 0 is the worst value and 1 or 10 is the best) [35]. With the support of the value functions generated with the knowledge shared by experts or the experiences detected by other researchers, it is possible to move from performance to value. The "suitability score" refers to the aggregated, weighted sum of these value maps, indicating suitability for adaptive reuse (higher scores denote more favorable conditions for intervention). Figure 3 presents an example of the three-stage maps generated.

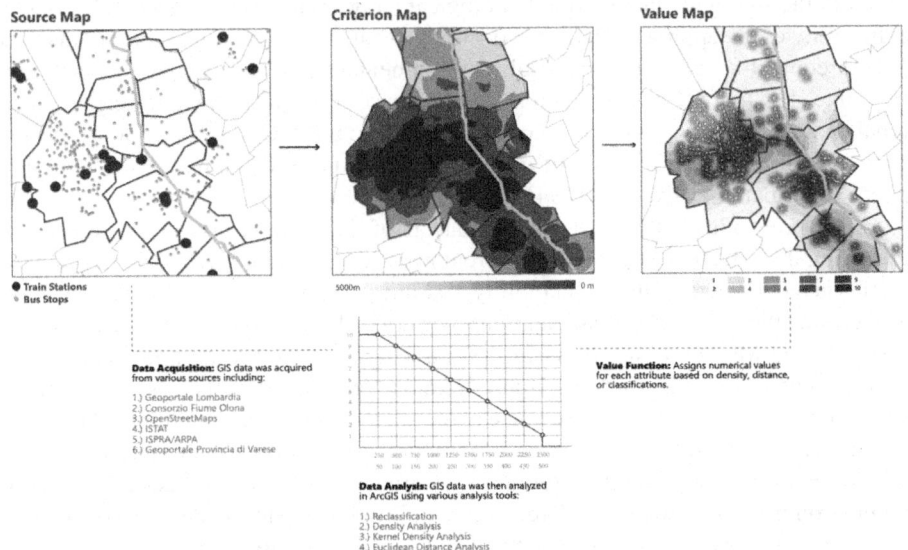

Fig. 3. Example of Source Map, Criterion Map, and Value Map

The final stage of GIS + MCDA involves the creation of Partial and Final Value Maps and the overlay of data layers to facilitate spatial decision-making. In this phase, the standardized criteria, weighted according to their relative importance, are combined to produce an overall suitability score for each location or area under consideration. Often using Weighted Linear Combination (WLC) or similar methods, the data overlay technique integrates the different layers of spatial data, each representing a specific criterion, into a single composite map. This Composite Vulnerability map visually represents various areas' suitability based on the requirements of the earlier stages. It enables decision-makers to quickly identify optimal regions that align with the set objectives, highlighting zones with the highest suitability scores. Additionally, sensitivity analysis is often conducted at this stage to assess the robustness of the results by evaluating how changes in criteria weights or data accuracy affect the outcomes [31, 34]. The conclusions drawn from the overlay process offer actionable insights for planning and policy, guiding decisions in land use, urban regeneration, or environmental management by clearly illustrating the spatial patterns of suitability across the study area.

4.2 Building Level

After applying the GIS + MCDA methodology and subsequent regional-scale territorial analysis, individual industrial sites at the building scale can be selected for further investigation. The building-level MCDA outputs reveal each site's strengths and weaknesses across the four overarching dimensions (cultural-touristic, governance-social, economic-technological, and environmental-ecological), providing a clear basis for scenario development. Based on the MCDA scores, a set of preliminary adaptive reuse scenarios is drafted—each tailored to leverage a site's highest-scoring dimensions (for example, a cultural hub on a site with strong cultural-touristic potential, or a light-industrial incubator where economic-technological scores dominate). This relationship between territorial potential and building-specific characteristics will inform a differentiated approach to adaptive reuse. This methodological transition from territorial analysis to architectural intervention represents a critical contribution to the discourse on industrial heritage regeneration, demonstrating how multi-scalar approaches can inform more nuanced, contextualized, and sustainable adaptive reuse strategies. The importance of participatory processes has been underlined in the literature analyzed, and the model proposed by [8] could be taken as a reference since it can combine technical and social evaluation. This is possible by defining adaptive reuse scenarios coherently with the context analysis and the needs and expectations of different stakeholders and developing a Social Multi-Criteria Evaluation through the SOCRATES method [36–41]. By structuring the workflow in this way, the methodology maintains continuity—from broad territorial diagnostics to site-specific MCDA, then into the dual rigor of the technical and social (SOCRATES) analyses—ensuring that final design proposals are evidence-based and stakeholder-endorsed. This approach integrates technical compromise solutions with social compromise solutions, and it is particularly suggested to deal with public policy problems within an inter-multi-disciplinary, participatory, and transparent framework [7, 38]. The final aim consists of supporting decision-makers in making more conscious decisions and finding a trade-off among the values elicited by various groups of stakeholders while selecting a scenario of adaptive reuse.

5 Conclusions and Future Perspectives

This paper proposes a methodological framework for the strategic regeneration of industrial heritage assets through an innovative approach combining Geographic Information Systems (GIS) and Multi-Criteria Decision Analysis (MCDA) at the urban scale and a Social Multi-Criteria Evaluation method (technical and social analysis) at the building scale. The research addresses a significant gap in current practice: despite growing recognition of industrial heritage's value, decision-making processes regarding intervention locations, scope, and future uses have remained largely unsystematic.

A crucial direction for methodological refinement involves expanding the stakeholder engagement component [42], particularly in the criteria definition phase. Future research should integrate more robust participatory methods that capture local knowledge, community aspirations, and cultural values. Such enhanced stakeholder engagement could generate more innovative and contextually appropriate adaptive reuse scenarios and features of the territorial context. This expanded participatory approach would strengthen the social legitimacy of interventions while potentially revealing adaptive possibilities overlooked in expert-driven analyses.

The GIS + MCDA methodology is a potential path in addressing the complex challenge of adaptive reuse of industrial heritage. Its future application will demonstrate how systematic, multi-scalar analysis can transform what might otherwise be fragmented, suboptimal interventions into strategically coordinated revitalization efforts that honor historical significance while serving contemporary needs. The research opens several promising avenues for future theoretical development regarding the adaptive reuse of industrial heritage and strategic economic planning at the regional level.

Acknowledgments. The article is a research product of the project PRIN 2022 financed by the European Union – Next Generation EU (Missione 4 Componente 1) CUP D53D23014860006: "PLanETs. Production Landscapes through Energy Transitions: Industrial heritage preservation, socio-political processes and potential reuse in Lombardy, Sardinia, and Calabria."

Credit Author Statement. Conceptualization: M.D.O., O.C.T..; Data curation: J.C.S, F.C.M.; Formal analysis: J.C.S Methodology: M.D.O., J.C.S.; Project administration: O.C.T.; Software: M.D.O., J.C.S.; Supervision: O.C.T, R.G.; Validation: M.D.O., J.C.S., F.C.M., O.C.T., R.G. Visualization: M.D.O., J.C.S.; Writing – original draft: M.D.O., J.C.S.; Writing - Review & Editing: M.D.O., J.C.S., F.C.M.

Disclosure of Interests. The authors have no competing interests to declare that are relevant to the content of this article.

References

1. Bottero, M., Datola, G., Fazzari, D., Ingaramo, R.: Re-thinking detroit: a multicriteria-based approach for adaptive reuse for the Corktown district. Sustainability **14**, 8343 (2022). https://doi.org/10.3390/SU14148343
2. Hatuka, T., Ben-Joseph, E.: Industrial urbanism: typologies, concepts and prospects. Built Environ. **43**, 10–24 (2017). https://doi.org/10.2148/BENV.63.3.10
3. Assumma, V., De Luca, C.: Assessing the value of cultural landscapes through the integration of biophysical-economic valuation, risk assessment and cost-benefit analysis. In: Gervasi, O., Murgante, B., Garau, C., Taniar, D., Rocha, A.M.A.C., Faginas Lago, M.N. (eds.) ICCSA 2024. LNCS, vol. 14822, pp. 78–93. Springer, Cham (2024). https://doi.org/10.1007/978-3-031-65318-6_6
4. Protection and Reuse of Industrial Heritage: Dilemmas, Problems, Examples ICOMOS Slovenia
5. Robiglio, M.: Re-USA: 20 American Stories of Adaptive Reuse, A Toolkit for Post-industrial Cities. Jovis Verlag, Berlin (2017)
6. Ingaramo, R., Lami, I.M., Robiglio, M.: How to activate the value in existing stocks through adaptive reuse: an incremental architecture strategy. Sustainability **14**, 5514 (2022). https://doi.org/10.3390/SU14095514
7. Rossitti, M., Torrieri, F.: The THEMA tool to support heritage-based development strategies for marginal areas: evidence from an Italian inner area in Campania Region. REGION **9**, 109–129 (2022). https://doi.org/10.18335/region.v9i2.394
8. Dell'Ovo, M., Dell'anna, F., Simonelli, R., Sdino, L.: Enhancing the cultural heritage through adaptive reuse. A multicriteria approach to evaluate the Castello Visconteo in Cusago (Italy). Sustainability **13**, 4440 (2021). https://doi.org/10.3390/SU13084440
9. Coscia, C., Lazzari, G., Rubino, I.: Industrial heritage, adaptive reuse and sustainable redevelopment scenarios: including local communities' multiple values in the decision-making

process. In: Giuffrida, S., Trovato, M.R., Rosato, P., Fattinnanzi, E., Oppio, A., Chiodo, S. (eds.) Science of Valuations. Green Energy and Technology, Part F2560, pp. 347–360. Springer, Cham (2024). https://doi.org/10.1007/978-3-031-53709-7_24
10. Love, P.: Factors influencing the adaptive re-use of buildings. J. Eng. Des. Technol. **9**, 32–46 (2011). https://doi.org/10.1108/17260531111121459/FULL/PDF
11. Moroni, S., de Franco, A., Bellè, B.M.: Vacant buildings. distinguishing heterogeneous cases: public items versus private items; empty properties versus abandoned properties. Smart Innov. Syst. Technol. **168**, 9–18 (2020). https://doi.org/10.1007/978-3-030-35550-0_2
12. Abastante, F., Lami, I.M., Mecca, B.: Performance indicators framework to analyse factors influencing the success of six urban cultural regeneration cases. In: Bevilacqua, C., Calabrò, F., Della Spina, L. (eds.) NMP 2020. SIST, vol. 178, pp. 886–897. Springer, Cham (2021). https://doi.org/10.1007/978-3-030-48279-4_83
13. Yau, Y.: Multi-criteria decision making for urban built heritage conservation: application of the analytic hierarchy process. J. Build. Apprais. **4**, 191–205 (2009). https://doi.org/10.1057/jba.2008.34
14. Turskis, Z., Zavadskas, E.K., Kutut, V.: A model based on ARAS-G and AHP methods for multiple criteria prioritizing of heritage value. Int. J. Inf. Technol. Decis. Mak. **12**, 45–73 (2013). https://doi.org/10.1142/S021962201350003X
15. Oppio, A., Bottero, M.: Conflicting values in designing adaptive reuse for cultural heritage. a case study of social multicriteria evaluation. In: Gervasi, O., et al. (eds.) ICCSA 2017. LNCS, vol. 10406, pp. 607–623. Springer, Cham (2017). https://doi.org/10.1007/978-3-319-62398-6_43
16. Della Spina, L.: Multidimensional assessment for "culture-led" and "community-driven" urban regeneration as driver for trigger economic vitality in urban historic centers. Sustainability **11**, 1–20 (2019). https://doi.org/10.3390/SU11247237
17. Della Spina, L.: Adaptive sustainable reuse for cultural heritage: a multiple criteria decision aiding approach supporting urban development processes. Sustainability **12**, 1–20 (2020). https://doi.org/10.3390/su12041363
18. Haroun, H.A.A.F., Bakr, A.F., Hasan, A.E.S.: Multi-criteria decision making for adaptive reuse of heritage buildings: Aziza Fahmy Palace, Alexandria, Egypt. Alex. Eng. J. **58**, 467–478 (2019). https://doi.org/10.1016/j.aej.2019.04.003
19. Nesticò, A., Somma, P.: Comparative analysis of multi-criteria methods for the enhancement of historical buildings. Sustainability **11** (2019). https://doi.org/10.3390/su11174526
20. Oppio, A., Bottero, M., Ferretti, V., Fratesi, U., Ponzini, D., Pracchi, V.: Giving space to multicriteria analysis for complex cultural heritage systems: the case of the castles in Valle D'Aosta Region, Italy. J. Cult. Herit. **16**, 779–789 (2015). https://doi.org/10.1016/j.culher.2015.03.003
21. Della Spina, L., Lanteri, C.: A collaborative multi-criteria decision-making framework for the adaptive reuse design of disused railways. Land **13**, 851 (2024). https://doi.org/10.3390/LAND13060851
22. Coscia, C., De Filippi, F.: The use of collaborative digital platforms in the perspective of shared administration. The MiraMap project in Turin1. Territorio Italia, 61–104 (2016). https://doi.org/10.14609/Ti_1_16_4e
23. Coscia, C., Lazzari, G., Rubino, I.: Values, memory, and the role of exploratory methods for policy-design processes and the sustainable redevelopment of waterfront contexts: the case of Officine Piaggio (Italy). Sustainability **10**, 2989 (2018). https://doi.org/10.3390/SU10092989
24. Swensen, G., Granberg, M.: The impact of images on the adaptive reuse of post-industrial sites. Hist. Environ. Policy Pract. **15**, 101–129 (2024). https://doi.org/10.1080/17567505.2024.2311005

25. Vecco, M.: A definition of cultural heritage: from the tangible to the intangible. J. Cult. Herit. **11**, 321–324 (2010). https://doi.org/10.1016/J.CULHER.2010.01.006
26. Swensen, G., Sirowy, B.: Resilience thinking in museums: industrial heritage, urban regeneration and civic engagement. Mus. Soc. **21**, 36–56 (2023). https://doi.org/10.29311/MAS.V21I3.4408
27. Bottero, M., D'Alpaos, C., Oppio, A.: Ranking of adaptive reuse strategies for abandoned industrial heritage in vulnerable contexts: a multiple criteria decision aiding approach. Sustainability **11**, 785 (2019). https://doi.org/10.3390/SU11030785
28. Ferretti, V., Comino, E.: An integrated framework to assess complex cultural and natural heritage systems with multi-attribute value theory. J. Cult. Herit. **16**, 688–697 (2015). https://doi.org/10.1016/J.CULHER.2015.01.007
29. Gravagnuolo, A., Angrisano, M., Bosone, M., Buglione, F., De Toro, P., Fusco Girard, L.: Participatory evaluation of cultural heritage adaptive reuse interventions in the circular economy perspective: a case study of historic buildings in Salerno (Italy). J. Urban Manag. **13**, 107–139 (2024). https://doi.org/10.1016/J.JUM.2023.12.002
30. Coscia, C., Dalpiaz, P.E., parole chiave: candidatura UNESCO: Ivrea città Enrico Giacopelli***, Giulia Maria Infortuna** industriale del XX secolo, architetture olivettiane, valorizzazione, decision-making, metodo Delphi
31. Malczewski, J.: GIS-based land-use suitability analysis: a critical overview. Prog. Plan. **62**, 3–65 (2004). https://doi.org/10.1016/J.PROGRESS.2003.09.002
32. Watershed, M., Darwish, K.: GIS-based multi-criteria decision analysis for flash flood hazard and risk assessment: a case study of the Eastern Minya Watershed, Egypt. Environ. Sci. Proc. **25**, 87 (2023). https://doi.org/10.3390/ECWS-7-14315
33. Baser, V.: Effectiveness of school site decisions on land use policy in the planning process. ISPRS Int. J. Geo-Inf. **9**, 662 (2020). https://doi.org/10.3390/IJGI9110662
34. Malczewski, J., Rinner, C.: Multicriteria Decision Analysis in Geographic Information Science (2015). https://doi.org/10.1007/978-3-540-74757-4
35. Dell'Ovo, M., Capolongo, S., Oppio, A.: Combining spatial analysis with MCDA for the siting of healthcare facilities. Land Use Policy **76**, 634–644 (2018). https://doi.org/10.1016/j.landusepol.2018.02.044
36. Cerreta, M., Falotico, A., Poli, G., Grazioli, G., Laviola, F.: Adaptive reuse strategies for a regenerative design: a multi-methodological decision-making process for Montalbano Jonico. BDC. Bollettino Del Centro Calza Bini **19**, 515–535 (2019). https://doi.org/10.6092/2284-4732/7280
37. Panaro, S., Poli, G., Botte, M., Sacco, S., Cerreta, M.: Assessing the sustainability of the city-port transformations: multi-criteria decision analysis (MCDA) for alternatives portfolio selection
38. Munda, G., Azzini, I., Cerreta, M., Ostlaender, N.: SOCRATES manual software manual for social multi-criteria evaluation, version November 2022 (2022). https://doi.org/10.2760/015604
39. Integrated Approaches for the Management of Environmental Site Remediation Processes: A Baseline Report (2024). https://doi.org/10.61092/IAEA.NLIA-NILQ
40. Baron, V.M.R., Munda, G., Fuetterer, M., Aldave, D.L.H.L., Benes, O.: Multi-criteria decision support for small modular reactors (2025). https://publications.jrc.ec.europa.eu/repository/handle/JRC140704
41. Munda, G.: A NAIADE based approach for sustainability benchmarking. Int. J. Environ. Technol. Manag. **6**, 65–78 (2006). https://doi.org/10.1504/IJETM.2006.008253
42. Caprioli, C.: The integration of multi-agent system and multicriteria analysis for developing participatory planning alternatives in urban contexts. Environ. Impact Assess. Rev. **113**, 107855 (2025). https://doi.org/10.1016/J.EIAR.2025.107855

Undertourism and Destination Management in the Inner Areas. The Case of Locride, Reggio Calabria

Francesco Calabrò(✉), Immacolata Lorè, Giovanna Emanuela Minniti, and Rosa Maria Staropoli

Mediterranea University, Via dell'Università, 25, 89124 Reggio Calabria, Italy
francesco.calabro@unirc.it

Abstract. This work illustrates the first results of an experimental activity conducted in a territory characterized by a strong peripherality, located in the southern part of Calabria.

The study starts from an examination of the role of Cultural Heritage and Tourism for the development of Inner Areas. Among the tools identified to promote the triggering of processes of touristic enhancement of Cultural Heritage, Destination Management Organizations are identified, whose characteristics are outlined, highlighting their function in terms of Strategic Planning.

After recalling the process in which this type of process is usually articulated and the fundamental role of Evaluation, the territory object of the case study is framed, especially in relation to the relevance of its Cultural Heritage.

The work concludes by illustrating the results of the first cognitive investigations conducted in the field through questionnaires administered to a group of tourist-cultural operators.

Keywords: Inner Areas · Cultural Tourism · Destination Management Organization · Strategic Planning · Economic Evaluation

1 Inner Areas, Cultural Heritage and Tourism

"Inner Areas are those that, failing to enhance the existing resources, are poorly responsive both to the impulses deriving from their integration into the national economy and to the solicitations expressed on them by interventions, especially those of an extraordinary nature" [1].

It was 1996, when Edoardo Mollica gave this definition in the study *"Typology of the Framework Plan for Inner Areas in Calabria"*, commissioned by the Calabria Region to the then PAU Department of the Mediterranea University of Reggio Calabria, a good 18 years before the Italian State equipped itself with the National Strategy for Inner Areas (SNAI), included in the National Reform Program (PNR) of 2014 and in the Partnership Agreements 2014–2020 and 2021–2027 [2, 3].

The poor reactivity of these areas to external stimuli recorded up to now has also been highlighted by other authors in more recent times, such as Bernard and Keim-Klärner, Kuhn and many others [4–6].

The definition given by the Department for Cohesion Policies and for the South – DPS, instead, defines Inner Areas as *"those areas characterized by a significant distance from the main service provision centers, in particular those relating to education, mobility and social and health services"*.

A further interpretative key to these territories is offered by the Public Investment Evaluation Unit - UVAL, which considers the considerable unused or underused "territorial capital", consisting of environmental resources (water resources, agro-forestry-pastoral systems, etc.), cultural resources (archaeological assets, historical settlements, defensive and religious architecture, small museums, etc.), disused building capital, underused accommodation facilities, traditional knowledge, etc. [7]; UVAL itself underlines their national importance in terms of "economic development potential", that is, *"how consistent is the development potential that they express today as a whole and how important is their contribution to stabilizing the trajectory of national economic development."* [7].

Whatever definition one wishes to consider, the Inner Areas still constitute a significant portion of Italy, they represent more than 60% of the national surface area, over half of the municipalities (53%) and approximately a quarter of the resident population (23%) [8].

In terms of underutilized territorial capital, cultural heritage stands out: in 2022, of the 4,416 structures open to the public, including museums, galleries, archaeological areas, monuments and public and private monumental complexes found in Italy, 1,740, equal to almost four out of 10 (39.4%), were located in the Municipalities of the Inner Areas. The heritage sites of the Inner Areas are mainly ethno-anthropological museums (19.2%), archaeological (17.6%), natural sciences or technological (17.0%) and thematic museums (14.9%); among the monumental complexes, castles and fortified buildings prevail (35.7%), as do churches and other religious buildings (33.2%) [9].

Such a substantial Cultural Heritage, however, struggles to express its full potential contribution to local development processes, especially from a tourism perspective: it is *"A widespread reality, where tourism still plays a modest role compared to the country's poles of attraction (sea and cities of art), and below the potential linked to the richness and variety of the cultural and environmental assets present and the availability of almost half of the Italian accommodation offer."* [10].

As perfectly highlighted by the above-mentioned definition of Inner Areas given by Mollica, one of the elements that characterizes them is precisely their poor reactivity: for this reason, the mere provision of resources is not sufficient to trigger development processes: *"The project areas of the National Strategy for Inner Areas are characterized by extreme diversity and variety within them […]. In order for these distinctive features to transform into a desire to travel, stay and/or enjoy, an effort is needed to identify the real vocations of the territory, to define the best differentiation strategies on the market and to develop specific interventions and product ideas, with respect to which to also evaluate the possibility of forming local (and/or supra-local) alliances and implementing any system actions."* [10].

2 Organization of the Tourist-Cultural Offer: Destination Management Organizations

The ICOMOS International Charter for Cultural Heritage Tourism "Reinforcing cultural heritage protection and community resilience through responsible and sustainable tourism management", adopted by the ICOMOS Annual General Assembly (Bangkok, Thailand) in November 2022, provides useful principles to guide Cultural Tourism policies towards sustainability [11].

In particular, Principle 5 *"Raise awareness and reinforce cultural heritage conservation"*, pushes towards organizational forms of the tourist offer that involve all stakeholders.

In literature and in Italian legislation, numerous references can be found to different forms of organization of the tourist offer; in literature, in particular, two different approaches to the topic of the organization of the tourist offer can be found [12, 13]:

- One that looks first of all at the territory and its components: forms such as Local Tourist Systems, introduced by Law 29 March 2001 n. 135 "Reform of the national tourism legislation", and the Tourist Districts, introduced by law 12 July 2011 n. 106 [14, 15];
- One that could be defined, instead, as demand-based, to which the DMO - Destination Management Organization tool can be traced back. This organizational form in Italy is not regulated at a national level, also in light of the attribution of Tourism to the Regions, as a "residual competence", while numerous Regions (among which, for example, Sicily, Tuscany, Veneto, Emilia Romagna and Campania) have legislated on the matter. Calabria has not yet issued any regulations on DMOs.

According to the UNWTO, the purpose of DMOs is: *"the coordinated management of all the elements that make up a destination (attractions, amenities, accessibility, human resources, image and price). [...] Its role is to lead and coordinate activities under a coherent strategy or plan, serving the interests of all stakeholders"*. [16].

2.1 DMO: Definition and Functions

According to the Department of Economic and Social Affairs Statistics Division of the United Nations: *"Destination (main destination of a trip): The main destination of a tourism trip is defined as the place visited that is central to the decision to take the trip. See also purpose of a tourism trip"* [17].

The answer becomes more complicated if the question becomes which territorial entity corresponds to a Destination. There is no univocal answer to this question, as there may be destinations corresponding to profoundly different territorial entities: cities, rural areas, regions or even entire nation states [18].

The legal forms that a DMO assumes can be equally differentiated: *"In some countries, destinations may be managed for tourism directly by the central or regional tourism authority, but the trend is towards decentralization and encouraging greater local involvement. [...] Often there is a need to create a new organization, or to strengthen an existing one, to undertake some functions that the partner organizations are not able to handle effectively."* [19].

About the functions performed by a DMO, instead, Carter and Nevill first propose a distinction between "core functions" (at two levels) and "enabling functions" [19]. The first ones include:

Level I:

- Strategic and operational planning
- Research & intelligence

Level II:

- Product and experience development
- Destination marketing and sales
- Visitor and destination services
- Events development
- Skills development

While the "enabling functions" include:

- Partner and stakeholder engagement
- Advocacy and corporate/ industry communication
- Fundraising and financial management
- Performance management
- Application of digital systems

In reality, even Research & intelligence can be considered enabling functions, therefore the true core function of Level I of DMOs is Strategic and Operational Planning.

3 Organization of the Tourist-Cultural Offer: The Strategic Planning

Strategic Planning, as is known, is a tool that was born in the military field and then adopted in the corporate field [20] to arrive, starting from the 80s, to the planning of cities and territories: in the latter case it is more correct to speak of Strategic Territorial Planning or Strategic Spatial Planning [21].

In the case of DMOs, given their nature and their purposes, we find ourselves in a hybrid situation, in which elements of Corporate Strategic Planning and Territorial Planning coexist, but the territorial dimension clearly prevails, since the ultimate goal is not the promotion of the development of the company-DMO but of the territory in which it operates. It is therefore to Strategic Territorial Planning that we will refer for the rest of the article, keeping in mind, however, the conditions of budgetary balance necessary to guarantee the sustainability of DMOs over time [22, 23].

Among the many definitions of Strategic Planning, the following is given by Albrechts: "[…] *strategic planning can be defined as a public sector-led process through which a vision, actions and means of implementation are formulated, shaping and framing what a place is and can become*". In other words, strategic planning [22]:

- Focuses attention on a limited number of key issues;
- Critically addresses the environment, assessing its strengths and weaknesses, as well as threats and opportunities;

- Evaluates external trends, forces and available resources;
- Identifies and groups the main interests (stakeholders), both public and private;
- Allows for broad (at various administrative levels) and diversified (public sector, private sector, civil society) involvement during the planning process;
- Develops a vision/perspective – realistic and long-term – and strategies, at different administrative levels, considering the power structure, uncertainties and different competing values;
- Designs structures for the preparation of plans and develops contents, images and decision-making frameworks to direct and manage territorial transformations;
- Builds new ideas and the processes that can bring them forward, generating ways to understand, to build consensus, to organize and mobilize opinion and to exert influence in different arenas;
- Focuses attention, both in the short and long term, on decisions, actions, results and implementation, incorporating monitoring, feedback and review procedures.

This last point, by emphasizing the characteristic of the Strategic Plan of being a goal-oriented process, also implicitly highlights the need for the entire process to be permeated by evaluation activities.

3.1 Strategic Planning and Demand for Evaluations

In light of the last consideration, the most generic Strategic Planning scheme, shown in Fig. 1, sees the process divided into 3 phases, connected to each other by the different types of evaluation required by the corresponding phase [24]:

- Phase 1: Cognitive
- Phase 2: Proposal
- Phase 3: Implementation

In the transition from the Cognitive Phase to the Proposal Phase, the Evaluation is necessary to understand the strengths, weaknesses, opportunities and threats (typical action of the SWOT Analysis), but also what are the points of view of the stakeholders and, more generally, of the Community: the result of this first evaluation activity is the vector of the objectives of the Plan, based on the Priority criterion.

The next step is the selection of the actions, based on the criteria of Effectiveness, Feasibility and Sustainability: through both monetary and non-monetary evaluations.

Once the Proposal Phase is concluded, it is possible to move on to the implementation of the Strategic Plan; during this phase, a constant monitoring action is carried out, which provides the information necessary for the ongoing evaluation; the outcome of this evaluation activity allows any corrections to be made to the Plan.

At the end of the planning cycle, it is necessary to draw up a balance of the path, through the ex post evaluation: the results thus obtained will allow the start of a new programming cycle, which will be able to capitalize on the experience conducted previously.

The entire process is accompanied by two types of transversal activities: research and development activities and community involvement, starting with stakeholders.

In the specific case of Strategic Planning applied to DMOs, the Knowledge Phase includes:

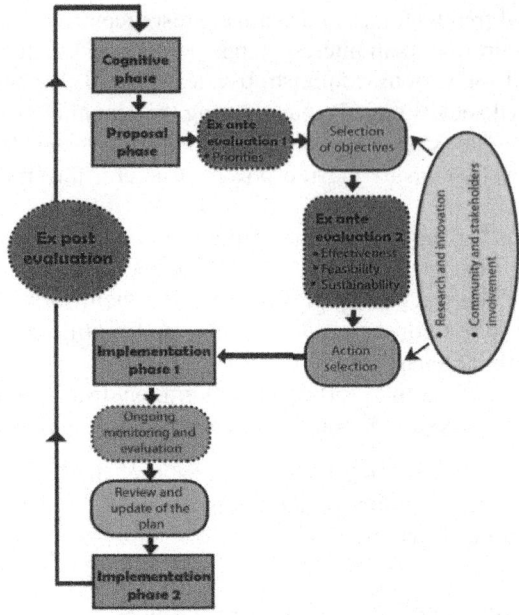

Fig. 1. Strategic plan scheme

- Stakeholder Analysis
- Reconnaissance of Attractors
- Reconnaissance of existing services
- Reconnaissance of the already expressed planning
- Market research
- Benchmark

3.2 Strategic Planning and Demand for Evaluations

In this phase, apart from the estimate of the costs necessary for the implementation of the actions, it may be useful in some cases to also verify the economic feasibility/sustainability in the management phase of the planned interventions, through the use of the Discounted Cash Flow Analysis - DCFA or the Cash Flow Analysis – CFA [25–27].

Similarly, the set of Key Performance Indicators (KPI) will be built to measure the effectiveness of the planned interventions: in the ex-ante, planning phase, in terms of expected results; in the ex post phase, in terms of results achieved [28–30].

> *"Enterprises and institutions need to evaluate their activity in order to determine the extent to which their goals have been achieved. One possible way to carry out this evaluation is to measure performance, for which organizations rely on metrics known as Key Performance Indicators (KPI)."* [31].

> *"Indicators are considered as useful tools that allow tourism managers to diagnose the situation of the destination, and to identify and evaluate issues that require addressing to improve the level of sustainability of the tourist activities."* [32].

The United Nations World Tourism Organization - UNWTO identifies 42 key indicators, grouped into 13 thematic areas, to measure tourism performance from a sustainability perspective: Wellbeing of Host Communities (5 indicators); Sustaining Cultural Assets (1 indicator); Community Participation in Tourism (1 indicator); Tourist Satisfaction (2 indicators); Health and Safety (4 indicators); Capturing Economic Benefits from Tourism (7 indicators); Protection of Valuable Natural Assets (2 indicators); Managing Scarce Natural Resources (4 indicators); Limiting Impacts of Tourism Activity (5 indicators); Controlling Tourist Activities and Levels (2 indicators); Destination Planning and Control (4 indicators); Designing Products and Services (4 indicators); Sustainability of Tourism Operations and Services (1 indicator) [33].

4 Cultural Tourism in Italy and Calabria

With the profound transformation of production systems underway, which has affected almost all industrial sectors, tourism has become increasingly important in the Italian economic system. According to the study conducted in 2023 by OpenEconomics and Fondazione Tor Vergata for the Ministry of Tourism, given the direct impact produced by an annual expenditure on tourism consumption of 100 billion euros (in 2022), the overall impact on national GDP, also considering the indirect impacts (i.e. the increase in supply and demand in the activated supply chains) and induced impacts (re-injection of income from work received by families in the form of consumption and re-investment of tax revenues in the form of public spending) is equal to 255 billion euros, equal to 13% of total GDP [34]. According to other studies [35], however, the added value activated by tourism spending is approximately 7% of GDP.

It should be noted that these data are affected by the so-called "COVID effect": in 2020, in fact, due to the pandemic, Italy recorded a 48.6% drop in tourism spending [35]. After the 2020 crisis, there was a progressive recovery in the sector, which, in 2023, recorded a full recovery, even exceeding the 2019 data, at least as far as tourist presences are concerned: with 133.6 million arrivals and 447.2 million presences recorded in accommodation facilities, the absolute peak recorded previously in 2019 was exceeded, when arrivals were 131.4 million and presences 436.7 [36].

As is known, Cultural Tourism is the prevalent type of tourism in Italy. According to ISTAT, 61.8% of national tourist flows are linked to the use of cultural attractions [37].

In order to identify the specific vocations of each territory, ISTAT has proceeded to classify Italian municipalities based on the geographical and/or anthropic characteristics [38]:

– **Municipalities with cultural, historical, artistic and landscape resources**
– **Municipalities with maritime facilities**
– **Municipalities with lake facilities**
– **Municipalities with mountain facilities**
– **Municipalities with thermal facilities**
– **Municipalities with two or more facilities**

of which: Maritime and cultural-landscape; Mountain and cultural-landscape; More than two facilities of which one cultural-landscape; Two or more facilities other than cultural-landscape.

– **No specific facilities**

From this classification it emerges that, of the 7926 Italian Municipalities, 1026 (12.95%) have vocations connected, in various ways, with cultural tourism, 1182 (14.91%) refer to other categories, 4014 (50.64%) do not belong to a specific category and 1704 (21.50%) cannot be classified as "Tourist Municipalities".

In Calabria, of the 404 Municipalities into which the regional territory is divided, 39 (9.65%) are characterized by cultural tourism flows, 68 (16.83%) by other types of tourism, 114 (28.22%) do not belong to a specific category and 183 (45.30%) are not considered tourist.

It is important to compare the regional data with the national one, as the percentage of non-tourist Municipalities in Calabria is more than double the national one, including almost half of the total number of Municipalities.

If the analysis of the tourist characterization of the Municipalities is limited only to the "tourist" ones, the proportions vary significantly, as can be seen from Table 1:

Table 1. Classification of Calabrian municipalities by type of tourism (Source: ISTAT)

	Municipalities with Cultural Tourism categories		Municipalities with other categories		Municipalities not belonging to specific categories		Total Tourist Municipalities
Italy	1026	16,49%	1182	19,00%	4014	64,51%	6222
Calabria	39	17,65%	68	30,77%	114	51,59%	221

As can be seen, in Calabria the data on cultural vocation is slightly higher than the national average, while the substantial difference concerns the other types of tourism which, based on empirical evidence, should be mainly traced back to seaside tourism.

5 The Case Study Territory: Inner Areas, Calabria, Locride

The Inner Areas are the element that most characterizes the territory of Calabria, as confirmed by the classification carried out by the DPS: out of 404 Municipalities present in Calabria, 326 (80.69%) are classified as Inner Areas, with varying degrees of peripherality [39].

Of the 97 Municipalities falling within the territory of the Metropolitan City of Reggio Calabria, 75 (77.32%) are classified as Inner Areas; in Locride, the area that is the subject of the case study illustrated in this contribution (highlighted with a black border in Figs. 2 and 3), the Municipalities included among the Inner Areas are 31 out of 42 (73.81%) [39, 40].

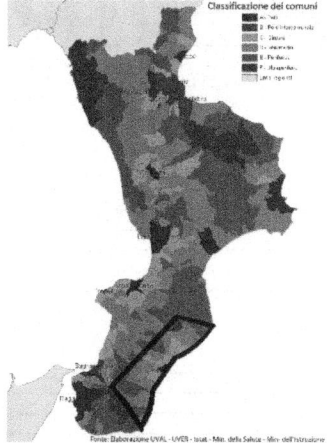

Fig. 2. Calabria Region – Territory classification 2014–2020 (Source: Elaboration of UVAL – UVER – ISTAT – Ministry of Health – Ministry of Education)

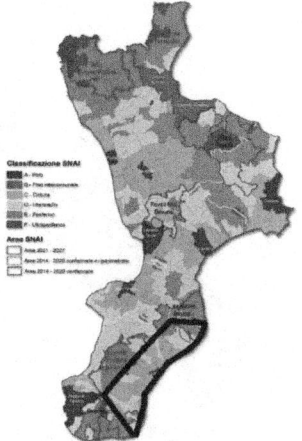

Fig. 3. Calabria Region – Territory classification 2021–2027

As regards cultural endowment, if we refer for example to the density of museums and similar structures in relation to the resident population, Calabria is slightly above the national average, with 2.8 institutions per 10,000 inhabitants compared to the Italian average of 2.7, as can be seen from Table 3 [9] (Fig. 4):

The case study that is the subject of this article concerns the eastern area of the Metropolitan City of Reggio Calabria: the area, called Locride, includes 42 municipalities and is bordered to the east by the Ionian Sea and to the west by the Aspromonte National Park (Fig. 5).

Regioni	Numero di istituzioni per 10.000 abitanti
Valle d'Aosta/Vallée d'Aoste	13,0
Piemonte	6,5
Friuli-Venezia Giulia	6,3
Liguria	5,5
Marche	5,2
Sardegna	5,1
Trento	4,8
Molise	4,4
Bolzano	3,5
Umbria	3,3
Lombardia	3,3
Toscana	3,2
Calabria	2,8
Veneto	2,7
Italia	**2,7**
Emilia-Romagna	2,3
Campania	2,1
Abruzzo	2,0
Basilicata	2,0
Lazio	1,9
Sicilia	1,2
Puglia	0,7

Fig. 4. Density of museums and similar institutions in the Municipalities of the Inner Areas in relation to the population. Year 2022, values per 10 thousand inhabitants. (Source: ISTAT)

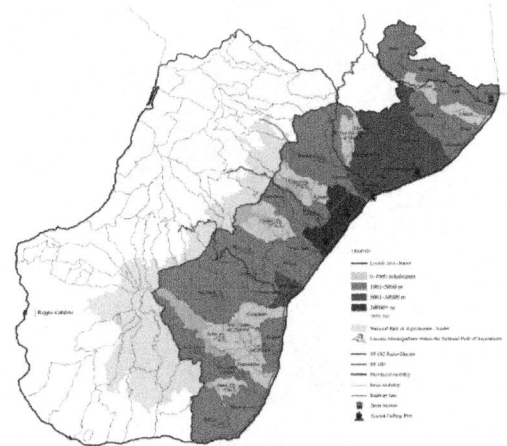

Fig. 5. The territory under study (Source: authors' elaboration)

6 The Initial Process for the Construction of a DMO for Locride

The Municipalities of Locride have been working for a long time to promote the tourism development of the territory. Numerous experiences have been conducted in the past, both individually and in aggregate form, starting from the Integrated Local Development Projects, promoted in 2013 by the Calabria Region and also dedicated to Tourism, and from the Local Action Plans developed over time by the GAL of Locride, just to name a few.

The results, however, are currently unsatisfactory, Locride is struggling to trigger tourism development processes: it is from this condition that the hypothesis of a new initiative is born that allows to overcome the difficulties encountered by the previous ones and manages to achieve the desired results.

With this spirit, four entities operating in the field of Tourism Services (Tourlallà), Digital Solutions for Companies (Evermind s.r.l. Benefit Company), Training (Farimpresa srl) and Research (Mediterranea University of Reggio Calabria - ECHE Lab Laboratory), have decided to start an experimental path aimed at the creation of a DMO of Locride.

6.1 The Cognitive Activities of the DMO

In February 2025, the four promoting entities started a preliminary cognitive phase, aimed at identifying:

- the enhancing resources, cultural and natural;
- the stakeholders;
- the existing activities and services (accommodation, transport and infrastructure, use of attractions, catering, typical products, complementary services, etc.);
- the planning already expressed by the territory;
- the existing tourist flows and potential demand;
- any benchmarks.

6.2 The Enhancing Resources, Cultural and Natural

This is an area with a cultural and natural heritage of great importance; in addition to the aforementioned National Park, among the cultural sites open to the public there are 14 Defensive Architectures, 10 Historic Palaces, 8 Historic Centers, 7 Archaeological Areas, 5 Places of Pilgrimage and 5 Rock Sites [41] (Fig. 6).

The Locride area also has a very rich intangible heritage, made up of rites, traditions, peasant and artisan knowledge, as well as highly appreciated food and wine products, among which it is worth mentioning the wines (IGT Mantonico Bianco, and DOC Rosso di Bivongi), the cheeses (caciocavallo di Ciminà) and much more, currently the subject of detailed cataloguing by the working group [42].

6.3 Stakeholder Analysis

Given the limited availability of information referring to levels of territorial aggregation lower than the Region, the start of the knowledge activities consisted of audits with sixteen private operators, which allowed us to have an initial picture, certainly not exhaustive, on the origin of the current tourists of Locride and on the main existing critical issues.

These interviews are part of the broader stakeholder analysis that will be conducted during the knowledge phase. Stakeholder analysis identify and analyze the more relevant actors of a strategic planning process. It involves understanding their interests, influence, and potential impact on the plan [43, 44].

The sixteen tour operators carry out very heterogeneous work activities. The most represented category is that of the managers of accommodation facilities (ten); of these,

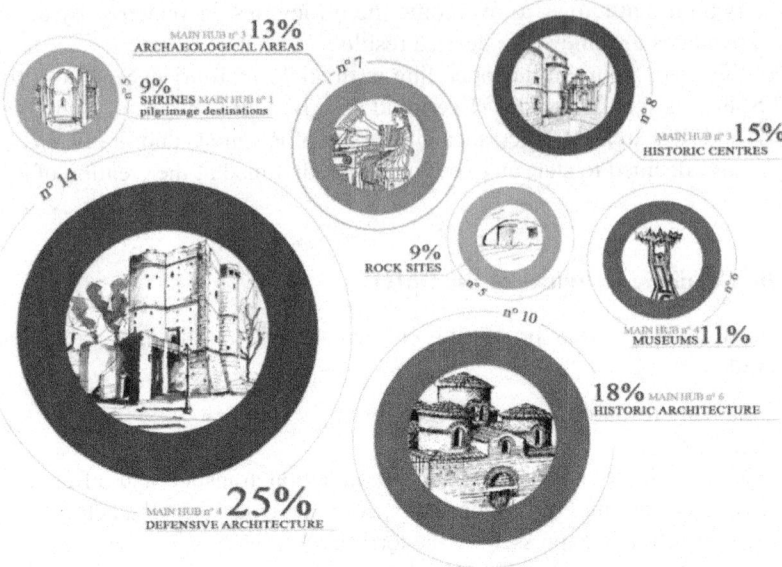

Fig. 6. The Cultural Heritage of the area under study (Source: authors' elaboration)

three are also hiking guides, two of whom are also organizers of events and shows. Two operators carry out activities related to the sea: one organizes boat trips, the other manages a buoy field and water sports. Other categories represented by an operator are: travel agent; manager of a civic museum; hiking guide; organizer of outdoor sports activities (climbing, paragliding, etc.).

From a methodological point of view, the interview was divided into two parts, the first aimed at identifying the origin of current tourists, the second aimed at knowing the main critical issues encountered by professionals. Both parts were structured with open answers, but as regards the origin, there were three questions:

- among your customers, what is the percentage ratio between Italian and foreign tourists?
- among Italian tourists, what is the region of origin?
- among foreign tourists, what is the country of origin?

The results of the interviews are shown in Tables 2, 3, 4 and 5.

Table 2. Origin of tourists of Locride (Source: field survey and processing by the authors)

Origin	%
Italians	40%
Foreigners	60%

Table 3. Regions of origin of tourists (Source: field survey and authors' processing)

Origin	%
Piedmont	15%
Lombardy	10%
Sicily	10%
Lazio	10%
Veneto	5%
Emilia-Romagna	5%
Tuscany	5%
Other Regions	40%

Table 4. Countries of origin of tourists (Source: field survey and authors' processing)

Origin	%
France	15%
U.K	15%
Germany	10%
U.S.A	10%
Switzerland	5%
Poland	5%
Other countries (Canada, Australia, Argentina, Scandinavia, Belgium, Netherlands, Luxembourg, Eastern countries, Austria, Greece, Spain, Portugal)	40%

From the interview with the operators it was also possible to obtain a first picture of the critical issues that hinder the tourist development of the territory. The questionnaire was open-ended but, despite their heterogeneity, the answers can be traced back to eight thematic areas:

The percentages reported for each area indicate the percentages of operators who have identified that area as a priority.

It is clear that the priority issue concerns transport, in terms of accessibility to the area but, above all, in terms of internal mobility, especially towards areas far from the coast.

The data that is in some ways the most surprising is the self-criticism that entrepreneurs make: the most frequent answers concern above all the difficulties in creating synergy, in dialoguing with operators from other sectors, such as food and wine producers, in operating by giving themselves medium-long term visions and horizons without privileging immediate results.

As regards the Communication Area, the observations concern above all the quality of some communication campaigns, their effectiveness in changing the stereotyped image

Table 5. Thematic areas that hinder the tourist development of Locride (Source: field survey and authors' elaboration)

A	Community	37,50%
B	Politics and Local Institutions	37,50%
C	Communication	62,50%
D	Transport	75,00%
E	Entrepreneurship	68,70%
F	Skills and Education	50,00%
G	Tourist Offer	31,20%
H	Complementary Services	18,70%

of Calabria, but also aspects such as the availability of information on institutional websites or the poor dissemination at local level of information on events and initiatives organized in the area.

Skills are also one of the most felt vulnerabilities: in particular with regard to linguistic skills, but in general there is a lack of professionalism on the part of many operators (both business owners and employees) and a certain propensity to improvise. The education system also does not help, by not providing students with almost any information regarding the huge cultural heritage, both tangible and intangible, that Locride is endowed with, thus not allowing the Community to acquire full awareness of the importance of the existing heritage.

The Communities themselves, for their part, are called into question especially with regard to the widespread mentality, oriented towards pessimism, welfare, lack of initiative and, above all, finding in emigration the answer to the problems of personal fulfillment.

In this context, Politics and Local Institutions could certainly not be missing, even if they are not in first place: the lack of effective planning, capable of truly responding to the needs of citizens, the incorrect use of the huge resources spent in recent decades, the lack of institutional support for businesses in terms of advanced services and, above all, administrative simplifications, represent obstacles that sometimes appear insurmountable [45].

The operators' responses also concerned the Tourist Offer Area: in this field, it is reported that the quality of services is often inadequate, which sometimes, in proportion, corresponds to excessive prices, the lack of innovation and originality of products and, above all, the lack of effective organizational forms, capable of conveying the territory's offer in a unitary manner.

Finally, a non-negligible share of responses also concerned complementary services: the lack of essential services in some places such as pharmacies, ATMs, etc.; the poor accessibility and usability of many cultural sites; the lack of attention to accessibility and usability by people with disabilities; the scarcity of complementary services such as, for example, equipment rental and, more generally, experiential activities; the lack of attention to the quality of the environment, both in terms of cleanliness of public spaces and urban decorum [46].

6.4 Provisional Strategic Objectives

This Survey has therefore allowed us to define a provisional vector of strategic objectives, which will serve as a basis for comparison with other stakeholders and will guide subsequent knowledge-gathering activities:

Objective 1: build the "products" of the Locride Destination, thematic itineraries that consider the resources to be enhanced, existing accessibility and other available services;
Objective 2: enrich the offer of "complementary" services, such as events (musical, cultural, sporting, etc.) and experiences, with the involvement of companies operating in the area;
Objective 3: promote knowledge of the Locride Destination: develop innovative and effective communication and marketing tools, also through the use of digital technologies and social media;
Objective 4: improve the quality of services offered to tourists;
Objective 5: increase the skills of operators;
Objective 6: improve internal mobility in the area through innovative forms of transport;
Objective 7: increase community empowerment;
Objective 8: promote synergies between operators.

7 Conclusions

The cognitive activities for the establishment of the DMO of Locride have just begun. The results obtained from the responses of the interviewed operators constitute a starting point for the subsequent cognitive activities and will allow to start the comparison with the stakeholders and the involvement of the Community.

The outcome of this participatory process will allow to identify the real priority objectives of the Strategic Plan of the Locride Destination and, subsequently, to hypothesize the actions to be undertaken, to be subjected to evaluation of effectiveness, feasibility and sustainability.

In particular, the actions will concern:

– Product and experience development
– Destination marketing and sales
– Visitor and destination services
– Events development
– Skills development

The research activities will concern, in particular, the evaluation tools, starting from the identification of the set of Key Performances Indicators to be used for the purposes of the ex-ante and ex post evaluation of the actions of the Plan.

This aspect is particularly relevant in the strategic planning process of a tourist destination: it is the tool that, in addition to allowing us to understand the effectiveness of the plan, allows us to prevent overtourism phenomena, aiming at the sustainable growth of the destination, without ever exceeding its carrying capacity.

Disclosure of Interests. The authors have no competing interests to declare that are relevant to the content of this article.

References

1. Mollica, E.: Le Aree Interne della Calabria. Rubbettino Editore, Soveria Mannelli (CZ), Italy (1996)
2. Agenzia per la coesione territoriale. Accordo di Partenariato 2014–2020. Strategia nazionale per le Aree interne: definizione, obiettivi, strumenti e *governance*. Documento tecnico collegato alla bozza di Accordo di Partenariato trasmessa alla CE il 9 dicembre 2013 (2014)
3. Dipartimento per le politiche di coesione e per il sud. Accordo di Partenariato Italia 2021–2027, pp. 84–85 (2022)
4. Bernard, J., Keim-Klärner, S.: Disadvantaged and disadvantaging regions: opportunity structures and social disadvantage in rural peripheries. Tijdschr. Econ. Soc. Geogr. **114**(5), 463–478 (2023)
5. Kühn, M.: Peripheralization: theoretical concepts explaining socio-spatial inequalities. Eur. Plan. Stud. **23**(2), 367–378 (2015)
6. Torriani, C., Barreca, A., Rebaudengo, M., Rolando, D.: Projects and funding in Italian inner areas: learning from the 2014–2020 programming of the SNAI national strategy. In: Gervasi, O., et al. (eds.) Computational Science and Its Applications – ICCSA 2023 Workshops. ICCSA 2023. LNCS, vol. 14106. Springer, Cham (2023). https://doi.org/10.1007/978-3-031-37111-0_17
7. UVAL - Unità di valutazione degli investimenti pubblici. Strategia Nazionale per le Aree Interne: definizione, obiettivi, strumenti e governance. Materiali Uval, Numero 31 - Anno 2014, Roma, Italy (2014)
8. ISTAT. The geography of Inner Areas in 2020. Territories between potential and weaknesses. Statistiche Focus. Roma, Italy (2022)
9. ISTAT. Il Patrimonio Culturale nelle Aree Interne. Anno 2022. Statistiche Focus. Roma, Italy (2025)
10. MiBACT - Ministero dei beni e delle attività culturali e del turismo. Linee Guida per la Strategia Nazionale per le Aree Interne (2016). https://www.agenziacoesione.gov.it/wp-content/uploads/2020/07/Linee_guida_Mibact_v05122016.pdf
11. ICOMOS. International Charter for Cultural Heritage Tourism "Reinforcing cultural heritage protection and community resilience through responsible and sustainable tourism management" (2022). https://openarchive.icomos.org/id/eprint/2805/
12. Capone, F.: I sistemi locali turistici in Italia. Identificazione, misurazione ed analisi delle fonti di competitività. Firenze University Press (2005)
13. Franch, M.: Destination management: governare il turismo tra locale e globale. Giappichelli, Torino (2002)
14. Legge 29 marzo 2001, n. 135, Riforma della legislazione nazionale del turismo. (GU Serie Generale n.92 del 20-04-2001)
15. Legge 12 luglio 2011, n. 106, Conversione in legge, con modificazioni, del decreto-legge 13 maggio 2011, n. 70, concernente Semestre Europeo - Prime disposizioni urgenti per l'economia. (GU n.160 del 12-07-2011)
16. World Tourism Organization. A Practical Guide to Tourism Destination Management, UNWTO, Madrid (2007). https://doi.org/10.18111/9789284412433, https://www.e-unwto.org/doi/book/10.18111/9789284412433

17. United Nations, Department of Economic and Social Affairs Statistics Division. International Recommendations for Tourism Statistics 2008. Studies in Methods Series M No. 83/Rev.1. New York, USA (2010). https://unstats.un.org/unsd/publication/Seriesm/SeriesM_83rev1e.pdf#page=24
18. Viglianisi, A., Calabrò, F.: The management models of a tourist destination in Italy. In: Calabrò, F., Della Spina, L., Piñeira Mantiñán, M.J. (eds.) New Metropolitan Perspectives. NMP 2022. LNNS, vol. 482, pp. 2325–2334, 2022. Springer, Cham (2023). https://doi.org/10.1007/978-3-031-06825-6_223
19. Carter, R., Nevill, H.: Destination management handbook. a guide to the planning and implementation of destination management. World Bank Group, Washington DC, USA (2022)
20. Martinelli, F.: La pianificazione strategica in Italia e in Europa. FrancoAngeli, Milano, Italy (2005)
21. Albrechts, L.: Strategic (Spatial) planning reexamined. Environ. Plann. B. Plann. Des. **31**(5), 743–758 (2004). https://doi.org/10.1068/b3065
22. Albrechts, L.: Alcune riflessioni sul "cosa" e sul "come" della pianificazione strategica. In: Martinelli, F. (ed.) La pianificazione strategica in Italia e in Europa. FrancoAngeli, Milano, Italy (2005)
23. Spatari, G., Lorè, I., Viglianisi, A., Calabrò, F.: Economic feasibility of an integrated program for the enhancement of the byzantine heritage in the aspromonte national park. the case of staiti. In: Calabrò, F., Della Spina, L., Piñeira Mantiñán, M.J. (eds.) New Metropolitan Perspectives. NMP 2022. LNNS, vol. 482, pp. 313–323. Springer, Cham (2022). https://doi.org/10.1007/978-3-031-06825-6_30
24. Calabrò, F., Mafrici, F., Meduri, T.: The valuation of unused public buildings in support of policies for the inner areas. The application of SostEc model in a case study in Condofuri (Reggio Calabria, Italy). In: Bevilacqua C., Calabrò F., Della Spina L. (eds.) New Metropolitan Perspectives. Smart Innovation, Systems and Technologies, vol. 178, pp. 566–579; Springer (2021). https://doi.org/10.1007/978-3-030-48279-4_54; Scopus ID: 2-s2.0–85091316344
25. Nesticò, A., Maselli, G., Ghisellini, P., Ulgiati, S.: A dual probabilistic discounting approach to assess economic and environmental impacts. Environ. Resource Econ. **85**(1), 239–265 (2023). https://doi.org/10.1007/s10640-023-00766-6
26. Nesticò, A., Galante, M.: An estimate model for the equalisation of real estate tax: a case study. Int. J. Bus. Intell. Data Min. **10**(1), 19–32 (2015). https://doi.org/10.1504/IJBIDM.2015.069038
27. Sica, F., Tajani, F., Cerullo, G.: An evaluation model for an optimal decarbonisation process in the built environment. Built Environ. Project Asset Manage. **15**(1), 51–66 (2025). https://doi.org/10.1108/BEPAM-05-2024-0126
28. Rasoolimanesh, S.M., Ramakrishna, S., Hall, C.M., Esfandiar, K., Seyfi, S.: A systematic scoping review of sustainable tourism indicators in relation to the sustainable development goals. J. Sustain. Tour. **31**(7), 1497–1517 (2020). https://doi.org/10.1080/09669582.2020.1775621
29. Stankulova, A., Barreca, A., Rebaudengo, M., Rolando, D.: The quantitative indicator-based evaluation for rural development. Int. Regio. Sci. Rev. 01600176241268028 (2024)
30. Aulisio, A., Barbero, S., Barreca, A., Malavasi, G., Rolando, D.: From data collection to a cross-cutting analysis visualisation: territorial complexity overview to foster responsible tourism in rural areas. In: Gervasi, O., Murgante, B., Garau, C., Taniar, D., C. Rocha, A.M.A., Faginas Lago, M.N. (eds.) Computational Science and Its Applications – ICCSA 2024 Workshops. ICCSA 2024. LNCS, vol. 14819. Springer, Cham (2024). https://doi.org/10.1007/978-3-031-65282-0_3
31. Domínguez, E., Pérez, B., Rubio, A.L., Zapata, M.A.: A taxonomy for key performance indicators management. Comput. Stand. Interfaces **64**(2019), 24–40 (2019). https://doi.org/10.1016/j.csi.2018.12.001

32. Lozano-Oyola, M., Blancas, F.J., González, M., Caballero, R.: Sustainable tourism indicators as planning tools in cultural destinations. Ecol. Ind. **18**(2012), 659–675 (2012). https://doi.org/10.1016/j.ecolind.2012.01.014
33. World Tourism Organization. Indicators of Sustainable Development for Tourism Destinations A Guidebook (English version), UNWTO, Madrid (2004). https://doi.org/10.18111/9789284407262
34. OpenEconomics, Fondazione Tor Vergata. Il turismo in Italia. Impatto della spesa turistica sull'economia (2023). https://www.openeconomics.eu/2023/12/04/turismo-in-italia-analisi-di-impatto-economico/
35. Marasco, A., Maggiore, G., Morvillo, A., Becheri, E.: Rapporto sul Turismo italiano - XXV edizione, 2020–2022. CNR Edizioni, Roma, Italy (2022)
36. ISTAT. I flussi turistici nel 2023. Statistiche today (2024). https://www.istat.it/wp-content/uploads/2024/11/Statistica-Today_Turismo-2023_rev.pdf
37. ISTAT. Il Turismo Culturale in Italia. Analisi territoriale integrata dei dati. Letture Statistiche - Territori. Roma, Italy (2023)
38. ISTAT. Classificazione dei Comuni in base alla densità turistica come indicato dalla Legge 17 luglio 2020, n. 77, art. 182 (2022). https://www.istat.it/it/files/2020/09/classificazione-turistica-comuni.Istat_.pdf
39. Agenzia per la Coesione Territoriale. Dossier_DPS_Calabria (2015). https://www.agenziacoesione.gov.it/wp-content/uploads/2020/07/Dossier_DPS_Calabria.pdf
40. Formez PA & Dipartimento per le politiche di coesione e per il sud – DPS. SNAI Dossier Regione Calabria (2022). https://politichecoesione.governo.it/media/3166/snai-dossier-regionale-calabria.pdf
41. Calabrò, F., Cassalia, G., Lorè, I.: A project of enhancement and integrated management: the cultural heritage agency of locride. In: Calabrò, F., Della Spina, L., Piñeira Mantiñán, M.J. (eds.) New Metropolitan Perspectives. NMP 2022. LNNS, vol. 482, pp. 278–288. Springer, Cham (2022). https://doi.org/10.1007/978-3-031-06825-6_27
42. Calabrò, F., Campolo, D., Cassalia, G.: a cultural route on the trail of greek monasticism in calabria. In: Calabrò F., Della Spina L., Bevilacqua C. (eds.), New Metropolitan Perspectives. Smart Innovation, Systems and Technologies, vol. 101, pp. 475–483, Springer, ISBN: 978-3-319-92098-6, ISSN: 2190-3018 (2019). https://doi.org/10.1007/978-3-319-92102-0_50
43. Malavasi, G., Barreca, A., Rebaudengo, M., Rolando, D.: A stakeholder analysis to support resilient strategies in the Alta Valsesia inner area. n: Gervasi, O., et al. (eds.) Computational Science and Its Applications – ICCSA 2023 Workshops. ICCSA 2023. LNCS, vol. 14106. Springer, Cham (2023). https://doi.org/10.1007/978-3-031-37111-0_19
44. Tajani, F., Manganelli, B., Cerullo, G., Morano, P., Morente, M.A.: The student housing as a catalyst for virtuous processes of "win-win" revitalization of property assets in disuse. Lecture Notes in Computer Science (including subseries Lecture Notes in Artificial Intelligence and Lecture Notes in Bioinformatics), 14109 LNCS, pp. 387–400 (2023). https://doi.org/10.1007/978-3-031-37120-2_25
45. Forte, F., Antoniucci, V., De Paola, P.: Immigration and the housing market: the case of castel volturno, in campania region Italy. Sustainability **10**, 343 (2018). https://doi.org/10.3390/su10020343
46. Del Giudice, V., Massimo, D.E., De Paola, P., Del Giudice, F.P., Musolino, M.: Green buildings for post carbon city: determining market premium using spline smoothing semiparametric method. In: Bevilacqua, C., Calabrò, F., Della Spina, L. (eds.) New Metropolitan Perspectives. NMP 2020. Smart Innovation, Systems and Technologies, vol. 178. Springer, Cham (2021). https://doi.org/10.1007/978-3-030-48279-4_114

Econometric and Multidimensional Evaluation in Urban Environment (EMEUE 2025)

The Urban One Health Approach for the Planning of Effective Interventions on Territory: A Systematic Analysis of the Scientific Literature

Pierluigi Morano[1], Felicia Di Liddo[1], Marco Locurcio[1], Francesca Fariello[2(✉)], and Debora Anelli[2]

[1] Department of Civil, Environmental, Land, Building Engineering and Chemistry (DICATECh), Polytechnic University of Bari, 70126 Bari, Italy
{pierluigi.morano,felicia.diliddo,marco.locurcio}@poliba.it
[2] Department of Architecture and Design, "Sapienza" University of Rome, 00196 Rome, Italy
{francesca.fariello,debora.anelli}@uniroma1.it

Abstract. The aims of this research is to conduct an analysis of the existing scientific literature on the concept of Urban One Health that is an innovative and integrated approach that connects human, animal and environmental health within urban planning and development processes. This multidisciplinary paradigm is a concrete and necessary response to the challenges posed by contemporary urbanisation, environmental sustainability and the well-being of populations.

The Urban One Health approach promotes an holistic vision that recognises the interconnection between urban ecosystems and public health.

The main purpose of this study is to expand the theoretical and practical knowledge and understanding of the Urban One Health concept, highlighting its main implications for contemporary urban planning. For this scope, the analysis focuses on identifying interdisciplinary tools, strategies and methodologies that can support a more resilient, inclusive and conscious urban transformation in line with the principles of sustainability.

Through the examination of the scientific literature, it was possible to identify three criteria that characterise the Urban One Health approach: firstly, the definition of specific research objectives focused on the integration of health and urban planning; secondly, the analysis of the context as a field of interaction between biological, social and environmental factors; and finally, the use of interdisciplinary research methodologies, capable of understanding the complexity of the issue.

Keywords: One Health · Urban One Health · Sustainable Cities · Urban planning · Review

1 Introduction

In the 20th century the exponentially growing world population connected to the increasing urbanization have profoundly transformed the cities and have proposed new challenges for the management of public health and environmental sustainability.

Demographic surveys show that by 2050 the world population could exceed 9.7 billion people, with over 70% of the global community concentrated in urban areas [1]. It is currently evident that the intensive expansion of the territories causes different socio-environmental critical issues that require rethinking urban planning strategies and health policies, in order to ensure more sustainable, healthy and resilient cities. In this framework, the concept of One Health is increasingly crucial. In particular, this innovative model addresses the interconnections between human health, animal health and environmental health, highlighting the need for territories governance of the interventions to be carried out that is integrated with multidisciplinary measures. In 2021, the World Health Organization (WHO) defines the health as the result of a holistic balance between people and environment, in natural terms but also in the urban dimension. This notion is consistent with the attested increase in awareness of necessarily redesigning cities by ensuring more sustainable and healthy living conditions.

Furthermore, in 2015, the United Nations has pointed out the urge of introducing among the 17 Sustainable Development Goals (SDGs) a specific objective aimed at transforming cities in order to make them more inclusive, sustainable and safe, emphasizing the simultaneous need to analyze and manage progressive urbanization [2].

In this sense, effective strategic actions on the territories able to address the global issues in a systematic manner for the increase of communities well-being should be implemented. Among them, the strengthening of public health on a international, national, regional and local scale represents a key factor to prevent future pandemics and support scientific research for creating safer and more resilient perspectives. To ensure the development of urban environments (built and unbuilt) as a generator of factors of well-being in line with a salutogenic approach [3], the promotion of a holistic vision for a effective balance between human, environmental and animal health is essential. From this point of view, cities should be rethought to reduce environmental risk and improve air quality in a context of healthy lifestyles.

Moreover, the establishment of successful collaborations between government entities, local authorities, health agencies, academics, public and private research institutes, professionals and companies becomes a fundamental pillar. These synergies are central to address critical phenomena such as the increased contact between wildlife and population in urban areas, climate change and pressure on biodiversity. Through the application of a multidisciplinary criterion, it will be possible to identify and control, since the beginning, the emergence and spread of new infectious agents, in order to limit the risk of new pandemics and protect global health.

In addition, urban health should be oriented to equal access to care, diagnostics and health treatments for the entire population: territorial inequalities in health care cause relevant questions that are reflected also in waiting times and perceived quality of health services, especially for the most vulnerable population groups. During the last decades, the strengthening of the prevention of chronic non-communicable diseases (tumors, diabetes, cardiovascular, respiratory and neurodegenerative diseases) has assumed a significant role in the debates on human health. A key policy to be applied in all urban areas can be the creation of a broad and homogeneous care network: this strategic measure would reduce the financial burden of chronic diseases on public health expenditure, over and above the improvement of communities life quality.

The definition of social and health policies for fovouring the health as a 'common good' and its integration into all development sustainable cities initiatives is the main aspect on which the Urban One Health approach is based.

For raising awareness among the population to contribute to the creation of a preventive culture consistently with the One Health principles, the implementation of multidisciplinary training of health professionals, urban planners and public administrators should be promoted. Given the close relationship between population health and urban territories in which the people live, the scientific debates on the topic are mainly focalized on the definition of guidelines for interventions able to improve the citizens weel-being (of which the health represents a essential sphere).

For exemple in the reference literature, [4] highlights that the emergence of new infectious diseases (such as zoonosis) is greatly linked to urbanization, changes in land use and the loss of biodiversity. According to [5], the adoption of the One Health approach has accelerated due to the increase in global health crises (especially the last caused by the COVID-19 pandemic). The emergencies have confirmed the strong interconnession between people, animals, plants and envirorment into the macrosystem in which are included and that the single elements health depends on from that of all the others. In 2022 the Food and Agriculture Organization (FAO), the United Nations Environment Programme (UNEP), the World Health Organization (WHO) and the World Organisation for Animal Health (WOAH) have developed a joint and participation-based action plan to address threats to the ecosystems health (of humans, animals, plants and environment) aimed at creating a framework in which systems and capabilities to better prevent, predict, detect and respond to crisis are integrated. Thus, the plan focuses on the strengthening of the fair international cooperation between all sectors that involve the global health [6], setting operational goals and collective actions to be taken.

In this scenario, the Urban One Health approach should guide the correct management of the territories, stimulating the implementation of regeneration strategies targeted at rehabilitating the urban ecosystem of future cities, focusing on biodiversity and ecosystem services within the design of healthy and sustainable urban spaces.

Currently, the Urban One Health application faces some important obstacles from an operational point of view: legislative fragmentation, difficulties in coordination between different sectors and scarce awareness of this importance by citizens [7]. Furthermore, [8] underlines that the transition towards the urban models from the prespective of One Health implies significant initial investments, although economic and health benefits high and considerable.

The definition of public policies in line with this approach presupposes the integration between science, technology and political decisions [9] in order to guarantee healthy and resilient cities ready to face the global challenges of the 21st century.

2 Aim

The research is part of the outlined framework. In particular, the work aims to provide an analytic framework of the main aspects connected to the notion of Urban One Health covered by the reference literature. The analysis intends to highlight the ever-increasing role of the approach in the development of strategic urban policies for the effective management of the cities with a view of a synergistic integration between public health, environmental sustainability and communities quality of life [10, 11].

The Urban One Health approach represents a holistic model of contemporary city planning. It includes an innovative paradigm that redefines the notion of health related to urban design, overcoming the ordinary sectoral vision to encompass a multidisciplinary approach in which urban planning, epidemiology, ecology and governance are projected towards the creation of healthier and more resilient cities.

Through the analysis of the reference literature, in the present research the interpretation of the looking for healthy urban governance models is carried out, to point out the the benefits deriving from the adoption of One Health-based tools and to provide evidence for supporting the planning oriented towards the communities well-being improvement [13]. The identification of factors and best practices from the literature contributes to outlining the interventions capable of directing wider urban strategies, improving their effectiveness and promoting models of sustainable development. The high attention of the scientific and institutional community towards Urban One Health confirms, in fact, the need to implement and favour innovative approaches aimed at addressing the challenges of urban health, with particular attention to climate change, socio-economic inequalities and equitable access to territorial resources (i.e. the available environmenatal, cultural, social, economic factors) [9, 12].

In this sense, this study tries to provide an additional contribution to the existing knowledge on the topic, for the future development of methodological and operational tools to support urban management as well as to promote a more holistic vision of health as a fundamental element in planning policies and the consequent development of cities [7].

The following part of the paper is organized as described below. Section 3 describes the methodology developed for the systematic analysis of the relevant literature, with the aim of selecting the contributions that discuss the main aspects in the various geographical contexts to investigate the topic. Section 4 is dedicated to the presentation of the results and a summary of the main issues deal with by the different Authors is outlined; in addition, the main trends and critical issues in the relationship between urban planning and health are highlighted. Finally, in Sect. 5 the conclusions are discussed. Therefore, the practical implications of the research and further insights are illustrated.

3 The Methodology Adopted for the Literature Review Development

In order to carry out a systematic analysis of the scientific literature related to the concept of Urban One Health, 57 documents [14–70] have been collected and chosen through the consultation of the main academic databases, including Scopus and Google Scholar.

Urban One Health is part of an emerging research field that connects territorial planning, public health and environmental sustainability, recognizing the crucial role of the urban space on the well-being of communities [14, 15]. The exponential increase in the urban population – associated with a growing exposure to pollutants - has made the need for integrated approaches to mitigate the connected risks and improve the quality of life in cities, evident. During the last decades, the health implications of urban planning have been particularly recognized as a priority within the public policies. Furthermore, the focus on the strategies for adaptation and reduction of environmental impacts of interventions on territories has assumed a fundamental importance, by attesting the urge to implement solutions based on urban sustainability and resilience [16, 17].

To ensure a wide and in-depth analysis of the scientific literature consistent with the general topic covered in the present research, the keywords representative of the question have been identified. These are: *urban one health, urban health, urban sustainability, environmental health, public health policies, urban planning and well-being, ecosystem services in cities, green infrastructure and health, climate change and urban health, socio-environmental determinants of health*. The synergic and combined use of these keywords in the consulted databases have allowed to select several scientific contributions, guaranteeing a broad and representative coverage of the different disciplines involved in the discussion, including the environmental epidemiology, the territorial planning and the Medicine. In Fig. 1 a scheme of the main keywords used for the papers selection is shown.

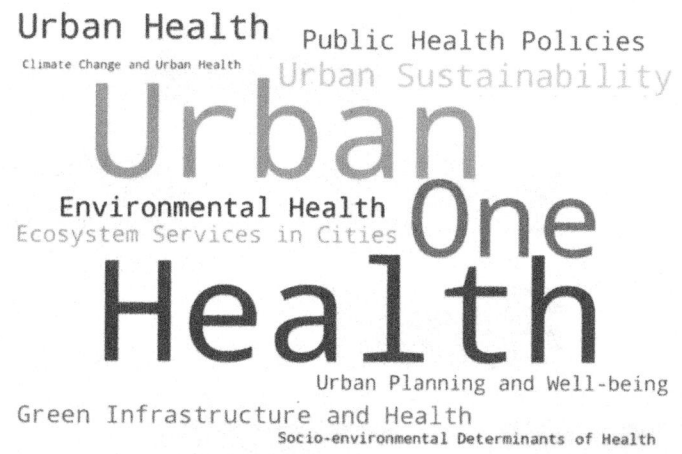

Fig. 1. Keywords used for the collection of the papers analysed in the review

From the first set of 187 papers collected through the databases consultation, only the contributions with scientific relevance and thematic consistency have been selected. In particular, the studies that addressed the interconnections between human, environmental and animal health within urban contexts, with reference to planning strategies or sustainability goals, have been included in the final papers set. Conversely, off-topic documents or focused exclusively on rural contexts, or lacked an interdisciplinary perspective, or not available in full text, have been excluded.

Figure 2 shows the flow chart of the phases carried out for the contributions selection process.

The identified literature articles are referred to a publication period of the last two decades and include different documents aimed at highlighting the role of environmental, social and economic factors in determining urban health.

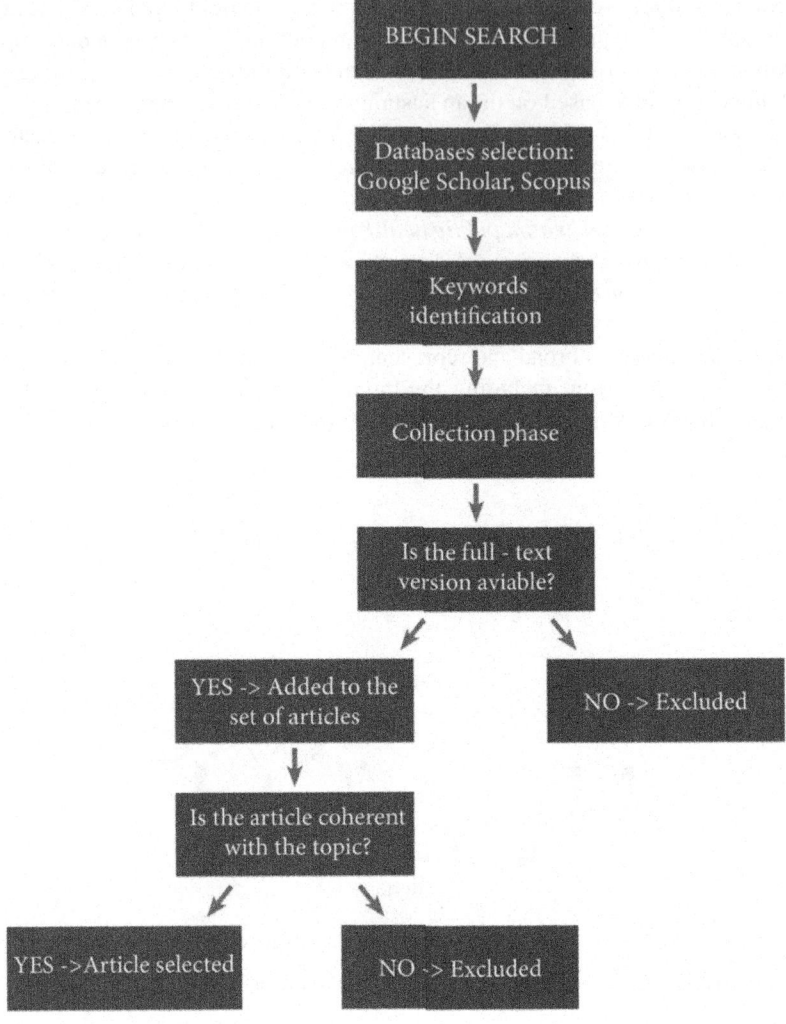

Fig. 2. Main steps for the selection of the 57 papers analysed in the review

By recalling the aim of the research (i.e. to investigate the scientific literature on the topic of Urban One Health), three main criteria have been identified to classify and examine the selected records: i) the specific research objectives, ii) the context of analysis, iii) the methodologies adopted. This tripartite classification has led to a structured interpretation of the literature results, highlighting recurring patterns and emerging directions in the field.

Specifically, the analysis of the research objectives allows to focus the several purposes for which each study has been developed, in terms of innovative contribution to the existing knowledge and of practical implications, as the definition of new tools to be used in the decision-making processes related to the urban interventions.

The identification of the contexts of analysis is connected to the different aspects on which the academic has placed greater attention, highlighting the issues related to the general topic of Urban One Health mostly discussed within various geographical territories.

The investigation of the methodological approaches implemented in the selected papers for specific objectives allows to identify any recurring techniques applied with reference to targeted goals and contexts (Fig. 3).

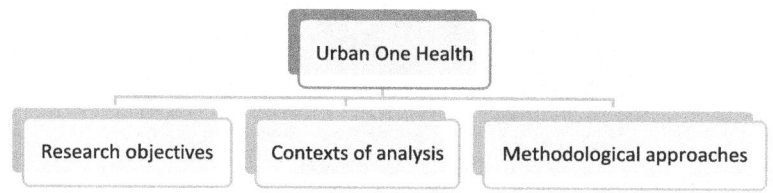

Fig. 3. Criteria used for the classification and the analysis of the collected papers

4 Results

Based on the three criteria used for the classification and analysis of the papers collected for this literature review, the discussion of the results is structured into the three main sections outlined below: research objectives, contexts of analysis and methodological approaches.

4.1 Research Objectives

In general terms, the research objectives of the collected 57 papers are all linked to highlight the relevance of the inclusion of the Urban One Health approach in the urban planning operations. The most frequent goal identified in the literature papers sample concerns the analysis of how the urban environment influences public health. In this sense, integrated strategies can promote equitable and sustainable communities well-being. The most recent studies point out the role of local governance in the urban health policies management, and underline the importance of evaluation tools - such as the Health Impact Assessment (HIA) - to promote informed decisions based on scientific evidence [18]. Furthermore, a growing interest for the synergic integration between urban planning, public health and ecology is attested, with the aim of developing territorial strategies targeted to sustainable and resilient cities [19].

Furthermore the influence of the environment on public health is increasingly acknowl-edged through studies emphasizing how air quality, green spaces, accessibility to resources, and built environment characteristics significantly impact on physical and mental health outcomes. Addressing environmental determinants such as pollution, urban heat islands, and noise exposure through integrated urban planning strategies not only improves overall community health but also contributes to reducing health inequities among urban populations. Consequently, multidisciplinary approaches that connect urban design with environmental health considerations emerge as essential for achieving healthier, more inclusive urban settings [17].

Figure 4 summarizes the main research objectives of the 57 studies of the detected sample.

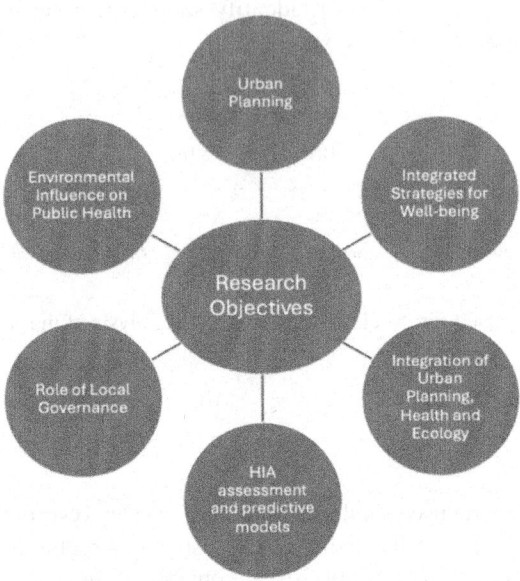

Fig. 4. Research objectives of the analysed studies

4.2 Contexts of Analysis

With regard to the contexts of analysis examined by the 57 researches, several key themes are found.

The aspects mostly deal with within each study represent the main declinations of the more general topic of the Urban One Health. Among the issues, the relationship between access to green spaces and mental health, the role of urban pollution on the human health, the socio-spatial inequalities in determining the communities well-being, the importance of urban planning focusing on public health constitute the most common questions of the relevant literature [20–22]. In this framework, different Authors conclude that air pollution, soil degradation and the lack of green spaces are the main factors that influence the spread of chronic diseases, with a greater impact on the most vulnerable population groups. Moreover, the role played by air quality, noise pollution and urban heat islands is explored as determinant variable of public health [23, 24].

The case studies of the different analyzed researches show that prolonged exposure to high levels of air pollution is associated with an increased risk of cardiovascular and respiratory diseases [15, 25]. In addition, the lack of green infrastructure in cities contributes to the increase in stress-related disorders, obesity and metabolic diseases

[26, 27]. In this sense, the socio-spatial inequalities are also relevant in the relationship between the human health and urban planning, as the uneven distribution of green spaces and health services significantly affects the territorial gap in urban health [28]. Moreover, recent studies indicate more equitable levels of well-being in cities with planning focalized on health and social inclusion [29].

Among the urban factors examined in the set of papers related to the Urban One Health approach, housing quality and sustainable mobility are fundamental aspects of quality of life in urban areas. Building density and traffic conditions have a direct influence on the perception of well-being and the risk of exposure to pollutants [30]. At the same time, recent studies have highlighted how an active integration between sustainable transport and territorial planning can drastically reduce toxic gas emissions, improving public health [31]. From a practical point of view, numerous examples demonstrate the effectiveness of the Urban One Health approach in different urban contexts. Lyon (France) leads the One Health 4 Cities network, which develops tools to increase the positive impact of urban projects on the health of people, animals and the environment [32]. Lahti (Finland) has implemented the Nature Step to Health program, which integrates health into urban policies through initiatives such as the Health Forest that promotes the mental and phisical well-being of the visitors through sensorial paths [33]. Accra (Ghana) shares the WHO Urban Health Initiative [34], adopting measures to reduce deaths and diseases associated with air and climate pollutants. Kathmandu (Nepal) is involved in a pilot project that monitors the health and economic burden of air pollution for improving urban health [35] (Fig. 5).

Fig. 5. Main topics addressed in the analyzed papers

4.3 Methodological Approaches

The documents examined in the reference literature implement a variety of methodological attitudes to analyze the Urban One Health approach in line with specific objectives. These methodologies reflect the multidisciplinary nature of Urban One Health, integrating perspectives from urban planning, epidemiology, environmental sciences, and public health policies.

A significant number of studies develop systematic reviews on the topic to provide a critical overview of the scientific debate and to define the main conceptual and applicative models related to Urban One Health [16, 18, 19, 28, 36, 37]. These reviews highlight the multidisciplinarity as a central aspect for the study of interactions between the urban environment and public health. By analyzing a broad set of scientific suggestions, they contribute to establishing a solid theoretical framework that allows the creation of interpretative and predictive models, as well as operational guidelines to support urban policies [38]. The systematic literature reviews serve as an essential reference for identifying best practices, common challenges, and emerging research trends in the field of Urban One Health.

In addition to systematic reviews, many studies apply quantitative and empirical analyses by using environmental, epidemiological, and socioeconomic datasets to investigate the relationship between urban factors and public health [20]. The integration of big data analytics and machine learning algorithms has enabled researchers to extract insights from large-scale datasets, identifying hidden patterns and correlations between urban design and health outcomes [39–41]. For instance, statistical models applied to air pollution data have demonstrated a strong link between urban emissions and increased rates of respiratory and cardiovascular diseases, reinforcing the necessity of policy interventions [31].

Among the most widely used analytical tools, Geographic Information System (GIS) techniques play a crucial role in understanding spatial dynamics in urban health. Spatial regression models and time series analysis allow researchers to identify spatial patterns, long-term trends, and geographic disparities in exposure to environmental risk factors [31, 42]. These approaches facilitate the development of forecasting tools that can be used to monitor health and environmental risks in cities, providing decision-makers with evidence-based information for urban planning and public health management [22]. The integration of remote sensing technologies and satellite imagery further enhances the ability to track urban environmental changes in real time, enabling the rapid assessment of interventions' effectiveness [43].

The development of experimental approaches in some research is intended to test innovative strategies aimed at managing air quality, sustainable mobility, and green infrastructures [26]. These experiments include the implementation of urban pilot projects to evaluate the impact of green urban designs, low-emission zones, and renewable energy-based transportation systems on public health [44]. Additionally, some studies use behavioral experiments to understand how urban residents respond to environmental changes, such as the introduction of pedestrian-friendly areas or expanded cycling networks.

A particularly increasing area of research focuses on the validation of Nature-Based Solutions (NBS) as an effective means of promoting urban health and sustainability.

NBS refer to strategies that leverage on natural processes and ecosystem services to address urban challenges while providing social, environmental, and economic benefits. Studies have demonstrated that interventions such as the creation of urban forests, green roofs, vertical gardens, and permeable pavements can significantly reduce air pollution, mitigate urban heat islands, and enhance mental well-being [27]. Furthermore, urban planning strategies incorporating green corridors, wetlands restoration, and biodiversity conservation have been shown to increase resilience to climate change while fostering a healthier urban environment [40, 41, 45, 46].

A significant contribution to the understanding of Urban One Health comes from studies on the evaluation of urban ecosystems' health, which propose a series of indicators to measure the social and ecological well-being of cities [17]. These indicators can be grouped into three main categories: environmental indicators (assessment of air and water quality, urban biodiversity, and pollution levels), economic indicators (analysis of public health expenditures, cost of urban interventions, and financial efficiency of green projects), social indicators (evaluation of healthcare accessibility, quality of public spaces, urban mobility infrastructure, and socio-spatial inequalities) [20, 43, 47, 48].

By integrating these indicators into urban policies, researchers propose new frameworks based on the One Health approach, emphasizing the synergistic relationship between biodiversity, green infrastructures, and sustainable urban planning [49, 50].

A further methodological aspect concerns the evaluation of the Health Impact Assessment (HIA), an analytical tool designed to connect health with environmental sustainability and urban planning [38]. Despite its effectiveness in informing evidence-based decision-making, its application remains limited in practice due to regulatory barriers and lack of standardized assessment criteria [51]. To address these challenges, researchers advocate for greater integration of HIA into policy frameworks, emphasizing its role in evaluating the health consequences of urban development projects before their implementation. [52–54].

Finally, to obtain a dynamic and predictive vision of the health of cities, advanced mathematical models are proposed to track trends, anticipate health risks, and identify critical issues over time [22]. These models use longitudinal data, multi-variable forecasting algorithms, and real-time environmental monitoring to assess the complex interactions between society, the environment, and the economy. The adoption of artificial intelligence (AI)-driven analytics is further expanding the possibilities of real-time health risk assessment, allowing urban planners to design proactive rather than reactive health policies [41, 55, 56].

The combined use of these methodologies confirms that Urban One Health is not just a theoretical framework but an operational approach capable of guiding concrete urban interventions. The growing body of research supports the adoption of holistic planning models, where public health considerations are integrated with ecological and urban development strategies [57, 58].

In Fig. 6, the main methodological approaches used for the analysis of Urban One Health concepts in the analyzed research are summarized.

A cross-analysis of the reviewed studies reveals that empirical and spatially-based methods - such as GIS modelling - are mainly used in the documents that seek to inform

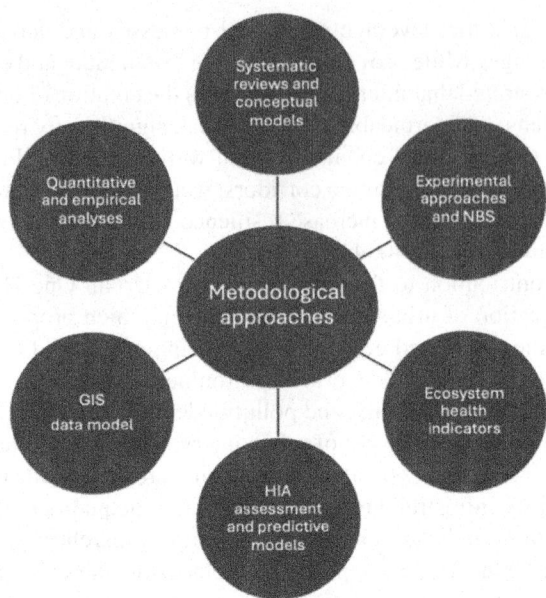

Fig. 6. Methodological approaches mostly implemented in the collected studies

planning and policy decisions. In contrast, conceptual contributions often rely on systematic reviews and theoretical frameworks to consolidate the epistemological foundations of Urban One Health. This dual orientation confirms the progressive integration between research and practice, where interdisciplinary approaches are increasingly adopted to connect scientific evidence with territorial governance. The most effective contributions emerge from hybrid approaches that link spatial, social and health data, paving the way for future experimentation.

5 Conclusions

Within the definition of public policies for the cities development, the adoption of the Urban One Health approach is no longer an optional choice. It represents an essential strategy to address the actions of territorial governance and health protection by promoting the regeneration processes. Cities, from simple agglomerations of infrastructures and buildings, should be converted into resilient ecosystems, capable of fitting to environmental changes, by successfully ensuring the communities well-being. This requires an innovative paradigm in urban management that overcomes the traditional separation between sectors in favor of integrated models.

In this context, the role of digital technologies and big data in monitoring urban health becomes crucial. Environmental sensors, artificial intelligence systems for the adequate urban resources use and forecasting analysis platforms allow to facilitate informed and timely decisions. The creation of virtual models for simulating the impact of urban policies on public health constitutes a turning point for evidence-based planning, that ismainly aimed at improving the citizies well-being [71].

Furthermore, the communities involvement in decision-making mechanisms for urban planning, through participatory tools and urban co-design initiatives, favours the implementation of strategies targeted for health and for the creation of more liveable cities. The empowerment of the population in identifying healthy options – from sustainable mobility to the use of green spaces – assumes a relevant role to making Urban One Health approach effective.

A critical point currently widely debated concerns the operational implementation of this approach. In this sense, the integration between public and private sectors, the activation of financial incentives for cities that adopt One Health models and the development of regulatory tools for making these principles mandatory are decisive elements in moving from theory to practice [72]. Without an adequate economic and legislative formalized support, the risks of remaining applied only to experimental projects without structural impact are significant.

In addition, the challenge of integrating the One Health approach into educational models is still open [73]. The training of multidisciplinary professionals should be combined with the active participation of citizens in new models of coexistence with the surrounding urban environment and biodiversity. The inclusion of the Urban One Health approach into the schools and universities formation could help to build more aware communities able to face the urban health challenges.

In future, the positive outcome of Urban One Health application to the urban policies will depend on the ability of cities to experiment it, with integrated and flexible solutions based on a holistic vision of human, animal and environmental health [74]. Therefore, the future of urban areas should be based on a dynamic balance between environment, health and economic development [75].Through the analysis of the reference scientific literature, the present research has aimed to highilight the increasing importance assumed by the Urban One Health concept for the definition of tools to support the territorial governance [76]. The decision-making processes related to the operations of urban interventions planning should be based on a effective cooperation between different disciplines (including human health, veterinary medicine, environmental sciences, social science, etc.) for tacking the most urgent, relevant and complex current issues (dense population, pollution, close human-animal interaction, shared environmental spaces, climate changing, etc.) for building more resilient, inclusive and sustainable communities [77]. The results of the present literature review confirms the growing integration between urban planning and health issue, especially through methods that combine spatial analysis, environmental monitoring, and interdisciplinary approaches. Nonetheless, the review has some limitations, including the exclusion of non-peer-reviewed sources and the lack of standardised evaluation criteria. Future research may explore how Urban One Health can be applied in concrete situations, through pilot projects, cross-sectoral governance and participatory planning with local communities.

Note: The research has been developed within the project "MISTRAL - a toolkit for dynaMic health Impact analysiS to predicT disability-Related costs in the Ag"- HORIZON-HLTH-2022-ENVHLTH04 - Grant Agreement Project n. 101095119 of the Polytechnic of Bari (Italy).

References

1. Focus: Le previsioni dell'ONU sulla popolazione mondiale, 17 July 2022. https://www.focus.it/scienza/scienze/previsioni-onu-popolazione-mondiale. Accessed 3 Dec 2025
2. UN General Assembly, Transforming our world : the 2030 Agenda for Sustainable Development, 21 October 2015, A/RES/70/1. https://www.refworld.org/docid/57b6e3e44.html. Accessed 3 Dec 2025
3. Mittelmark, M.M., Daniel, M., Urke, H.B.: Risorse Specifiche di Resistenza nel Modello Salutogenico di Salute. In Salutogenesi (Cap. 13). University of Bergen, Faculty of Psychology (2024)
4. Mackenzie, J.S., Jeggo, M.: The one health approach—why is it so important? Trop. Med. Infect. Disease **4**(Article 88) (2019) (MDPI, Basel)
5. Nzietchueng, S., Kitua, A., Nyatanyi, T., Rwego, I.B.: Facilitating implementation of the one health approach: a definition of a one health intervention. One Health **16**, Article 100491 (2023) (Elsevier)
6. Dafne: One Health: FAO, UNEP, OMS, WOAH e SACRU insieme per la salvaguardia della salute umana, animale, vegetale e degli ecosistemi. https://consorziodafne.com/notizie/one-health-fao-unep-oms-woah-e-sacru-insieme-per-la-salvaguardia-della-salute-umana-animale-vegetale-e-degli-ecosistemi/. Accessed 3 Dec 2025
7. Pepin, K.M., et al.: Steps towards operationalizing one health approaches. One Health **18**, Article 100740 (2024) (Elsevier)
8. Falzon, L.C., et al.: Quantitative outcomes of a one health approach to study global health challenges. EcoHealth **15**(4) (2018) (Springer)
9. World Health Organisation: one health joint plan of action (2022–2026): working together for the health of humans, animals, plants and the environment (2022). https://www.who.int/publications/i/item/9789240059139. Accessed 3 Dec 2025
10. Kent, J.L., Thompson, S.: The Three domains of urban planning for health and well-being. J. Plan. Literat. **29**(3) (2014) (SAGE Publications)
11. Winkler, M.S., Krieger, G.R., Divall, M.J., et al.: Untapped potential of health impact assessment. Bull. World Health Organ. **91** (2013) (World Health Organization)
12. Nieuwenhuijsen, M.J.: Urban and transport planning, environmental exposures, and health - new concepts, methods, and tools to improve health in cities. Environ. Health **15**(Suppl. 1) (2016) (BioMed Central)
13. Barton, H.: A health map for urban planners: towards a conceptual model for healthy, sustainable settlements. Built Environ. **31**(4) (2005) (Alexandrine Press)
14. Galea, S., Vlahov, D.: Urban health: evidence, challenges, and directions. Ann. Rev Public Health **26** (2005) (Annual Reviews)
15. Nieuwenhuijsen, M.J., Khreis, H., Verlinghieri, E., Mueller, N., Rojas-Rueda, D.: Participatory quantitative health impact assessment of urban and transport planning in cities: a review and research needs. Environ. Int. **103** (2017) (Elsevier)
16. Pineo, H., Glonti, K., Rutter, H., Zimmermann, N., Wilkinson, P., Davies, M.: Urban health indicator tools of the physical environment: a systematic review. J. Urban Health **95** (2018) (Springer)
17. Su, M., Fath, B.D., Yang, Z.: Urban ecosystem health assessment: a review. Sci. Total Environ. **408**(12) (2010) (Elsevier)
18. Dannenberg, A.L.: Effectiveness of health impact assessments: a synthesis of data from five impact evaluation reports. Prevent. Chronic Disease **13** (2016) (Centers for Disease Control and Prevention)
19. Harris-Roxas, B., et al.: Health impact assessment: the state of the art. Impact Assessment and Project Appraisal, vol. 30, no. 1. Taylor & Francis (2012)

20. Takano, T., Nakamura, K.: An analysis of health levels and various indicators of urban environments for healthy cities projects. J. Epidemiol. Commun. Health **55** (2001) (BMJ Publishing Group)
21. Nutsford, D., Pearson, A.L., Kingham, S.: An ecological study investigating the association between access to urban green space and mental health. Public Health **127** (2013) (Elsevier)
22. Kondo, M.C., Fluehr, J.M., McKeon, T., Branas, C.C.: Urban green space and its impact on human health. Int. J. Environ. Res. Public Health **15**, Article 445 (2018) (MDPI)
23. van den Bosch, M., Ode Sang, Å.: Urban natural environments as nature-based solutions for improved public health – a systematic review of reviews. Environ. Res. **158** (2017) (Elsevier)
24. Ebi, K.L., Harris, F., Sioen, G.B., et al.: Transdisciplinary research priorities for human and planetary health in the context of the 2030 agenda for sustainable development. Int. J. Environ. Res. Public Health **17**, Article 8890 (2020) (MDPI)
25. Jackson, L.E.: The relationship of urban design to human health and condition. Landscape Urban Plan. **64**(4) (2003) (Elsevier)
26. Shanahan, D.F., Lin, B.B., Bush, R., et al.: Toward improved public health outcomes from urban nature. Am. J. Public Health **105**(3) (2015) (American Public Health Association)
27. Larson, L.R., Jennings, V., Cloutier, S.A.: Public parks and wellbeing in urban areas of the united States. PLoS ONE **11** (2016) (Public Library of Science)
28. Cole, B.L., Fielding, J.E.: Health impact assessment: a tool to help policy makers understand health beyond health care. Ann. Rev. Public Health **28** (2007) (Annual Reviews)
29. Greer, S.L., Falkenbach, M., Siciliani, L., McKee, M., Wismar, M., Figueras, J.: From health in all policies to health for all policies. Lancet Public Health **7** (2022) (Elsevier)
30. Chen, W., Wang, Y., Ren, Y., Yan, H., Shen, C.: A novel methodology (WM-TCM) for urban health examination: a case study of wuhan in China. Ecol. Indicat. **136** (2022) (Elsevier)
31. Alipour, D., Dia, H.: A systematic review of the role of land use, transport, and energy-environment integration in shaping sustainable cities. Sustainability **15** (2023) (MDPI)
32. URBACT: One health 4 cities network: strengthening health-oriented urban planning in lyon. URBACT Programme (2024)
33. URBACT: Nature step to health: integrating health and urban planning in lahti. URBACT Programme (2024)
34. Organizzazione Mondiale della Sanità (OMS): Implementing the urban health initiative: reducing pollution and health risks in accra. OMS (2024)
35. Organizzazione Mondiale della Sanità (OMS): Urban air pollution and health: a pilot project in kathmandu. OMS (2024)
36. Siri, J.G., Geddes, I.: Mainstreaming health in urban design and planning: advances in theory and practice. Cities Health **6**(5) (2022) (Taylor & Francis)
37. Vlahov, D., Galea, S., Freudenberg, N.: The urban health "Advantage". J. Urban Health **82**(1) (2005) (Springer)
38. McDermott, R., Douglas, M.J., Haigh, F., Takemon, N., Green, L.: A systematic review of whether health impact assessment frameworks support best practice principles. Public Health **233** (2024) (Elsevier)
39. Jiang, X., Ye, D., Lan, W., Luo, Y.: Epidemic, urban planning and health impact assessment: a linking and analyzing framework. Buildings **14**, Article 2141 (2024) (MDPI)
40. Kemm, J.: Health impact assessment: a tool for healthy public policy. Health Promot. Int. **16**(1) (2001) (Oxford University Press)
41. Parry, J.M., Kemm, J.R.: Criteria for use in the evaluation of health impact assessments. Public Health **119**(12), 1122–1129 (2005) (Elsevier)
42. Lock, K.: Health impact assessment. British Med. J. **320**(7246), 1395–1398 (2000) (BMJ Publishing Group)

43. Thomson, H., Atkinson, R., Petticrew, M., Kearns, A.: Do urban regeneration programmes improve public health and reduce health inequalities? A synthesis of the evidence from UK policy and practice (1980–2004). J. Epidemiol. Commun. Health **60** (2006) (BMJ Publishing Group)
44. Bruno, A., Arnoldi, I., Barzaghi, B., et al.: The one health approach in urban ecosystem rehabilitation: an evidence-based framework for designing sustainable cities. iScience (2024) (Cell Press)
45. Dye, C.: Health and urban living. Science **319** (2008) (American Association for the Advancement of Science)
46. Kadakia, K.T., Galea, S.: Urbanization and the future of population health. Milbank Quar. **101**(S1) (2023) (Wiley)
47. Bai, X., Nath, I., Capon, A., Hasan, N., Jaron, D.: Health and wellbeing in the changing urban environment: complex challenges, scientific responses, and the way forward. Curr. Opin. Environ. Sustain. **4** (2012) (Elsevier)
48. Perera, A.C.S., Davies, P.J., Graham, P.L.: A global review of urban blue-green planning tools. Land Use Policy **140** (2024) (Elsevier)
49. Seraphim, A.P., Niu, H., Morgado, P., Miranda, B., Silva, E.A.: Mapping urban health policies: a scoping review of environmental, behavioural and socioeconomic determinants of health. Progress Plan. **193** (2025) (Elsevier)
50. Sturm, R., Cohen, D.: Proximity to urban parks and mental health. J. Mental Health Policy Econ. **17** (2014) (International Center of Mental Health Policy and Economics)
51. Dyer, G.M.C., Khomenko, S., Adlakha, D., et al.: A road map for future data-driven urban planning and environmental health research. Cities **155** (2024) (Elsevier)
52. Bonilla-Aldana, D.K., Dhama, K., Rodriguez-Morales, A.J.: Revisiting the one health approach in the context of COVID-19: a look into the ecology of this emerging disease. Adv. Animal Veterin. Sci. **8**(3), 234–237 (2020) (Academic Publishers)
53. De Angelis, M.: Uno Sguardo all'Urban Health: Città e Benessere fra Esigenze Locali e Salute Globale. Atti del XXXIII Congresso ALASS, Città del Messico (2023)
54. Cubadda, F., Mantovani, A., Aquilina, G., Marcon, F.: Valutazione Rischio-Beneficio delle Sostanze Usate nell'Alimentazione Animale. Istituto Superiore di Sanità, Italia (2022)
55. Ministero della Salute - Direzione Generale della Prevenzione Sanitaria: Documento di Indirizzo per la Pianificazione Urbana in un'Ottica di Salute Pubblica. Ministero della Salute, Italia (2021)
56. Puig-Ribera, A., Rofin, M., Bort-Roig, J., et al.: Integrating health into the urban master plan of vic, barcelona: a comprehensive approach. Urban Plan. **7**(4) (2022) (Cogitatio Press)
57. Capolongo, S., Lemaire, N., Oppio, A., Buffoli, M., Roue Le Gall, A.: Action planning for healthy cities: the role of multi-criteria analysis, developed in italy and france, for assessing health performances in land-use plans and urban development projects
58. Vlahov, D., Freudenberg, N., Proietti, F., et al.: Urban as a determinant of health. J. Urban Health: Bull. New York Acad. Med. **84**(1) (2007) (Springer)
59. Krieger, N., et al.: Assessing health impact assessment: multidisciplinary and international perspectives. J. Epidemiol. Commun. Health **57** (2003) (BMJ Publishing Group)
60. Abejirinde, I.-O.O., Gwacham-Anisiobi, U., Affun-Adegbulu, C., Vanhamel, J., Van Belle, S., Marchal, B.: A perspective on urban health systems and research for equitable healthcare in Africa. BMJ Global Health **7** (2022) (BMJ Publishing Group)
61. Quigley, R.J., Taylor, L.C.: Evaluating health impact assessment. Public Health **118** (2004) (Elsevier)
62. Moore, M., Gould, P., Keary, B.S.: Urban health and environmental risks. Int. J. Hygiene Environ. Health **206** (2003) (Elsevier)
63. Amado, M.P., Santos, C.V., Moura, E.B., Silva, V.G.: Public participation in sustainable urban planning. Int. J. Urban Sustain. Develop. **12** (2023) (Taylor & Francis)

64. McMichael, A.J.: The urban environment and health in a world of increasing globalization: issues for developing countries. Bull. World Health Organ. **78**(9) (2000) (World Health Organization)
65. Hensher, M.: Incorporating environmental impacts into the economic evaluation of health care systems: perspectives from ecological economics. Resources Conserv. Recycl. **154** (2020) (Elsevier)
66. Ramirez-Rubio, O., Daher, C., Fanjul, G., et al.: Urban health: an example of a "health in all policies" approach in the context of SDGs implementation. Global. Health **15** (2019) (BioMed Central)
67. Li, O.Y., Wang, X., Yang, K., et al.: The approaching pilot for one health governance index. Infect. Diseases Poverty **12** (2023) (BioMed Central)
68. Tarricone, R.: Cost-of-illness analysis: what room in health economics? Health Policy **77**, 51–63 (2006) (Elsevier)
69. Mersal, A.: Sustainable urban futures: environmental planning for sustainable urban development. Procedia Environ. Sci. **34** (2016) (Elsevier)
70. Douglas, I.: Urban ecology and urban ecosystems: understanding the links to human health and well-being. Curr. Opin. Environ. Sustain. **4** (2012) (Elsevier)
71. Di Liddo, F., Morano, P., Tajani, F., Torre, C.M.: An innovative methodological approach for the analysis of the effects of urban interventions on property prices. Valori e Valutazioni, No. 26. Società Italiana di Estimo e Valutazione (2020)
72. Morano, P., Anelli, D., Tajani, F., Roma, A.: The real estate risk assessment: an innovative methodology for supporting public and private subjects involved into sustainable urban interventions. In: Gervasi, O., et al. (eds.) Computational Science and Its Applications – ICCSA 2023 Workshops. ICCSA 2023. LNCS, vol. 14109. Springer, Cham (2023). https://doi.org/10.1007/978-3-031-37120-2_27
73. Anelli, D., Sica, F.: The financial feasibility analysis of urban transformation projects: an application of a quick assessment model. In: Bevilacqua, C., Calabrò, F., Della Spina, L. (eds.) New Metropolitan Perspectives. NMP 2020. Smart Innovation, Systems and Technologies, vol 178. Springer, Cham (2020). https://doi.org/10.1007/978-3-030-48279-4_44
74. Tajani, F., Morano, P., Di Liddo, F., La Spina, I.: An evaluation methodological approach to support the definition of effective urban projects: a case study in the city of Rome (Italy). Sustain. Develop. **33**(1), 771–793 (2025) (Wiley)
75. Locurcio, M., Tajani, F., Morano, P., Torre, C.M.: A fuzzy multi-criteria decision model for the regeneration of the urban peripheries. In: New Metropolitan Perspectives: Local Knowledge and Innovation Dynamics Towards Territory Attractiveness Through the Implementation of Horizon/E2020/Agenda2030 – vol. 1, pp. 681–690. Springer International Publishing (2019)
76. Guarini, M.R., Locurcio, M., Battisti, F.: GIS-Based Multi-Criteria Decision Analysis for the "Highway in the Sky". In: Gervasi, O., et al. (eds.) Computational Science and Its Applications – ICCSA 2015. ICCSA 2015. LNCS, vol 9157. Springer, Cham (2015). https://doi.org/10.1007/978-3-319-21470-2_11
77. Morano, P., Guarini, M.R., Tajani, F., Anelli, D.: Sustainable redevelopment: the cost-revenue analysis to support the urban planning decisions. In: Gervasi, O., et al. (eds.) Computational Science and Its Applications – ICCSA 2020. ICCSA 2020. LNCS, vol. 12251. Springer, Cham (2020). https://doi.org/10.1007/978-3-030-58808-3_69

Urban Green Spaces and Housing Prices: The Impact of Metric Choice on Econometric Models

Pierluigi Morano[1], Debora Anelli[2], Francesca Fariello[2(✉)], Marco Locurcio[1], and Felicia Di Liddo[1]

[1] Department of Civil, Environmental, Land, Building Engineering and Chemistry (DICATECh), Polytechnic University of Bari, 70126 Bari, Italy
{pierluigi.morano,marco.locurcio,felicia.diliddo}@poliba.it
[2] Department of Architecture and Design, "Sapienza" University of Rome, 00196 Rome, Italy
{debora.anelli,francesca.fariello}@uniroma1.it

Abstract. It is widely recognized that green urban areas play a significant role in enhancing environmental quality, social and economic well-being within cities. In the context of urban planning and sustainable development, the study of their impact on housing prices can guide administrations more effectively in the design and allocation of green spaces. However, the choice of metrics for this purpose has the potential to influence the results. The present study aims to investigate how the choice of urban green space metrics influences the econometric analysis of real estate prices in a densely populated Italian city. The case study focuses on the city of Rome, which, being one of the European capitals with the largest extension of green urban surface, represents a particularly relevant context for investigating the effects on real estate values. The investigation employs a regression-based methodology, utilizing three green space metrics: total absolute surface, percentage coverage, and the presence or absence of green areas. The dependent variable in this study is housing prices, while the independent variables relate to socio-economic and environmental issues, including construction and social quality. The findings of this study underscore the significance of judicious selection of metrics in order to achieve reliable results. In contrast to the extant literature, which has hitherto concentrated exclusively on the presence of green spaces, this research examines how different metrics influence their estimated impact on property values. The findings offer valuable insights for urban planners and policymakers in optimizing the integration of green spaces into urban valuation models.

Keywords: housing prices · econometric analysis · urban green space metrics · decision support tools · spatial configuration · housing prices

1 Introduction

The analysis of real estate prices is a central theme in urban economics and spatial planning, as it enables a deeper understanding of market dynamics and supports strategic decision-making in investment and sustainable development. Various factors influence property values, including socio-economic, infrastructural, and environmental variables.

Among these, the quality of the urban environment has become increasingly relevant, in line with the growing focus on sustainability and public well-being [1]. In particular, the availability of urban green spaces is considered a key element in enhancing quality of life and attracting investments in the real estate sector. In order to ensure that these benefits translate into a sustainable increase in property values, public policies must promote the creation and optimal management of green spaces through appropriate regulations. The regulatory framework plays a crucial role in urban green space management, as it impacts both spatial planning and real estate valuation. Several policy guidelines have been introduced to preserve and incentivize the creation of green areas in urban environments. At the European level, the EU Green Infrastructure Strategy promotes the integration of green spaces into spatial planning [2].

At a national level, various countries have implemented regulations to manage and enhance urban greenery. In Italy, Legislative Decree 152/2006 introduced environmental criteria into spatial planning, while the National Recovery and Resilience Plan (PNRR) allocated funds for urban regeneration, with a particular focus on creating new green spaces and protecting landscapes [3]. Some cities have adopted more advanced urban planning tools, such as Urban Green Plans, which assign specific ecological functions to green areas, or the concept of Urban Forestry, which involves the strategic planting of trees to counteract the urban heat island effect and improve air quality [4].

Further confirmation of the importance of green spaces in urban dynamics comes from Report [5], which analyzed the environmental performance of Italian cities. The report highlights the growing attention of local administrations toward increasing pedestrian areas and green spaces factors that enhance quality of life and, consequently, the real estate attractiveness of affected areas. Additionally, the report indicates that in several Italian cities, the expansion of green spaces has coincided with an increase in both housing demand and average residential property prices.

Environmental certifications in the real estate sector are also playing an increasingly significant role. Systems such as LEED (Leadership in Energy and Environmental Design) and BREEAM (Building Research Establishment Environmental Assessment Method) accredit higher scores to buildings located near green areas or integrated with private green spaces, thereby increasing the market value of certified properties [6]. This aspect has direct implications for the real estate market, as environmental certifications are becoming a competitive factor for new developments and the renovation of existing building stock.

However, to ensure the effectiveness of these policies, it is essential to understand how the measurement of green spaces influences econometric estimates of property values. This study examines how different metrics used to quantify urban greenery affect econometric analyses of real estate values, identifying the most effective measures in capturing the relationship between green spaces and housing prices in high-density urban contexts.

2 Aim

The aim of the work is to analyze how different metrics for measuring urban green spaces affect econometric models of housing prices, focusing on the city of Rome. As one of the greenest European capitals in terms of total urban surface, Rome offers an ideal context to assess the impact of greenery on real estate dynamics. The city's urban complexity and environmental policies make it a valuable case for understanding how metric choice influences valuation outcomes. In order to understand this, a case study application with multiple regression analysis is proposed. Through the application of a linear regression model to a dataset related to a city in central Italy, three metrics are compared to quantify the presence of urban green spaces: absolute surface area in square meters, percentage incidence on the territorial surface of the considered urban areas, and the presence or absence of green areas (dummy variable). The objective is to assess whether and how the choice of metric affects the significance of the urban green space variable and the robustness of econometric estimates. Comparing the regression results across the three different metrics will allow for an evaluation of whether the urban green space variable is significant in predicting real estate prices and which metric is most effective in capturing its impact in the case under study.

The reminder of the work is as follows: Sect. 3 analyses literature, underlining the different metrics for measuring urban greenness and their effect on econometric estimates; Sect. 4 describes the sample dataset and the case study; Sect. 5 presents the discussion of the obtained results; Sect. 6 outlines the conclusions of the work and the future possible insights.

3 Background

In recent years, econometrics applied to the real estate sector has developed various regression models to identify the key factors influencing property prices. Hedonic analysis is one of the most robust methods for determining the market value of residential properties, assigning specific weights to each characteristic of the property and its surrounding area [7].

Traditional econometric models, such as the Hedonic Pricing Model (HPM) and Spatial Regression Models (SRM), are commonly used to estimate the impact of socioeconomic, environmental, and infrastructural factors. Additionally, non-linear models are sometimes employed when a more detailed identification of the functional relationship between urban green spaces and property values is required [8–10].

Socio-economic variables include indicators such as the average income of the area, the education level of the resident population, and the employment rate. Average income is considered a key determinant of property prices, as higher purchasing power among residents tends to drive up housing values in the area [11]. Education levels also have a significant impact: areas with a more educated population attract buyers with higher purchasing power, contributing to real estate market appreciation [12]. Furthermore, the employment rate is closely linked to housing demand and can influence price dynamics, particularly in areas characterized by high job stability [13].

Among environmental factors, the presence of urban green spaces has been widely analyzed in the literature [14]. The predominant variable considered in determining real estate prices encloses a broad range of urban greenery types, including public parks, wooded areas, community gardens, tree-lined avenues, and green roofs. In the article by [15], it is highlighted that the economic and social value of green spaces depends not only on their size but also on maintenance quality, accessibility, and their ability to integrate with the surrounding urban fabric, an idea also restated in the study by [16].

The presence of well-maintained green areas is associated with an increase in property values, due to benefits such as urban temperature reduction, improved air quality, and the creation of spaces for social interaction and physical activity. Empirical studies confirm this relationship: in Seville, an increase of one square meter of green space per inhabitant led to an average rise of €120/m² in housing values, while in Los Angeles, greater tree cover resulted in an 8% increase in real estate prices [11, 13]. A study on urban regeneration in Milan highlights a positive correlation between the expansion of green areas and property appreciation in certain microzones [9].

Recent research has expanded this perspective by including blue spaces (urban water bodies, lakes, rivers, fountains), emphasizing their beneficial effects on health and psychological well-being. The combined access to green and blue spaces not only enhances quality of life but also helps reduce inequalities, promoting greater stability in real estate values in areas where these features are present [17].

However, the impact of urban green spaces varies depending on their type and maintenance. A study conducted in San José, Costa Rica, found that metropolitan parks have a stronger positive effect on real estate prices compared to neighborhood parks, whose impact depends more on size and quality than on mere proximity. Conversely, undeveloped natural areas, such as riverbanks and urban forests, can have negative effects if perceived as degraded or unsafe [18–20].

A similar dynamic was observed in Beijing, where proximity to parks is beneficial only within an optimal distance of 850–1,604 m; beyond this range, issues such as overcrowding and degradation may arise [21, 22].

Finally, the presence of poorly maintained, dimly lit, or unsafe green spaces can generate negative perceptions, leading to a devaluation of residential properties [23]. Similarly, excessively dense tree cover can reduce natural light and the perception of safety, negatively impacting real estate prices [12].

Understanding the effect of metric selection on econometric estimates is not just a methodological issue but has direct implications for urban planners, investors, and public administrators. As reported by [5, 9], if the presence of green spaces is measured inconsistently, there is a risk of over- or underestimating its impact on the real estate market, compromising the effectiveness of urban enhancement policies. Moreover, professionals in the sector may prefer one metric over another depending on the territorial context or the objective of the analysis, assigning different levels of importance based on the socio-economic characteristics of the study area.

Among the key measurement variables, additional factors can be considered, such as the absolute surface area of green spaces in m² or km², the percentage of urban greenery relative to the total reference area [24], the distance to green spaces measured in meters or walking time [11], perceived accessibility to green spaces [21], maintenance quality, and perceived safety of green areas [25].

The choice of metric can significantly influence the results: while absolute surface area emphasizes the total amount of greenery available, it does not account for its spatial distribution or accessibility for residents. In reverse, the percentage of green cover relative to the urban surface may better capture the actual usability of green spaces in high-density cities. The literature has proposed different metrics to quantify green space presence, including both absolute extension in square meters or kilometers and the percentage of green space relative to total urban area [7, 8].

Recent studies have introduced quantitative and qualitative indices to support the evaluation of green spaces impacting real estate prices. These indices include Urban Green Index (UGI) which measures the percentage of urban surface covered by vegetation [26], Normalized Difference Vegetation Index (NDVI) which uses satellite imagery to quantify urban vegetation density [8], Green Space Ratio (GSR) which calculates the percentage of green space relative to the total surface of an urban area [1].

The heterogeneity of results found in the literature highlights the need for a careful selection of measurement metrics in econometric analyses. Differences in metric choice can lead to divergent results, making comparisons between studies challenging.

4 Sample Dataset and Case Study

The empirical analysis was conducted in the city of Rome, selected due to its extensive urban green infrastructure and high spatial variability among neighborhoods. With over 30% of its territory covered by green areas, including parks, historical gardens, and ecological corridors, Rome represents a highly relevant case for examining how greenery affects housing prices. Its socio-economic heterogeneity and current environmental planning strategies further support the city's suitability as a case study in this domain. In the present research a sample dataset is constructed. The unique difference is in the metric used for taking into account the extent of the urban green spaces. In Table 1 the independent and dependent variables considered with their metrics, the employed acronym, the description and main descriptive statistics (minimum value, maximum value and standard deviation) are reported.

Table 1. Independent and dependent variables' main features

Variable	Dependent/Independent variable	Metric	Acronym	Min	Max	Standard Deviation
Average housing value	Dependent	€/m²	Y	1,125	1,125	1,066.48
Population	Independent	Inhabitants/km²	Po	536	79,837	14,352.58
Disposable per-capita income	Independent	€/per person/per year	Di	8,837	57,571	7,526.26
Abandoned spaces	Independent	Km²	As	8,837	57,571	1.11
Social disease	Independent	Score	Sd	1.06	4140	6.04
Building disease	Independent	Score	Bd	1.12	5.95	1.55
Urban green spaces	Independent	m²	Gsm	0	3.51	0.51
	Independent	Percentage incidence (on total territorial surface)	Gsi	0	0.64	0.14
	Independent	Dummy	Gsd	0	1	0.4

Each variable refers to a specific sub-urban area of the Italian city. Specifically, they refer to 117 out of 155 of the homogeneous zones defined by the Real Estate Market Observatory of the Italian Revenue Agency for the first semester of 2024. The excluded zones have no retrievable housing values data, due to their tertiary and productive vocation, therefore they could not be considered in this work.

The dependent variable (Y) is the average housing selling value per each homogeneous zone expressed in €/sqm and its source is the Real Estate Market Observatory's quotations updated to the first semester of 2024 (last available update).

Among the independent variables, the population (Po) and the disposable per-capita income (Di) represent, respectively, the number of individuals that live per square kilometer of the homogeneous zone and the gross domestic product potentially produced by an individual within it. The employed sources of data are the population census of 2011 of the Italian Statistic Institute (ISTAT) and the socio-economic database of *Urbistat Geosoftware*.

The independent variables related to the social disease (Sd) expresses the weighted average of the rate' deviations of unemployment, employment, youth concentration and education values, referring to the second semester of 2023, from the national average values, detected by the ISTAT census.

The building disease (Bd) derives from the comparison of maintenance state of buildings in each homogeneous area with the national average value, considering the residential buildings in very bad conditions and in mediocre conditions and the total residential buildings of each zone, detected by the ISTAT census.

The variable of abandoned spaces (As) represents the square kilometers of each homogenous zone characterized by critical presence of degradation in both un-built and built environments. It is calculated by ISTAT for the "Call for the submission of proposals for the preparation of the national plan for the social and cultural redevelopment of degraded urban areas (DPCM 21 October 2015)".

The independent variable related to the extent of green space (Gs) is the one for which the metrics will vary according to as follows: in the first case it is calculated as the square meters of each homogeneous zone occupied by green surfaces likes declared public parks; instead in the second case the used metric is the percentage incidence of the surface occupied by green public parks within the entire territorial extension of the homogeneous zone. In the third case, the dummy variable is used for checking the presence or the absence of green spaces in the urban area. The source of data is https://download.geofabrik.de/europe/italy.html.

The performed correlation analysis shows a weak level of interdependence of the set of chosen variables. In the first case – when the presence of green urban area is calculated through square kilometers of surface -, only for the variable Di and the dependent one (Y) the Pearson coefficient is equal to 0.93 with a positive sign. Other correlation levels are between the variables Di and As (-0.18), Po with Sd (-0.06) and Po with Bd (-0.05). Similar correlation levels figure for the second case – when the presence of green urban area is expressed as incidence on total territorial surface -.

5 Regression Results

Through a multiple regression analysis, three different methods for measuring and quantifying urban green spaces were tested: i) Gsm: surface area measured in square meters; ii) Gsi: surface area expressed as a percentage of the total urbanized area; iii) Gsd: binary variable indicating the presence or absence of urban greenery.

Multiple regression was chosen for its ability to isolate the specific effect of explanatory variables on real estate value, ensuring interpretability and robustness in the results.

The following Tables 2, 3 and 4 present the coefficient values, standard errors, t-statistic, and significance levels of each independent variable, based on the selected method for measuring urban green space.

Table 2. Regression Results with Gsm

Regression results with Gsm: surface area measured in square meters				
$R^2 = 0.8734$	Coefficients	Standard errors	T-stat	p-value
Intercept	50.344	132.244	0.381	0.704
Sd	−450.849	246.992	−1.825	0.071
Bd	33.490	144.386	0.232	0.817
Po	248.486	200.560	1.239	0.218
Di	7396.199	280.252	26.391	0.000
As	−577.902	205.883	−2.807	0.006
Urban green spaces (m^2)	211.453	242.488	0.872	0.385

Table 3. Regression Results with Gsi

Regression results with Gsi: surface area expressed as a percentage of the total urbanized area				
$R^2 = 0.8751$	Coefficients	Standard errors	T-stat	p-value
Intercept	50.750	131.059	0.387	0.699
Sd	−435.441	245.703	−1.772	0.079
Bd	31.129	143.453	0.217	0.829
Po	227.855	199.195	1.144	0.255
Di	7343.208	281.035	26.129	0.000
As	−544.960	206.315	−2.641	0.009
Urban green spaces (%)	248.506	166.525	1.492	0.138

Table 4. Regression Results with Gsd

Regression results with Gsd: binary variable indicating the presence or absence of urban greenery				
$R^2 = 0.8746$	Coefficients	Standard errors	T-stat	p-value
Intercept	−26.728	146.505	−0.182	0.856
Sd	−433.127	246.452	−1.757	0.082
Bd	70.866	146.211	0.485	0.629
Po	152.168	218.430	0.697	0.487
Di	7303.585	288.367	25.327	0.000
As	−524.665	211.079	−2.486	0.014
Urban green spaces (dummy)	146.679	110.268	1.330	0.186

The analysis of the three regressions shows how the measurement of urban green space influences the predictive power of the model and the relationships with real estate values. The F-statistic is very high in all three models, with values exceeding 134, indicating that at least one of the independent variables is significantly different from zero and contributes to explaining the dependent variable. The model with green space measured as a percentage (Gsi) presents the best balance between the quality of explanation (highest F) and prediction accuracy (lowest standard error). The use of green space in square meters (Gsm) is the least effective specification, with the highest standard error and the lowest F-value. The F-significance (p-value of the F-test) is extremely low ($< 10^{-48}$), suggesting that all models are highly significant overall. This means that, although some individual variables may not be significant, the overall model is statistically robust. The Variance Inflation Factor (VIF) shows the absence of multicollinearity for all cases considered.

From the perspective of model quality, the relative measurement of green space (Gsi) delivers the best performance, with a higher adjusted R^2 (0.8751) and a lower standard error (376.91) compared to the measurement in square meters (Gsm) and the dummy variable (Gsd). Similarly, the model's standard error decreases from 379.40 (Gsm) to 376.91 (Gsi) and 377.68 (Gsd).

Analyzing the coefficients of the green variable, it is observed that property values increase with the expansion of green space, regardless of the measurement method. However, only the percentage-based measurement (Gsi) approaches statistical significance (p-value = 0.138), while the other two methods are not significant (p-value > 0.18). The results indicate that the incidence of green space on the urbanized area is a more representative measure of its influence on property values than the absolute quantity or mere presence/absence. This implies that buyers place greater value on the proportional distribution of green space rather than on its mere territorial extent. This result aligns with the principle that the perception of green space is more closely tied to its accessibility and distribution than to the absolute amount available.

The change in the measurement of green space not only affects model quality but also alters the strength and significance of the other independent variables. The other variables confirm some of the expected trends.

Social degradation (Sd) exhibits consistent behavior across the different models, with a p-value ranging between 0.070 and 0.081, always close to the significance threshold. However, the introduction of the relative measure of green space (Gsi) tends to diminish its importance. This could suggest that the presence of urban green space and social degradation share a certain degree of correlation, whereby the percentage-based measurement of green space absorbs part of the effect of social degradation on the dependent variable. Social degradation (Sd) shows a negative effect on property values.

Building degradation (Bd) is never significant in any model (p-value > 0.6–0.8). This result suggests that the state of the building stock does not directly affect the average unit sale price, at least not within the context of this analysis. Moreover, the method of measuring urban green space does not appear to alter the role of this variable in the model.

The resident population (Po) is never significant in the model (p-value > 0.2), but its p-value increases when moving from an absolute to a relative measurement of green space (Gsi, Gsd). This might indicate that the resident population has a lesser influence on property values when green space is measured in percentage or binary terms.

Disposable income (Di) is the most stable and significant variable in all models (p-value < 0.001). The coefficient ranges between 7,300 and 7,400, indicating a strong positive effect on property values. This result confirms that income is the primary predictive factor for the value of residential properties.

The area of degraded urban space (As) is always significant (p-value < 0.05) and shows a negative coefficient in all models, confirming that an increase in degraded area reduces property values. However, its p-value increases slightly when green space is measured using Gsi or Gsd, suggesting that the relative measurement of green absorbs part of the negative effect of degraded areas.

The economic interpretation of the regression coefficients allows for an estimation of the marginal price associated with the presence of urban green space. When green space is measured in square meters (Gsm), an increase of 1 m^2 of urban green area is associated with an average increase of €211.45/m^2 in property values.

In contrast, when considering the relative metric (Gsi), the results show that a 1% increase in the territorial area covered by urban green corresponds to an average increase of €248.51/m^2 in property values. The analysis of marginal prices provides concrete insights for urban planning, demonstrating how policies aimed at increasing urban green space can have positive effects on property values and, consequently, on investments in the residential sector.

These results are consistent with the study by [24], which highlights that the density of urban green has a greater impact than its absolute extent.

6 Conclusions

This study addresses the topic of urban green spaces and their influence on property values, highlighting how the choice of metric significantly affects the results. In particular, it has been emphasized that the presence of urban green areas improves quality of life and increases the attractiveness of residential zones, but it is crucial to select the most appropriate metric to evaluate its effects on real estate prices.

The objective of the present study was to analyze how the choice of metric used to measure urban green space influences the outcomes of econometric analyses. To this end, a linear regression model was applied to a dataset of socio-economic, environmental, and real estate data related to a city in central Italy, comparing three metrics: the total green area calculated in absolute terms (m^2), its percentage incidence relative to the total territorial surface of each suburban area, and its presence and/or absence as a dummy variable.

The study demonstrated that the way green space is measured can alter the result of the econometric analysis; indeed, when using either the variable representing total area or its presence/absence, the results are less precise, whereas using the percentage of urban green leads to more accurate predictions of real estate prices, concluding that the more evenly distributed the green space is, the more valued the properties become. The results of this study offer valuable insights for urban planners and policymakers in the design and management of urban green spaces. The analysis shows that the proportional distribution of green within the urban fabric is more relevant than its mere absolute extent in determining property value. This suggests that targeted interventions aimed at the redevelopment and optimization of green distribution could have a more significant impact than simply creating new, large green areas. A strategic planning approach to green distribution, taking into account population density and accessibility, could maximize both economic and social benefits.

Furthermore, the results highlight that the quality and perceived safety of green spaces play a crucial role: policies of regular maintenance, adequate lighting, and integration with pedestrian infrastructures could promote greater usability, reinforcing the positive effect of urban green on property values.

These findings can support environmental offset policies, where local administrations encourage urban forestry and the improvement of public green areas in under-served neighborhoods, contributing to greater territorial equity. Moreover, the results could be integrated into environmental impact assessment processes and urban regeneration strategies, guiding both public and private investments toward more effective solutions for sustainability and real estate enhancement [27, 28].

For future developments, the proposed model could be applied in additional urban contexts, both nationally and internationally, in order to verify the standardization of the relationship between the distribution of urban green and property values. Nevertheless, it is essential to consider some limitations: for example, the analysis does not examine the quality of green spaces, their actual accessibility, or the perception of safety, factors that may further influence property values. Future insights could expand to include additional variables and compare the implementation of machine learning methodologies to further improve predictions [29–33]. From a decision-making perspective, the results of this study underline the importance of selecting the most appropriate metric for evaluating the impact of green spaces on property values. The superior performance of the percentage-based metric (Gsi) suggests that spatial policies should prioritize the relative distribution of greenery across districts, rather than focusing solely on the overall surface. These insights can inform urban regeneration plans, green infrastructure investments, and environmental offset strategies aimed at maximizing both economic value and urban equity.

References

1. Gibbons, S., Mourato, S., Resende, G.M.: The amenity value of english nature: a hedonic price approach. Environ. Resource Econ. **57**(2), 175–196 (2014) (Springer)
2. Commissione Europea: Strategia dell'Unione Europea per le Infrastrutture Verdi. Commissione Europea, Bruxelles (2020)
3. Ministero della Transizione Ecologica: Piano Nazionale di Ripresa e Resilienza (PNRR) e Rigenerazione Urbana. Ministero della Transizione Ecologica, Roma (2022)
4. ISPRA: I Piani Comunali del Verde: Strumenti per Riportare la Natura nella Nostra Vita? Istituto Superiore per la Protezione e la Ricerca Ambientale, Roma (2024)
5. Legambiente: Ecosistema Urbano 2024: Rapporto sulla Qualità Ambientale delle Città Italiane. Legambiente, Roma (2024)
6. Rebuild Italia, CBRE, GBCI Europe: L'Impatto della Certificazione LEED sul Valore degli Immobili. Green Building Council Italia (2021)
7. Mauri, F.: La Valutazione Economica di Grandi Progetti Urbani: La Metodologia dei Prezzi Edonici. Politecnico di Milano, Facoltà di Ingegneria, Corso di Laurea Magistrale in Gestione del Costruito (2011)
8. Acierno, A., Coppola, E.: Tools for green cities in urban planning: building sustainable and livable urban environments. Territory Res. Settle. Environ. **16**(1) (2023) (Federico II University Press)
9. Massimo, D.E., De Paola, P., Musolino, M., Malerba, A., Del Giudice, F.P.: Green and gold buildings? Detecting real estate market premium for green buildings through evolutionary polynomial regression. Buildings **12**(5), Article 621 (2024) (MDPI)
10. Xu, Y., Chen, R., Du, H., Chen, M., Fu, C., Li, Y.: Evaluation of green space influence on housing prices using machine learning and urban visual intelligence. Cities **158**, Article 105661 (2024) (Elsevier)
11. Wen, H., Jia, S., Guo, X.: Hedonic price analysis of urban housing: an empirical research on Hangzhou, China. J. Zhejiang Univ. Sci.. **6A**(8), 907–914 (2005) (Springer)
12. Saphores, J.D., Li, W.: Estimating the value of urban green spaces: a hedonic approach. Ecol. Econ. **79**, 92–102 (2012) (Elsevier)
13. Ramírez-Juidías, E., Sánchez-García, A., García-Pérez, J.: Urban green spaces and real estate market: empirical evidence from seville. J. Housing Econ. **51**, 101–116 (2022) (Elsevier)
14. Brander, L.M., Koetse, M.J.: The value of urban green space: a meta-analysis of the economic valuation literature. Environ. Resource Econ. **50**(3), 365–393 (2011) (Springer)
15. Liebelt, V., Bartke, S., Schwarz, N.: Urban green spaces and housing prices: an alternative perspective. J. Environ. Econ. Manage. **85**, 110–129 (2019) (Elsevier)
16. Setiowati, R., Koestoer, R.H., Andajani, R.D.: Valuation of urban green open space using the hedonic price model. Global J. Environ. Sci. Manage. **10**(2), 451–472 (2024) (GIAP Journals)
17. Georgiou M., Morison, G., Smith, N., Tieges, Z., Chastin, S.: Mechanisms of impact of blue spaces on human health: a systematic literature review and meta-analysis. Int. J. Environ. Res. Public Health **18**(5), Article 2486 (2021) (MDPI)
18. Piaggio, L.: Green space and housing prices: evidence from san josé, costa rica. Land Econ. **98**(2), 278–295 (2022) (University of Wisconsin Press)
19. Panduro, T.E., Veie, K.L.: The amenity value of green urban spaces: evidence from a hedonic pricing model. Landscape Urban Plan. **113**, 62–69 (2013) (Elsevier)

20. Baró, F., Calderón-Argelich, A., Langemeyer, J., Connolly, J.J.: Under one canopy? Assessing the distributional environmental justice implications of street tree benefits in barcelona. Environ. Sci. Policy **47**, 10–21 (2015) (Elsevier)
21. Zhang, B., Xie, G., Xia, B., Zhang, C.: The effects of public green spaces on residential property value in Beijing. J.. Resources Ecol. **3**(3), 243–252 (2012) (Institute of Geographic Sciences and Natural Resources Research, CAS)
22. Szczepańska, A., Krzywnicka, I., Lemański, G.: Urban greenery as a component of real estate value. Real Estate Manage. Valuat. **24**(4), 79–87 (2016) (De Gruyter)
23. Troy, A., Grove, J.M.: Property values, parks, and crime: a hedonic analysis in baltimore, MD. Landscape Urban Plan. **87**(3), 233–245 (2008) (Elsevier)
24. Sim, J.: Seeing impacts of park design strategies on local economy through big data: a case study of gyeongui line forest park in seoul. Sustainability **12**(17), Article 6722 (2020) (MDPI)
25. Lee, C.-C., Liang, C.-M., Yeh, W.-C., Hu, Z.: The impact of urban renewal on neighboring housing prices: an application of hierarchical linear modeling. Int. J. Strat. Property Manage. **26**(1) (2022) (Taylor & Francis)
26. Li, H., Zhou, Y., Li, X., Meng, L., Wang, X., Wu, S., Sodoudi, S.: A new method to quantify surface urban heat island intensity. Sci. Total Environ. **624**, 262–272 (2018) (Elsevier)
27. Morano, P., Tajani, F., Anelli, D.: Urban planning variants: a model for the division of the activated "plusvalue" between public and private subjects. Valori e Valutazioni **28**, 31–47 (2021)
28. Locurcio, M., Tajani, F., Anelli, D.: Sustainable urban planning models for new smart cities and effective management of land take dynamics. Land **12**(3), 621 (2023)
29. Di Liddo, F., Morano, P., Tajani, F., Torre, C.M.: An innovative methodological approach for the analysis of the effects of urban interventions on property prices. Valori e Valutazioni, No. 26. Società Italiana di Estimo e Valutazione (2020)
30. Morano, P., Guarnaccia, C., Tajani, F., Di Liddo, F., Anelli, D.: An analysis of the noise pollution influence on the housing prices in the central area of the city of Bari. J. Phys. Conf. Ser. **1603**(1), 012027 (2020) (IOP Publishing)
31. Morano, P., Guarini, M.R., Tajani, F., Di Liddo, F., Anelli, D.: Incidence of different types of urban green spaces on property prices: a case study in the Flaminio District of Rome (Italy). In: Gervasi, O., et al. (eds.) Computational Science and Its Applications – ICCSA 2019, LNCS, vol. 11622, pp. 23–34. Springer, Cham (2019)
32. Morano, P., Guarini, M.R., Tajani, F., Anelli, D.: Sustainable redevelopment: the cost-revenue analysis to support the urban planning decisions. In: Gervasi, O., et al. (eds.) Computational Science and Its Applications – ICCSA 2020, LNCS, vol. 12253, pp. 968–980. Springer, Cham (2020)
33. Locurcio, M., Tajani, F., Anelli, D., Ranieri, R.: A multi-criteria composite indicator to support sustainable investment choices in the built environment. Valori e Valutazioni **30**, 85–100 (2022)

Reliable Evaluation Methods for Effective Urban Planning Initiatives: The Case Study of the Agro-Food Center of Rome (Italy)

Francesco Tajani[1], Pierluigi Morano[2], Debora Anelli[1], Giuseppe Cerullo[1](✉), and Melania Arenas Morente[3]

[1] Department of Architecture and Design, "Sapienza" University of Rome, 00196 Rome, Italy
giuseppe.cerullo@uniroma1.it

[2] Department of Civil, Environmental, Land, Building Engineering and Chemistry (DICATECh), Polytechnic University of Bari, 70126 Bari, Italy

[3] School of Engineering, University of Basilicata, 85100 Potenza, Italy

Abstract. The extraordinary urbanization contribution (EUC) constitutes a mechanism for urban equalization between private stakeholders and the Public Administration, designed to redistribute a portion of the land surplus value generated by territorial initiatives. This study introduces an evaluation approach applied to the case study of the Rome Agro-Food Centre (Italy), that, rather than relying on the static formula traditionally prescribed by local regulations, employs a dynamic method based on the implementation of the Discounted Cash Flow Analysis (DCFA). This method enables a more accurate assessment of the value increase arising from the urban planning amendment, thereby improving the effectiveness of the calculation of the EUC. The analysis demonstrates the potential of the DCFA in Public-Private Partnership initiatives, providing a replicable model for the economic-financial assessment of urban transformation processes.

Keywords: Urban Transformation Feasibility · Extraordinary Urbanization Contribution · Public-private Partnership · Public Compensation

1 Introduction

In the context of contemporary urban transformation processes, the implementation of value recapture mechanisms has become increasingly relevant, particularly in light of the financial constraints facing Public Administrations and the global push towards sustainable development [1, 2]. The Extraordinary Urbanization Contribution (EUC) is one of the most significant instruments introduced in Italy to regulate the redistribution of the capital gains generated by planning derogations and urban variants, established by Law No. 164/2014 and later amended by Law No. 76/2020. According to Article 16, paragraph 4, letter d-ter) of Presidential Decree No. 380/2001, private developers requesting urban planning variants are required to pay to the Public Administration (PA) a share of no less than 50% of the additional value generated by such interventions. This surplus value must be calculated by the municipal authority and is "tied to a specific cost center for the construction of public works and services to be carried out in the context in which the intervention is located" [3]. The municipal authority is responsible for calculating this surplus value, which is intended to finance public works and services within the intervention area, including infrastructure, public facilities, and social housing.

EUC represents a pivotal tool for regulating private benefits arising from urban transformation initiatives, aligning with overarching international principles of value recapture and value sharing [4, 5]. The overarching objective of these principles is to ensure that a proportion of the surplus value generated by planning decisions and infrastructure investments is redistributed to the community, thereby mitigating speculative behaviors and promoting more equitable urban development [6]. In light of the expanding budgetary constraints of public financial resources in many countries, including Italy, and the increasing urban infrastructure needs that have arisen in the aftermath of the 2008 financial crisis, the COVD-19 pandemic, and recent geopolitical instability, the EUC could constitute an essential instrument for many nations [7, 8]. Despite its strategic importance, implementing EUC has revealed significant challenges in the development of standardized and effective procedures for calculating the surplus value and determining the appropriate share to be transferred to the PA. The regulatory framework has been interpreted and implemented inconsistently across Italian regions, leading to fragmented practices and uncertainty in the application of the contribution. This has resulted in difficulties for both the public and private sectors in assessing the financial feasibility of transformation interventions and in ensuring a balanced distribution of costs and benefits.

Recent studies have proposed rational and replicable procedures for assessing the EUC, grounded in robust valuation methods and supported by mathematical optimization models. These models seek to delineate the pivotal urban parameters – including gross floor areas, land use allocations, and urban planning indices – that exert influence on the transformation value prior to and following the implementation of the planning variant [9]. The use of these models facilitates the identification of solutions that ensure the financial viability of private investment, while ensuring the availability of adequate resources for public urban development. Furthermore, these procedures incorporate real estate market data and regulatory constraints, allowing public authorities to adopt evidence-based criteria in the negotiation and the definition of urban planning agreements [10, 11]. Hence, although the present study is focused on a specific case, the proposed methodological framework lends itself to broader applicability, offering a flexible tool for supporting public decision-making in diverse contexts involving urban redevelopment, infrastructure planning, and value-sharing negotiations.

In the determination of the EUC, a significant development has been represented by the incorporation of temporal and risk-related dimensions, through the utilization of the Discounted Cash Flow Analysis (DCFA). This method enhances the ability of the Public Administrations to evaluate the sustainability of the proposed interventions over time, adjusting the EUC accordingly to reflect varying market conditions and ensuring that the redistribution of benefits remains fair and economically sound.

However, in many Italian municipalities the urban planning regulations for the determination of the EUC provide a conventional method based on a *static* analysis, i.e. the difference between the revenues and the costs of the urban variant without taking into account their actual temporal distribution over time: this situation could generate an inappropriate assessment of the EUC, that can determine economic - especially in public-private partnership initiatives - damages for the (public and private) parties involved in the transformation process.

With reference to a public property located in the Italian territory, for which an urban variant is provided, this study aims to verify the application of a *dynamic* model, through the implementation of a DCFA, for determining the market value of the property to be used in the EUC assessment, and to compare the obtained outputs with those generated by the application of the *static* method provided by the urban planning regulations. The proposed methodology aims to enhance transparency, equity, and replicability in the economic-financial assessment of urban transformation initiatives.

The research is organized as follows. In Sect. 2, a framework of the DCFA as a relevant method for public-private partnerships initiative is drawn. In Sect. 3, the case study represented by the public Agro-Food Center of Rome (Italy) is illustrated. In Sect. 4, the DCFA for the assessment of the post variant market value of the property is applied, the EUC is determined and the differences with a static assessment according to the current urban planning regulations are highlighted. Finally, the conclusions of the work are discussed.

2 The Role of Public-Private Partnerships

The development of a territory does not depend solely on the availability of natural resources or capital accumulation but is closely tied to the ability of both public and private actors to promote targeted investment strategies capable of generating economic and social progress. In this perspective, urban transformations represent a key element for ensuring a sustainable evolution of cities, through interventions that are adapted to meet the emerging needs of the community [12].

The current economic and urban context is characterized by a growing demand for modern and efficient initiatives, necessary to support strategic productive sectors and improve territorial competitiveness [13]. However, in a context of limited public resources, it is essential to rely on urban planning aimed at identifying fair mechanisms for the distribution of costs and benefits generated by transformations [14–16], avoiding the sole burden falling on the public sector or, conversely, the privatization of benefits without adequate returns for the community. In this context, the EUC plays a central role, representing a fundamental tool to ensure that the advantages generated by transformation operations are not concentrated solely in the private sector but are redistributed for the benefit of the entire community [17].

In this regard, the adoption of Public-Private Partnerships (PPPs) [18] has found wide application in urban transformation projects for reasons related to improving urban quality despite the scarcity of public financial resources. Involving private entities in this type of operation allows public administrations to leverage private managerial and entrepreneurial expertise, as well as financial resources [19]. In order for PPPs to generate benefits for the entire community, it is essential to ensure a fair distribution of the value created by the interventions, ensuring that the benefits generated are not exclusively captured by the private sector, while the costs do not fall entirely on the community

[20]. For interventions carried out under PPPs, it is therefore essential, in addition to a regulatory recovery of the value, to ensure a fair distribution of such value, also known as the land surplus value. In this context, the negotiating activity of the PA must allow the regulation of the privatization of the generated value by creating equitable conditions for its distribution, identifying win-win solutions between the public and private sectors [21].

In this context, the analysis of cash flows through the DCFA emerges as a fundamental approach for evaluating the economic sustainability of urban interventions carried out within the framework of a PPPs. This method allows for the examination of the financial feasibility of investments, forecasting transformation and management costs, and estimating expected revenues. Key performance indicators, such as Net Present Value (NPV) and Payback Period (PbP), provide crucial information to understand the long-term sustainability of the intervention, both from a financial and economic perspective [22].

3 Case Study

The Rome Agro-Food Centre (CAR) is a public property that represents one of the most important European facilities dedicated to the commercialization, distribution, and processing of fruit, vegetable, fish, and agro-food products in general.

Located in the municipality of Guidonia Montecelio, with a population of 89,153 inhabitants [23], within the Metropolitan City of Rome (Italy), the CAR plays a key role not only locally but also regionally and nationally, acting as a strategic hub for the agro-food supply chain. Currently, given the growing demand for services, in line with the expansion dynamics of major European markets, the CAR is facing the saturation of available spaces, both in terms of built volumes and deployable areas within the original site.

In this context, the area under analysis is represented by the *"Comparto B"* (62.5 ha), which represents an expansion and completion of the original CAR areas (140 ha). This development is seen as a strategic integration with the existing productive zones, aiming to create multifaceted systems that are efficiently integrated with the surrounding areas. The goal is to promote the establishment of new innovative functions internally—such as production, sales, and logistics—and externally—covering social and service areas.

The expansion of CAR (*Comparto B*) complies with the urban planning provisions, by transforming an agricultural area enclosed between *Via Tiburtina*, and the CAR itself. The aim is to integrate the existing industrial system into a single productive area.

Comparto B is divided into several sub-compartments (Fig. 1.), each serving specific functions:

- The *"Sub-Comparto 1"* encompasses areas adjacent to *Via Tiburtina*, where the construction of a large roundabout has been planned. This roundabout facilitates the inclusion of additional functions, which have been further identified within a specific sub-compartment (*Sub-Comparto 2*), serving both CAR and the surrounding area.
- The large roundabout containing *"Sub-Comparto 2"* also provides access, at multiple points, to *"Sub-Comparto 3"*, which, as part of the new Food Hub, may have been developed further to meet the demand for additional specific functions.

- The *"Sub-Comparto 4"* comprises available land areas for the potential establishment of functions that may have become necessary to complete the services offered by the CAR.
- In direct connection with the administrative and accomodation facilities of the existing CAR, *"Sub-Comparto 5"* is situated, which may also enable the establishment of functions aimed at integrating and complementing the existing industrial structures, directional buildings and accomodation facilities.

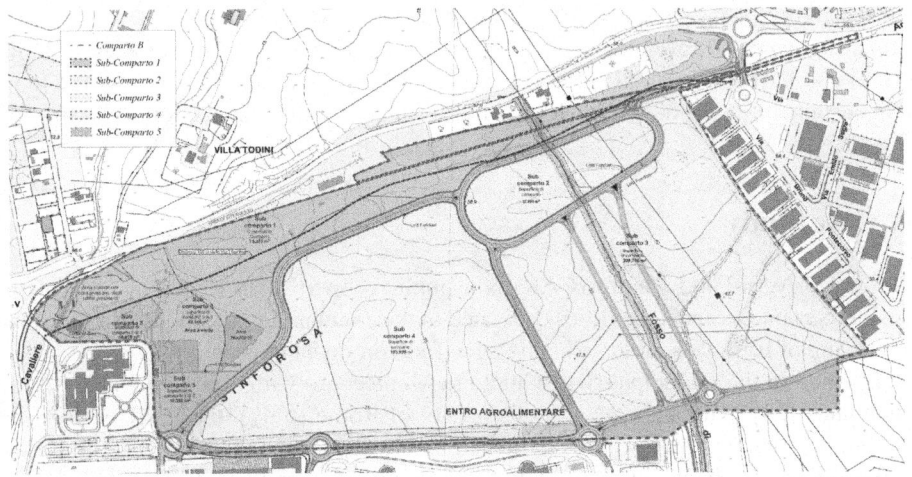

Fig. 1. Delimitation of *Comparto B* and its associated functional areas.

4 Method

4.1 Application of the DCFA

This study aims to verify the application of a *dynamic* model - through the implementation of a DCFA - for determining the real estate value to be used in calculating the EUC, with specific reference to the regulatory framework established by the municipality of Guidonia Montecelio (Rome).

Currently, the applicable legislation prescribes the exclusive adoption of a *static* analysis, an approach that proves inadequate when the intervention extends beyond a single year and instead takes the form of a transformation process unfolding over time. It is therefore essential to explore the possibility of adopting a procedure that fully integrates the time factor as a fundamental component of the appraisal process. In this regard, the present work proposes the adoption of a dynamic method, such as the DCFA, which can more accurately represent the evolutionary nature of the intervention.

With reference to the calculation of the EUC, the Italian legislation delegates urban planning competencies to the Regional Authorities (D.P.R. no. 616/1977). Specifically, considering that the contribution is calculated for the municipality of Guidonia Montecelio, the regulatory framework refers to the Regional Law no. 21/2009, which in turn refers to the provisions of D.P.R. no. 380/2001. The latter decree stipulates that the determination of the contribution's amount, the application methods, and related guarantees are defined by the competent municipality.

Consequently, the municipality of Guidonia Montecelio has established – pursuant to Art. 16, paragraph 4, letter d-ter of D.P.R. no. 380/2001, and as provided for in Art. 14, paragraph 16, letter f) of Decree-Law no. 78 of 31 May 2010, converted into Law no. 122 of 30 July 2010 – an EUC equal to a minimum percentage of 50%. This percentage is applied to the higher value generated by interventions on land or buildings undergoing an urban planning variant, derogation, or change of use, for which a percentage increase is expected equal to:

- Increase from 1.3 to 1.50 = partial compliance with higher-level and/or sectoral planning instruments in the presence/absence of landscape/environmental constraints, with the following specifications.

The highest value generated by the urban planning variant, on which the EUC is calculated, is obtained by determining the difference (Δ) between the "post" variant market value (Vm_{post}) and the "ante" variant market value (Vm_{ante}) of the property (Eq. 1). Formally:

$$D = Vm_{post} - Vm_{ante} \qquad (1)$$

Taking into account that the application of the DCFA is performed for the determination of the market value of the property in the "post" variant condition (Vm_{post}), an analysis period of seven years has been considered for the allocation of costs and the revenues over a time horizon, subdivided into fourteen semesters. The construction of the financial cash flows has been performed by taking into account the following cost and revenue items.

Costs. The costs considered for the evaluation of the intervention include the following items:

- K_{constr}: construction cost of the building units;
- K_{duty}: legal expenses;
- K_{tech}: technical fees for the professional works;
- K_{urb}: urbanization charges (primary, secondary and of construction);
- K_{contr}: contribution to the construction cost;
- K_{adapt}: land adaptation costs and connections;
- $K_{management}$: management expenses of the intended uses;
- $K_{marketing}$: commercialization costs of the building units;
- K_{prof}: profit of the entrepreneur.

Construction Cost of the Building Units (K_{constr}): This is the sum of the costs related to the three different intended uses (Table 1) identified in the urban variant: industrial structures ($K_{industrial}$), directional buildings ($K_{directional}$), and accomodation facilities ($K_{accomodation}$). This cost has been determined on a parametric basis, or in €/m², derived from the price list of the Milan Engineers and Architects Association (DEI) [24], appropriately adjusted using adjustment coefficients derived from market analysis.

- *Industrial structures ($K_{industrial}$)*: With regard to industrial structures, reference has been made to category E5 [25]. Following percentage adjustments derived from market analysis, a unitary value of 400 €/m^2 has been established. Given the total surface area of 203,975.00 m^2, the total construction cost for this category of work amounts to 81,590,000.00 €.
- *Directional buildings ($K_{directional}$)*: For the determination of the construction cost of office buildings, the reference value of category D16 [25] has been considered. Following percentage adjustments based on market dynamics, the unitary construction cost has been estimated at 1,500 €/m^2. Given a total surface area of 5,000 m^2, the total construction cost for the office buildings amounts to 7,459,202.90 €.
- *Accomodation facilities ($K_{accomodation}$)*: For the evaluation of accomodation structures, characterized by features similar to office buildings but with higher quality finishes, a unitary value of 1,600 €/m^2 has been adopted following a market analysis. Given a total surface area of 5,000 m^2, the total construction cost for this category of work has been calculated at 8,000,000 €.

Legal Expenses (K_{duty}): These include registration taxes and notary fees. They have been calculated based on an incidence of 13% of the market value (Vm_{post}) of the property, for a total amount of 1,012,582 €. The payment has been expected to be made during the third semester (start of construction) and will have been completed by the fourth semester.

$$K_{duty} = 13\% \cdot V_m = 1{,}012{,}582 \text{ €} \tag{2}$$

Technical Fees (K_{tech}): This item includes the costs related to the technical commitments (design, construction management, etc.) required for the transformation intervention. In this case study, these costs have been determined by applying a rate of 10% to the sum of the construction costs (K_{constr}) and the land adaptation costs (K_{adapt}), totaling 10,044,593.00 €. The time distribution of this cost item has been based on an incidence of 5% in the first two semesters, followed by a share of 10% for each subsequent semester until the twelfth semester, which has coincided with the completion of the works. Therefore, the technical costs amount to:

$$K_{tech} = 10\% \cdot (K_{constr} + K_{adapt}) = 10{,}044{,}593 \text{ €} \tag{3}$$

Total Urbanization Fees (K_{fees}): This item includes the primary and secondary urbanization charges (K_{urb}), calculated as 8% of the total construction cost, and the contribution to the construction cost (K_{contr}), amounting to 5% of the construction cost. The total amount is 12,616,396.00 €. The expenditure begins with the commencement of the works – in the second year – and continues until the completion of the intervention – in the sixth year – with annual payments distributed in equal installments, each amounting to 20% of the total amount.

$$K_{fees} = (K_{urb} + K_{contr}) = (8\% \cdot K_{constr}) + (5\% \cdot K_{constr}) = 12{,}616{,}396 \text{ €} \tag{4}$$

Reliable Evaluation Methods for Effective Urban Planning Initiatives 339

Land Adaptation Costs and Connections (K_{adapt}): This item includes all remediation works, site preparation, connections, and the related archaeological and geological surveys. In this case, it is calculated by applying an incidence of 3.5% of the total construction cost, for a total amount of 3,396,722.00 €. Similarly, the disbursement of this amount begins with the commencement of the works – in the second year – and is evenly distributed until the completion of the intervention – in the sixth year – with an annual expenditure equal to 20% of the total amount.

$$K_{adapt} = 3.5\ \%\cdot k_{constr} = 3,396,722\ \text{€} \tag{5}$$

Management Costs ($K_{management}$): This is the cost of managing the entire operation. This item has been calculated as a percentage – fixed at 2% – of the total construction costs, for a total amount of 1,940,984.00 €. The disbursement has been spread evenly over the entire duration of the intervention, from the first semester to the thirteenth semester, corresponding to the completion of the works.

$$K_m = 2\ \%\cdot k_{constr} = 1,940,984\ \text{€} \tag{6}$$

Commercialization Costs ($K_{marketing}$): These are the costs representing the amounts necessary for the advertising and marketing the buildings of the intervention, amounting to 2.5% of the estimated and obtainable revenues (V_{mt}). The total amount has been calculated at 4,132,063.00 €.

$$K_{marketing} = 2.5\ \%\cdot V_{mt} = 4,132,063\ \text{€} \tag{7}$$

Profit of the Entrepreneur (K_{prof}): This represents the total profit obtained by the promoter from the use of the capital invested in the real estate operation. In accordance with current regulations, the profit margin ranges from a minimum of 15% to a maximum of 25% of the market value of the property units obtained by the transformation (V_{mt}). In this case, by applying the lower limit of 15%, the profit has been calculated at 24,792,375.00 €.

$$K_{prof} = 15\ \%\cdot V_{mt} = 24,792,375\ \text{€} \tag{8}$$

The total construction cost (Eq. 9) of the buildings has been calculated at 97,049,203.00 €.

$$K_{constr} = k_{industrial} + k_{directional} + k_{accomodation} = 97,049,203\ \text{€} \tag{9}$$

In Table 1 the Costs of the transformation initiative have been reported and temporally distributed over the analysis period. The profit of the entrepreneur has not been indicated, as it will constitute a boundary for the determination of the market value of the property.

Revenues. Regarding the determination of revenues, in accordance with current regulations, reference is made to the most up-to-date quotations provided by the Real Estate Market Observatory (OMI) of the Italian Revenue Agency [25]. The analysis of the relevant OMI area has allowed for the identification of the following parameters:

Table 1. Temporal distribution (for semesters) of the costs.

Semesters	1	2	3	12	13	14
Industrial structures [€]	0	0	12,238,500	4,079,500	0	0
Directional buildings [€]	0	0	1,118,880	372,960	0	0
Accomodation facilities [€]	0	0	1,200,000	400,000	0	0
Legal expenses [€]	0	0	202,516	0	0	0
Technical fees [€]	0	502,230	502,230	1,004,459	0	0
Urbanization charges [€]	0	0	1,552,787	0	0	0
Contribution to the construction cost [€]	0	0	970,492	0	0	0
Land adaptation costs and connections [€]	0	0	679,344	0	0	0
Management expenses [€]	0	161,749	161,749	161,749	0	0
Commercialization costs [€]	0	82,641	123,962	619,809	82,641	82,641

- *Industrial structures ($R_{industrial}$)*: a market value of 700 €/m² has been assessed. By applying this value to the surface area under consideration, a total value of 142,782,500 € is obtained.
- *Directional structures ($R_{directional}$)*: a market value of 2,000 €/m² has been assessed, corresponding to a total value of 10,000,000 €.
- *Accomodation structures ($R_{accomodation}$)*: From the market analysis, a unitary value of 2,500 €/m² has been derived, which, when applied to the reference surface area, results in a total value of 12,500,000 €.

The total revenues (Eq. 10) obtainable from the real estate units amount to 165,282,500 €.

$$R_{tot} = R_{industrial} + R_{directional} + R_{accomodation} = 165,282,500€ \quad (10)$$

The total revenues (Table 2) have been spread over a 14-semester period, in line with the project's construction and commercialization timelines, assuming a sales hypothesis characterized by a 15% peak in the first and second years, followed by a gradual reduction until the final year of the analysis. This distribution is based on a market analysis that highlights how, in similar contexts, the initial phase of commercialization is supported by strong initial demand, stimulated by more favourable conditions. Subsequently, the market absorption rate tends to decrease gradually, due to the contraction of the pool of interested buyers and the increased selectivity remaining in the available offer.

Table 2. Revenues.

Semesters	1	2	3	12	13	14
Industrial structures [€]	2,855,650	4,283,475	21,417,375	2,855,650	2,855,650	2,855,650
Directional buildings [€]	200,000	300,000	1,500,000	200,000	200,000	200,000
Accomodation facilities [€]	250,000	375,000	1,875,000	250,000	250,000	250,000

4.2 Results

The main indicator of the project's financial profitability is represented by the Net Present Value (NPV), using a discount rate of 4.5% which excludes the compensation for the entrepreneur's risk and takes into account the financial charges related to the cost of money for a loan. Moreover, the financial statements carefully consider the tax liabilities of the private promoter, such as the corporate income tax (IRES), set at 24%, and the regional tax on productive activities (IRAP), equal to 4.82% of net revenues. In order to guarantee a profit for the entrepreneur equal to 24,792,375 € (i.e. 15% of the market value of the units to be realized), an iterative process has been carried out for determining the market value of the property (Vm_{post}) able to ensure the equalization of the NPV and the profit expected by the entrepreneur as the ordinary compensation for the risk assumed in the transformation initiative.

Therefore, the implementation of the DCFA and the iterative process described above have allowed to determine a post variant market value of the property (Vm_{post}) equal to 7,789,094 € (Table 3).

Table 3. Implementation of the DCFA.

Semesters		1	2	3	12	13	14
Post variant market value	7,789,094 €						
Total costs [€]		1,802,209	2,345,759	20,804,127	6,101,309	82,641	82,641
Total revenues [€]		3,305,650	4,958,475	24,792,375	3,305,650	3,305,650	3,305,650
Cash Flow [€]		1,503,441	2,612,716	3,988,248	-2,795,659	3,223,009	3,223,009
Discount rate	4,50%						
Discounted cash flow [€]		1,470,714	2,500,207	3,733,428	-2,146,775	2,421,060	2,368,359
NPV	24,792,375 €						

For the determination of the value of the area "ante intervention" (Vm_{ante}), it should be considered that, in its current condition, the property is classified as agricultural land. Through a market analysis, a unitary value of 33,00 €/ha has been assessed. Therefore, the market value of the property "ante intervention" by relating this value to the size of the area under study, a "pre-intervention" is equal to 2,062,500 €.

Therefore, according to Eq. (1), the highest value generated by the urban planning variant (Δ) can be obtained through Eq. (11):

$$\Delta = 7,789,094 \text{ €} - 2,062,500 \text{ €} = 5,726,594 \text{ €} \tag{11}$$

Determination of the EUC. For the calculation of the EUC, in accordance with the regulatory provisions, a 1.3 multiplier is applied to the minimum percentage of 50%. This increase is justified by the fact that the intervention concerns undeveloped or not yet urbanized areas and involves an area larger than 40 ha. Consequently, the percentage to be applied to the added value is 65%. Applying this percentage to the value obtained in Eq. (11), the EUC amounts to:

$$\text{EUC} = 5,726,594 \cdot 65\% = \mathbf{3,722,286 \text{ €}} \tag{12}$$

Table 4. Determination of the EUC.

Post variant market value of the property (Vm_{post})	7,789,094 €
Ante variant market value of the property (Vm_{ante})	2,062,500 €
Reference value for the assessment of the EUC ($\Delta = Vm_{post} - Vm_{ante}$)	5,726,594 €
Percentage to be considered for the assessment of the EUC	50% · 1.3 = 65%
EUC	**3,722,286 €**

In Table 4 the items for the determination of the EUC have been reported.

By comparing the post variant market value of the property obtained through the dynamic analysis (i.e. the implementation of the DCFA) with the market value generated from a static analysis (as provided the current urban planning regulations), a significant differential can be observed. Specifically, the dynamic method, based on the DCFA, returned a value of 7,789,093.68 €, while the static approach - i.e. by performing the difference between the revenues and the costs without considering the temporal distribution of these items over time - assesses a post variant market value equal to 8,226,336.56 €, with a differential amount between the two methods equal to 437,242.56 € (i.e. in percentage, about 5.61%). This output points out that the static analysis tends to overestimate the market value of the intervention: a contingence that could lead to the application of an unfair EUC, that is based on an unrealistically higher value than the market one. In practice, this would result in disproportionate financial burdens, potentially reducing the intervention's profitability or even compromising its viability for a private investor initially interested in performing the initiative.

From the public operator's perspective, the 5.61% deviation between the static and dynamic methods highlights the importance of the implementation of an evaluation model that realistically reflects the market dynamics. An assessment based on the DCFA allows for the definition of sustainable and consistent urban planning charges, promoting the realization of economically viable interventions for the private investors, while ensuring reliable public incomes for the planning and the realization of public works. Additionally, the dynamic method can reduce the risk of disputes and encourages a virtuous negotiation between the public and private subjects, fostering competitive and sustainable urban development. It is, however, not to be overlooked that the dynamic analysis also entails limitations, such as the uncertainty and potential inaccuracy of input variables under unforeseeable market conditions.

5 Conclusions

In a context where the need to mobilize resources for the achievement of the Sustainable Development Goals – particularly Goal 11, which aims to promote inclusive, safe, resilient, and sustainable cities – is becoming increasingly urgent, the Extraordinary Urbanization Contribution (EUC) emerges as an indispensable tool for ensuring equity in the redistribution of the economic benefits generated by urban transformations. However, the effectiveness of this tool lies in the ability of Public Administrations to effectively manage negotiation processes with private actors, enhancing public-private partnership models that are transparent and oriented towards collective welfare [26].

The analysis conducted on the case of the Rome Agro-Food Centre (Italy) provided a concrete application of the principles of value recovery and sharing, demonstrating how, through a precise determination of the land surplus value resulting from a change of the eligible intended use resulting by the transformation of the property, it is possible to generate resources to be allocated to the improvement of infrastructures and public services. This mechanism, when implemented with accuracy and foresight, initiates a virtuous cycle that integrates public and private interests: the investor benefits from the increase in real estate value, while the community receives additional resources for interventions that can enhance urban life quality and territorial attractiveness.

The contribution of this research goes beyond theoretical elaboration, providing practical guidelines that can steer both administrative practices and negotiation dynamics within public-private partnerships. The proposed method stands out for its ease of application and replicability, responding to the needs for standardization and simplification in the management of complex operations. In particular, the dynamic reinterpretation of the EUC regulation, through the development of the Discounted Cash Flow Analysis (DCFA), introduced updated and adaptable criteria for different territorial contexts. The methodological framework proposed in this study aligns with a broader systemic perspective for integrating evaluation processes within sustainable urban planning strategies [27, 28].

Future insights can concern the verification of the reliability of the dynamic method in other territorial contexts, by comparing the outputs obtained by the implementation of the DCFA with those generated by the use of the conventional method for estimating the EUC provided by the local urban planning regulations: in this way, it will be possible to define a reference framework that can constitute a valid support for Public Administrations in the decisions regarding possible improvements in the evaluation criteria applied for the EUC assessment [29].

Note. The current study has been developed within the current research P.R.I.N. Project 2022: "INSPIRE—Improving Nature-Smart Policies through Innovative Resilient Evaluations", Grant number: 2022J7RWNF.

References

1. UN-Habitat: The new urban agenda, Nairobi, Kenya (2016)
2. United Nations: Transforming our world: the 2030 Agenda for Sustainable Development (2016)
3. Morano, P., Tajani, F., Anelli, D.: Urban planning variants: a model for the division of the activated "plusvalue" between public and private subjects. Valori e Valutazioni, pp. 31–47 (2021)
4. Camagni, R.: Urban form and sustainability: value recapture tools in urban transformation (2016)
5. Smolka, M.: Implementing land value recapture instruments: global lessons and challenges (2019)
6. Morano, P., Tajani, F., Anelli, D.: The value recapture of complex urban transformation interventions: a rational procedure for the fair share of public and private benefits. Valori e Valutazioni. **16**, 47–64 (2023)

7. Allam, Z., Newman, P.: Economics of urban regeneration: recent developments and future directions (2018)
8. Gielen, D., Tasan-Kok, F.: Renewing the public city through value sharing (2017)
9. Di Liddo, F., Morano, P., Tajani, F., Torre, C.M.: an innovative methodological approach for the analysis of the effects of urban interventions on property prices. Valori e Valutazioni (2020)
10. Morano, P., Tajani, F., Anelli, D., Sabatelli, E.: The assessment of the public and private conveniences in the urban transformation interventions: an optimization model for the value recapture adoption. Wseas Trans. Environ. Develop. **19**, 863–872 (2023). https://doi.org/10.37394/232015.2023.19.82
11. Guarini, M.R., Morano, P., Micheli, A., Sica, F.: Public-private negotiation of the increase in land or property value by urban variant: an analytical approach tested on a case of real estate development. Sustainability **13**, 10958 (2021). https://doi.org/10.3390/su131910958
12. Della Spina, L., Calabrò, F.: The evaluations of private and public conveniences in the complex urban programs: support activities of the municipality of Reggio Calabria. LaborEst. **5**, 5–11 (2010)
13. Anelli, D., Morano, P., Tajani, F., Sabatelli, E.: Impacts of urban decay on the residential property market: an application to the city of Rome (Italy). In: Gervasi, O., Murgante, B., Garau, C., Taniar, D.C. Rocha, A.M.A., Faginas Lago, M.N. (eds.) Computational Science and Its Applications – ICCSA 2024 Workshops, pp. 36–48. Springer Nature Switzerland, Cham (2024). https://doi.org/10.1007/978-3-031-65318-6_3
14. Camagni, R.: Perequazione urbanistica "estesa", rendita e finanziarizzazione immobiliare: un conflitto con l'equità e la qualità territoriale. Scienze regionali **2014**(2), 29–44 (2014)
15. Calabrò, F., Mafrici, F., Meduri, T.: The valuation of unused public buildings in support of policies for the inner areas. the application of SostEc Model in a case study in Condofuri (Reggio Calabria, Italy). In: Bevilacqua, C., Calabrò, F., and Della Spina, L. (eds.) New Metropolitan Perspectives, pp. 566–579. Springer, Cham (2021). https://doi.org/10.1007/978-3-030-48279-4_54
16. Spatari, G., Lorè, I., Viglianisi, A., Calabrò, F.: Economic feasibility of an integrated program for the enhancement of the byzantine heritage in the aspromonte national park. the case of staiti. In: Calabrò, F., Della Spina, L., and Piñeira Mantiñán, M.J. (eds.) New Metropolitan Perspectives, pp. 313–323. Springer, Cham (2022). https://doi.org/10.1007/978-3-031-06825-6_30
17. Morano, P., Tajani, F., Anelli, D.: A decisions support model for investment through the social impact bonds. The case of the city of Bari (Italy). Valori e Valutazioni, pp. 163–179 (2020)
18. Morano, P., Tajani, F., Di Liddo, F., Amoruso, P.: The public role for the effectiveness of the territorial enhancement initiatives: a case study on the redevelopment of a building in disuse in an Italian small town. Buildings **11**, 1–22 (2021). https://doi.org/10.3390/buildings 11030087
19. Copiello, S.: Progetti urbani in partenariato. Studi di fattibilità e piano economico finanziario. Alinea Editrice (2011)
20. Morano, P., Tajani, F., Anelli, D.: Urban planning decisions: an evaluation support model for natural soil surface saving policies and the enhancement of properties in disuse. Prop. Manag. **38**, 699–723 (2020). https://doi.org/10.1108/PM-04-2020-0025
21. Morano, P., Tajani, F., Del Giudice, V., De Paola, P., Anelli, D.: Urban transformation interventions: a decision support model for a fair rent gap recapture. In: Gervasi, O., et al. (eds.) Computational Science and Its Applications – ICCSA 2021, pp. 253–264. Springer, Cham (2021). https://doi.org/10.1007/978-3-030-86979-3_19
22. Morano, P., Tajani, F., Di Liddo, F.: Iniziative di riqualificazione urbana in partenariato pubblico-privato: un modello per la definizione di liste di priorità temporale. LaborEst, pp. 50–56 (2020). https://doi.org/10.19254/LaborEst.20.08

23. Guidonia Montecelio - Popolazione | Dinamica demografica e territorio, https://ottomilac ensus.istat.it/sottotema/058/058047/1/. Accessed 16 March 2025
24. Collegio degli Ingegneri e Architetti di Milano ed: Prezzi Tipologie Edilizie 2024
25. Geopoi. https://www1.agenziaentrate.gov.it/servizi/geopoi_omi/index.php. Accessed 16 March 2025
26. Guarini, M.R., Morano, P., Micheli, A.: A procedure to evaluate the extra-charge of urbanization. In: Gervasi, O., et al. (eds.) Computational Science and Its Applications – ICCSA 2020, pp. 981–999. Springer, Cham (2020). https://doi.org/10.1007/978-3-030-58808-3_70
27. Scorza, F., Santopietro, L.: A systemic perspective for the Sustainable Energy and Climate Action Plan (SECAP). Eur. Plan. Stud. **32**, 281–301 (2024). https://doi.org/10.1080/09654313.2021.1954603
28. Santopietro, L., Solimene, S., Lucchese, M., Di Carlo, F., Scorza, F.: An economic appraisal of the SE(C)AP public interventions towards the EU 2050 target: the case study of Basilicata region. Cities **149**, 104957 (2024). https://doi.org/10.1016/j.cities.2024.104957
29. Locurcio, M., Tajani, F., Anelli, D.: Sustainable urban planning models for new smart cities and effective management of land take dynamics. Land **12**, 621 (2023)

The Implementation of Multicriteria Analysis for Heritage Assets Enhancement: An Application for the HBU Identification of a Historical Building in an Italian Municipality

Marco Locurcio[1], Felicia Di Liddo[1], Laura Tatulli[1(✉)], Pierluigi Morano[1], and Debora Anelli[2]

[1] Department of Civil, Environmental, Land, Building Engineering and Chemistry, Polytechnic University of Bari, Via Orabona 4, 70125 Bari, Italy
`laura.tatulli@poliba.it`
[2] Department of Architecture and Design, "Sapienza" University of Rome, Via Flaminia 359, 00196 Rome, Italy
`debora.anelli@uniroma1.it`

Abstract. The enhancement of properties with historical and cultural value should be consistent with the need for their preservation, the interests of stakeholders and the urge of obtaining public and/or private funding. These aspects, defined through both qualitative and quantitative criteria, can be simultaneously considered by implementing Multi-Criteria Decision Analysis (MCDA). In the present work, through the application to a case study concerning a building located in the ancient part of a municipality in Southern Italy, the potential of MCDA is tested as a support tool for evaluations related to the functional reconversion of heritage assets aimed at identifying the Highest and Best Use.

Keywords: Real estate heritage · MCDA · AHP · TOPSIS · HBU

1 Introduction

The definition of methodological approaches aimed at the efficient management of public resources represents a topic that is both highly complex and an issue of current relevance. Recent developments in decision support tools for public administration have increased interest in strategies for the optimal allocation of resources. In particular, the evaluation techniques adopted by public sector are not always able to adequately account for all the fundamental aspects involved in choices processes, specifically when these relate to the social, economic, and environmental impacts of interventions on the territory. Public assets constitute a heterogeneous patrimony belonging to a public legal entity, which manages them for the purpose of achieving specific objectives. Within these properties, attention should be paid to buildings with historical and cultural significance. In this sense, the present work focuses on real estate heritage assets, that are characterized by two aspects:

1. the purpose of ownership is primarily aimed at spreading knowledge, education or culture;
2. it is possible to circumscribe the asset, i.e. define its physical boundary.

The growing awareness of the central role of historical and artistic assets has led public administrations to seek efficient strategies for their management and use; to this end, they must implement qualitative and quantitative approaches capable of overcoming traditional ones, which are often inadequate as these are strictly focused on the financial aspects.

The proper enhancement and management of existing heritage is essential in light of their significant implications for both local and national development and economies. Indeed, these assets have a strong capacity to attract tourism flows and to provide intangible benefits to the population. Of course, the use of such assets should be compatible with conservation and protection requirements, so that they may also be used by future generations. From this perspective, it is fundamental to identify targeted intended uses that allow to benefit from both public and private funding, and, at the same time, to preserve the identity, social, cultural, and economic value of these properties [1–3].

In view of the recognized importance of cultural assets preservation and the widespread presence of numerous underutilized and/or abandoned historical and cultural buildings - often due to their degraded condition – the definition of effective strategies to ensure their conservation and valorization, is needed. The limited monetary resources of public entities represent a significant limit on these assets' requalification, and the involvement of private investors through forms of cooperation has proven to be a viable and solution. However, the integration of private funding entails the inclusion of interests and objectives that often differ from the more "passive" protection goals traditionally pursued by public bodies [4], incorporating also conflicting targets of the stakeholders.

The tendency of the public administrations towards new policies that incentivize private sector participation makes it necessary to introduce tools capable of coordinating public and private interests in the development of efficient and sustainable management interventions for heritage assets. Furthermore, in order to encourage private involvement, it is often necessary to implement functional reconversion initiatives aimed at introducing new uses that are consistent with the community needs, and possibly even different from the original ones. In this context, Multi-Criteria Decision Analysis (MCDA) represents an adequate tool for identifying the most appropriate function among different alternatives. These approaches, in fact, allow for the simultaneous consideration of different aspects that can be translated by i) quantitative criteria, among which those linked to the expectations of profitability by the private operator, and ii) qualitative ones, such as those related to compatibility with the surrounding context and with the socio-economic tissue in which the property is located.

MCDA techniques are effective for supporting investment decision-making in contexts characterized by high uncertainty [5, 6] by guarantying transparency to the entire mechanisms for the selection of "the best" project solution. In fact, they allow for: i) the reconstruction of the Decision Maker's (DM) choice process; ii) the development of a shared foundation among the various involved stakeholders; and iii) the clear and unambiguous representation of the selected option through the use of a synthetic numerical indicator and graphical outputs.

2 Aim

The several challenges associated with the heritage asset repurposing derive primarily from their peculiar specificities and the need to define interventions capable of generating positive impacts in social, economic, and environmental terms, while also ensuring the financial sustainability of the initiative [7–9] and the properties protection. To this end, appropriate tools are required to identify "the best" alternative among different potential uses, based on specific predetermined criteria [10, 11].

The reference literature includes numerous studies that explore the use of these techniques for selecting optimal solutions, i.e. to be preferred. Ribera et al. (2019), for instance, highlight how the choice of the HBU (Highest and Best Use) requires a rational approach that must be supported by appropriate tools. Among these, the study promotes the AHP (Analytic Hierarchy Process) implementation, as it allows to take into account both financial performance and the project's effects on the territory, including its ability to foster cultural development while respecting building historical and architectural characteristics [1]. Similarly, the research carried out by Nesticò et al. (2019) points out the key role of MCDAs, as these are capable of accounting for the multiple effects -financial, social, cultural, and environmental - generated by an enhancement project. In particular, the Authors develop a comparison between different multicriteria techniques, confirming the validity of AHP due to its usefulness in decomposing the problem and identifying its essential aspects [2]. In line with this framework, the work by Claver et al. (2015) examines the suitability of multicriteria techniques as part of a comprehensive methodology for analysing assets of Spanish industrial heritage, specifically as decision-support tools for assessing their potential new uses [12]. Bottero et al. (2019) propose a multicriteria decision-support approach for classifying adaptive reuse strategies for cultural heritage assets [13]. The article by Mohamed et al. (2025) aligns with this line of research, suggesting the integration of fuzzy logic with MCDA for a case study focused on the development of the built heritage in Egypt [14].

In accordance with the overview of existing scientific literature, the present work explores the role of MCDA in identifying the HBU of historically and culturally significant properties to be redeveloped. The aim of the research concerns the application of MCDA techniques to a case study relating to a functional repurposing project of a historic building located in a municipality in Southern Italy.

3 Methodological Approach

In general, MCDA approaches are structured into the following phases: i) definition of the goal; ii) construction of the criteria matrix; iii) determination of the local weights of the criteria; iv) normalization and elaboration of the alternatives matrix; v) computation of the global weights; and vi) aggregation of the weights and identification of "the best" alternative. To successfully achieve the objective, among the various existing MCDA techniques, this study adopts a combined use of the Analytic Hierarchy Process (AHP) and the Technique for Order of Preference by Similarity to Ideal Solution (TOPSIS).

The AHP is based on the concept of criteria pair-wide comparing to determine their respective weights, and among alternatives for each criterion, to establish their relative importance. The final result is obtained by aggregating the weights of criteria and the scores assigned to each alternative through the Weighted Sum Model (WSM) approach. In particular, in this study, the AHP is employed for determining the weights of the criteria (phase iii), as the presence of a consistency measure allows to verify the consistency of the pair-wise comparisons by decreasing the arbitrariness of the judgments in the weights assignment [15]. On the other hand, the fundamental idea of the TOPSIS is that "the best" solution is characterized by the minimum distance to the ideal solution and the furthest distance from the anti-ideal solution. The TOPSIS technique proves to be particularly useful in phases iv), v), and vi), as it generates four different orders depending on the type of applied normalization and the approach used to identify the ideal and anti-ideal solutions. This contributes to the robustness of the final result by making it as independent as possible from the specific adopted normalization rules, thereby overcoming one of the main limitations associated with MCDAs. The integration of these two techniques combined is a key aspect of the present analysis, as it ensures a structured and balanced approach that facilitates the decision-making process by combining a subjective approach with a rigorous analytical one. As previously described, the AHP determines the weight of each criterion based on the preferences of the DM, which reflects the individual perception as well as the social and cultural context. Complementarily, TOPSIS method uses unbiased numerical data, enabling the calculation of distances from ideal solutions and similarity coefficients through the decision matrix and data normalization process. In light of this, the application of the AHP for assigning weights to the criteria used in the TOPSIS allows the incorporation of subjective preferences and DM requirements into an objective evaluation, thereby balancing community opinions with analytical rigor in identifying the HBU. In addition, the inclusion of the Consistency Index (CI) into AHP and the data normalization in TOPSIS contribute to reduce of the subjectivity of the methods, ensuring more coherent and reliable outcomes.

This integrated approach therefore enables the DM to manage both qualitative judgment and quantitative data, providing a more efficient assessment of the alternatives. Furthermore, while the AHP facilitates the involvement of multiple DMs through the hierarchical structuring of criteria and the collection of their points of view, TOPSIS offers a clear ranking of the alternatives. Together, these techniques support participatory, transparent, and data-driven decision-making processes, enhancing acceptability, legitimacy and transparency of the final decisions.

4 The Case Study

The case study of this work concerns a building of historical and cultural significance located in the ancient part of a municipality in Southern Italy. The building first floor is currently mainly intended for a library while the largest rooms in the same floor are occasionally used for conferences and meetings. However, the local public administration (DM) recognises the current use as limited if compared to the property potentialities. In consideration of a series of funded restoration and consolidation interventions, the objective of the present analysis is to identify the HBU of the property, starting from a set of repurposing proposals suggested by the local population, professional association and representatives of local public entities.

The building was founded in 1270 as a noble residence; according to some sources, the property was originally organized *a curtis*, that is, it featured a large space enclosed by walls, with towers and *lamie* arranged at its center. Over time, several phases of transformation and expansion have occurred, each of which was driven by the urban development dynamics that encompassed different parts of the municipality historic center. Of all the transformations, the widening of the main streets of the city during the 17th century has played a major role; indeed, in 1650, with the enlargement of the street facing the main front of the building, the *a curtis* configuration was modified: the entire medieval complex was restructured together with the church. Furthermore, the entrance was set back by approximately one and a half meters. At the end of the 1600s, due to the continuous changes affecting the city's socio-economic conditions, a significant urban transformation took place: noble residences were renovated with the construction prestigious façades. After a fire that occurred at the beginning of the 18th century, the front and part of the building were rebuilt. In 1920 a partial renovation took place, more specifically, the first floor was designated as the Municipal Tax Office (Ufficio Esattoriale delle Imposte Comunali), which led to some modifications. The family residence was thus moved to the second floor, which was adapted to its new function through the addition of partition walls and independent vaulted ceilings. More recently, the deteriorated roof structures have been replaced. The portion of the façade aligned with the main entrance portal was completely rebuilt (set back by 1.5 m) in 1965, following the removal of dilapidated elements. This reconstruction was executed on behalf of the Municipal Technical Office and coincided with the donation to the municipality of the entire first floor and part of the ground floor. The building has a highly complex planimetric articulation: it is organized around three courtyards, one of which - the main one - is directly connected to the only current entrance. On the left side of this entrance there is the deconsecrated medieval chapel of Sant'Anna. The current façade is articulated into three levels: the base level, the main floor (piano nobile) and the service floor. In Fig. 1 the plan of the first floor of the case study property is reported and in Fig. 2 the main façade of the building is shown.

4.1 Building Surface Restoration and Consolidation Project

The designed restoration intervention for the building consists of a systematic set of conservation operations. In response to the observed structural and surface degradation phenomena, the project proposes technical solutions aimed at surface treatment and structural consolidation. The analysis of the ante-intervention building conditions reveals several structural damages, which are hypothesized to derive primarily from two conditions: the first is the differential settlement of the foundation segments beneath the façade of the annexed church and the main entrance portal; the second is the overturning tendency of the left-hand corner of the façade. In addition to these primary causes, successive modifications to the masonry over time has a key-role. In the light of the detected cracking patterns, different structural restoration measures have been planned, including consolidation through injections of hydraulic lime-based mortar [16, 17]. To compensate the differential settlement of the foundations, the consolidation project aims to enhance their load-bearing capacity through a series of targeted interventions. These include the insertion of carbon fiber ties (diatoni) to improve overall structural resistance;

Fig. 1. Plan of the first floor of the case study building. Floor plan based on the metric survey, for the purpose of seismic vulnerability analysis, made by Ing. Paolo Dellorusso, Studio Tecnico D'Ambrosio & Associati, Studio Pazienza-De Rienzio & Associati, Studio SIGMA srl, Architetto Antonio Maria Maffiola, Ing Saverio Catena, Ing. Francesco Glardino

Fig. 2. Main façade of the building

injections of hydraulic lime-based mortars to increase the strength of the masonry wall; and jet grouting with nanolime injections at the foundation level, intended to improve soil compaction and load-bearing capacity. The set of cracks found on the corner portion of the building's main façade is hypothesized to be caused by the outward thrust of the corner, which tends to project into the void. The restoration project addresses this issue by inserting two steel tie rods arranged in a pseudo-orthogonal configuration, allowing the retention of the wall section that shows a tendency to overturn.

The façades of the building are characterized by various forms of surface degradation, affecting both stone and plastered elements. Among the most prevalent phenomena identified in the case study there are alveolization, efflorescence, biological patina, surface deposits, and crust formations. The restoration of the deteriorated surfaces involves a range of steps, including cleaning, consolidation, recovery, replacement, finishing, and targeted specific treatments.

Among the designed operations, the most significant ones include: the removal of incoherent surface deposits, crusts, and biological patinas and the consolidation of eroded parts and of areas characterized by material loss through reintegration using materials that are either analogous or compatible with the original ones, while remaining distinguishable through chromatic differentiation. For plastered surfaces affected by phenomena such as material loss, exfoliation, or washout, restoration regards the use of a lime-based plaster with a slightly recessed finish in relation to the original material [18].

4.2 Description of the Criteria and Identification of Their Weights

The objective of the present analysis concerns the identification of the HBU of the considered property, i.e. "the best" alternative to be preferred among the proposed project hypotheses. This goal is declined through a set of criteria that represent the various aspects to be taken into account for the HBU determination, in accordance with the logic of the DM, that is the technical office of the public administration (property owner). In particular, the technical office is composed of various professionals, such as architects, engineers, urban planners, and economic-financial consultants, who perform different functions to ensure compliance with regulations and the achievement of an adequate level of goal fulfillment across different sectors.

The involvement of different actors, in the roles of decision makers, stakeholders and users, is fundamental to guarantee a certain degree of sustainability of the repurposing project. Indeed, broad acceptance of the selected function and an adequate level of profitability contribute to reducing the risk of abandonment, vandalism, while also promoting the development of spaces with comparable uses and socio-cultural significance. Specifically, several stakeholders have been considered for this analysis and among them a key role is assigned to heritage protection and urban planning authorities, private investors, residents and involved professionals.

The criteria aim to consider, within the evaluation, the need to preserve and enhance the asset, the economic and financial aspects, the private sector level involvement, the needs of the population, and the social implications of each project alternative.

The criteria identified are:

1. Net income, defined as the difference between the total revenues and all expenses borne by the property owner for the reconversion intervention.

2. Riskiness, assessed qualitatively in terms of the likelihood of not achieving the expected net income, through a comparison of the intervention with similar ones within the same context.
3. Structural compatibility, defined on the basis of the impact of the proposed uses on the static functionality and load-bearing capacity of the building or its components.
4. Compatibility with the historical and artistic features, that is, its aptitude for conservation and protection of the property.
5. Compatibility with the surrounding context, which includes the accessibility of the building, the proximity to services and spaces with functions similar to those hypothesized for the property, and the compatibility with the land use designation of the area in which the property is located.
6. Alignment with the interests of the local population, which - given the need to maintain the public nature of the asset - assesses how the functional reconversion impacts community demand and its needs.

In Fig. 3 a summary of the evaluation criteria selected for the analysis is reported.

Evaluation criteria

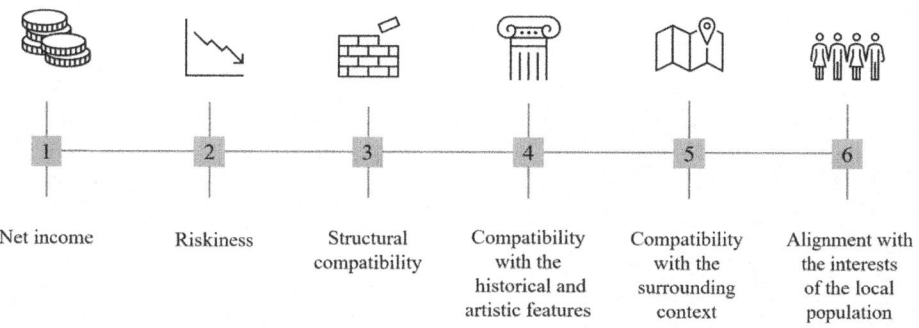

Fig. 3. Evaluation criteria used for determining the HBU

The weight of each criterion is determined starting from the opinions expressed by DM through the application of AHP, as described below. In particular, in order to gather community opinions, questionnaires are administered to the local residents, while to take professional opinions into account, consultations among experts are conducted. As a result of applying the AHP method, it is observed that the most influential criterion is the "Structural compatibility", which accounts for 39.1%. In particular, the preservation of building static functionality represents an essential requirement to ensure the long-term conservation of the asset and the proper performance of the intended uses. The adoption of alternatives that could potentially damage the load-bearing capacity may, in fact, severely compromise the maintaining of the property, as well as nullify the effects of restoration interventions. The criterion of "Compatibility with the historical and artistic features" plays a fundamental role in the decision-making process (weight of 28.5%), as it is linked to the necessity of safeguarding these characteristics, which serve as catalysts for the cultural and identity value of the asset. Less relevant is the criterion related to the "Net income" (11.1%): although it is necessary to identify financially sustainable function, this objective remains subordinate to the overarching goals of preservation property structural and historical-artistic aspects.

"Compatibility with the surrounding context" is considered only moderately relevant (influence of 8%) compared to the previous criteria: this is due to the lower importance assigned to the alignment with the characteristics of the reference area, in relation to the structural requirements and usability of the project alternative. A similar level of priority is attributed to the criteria of "Riskiness" and "Alignment with the interests of the local population" (6.8% and 6.5%, respectively). Indeed, a low risk of intervention or a high compatibility with the community needs do not justify a functional repurposing that have a negative impact on the building structural elements or on its historic-artistic value. Moreover, the medium- and long-term sustainability perspective, that is fundamental for the heritage management, often does not align well with the immediate and current needs of the population.

The Consistency Ratio (CR), equal to 2.9%, is particularly low, indicating adherence to the transitivity principle, coherence in the expressed judgments, and, ultimately, the care with which the DM carried out the pair-wise comparisons. In Fig. 4 the different weights of the identified criteria are shown.

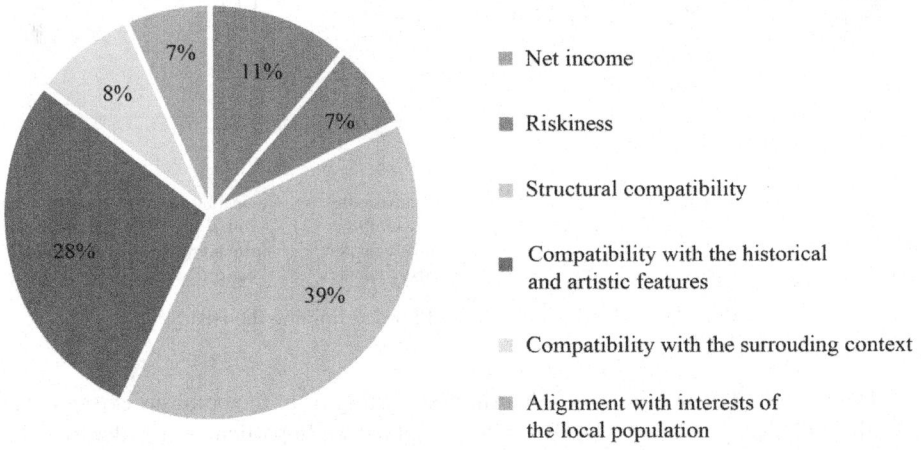

Fig. 4. Weights of the criteria

4.3 Description of the Repurposing Alternatives and Their Relative Importance

Following the described restoration and structural consolidations interventions - necessary to eliminate phenomena of degradation and to ensure proper building structural functionality - a project for the adaptive reuse of the first-floor spaces is developed. Currently, the building is only partially in use and serves as a library, study hall, and conference room for citizens and public institutions. In the functional reconversion proposal, it is planned to use of the entire surface area (approximately 550 square meters), and five alternative options are determined:

1. Conference rooms designated to host events organized by public and private entities, subject to the payment of an hourly fee. This alternative also includes the provision of complementary services such as coffee breaks, light lunches, event promotion through social media channels, press review, event recording, and photo/video services.
2. Art exhibition spaces for temporary displays by emerging contemporary artists, subject either to the payment of a fixed fee by the event organizer or to a ticketing system for visitors, depending on the resonance. Additional services are also envisaged, such as event promotion through posters and social media channels, as well as the management of lighting and, where applicable, audiovisual elements.
3. Coworking spaces to support startups, professional firms, and companies. In particular, the proposal includes the availability of rooms of various sizes, as well as larger rooms that can be reserved for meetings and other events. The service fee includes costs for cleaning and utilities.
4. Restaurant/cafeteria. This alternative involves targeted transformation works to make the spaces compliant from both regulatory and technical standpoints, through the installation of appropriate systems and equipment. A sustainable lease agreement is proposed, consisting of a fixed component - based on the estimated total annual revenue - and a variable component linked to any potential increases in that revenue over time.
5. Non-intervention alternative, or "use as is" scenario, which entails the continuation of the current functions as a library and study hall, with the possibility of using some rooms for conferences.

Figure 5 shows the different uses of the project alternatives.

Functional repurposing proposals

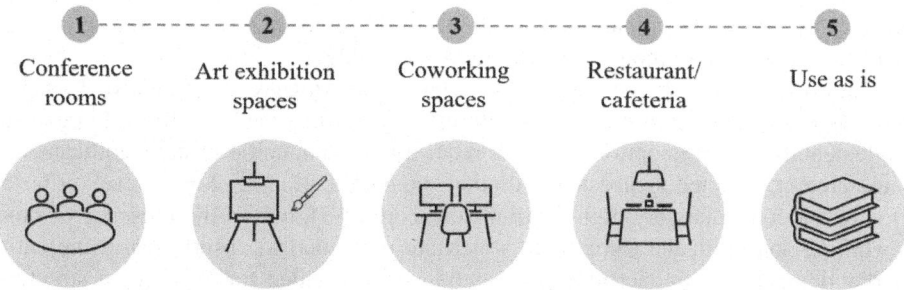

Fig. 5. Functional repurposing proposals

For each of the five alternatives a score from 0 to 10 is assigned, representing the level of satisfaction with respect to the identified six criteria. The value of 0 indicates a complete absence of satisfaction; a score of 1 corresponds to an extremely unsatisfied criterion, 2 to very poorly satisfied, 3 to poorly satisfied, and 4 to insufficient. The score of 5 represents an averagely satisfied or acceptable criterion. A score of 6 is attributed to sufficiently satisfied criteria, 7 to more than sufficiently satisfied; 8 indicates a good level of satisfaction, 9 a very good level and 10 the maximum level of satisfaction with the criterion.

The assignment of scores within the evaluation matrix takes into account the aspects previously specified for each of the proposed design alternatives. The assessments carried out for each hypothesis of re-functionalization concerning the first-floor spaces of the building are described below.

For the conference rooms conversion option (alternative 1), the level of satisfaction with respect to the first criterion ("Net income") is considered acceptable, with a score of 5. This score is assigned by considering both the relatively low adaptation costs and the expected modest revenues, given the limited demand in the target market for conference spaces. Furthermore, this function is associated with a high level of risk ("Riskiness" criterion) due to the presence of the Diocesan Museum located in the municipality, which already includes five conference rooms with a capacity of up to 200 people, making the market nearly saturated.

With regard to the use "art exhibition spaces" (alternative 2), a score of 7 is assigned for the satisfaction of the first criterion ("Net income"). This score is given according to the presence of tourists in the city, and therefore potential of exhibition visitors. However, the costs associated with managing the lighting aspects linked to this use, are considered and covered in this score. The riskiness connected to this function is evaluated as high (with a normalized score of 2), in consideration of the presence of other buildings nearby that host permanent exhibitions, as well as additional facilities that offer their spaces for temporary exhibitions. The compliance with criteria 3 ("Structural compatibility") and 4 ("Compatibility with the historical and artistic features") for the proposed use is high, with scores of 9 and 8 respectively. Indeed, no significant structural modifications are foreseen that would affect the building's stability or compromise its historical and artistic value. The "Compatibility with the surrounding context" is likewise high (score of 10), given the presence of similar activities and services aligned with the tourist flows attracted by the exhibition function. Similarly, this intended use is assumed to be well-received by the local population, as it allows to maintain the access to the spaces and their use for activities recognized as culturally valuable.

The conversion of the building's spaces into coworking areas (alternative 3) is evaluated as moderately consistent with criterion 1 ("Net income"). In fact, although the implementation of this option does not require high adaptation costs, significant revenues are not expected. Consistent with this, the intervention's riskiness level (criterion 2) is considered relatively high (normalized score of 3), due to the presence of other coworking spaces in the same area, which are presumed to absorb nearly the entire market demand. No impactful transformations are provided for in terms of structural aspects or the building's historical and artistic features; therefore, the satisfaction of criteria 3 and 4 is evaluated as optimal, with a score of 10. The compatibility with the surrounding context (criterion 5) is considered more than sufficient (score of 7), as - despite the building's limited accessibility by private vehicles or public transportation - this type of activity is consistent with the uses in the surrounding area. The level of public appreciation (criterion 6) is assumed to be insufficient (score of 4), given that this function would effectively privatize the use of the building.

For the implementation of a restaurant or a cafeteria (alternative 4), the expected net income (criterion 1) is assessed as sufficient (score of 6), and the riskiness (criterion 2) associated with the conversion is evaluated with a normalized score of 4. These assessments are based on the significant expenses required for the transformation project, compared to the relatively modest expected revenues. Additionally, the presence of similar uses in the surrounding area is taken into account, although these have lower attractive potential as the analysed building is characterized by a high historical and artistic value. "Structural compatibility" levels are lower than those of the other alternatives (score of 7), as moderate structural impacts are planned. "Compatibility with the historical and artistic features" (criterion 4) is assessed as low (score of 5), since the designed modifications, the expected number of users, and exposure to fumes from typical restaurant activities may have negative effects on valuable architectural elements. For criterion 5 ("Compatibility with the surrounding context"), the maximum score is assigned, in light of the strong alignment with existing activities in the area. Similarly, the "Alignment with the interests of the local population" (criterion 6) is highly rated, as this option allows to maintain public access without privatizing the spaces.

With reference to the alternative "use as is" (alternative 5), that provides the absence of functional reconversion interventions and, thus, the current library intended use, a low score is assigned for expected "Net income" (score of 3). Indeed, while no transformation costs are involved, the building in its current state does not generate any revenue. Furthermore, this function is associated with a moderate riskiness (criterion 2), given the absence of other libraries within the territory. The "Structural compatibility", the "Compatibility the with the historical and artistic features" and "the surrounding context" (criteria 3, 4 and 5), are assessed as optimal, due to the lack of modifications or interventions that could impact the building's static or architectural integrity. In addition, a limited flow of users is assumed, along with the absence of activities that could potentially damage the valuable decorative elements. Moreover, the use of the building as a municipal library appears well-suited to the surrounding context and it is positively received by the local population (criterion 6), also thanks to a perception that has become well-established over time as public space.

The evaluation matrix of the criteria and alternatives is elaborated in the following Table 1.

4.4 Identification of the HBU

To identify the HBU, the determination of the synthetic numerical indicator, that is the TOPSIS closeness coefficient, is carried out. In particular, the coefficients obtained for each of the four different orders - depending on the type of applied normalization and the approach used to identify the ideal and anti-ideal solutions - point out that in three out of four cases, the HBU corresponds to the "coworking spaces" alternative (alternative 3). Only in one case the project solution to be preferred is the current intended use (alternative 5, i.e. "use as is"). In all scenarios, the "restaurant/cafeteria" option (alternative 4) ranks as the least favorable. The "coworking spaces" solution is highly compatible with structural and historical-architectural aspects (criteria 3 and 4), which

Table 1. Criteria and alternatives evaluation matrix

	j	1	2	3	4	5	6
i		Net income	Riskiness	Structural compatibility	Compatibility with the historical and artistic features	Compatibility with the surrounding context	Alignment with interests of the local population
	Weight	11%	7%	39%	28%	8%	7%
1	Conference rooms	4	2	10	10	6	4
2	Art exhibition spaces	7	2	9	8	10	10
3	Coworking spaces	5	3	10	10	7	4
4	Restaurant/ cafeteria	6	4	7	5	10	8
5	Use as is	3	5	10	10	9	9

are the most important (with respective weights of 39% and 28%) for achieving the set goal. In contrast, although the "restaurant/cafeteria" alternative aligns well with the context and community interest (criteria 5 and 6), it entails moderately impactful transformations on structural aspects and potential damages to historically and artistically valuable elements.

The adaptive reuse of the building as "art exhibition spaces" (alternative 2) is, in all four cases, considered a more favorable option than the creation of a restaurant/cafeteria, yet less preferable compared to the other three alternatives. This is due to the need to install systems and facilities to support exhibitions, which have an impact - although less severe than that caused by converting the spaces for restorative use - on structural elements and artistic features (i.e., criteria 3 and 4, which are the most influential). The maintenance of the current function (alternative 5) and the conversion into conference rooms (alternative 1) are evaluated as nearly equally valid solutions in two of the four orders, and similarly acceptable in the remaining cases. This outcome reflects analogous levels of compatibility with the criteria 3 and 4 (the most influential), and only moderately different values for the criteria related to compatibility with the context and population interests (criteria 5 and 6 that are less influential compared to the others), for which the non-transformation scenario is slightly more favorable. In Fig. 6 the orders obtained by the TOPSIS technique implementation are reported.

As previously mentioned, the selection of the HBU does not represent the identification of the best alternative in absolute terms, but rather a form of compromise that balances to the satisfaction of different selected criteria. In fact, the functional conversion of a historical building into coworking spaces presents certain limitations. In this sense, the expected net income may not adequately meet economic expectations and needs, especially when considering the associated risk levels of the intervention.

5 Results Analysis

The combination of the AHP and TOPSIS techniques offers a structured and balanced decision-making approach by integrating subjective judgments evaluated in the AHP with objective analysis carried on in the TOPSIS method. In particular, the AHP assign

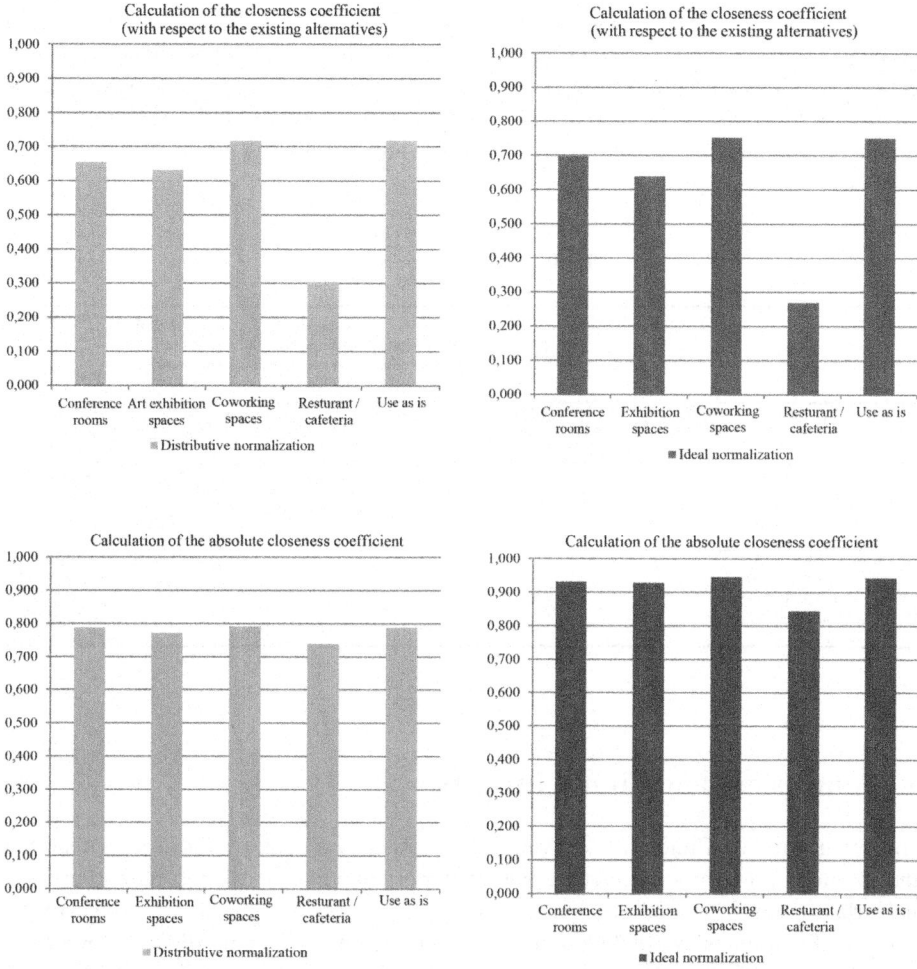

Fig. 6. Orders obtained by the TOPSIS technique implementation

criterion weights based on the decision maker's preferences, while TOPSIS uses normalized numerical and unbiased data to rank alternatives. The implementation of these two approaches, therefore, enhances the consistency and reliability of results integrating the DM preferences in a rigorous evaluation. Moreover, the AHP facilitates stakeholder participation, while TOPSIS ensures transparency through clear rankings. Together, they support participatory and data-driven decisions.

Despite these strengths, it is important to acknowledge some limitations. The main one, typical of the multicriterial approaches, derives from the subjectivity of the judgements expressed by the DM. Although this is partially overcome by i) the involvement of several stakeholders, ii) the use of the CI and iii) the normalization of the data typical of the TOPSIS method, subjectivity still remains an intrinsic aspect of these approaches.

Furthermore, through a correlation analysis (Table 2), a strong positive correlation has been identified between the criterion of compatibility with the historical and artistic features and that of structural compatibility, as well as between the criteria of compatibility with the surrounding context and alignment with interests of local population. These correlations suggest that certain criteria may provide information that are not sufficiently independent.

Table 2. Correlation matrix

	Net income	Riskiness	Structural compatibility	Compatibility with the historical and artistic features	Compatibility with surrounding context	Alignment with interests of the local population
Net income	1,00	-0,49	-0,61	-0,65	0,52	0,34
Riskiness		1,00	-0,18	-0,14	0,38	0,34
Structural compatibility			1,00	1,00	-0,68	-0,41
Compatibility with the historical and artistic features				1,00	-0,70	-0,44
Compatibility with surrounding context					1,00	0,92
Alignment with interests of the local population						1,00

6 Conclusions and Future Insights

The enhancement of underutilized real estate assets - particularly those with historical and architectural significance - represents an important opportunity to revitalize buildings and urban areas from both a social and economic perspective [19–22]. However, the scarcity of resources available to public administrations, which are often the owners of such properties, the constraints to ensure the heritage protection and the lack of interest from private investors - discouraged by restrictions on potential uses - make it challenging to define new functions that can give new life to these properties.

MCDA techniques allow to overcome these obstacles by establishing a shared platform among the various stakeholders involved in the valorisation process. In this research, through a case study focused on identifying the optimal use for a historic building located in a municipality in Southern Italy, the application of these tools in decision-making processes has been tested. Specifically, the implementation of two different multicriteria approaches (AHP and TOPSIS) has enabled to carry out a clear and transparent identification of the HBU by the DM, while reducing the uncertainty typically associated with such procedures and the resulting difficulties.

As described before, the combination of these two techniques in the present work has some limitations; indeed, while the consistency index and data normalization contribute into reducing subjectivity, the intrinsic subjectivity of multicriteria approaches, which may introduce bias, is still present. In addition to this critical issue the correlation matrix in Table 2 identifies a strong positive correlation between some of the criteria suggesting that provided information are not sufficiently independent. In the light of these considerations, future developments of this approach applied to the specific case study may include the quantitative definition of certain criteria, such as net income and investment riskiness (the latter being analysable through the study of volatility in similar investments). In fact, the inclusion of less subjective criteria and of indicators already used in academic works with similar purposes could contribute to a more robust and efficient evaluation based on accurate and reproducible calculation. Furthermore, through a more refined differentiation, reformulation, merging, or restructuring of these criteria the reduction of redundancy and improvement of the consistency of the DM choices could be obtained.

Note: The current study has been developed within the current research P.R.I.N. Project 2022: "INSPIRE—Improving Nature-Smart Policies through Innovative Resilient Evaluations", Grant number: 2022J7RWNF.

References

1. Ribera, F., Nesticò, P., Cucco, P., Maselli, G.: A multicriteria approach to identify the Highest and Best Use for historical buildings. J. Cult. Herit. **41**, 166–177 (2020)
2. Nesticò, A., Somma, P.: Comparative analysis of multi-criteria methods for the enhancement of historical buildings. Sustainability **11**(17), 4526 (2019)
3. Mısırlısoy, D., Günçe, K.: Adaptive reuse strategies for heritage buildings: a holistic approach. Sustain. Cities Soc. **26**, 91–98 (2016)
4. Locurcio, M., Morano, P., Tajani, F.: Un modello di supporto alle decisioni per la riconversione funzionale di immobili pubblici dismessi. LaborEst **13**, 28–33 (2016)
5. Chen, O., Han, D.: A participatory multiple criteria decision analysis to tackle a complex environmental problem involving cultural water heritage and nature. Water **10**(12), 1785 (2018)
6. Ferretti, V., Bottero, M., Mondini, G.: Decision making and cultural heritage: An application of the Multi-Attribute Value Theory for the reuse of historical buildings. J. Cult. Herit. **15**(6), 644–655 (2014)
7. Wang, H.J., Zeng, Z.T.: A multi-objective decision-making process for reuse selection of historic buildings. Expert Syst. Appl. **37**(2), 1241–1249 (2010)
8. Maselli, G., Cucco, P., Nesticò, A., Ribera, F.: Historical heritage–MultiCriteria Decision Method (H-MCDM) to prioritize intervention strategies for the adaptive reuse of valuable architectural assets. MethodsX **12**, 102487 (2024)
9. Cao, Z., Huang, L., Mao, Y., Mustafa, M., Isa, M.H.M.: Navigating complexity in sustainable conservation: a multi-criteria decision making of architectural heritage in urbanizing China. J. Build. Eng. 111906 (2025)
10. Della Spina, L.: Adaptive sustainable reuse for cultural heritage: a multiple criteria decision aiding approach supporting urban development processes. Sustainability **12**(4), 1363 (2020)
11. Pavlovskis, M., Migilinskas, D., Antucheviciene, J., Kutut, V.: Ranking of heritage building conversion alternatives by applying BIM and MCDM: a case of Sapieha Palace in Vilnius. Symmetry **11**(8), 973 (2019)
12. Claver, J., Sebastián, M.A., Sanz-Lobera, A.: Opportunities of the multicriteria methods in the study of immovable assets of the Spanish industrial heritage. Procedia Eng. **132**, 175–182 (2015)

13. Bottero, M., D'Alpaos, C., Oppio, A.: Ranking of adaptive reuse strategies for abandoned industrial heritage in vulnerable contexts: a multiple criteria decision aiding approach. Sustainability **11**(3), 785 (2019)
14. Mohamed, B., Marzouk, M.: Post-adaptive reuse evaluation of heritage buildings using multi-criteria decision-making techniques. J. Build. Eng. **99**, 111485 (2025)
15. Morano, P., Locurcio, M., Tajani, F.: Cultural heritage valorization: an application of AHP for the choice of the highest and best use. Procedia Soc. Behav. Sci. **223**, 952–959 (2016)
16. Carbonara, G.: Trattato di restauro architettonico. Terzo Aggiornamento. Grandi temi di restauro (2008)
17. Franceschi, S., Germani, L., Cruciani Fabozzi, G. Manuale operativo per il restauro architettonico. In: Manuale operativo per il restauro architettonico (2007)
18. Lazzarini, L., Laurenzi, T. M. Il restauro della pietra (2009)
19. Tajani, F., Morano, P., Di Liddo, F.: The optimal combinations of the eligible functions in multiple property assets enhancement. Land Use Policy **99**, 105050 (2020)
20. Morano, P., Tajani, F., Di Liddo, F., Amoruso, P.: The public role for the effectiveness of the territorial enhancement initiatives: a case study on the redevelopment of a building in disuse in an Italian small town. Buildings **11**(3), 87 (2021)
21. Tajani, F., Morano, P., Di Liddo, F., Locurcio, M.: An innovative interpretation of the DCFA evaluation criteria in the public-private partnership for the enhancement of the public property assets. In: New Metropolitan Perspectives: Local Knowledge and Innovation Dynamics Towards Territory Attractiveness Through the Implementation of Horizon/E2020/Agenda2030–Volume 1, pp. 305–313. Springer International Publishing (2019)
22. Tajani, F., Morano, P.: Concession and lease or sale? A model for the enhancement of public properties in disuse or underutilized. WSEAS Trans. Bus. Econ. **17**, 18 (2014)

Quantifying the Priceless: A Methodological Approach to the Evaluation of Historical-Architectural Heritage

Benedetto Manganelli[1(✉)], Francesco Tajani[2], Pierfrancesco De Paola[3], and Francesco Paolo Del Giudice[1]

[1] Department of Engineering, University of Basilicata, Ateneo Lucano Avenue 10, 85100 Potenza, Italy
{benedetto.manganelli,francesco.delgiudice}@unibas.it

[2] Department of Architecture and Design, Sapienza University of Rome, Via Flaminia 359, 00196 Rome, Italy
francesco.tajani@uniroma1.it

[3] Department of Industrial Engineering, University of Naples "Federico II", Vincenzo Tecchio Sq. 80, 80125 Naples, Italy
pierfrancesco.depaola@unina.it

Abstract. That humor is invaluable is absolutely evident, but that it is also a characteristic of a property, given the advances in the discipline of Real Estate Appraisal, is today more difficult to sustain. Today, the valuation of historical-architectural properties requires rigorous methodologies that go beyond merely qualitative and subjective approaches, moving toward valuation models capable of precisely quantifying the contribution that elements of historical value bring to the overall worth. The historical-architectural heritage of Italian cities, conceived as a resource to be preserved for future generations, requires adequate appraisal tools that recognize its intrinsic complexity, connected not only to the physical characteristics of the property but also to its cultural context and its ability to generate positive externalities. The methodological challenge consists of integrating both tangible and intangible aspects into the valuation analysis, developing models that can be applied with consistency and scientific rigor even in contexts characterized by high variability and specificity, such as properties used for tourism and hospitality. This research analyzes the impact of historical-architectural value on the market value of properties used for tourism and hospitality, with specific regard to the city of Rome. Unlike previous studies, where econometric models were implemented with reference to samples of historical price data, in this case the analysis will reference samples of forecast data concerning the profitability of hospitality structures characterized by different historical-architectural values. The adopted methodology integrates the Analytic Hierarchy Process (AHP) with multiple linear regression models, allowing consideration of both qualitative and quantitative variables in real estate valuation.

Keywords: Historical–architectural significance · Marginal prices · Property values

1 Introduction

The historical-architectural heritage of Italian cities represents an invaluable treasure that encapsulates the essence of human cultural evolution. Through its physical manifestations – tangible works created over centuries – it embodies social values of extraordinary uniqueness and relevance. The definition of real estate property with historical and architectural significance goes beyond the simple cataloging of museum buildings or places of worship, extending to entire neighborhoods of historical importance. This heritage constitutes an inheritance not oriented toward the market but rather conceived as precious capital to be preserved for present and future generations [1]. The evaluation of such "special assets" presents numerous complexities, deriving not only from the intrinsic nature of the property, but also from its broader natural and cultural context, from its ability to attract visitors, as well as from its contribution to socioeconomic and sustainable development. The valuation of real estate property with historical-architectural significance presents significant challenges on the methodological level. To determine the most probable market value, it is necessary to identify and make explicit the specific contribution that historical and architectural elements bring to the overall value [2]. The appraisal process requires solving three distinct problems: *i)* accurate measurement of the qualitative and quantitative characteristics of the property being appraised; *ii)* their appropriate weighting; *iii)* determination of the marginal price attributable to specific qualitative and quantitative variables. Only through an analysis that methodically addresses these three dimensions is it possible to arrive at an estimate that adequately reflects the market value of a property with historical-architectural significance. The literature has already defined the marginal contribution of historical-architectural value for properties used purely for residential purposes. This study intends instead to determine this contribution with specific regard to properties used for tourism and hospitality, evaluating the weight that this variable under study assumes in the formation of the most probable market value [3]. Unlike studies conducted until now, where econometric models were implemented with reference to samples of historical data (prices), in this case such analysis will reference samples of forecast data (the values of hotel rooms) concerning the profitability of hospitality structures characterized by different historical-architectural values. In this way, arriving at the estimate of the marginal contribution of the value under study, in terms of willingness to pay by users of such structures. The methodology used combines the AHP (Analytic Hierarchy Process) multicriteria analysis, which employs the pairwise comparison developed by T.L. Saaty, with multiple linear regression models to incorporate both qualitative and quantitative property characteristics in the estimation. The case study focuses on the city of Rome, a capital with high tourist flow and numerous hotels of historical interest. The results of the study will constitute a valid evaluative reference for resolving valuation issues related to properties with different historical-architectural values. The study develops through a methodical and coherent path, structured in the following sections: the Sect 2 is dedicated to an in-depth analysis of the scientific literature concerning the impact of historical-architectural component on property values, both from an intrinsic point of view, understood as the weight that such value assumes in relation to the value of the individual property, and from an extrinsic point of view, understood as externalities - positive or negative - that the neighborhood as a historical district exerts on the value of properties within it. The Sect. 3

presents the methodological model developed for the research. The integrated approach that combines the Analytic Hierarchy Process (AHP) with multiple linear regression is illustrated, highlighting how this integration allows for capturing both qualitative and quantitative aspects of the evaluation. The Sect. 4 presents the empirical results obtained from applying the model to the Rome case study. The Sect. 5 gathers the conclusions of the study, synthesizing the main theoretical and practical contributions of the research, as well as outlining the future research developments.

2 Literature Review

In the following section, a comprehensive overview is presented of the main literature concerning the impact of historical-architectural component on the market value of residential properties. The analysis is structured on two levels: *i)* the first considers the influence of this characteristic on the value of the individual property; *ii)* the second explores the "spatial effects" – the positive or negative externalities – that neighborhoods of historical-architectural significance generate on property values, the latter being devoid of the studied value but falling within the perimeter of historical districts. The investigation aims, therefore, to define the impact in percentage terms of the historical-architectural significance both from a purely intrinsic point of view, referring to the individual property, and from an extrinsic point of view, connected to the dynamics of valorization that the historical district exerts on the properties that belong to it.

2.1 Intrinsic Effects of Historical-Architectural Significance on Property Values

The American context offers a rich panorama of empirical studies documenting how the architectural style and historical designation of properties positively influence their market value, highlighting a clear economic premium associated with these characteristics. Asabere et al. (1989) conducted a pioneering study in Newburyport, Massachusetts, analyzing 520 properties from 1983–1985. The research demonstrated that Garrison, Federal, Victorian, and Colonial architectural styles generate substantial premiums on property values, with increases around 20–21%. The authors conclude that buyers are willing to pay higher prices for architecturally significant buildings compared to similar but stylistically inferior structures [4]. Expanding the research to a territorial level, Leichenko et al. (2001) extended the analysis to nine Texas cities, finding that historical designation produces positive effects on property values in all locations examined. The increases range from 4,9% in Dallas (equivalent to about $3.200 per property) to 20,1% in Nacogdoches, with San Antonio recording an increase of 18,6% (equivalent to an average property value increase of $8.900) [5]. Bergen (2015) examined the impact of historical-architectural significance in Tacoma, Washington, where single-family properties historically designated at the local level by the Tacoma Register of Historic Places show an average market value increase of 12,35%, corresponding to an average property value increase of about $23.600. To obtain such designation, properties must be at least 50 years old and maintain a significant original context [6]. In the historic city of Atlanta, Georgia, Oba et al. (2017) analyzed the impact of local historical designation on property values from 2000–2010, highlighting an average market value increase of 12,1%

[7]. In the same state, Cebula (2009) documented a more modest but still positive effect of 1,7% for nationally designated properties in Savannah [8]. In California, Narwold et al. (2008) studied the impact of local historical designation on single-family home values in San Diego from 2000–2006, estimating a price differential of 16% between properties covered by Mills Act contracts and those with similar characteristics but without such designation [9]. In Abilene, Texas, Coulson et al. (2001) examined a large sample of approximately 7.600 single-family properties, of which 160 were historically designated at the local level. Results indicate a market value increase of 17,6% compared to non-designated properties, equivalent to about $7.040 on a $40.000 property [5]. In Baton Rouge, Louisiana, Zahirovic-Herbert et al. (2012) evaluated the effects of historical-architectural significance on single-family residential property values using real estate transaction data from 1984 to 2005, finding increases between 5% and 8% [10]. In the northeastern United States, Vandell et al. (1989) examined the impact of historical-architectural significance on single-family home values in Boston and Cambridge, Massachusetts, documenting a notable market value increase of 22% [11]. The Australian continent offers further evidence of the studied phenomenon. Jeffries (2012) analyzed the impact of historical-architectural significance in Mosman, one of Sydney's oldest and most prestigious suburbs, finding that locally historically designated properties record an average market value increase of 17,9% [12]. In contrast, some research has shown that this studied value can also cause a decrease in property market value, highlighting the complex and multifaceted nature of the phenomenon. Not surprisingly, Asabere et al. (1994) documented a negative impact of local historical designation on property values in Philadelphia, with a 24% reduction for properties located in condominiums. This negative effect is attributed to excessively rigid and restrictive programs, limited state incentives [13].

2.2 Extrinsic Effects of Historical-Architectural Significance on Property Values

The designation of neighborhoods as historical districts generates complex and sometimes contradictory effects on property values, with dynamics that vary significantly depending on the level of recognition - national or local - and the specific regulations in different territorial contexts. Research conducted in various US metropolitan areas shows that the national designation of a historical district generally tends to produce a significant appreciation in property values. In Atlanta, properties located within national historical districts registered an average increase of 15% in their market value [14], while in Savannah, Georgia, residential properties in the Savannah Historic Landmark District benefited from an increase of 20–21% [8]. Similarly, in Philadelphia, Pennsylvania, national recognition resulted in an appreciation of 26% [15], and in Chicago, Illinois, the Ridge Historic District saw increases of 24%, with peaks of 53% in the historic districts of Longwood Drive and 104th Place [16]. These positive effects primarily derive from the prestige conferred by national recognition and the related tax benefits. The picture appears more complex when considering locally designated historical districts. In Atlanta, such properties experienced an average reduction of 3% in their market value [14], while in Massachusetts (Boston, Cambridge, and Quincy), local designation is associated with decreases between 11,6% and 15,5% [17]. In Illinois (Aurora and Elgin), on the contrary, increases of 6–7% were recorded [18], and in six different

US locations (Atlanta, Dallas, Phoenix, Cincinnati, Cleveland, and Pittsburgh), a study found an average increase of 9,5% [19]. The divergence in results reflects the diversity of local regulations: particularly severe and restrictive regulations can lead to a devaluation of properties, while policies that balance conservation constraints with adequate tax incentives tend to produce positive effects. The complex relationship between historical designation and property values finds further confirmation in the analysis of emblematic cases such as Louisville (Kentucky), Sacramento (California) and Washington DC, whose peculiarities illustrate the multiple facets of the phenomenon. Kentucky, considered among the national leaders in the preservation of historically significant buildings, represents a paradigmatic case of how targeted policies can generate particularly beneficial effects on market values. The city of Louisville, founded in 1778 and rich in architectural testimonies of the past, hosts numerous historical districts, including Old Louisville, the nation's largest Victorian-era neighborhood. The peculiarity of the Kentucky context lies in the system of federal tax incentives for national-level historical designation, coordinated by the Kentucky Heritage Council, which provides state tax credits of 30% for residential properties and 20% for commercial ones on rehabilitation and conservation investments. Since 1976, this policy has allowed the restoration of approximately 34.000 structures located within national historical districts, with a total investment of over $40 billion. The effectiveness of these measures is confirmed by the average 58% increase in market value of properties located in Louisville's ten nationally designated neighborhoods, examined in the period 2000–2006 [20]. Similarly, Sacramento's Conservation Program, established in 1975, illustrates how rigorous regulations can translate into property appreciation when accompanied by adequate tax incentives. The program, aimed at protecting structures built between 1848 and 1920, imposes significant restrictions on external alterations of buildings, regulating building materials, color tones, and architectural details. At the same time, it provides reductions of up to 20% in taxes for owners for improvements made to properties dating before 1936. This balanced approach between constraints and incentives has resulted, as evidenced by a 1997 study, in an average increase of 17,32% in the market value of properties located within Sacramento's six historical districts, suggesting the predominance of positive externalities over negative ones derived from strict restrictions [21]. The case of Washington, DC also offers a further perspective on the impact of historical-architectural significance in relation to building typology. From the first historical district of Georgetown, designated in 1950, the federal capital has progressively extended protection to include 37 historical districts, which currently comprise 4,2% of the city's residential properties. An analysis of real estate sales between 1992 and 2019 revealed that, while single-family properties and townhouses located within historical neighborhoods register an average increase in market value of 9%, condominiums experience an average reduction of 6,3%. This divergence is attributed to the higher maintenance costs associated with condominiums and their lesser historical-architectural significance, being generally more recent buildings compared to single-family properties [22].

3 Methodology

The present study has developed a logical-evaluative model capable of addressing the problem concerning the measurement and weighting of qualitative variables, allowing for the explicit determination of the monetary value of the historical-architectural significance of real estate properties.

The methodological development of the model is articulated in three distinct phases:

I. Definition of the research scope and selection of the data sample under study, composed of thirteen properties for tourist-hospitality use classified as historical by "Federalberghi Rome" and their comparable units. For the entire data sample, the most probable market value of the hotel room was determined through a direct monoparametric estimation procedure.
II. Development of a questionnaire submitted to experts in the field, invited to evaluate the thirteen historical properties according to four criteria defined based on the reference literature. The criteria were subsequently weighted through the implementation of the AHP (Analytic Hierarchy Process) method.
III. Application of a specific econometric analysis, based on the hedonic pricing technique, aimed at determining the marginal contribution made by the historical-architectural significance in the formation of the property price.

3.1 Data Sample

Assuming that the purpose of the work is to explicitly determine the monetary value of the historical-architectural characteristic of real estate properties, that is, the "weight" that this variable assumes in the formation of the property's market value, the preliminary phase of the analysis consists of defining an appraisal sample that includes both properties of historical significance and comparable structures lacking this value. The sample of historical properties consists of thirteen hotel structures recognized as having particular historical value by the Historical Hotels Committee of "Federalberghi Rome" and listed on the tourist portal of the city of Rome: *1. Eitch Borromini, 2. Hotel Vilòn, 3. Donna Camilla Savelli, 4. Hotel Principe Torlonia, 5. Villa Laetitia Roma, 6. Albergo Del Sole Al Pantheon, 7. Grand Hotel De La Minerve, 8. Albergo D'Inghilterra, 9. Grand Hotel Plaza, 10. Hotel Hassler Villa Medici, 11. Hotel Ambasciatori Palace, 12. Hotel Eden, 13. The St. Regis Rome.* To obtain the designation of "historical hotel" from "Federalberghi Rome", a structure must satisfy the following requirements: *i) Construction date*, the hotel must have been operational at least since 1950 and situated in a building of notable historical-architectural significance, generally built no less than seventy years ago. *ii) Historical-cultural relevance*, the structure must possess significant historical value, such as having hosted events of local or national importance, illustrious personalities, or having been designed by renowned architects. *iii) Preservation of authenticity*, the property must preserve intact the original architectural and decorative elements representative of a specific historical period or distinctive architectural style. *iv) Privileged location*, the hotel must be located in an area of the city of particular historical or cultural relevance. For evaluation purposes, for each property used as a hotel designated as historically significant, a variable number of comparables was considered, from a minimum of one to a maximum of seven units, for a total of forty-one comparable properties. Overall, the data sample, including both historical hotels and "comparable" properties lacking significance, consists of fifty-four properties (see Table 1). The comparable properties were selected based on specific productive characteristics, such as the hotel's star rating (taken as a proxy variable for the services offered by the structure); intrinsic positional characteristics, such as the advertised area of suites expressed in square meters (sqm); extrinsic positional characteristics, such as macro-location in homogeneous territorial zones (OMI zone); technological characteristics related to the state of preservation and maintenance of the property.

Determination of Individual Hotel Room Value

Once the data sample was selected, the market value of the individual hotel room was estimated for the fifty-four properties through a direct monoparametric procedure. This was done to provide an econometric measure of the higher price paid for a room offered by a historical accommodation structure compared to a similar one without that significance. For the purpose of estimating the market value of the hotel room, it was necessary to previously define the *gross annual revenue of the room* (R_{LC}), obtained as the product of: the average cost of the room (C_c) calculated as the average between low, medium and high season rates; the annual occupancy rate (t_0), which varies depending on the number of stars of the hotel, and the number of days in the year.

Therefore:

$$R_{LC} = C_C \cdot t_0 \cdot 365 \qquad (1)$$

This gross annual revenue of the room must then be multiplied by a rate (k) that expresses the remuneration due to the property owner (remuneration of real estate capital), thus obtaining the *gross rental value* or the market rental rate of the room (V_{LC}):

$$V_{LC} = R_{LC} \cdot k \qquad (2)$$

Finally, to estimate the market value of the hotel room (V_C), the aforementioned gross rental value must be "capitalized" using a suitable rate (r_c):

$$V_C = V_{LC}/r_c \qquad (3)$$

In this way, we arrive at the determination of the values attributable to the rooms of historically designated hotels and comparable similar structures. (see Table 2).

3.2 Implementation of the AHP Method

In the second phase, a questionnaire was submitted to sector experts to evaluate, according to four appropriate criteria (defined based on the reference literature), the data sample consisting of only thirteen hotels with historical-architectural significance located in the city of Rome. Obviously, the "weight" that each of these criteria can express in the experts' judgment is capable of influencing the value differences found between historically designated properties and properties lacking this characteristic. Objectifying this weight becomes fundamental for the purpose of estimating these value differences. In other words, it becomes essential to establish a set of rules that make transparent

Table 1. Summary of historical units with their comparable units.

Historical units	Comparable unit 1	Comparable unit 2	Comparable unit 3	Comparable unit 4	Comparable unit 5	Comparable unit 6	Comparable unit 7
1. Eitch Borromini	Lifestyle Suites Rome	Bio Hotel Raphael	–	–	–	–	–
2. Hotel Vilòn	Fendi Private Suites	Hotel J.K. Place Roma	–	–	–	–	–
3. Donna Camilla Savelli	Hotel Horti 14 Borgo Trastevere	Hotel la Rovere	–	–	–	–	–
4. Hotel Principe Torlonia	Mercure Roma Corso Trieste	Hotel Villa Torlonia	Hotel Fenix	–	–	–	–
5. Villa Laetitia Roma	Albergo Etico Roma	Roma in una stanza	Ferrari Home – Guesthouse	–	–	–	–
6. Albergo Del Sole Al Pantheon	Pantheon Royal Suite	Hotel Pantheon	Hub Pantheon	Terrace Pantheon Relais	–	–	–
7. Grand Hotel De La Minerve	The Pantheon Iconic Rome Hotel	Singer Palace Hotel	–	–	–	–	–
8. Albergo D'Inghilterra	Portrait Roma	–	–	–	–	–	–
9. Grand Hotel Plaza	Fendi Private Suites	J.K. Place Roma	The First Roma Dolce	–	–	–	–
10. Hotel Hassler Villa Medici	Hotel de la Ville	–	–	–	–	–	–
11. Hotel Ambasciatori Palace	Hotel Sofitel Roma Villa Borghese	Baglioni Hotel Regina	Hotel The Westin Excelsior	Grand Hotel Palace	Aleph Rome Hotel	Hotel Sina Bernini Bristol	Hotel Splendide Royal
12. Hotel Eden	Hotel The Westin Excelsior	Aleph Rome Hotel	Hotel Splendide Royal	Hotel Sofitel Roma Villa Borghese	Baglioni Hotel Regina	Grand Hotel Palace	Hotel Sina Bernini Bristol
13. The St. Regis Rome	Baglioni Hotel Regina	Hotel The Westin Excelsior Roma	Hotel Sina Bernini Bristol	Hotel Splendide Royal	–	–	–

the process of assigning weights to the evaluation criteria considered in the questionnaire. This set of rules should conform to the typical approach of non-monetary evaluation techniques often used to support decision-making processes involving goods and resources characterized by qualitative aspects [23, 24]. For this reason, the evaluative approach underlying the "multicriteria" analysis technique called Analytic Hierarchy

Quantifying the Priceless   371

Table 2. Summary of individual hotel room values for historical units and their comparable units.

Historical units	V(x)	V(x) Comparable unit 1	V(x) Comparable unit 2	V(x) Comparable unit 3	V(x) Comparable unit 4	V(x) Comparable unit 5	V(x) Comparable unit 6	V(x) Comparable unit 7
1. Eitch Borromini	€ **1.073.627,79**	€ 891.064,30	€ 909.264,73	–	–	–	–	–
2. Hotel Vilòn	€ **2.465.550,94**	€ 1.512.934,64	€ 1.959.648,39	–	–	–	–	–
3. Donna Camilla Savelli	€ **555.595,49**	€ 372.154,06	€ 214.806,26	–	–	–	–	–
4. Hotel Principe Torlonia	€ **444.669,38**	€ 175.615,04	€ 188.729,16	€ 115.461,16	–	–	–	–
5. Villa Laetitia Roma	€ **257.964,84**	€ 111.985,18	€ 70.430,87	€ 61.846,55	–	–	–	–
6. Albergo Del Sole Al Pantheon	€ **615.207,98**	€ 261.384,23	€ 478.473,16	€ 285.564,60	€ 289.941,40	–	–	–
7. Grand Hotel De La Minerve	€ **1.058.906,86**	€ 866.597,30	€ 674.295,89	–	–	–	–	–
8. Albergo D'Inghilterra	€ **1.086.738,76**	€ 842.141,36	–	–	–	–	–	–
9. Grand Hotel Plaza	€ **5.129.161,02**	€ 1.512.940,48	€ 1.959.654,22	€ 1.279.236,05	–	–	–	–
10. Hotel Hassler Villa Medici	€ **982.207,31**	€ 856.711,28	–	–	–	–	–	–
11. Hotel Ambasciatori Palace	€ **1.043.948,80**	€ 671.951,86	€ 839.011,72	€ 846.436,61	€ 599.243,71	€ 680.304,86	€ 821.377,63	€ 881.704,80
12. Hotel Eden	€ **1.014.046,33**	€ 846.436,61	€ 680.304,86	€ 881.704,80	€ 671.951,86	€ 839.011,72	€ 599.243,71	€ 821.377,63
13. The St. Regis Rome	€ **5.366.540,09**	€ 839.011,72	€ 846.436,61	€ 821.377,63	€ 881.704,80	–	–	–

Process (AHP), which uses pairwise comparison, appears entirely suitable for "weighting" the criteria considered. The implementation of a model whose formalization is based on the pairwise comparison technique has made it possible to transform qualitative variables, apparently expressible only on nominal or ordinal scales, into variables measurable on interval scales. The advantages of this approach lie in the creation of a flexible and universally valid logical-evaluative framework, optimally adaptable to specific decision-making contexts. From an operational point of view, four criteria were defined to encompass the peculiarities or distinctive characteristics of the historical properties examined: *i) Historical-Artistic Importance Criterion*, criterion related to the building's connection with historical events or famous guests who have stayed there; *ii) Architect*

Criterion, criterion related to the prestige of the Architect who designed and/or oversaw the construction of the building; *iii) Preservation of Original Appearance Criterion*, criterion related to the preservation of the original appearance of the building and the significant elements that reflect its history; *iv) Cultural Importance Criterion*, criterion related to the integration of the hotel with the surrounding architectural and cultural context. Therefore, pairwise comparison was applied to the thirteen tourist accommodation properties under study, with reference to the four criteria. The results obtained, the product of a series of multiple comparisons based on subjective judgments formulated by sector experts - particularly architects - can be summarized in a matrix, called the *ratio matrix* or *pairwise comparison matrix*.

In particular, four ratio matrices are defined, each associated with one of the established criteria (Figs. 1, 2, 3 and 4):

A - Historical-Artistic Importance Criterion													
	H1	H2	H3	H4	H5	H6	H7	H8	H9	H10	H11	H12	H13
H1	1	9	7	3	9	1	7	3	5	9	5	7	3
H2	0,111	1	3	0,143	5	0,143	0,143	0,143	0,143	5	0,2	3	0,111
H3	0,143	0,333	1	0,143	3	0,111	0,111	0,143	0,2	0,333	0,333	3	0,1429
H4	0,333	7	7	1	7	0,143	0,143	3	3	5	3	7	0,2
H5	0,111	0,2	0,333	0,143	1	0,111	0,111	0,143	0,143	0,2	0,143	0,333	0,143
H6	1	7	9	7	9	1	3	5	5	7	5	7	3
H7	1	7	9	7	9	0,333	1	3	5	5	1	5	7
H8	0,333	7	7	0,333	7	0,2	0,333	1	3	5	7	0,2	7	0,2
H9	0,2	7	5	0,333	7	0,2	0,2	0,2	1	5	0,333	7	0,2
H10	0,2	0,2	3	0,2	5	0,143	0,2	0,143	0,2	1	0,143	3	0,111
H11	0,2	5	3	0,333	7	0,2	1	5	3	7	1	7	0,333
H12	0,143	0,333	0,333	0,143	3	0,143	0,143	0,143	0,143	0,333	0,143	1	0,111
H13	0,333	9	7	5	7	0,333	0,333	5	5	9	3	9	1

Fig. 1. Matrix A synthesizes the pairwise comparisons between the thirteen historically significant tourist accommodation properties, examined in relation to the Historical-Artistic Importance criterion.

B Architect Criterion													
	H1	H2	H3	H4	H5	H6	H7	H8	H9	H10	H11	H12	H13
H1	1	3	1	5	7	9	9	5	5	9	7	9	7
H2	0,333	1	0,333	3	7	9	9	5	9	9	7	9	5
H3	1	3	1	5	7	9	9	5	9	9	7	9	7
H4	0,2	0,143	0,2	1	7	9	9	3	9	9	5	9	3
H5	0,143	0,143	0,143	0,143	1	9	9	0,2	3	9	0,333	3	0,2
H6	0,111	0,111	0,111	0,111	0,111	1	1	0,111	1	1	0,111	0,111	0,111
H7	0,111	0,111	0,111	0,111	0,111	1	1	0,111	1	1	0,111	0,111	0,111
H8	0,2	0,2	0,2	0,333	5	9	9	1	7	9	5	7	3
H9	0,111	0,111	0,111	0,111	0,333	1	1	0,143	1	1	0,2	0,333	0,143
H10	0,111	0,111	0,111	0,111	0,111	1	1	0,111	1	1	0,111	0,111	0,111
H11	0,143	0,143	0,143	0,2	3	9	9	0,2	5	9	1	5	0,333
H12	0,111	0,111	0,111	0,111	0,333	9	9	0,143	3	9	0,2	1	0,2
H13	0,143	0,2	0,143	0,333	5	9	9	0,333	7	9	3	5	1

Fig. 2. Matrix B synthesizes the pairwise comparisons between the thirteen historically significant tourist accommodation properties, examined in relation to the Architect criterion.

At this point, to calculate the weights w of the four criteria, the elements of the ratio matrices were normalized by dividing the same elements by their sum, thus obtaining matrices characterized by the reciprocal property (Figs. 5, 6, 7, and 8):

Subsequently, the "weights" of each individual criterion were calculated as the ratio between the sum of the row elements and the sum of all elements of the normalized matrix, arriving at the determination of the weight related to the four criteria for each of the thirteen hotels under study (Fig. 9):

Quantifying the Priceless

C - Preservation of Original Appearance Criterion

	H1	H2	H3	H4	H5	H6	H7	H8	H9	H10	H11	H12	H13
H1	1	7	5	9	7	7	5	3	0,333	5	5	7	0,2
H2	0,143	1	0,333	5	5	0,2	3	0,333	0,143	3	3	5	0,143
H3	0,2	3	1	7	5	3	3	0,2	0,143	3	3	5	0,143
H4	0,111	0,2	0,143	1	0,200	0,143	0,2	0,143	0,111	0,2	0,2	0,333	0,111
H5	0,143	0,2	0,2	5	1	0,2	3	0,143	0,111	0,2	0,2	3	0,111
H6	0,143	5	0,333	7	5	1	5	0,333	0,143	5	5	7	0,143
H7	0,2	0,333	0,333	5	0,333	0,2	1	0,143	0,1	0,2	0,2	3	0,111
H8	0,333	3	5	7	7	3	7	1	0,2	5	5	7	0,143
H9	3	7	7	9	9	7	7	5	1	7	7	9	0,333
H10	0,2	0,333	0,333	5	5	0,2	5	0,2	0,143	1	1	5	0,143
H11	0,2	0,333	0,333	5	5	0,2	3	0,2	0,143	1	1	5	0,143
H12	0,143	0,2	0,2	3	0,333	0,143	0,333	0,143	0,111	0,2	0,2	1	0,111
H13	5	7	7	9	9	7	9	7	3	7	7	9	1

Fig. 3. Matrix C synthesizes the pairwise comparisons between the thirteen historically significant tourist accommodation properties, examined in relation to the Preservation of Original Appearance criterion.

D - Cultural Importance Criterion

	H1	H2	H3	H4	H5	H6	H7	H8	H9	H10	H11	H12	H13
H1	1	5	7	9	7	3	5	5	5	1	5	5	7
H2	0,2	1	7	7	7	0,2	5	0,333	0,333	0,143	5	5	5
H3	0,143	0,143	1	3	0,333	0,143	0,143	0,143	0,143	0,111	0,143	0,143	0,2
H4	0,111	0,143	0,333	1	0,333	0,143	0,143	0,143	0,143	0,111	0,143	0,143	0,2
H5	0,143	0,143	3	3	1	0,143	0,143	0,143	0,143	0,111	0,143	0,143	0,2
H6	0,333	5	7	7	7	1	3	5	3	0,2	5	3	7
H7	0,333	5	7	7	7	0,333	1	3	0,333	0,2	5	5	7
H8	0,2	3	7	7	7	0,2	0,333	1	0,333	0,2	5	5	7
H9	0,2	3	7	7	7	0,333	3	3	1	0,2	7	7	9
H10	1	7	9	9	9	5	5	5	5	1	5	7	9
H11	0,2	0,2	7	7	7	0,2	0,2	0,2	0,143	0,2	1	3	5
H12	0,2	0,2	7	7	7	0,2	0,2	0,2	0,143	0,143	0,333	1	5
H13	0,143	0,2	5	5	5	0,143	0,143	0,143	0,111	0,111	0,2	0,2	1

Fig. 4. Matrix D synthesizes the pairwise comparisons between the thirteen historically significant tourist accommodation properties, examined in relation to the Cultural Importance criterion.

A - Normalized matrix

	H1	H2	H3	H4	H5	H6	H7	H8	H9	H10	H11	H12	H13
H1	0,196	0,150	0,114	0,121	0,114	0,246	0,130	0,116	0,152	0,088	0,256	0,102	0,260
H2	0,022	0,017	0,049	0,006	0,063	0,035	0,019	0,006	0,004	0,088	0,010	0,044	0,010
H3	0,028	0,006	0,016	0,006	0,038	0,027	0,014	0,006	0,006	0,006	0,017	0,044	0,012
H4	0,065	0,117	0,114	0,040	0,089	0,035	0,019	0,116	0,091	0,088	0,154	0,102	0,017
H5	0,022	0,003	0,005	0,006	0,013	0,027	0,014	0,006	0,004	0,004	0,007	0,005	0,012
H6	0,196	0,117	0,146	0,283	0,114	0,246	0,389	0,193	0,152	0,123	0,256	0,102	0,260
H7	0,196	0,117	0,146	0,283	0,114	0,082	0,130	0,116	0,152	0,088	0,051	0,102	0,260
H8	0,065	0,117	0,114	0,013	0,089	0,049	0,043	0,039	0,152	0,123	0,010	0,102	0,017
H9	0,039	0,117	0,081	0,013	0,089	0,049	0,026	0,008	0,030	0,088	0,017	0,102	0,017
H10	0,039	0,003	0,049	0,008	0,063	0,035	0,026	0,006	0,006	0,018	0,007	0,044	0,010
H11	0,039	0,083	0,049	0,013	0,089	0,049	0,130	0,193	0,091	0,123	0,051	0,102	0,029
H12	0,028	0,006	0,005	0,006	0,038	0,035	0,019	0,006	0,004	0,006	0,007	0,015	0,010
H13	0,065	0,150	0,114	0,202	0,089	0,082	0,043	0,193	0,152	0,158	0,154	0,132	0,087
	1	1	1	1	1	1	1	1	1	1	1	1	1

Fig. 5. Normalized matrix of ratios for the Historical-Artistic Importance criterion.

Finally, the quality of the weight estimation was verified in terms of measuring the consistency of the ratio matrices A, B, C, D. The pairwise comparison matrix is consistent only if the maximum eigenvalue λ_{max} is equal to the order of the matrix n. A small error in the estimation of the ratios results in a variation of λ_{max}, where the deviation of the latter from n involves an inconsistency error that can be represented by the ratio $(\lambda_{max} - n)/(n - 1)$, defined as the *consistency index* (C.I.). Therefore, once the consistency index (C.I.) has been calculated using the maximum eigenvalue (λ_{max}) for

B - Normalized matrix

	H1	H2	H3	H4	H5	H6	H7	H8	H9	H10	H11	H12	H13
H1	0,2690009	0,3498704	0,2690009	0,3212319	0,1627907	0,1058824	0,1058824	0,2456715	0,1384615	0,1058824	0,194085	0,1560694	0,2572629
H2	0,089667	0,1166235	0,089667	0,1927391	0,1627907	0,1058824	0,1058824	0,2456715	0,1384615	0,1058824	0,194085	0,1560694	0,1837592
H3	0,2690009	0,3498704	0,2690009	0,3212319	0,1627907	0,1058824	0,1058824	0,2456715	0,1384615	0,1058824	0,194085	0,1560694	0,2572629
H4	0,0538002	0,0388745	0,0538002	0,0642464	0,1627907	0,1058824	0,1058824	0,1474029	0,1384615	0,1058824	0,1386322	0,1560694	0,1102555
H5	0,0384287	0,0166605	0,0384287	0,0091781	0,0232558	0,1058824	0,1058824	0,0098269	0,0461538	0,1058824	0,0092421	0,0520231	0,0073504
H6	0,029889	0,0129582	0,029889	0,0071385	0,002584	0,0117647	0,0117647	0,0054594	0,0153846	0,0117647	0,0030807	0,0019268	0,0040835
H7	0,029889	0,0129582	0,029889	0,0071385	0,002584	0,0117647	0,0117647	0,0054594	0,0153846	0,0117647	0,0030807	0,0019268	0,0040835
H8	0,0538002	0,0233247	0,0538002	0,0214155	0,1162791	0,1058824	0,1058824	0,0491343	0,1076923	0,1058824	0,1386322	0,1213873	0,1102555
H9	0,029889	0,0129582	0,029889	0,0071385	0,0077519	0,0117647	0,0117647	0,0070192	0,0153846	0,0117647	0,0055453	0,0057803	0,0052503
H10	0,029889	0,0129582	0,029889	0,0071385	0,002584	0,0117647	0,0117647	0,0054594	0,0153846	0,0117647	0,0030807	0,0019268	0,0040835
H11	0,0384287	0,0166605	0,0384287	0,0128493	0,0697674	0,1058824	0,1058824	0,0098269	0,0769231	0,1058824	0,0277264	0,0867052	0,0122506
H12	0,029889	0,0129582	0,029889	0,0071385	0,0077519	0,1058824	0,1058824	0,0070192	0,0461538	0,1058824	0,0055453	0,017341	0,0073504
H13	0,0384287	0,0233247	0,0384287	0,0214155	0,1162791	0,1058824	0,1058824	0,0163781	0,1076923	0,1058824	0,0831793	0,0867052	0,0367518
	1	1	1	1	1	1	1	1	1	1	1	1	1

Fig. 6. Normalized matrix of ratios for the Architect criterion.

C - Normalized matrix

	H1	H2	H3	H4	H5	H6	H7	H8	H9	H10	H11	H12	H13
H1	0,0924567	0,2023121	0,1837592	0,1168831	0,1189128	0,2390244	0,0933998	0,1681794	0,0582363	0,1322751	0,1322751	0,1055276	0,0705487
H2	0,0132081	0,0289017	0,0122506	0,0649351	0,0849377	0,0068293	0,0560399	0,0186866	0,0249584	0,0793651	0,0793651	0,0753769	0,0503919
H3	0,0184913	0,0867052	0,0367518	0,0909091	0,0849377	0,102439	0,0560399	0,011212	0,0249584	0,0793651	0,0793651	0,0753769	0,0503919
H4	0,010273	0,0057803	0,0052503	0,012987	0,0033975	0,004878	0,003736	0,0080085	0,0194121	0,005291	0,005291	0,0050251	0,0391937
H5	0,0132081	0,0057803	0,0073504	0,0649351	0,0169875	0,0068293	0,0560399	0,0080085	0,0194121	0,005291	0,005291	0,0452261	0,0391937
H6	0,0132081	0,1445087	0,0122506	0,0909091	0,0849377	0,0341463	0,0933998	0,0186866	0,0249584	0,1322751	0,1322751	0,1055276	0,0503919
H7	0,0184913	0,0096339	0,0122506	0,0649351	0,0056625	0,0068293	0,01868	0,0080085	0,0249584	0,005291	0,005291	0,0452261	0,0391937
H8	0,0308189	0,0867052	0,1837592	0,0909091	0,1189128	0,102439	0,1307597	0,0560598	0,0349418	0,1322751	0,1322751	0,1055276	0,0503919
H9	0,2773701	0,2023121	0,2572629	0,1168831	0,1528879	0,2390244	0,1307597	0,280299	0,1747088	0,1851852	0,1851852	0,1356784	0,1175812
H10	0,0184913	0,0096339	0,0122506	0,0649351	0,0849377	0,0068293	0,0933998	0,011212	0,0249584	0,026455	0,026455	0,0753769	0,0503919
H11	0,0184913	0,0096339	0,0122506	0,0649351	0,0849377	0,0068293	0,0933998	0,011212	0,0249584	0,026455	0,026455	0,0753769	0,0503919
H12	0,0132081	0,0057803	0,0073504	0,038961	0,0056625	0,004878	0,0062267	0,0080085	0,0194121	0,005291	0,005291	0,0150754	0,0391937
H13	0,4622835	0,2023121	0,2572629	0,1168831	0,1528879	0,2390244	0,1681196	0,3924186	0,5241265	0,1851852	0,1851852	0,1356784	0,3527436
	1	1	1	1	1	1	1	1	1	1	1	1	1

Fig. 7. Normalized matrix of ratios for the Preservation of Original Appearance criterion.

D - Normalized matrix

	H1	H2	H3	H4	H5	H6	H7	H8	H9	H10	H11	H12	H13
H1	0,2377358	0,1665081	0,0941704	0,1139241	0,0976744	0,271786	0,1817657	0,2145484	0,3159478	0,2680851	0,1283305	0,1146038	0,1118211
H2	0,0475472	0,0333016	0,0941704	0,0886076	0,0976744	0,0181191	0,0121177	0,0143032	0,0210632	0,0382979	0,1283305	0,1146038	0,0798722
H3	0,0339623	0,0047574	0,0134529	0,0379747	0,0046512	0,0129422	0,0086555	0,00613	0,0090271	0,0297872	0,0036666	0,0032744	0,0031949
H4	0,0264151	0,0047574	0,0044843	0,0126582	0,0046512	0,0129422	0,0086555	0,00613	0,0090271	0,0297872	0,0036666	0,0032744	0,0031949
H5	0,0339623	0,0047574	0,0403587	0,0379747	0,0139535	0,0129422	0,0086555	0,00613	0,0090271	0,0297872	0,0036666	0,0032744	0,0031949
H6	0,0792453	0,1665081	0,0941704	0,0886076	0,0976744	0,0905953	0,1817657	0,2145484	0,1895687	0,053617	0,1283305	0,1146038	0,1118211
H7	0,0792453	0,1665081	0,0941704	0,0886076	0,0976744	0,0301984	0,0605886	0,1287291	0,0210632	0,053617	0,1283305	0,1146038	0,1118211
H8	0,0475472	0,0999049	0,0941704	0,0886076	0,0976744	0,0181191	0,0201962	0,0429097	0,0210632	0,053617	0,1283305	0,1146038	0,1118211
H9	0,0475472	0,0999049	0,0941704	0,0886076	0,0976744	0,0301984	0,1817657	0,1287291	0,0631896	0,053617	0,1796627	0,1604453	0,14377
H10	0,2377358	0,2331113	0,1210762	0,1139241	0,1255814	0,4529767	0,3029429	0,2145484	0,3159478	0,2680851	0,1283305	0,1604453	0,14377
H11	0,0475472	0,0066603	0,0941704	0,0886076	0,0976744	0,0181191	0,0121177	0,0085819	0,0090271	0,053617	0,0256661	0,0687623	0,0798722
H12	0,0475472	0,0066603	0,0941704	0,0886076	0,0976744	0,0181191	0,0121177	0,0085819	0,0090271	0,0382979	0,0085554	0,0229208	0,0798722
H13	0,0339623	0,0066603	0,0672646	0,0632911	0,0697674	0,0129422	0,0086555	0,00613	0,0070211	0,0297872	0,0051332	0,0045842	0,0159744
	1	1	1	1	1	1	1	1	1	1	1	1	1

Fig. 8. Normalized matrix of ratios for the Cultural Importance criterion.

the four criteria, it can be compared with random indices (R.I.) calculated from matrices generated randomly through software, such as "Expert Choice". If the consistency ratio (C.R.) is less than or equal to the random index x corresponding to the specific order of the matrix (C.R. $\leq$ x), the weights assigned to the criteria can be considered consistent, thereby attesting to the "consistency" of the system. In the case under examination, all four criteria passed the consistency check, thus proving to be fully coherent.

A	B	C	D
0,81706	1,00000	0,51677	0,82996
0,15402	0,70389	0,18706	0,29325
0,09378	1,00000	0,24849	0,06552
0,50006	0,51545	0,04646	0,05749
0,06200	0,21193	0,09771	0,08310
1,00000	0,05508	0,28379	0,57688
0,71036	0,05508	0,08275	0,41002
0,31469	0,41527	0,33451	0,31527
0,26632	0,06039	0,72887	0,50113
0,13019	0,05508	0,16077	1,00000
0,39095	0,26378	0,14226	0,20857
0,07587	0,18227	0,05615	0,20150
0,66461	0,33055	1,00000	0,12634

Fig. 9. Weight vectors related to the criteria of (A) Historical-Artistic Importance, (B) Architect, (C) Preservation of Original Appearance, (D) Cultural Importance for each of the thirteen historic hotels

3.3 Implementation of Econometric Analysis

Once the weights attributable to the four criteria have been determined through the Analytic Hierarchy Process (AHP), it is necessary to understand to what extent these weights influence the price of historic hotels, that is, how they contribute to determining the price of these properties [25, 26]. Therefore, one can proceed with the implementation of the multiple linear regression model which, with specific regard to the case under examination, can be schematized as follows:

$$\Delta V = \beta_0 + \beta_A w_A + \beta_B w_B + \beta_C w_C + \beta_D w_D + \varepsilon \qquad (4)$$

In which, ΔV represents the *dependent variable*, that is, the difference in value between the room of the historic hotel and the room of the comparable hotel (without the historical-architectural significance); obviously, in the case of a historic hotel that has multiple "comparables", the ΔV will consist of the difference between the value of the historic hotel room and the arithmetic mean of the values of the rooms of the comparable structures; conversely $\{w_A, w_B, w_C, w_D\}$ define the *independent variables* consisting of the "weights" respectively attributed to the four criteria obtained through the implementation of the AHP. Therefore, the dependent variable, together with the independent variables incorporated in the model, are configured as follows (Fig. 10):

Based on the sample data, the following algebraic model is determined through multiple linear regression analysis:

$$\Delta V = 0,51987 + 0,03440 \cdot A - 0,18125 \cdot B + 0,44832 \cdot C - 0,51396 \cdot D \qquad (5)$$

The results of which and the main statistical verification indices are shown in the following figures (Figs. 11, 12, and 13).

4 Results

From the results of the multiple regression model, an R-squared value of 72,27% emerges, indicating a significant relationship between the dependent variable and the group of selected independent variables. This value attests that a share equal to 72,27%

Value difference	A	B	C	D
0,16000	0,81706	1,00000	0,51677	0,82996
0,30000	0,15402	0,70389	0,18706	0,29325
0,47000	0,09378	1,00000	0,24849	0,06552
0,64000	0,50006	0,51545	0,04646	0,05749
0,68000	0,06200	0,21193	0,09771	0,08310
0,47000	1,00000	0,05508	0,28379	0,57688
0,27000	0,71036	0,05508	0,08275	0,41002
0,23000	0,31469	0,41527	0,33451	0,31527
0,69000	0,26632	0,06039	0,72887	0,50113
0,13000	0,13019	0,05508	0,16077	1,00000
0,25000	0,39095	0,26378	0,14226	0,20857
0,27000	0,07587	0,18227	0,05615	0,20150
0,84000	0,66461	0,33055	1,00000	0,12634

Fig. 10. Summary of the dependent variable and independent variables entered as input in the multiple linear regression model.

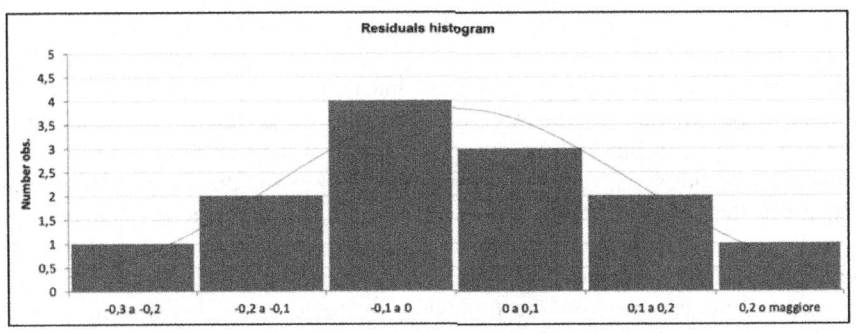

Fig. 11. Model verification results and statistical indices.

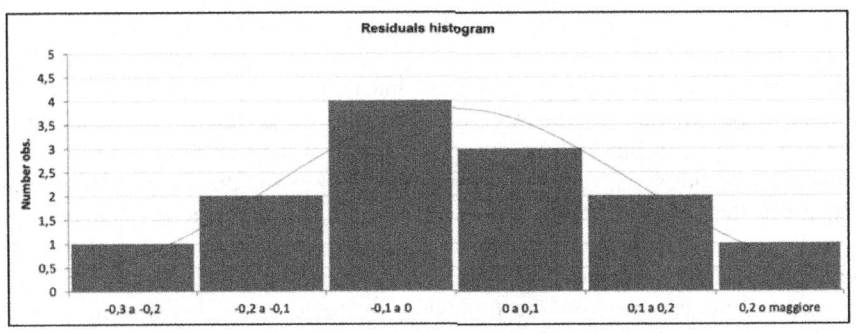

Fig. 12. Residuals histogram.

of the dependent variable can be explained by the set of independent variables included in the model, suggesting a good explanatory capacity of the adopted regression. From the analysis of the coefficients, it is noted that the independent variables A and B (i.e., historical-artistic importance and the prestige of the architect) are not significant in determining the value delta ΔV, which is the differential between the value of historic hotel rooms and the value of comparable hotel rooms. On the contrary, the coefficients of variables C (preservation of the original appearance) and D (cultural importance, understood as integration with the surrounding architectural context) are statistically

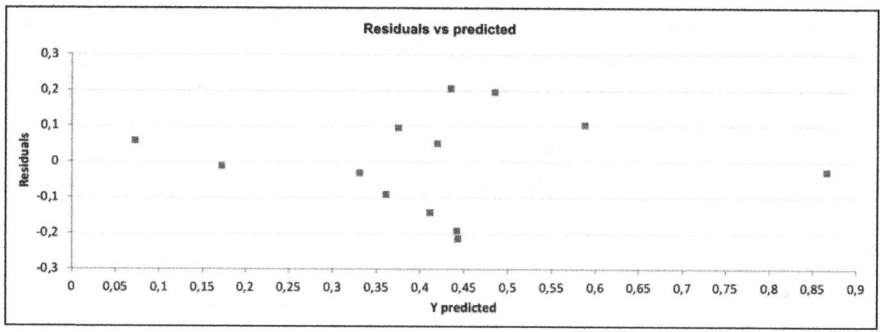

Fig. 13. Residuals vs predicted histogram.

significant, demonstrating a concrete explanatory capacity with respect to the dependent variable. Not surprisingly, for these significant variables, the standard error also appears statistically significant, thereby confirming a low dispersion of data around the regression line and indicating a good adherence between observed values and estimated values (see Fig. 14). This data underscores the high precision of the model in providing reliable estimates of the coefficients, as a more contained standard error is correlated with greater accuracy in the estimation.

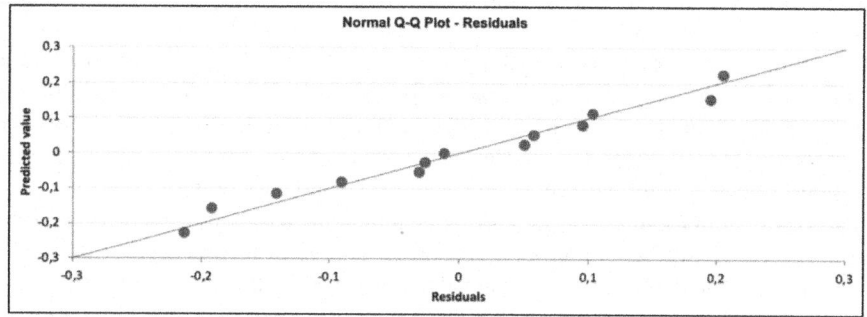

Fig. 14. Dispersion of data around the regression line.

Moreover, the Student's t-test relating to the significance of the explanatory variables C and D produced values within the range of statistical significance (> 2 or < -2), demonstrating that, for the independent variables considered, the test is significant. The p-value also respected the threshold of statistical significance (less than 0,05), further consolidating the robustness of the model. Specifically, variable C (preservation of the original appearance) has a positive coefficient, indicating that a 10% increase in this variable is associated with a 4,5% increase in the dependent variable represented by the value delta indicated by ΔV. This suggests that the preservation of the original appearance of the historic hotel translates into greater appreciation, giving the property a surplus value compared to non-historic hotels. Conversely, variable D (cultural importance) presents a negative coefficient. A 10% increase in the integration of the historic hotel with the surrounding architectural and cultural context is associated with a 5,1% decrease in the dependent variable ΔV. This inverse relationship indicates that greater harmonization with the surrounding environment tends to reduce the perceived distinction between the historic hotel and the comparable hotels without such significance under study, thus reducing the value differential. In other words, the more the historic hotel blends into the cultural and architectural context, the less the surplus value appears compared to accommodation facilities of the same category but without historical character.

5 Conclusions

The results that emerged are indicative of an interesting phenomenon: the perceived added value of historic hotels derives not so much from their historical-artistic importance or the architect's signature, but rather from the preservation of their original architectural characteristics and their relationship with the surrounding cultural-architectural environment. This suggests some fundamental considerations about the relationship between historical real estate heritage and the economic value perceived by its users:

- *Enhancement through authenticity*: Variable C (preservation of the original appearance) shows a significantly positive impact on the value delta ΔV. This means that visitors and customers are attracted by the tangible authenticity of the historic structure, that is, by those visible characteristics that refer to a past era and give the place a unique and distinctive atmosphere. In other words, it is not so much the "history" in an abstract sense or past events that enhance the hotel, but rather the visual and sensory perception of a structure that has remained faithful to its era of construction.
- *The architect and historical importance as peripheral elements*: The non-significance of variables A (historical-artistic importance) and B (architect) suggests that these factors are less perceptible or appreciable. The identity of an architect, however famous, and the historical events that may have marked a building are information that requires prior knowledge and are often appreciated only by a niche of experts or enthusiasts. Therefore, while being important factors in the history of the building, they do not directly contribute to the value perceived by the average clientele.
- *Integration with the cultural context:* Variable D (integration with the cultural context), while significant, exerts a negative effect on the perceived value. This can be interpreted to mean that if a historic hotel is too harmonized with the surrounding environment, it loses part of its distinction as a "special" or iconic reference point. When a building completely blends with the urban or cultural landscape, its uniqueness is attenuated, and this can lead to a reduction in the value perceived by visitors, who seem to appreciate more a building that, while integrating, maintains a distinctive character that visually separates it from surrounding buildings.

In conclusion, it appears evident that the value delta ΔV, that is, the difference in value between the room of the historic hotel and the room of the comparable hotel (without the historical-architectural significance), does not reside so much in the intangible cultural heritage of the building—such as the historical events that have distinguished it or the prestigious signature of its Architect—but rather in elements capable of evoking authenticity and uniqueness of the property, such as the preservation of its original appearance. The practical implications of the research conducted concern the usefulness of the outputs, as a valid evaluative reference, in resolving estimation issues connected to urban properties with historical-architectural significance. Future developments of the work could consist of expanding the analysis to additional urban contexts, integrating and systematizing this methodology.

References

1. Deodhar, V.: Does the housing market value heritage? some empirical evidence. Macquarie Econ. Res. Papers **3**, 1–31 (2004)
2. Forte, F., Del Giudice, V., De Paola, P., Del Giudice, F.P.: Cultural heritage and seismic disasters: assessment methods and damage types. In: Morano, P., Oppio, A., Rosato, P., Sdino, L., Tajani, F. (eds.) Appraisal and Valuation, Green Energy and Technology, pp. 163–175. Springer, Cham (2021)
3. Manganelli, B., Tajani, F., De Paola, P., Del Giudice, F.P.: The impact of the historical-architectural component on property value. Heritage **6**, 4934–4955 (2023)
4. Asabere, P.K., Hachey, G., Grubaugh, S.: Architecture, historic zoning, and the value of homes. J. Real Estate Financ. Econ. **2**, 181–195 (1989)
5. Leichenko, R.M., Coulson, N.E., Listokin, D.: Historic preservation and residential property values: an analysis of texas cities. Urban Stud. **38**, 1973–1987 (2001)
6. Bergen, P.: The Effect of Historic Designation on the Value of Single-Family Homes in Tacoma. https://studylib.net/doc/12174347/fifth-draft-second-full-draft. Accessed 15 Feb 2025
7. Oba, T., Noonan, D.S.: The many dimensions of historic preservation value: national and local designation, internal and external policy effects. J. Prop. Res. **34**, 211–232 (2017)
8. Cebula, R.J.: The hedonic pricing model applied to the housing market of the city of savannah and its savannah historic landmark district. Rev. Reg. Stud. **39**, 9–22 (2009)
9. Narwold, A., Sandy, J., Tu, C.: Historic designation and residential property values. Int. Real Estate Rev. **11**, 83–95 (2008)
10. Zahirovic-Herbert, V., Chatterjee, S.: Historic preservation and residential property values: evidence from quantile regression. Urban Stud. J. Ltd. **49**, 369–382 (2012)
11. Vandell, K.D., Lane, J.S.: The economics of architecture and urban design: some preliminary findings. Real Estate Econ. **17**, 235–260 (1989)
12. Jeffries, W.: Does Heritage Listing have an Effect on Property Prices in Australia? Evidence from Mosman, Sydney. Bachelor's Thesis, The University of New South Wales UNSW, 1 (2012)
13. Asabere, P.K., Huffman, F.E., Mehdian, S.: The adverse impacts of local historic designation: the case of small apartment buildings in Philadelphia. J. Real Estate Financ. Econ. **8**, 225–234 (1994)
14. Oba, T., Noonan, D.S.: The price of preserving neighborhoods: the unequal impacts of historic district designation. Econ. Dev. Q. **34**, 343–355 (2020)
15. Asabere, P.K., Huffman, F.E.: Historic designation and residential market values. Apprais. J. **62**, 396 (1994)
16. Schaeffer, P.V., Millerick, C.A.: The impact of historic district designation on property values: an empirical study. Econ. Dev. Q. **5**, 301–312 (1991)
17. Heintzelman, M.D., Altieri, J.A.: Historic preservation: preserving value? J. Real Estate Financ. Econ. **46**, 543–563 (2013)
18. Coffin, D.A.: The impact of historic districts on residential property values. East. Econ. J. **15**, 221–228 (1989)

19. Ijla, A., Ryberg, S., Rosentraub, M.S., Bowen, W.: Historic designation, and the rebuilding of neighborhoods: new evidence of the value of an old policy tool. J. Urban. Int. Res. Placemaking Urban Sustain. **4**, 263–284 (2011)
20. Gilderbloom, J.I., Hanka, M.J., Ambrosius, J.D.: Historic preservation's impact on job creation, property values, and environmental sustainability. J. Urban. **2**, 83–101 (2009)
21. Clark, D.E., Herrin, W.E.: Historical preservation districts and home sale prices: evidence from the sacramento housing market. Rev. Reg. Stud. **27**, 29–48 (1997)
22. Klarnet, L.: Preserving history or property values: historic preservation and housing prices in Washington DC. Undergrad. Econ. Rev. **17**, 1 (2020)
23. Massimo, D.E., Del Giudice, V., Musolino, M., De Paola, P., Del Giudice, F.P.: Green building to overcome climate change: the support of energy simulation programs in Gis environment. In: Calabrò, F., Della Spina, L., Piñeira Mantiñán, M.J. (eds.) New Metropolitan Perspectives. NMP 2022, Lecture Notes in Networks and Systems, vol. 482, pp. 1–13. Springer, Cham (2022)
24. Massimo, D.E., Del Giudice, V., Musolino, M., De Paola, P., Del Giudice, F.P.: A bio ecological prototype green building toward solution of energy crisis. In: Calabrò, F., Della Spina, L., Piñeira Mantiñán, M.J. (eds.) New Metropolitan Perspectives. NMP 2022, Lecture Notes in Networks and Systems, vol. 482, pp. 1–13. Springer, Cham (2022)
25. Salvo, F., De Ruggiero, M., Tavano, D., De Paola, P., Del Giudice, F.P.: Analytical implications of mortgage lending value and bottom value. Buildings **12**, 799 (2022)
26. Del Giudice, V., De Paola, P., Morano, P., Tajani, F., Del Giudice, F.P.: A multidimensional evaluation approach for the natural parks design. Appl. Sci. **11**, 1767 (2021)

Environmental Impacts and Housing Deprivation: A Study of the Effects of Industrial Polluting Sites in the Italian Context

Debora Anelli[1(✉)], Pierluigi Morano[2], Francesco Tajani[1], Felicia Di Liddo[2], and Marco Locurcio[2]

[1] Department of Architecture and Design, "Sapienza" University of Rome, 00196 Rome, Italy
{debora.anelli,francesco.tajani}@uniroma1.it
[2] Department of Civil, Environmental, Land, Building Engineering and Chemistry (DICATECh), Polytechnic University of Bari, 70126 Bari, Italy
{pierluigi.morano,felicia.diliddo,marco.locurcio}@poliba.it

Abstract. The disadvantaged populations often bear a disproportionate burden of environmental pollution, especially when air quality exceeds regulatory standards. This link is particularly pronounced in areas with housing deprivation. As deprivation levels rise, the number of people exposed to excessive pollution increases. The industrial sector is one of the major contributors to air pollution and greenhouse gas emissions. Given the close relationship between industrial sites and socioeconomic, environmental, and health factors in cities, analyzing the real estate market can provide valuable insights for guiding sustainable development strategies. The present research aims to determine if a correlation exists between residential property prices and polluting sites, by considering factors that could represent housing deprivation. By examining the type of relationship and changes in property prices, the study intends to inform decision-making on housing deprivation policies. Through a genetic algorithm (Multi-Case Strategy of Evolutionary Polynomial Regression) applied to a sample of a limited available sample of polluting sites in Italy, first results have been obtained, that align with empirical observations and local user expectations. The results highlight the importance of implementing effective housing deprivation policies that address the environmental impacts of polluting industrial sites on real estate market dynamics. The innovative contribution of this work lies in identifying critical 'pollution-poverty' areas that require urgent remedial action.

Keywords: environmental pollution · sustainable city · real estate market · industrial sites · socio-environmental vulnerability · housing deprivation

1 Introduction

Housing deprivation, a condition where individuals lack adequate and affordable housing, is intricately linked to environmental degradation, particularly in areas surrounding industrial polluting sites. The relationship between these two issues is deeply intertwined, as the proximity to industrial sites often correlates with poor housing conditions, contributing to social inequalities and exacerbating environmental injustices. In both international and Italian contexts, comprehensive policies that address both housing and environmental issues are crucial to mitigating the impacts on marginalized populations and creating more equitable urban environments. Industrial polluting sites, particularly those in urban and semi-urban areas, significantly impact the environment, and their presence often correlates with the most disadvantaged communities. These industrial zones emit hazardous pollutants into the air, water, and soil, resulting in long-term health consequences for residents. According to the World Health Organization, exposure to pollutants like particulate matter and nitrogen dioxide can cause respiratory diseases, cardiovascular problems, and even premature death [1]. This is often compounded by the fact that low-income populations, who face housing deprivation, are more likely to live near such hazardous sites. Countries such as the United States and China have seen clear links between environmental degradation and housing inequality. In the U.S., for instance, neighborhoods near polluting industries, often inhabited by minority and low-income groups, face higher levels of exposure to toxic chemicals, a phenomenon sometimes referred to as "environmental racism" [2]. Similar patterns are seen in developing countries where rapid industrialization has led to the creation of informal settlements close to polluting industries. These residents live in substandard housing, face environmental health risks, and suffer from systemic neglect by both market forces and policy-makers.

Addressing housing deprivation and its links to environmental degradation require comprehensive policy action. On an international level, organizations like the United Nations have emphasized the need for sustainable urban development, which incorporates both affordable housing and environmental protection. Italy has also begun to take steps to address these issues. The European Union's Green Deal and Italy's National Recovery and Resilience Plan (PNRR) aim to promote sustainable industry while addressing environmental injustices by improving housing conditions and reducing pollution. The Italian context mirrors many of these international trends. Industrial hubs such as Taranto in southern Italy, which hosts one of Europe's largest steel plants, have long been associated with both pollution and housing challenges. The "Ilva" steel plant in Taranto has been a notorious source of air and soil contamination, contributing to higher cancer rates and respiratory diseases among the local population. In evaluating the literature surrounding the environmental and health impacts of the Ilva steel plant, [3] have analyzed the linkages between pollution from the industrial site and adverse health outcomes, such as increased cancer rates and respiratory diseases. This work aligns with other studies that have examined the broader environmental crisis in Taranto, particularly the SENTIERI report, which also found elevated mortality rates linked to industrial pollutants in the area. Local residents, often from lower socioeconomic backgrounds, live in deteriorating housing conditions, trapped in a cycle where property values have plummeted due to environmental degradation, making relocation unaffordable. However, there are diverging perspectives regarding the socioeconomic trade-offs. Some literature highlights the tension between economic dependence on the Ilva plant and the public health crisis it has caused. For example, [4] describes a polarized debate between those prioritizing jobs and those advocating for environmental health. This dichotomy often complicates policy responses, as both health and economic stability are essential for local residents.

Housing markets play a significant role in perpetuating environmental inequalities. In many urban areas, real estate prices tend to be lower near industrial zones, making such locations more accessible to economically disadvantaged populations. For instance, in many cities, properties located near highways or industrial zones are cheaper due to pollution, noise, and other environmental nuisances. As a result, low-income households tend to live in these areas, despite the associated health risks.

A good key for studying and interpreting the effects of the environmental impacts produced by industrial polluting sites on the housing deprivation issues is represented by the analysis of the variation of the residential market dynamics due to the presence of polluting activities. The present research aims to determine if a correlation exists between residential property prices and 41 industrial polluting sites located in the Italian territory, by considering different factors of local housing deprivation conditions. The presence and the type of the functional relationships are investigated through the implementation of a genetic algorithm based on a multi-case strategy (Multi-Case Strategy of Evolutionary Polynomial Regression), that is able to provide a unique generalized interpretative model for the following three case studies: i) 11 still active industrial plants, ii) 23 dismissed industrial polluting sites and iii) 7 partially dismissed industrial polluting sites. Even if the total sample is limited for a statistical reliability of the model obtained, by using the property prices as a proxy of the inhabitants' preferences, the outputs allow to raise first but relevant considerations concerning the qualitative effects of different typologies of industrial polluting sites on the local housing deprivation. According to the mentioned subdivision, the genetic algorithm searches for the existing relationships and their typology between the dependent variable, that is the differential between the municipal average residential prices and the average property selling prices detected in the urban area in which the industrial site is located, and a set of seven housing deprivation factors as independent variables.

The sections of the work are articulated as follows. Section 2 consists of a review of the main literature on the environmental impacts and housing deprivation issues, in order to justify the choice of specific explanatory variables in the next step of the elaboration. Section 3 describes the methodology based on the application of a multi-case strategy genetic algorithm to the Italian territory and it presents the case study. Section 4 provides the discussion of the results obtained. Section 5 contains the conclusions and future insights of the research.

2 Literature Review

The relationship between environmental impacts and housing deprivation has been explored extensively in academic literature, revealing a complex interaction that often results in severe social and health consequences. Housing deprivation, defined as inadequate, insecure, or unaffordable housing, often coexists with environmental degradation, particularly in areas near industrial sites and other polluting activities. This issue is well-documented both in developed and developing countries, illustrating global environmental inequality.

A significant body of research highlights the disproportionate burden of environmental hazards on marginalized populations. [2] coined the term "environmental racism" to describe the phenomenon in which racial minorities and low-income populations bear the brunt of industrial pollution. Bullard's research in the United States revealed that low-income African American and Latin communities are more likely to live near hazardous waste sites, which correlates with higher rates of respiratory diseases and cancers. This environmental inequality is rooted in historical and systemic discrimination in housing markets, which forces marginalized groups to live in less desirable and more polluted areas.

Internationally, studies in both the Global North and South reinforce this trend. [5] found that industrial zones, particularly in urban areas, are often situated near poor neighborhoods where housing conditions are inadequate. These communities are exposed to pollutants from factories, vehicle emissions, and contaminated water sources, which exacerbate housing deprivation and contribute to long-term health issues, such as cardiovascular diseases and asthma. The Authors emphasize that the health risks are not only related to physical proximity to pollution but are also magnified by poor housing conditions, such as lack of insulation, overcrowding, and poor ventilation, which increase the vulnerability to environmental hazards.

The role of the housing market in perpetuating environmental injustice has been widely studied. Scholars such as [6] argue that housing affordability often dictates where vulnerable populations live, with the cheapest properties frequently located in environmentally degraded areas. As property values decline near polluting sites, low-income residents are disproportionately exposed to environmental hazards. In regions like the Po Valley in Italy, known for its high levels of air pollution, housing is more affordable, but residents face significant health risks due to poor air quality [3]. This trend is also seen in rapidly urbanizing cities in developing countries, where informal settlements emerge near industrial areas due to the lack of affordable housing options.

Literature consistently links environmental impacts and housing deprivation to increased mortality rates. The [1] has highlighted how inadequate housing in polluted areas contributes to a range of health issues, including respiratory diseases, cardiovascular problems, and premature death. Studies like those by [7] show that areas with high levels of air pollution, often corresponding with low-income housing, experience significantly higher mortality rates due to chronic exposure to harmful pollutants. Supporting Lelieveld et al.'s findings, several studies highlight the severe health impacts of air pollution, including cardiovascular and respiratory diseases. For instance, [8] applied the Global Exposure Mortality Model (GEMM), showing that air pollution causes an even greater global mortality burden than previously thought, with 8.9 million deaths annually. Similar to Lelieveld's work, Burnett also underscored the cardiovascular system's vulnerability to particulate matter exposure.

The literature on environmental impacts and housing deprivation illustrates a clear link between social inequality and environmental injustice. Marginalized populations, confined to substandard housing near industrial zones, experience heightened exposure to pollution, leading to adverse health outcomes and higher mortality rates. The intersection of these two issues requires comprehensive policy interventions that address both environmental and housing inequities.

3 Methodology and Case Study

The present research focuses on a case study that concerns the 41 Italian Sites of National Interest (SIN), according to the classification provided by the Ministry of Ecological Transition (MiTE). SIN are characterized by the presence of significant levels of hazardous pollutants that lead to high environmental and health impacts on the surrounding neighborhoods. They include abandoned, active and partially dismissed industrial areas, nor ports, former mines, illegal landfills, sites affected by asbestos production and extraction activities. On these sites, the main exposure is to pollutants like heavy metals and organochlorinated solvents, dioxins, polychlorinated biphenyls and polycyclic aromatic hydrocarbons. After several process of remediation, the SIN are actually – second semester 2023 – 41 and cover a total surface area equal to 248,000 hs, of which 170,000 on land and 78,000 on sea. In all Italian regions there is at least one SIN and the ones with the largest contaminated area are Campania and Sardinia with, respectively, 345,000 and 445,000 hs.

The proposed methodology applies a genetic algorithm (Multi-Case Strategy of Evolutionary Polynomial Regression) for investigating the effects that presence of SIN have on urban environments in the residential market where they are located. In order to perform this output, the selected dependent variable is the differential between the municipal average residential prices and the average property selling prices detected in the urban area in which the SIN is found. This variable has been used as a proxy of the inhabitants' preferences, which change according to the local context considered. It is calculated by consulting the selling price quotations of the second semester 2023 provided by the Real Estate Market Observatoy of the Italian Revenue Agency for each of the trade area to which every SIN pertains. The assumption underlying the work is that the gap (Y) detected between the average real estate values in the reference context and those of the specific urban area in which the SIN is located is associated with the presence of the contaminated site and its specific characteristics. The independent variables chosen are seven, following described:

- age of the industrial plant, computed as the difference between the year (2023) and the construction one (C);
- total surface area of the SIN, expressed in hectares (Su);
- distance from the nearest urban green area, calculated in km on foot (G)
- accessibility degree, considering the distance from the nearest entrance to the high-speed road and calculated in km by car (Ac).
- distance from the city-center, calculated in km on foot (Ce);
- mortality rate from cancer (Mc), expressed in percentage;
- mortality rate from diseases of the nervous system (Mn), reported in percentage.

As illustrated in the previous review of the literature, these variables have been selected in order to effectively represent the possible interactions between environmental impacts of SIN and housing deprivation. Except the construction date (C) and the total surface area of the SIN (Su), the variables related to the distance from the city center (Ce), the nearest urban green area (G) and the accessibility degree (Ac) represent the level of urban facilities of the housing market. Both the mortality rates (Mc and Mn) express the intricate connections among housing deprivation, environmental degradation, and health impacts. People living in inadequate housing often face greater exposure to environmental hazards, which in turn leads to higher mortality rates. This issue is evident both internationally and within Italy, where the interplay of industrial pollution, housing market dynamics, and social inequality has created severe public health challenges. According to a study by the European Environment Agency (EEA), people living in close proximity to such areas experience a higher risk of respiratory diseases, cardiovascular issues, and cancer, all of which contribute to increased mortality rates [9]. For example, in Italy, a study by the European Heart Journal found that air pollution was responsible for about 80,000 premature deaths annually [7]. These deaths disproportionately affect those living in deprived housing conditions near polluting industries. Starting from the sample data, the technique implemented to identify the effects of the SIN on the residential market prices is represented by the Evolutionary Polynomial Regression (EPR). The technique implements a genetic algorithm to combine numerical and symbolic regression methods using polynomial structures [10–13]. In particular, in the present research a further evolution of EPR that develops generalized prediction models to identify the functional relationships able to simultaneously describe the selling prices mechanism in different study samples (for example, in different territorial contexts), is used. The employed technique is the Multi-Case Strategy of the Evolutionary Polynomial Regression (MCS-EPR). The mathematical logic of the MCS-EPR technique applies a genetic algorithm to identify the polynomial coefficient values for all considered data samples that simultaneously satisfy the three objective functions - maximization of statistical performance, minimization of the number of coefficients and minimization of the number of variables - for all analyzed case studies. It is implemented by taking into account a subdivision of the 41 considered SIN that, according to their activity status, are divided into: i) 11 active ones, ii) 23 dismissed ones and iii) 7 partially dismissed ones. As the total sample is limited for a statistical reliability of the model obtained, the outputs will be analyzed for first considerations about the qualitative effects of different typologies of industrial polluting sites on the local housing deprivation.

The application of the technique has generated several functions. Among them, the generalized model selected is reported in Eq. (1).

$$\begin{aligned}Y = &+a_1 \times Ce \times Ac^{0.5} \times Mn^2 + a_2 \times Su \times G^{0.5} \times Ce \times Ac^2 + a_3 \times Su \times G^2 \times Ce \times Mc^{0.5} \\ &\times Mn^2 + a_4 \times Su^2 \times Ce^2 + a_5 \times C \times S^{0.5} \times Mc^2 \times Mn^{0.5} + a_6 \times C^2 \times Ce \times Ac^2 \\ &+ a_7 \times C^2 \times Su^{0.5} Ce^2 \times Ac + a_8 \times C^2 \times Su^{0.5} \times G \times Ce^2 + \\ &a_9 \times C^2 \times Su^2 \times G \times Ce^2 \times Ac^2 \times Mn + a_0\end{aligned} \quad (1)$$

The parameters of the model for the three case studies are reported in Table 1.

4 Results

The obtained results confirm the empirically expected correlations between environmental impacts and housing deprivation factors selected by the multi-strategy technique. In Table 2 a summary of the correlations between the dependent and independent variables and the effects of the explanatory factors on the differential between the municipal average residential prices and the average property selling prices detected in the urban

Table 1. Values of the parameters of the model for each case study

	a_0	a_1	a_2	a_3	a_4	a_5	a_6	a_7	a_8	a_9
Active SIN	−0.10	3.18	5,290.4	−878.28	−2,393.5	14.02	−42.79	−1,566.0	705.68	−32,078.63
Dismissed SIN	−0.13	−2.96	132.16	0	−1,481.8	1.45	9.53	0	1,057.7	0
Partially dismissed SIN	0.00	6.63	449.10	−13,009	8,583.1	−2.56	−35.13	998.83	214.34	−140,143.76

area in which the SIN is located, is reported. By analyzing the observed results, there are substantial differences among the study cases considered. Only for the accessibility level the same type of correlation (proportionally direct) links the dependent variable with the independent ones in all the three study cases. Five times out of seven the analyzed variables have the same type of correlations in the case where the SIN is active and in those in which it is dismissed. This condition is also found when the SIN is dismissed or partially dismissed (three times out of seven) and when it is active or partially dismissed (one time out of seven). The analysis of the individual results for each independent variable in the three case studies considered is developed in detail as follows to understand the reasons for these situations and verify their consistency with empirical evidence.

4.1 Industrial Plant Age (C)

When the SIN is still active and it is constructed after 1910, the differential is positive. It means that the average property selling prices of the urban area in which the SIN is found are minor than the municipal ones, therefore the presence of active SIN negatively affects the housing real estate market near the industrial active plants. Instead, when the SIN is dismissed or partially dismissed, in the first case, recent industrial plants lead to a negative differential given by the high housing prices of neighboring districts; in the second case, the differential is always negative and, as in the previous case of the SIN dismissed, therefore, the prices are higher than the municipal average and the partially dismissed plant is not perceived negatively by the local real estate market.

4.2 Total Surface Area (Su)

If the surface areas of active and dismissed SIN increase, the dependent variable decreases and, in particular, the differential of housing quotations is always negative, therefore higher selling prices pertain to the area of the SIN. It can happens when the industrial plant's area has become fully urbanized and integrated with the surrounding urban conurbation due to the increase in services and real estate demand over time. The situation is different for the partially dismantled SIN: it is observed that the housing prices are minor than those at the municipal level so maybe the perception of a reduction in the industrial activities causes lower attraction for the surrounding area.

Table 2. Main findings from the application of the MCS-EPR

Variable	Study case					
	Active SIN		Dismissed SIN		Partially dismissed SIN	
	Correlation	Effects on the dependent variable	Correlation	Effects on the dependent variable	Correlation	Effects on the dependent variable
Industrial age	Proportionally direct	Recent SIN increase the differential	Inverse proportionality	Every considered construction date decrease the differential	Inverse proportionality	Every considered construction date decrease the differential
Total surface area	Inverse	Major surface areas of active SIN reduce the differential	Inverse	Major surface of dismissed SIN reduce the differential	Proportionally direct	Major surface areas of partially-dismissed SIN increase the differential
Distance from urban green area	Proportionally direct	If the green area is within 11.39 km, the differential increases	Proportionally direct	Major distance from the green area increases the differential	Inverse proportionality	Major distance of the SIN from the green area decreases the differential
	Inverse	If the green area is over 11.39 km, the differential decreases				
Accessibi-lity degree	Proportionally direct	Major distance from high-speed road increases the differential	Proportionally direct	Major distance of dismissed SIN from high-speed road increases the differential	Proportionally direct	Major distance of partially dismissed SIN from high-speed road increases the differential
Distance from city-center	Inverse	Major distance from city center reduces the differential	Proportionally direct	Major distance of dismissed SIN from city-center rises the differential	Proportionally direct	Major distance of SIN from city-center makes the differential grow
Cancer mortality	Proportionally direct	Higher mortality rate lead to significant differential	Proportionally direct	Higher mortality rate lead to significant differential	Inverse proportionality	Higher mortality rate lead to significant reduction of differential
Neurologi-cal mortality	Inverse	If the rate increases the differential decreases	Inverse	If the rate increases the differential decreases	Direct	A growth of mortality rate increases the differential

4.3 Distance From Urban Green Area (G)

If the green urban area is about 12 km from an active or dismantled SIN, the dependent variable grows. More precisely, the housing quotations of the active SIN's area are greater than the municipal ones when the distance is lower than 5 km. If it is between 5 km and 12 km the municipal quotations are greater than those of the industrial area. Instead, if the distance is more than 12 km the differential remains positive but it is reduced, so the housing prices even if greater than the municipal average, appear to be slighlty affected by the distance. In the case of dismissed SIN the treshold distance is equal to about 6 km: closer green areas increase the prices of the residential market in the SIN area, and vice versa. The independent variable has an inverse proportionality when the SIN is partially dismissed. In fact, a negative differential is observed therefore, even if the distance increases the quotations near the industrial plant are always greater than the municipal average. This can be due to the influence of other factors not included in the present analysis or the scarce importance of green spaces for the housing market when the industrial plant is partly active.

4.4 Distance from City-Center (Ce)

The situations in which the SIN is dismissed or partially dismissed register the same effects on the dependent variable if an increase of the distance from the city center occurs. Higher and positive differential is observed in both cases; therefore the average municipal quotations are greater than those of the SIN's area. If the SIN is active and the distance from the city center is lower than 8 km, the differential is positive, instead it becomes negative when the distance is greater than 8 km. This phenomenon can be caused by several factors: there are cases in which the industrial plants have been constructed very near the urban centers and other cases where they have been surrounded by a full urbanization that could reduce the appreciation of staying in the city center. Moreover, sometimes the urban centers are degraded or abandoned, and this can affect the housing conditions.

4.5 Cancer Mortality (Mc)

Higher mortality rate of cancer increases the value of the dependent variable when the SIN is active or dismissed. In both cases the average municipal quotations are higher than those of the SIN's area because the differential is always positive. However, this results suggest that health diseases can be reconducted to the industrial plant activities. If the SIN is currently closed, it could be possible that the health effects are still evident from the presence of pollutants in the soil or groundwater. In the case where the SIN is partially dismantled, a reduction in the dependent variable is observed when the mortality rate grows. The differential remains negative so when the mortality rate is low housing prices in the SIN area are much higher than the municipal average when the recorded mortality rate is highest. This means that when mortality is high the attractiveness of other residential areas increases, matching the gap with those near the industrial plant.

4.6 Neurological Mortality (Mn)

A high neurological mortality rate is linked to small differences between the housing quotations of the active and dismissed SIN and the average municipal ones. Vice versa it happens when the SIN is partially dismissed, or a positive differential is observed, and the average municipal quotations are higher than the those of the SIN's area. This can be due to several reasons that takes into account also other factors not included in the present work (e.g. perceived diseases, proximity to other potential source of health damages, type of industrial activity that involve the neurological system etc.).

5 Conclusions

This study explored the correlation between housing deprivation and environmental degradation, particularly in areas near industrial polluting sites. This connection often results in significant social and health inequalities, especially in urban and semi-urban regions where industrial activity is prevalent.

The analysis reveals significant differences in the correlations between the studied variables across the three cases, with only the accessibility level demonstrating a consistently direct relationship with the dependent variable (the "delta" of the market quotations) across all cases. In five out of seven variables, similar relationships exist whether the SIN are active or dismissed. This consistency is observed when the SIN are either dismissed or partially dismissed (three out of seven times) and when active or partially dismissed (one out of seven times). These findings underscore the importance of further analyzing individual variables to assess their empirical consistency. For instance, the age of industrial plants significantly affects housing prices. Active SIN constructed after 1910 tends to negatively impact nearby real estate values, as industrial activity reduces property desirability. Conversely, dismissed or partially dismissed SIN are associated with higher housing prices, suggesting that reduced industrial activity or plant closure may improve the area's perception, leading to increased property demand. Similarly, the total surface area of the SIN also plays a crucial role. Larger SIN, whether active or dismissed, tend to positively affect local property values when they are fully urbanized and integrated into the surrounding city. However, in partially dismantled SIN, housing prices remain lower than the municipal average, possibly due to the perception of ongoing industrial decline. Green spaces also affect housing markets, particularly in active and dismissed SIN areas. Proximity to urban green areas increases housing prices, particularly when the SIN are active, up to a threshold of 12 km. However, this relationship is less pronounced in partially dismantled SIN, where other factors may play a larger role. In contrast, distance from the city center demonstrates a mixed impact. Active SIN located within 8 km of the center negatively impact property values as distance increases, while dismissed or partially dismantled SIN result in a positive differential, with municipal prices exceeding those near the industrial site. Health-related variables such as cancer and neurological mortality further reinforce the complexity of relationships. High cancer mortality rates, particularly in active or dismissed SIN, consistently lead to lower property values, reflecting the perceived health risks associated with industrial pollution. Neurological mortality shows mixed effects, with smaller price differentials for active or dismissed SIN but larger differentials in partially dismantled SIN, highlighting the need for further exploration of these health-related factors.

Even if the total sample is limited for a statistical reliability of the market price function obtained, the outputs allow to raise the previous considerations concerning the qualitative effects of different typologies of industrial polluting sites on the local housing deprivation. Overall, the findings suggest that housing markets are highly sensitive to the presence and status of SIN, influenced by factors such as the plant's operational status, environmental conditions, and health risks. These insights can inform policy interventions aimed at improving environmental quality and public health in industrial areas while addressing housing market disparities. The innovative contribution of this work lies in identifying critical 'pollution-poverty' areas that require urgent remedial action [14–18].

Note: The current study has been developed within the current research P.R.I.N. Project 2022: "INSPIRE—Improving Nature-Smart Policies through Innovative Resilient Evaluations", Grant number: 2022J7RWNF.

References

1. World Health Organization (WHO): WHO guidelines on health policy and system support to optimize community health worker programmes, pp. 1–116. WHO, Geneva (2018)
2. Bullard, R.D.: Dumping in dixie: race, class, and environmental quality. Westview Press, Boulder (1990)
3. Forastiere, F., et al.: Health impact of the Ilva steel plant in Taranto Italy. Epidemiol. Prevent. **43**(3–4), 201–208 (2019)
4. Greco, L., Bagnardi, F.: State-corporate legal symbiosis and social harm: The case of the steel factory 'Ilva' in Taranto, Italy. Crime Law Soc. Chang. **70**(4), 473–492 (2018)
5. Mitchell, G., Chakraborty, J.: Urban inequality and environmental justice: Do US cities exhibit environmental injustice? Environ. Res. Let. **13**(7) (2018)
6. Mukhija, V.: The informal american city: beyond taco trucks and day labor. MIT Press, Cambridge (2014)
7. Lelieveld, J., et al.: Cardiovascular disease burden from ambient air pollution in Europe reassessed using novel hazard ratio functions. Eur. Heart J. **40**(20), 1590–1596 (2019)
8. Burnett, R.T., et al.: Global estimates of mortality associated with long-term exposure to outdoor fine particulate matter. Proc. Natl. Acad. Sci. **115**(38), 9592–9597 (2018). https://doi.org/10.1073/pnas.1803222115
9. European Environmental Agency (EEA): La sfida per ridurre l'inquinamento industriale. European Environmental Agency (2021). https://www.eea.europa.eu/it/segnali/segnali-2020/articles/la-sfida-per-ridurre-l2019inquinamento-industriale. Accessed 18 Dec 2024
10. Giustolisi, O., Savic, D.A.: Advances in data-driven analyses and modelling using EPR-MOGA. J. Hydroinf. **11**(3–4), 225–236 (2009)
11. Morano, P., Guarnaccia, C., Tajani, F., Di Liddo, F., Anelli, D.: An analysis of the noise pollution influence on the housing prices in the central area of the city of Bari. J. Phys.: Conf. Ser. **1603**(1), 012027 (2020)
12. Morano, P., Tajani, F., Guarini, M.R., Di Liddo, F., Anelli, D.: A multivariate econometric analysis for the forecasting of the interdependences between the housing prices and the socio-economic factors in the city of Barcelona (Spain). In: Gervasi, O., et al. (eds.) Computational Science and Its Applications – ICCSA 2019, LNCS, vol. 11622, pp. 13–22. Springer, Cham (2019)
13. Morano, P., Tajani, F., Di Liddo, F., Anelli, D.: A feasibility analysis of the refurbishment investments in the Italian residential market. Sustainability **12**(6), 2503 (2020)
14. Tajani, F., Anelli, D., Di Liddo, F., Morano, P.: An innovative methodology for the assessment of the social discount rate: an application to the European states for ensuring the goals of equitable growth. Smart Sustain. Built Environ. **13**(5), 1281–1309 (2024). https://doi.org/10.1108/SASBE-12-2022-0274
15. Locurcio, M., Tajani, F., Anelli, D.: Sustainable urban planning models for new smart cities and effective management of land take dynamics. Land **12**(3), 621 (2023)
16. Gabrielli, L., Bottarelli, M.: Financial and economic analysis for ground-coupled heat pumps using shallow ground heat exchangers. Sustain. Cities Soc. **20**, 71–80 (2016)

17. Morano, P., Tajani, F., Anelli, D.: Urban planning variants: a model for the division of the activated "plusvalue" between public and private subjects. Valori e Valutazioni **28**, 31–47 (2021)
18. Torre, C.M., Balena, P., Ceppi, C.: The devaluation of property due to the perception of health risk in polluted industrial cities. Int. J. Bus. Intell. Data Min. **9**, 74–90 (2014). https://doi.org/10.1504/IJBIDM.2014.062885

Student Housing Market: An Evaluation Model for the Identification of the Investment Opportunities in the Major European Cities

Debora Anelli[1(✉)], Pierluigi Morano[2], Maria Rosaria Guarini[1], and Francesco Tajani[1]

[1] Department of Architecture and Design, "Sapienza" University of Rome, 00196 Rome, Italy
{debora.anelli,mariarosaria.guarini,
francesco.tajani}@uniroma1.it
[2] Department of Civil, Environmental, Land, Building Engineering and Chemistry (DICATECh), Polytechnic University of Bari, 70126 Bari, Italy
pierluigi.morano@poliba.it

Abstract. The student housing market is emerging as a strategic sector for real estate investment in Europe, driven by an increase in demand for international and local student accommodation. This study proposes a valuation model based on the analysis of the break-even point for the rentable surface to determine the economic feasibility of projects for the redevelopment of existing buildings into student housing units. The approach was applied to 15 selected European university cities, given to local specificities in terms of costs. The results demonstrate that break-even points exhibit considerable variation between cities, shaped by factors such as labour costs, property values and rents. This study presents a replicable methodological framework for identifying the most attractive investment prospects and underscores the value of comprehensive local analysis in the planning of student housing projects. The practical implications extend to real estate investors, policy makers and stakeholders engaged in urban regeneration within a European context.

Keywords: student housing · financial feasibility · real estate investments · purpose-built student accommodation · evaluation model · break-even analysis · optimal rent

1 Introduction

The student housing market in Europe has undergone a significant transformation in recent years, becoming one of the most strategic sectors for property investment. According to recent data, the volume of investment in the sector will exceed €9 billion in 2019, demonstrating growing interest from institutional and private investors [1]. The European student population has more than 20 million students enrolled in higher education institutions, a number that is steadily increasing thanks to international mobility promoted by pro-European programmes such as Erasmus+ and the attractiveness of European universities to students from all over the world.

Over the last six years, more than 400 student accommodation projects have been implemented in Europe, responding to the growing demand for adequate student accommodation. This expansion has led to increased competition in the sector, making it essential to analyse key issues such as the sustainability of business models, innovation in services offered and understanding local market dynamics [2].

A key element to examine is the change in the nature of services provided by student accommodation facilities over the years. Whereas in the past student accommodation was limited to providing essential rooms and basic services, today we are witnessing a move towards facilities that offer a complete living experience. Modern student residences include facilities such as communal study and leisure areas, gyms, co-working spaces, high-speed internet connectivity, advanced security services and social activity programmes. This evolution responds to the needs of a more demanding generation of students who seek not only accommodation, but an environment conducive to personal and academic growth.

The sector offers many opportunities, including stable returns estimated at between 4% and 7%, steady demand fuelled by a growing student population and the potential to contribute to urban regeneration through the redevelopment of existing buildings. However, there are also significant limitations and risks. Market saturation in some cities, the variability of local regulations, the challenges of acquiring suitable property and the impact of global factors such as pandemics or changes in migration policies can all have a negative impact on returns [3].

Another important consideration is the scale of student projects. While large cities offer larger markets that allow for the development of larger facilities, smaller university towns may offer attractive opportunities for smaller but less competitive projects. Investors should therefore carefully consider the optimal size of the project in relation to the local market, student needs and available resources.

In terms of regulatory and financial support, there are European programmes that can co-finance interventions in the field of student housing, although there is no specific legislation dedicated exclusively to this area. For example, the European Regional Development Fund (ERDF) and the European Social Fund Plus (ESF+) provide funding for projects that promote social cohesion, inclusion and sustainable development. These funds can be used to co-finance the upgrading of buildings for student education, especially if the projects contribute to wider objectives such as energy efficiency, social innovation and urban regeneration.

The European Investment Bank (EIB) also provides financing and technical assistance for infrastructure projects, including education and student housing. These financial instruments can reduce the cost of capital for investors and improve the economic viability of projects.

In conclusion, the student housing market in Europe offers significant opportunities, but requires careful analysis of several key issues. Understanding market trends, such as the evolution of services offered and student expectations, is crucial to developing successful projects. Investors need to consider the limitations and associated risks, including regulatory changes, competition and demographic dynamics. The proposal of an evaluation model based on break-even point analysis represents a useful tool to support strategic decisions in the real estate sector, with particular reference to the planning of investments in student housing.

Determining the financial feasibility of interventions in this area requires the application of advanced valuation techniques that allow an accurate analysis of the costs, revenues and risks associated with the projects [4, 5].

One of the most widely used techniques is net present value (NPV) analysis, which makes it possible to assess the return on an investment by calculating the difference between the present value of expected cash flows and the initial investment [6]. For example, [7] describe the application of NPV in the context of real estate investments, including student housing projects.

The internal rate of return (IRR) is another basic tool used to compare the profitability of different projects or to assess whether an investment meets the minimum return required by investors [8–10]. In the context of student housing, IRR helps to understand the potential for returns compared to other types of property investment.

Cash discount analysis has been used in many studies to assess the financial feasibility of student housing projects. [11] use this method to analyse the investment performance of student housing in Australia, highlighting the stable returns and risk-return characteristics of the industry.

Sensitivity analysis is essential for understanding how variations in key parameters affect the profitability of a project. [12] highlight the importance of this technique in assessing the impact of factors such as employment rates, rents and construction costs on the financial viability of real estate projects.

The break-even point analysis can be used to determine the level of employment or rent required for revenues to cover total costs. [13] stress the importance of this technique for investors wishing to understand where a project becomes profitable.

The academic literature has also explored the application of more flexible methods, such as real options, to assess management flexibility in property development projects. [14] discuss the use of real options to incorporate uncertainty and the possibility of adapting decisions based on market developments.

Risk assessment through probabilistic analysis and scenarios has been used to address the uncertainty associated with student accommodation projects. [15] highlight the importance of incorporating risk analysis into financial assessments in order to improve forecasting accuracy.

Concrete examples of the application of these techniques can be found in experimental studies. [16] analysed the financial feasibility of sustainable student housing projects using discounted cash flow analysis, taking into account environmental and economic benefits. Another important contribution is that of [17], who examined the impact of sustainability certificates on the profitability of property investments, including student housing, highlighting how they can positively affect long-term returns. Research from Jones [18] provides an in-depth analysis of the European student housing market, using valuation techniques to identify investment opportunities and emerging trends in the sector. [19] uses data analytics to assess the performance of the UK student housing sector, providing insights into returns, employment rates and future prospects. [20] has analysed the student housing market in continental Europe, applying financial valuation techniques to identify cities with the best investment opportunities. In the academic sphere, [21] examined the impact of student demand on the housing market, using econometric models to assess the financial implications for investors. Finally, [22–24] examined investment strategies in the student housing sector, discussing the challenges and opportunities associated with financial valuation and risk management.

2 Aim

This study provides a useful tool for determining the economic viability of existing student housing refurbishment projects through an evaluation model based on break-even analysis. The starting point is a common case study with known parameters which, depending on the local characteristics of 30 selected European cities in terms of fixed costs, variable costs and unit revenues, enables investors to identify the most profitable investment opportunities and develop targeted risk mitigation strategies. In order to determine the optimal area for renting and allocating student rooms in 30 European cities, this work examines the impact of costs and revenues on the determination of the break-even area. It also indicates the amount of optimal annual revenue, i.e. the amount that would ensure the break-even point is reached, while maintaining the rental area and investment in the cities considered. In this sense, a scenario analysis is carried out based on the difference between the estimated annual revenue and the optimal annual revenue for student housing projects with a rental area of 2,472 square metres.

This approach makes it possible to determine the minimum level of occupancy required for the rental income to fully cover the total costs, thus avoiding the risk of an operating deficit. Particularly in the context of a competitive and fragmented market such as that for student accommodation, the break-even point (BEP) allows technical considerations to be integrated with local specificities in terms of housing demand and rent levels.Understanding the break-even point is crucial for making strategic decisions on production, pricing and resource management.

The practical implications of this research go beyond investors. Policy makers and stakeholders interested in urban regeneration can use this information to promote policies and initiatives that support the sustainable development of the sector. Public-private partnerships, facilitated by European co-financing programmes, can help speed up the implementation of projects that not only meet the needs of students, but also contribute to the economic and social vitality of European cities.

3 Case Study

A building of about 7 floors and 2,678 sqm should be realized for student housing. The project identified consists of the refurbishment of an existing disused building of the same size in a semi-central urban area of each of the major 15 universities European city. The project provides medium quality spaces for rooms, study rooms, restaurant, gym, hall, laundry, terrace and garden. The assumptions made are:

- The building to be renovated is bought by the private investor involved in the intervention considering a share of public co-financing equal to the 50% of the acquisition cost;
- The entire refurbishment is concluded within 1 year, so the time effects are not considered;
- The surfaces of the building are established according to Table 1.

Table 1. parameters of the renovation building

Surface	Sqm
Total	2,678
Rooms	2,142
Restaurant	107
Gym	54
Hall	80
Laundry	54
Study rooms	107
Terrace	54
Garden	80

3.1 Analysis of Demand and Offer in the Considered European Cities

The student accommodation market in major European cities is growing strongly, with increasing demand and diversifying supply. This is being driven by a number of factors, including increased international student mobility, the attractiveness of European universities and changing housing preferences. Demand for student accommodation has grown exponentially in recent years. Cities such as London, Paris, Berlin and Amsterdam attract large numbers of international students due to the presence of world-renowned universities.

London, for example, has more than 400,000 university students, while Paris has more than 330,000. However, the availability of beds in halls of residence does not match demand: London has around 96,000 beds, while Paris has around 75,000, with a coverage rate of 24% and 22% respectively. By comparison, cities such as Rome and Lisbon suffer from a much lower supply of less than 10%, forcing most students to turn to the private rental market, which is often expensive and not suited to their specific needs. This imbalance forces many students to turn to the private market, which is often characterised by high costs and inadequate infrastructure. The graph in Fig. 1 shows the student population, the number of beds available and the supply deficit to be covered in the 30 European cities considered in this work.

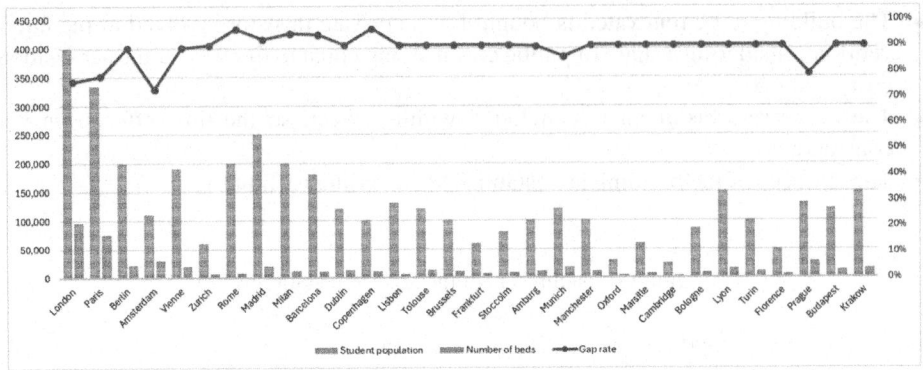

Fig. 1. Student population, number of beds available and supply gap to be covered

It can be seen that there are only 16,672 beds available for an average student population of 135,167, resulting in an average supply shortfall of 89% in the cities surveyed.

To meet their housing needs, a large proportion of Europe's student population looks for private rental accommodation, which is not available in the public sector. Private rentals offer more options in terms of location and size, but can be more expensive and less suited to the specific needs of students. In terms of accessibility, student accommodation is often close to universities or well served by public transport, reducing travel time and costs. On the contrary, cheaper private rentals are often located far from universities, in suburban or peripheral areas, increasing travel times and reducing student mobility. Modern student accommodation offers a range of services designed to meet the needs of students. Private operators such as The Student Hotel, Scape and DoveVivo have introduced innovative housing models that combine accommodation with shared spaces, premium services (gym, co-working, leisure areas) and advanced technological infrastructure. The Student Hotel, for example, has opened facilities in Paris and Amsterdam that provide students with modern and multifunctional spaces. These models are changing the perception of student accommodation, making it more of a community and learning space than a dormitory. However, private rentals can offer more privacy and flexibility in terms of guests and house rules.

New student accommodation tends to be more sustainable, built with ecological materials and with green certifications. Private rented accommodation, especially in cities with mature housing markets such as Vienna or Barcelona, often does not meet the same environmental standards.

In cities such as Berlin and Munich, the growing demand for student accommodation has led to intense competition for access to public housing, which offers lower costs than private accommodation. In response, many local governments are promoting initiatives to encourage the construction of new housing, but expansion is often hampered by a lack of building land and high construction costs.

The cost of student accommodation varies considerably from city to city. In cities with mature property markets, such as Amsterdam, London and Zurich, the price of a room in a premium private residence can exceed €1,000 per month, while in public or subsidised residences, such as those run by the CROUS in Paris, the cost can fall to €250-€400. In cities such as Milan, the average cost of a room in a private residence is around €600-800, a low price that reflects the scarcity of supply. On the other hand, cities such as Krakow and Budapest offer significantly lower costs, making them particularly attractive to students on a limited budget.

Key challenges in the student housing market include affordability, sustainability and the need for flexible solutions for international students. For example, while Amsterdam and Dublin are known for their high housing costs, innovative solutions such as hybrid residences combining shared accommodation and student housing are emerging. At the same time, the environmental impact of buildings has become a key issue: many new buildings, such as those in Berlin and Copenhagen, are designed with sustainability certificates and environmentally friendly materials.

In terms of opportunities, cities such as Lisbon, Budapest and Krakow represent emerging markets with great development potential. Demand is growing but supply is still limited, making these cities particularly attractive to investors. Milan, despite its competitive property market, is experiencing significant growth in the private student housing sector, with operators such as Camplus expanding their presence.

3.2 Methodology

In the design of European student housing projects, break-even analysis is a crucial tool for determining the minimum floor area to be built and rented in order to make the project financially sustainable. To calculate the break-even point (BEP), two main categories of costs are distinguished: fixed costs and variable costs. Fixed costs are those that remain the same regardless of the rental of the premises, such as the purchase cost of the building to be refurbished, technical and general expenses, legal fees and renovation costs [25, 26]. Variable costs, on the other hand, vary in direct proportion to the rental area of the premises, such as cleaning costs, maintenance and the normal profit of the entrepreneur. The calculation of the BEP in this case can be expressed in terms of the net rental area required, which is obtained by the equation:

$$Break-even\ point = total\ fixed\ costs/(Monthly\ unit\ revenue\ per\ room - Monthly\ variable\ unit\ cost\ per\ room)$$

In this equation, the denominator is the contribution margin per unit, i.e. the part of the unit revenue that helps to cover fixed costs after deducting variable costs. Total fixed costs include the purchase cost of the building to be refurbished, technical and overhead costs and legal fees. Variable costs, on the other hand, include expenses such as utilities, routine maintenance and cleaning costs, which are proportional to the area actually occupied. The numerator therefore reflects the need to cover non-letting costs, while the denominator represents the net margin per unit area, which is the difference between the average achievable rent and the variable costs.

The use of breakeven analysis in this context allows key operational questions to be answered for strategic planning. For example, it can be used to estimate the minimum employment rate as a function of the built up area and local economic parameters. It also shows how variations in rents or operating costs can affect the sustainability of the project.

The analysis is particularly useful in scenarios characterised by high uncertainty, such as those resulting from fluctuations in student housing demand in relation to external factors such as university policy or demographic dynamics. However, the use of breakeven analysis in the student housing sector has some critical features. The assumption of linearity in variable costs and revenues can be restrictive, given that the size of the project may generate economies of scale or diseconomies of scale. The heterogeneity of the European market also requires careful contextualisation of the economic parameters used. Break-even analysis should therefore be complemented by forecasting tools that take into account risk scenarios and demand variability.

3.3 Data Collection

In the application of break-even analysis to the economic evaluation of property refurbishment projects for student accommodation, the collection and preliminary analysis of data is a crucial stage in ensuring the accuracy of the estimates and the validity of the conclusions (Table 2). The key data include the unit market value of the building to be refurbished, expressed in €/m², determined by analysing the local property market and taking into account quotations of properties similar to the one under study and located in semi-urban areas of the 30 selected cities. This value is used to calculate the incidence of technical, general and legal costs. These components include the cost of design, technical and administrative advice and the cost of formalising the sales documents. To these are added the unit renovation costs, calculated in €/m², which summarise the expenditure required to bring the property up to a standard appropriate to its specific use as student accommodation. These parameters are the main inputs for determining the total fixed costs.

For the unitary variable costs, defined on a monthly basis per room (€/room/month), it is essential to include all recurring costs associated with the routine management and maintenance of the property. These costs include cleaning, utilities (electricity, water, gas and connectivity), routine maintenance (routine repairs) and administrative management (e.g. staff costs or any outsourcing of management). This data was collected through market research in each of the selected cities, taking into account local characteristics such as cost levels, regulations and differences in energy consumption related to the local climate. Data was collected and analysed from sector reports and professional associations, documentation of projects already carried out, local and national observatories, public databases and local reports.

The integration of these variables makes it possible to adapt the analysis to territorial and sectoral specificities, improving the model's ability to reflect real market conditions. The data collected thus form a coherent framework for calculating the break-even point, the basis for a robust economic evaluation and for optimising design and management decisions.

The unit fee was determined as the average of the monthly fees charged by comparable institutions already operating in the cities surveyed. The analysis was based on a representative sample of 30 European cities, selected on the basis of academic relevance, student market dynamics and availability of reliable data. Data was collected through detailed market research, including analysis of digital rental platforms (e.g. specialist student accommodation portals), sector reports and direct checks with local operators.

The primary objective was to obtain a realistic picture of the average rent in each city by normalising the data to take into account factors such as location, room size, services offered and maintenance status. This approach has enabled the creation of a reliable and standardised database, which is necessary to ensure the comparability of results between different geographical areas. The unit rent taken into account also takes into account the rental of rooms to tourists during certain periods of the year (summer, Christmas and Easter holidays).

The average of the rents recorded was calculated with particular attention to the statistical representativeness of the sample, excluding abnormal or non-periodic data. In addition, the effect of local variables, such as university policy and public or private housing supply, which can have a significant impact on price levels, was taken into account. This methodology has allowed the definition of a key parameter for the calculation of the unitary contribution margin, which is fundamental for the estimation of the area needed to reach the break-even point (break-even point).

The use of an average fee based on current and localised market data is a key element in ensuring the accuracy of economic assessments. Rigorous data collection not only ensures that assumptions are realistic, but also allows the analysis to be adapted to the specificities of the local context, thereby improving the robustness of project conclusions.

Cities such as Zurich (14,000 €/m^2) and Paris (12,500 €/m^2) have significantly higher property market values than Eastern European cities such as Krakow (2,600 €/m^2) and Budapest (2,850 €/m^2). This reflects increased housing pressure and strong demand in economically advanced cities. However, cities such as London (10,000 €/m^2) and Amsterdam (10,500 €/m^2) remain high, but in line with their strategic location and service offering.

Restructuring costs tend to be homogeneous in mature markets, averaging around 1,400–1,700 €/m^2. However, cities such as Zurich (1,785 €/m^2) and London (1,728 €/m^2) have the highest costs, reflecting the high value of the property market. Emerging markets, on the other hand, have significantly lower costs, such as Krakow (880 €/m^2) and Budapest (912 €/m^2), which can attract investment in high-return projects.

Technical and general costs vary considerably in percentage terms, from a minimum of 18% in Berlin and Hamburg to a maximum of 25% in Italian cities such as Rome and Bologna. This may indicate regulatory or structural differences in the management of refurbishment projects.

Legal fees vary widely, with cities such as Zurich (0.3%) having the lowest costs, while others such as Brussels (13%) and Rome (9.5%) have much higher rates. This may reflect differences in national regulatory requirements.

Operating and maintenance costs are significantly higher in the city of Zurich (275 €/ m^2) and London (250 €/m^2), probably due to the high quality of services required. Eastern cities such as Krakow (125 €/m^2) and Budapest (125 €/m^2) keep maintenance costs very low, favouring projects with lower running costs.

Figure 2 shows the impact of the various items used to calculate fixed costs in the 30 selected cities.

The figure shows how the economic and regulatory environment of each city has a significant impact on the structure of fixed costs. These data are essential for assessing the economic viability of student housing projects in different markets and for identifying

Table 2. Sample of data used in the analysis

City	Unit market value of the property [€/m²]	Unit cost of refurbishment [€]	Technical and general expenses [%]	Legal fees [%]	Unit average management and maintenance cost [€/month/room]
London	10,000.00	1,728.13	24	1.8	250
Paris	12,500.00	1,595.63	22	6.9	215
Berlin	6,000.00	1,448.75	18	7.5	175
Amsterdam	10,500.00	1,575.00	22	6.5	225
Vienne	7,000.00	1,461.88	19	5.0	175
Zurich	14,000.00	1,785.63	24	0.3	275
Rome	5,000.00	1,360.00	25	9.5	175
Madrid	6,000.00	1,423.75	21	7.5	150
Milan	7,000.00	1,448.13	25	7.5	185
Barcellona	6,000.00	1,423.75	21	1.5	170
Dublin	5,250.00	1,350.94	23	1.5	235
Copenhagen	6,000.00	1,432.81	22	0.8	215
Lisbon	3,750.00	1,082.19	20	6.5	150
Tolouse	3,500.00	1,164.06	22	6.8	150
Bruxelles	4,500.00	1,275.00	22	13.0	175
Francoforte	5,800.00	1,330.63	18	7.5	215
Stoccolm	6,200.00	1,452.19	22	3.5	225
Amburg	5,000.00	1,330.63	18	7.5	210
Munich	6,500.00	1,425.00	24	7.5	235
Manchester	4,000.00	1,275.63	24	1.8	185
Oxford	5,000.00	1,370.00	24	1.8	215
Marsille	3,150.00	1,164.06	22	6.8	150
Cambridge	5,200.00	1,320.00	24	1.8	215
Bologne	3,500.00	1,085.00	25	9.5	150
Lyon	3,750.00	1,154.69	22	6.8	150
Turin	3,150.00	1,041.25	25	9.5	150
Florence	4,250.00	1,116.88	25	9.5	150
Prague	3,350.00	969.06	19	4.5	125
Budapest	2,850.00	912.19	19	4.5	125
Cracovia	2,600.00	880.94	19	2.5	125

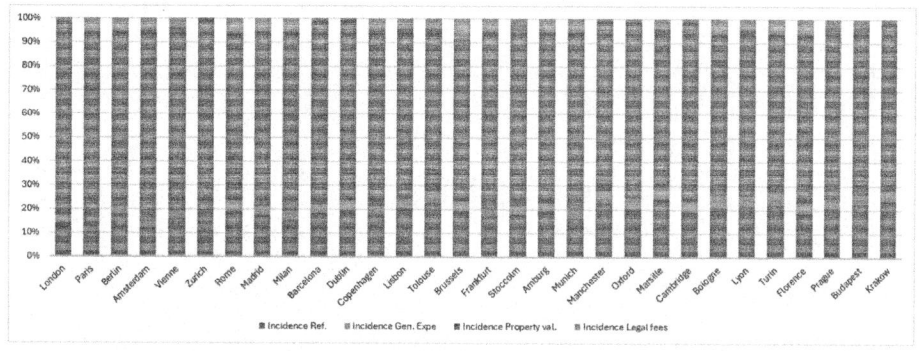

Fig. 2. Incidence of the items considered for the calculation of fixed costs in the 30 selected cities

cities that offer more favourable investment opportunities in terms of total costs. Cities in Northern Europe, such as Copenhagen and Stockholm, have a more balanced distribution between the different components, but with a lower incidence of overheads than markets in Southern Europe. Cities with relatively low property costs, such as Marseille, Lyon and Toulouse, appear to have a better balance of fixed costs between the different components, with a relatively higher weight of renovation costs compared to property value.

Property value (in green) is the dominant component in almost all cities, reflecting the importance of the local property market in total costs. Cities such as Zurich, Paris and London show a high incidence of this component, in line with their high cost property markets. In Eastern European cities such as Krakow, Budapest and Prague, this influence is relatively small.

Restructuring costs (in blue) and overheads (in orange) show significant variability, with a generally higher incidence in Italian cities such as Rome, Bologna and Florence, where the percentage of overheads is higher than average.

Legal fees (in light blue) show high variability: they are particularly low in cities such as Zurich and Copenhagen, probably due to more favourable or simpler regulations. On the contrary, cities such as Brussels show a significant incidence of this component, well above the average.

Figure 3 shows the monthly unit rent per room recorded in the 30 selected cities.

This chart provides a clear picture of the market differences in student housing across Europe. Cities with higher prices require innovative management strategies to attract students, while those with lower prices offer investment opportunities for low-cost housing projects. In addition, the concentration around certain averages suggests the existence of well-defined market segments, useful for the strategic positioning of new student housing projects.

The highest monthly room prices are found in London (€1,823) and Zurich (€1,553), confirming the strong demand in highly urbanised cities with high student densities. Eastern cities such as Krakow (€675) and Budapest (€675) have the lowest values, in line with lower living costs and economic demand. Cities in southern Europe, such as Marseille (€810) and Lisbon (€810), also have relatively low prices, suggesting investment opportunities in less saturated markets. Cities such as Paris (€1,350), Amsterdam

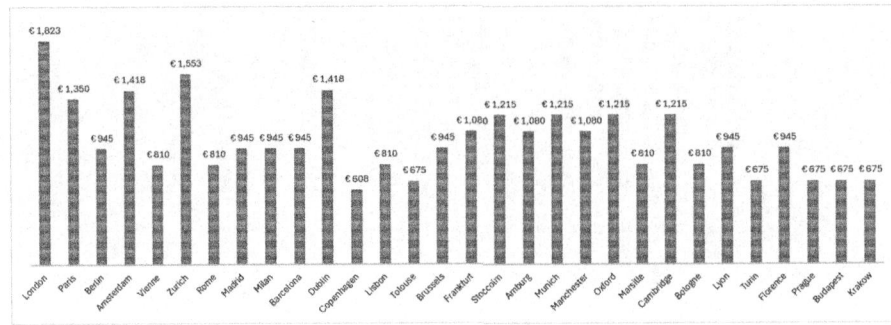

Fig. 3. Monthly unit rent per room in 30 selected cities

(€1,418) and Copenhagen (€1,418) are in the mid-to-high range, indicating a combination of high quality of life and moderate availability of student accommodation. The analysis shows a significant concentration of cities in the price range around €945 (e.g. Berlin, Milan, Madrid, Barcelona and Brussels), suggesting that this is the most common threshold for urban markets with a balanced combination of supply and demand.

3.4 Application and Results Discussion

The results of the break-even analysis in the 30 European cities considered show how different market dynamics and economic parameters affect the amount of land required to balance costs and revenues. Figure 4 shows the results obtained: the horizontal axis shows the value of the normalised area, while the size of the circles represents the actual amount of land required.

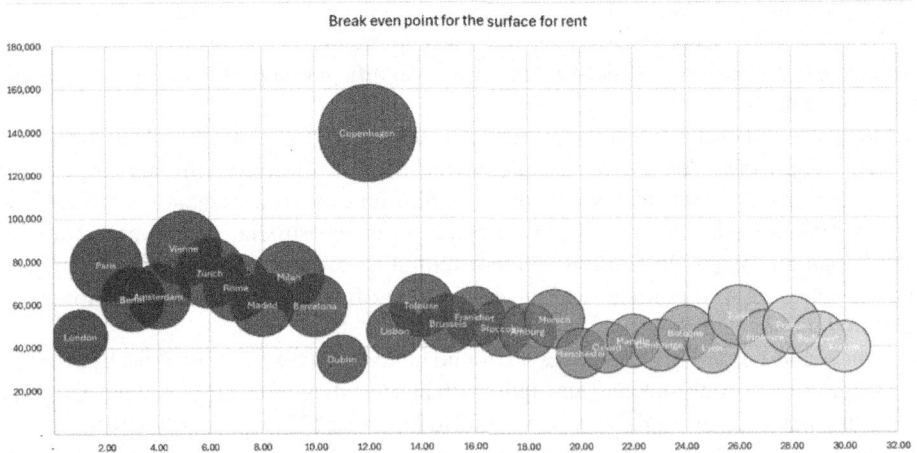

Fig. 4. Variation of the break-even rentable surface in the 30 cities

The cities of Western and Northern Europe (London, Zurich, Amsterdam) are in the low floor area requirement range, indicating markets where high yields are generated by the density of space per square metre.

The cities of Eastern and Southern Europe (Krakow, Budapest, Marseille) are grouped on the right, with a larger floor area required to compensate for the gap between average costs and rents. London, Paris, Zurich and Amsterdam are on the left of the graph. These cities require less space to break even, thanks to higher rents that allow fixed and variable costs to be covered by lower rental volumes.

The relatively small circles indicate the feasibility of small-scale housing projects in these cities, despite the high initial costs associated with land values.

Cities such as Milan, Barcelona, Madrid and Vienna show average values for the area required. These cities belong to moderate rental markets that require investment in larger projects than London, but are still competitive in terms of scale and cost.

The size of the circles suggests that these markets can support medium-sized projects, which are particularly attractive to investors with a medium-term horizon.

Copenaghen rappresenta un caso unico, con una superficie da realizzare e affittare significativamente maggiore rispetto ad altre città. Questo potrebbe derivare da un mix di costi elevati di costruzione e gestione combinati con canoni di locazione relativamente bassi rispetto ai mercati ad alto reddito.

Other cities such as Toulouse, Prague, Budapest and Krakow also require large areas to break even. However, their position on the right-hand side of the graph reflects lower unit costs and a reliance on economies of scale to compensate for reduced margins.

Cities with small areas offer investment opportunities for targeted housing projects, which require higher initial capital but generate a rapid return thanks to high rents.

Large cities require long-term strategies based on economies of scale, with larger but potentially less risky investments at lower cost per unit area.

3.5 Scenario Analysis and Discussion

The graph shows a scenario analysis based on the difference between the estimated annual revenue and the optimal annual revenue for student housing projects with a fixed rental area of 2,472 square metres in the 30 European cities concerned. The circles are grouped into clusters (cluster 1, cluster 2 and cluster 3) reflecting different market dynamics and levels of difference between estimated and optimal revenues. The map in Fig. 5 shows how this difference varies geographically and highlights relevant trends.

Cities in Cluster 1 (light yellow), such as Lisbon, Madrid, Tolosa, Prague and Budapest, show a relatively small difference between estimated and optimal revenues. This suggests that in these markets the economic conditions (rents and unit costs) allow costs to be covered with a floor area close to break-even. These cities are attractive for investment in emerging or less saturated markets. However, revenue growth in these markets may be constrained by moderately low fees.

Cities such as Amsterdam, Berlin, Brussels, Copenhagen and Stockholm fall into an intermediate (blue) cluster. Here the difference between estimated and optimal revenues is more significant than in cluster 1, probably due to higher fixed and variable costs compared to Southern and Eastern European markets. These cities have mature markets with

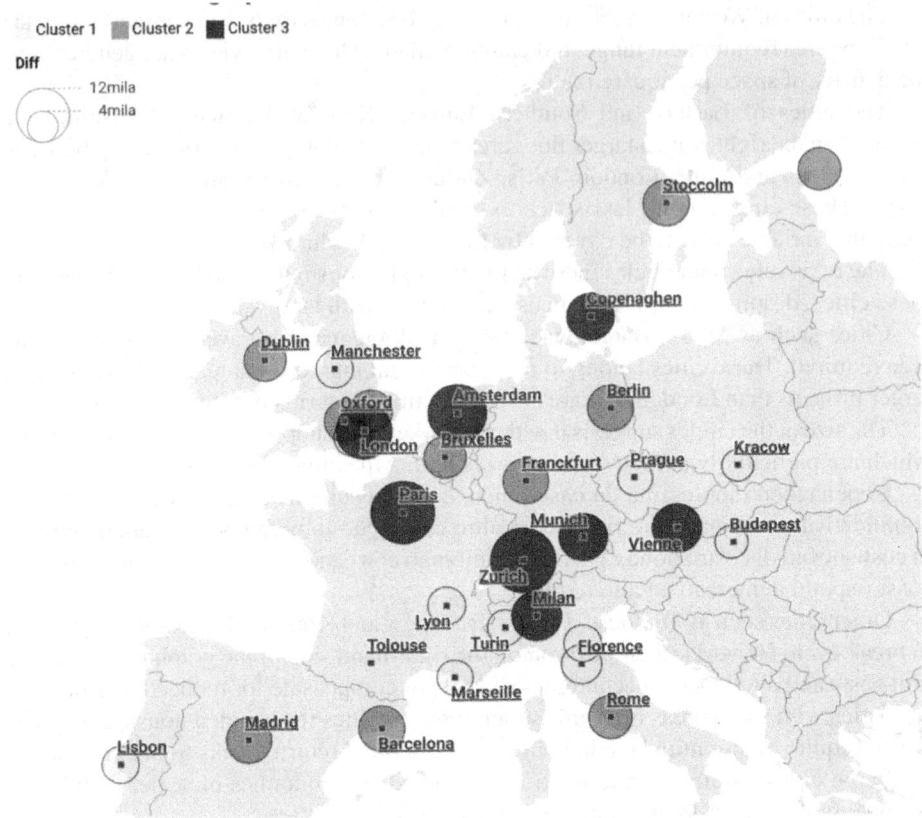

Fig. 5. Student housing optimal annual revenues differences

high entry costs, but also sustainable revenue opportunities if projects are implemented on a larger scale.

Within Cluster 3 (blue), cities such as London, Zurich, Paris, Milan, Munich and Oxford show a large difference between estimated and optimal revenues. In these markets, unit costs (especially fixed costs) are very high, requiring a significant increase in revenues to reach optimal levels of economic sustainability. Although these markets are characterised by high rents, high property pressures and development costs require aggressive strategies to maximise employment and reduce unit costs.

Cluster 1 represents an attractive opportunity for low-risk investment, with relatively stable markets and less exposure to high property costs. Cluster 3, on the other hand, requires more sophisticated investment strategies and greater scale to maximise returns and achieve economic equilibrium. Cities in Western and Northern Europe, such as London, Zurich and Copenhagen, are in the area with the largest difference between estimated and optimal income due to higher costs that are not fully offset by rents. Cities in Eastern and Southern Europe, such as Prague, Budapest and Marseille, show a much smaller difference, reflecting cheaper markets and more favourable dynamics for student housing projects.

4 Conclusions

The student housing market in Europe has developed significantly in recent years, becoming a key sector for property investment. In 2019, the volume of investment will exceed €9 billion, reflecting growing interest from institutional and private investors. There are more than 20 million students in higher education in Europe, a number that is constantly growing thanks to international mobility encouraged by programmes such as Erasmus+ and the attractiveness of European universities to students from all over the world. The present work provided a useful tool for determining the economic viability of existing student housing refurbishment projects through an evaluation model based on break-even analysis. The starting point was a common case study with known parameters which, depending on the local characteristics of 30 selected European cities in terms of fixed costs, variable costs and unit revenues, enabled investors to identify the most profitable investment opportunities and develop targeted risk mitigation strategies. The analysis of the results obtained highlights the differences in the economic dynamics of student housing projects in Europe, with particular attention to the variability of costs, rents and floor space required to break even. In terms of EU policy implications, the outcomes could suggest to stimulate sustainable investment in the sector with a share of public co-financing in order to increase the spread of this type of intervention. However, the break-even model has limitations related to simplified assumptions, such as the use of historical data and linearity of costs and revenues, which do not always reflect the complexity of the student housing market. Additional challenges arise from external factors such as fluctuations in demand, economies of scale and local regulations, as well as the lack of quality elements such as student preferences and competition from other housing solutions.

Future research developments could include dynamic evaluation techniques based on simulations of multiple scenarios and the use of geospatial tools to assess the economic viability of projects according to their location. In addition, the analysis could be extended to other property sectors such as offices and retirement homes. Finally, the applicability of the model in non-European contexts requires adjustments for regulatory and economic differences. Although useful for planning European funding policies, the breakeven model is only a starting point for a more in-depth and multi-dimensional analysis of the sector. The present study is consistent with the objectives of the *PRIN 2022 project INSPIRE – Improving Nature-Smart Policies through Innovative Resilient Evaluations*, as it develops a methodological framework for supporting resilient and sustainable investment decisions in urban contexts. By focusing on student housing, the research addresses key themes such as the adaptive reuse of existing buildings, the efficient allocation of resources, and the assessment of economic sustainability through dynamic and replicable tools. These aspects are consistent with the INSPIRE project's aim of improving policy effectiveness through nature-smart and innovation-driven evaluation approaches, especially in relation to urban regeneration and inclusive development policies.

Note: The current study has been developed within the current research P.R.I.N. Project 2022: "INSPIRE—Improving Nature-Smart Policies through Innovative Resilient Evaluations", Grant number: 2022J7RWNF.

References

1. BONARD: Student Housing 2022 – Europe Outlook (2022). https://www.bonard.com/insights/student-housing-2022-europe-outlook. Access on 19 Dec 2024
2. European Commission: Directorate-General for Education, Youth, Sport and Culture, Erasmus+ annual report 2023, Publications Office of the European Union (2024). https://data.europa.eu/doi/10.2766/833629
3. Assoimmobiliare: European student housing: The growing demand for PBSA in a constrained market. https://www.assoimmobiliare.it/wp-content/uploads/2024/12/European-student-housing_-The-growing-demand-for-PBSA-in-a-constrained-market.pdf. Accessed 2 Dec 2024
4. Locurcio, M., Tajani, F., Anelli, D.: Sustainable urban planning models for new smart cities and effective management of land take dynamics. Land **12**(3), 621 (2023)
5. Morano, P., Guarini, M.R., Tajani, F., Anelli, D.: Sustainable redevelopment: the cost-revenue analysis to support the urban planning decisions. In: Gervasi, O., et al. (eds.) *Computational Science and Its Applications – ICCSA 2020*, LNCS, vol. 12253, pp. 968–980. Springer, Cham (2020)
6. Locurcio, M., Tajani, F., Anelli, D., Ranieri, R.: A multi-criteria composite indicator to support sustainable investment choices in the built environment. Valori e Valutazioni **30**, 85–100 (2022)
7. Manganelli, B., Anelli, D., Tajani, F., Morano, P.: Capitalization rate and real estate risk factors: an analysis of the relationships for the residential market in the city of Rome (Italy). Real Estate Manage. Valuat. **32** (2024)
8. Brueggeman, W.B., Fisher, J.D.: Real estate finance and investments 14th edn. McGraw-Hill Irwin (2011)
9. Geltner, D., Miller, N.G., Clayton, J., Eichholtz, P.: Commercial real estate analysis and investments, 3rd edn. OnCourse Learning (2014)
10. Newell, G., Marzuki, M.J.: The emergence of student accommodation as an institutionalised property sector. J. Property Invest. Finan. **36**(6), 523–538 (2018)
11. Brounen, D., de Koning, S.: 50 years of real estate investment trusts: an international examination of the rise and performance of REITs. J. Real Estate Lit. **21**(2), 197–223 (2013)
12. Wurtzebach, C.H., Miles, M.E.: Modern real estate, 5th edn. Wiley (1995)
13. Trigeorgis, L., Tsekrekos, A.E.: Real options in operations research: a review. Eur. J. Oper. Res. **270**(1), 1–24 (2018)
14. Heijs, W., Stringer, C., Dijkstra, J.: The added value of student housing: a Dutch case study. J. Housing Built Environ. **31**(3), 495–508 (2016)
15. Byrne, P., Lee, S.: Real estate investment: a strategic approach, 2nd edn. Routledge (2011)
16. Wilkinson, S., Reed, R.: The business case for incorporating sustainability in office buildings: the adaptive reuse of existing buildings. In: 19th Annual Pacific Rim Real Estate Society Conference. Sydney, Australia (2008)
17. Oyedele, L.O., Ajayi, S.O., Kadiri, K.O.: Use of recycled products in UK construction industry: an empirical investigation into critical impediments and strategies for improvement. Resour. Conserv. Recycl. **73**, 177–186 (2013)
18. JLL. European student housing report. Jones Lang LaSalle (2019)
19. Knight Frank. UK student housing investment update. Knight Frank (2020)
20. Colliers International. The student housing market in continental Europe. Colliers International(2018)
21. Chatterton, P.: The student city: an ongoing story of neoliberalism, gentrification, and commodification. Environ. Plan A **42**(3), 509–514 (2010)
22. Munro, M., Turok, I., Livingston, M.: Students in cities: a preliminary analysis of their patterns and effects. Environ. Plan A **41**(8), 1805–1825 (2009)

23. Hubbard, P.: Regulating the social impacts of studentification: a Loughborough case study. Environ. Plan A **40**(2), 323–341 (2008)
24. Smith, D.P., Holt, L.: Studentification and 'apprentice' gentrifiers within Britain's provincial towns and cities: extending the meaning of gentrification. Environ. Plan A **39**(1), 142–161 (2007)
25. Anelli, D., Sica, F.: The financial feasibility analysis of urban transformation projects: an application of a quick assessment model. In: Calabrò, F., Della Spina, L., Bevilacqua, C. (eds.) *New Metropolitan Perspectives – NMP 2020*, LNCS, vol. 11786, pp. 462–474. Springer, Cham (2020)
26. Anelli, D., Ranieri, R.: Resilience of complex urban systems: a multicriteria methodology for the construction of an assessment index. In: Calabrò, F., Della Spina, L., Bevilacqua, C. (eds.) *New Metropolitan Perspectives – NMP 2022*, LNCS, vol. 482, pp. 690–701. Springer, Cham (2022)

Sustainable Real Estate in France: Impact of One-Stop Shop and Turnkey Contract Models on Energy Efficiency

Edda Donati[1](✉) and Dorothée Charlier[2]

[1] Department of Architecture and Arts, University IUAV of Venice, Santa Croce 191, 30135 Venice, Italy
`edonati@iuav.it`
[2] IREGE, Université Savoie Mont-Blanc, 4 chemin de Bellevue, 74940 Annecy-le-Vieux, France

Abstract. This study examines the relationship between business models for energy efficiency projects and the measures implemented in renovation and new construction in France.

A Hierarchical Cluster Analysis (HCA) is applied to 20 case studies using the One-Stop Shop and Turnkey Contract models. To further explore correlations, Cramér's V-test assesses the relationships between climate zones, business models, and photovoltaic system installations.

Two clusters emerge: Cluster 1, in continental climate zones, includes renovated buildings under the One-Stop Shop model with public incentives. Cluster 2, in oceanic climates, consists of new constructions under the Turnkey Contract model, without government support. Significant differences are observed in costs, surface area, and technologies used.

Cramér's V-test confirms the link between climate zone, business model, and technology adoption, showing that solar radiation influences photovoltaic system installation. The oceanic climate's favorable conditions explain the higher use of such technologies in new constructions.

These findings highlight the need to adapt business models to the local climate and building conditions. The study proposes targeted measures for policymakers to optimize energy efficiency through differentiated approaches.

Keywords: Innovative Business Model · Energy efficiency · Climate influence

1 Introduction and Background Literature

The real estate sector is a major contributor to environmental emissions, largely due to the poor energy efficiency of existing buildings. In Europe, outdated real estate assets account for approximately 48% of total emissions, exacerbating climate change [1–4].

To address this, the EU has implemented directives since the early 2000s, promoting energy-efficient renovations and nearly zero-energy buildings [5–8] National policies and incentives have further driven sustainable business models focused on improving building efficiency [9–13].

The One-Stop Shop business model, and the Turnkey Contract business model fall under these innovative business models.

The first model, the One-Stop Shop was developed in accordance with Directive 2018/844/EU and is exclusively used for the renovation of existing buildings. It is a place, either physical or virtual, where owners can obtain all the information and services they need to realize their renovation project. The One-Stop Shop offers a wide range of services to help customers at every stage of the project. It can therefore be described as a communication channel for owners and service providers [14–19]. There are different types of One-Stop Shop linked to the project and to the needs and resources of the client who wants to carry out efficient work. The model considered in this research is like the all-inclusive model or Energy Service Company (ESCo) model, where the ESCo ensures full continuity for the owners during the project phase by taking over the execution of the efficiency work from planning to implementation. It also ensures that the work is completed within the agreed timeframe and covers the project budget upfront, with the client repaying the costs after the work is completed [20, 24, 25] (Fig. 1).

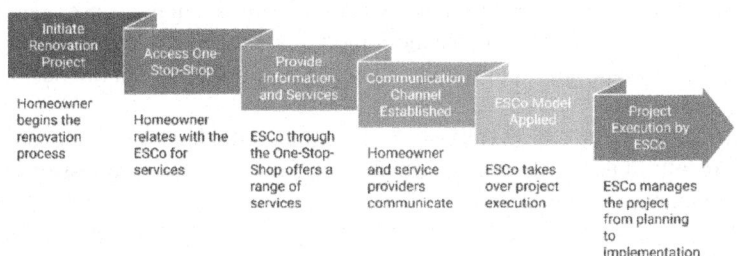

Fig. 1. One-Stop Shop (All-inclusive) business model process

The second business model, the Turnkey Contract, originated in the United States and is limited to the construction of new buildings. It requires the involvement of a large construction company that manages the design and the construction of the property on behalf of the client [20–22]. The Turnkey Contract model, which is used exclusively for newly constructed real estate, differs from the One-Stop Shop mainly in the relationship between the contractor and the client and in the commissioning of the project. With Turnkey Contract, the customer only defines the desired result, while the contractor develops the project, sets a fixed price and deadline. Finally, the project is awarded through a tendering process to select the most suitable contractor [20, 23] (Fig. 2).

Although 5 of the 20 case studies from the dataset have already been used to analyze the best practices that characterize the adopted business models and the associated economic figures, no study has yet focused on whether there is a direct link between the business model and the efficiency work performed [11, 19, 24].

This study aims to verify the existence or not of a significant relationship between the business model adopted and efficiency works promoted by analyzing 20 case studies on efficiency measures on the existing buildings and on the construction of new ones in

France, as it is one of the few European countries that has supported and promoted a policy aimed at making existing facilities more efficient [25–28].

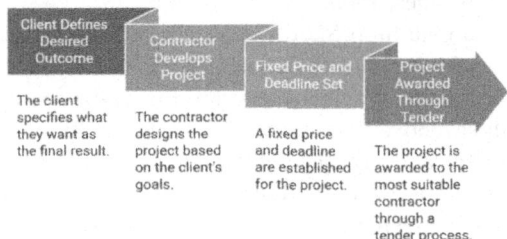

Fig. 2. Turnkey Contract business model process

The aim is to verify, using Hierarchical Cluster Analysis (HCA) and Cramer's V-test, whether the choice of business model can be considered as a characteristic element in the selection and promotion of the efficiency measures to be implemented.

The results obtained show that the two clusters identified differ not only in terms of the business model applied and the efficiency works promoted, but the subsequent Cramér's V-test between the variable of the business model and the works carried out underlines how much the installation of photovoltaic panels or not depends on the business model adopted in the project.

The article is organized as follows: Sect. 2 the methods adopted, Sect. 3 the data, Sect. 4 the results of the analyses performed, Sect. 5 contains their discussion and finally, Sect. 6 presents the conclusions.

2 Method

2.1 Hierarchical Clustering Analysis (HCA)

Hierarchical Cluster Analysis (HCA) is a widely used unsupervised learning technique for grouping similar objects into clusters.

It is particularly suitable for this study as it does not require specifying the number of clusters in advance and provides a hierarchical representation through a dendrogram, which helps interpret relationships within the data.

Given the dataset's characteristics, comprising only 20 observations with both continuous and categorical variables, HCA proves more effective than methods like K-Means, which is better suited for numerical data and larger datasets. Additionally, HCA allows for a flexible cluster structure without rigid assumptions about their shape. The quality of clustering can be evaluated using the Silhouette Score, which measures how well each observation fits within its assigned cluster compared to others, ensuring the robustness of the chosen methodology.

HCA builds a hierarchy of clusters using two main approaches: bottom-up (agglomerative) and top-down (divisive). This study adopts the divisive approach, where all observations start in a single cluster and are iteratively split into sub-clusters until a predefined number of clusters is reached or each object forms its own cluster. This approach is particularly useful for detecting natural separations within a dataset and provides a clear structure for interpreting clustering results [29–32].

Two fundamental concepts underlying the analysis method are the linkage criterion and the calculation of the distance between objects.

The linkage criterion defines how the distance between two clusters is calculated during the merging process in hierarchical clustering. There are different linkage criteria (e.g. simple linkage, complete linkage, etc.), but in this case, the focus will be on Single Linkage. [33].

Objects' distance, on the other hand, is a measure of dissimilarity that indicates how different two datasets (e.g. feature groups or objects) are. This concept is often used in clustering, especially when dealing with categorical or binary data.

Given two clusters C_1, C_2 and D as the distance between two objects x and y belonging to $C_1 and C_2$, the distance between the two clusters is expressed as:

$$D(C_1 C_2) = \frac{1}{|C_1| * |C_2|} \sum_{x \in C_1, y \in C_2} d(x, y) \quad (1)$$

where

- $|C_1|e|C_2|$ are the sizes (number of objects) of the clusters C_1 e C_2;
- $d(x, y)$ is the distance between two objects x and y that belong to the clusters respectively C_1 e C_2.

The sum is done on all possible pairs of objects, one for each cluster.

There are different types of distance measures, but this study will focus on the use of Jaccard distance which is a dissimilarity metric that quantifies the difference between two datasets [34, 35].

Given two sets A and B, the Jaccard similarity is defined as:

$$J(A, B) = \frac{|A \cap B|}{|A \cup B|} \quad (2)$$

where

- $|A \cap B|$ corresponds to the number of common elements between the two sets (the intersection);
- $|A \cup B|$ it is equal to the total number of elements joined between the two sets (union).

The Jaccard distance is the complement of the Jaccard similarity, and is therefore equal to:

$$D(A, B) = 1 - J(A, B) = 1 - \frac{|A \cap B|}{|A \cup B|} \quad (3)$$

2.2 Cramér's V-test

Cramér's V-test is a statistical measure to assess the strength of the relationship between two categorical variables. It is a normalized form of chi-square (X^2), that considers the sample size and the number of categories of the variables involved [36, 37].

The Cramér's V value varies between 0 and 1, where 0 means no association and 1 stands for a perfect association [38–42].

It is particularly useful when comparing contingency tables of different types. The following formula gives the value of Cramér's V:

$$V = \sqrt{\frac{X^2/n}{min(k-1, r-1)}} \qquad (4)$$

where:

- X^2 is the chi-squared test value calculated from the contingency table;
- n is the total number of observations;
- k is the number of columns in the contingency table;
- r is the number of rows in the contingency table;
- $min(k-1, r-1)$ is the smaller number between $k-1$ e $r-1$.

In this study, both analyses (HCA and Cramér's V-test) are conducted using the high-level programming language Python 3.0.

3 Data

The data analysis covers 20 case studies of projects involving the renovation of existing buildings or the construction of new ones, promoted through the One-Stop Shop or Turnkey Contract business model in France.

The collaborative web-based platform Construction21, which is aimed at all professionals in the construction sector and sustainable cities, is used to collect data. It presents numerous projects for the renovation and construction of new real estate that have taken place in Europe and beyond. Access to the platform is completely free and the content provided by users is moderated by recognized experts to ensure quality.

Although the web-based platform features numerous projects on the renovation of existing buildings and the construction of new ones in France, 20 case studies are selected as they focus on efficiency measures or new constructions promoted through business models classified under the One-Stop Shop and Turnkey Contract approaches. The first action performed is the naming and localization of the different cases. For each case, the identification code (ID), name (Name), business model adopted (BM) (One-Stop Shop or Turnkey Contract), Type of Intervention (IT), Construction Year (CY) and Investment Cost (IC) are recorded (Table 1). Once the naming is completed, it proceeds with the localization of the cases.

As can be seen in Fig. 3, the cases are divided according to the type of business model adopted: orange for the cases that use the One-Stop Shop business model and yellow for the cases that utilize the Turnkey Contract model.

Once this phase has been completed, the variables required for the HCA and the subsequent Cramér's V-test are determined (Table 2). They concern both the contractual aspect of the project (BM, IT, IC, INCEN) and the physical aspect of the building, which has been made more efficient or built from scratch (NFA, CY, ECb, ECa) and finally the climate in which the property has been improved or built from scratch (CZ).

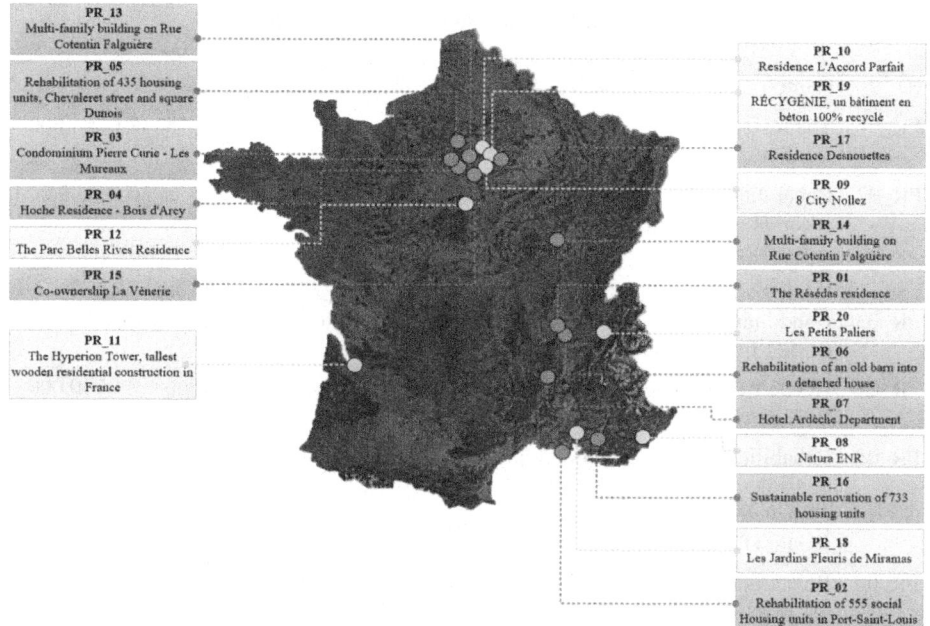

Fig. 3. Identification and localization of case studies

Great importance is given to the efficiency measures promoted, the type of heating, cooling and ventilation system installed (Heat, Vent, Cool) in addition to the installation or non-installation of photovoltaic systems (PVP). The installation or non-installation of insulation inside the building has not been considered, as in all cases have it included in the project.

The dataset consists of 20 case studies, 12 of which represent the One-Stop Shop business model and 8 Turnkey Contract model. The properties are evenly distributed between the Continental (8 out of 20), Oceanic (7 out of 20) and Mediterranean (5 out of 20) areas. The dataset shows an average investment cost (IC) of €6,574,236 and an average net floor area (NFA) of 9,884 m^2. In addition, most of the properties can be attributed to the condominium architectural typology (11 out of 20), most of which were built between 2019–2024 (6 out of 11) and between 1950–1976 (5 out of 11).

The Turnkey Contract business model is strongly linked to the installation of photovoltaic systems and the achievement of high levels of energy efficiency, as evidenced by the frequency of A and B class energy certificates in these buildings.

In contrast, the One-Stop Shop model is more common in buildings equipped with gas heating and alternative heating systems. This indicates a greater diversification of technological choices and management, which may be less focused on the implementation of sustainable technologies, such as photovoltaic systems.

The differences between the two business models are also reflected in the management strategies and energy efficiency outcomes.

The One-Stop Shop model shows greater variability in energy certification outcomes, including a significant percentage of buildings being categorized into energy

Table 1. Identification and coding of case studies

ID	Name	BM	IT	CY	IC
PR_01	The Résédas residence	One-Stop Shop	Renovation	1975	€1,800,000
PR_02	Rehabilitation of 555 social Housing units in Port-Saint-Louis (France)	One-Stop Shop	Renovation	1972	€16,400,000
PR_03	Condominium Pierre Curie - Les Mureaux	One-Stop Shop	Renovation	1974	€4,360,000
PR_04	Hoche Residence - Bois d'Arcy	One-Stop Shop	Renovation	1966	€1,700,000
PR_05	Rehabilitation of 435 housing units, Chevaleret street and square Dunois	One-Stop Shop	Renovation	1974	€18,295,000
PR_06	Rehabilitation of an old barn into a detached house	One-Stop Shop	Renovation	1940	€230,000
PR_07	Hotel Ardèche Department	One-Stop Shop	Renovation	1985	€3,400,000
PR_08	Natura ENR	Turnkey Contract	New Construction	2013	€4,200,000
PR_09	8 City Nollez	Turnkey Contract	New Construction	2022	€200,000
PR_10	Residence L'Accord Parfait	Turnkey Contract	New Construction	2022	€11,500,000
PR_11	The Hyperion Tower, tallest wooden residential construction in France	Turnkey Contract	New Construction	2019	€18,066,921
PR_12	The Parc Belles Rives Residence	Turnkey Contract	New Construction	2022	€4,174,695
PR_13	Multi-family building on Rue Cotentin Falguière	One-Stop Shop	Renovation	1950	€4,000,000
PR_14	20 dwellings Nuits-Saint-Georges	One-Stop Shop	Renovation	1972	€626,263
PR_15	Co-ownership La Vénerie	One-Stop Shop	Renovation	1976	€3,071,611

(*continued*)

Table 1. (*continued*)

ID	Name	BM	IT	CY	IC
PR_16	Sustainable renovation of 733 housing units	One-Stop Shop	Renovation	1975	€19,130,000
PR_17	Residence Desnouettes	One-Stop Shop	Renovation	1970	€2,950,000
PR_18	Les Jardins Fleuris de Miramas	Turnkey Contract	New Construction	2024	€9,800,000
PR_19	RÉCYGÉNIE, un bâtiment en béton 100% recyclé	Turnkey Contract	New Construction	2024	€9,869,070
PR_20	Les Petits Paliers	Turnkey Contract	New Construction	2022	€755,000

Table 2. List, description and values of variables

Variable	Description	Type	Code	Values
Business model adopted	Type of business model applied in the project	Categorical (Nominal)	BM	1: Turnkey Contract; 2: One-Stop Shop
Intervention typology	The intervention included renovation of the property or new construction	Categorical (Nominal)	IT	1: New construction 2: Renovation
Investment Cost	Total cost of the project	Categorical (Ordinal)	IC	1: €230,000 - €990,000; 2: €1,212,000 - €1,880,000; 3: €2,134,905 - €2,997,329; 4: €3,071,611 - €3.400,000; 5: €4,174,695 - €4,500,000; 6: €5,426,000 - €6,105,160; 7: €9,195,278 - €11,500,000; 8: €16,400,000 - €18,066,921

(*continued*)

Table 2. (*continued*)

Variable	Description	Type	Code	Values
Net Floor Area (m²)	Total area of the property	Categorical (Ordinal)	NFA	1: 162 – 516; 2: 1,119 – 2,948; 3: 3,420 – 5,760; 4: 6,372 – 9,138; 5: 12,343 – 56,000
Construction Year	Year of construction of the property	Categorical (Ordinal)	CY	1: 1890 – 1940; 2: 1950 – 1968; 3: 1970 – 1985; 4: 2003 – 2010; 5: 2011 – 2024
Building Typology	Architectural typology of the property studied	Categorical (Nominal)	BT	1: Office; 2: Condominium; 3: Single-detached house
Energy Certificate before	Energy performance certificate of the building before the efficiency measures	Categorical (Ordinal)	ECb	1: C; 2: D; 3: E; 4: F; 5: N/A
Energy Certificate after	Energy performance certificate of the building after the efficiency measures or new construction	Categorical (Ordinal)	ECa	1: A; 2: B; 3: C; 4: D
Heating system	The project includes efficiency measures on the building's heating system	Categorical (Nominal)	Heat	1: Central heating; 2: Heat pump; 3: Gas heating; 4: Other; 5: Electric heating
Ventilation system	The project includes efficiency measures related to the building's ventilation system	Categorical (Nominal)	Vent	1: Mechanical ventilation; 2: Natural ventilation; 3: No ventilation
Cooling system	The project includes efficiency measures related to the building's cooling system	Categorical (Nominal)	Cool	1: Active cooling; 2: Passive cooling; 3: No cooling

(*continued*)

Table 2. (continued)

Variable	Description	Type	Code	Values
Installation of photovoltaic panels	The project includes the installation of photovoltaic systems to generate electricity	Categorical (Nominal)	PVP	(Binary) 1: Yes
Incentives	Use of incentives for the realization of the project	Categorical (Nominal)	INCEN	(Binary) 1: Yes
Climate Zone	Climate zone in which the property is located	Categorical (Nominal)	CZ	1: Oceanic; 2: Continental; 3: Mediterranean

classes C and D. Post-intervention energy certification makes these differences even more pronounced.

Buildings managed under Turnkey Contract achieve better results in terms of energy efficiency, with the majority achieving an A or B class certification.

In contrast, the One-Stop Shop model, although successful in improving energy efficiency, does not achieve the highest scores as frequently, as shown by the presence of buildings certified in the lower energy classes.

4 Results

4.1 Hierarchical Clustering Analysis (HCA)

The analysis is performed using HCA to identify homogeneous groups within a dataset of categorical variables, and an initial dendrogram of the dataset was created (Fig. 4). To ensure an accurate representation of the relationships between observations, Jaccard distance and the average linkage method are applied, and the optimal number of clusters is set to two based on the characteristics of the dataset. The quality of clustering is assessed using the Silhouette score, which reached an average of 0.440 value. As can be seen in Appendix 1–2, the Silhouette score for two clusters proves to be the best, thus confirming the choice of the two clusters for the analysis, as the scores obtained for three or four clusters are worse and lower than the score of the two clusters.

A detailed description of the two identified clusters (Cluster 1 and Cluster 2) is then given. Since both clusters are represented by categorical variables, the description is made by calculating the mode of each variable to highlight the particular characteristics of each group (Table 3).

Cluster 1 comprises buildings in a continental climate zone that have been renovated on the basis of the One-Stop Shop business model and have benefited from government incentives. The average investment costs for these projects are between €16,400,000 and €18,066,921. The buildings in this cluster have a net floor area between 12,343 m² and 56,000 m², were built between 1970 and 1985 and are condominiums with an original energy rating of D and a final one equal to B. The efficiency measures in the renovation plan include the installation of a gas boiler and the introduction of a mechanical ventilation system, but cooling systems or photovoltaic panels are not included (Table 3).

Cluster 2 includes buildings in an oceanic climate zone that are built from scratch using the Turnkey Contract business model, with no government incentives for implementing the project. The average cost of these projects ranges between €9,195,278 and €11,500,000, with a net floor area that varies between 6,372 m² and 9,138 m². The buildings in this cluster were built between 2003 and 2010, belong to the condominium typology and have a final energy class of B. The planned efficiency measures include the installation of a mechanical ventilation system, a heat pump and photovoltaic systems, while a cooling system is not considered (Table 3).

This initial analysis shows that the only variables common to both clusters are the building typology of the condominium (BT = 2), a final energy class equal to B (ECa = 2), the installation of a mechanical ventilation system (Vent = 1) and the not installation of a cooling system (Cooling = 3).

Table 3. Clusters description

Variable	Cluster 1	Cluster 2
BM	2	1
IT	2	1
IC	8	7
NFA	5	4
CY	3	4
BT	2	2
ECb	2	5
ECa	2	2
Heat	3	2
Vent	1	1
Cooling	3	3
PVP	2	1
INCEN	1	2
CZ	2	1

4.2 Cramér's V-test

Although this initial analysis provides a clear distinction and description of the two characteristic clusters of the dataset, it does not yet answer the research question, i.e. whether the business model and the implementation of certain energy efficiency measures are correlated.

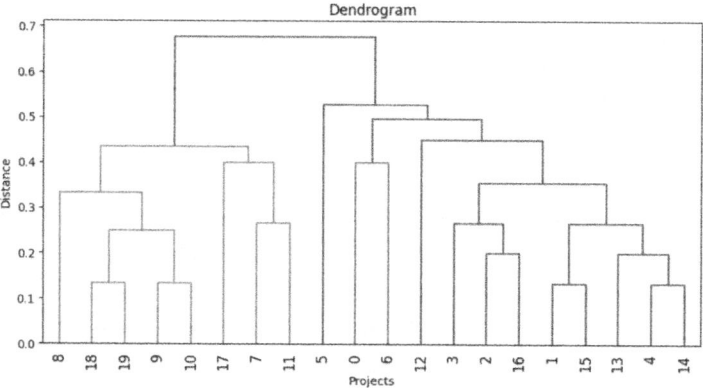

Fig. 4. Dendrogram representing the result of the hierarchical clustering analysis

To answer this question, Cramér's V-test is performed between the variables of the chosen business model (BM), the respective energy efficiency measures promoted in the projects (Heat, Vent, Cooling, PV) and also the variables related to the climate zone (CZ) and the use or non-use of government incentives (INCEN), as these also have a direct influence on the chosen energy efficiency measures or the type of business model.

The analysis of the correlations between the categorical variables using Cramér's V-test reveals significant results regarding the interactions between the chosen business model (BM) and some key variables of the energy efficiency measures. Table 4 shows the main results of the analysis.

The business model (BM) shows a moderate correlation with the installation of photovoltaic panels (PVP), with a Cramér's V of 0.578 and a p-value of 0.0098. The data suggests that the Turnkey Contract model is more frequently associated with the presence of PVP than the One-Stop Shop model. This correlation could be due to the nature of the Turnkey Contract model itself, which is more suited to new projects and major building interventions, while the One-Stop Shop model, which tends to focus on the renovation of existing buildings, demonstrates a tendency to exclude this technology from major interventions. Another significant correlation is found between the business model and access to public incentives (INCEN), with a Cramér's V of 0.636 and a p-value of 0.0045.

The results suggest that the One-Stop Shop model benefits more from the incentives, probably due to the greater compatibility of the renovation interventions with public financing programs for energy efficiency (as remarked in the existing literature).

This result is consistent with the role of incentives as a key element in stimulating investment in the sustainable renovation sector. A particularly strong and statistically significant correlation is found between the business model and the climate zone (CZ), with a Cramér's V value of 0.913 and a p-value of 0.0002.

This result shows how the choice of business models is influenced by the climatic context. In particular, the One-Stop Shop model is predominant in continental zones, where the harsher climate often requires interventions on existing buildings to improve their energy efficiency. In contrast, the Turnkey Contract model is more common in

Table 4. Cramér's V-test results

Variable 1	Variable 2	Cramer's_V	P-Value
BM	CZ	0.913	0.000
BM	Cooling	0.000	1.000
BM	Heat	0.441	0.421
BM	Vent	0.000	1.000
BM	PVP	0.578	0.010
BM	INCEN	0.636	0.004
CZ	Cooling	0.598	0.028
CZ	Heat	0.420	0.531
CZ	Vent	0.194	0.686
CZ	PVP	0.650	0.015
CZ	INCEN	0.674	0.011
Cooling	Heat	0.593	0.134
Cooling	Vent	0.000	1.000
Cooling	PVP	0.288	0.197
Cooling	INCEN	0.000	1.000
Heat	Vent	0.264	0.846
Heat	PVP	0.620	0.104
Heat	INCEN	0.351	0.652
Vent	PVP	0.000	1.000
Vent	INCEN	0.000	1.000
PVP	INCEN	0.348	0.120

oceanic zones, where more favorable climatic conditions facilitate the construction of new energy-efficient buildings. The relationship between CZ and the installation of PVP is also significant (Cramér's V = 0.650; p-value = 0.0147) and indicates that PVP are more frequently installed in oceanic zones, which are characterized by greater solar radiation and climatic conditions that favor the adoption of this technology.

5 Discussion

The HCA allows the identification of two different clusters reflecting significant differences between the buildings in terms of the chosen business model, energy efficiency measures and climatic context.

Cluster 1, characterized by buildings in continental climates renovated according to the One-Stop Shop model, shows a tendency to use public incentives for measures focused on thermal insulation and energy efficiency improvement.

In contrast, Cluster 2 includes buildings in oceanic climate zones that have been built from scratch using the Turnkey Contract model and are more inclined to use advanced technologies such as photovoltaic panels, despite the lack of government incentives.

Cramér's V-test assessed the significance of the relationships between the key variables and deepened the differences that emerged across the clusters. To aid interpretation, it is worth recalling that Cramér's V is a measure of association between categorical variables, with values ranging from 0 (no association) to 1 (perfect association). In this context, higher values indicate stronger links between variables such as the business model, climate zone, and adoption of technologies. The associated p-values show the statistical significance of these associations, with values below 0.05 indicating that the relationships are unlikely to be due to chance.

The strong correlation between business model and climate zone (Cramér's V = 0.913, p-value = 0.0002) indicates that climatic conditions directly influence the choice of operating model. Similarly, the significant relationship between the climatic zone and the installation of photovoltaic systems (Cramér's V = 0.650, p-value = 0.0147), which in turn are strongly correlated with the business model (Cramér's V = 0.578, p-value = 0.010) shows that local factors, such as greater solar radiation, are decisive for the adoption of certain technologies.

In France, the continental climate is characterized by cold winter temperatures, which prioritize measures to improve the energy efficiency of existing buildings. This context favors the adoption of the One-Stop Shop model, which focuses on energy-efficient renovations and is often supported by public incentives.

In contrast, the oceanic climate has milder temperatures and conditions that facilitate new construction projects. This suits the Turnkey Contract model, which is particularly suitable for the construction of energy-efficient buildings from the planning phase onwards. In addition, the greater solar radiation in some oceanic regions explains the significant correlation between the business model and the installation of photovoltaic systems (Cramér's V = 0.578, p-value = 0.0098).

The Turnkey Contract, associated with new projects, is suitable for more complex and technologically advanced measures, such as the introduction of photovoltaic systems and heat pumps.

The One-Stop Shop model, on the other hand, is geared towards measures that aim to significantly increase the energy class of existing buildings, such as the replacement of heating or ventilation systems.

This distinction is also in line with the characteristics of the French building stock: in the continental regions, the greater presence of buildings built between 1970 and 1985 requires renovation measures to bring them up to modern energy standards. In the oceanic regions, on the other hand, the availability of land and the absence of constraints linked to historical heritage favor the construction of new residential complexes.

The combination of HCA and Cramér's V-test offers valuable insights into the relationships between business models, technologies, and climatic factors. However, the results are influenced by the selected variables and the specific national context, which may limit broader applicability. Despite these limitations, the approach is effective for identifying patterns and informing targeted policy decisions.

6 Conclusions

This study investigates the correlation between business models and energy efficiency measures in 20 case studies of building renovations and new constructions across France. The case studies were selected based on geographic distribution (continental, oceanic or mediterranean climate), type of intervention (renovation vs. new construction), and the adopted business model (One-Stop Shop vs. Turnkey Contract).

The HCA clearly identifies two distinct clusters based on the business model, energy efficiency measures, and climatic contexts. The findings underscore the significant role of local climatic conditions in shaping the choice of business model and the technological measures implemented.

Cluster 1, representing buildings in continental climates, follows the One-Stop Shop model and relies on public incentives. The average investment costs for these projects range from €16,400,000 to €18,066,921, with a net floor area between 12,343 m^2 and 56,000 m^2. These buildings, primarily built between 1970 and 1985, undergo renovations that focus on improving energy efficiency but do not include advanced technologies like photovoltaic panels. Cluster 2, located in oceanic climates, includes new constructions under the Turnkey Contract model, with a focus on advanced energy solutions like heat pumps and photovoltaic panels. The costs for these projects range from €9,195,278 to €11,500,000, and they were built between 2003 and 2010.

The Cramér's V-test further strengthens the relationships between climate zone, business model, and technological adoption, revealing how solar radiation influences the decision to install photovoltaic systems. The oceanic climate's more favorable solar conditions explain the higher prevalence of such advanced technologies in new construction projects. While these results are insightful, several methodological considerations arise that could guide future research in this area.

First, local climate conditions appear to be a decisive factor in the selection of business models and technologies. Future research could replicate this study in different geographical areas or countries with varying climates to assess whether similar patterns emerge. This would help validate the findings and increase their applicability across different regions.

Second, a more qualitative approach could complement the findings. Interviews or surveys with industry professionals, such as building owners or developers, could provide deeper insights into the decision-making process behind the selection of business models and energy efficiency measures. Incorporating qualitative data would allow for a more nuanced understanding of the motivations, challenges, and constraints that influence these choices.

Based on the study's findings, policy makers are recommended to tailor energy efficiency programs to local climate conditions and building typologies. In continental climates, efforts should prioritize retrofitting and upgrading existing buildings, supported by business models such as the One-Stop Shop. In contrast, oceanic regions would benefit from promoting new energy-efficient constructions through models like the Turnkey Contract. Aligning energy efficiency initiatives with regional needs and characteristics would foster more effective implementation and adoption of sustainable measures.

Future research should expand the sample size and include a broader range of case studies to enable a more detailed examination of the relationship between climate, business model and technology adoption. In particular, research should explore adaptive business models tailored to regional climate variability to help policy makers, developers and investors make more informed decisions. This could accelerate the deployment of advanced technologies, such as photovoltaic panels and heat pumps, in regions where they are most effective.

Moreover, future studies should integrate quantitative variables—such as investment costs, renovation timelines, and energy performance indicators—together with qualitative insights gathered through interviews or focus groups with building owners and stakeholders. This mixed-method approach would significantly enrich the interpretation of the findings and provide a more comprehensive understanding of the motivations, constraints, and decision-making processes behind the adoption of energy efficiency strategies. It would also support clearer segmentation and comparison of case studies, contributing to more transparent and replicable methodologies. The methodology employed in this study is highly replicable in other regions or countries with similar climatic and regulatory contexts. The business model clustering technique can be applied to a wide range of energy efficiency initiatives across Europe and beyond, particularly where climate and technological factors influence real estate decisions. Applying this approach in diverse geographical areas would enhance the robustness of the results and increase their generalizability.

Disclosure of Interests. The authors have no competing interests.

Appendix

Appendix 1: Number of clusters and their different silhouette score

Number of clusters	Silhouette score
2	0.440
3	0.341
4	0.327

Appendix 2: Table number of cluster and their different silhouette score

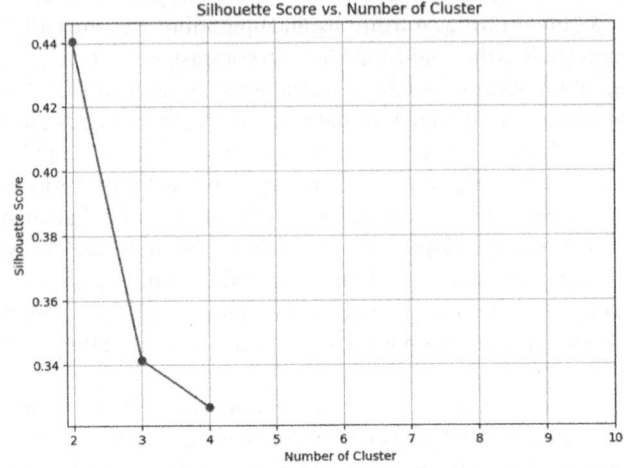

References

1. Maduta, C., Melica, G., D'Agostino, D., Bertoldi, P.: Towards a decarbonised building stock by 2050: the meaning and the role of zero emission buildings (ZEBs) in Europe. Energ. Strat. Rev. **44**, 101009 (2022). https://doi.org/10.1016/J.ESR.2022.101009
2. Miezis, M., Zvaigznitis, K., Stancioff, N., Soeftestad, L.: Climate change and buildings energy efficiency – the key role of residents. Environ. Climate Technol. **17**(1), 30–43 (2016). https://doi.org/10.1515/rtuect-2016-0004
3. Baglivo, C., Albanese, P.M., Congedo, P.M.: Relationship between shape and energy performance of buildings under long-term climate change. J. Build. Eng. **84** (2024). https://doi.org/10.1016/j.jobe.2024.108544
4. Xu, S., Fang, L., Govindan, K.: Energy performance contracting in a supply chain with financially asymmetric manufacturers under carbon tax regulation for climate change mitigation. Omega (Westport) **106**, 102535 (2022). https://doi.org/10.1016/J.OMEGA.2021.102535
5. I (Legislative acts) DIRECTIVES DIRECTIVE (EU) 2023/1791 OF THE EUROPEAN PARLIAMENT AND OF THE COUNCIL of 13 September 2023 on energy efficiency and amending Regulation (EU) 2023/955 (recast) (Text with EEA relevance)
6. DIRECTIVE (EU) 2018/844 OF the European Parliament and of the Council of 30 May 2018 amending Directive 2010/31/EU on the energy performance of buildings and Directive 2012/27/EU on energy efficiency (Text with EEA relevance)
7. Directive 2010/31/EU of the European Parliament and of the Council of 19 May 2010 on the energy performance of buildings
8. DIRECTIVE 2002/91/EC of the European Parliament and of the Council of 16 December 2002 on the energy performance of buildings.
9. Munaro, M.R., do Freitas, C.D., Tavares, S.F., Bragança, L.: Circular business models: current state and framework to achieve sustainable buildings. J. Constr. Eng. Manag. **147**(12), 04021164 (2021). https://doi.org/10.1061/(ASCE)CO.1943-7862.0002184
10. Zhao, X., Pan, W., Lu, W.: Business model innovation for delivering zero carbon buildings. Sustain. Cities Soc. **27**, 253–262 (2016). https://doi.org/10.1016/j.scs.2016.03.013

11. Copiello, S., Donati, E., Bonifaci, P.: Energy efficiency practices: a case study analysis of innovative business models in buildings. Energy Build. **313**, 114223 (2024). https://doi.org/10.1016/J.ENBUILD.2024.114223
12. Sinkovics, N., Gunaratne, D., Sinkovics, R.R., Molina-Castillo, F.J.: Sustainable business model innovation: an umbrella review, MDPI AG (2021). https://doi.org/10.3390/su13137266
13. Ensign, P.C.: business models and sustainable development goals MDPI (2022).https://doi.org/10.3390/su14052558
14. McGinley, O., Moran, P., Goggins, J.: Key considerations in the design of a one-stop-shop retrofit mode. Civil Engineering Research in Ireland, pp. 354–359 (2020)
15. Bagaini, A., Croci, E., Molteni, T.: Boosting energy home renovation through innovative business models: ONE-STOP-SHOP solutions assessment. J. Clean. Prod. **331**, 129990 (2022). https://doi.org/10.1016/J.JCLEPRO.2021.129990
16. Pardalis, G., Talmar, M., Keskin, D.: To be or not to be: the organizational conditions for launching one-stop-shops for energy related renovations. Energy Policy **159** (2021). https://doi.org/10.1016/j.enpol.2021.112629
17. Bjørneboe, M.G., Svendsen, S., Heller, A.: Using a one-stop-shop concept to guide decisions when single-family houses are renovated. J. Archit. Eng. **23**(2), 05017001 (2017). https://doi.org/10.1061/(ASCE)AE.1943-5568.0000238
18. Commission, E., Centre, J.R., Boza-Kiss, B., Bertoldi, P., Della Valle, N., Economidou, M.: One-stop shops for residential building energy renovation in the EU – analysis & policy recommendations. Publications Office (2021).https://doi.org/10.2760/245015
19. Donati, E., Copiello, S.: The one-stop shop business model for improving building energy efficiency: analysis and applications. In: Gervasi, O., et al. (eds.) Computational Science and Its Applications – ICCSA 2023 Workshops. ICCSA 2023. LNCS, vol. 14106. Springer, Cham (2023). https://doi.org/10.1007/978-3-031-37111-0_30
20. Doe, J., Nitek, D., Minamikata, N., Smith Freehills, H.: Construction Arbitration and Turnkey Projects, Construction Arbitration and Turnkey Projects (2021). https://globalarbitrationreview.com/guide/the-guide-construction-arbitration/fourth-edition/article/construction-arbitration-and-turnkey-projects
21. Schneider, M.E.: Turnkey contracts - Concepts, liabilities, claims. In: 4, vol. 3. London: LLYOD'S OF LONDON PRESS LTD (1986). https://www.lalive.law/wp-content/uploads/2019/10/mes_turnkey_contracts.pdf
22. Mimoso, M.J.: The Turnkey Contract and the Globalization Era
23. Merna, A., Smith, N.: Project managers and the use of turnkey contracts. Int. J. Project Manage. **8**(3), 183–189 (1990). https://doi.org/10.1016/0263-7863(90)90021-3
24. Donati, E., Copiello, S., Bonifaci, P.: Applications and economic profiles of the turnkey contract business model. In: Gervasi, O., Murgante, B., Garau, C., Taniar, D., Rocha, A.M.A.C., Faginas Lago, M.N. (eds.) Computational Science and Its Applications – ICCSA 2024 Workshops, pp. 143–161. Springer Nature Switzerland, Cham (2024)
25. Lévy, J.P., Belaïd, F.: The determinants of domestic energy consumption in France: energy modes, habitat, households and life cycles. Renew. Sustain. Energy Rev. **81**, 2104–2114 (2018). https://doi.org/10.1016/J.RSER.2017.06.022
26. Ravigné, E., Ghersi, F., Nadaud, F.: Is a fair energy transition possible? Evidence from the French low-carbon strategy. Ecol. Econ. **196**, 107397 (2022). https://doi.org/10.1016/J.ECOLECON.2022.107397
27. Sebi, C., Vernay, A.L.: Community renewable energy in France: the state of development and the way forward. Energy Policy **147**, 111874 (2020). https://doi.org/10.1016/J.ENPOL.2020.111874

28. Giraudet, L.G., Bourgeois, C., Quirion, P.: Policies for low-carbon and affordable home heating: a French outlook. Energy Policy **151**, 112140 (2021). https://doi.org/10.1016/J.ENPOL.2021.112140
29. Baker, F.B., Hubert, L.J.: Measuring the power of hierarchical cluster analysis. J. Am. Stat. Assoc. **70**(349), 31–38 (1975)
30. Schonlau, M.: Visualizing non-hierarchical and hierarchical cluster analyses with clustergrams. Comput. Stat. **19**, 95–111 (2004)
31. Köhn, H., Hubert, L.J.: Hierarchical cluster analysis. Wiley StatsRef: statistics reference online, pp. 1–13 (2014)
32. Contreras, P., Murtagh, F.: Hierarchical clustering. Handbook of cluster analysis, pp. 103–123 (2015)
33. Yim, O., Ramdeen, K.T.: Hierarchical cluster analysis: comparison of three linkage measures and application to psychological data. Quant. Method Psychol. **11**(1), 8–21 (2015)
34. Dolev, S., Ghanayim, M., Binun, A., Frenkel, S., Sun, Y.S.: Relationship of Jaccard and edit distance in malware clustering and online identification (Extended abstract). In: 2017 IEEE 16th International Symposium on Network Computing and Applications (NCA), pp. 1–5 (2017). https://doi.org/10.1109/NCA.2017.8171380
35. Mammone, N., Ieracitano, C., Adeli, H., Bramanti, A., Morabito, F.C.: Permutation jaccard distance-based hierarchical clustering to estimate EEG network density modifications in MCI subjects. IEEE Trans. Neural Netw. Learn. Syst. **29**(10), 5122–5135 (2018). https://doi.org/10.1109/TNNLS.2018.2791644
36. Gregory, G.G.: Key words: CRAMER-VON MISES TYPE TESTS FOR SYMMETRY (1977)
37. Rodriguez, J.C., Viollaz, A.J.: A cramer - von mises type goodness of fit test with asymmetric weight function. Commun. Stat. Theory Methods **24**(4), 1095–1120 (1995). https://doi.org/10.1080/03610929508831542
38. Taylor, H.M.W.A.T.C., Gusnanto, A.: Properties and approximate p-value calculation of the Cramer test. J. Stat. Comput. Simul. **90**(11), 1965–1981 (2020). https://doi.org/10.1080/00949655.2020.1754820
39. Laio, F.: Cramer-von Mises and Anderson-Darling goodness of fit tests for extreme value distributions with unknown parameters. Water Resour. Res. **40**(9) (2004). https://doi.org/10.1029/2004WR003204
40. Tamura, R.N., Faries, D.E., Feng, J.: Comparing time to onset of response in antidepressant clinical trials using the cure model and the Cramer-von mises test (2000). https://doi.org/10.1002/1097-0258(20000830)19:16<2169::AID-SIM513>3.0.CO;2-O
41. Tomizawa, S., Miyamoto, N., Houya, H.: Generalization of Cramer's coefficient of association for contingency tables: theory and methods. S. Afr. Stat. J. **38**(1), 1–24 (2004). https://doi.org/10.10520/EJC99072
42. Baker, R.D.: A new perspective on the cramér-von mises test. J. Nonparametr. Stat. **7**(3), 255–277 (1997). https://doi.org/10.1080/10485259708832703

An SMCE Approach for Developing Integrated and Shared Strategies for the Port City of Brindisi

Giuseppe Ciciriello[1](✉) [iD], Benedetta Ettorre[2], Carlotta Grandis[3], Sabrina Sacco[4] [iD], and Maria Cerreta[1] [iD]

[1] Department of Architecture, University of Naples Federico II, Naples, Italy
{giuseppe.ciciriello,cerreta}@unina.it
[2] Construction Technologies Institute (ITC), National Research Council of Italy (CNR), Naples, Italy
ettorre@itc.cnr.it
[3] AdSP, Western Ligurian Sea Port Authority, Naples, Italy
carlotta.grandis@portsofgenoa.com
[4] Department of Design, Polytechnic University of Milan, Milan, Italy
sabrina.sacco@polimi.it

Abstract. Within port cities, marine and coastal resources' exploitation is strongly influenced by interaction patterns existing among the actors living, working and managing such territories. This complexity raises questions about how the physical space can be regulated and how relational configurations between agents can be agreed and formalised.

In the port city of Brindisi (Southern Italy), strategic development and planning choices are marked by constant tensions: the community's aspiration to recover from decades of top-down industrialisation face the separation between port and urban planning policies, thus resulting in a conflictual decision-making. Port city planning and policymaking need to be supported by evaluation practices in order to face the complexity both in terms of sustainable port economy, coastal territory uses, and in terms of building a fair, participatory and effective decision-making process. The application of SOCRATES tool, implementing the principles of the Social Multi-Criteria Evaluation (SMCE) methodological framework, allows the identification of the most favourable sustainable development scenario for the Brindisi context, and takes into account the points of view and the possible alliances arising among the different social groups and actors involved. Adopting evaluation as an ex-ante support tool for spatial and maritime planning makes it possible to identify objectives, design site-specific scenarios and select the most preferable alternative. This valuation approach helps to combine a complex and multidimensional strategy, integrating economic, social, environmental and cultural values, and favours the building of shared transformative policies, engaging all actors involved into a participatory decision-making process.

Keywords: Port City Planning · SOCRATES · SMCE

© The Author(s), under exclusive license to Springer Nature Switzerland AG 2026
O. Gervasi et al. (Eds.): ICCSA 2025 Workshops, LNCS 15889, pp. 429–446, 2026.
https://doi.org/10.1007/978-3-031-97603-2_27

1 Introduction

The port city concept has evolved over time. Initially characterised by a spontaneous development symbiosis, it was transformed by the port industrialisation process, which resulted in the separation between settlements and coastal infrastructure [1, 2].

Despite their economic importance, port operations generate significant environmental externalities and pressure, including air and noise pollution, soil degradation, habitat loss, and traffic congestion [3–6]. The increasing functional specialization of ports has also led to a rupture in public perception, diminishing their recognizability and integration within the urban fabric. This detachment has contributed to a fragmentation in governance between ports and cities, intensifying conflicts among the various stakeholders who influence, or are affected by, port-driven transformations [7–11].

Port cities thus offer exemplary contexts for studying economic activities and anthropogenic effects on the natural environment, and at the same time considering public-private-social agreements through which coastal management and transformative decisions are taken. Consequently, port cities represent key areas for rethinking transformation and development paradigms, addressing the complexity of their dimensions and interests, and meeting international sustainability frameworks [12–14].

The International Association for Port Cities (AIVP) has specifically contextualized the SDGs, a comprehensive reference for reorienting development policies, for port cities' context, identifying key challenges and levers for promoting sustainability [15]. Among these are energy transition processes to safeguard natural resources and ecosystems–Goals 2; the development of soft mobility strategies enhancing access to port areas and supporting maritime cultural heritage valorisation–Goals 3 and 6; finally innovative, participatory governance models fostering joint pathways combining port and urban development–Goals 4 and 8.

Following the examination of sustainability frameworks in port cities, two key issues emerge: first, the economic models that underpin port productivity and efficiency; and second, the governance mechanisms through which stakeholders plan, manage, and make decisions affecting the broader coastal and urban territory.

The New Approach for a Sustainable Blue Economy in the EU (2021) proposes a novel economic model for ports, identifying sectors such as renewable marine energy, blue biotechnology, sustainable fisheries, aquaculture, and coastal tourism as main activities for the sustainable use of marine and coastal resources [16]. Among these, tourism could represent a strategic and socially favourable economic sector for coastal communities, although its uncontrolled spread could cause environmental degradation and tensions among residents [17]. In response, various studies [18–20] and international organizations [21], have proposed the concept of Circular Tourism, which seeks to minimize externalities and reorient port-city development strategies toward the enhancement of both tangible and intangible heritage.

Looking at port governance, ESPO [22] also emphasised the role of engagement and participation as crucial tools to improve the effectiveness and soundness of policy-making. Best practices include the use of public art, spatial activation, and multimedia communication to foster public support for port activities, strengthen citizen collaboration in improving port-city interface areas, and educate younger generations who may enter the maritime sector [23].

The wide range of emerging themes and strategic insights on the global stage contrasts with the still fragmented approach to port city planning, which oscillates between the imperative to maximise port productivity and the need to restore coastal and urban environments. Furthermore, the spatial scales at which these planning efforts operate are diverse, ranging from narrow, infrastructure-focused approaches to broader territorial considerations that account for the port's regional influence [24].

In this context, evaluation methods, particularly Multi-Criteria Decision Analysis (MCDA) [25–27], can serve as a valuable tool to reconcile competing planning objectives. By integrating economic, social, environmental, and cultural values, these methods support the ex-ante development of sustainable transformation scenarios [28]. In particular, this contribution intends to underline the valuable role that Social Multi-Criteria Evaluation (SMCE) [29] could play in port city planning. The SMCE framework enables the integration of operational evaluation criteria with the value preferences expressed by social groups engaged in the decision-making process. The objective is to explore how the inclusion of multiple actors and value systems [30] in a real-world context can generate synergistic, place-based, and sustainable solutions, challenging conventional development models and contributing to the innovation of urban-port policy. The main focus is on the ability to integrate SMCE into spatial planning in order to produce shared strategies for the transformation of complex port territories.

This research—part of the E.E.CO Culture Brindisine project, developed within the Second-Level Master's Program in Sustainable Planning and Design of Port Areas (MPPSAP) and doctoral research activities at the Department of Architecture, University of Naples "Federico II"—explores the opportunities offered by adopting an SMCE approach through the SOCRATES (Social Multi-Criteria Assessment of European Policies) tool [31], applied to the specific context of policy-making in Brindisi concerning port and city planning.

Brindisi, located in Southern Italy, is a significant case study, characterised by pronounced conflicts among stakeholders and the contradiction between coastal environment potential and industry-based port economy. Brindisi represents a potentially paradigmatic case for other Mediterranean port cities, that are currently struggling between maritime economic growth and enhancement of landscape and ecological heritage, as they address port-city interaction.

The contribution is structured as follows: Sect. 2 describes the case study of Brindisi; Sect. 3 focuses on the adopted methodology and its phases; Sect. 4 presents the results of the SMCE application; Sect. 5 offers a discussion of the findings and the conclusions.

2 Case Study: The Port City of Brindisi

In order to understand how evaluation can support the planning processes of port cities, contributing to the integration of different development objectives and considering the ambitions and trends expressed by the involved stakeholders, the SMCE evaluation model [29] has been applied to the case study of Brindisi, Apulia Region, Italy.

Brindisi is historically tied to its port, representing, since its pre-Roman origins, a strategic hub for Mediterranean maritime trade. In Roman times, the Via Appia reached its endpoint in the port of Brindisi, highlighting the port's commercial and military importance through the Middle Ages. In the 19th century, the port regained strategic relevance, becoming a main commercial hub for routes toward the Suez Canal and the East, strengthening connections between Europe and its Asian colonies [32, 33]. As a result, the city retains a rich historical-archaeological heritage, including evidence of urban settlement such as the historic center and the "Punta delle Terrare" archaeological area, as well as the rural masseria system. These heritage assets are currently threatened by industrial pressure and peripheral urban expansion.

From an environmental perspective, the territory of Brindisi features a flat, agriculturally oriented landscape shaped over time by waterways that have deeply carved the coastal profile, leading to the presence of coastal wetlands. The erosive action of these watercourses contributed to the formation of the port's unique configuration: an inner bifurcated basin surrounding the historic city. The hydrographic system of surface and groundwater is severely compromised by ecological degradation, morphological alteration, artificialization, and pollution, resulting in the port and its surrounding areas being designated as a Site of National Interest (SIN) [34, 35].

From an infrastructural standpoint, Brindisi has a complex intermodal system integrating the port, railway network, road arteries, and airport. The port is organized into three basins with distinct functions, serving passengers, recreational, logistical, and freight activities. It is supported by a specialized industrial hinterland focused on fossil-fuel energy and chemical production. The interface areas between port and city are partially compromised by military zones and airport facilities, limiting accessibility and the full enhancement of the urban waterfront and coastal landscape.

This case study was selected for its distinctive features, which make it particularly relevant for the adoption of evaluation tools and methods capable of capturing and enhancing its inherent complexity. Firstly, the implementation of industrialization policies from the second half of the 20th century, which led to a significant expansion of port infrastructure driven by top-down decisions, contributed to sea and coast pollution through predominantly fossil-fuel and chemical-based activities. Secondly, a high level of conflict among stakeholders is observed, both at an institutional level, between port and urban planning authorities, and at social one, as citizens tend to perceive port facilities as an environmental detractor and seek pathways toward more landscape, human health and ecosystem-oriented development. Moreover, the current progress of port sector planning, with the approval of the Port Regulatory Plan (PRP) scheduled for January 2025, has defined new infrastructure interventions aligned with operational forecasts [36].

In this complex panorama, Brindisi thus emerges as a city with a strong logistical and industrial identity, where recent transformations pose complex challenges linked to integrating economic development with environmental protection and historical-cultural heritage preservation.

3 Methodology

The methodological approach illustrated in this contribution is aimed at structuring a possible framework for the decision-making process related to the transformation of port cities. To this end, the approach is articulated in three distinct phases, with the objective

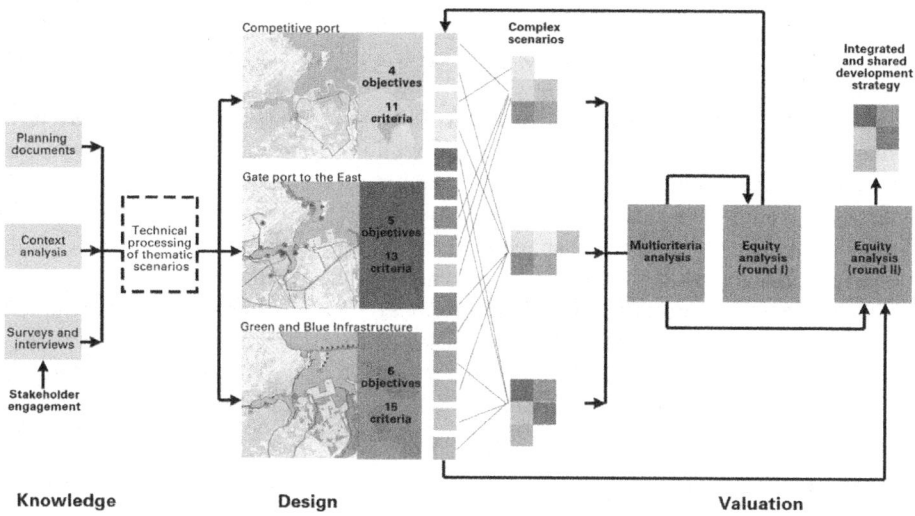

Fig. 1. Methodological scheme of the decision-making process

of implementing an evaluation model that is closely integrated into the planning process of the port city of Brindisi (Fig. 1).

The first phase consists of an in-depth understanding of the context, based on the analysis of territorial governance tools and official documents issued by sectoral institutions–such as the Port System Authority–as well as by public bodies– including the Apulia Region and the Municipality of Brindisi. These documents constitute the primary sources of institutional and regulatory knowledge. In parallel, more informal forms of knowledge were also considered, including non-scientific publications, online content, blogs, and social media platforms. These alternative sources were essential for empirically reconstructing a socio-economic and cultural profile of the case study. This knowledge phase includes the engagement of local stakeholders through a variety of methods aimed at capturing their opinions and preferences: an online survey; the observation of public meetings organised by actors within the port cluster—particularly during the final approval phase of the Port Regulatory Plan; and unstructured interviews [37] conducted with representatives of the Southern Adriatic Sea Port System Authority [38] and the Propeller Club Brindisi [39] between December 2024 and February 2025. This process of dialogue with territorial actors enabled the approximation of the viewpoints of various social groups, thereby contributing to the creation of a knowledge base that incorporates both expert and non-expert perspectives.

The second phase involved the design of preliminary alternative scenarios, developed through the technical elaboration of data gathered during the knowledge phase. Three mono-thematic scenarios were constructed, each focusing respectively on: the port's economic transition, the enhancement of mobility and attractiveness, and the environmental restoration of the sea and coastline. These scenarios represent distinct thematic clusters in which the main issues and critical elements identified in the previous phase are concentrated. A comparative analysis of these scenarios facilitated the construction of three more complex and integrated alternatives, which hybridise the elementary components of the mono-thematic dimensions based on their levels of compatibility and incompatibility.

Lastly, the evaluation phase enables the selection and articulation of a preferred scenario for the port city. The evaluation was conducted through a progressive process involving a multi-criteria analysis of the alternatives, followed by an initial multi-group assessment. Inconsistencies between the results of these two steps were addressed by conducting a second multi-group analysis focused on the elementary components of the scenarios. This allowed for a more nuanced interpretation of the preferences expressed by the different social groups and enabled a further recombination of the most favourable alternatives. The outcome of this decision-making process is a spatial planning strategy that integrates multidimensional development objectives, grounded in the preferences and values of the diverse social actors involved.

3.1 Knowledge Phase

The first methodological phase involves understanding the case study, aiming to formulate a framework of criticalities and potentials useful for defining strategic transformative objectives. Three types of knowledge sources were considered:

- Context analysis of the territory, especially regarding its environmental, historical-urban, and economic-infrastructural components, through the study of the Regional Territorial Landscape Plan (PPTR, 2015), and non-scientific sources such as newspapers, websites, and blogs;
- Review of projects and forecasts contained within the planning instruments and programming documents in force in the urban and port context;
- Information derived from stakeholder engagement, via informal and unstructured interviews, and data gathered from the compilation of a digital questionnaire.

The use of these diverse sources of knowledge has made it possible to highlight how the port city of Brindisi is currently engaged in a comprehensive planning and reorientation process concerning both port-related activities and urban economic development. Specifically, while the port development agenda includes infrastructure expansion, increased operations in logistics and cruise services, and the strengthening of linkages and functions supporting the industrial platform; the public sector is instead oriented toward de-industrialisation, urban regeneration, environmental restoration, and the enhancement of historical and architectural heritage.

Furthermore, the area's dense infrastructural network is widely recognised as a potential asset, not only for improving port and industrial logistics, but also for enhancing urban mobility and increasing the city's attractiveness as a tourist destination. This complex body of knowledge highlights the importance of adopting a transdisciplinary and integrated approach to address complex challenges [40], with the aim of designing strategic scenarios that both preserve the system's inherent complexity and support its interpretation, thereby facilitating informed decision-making.

3.2 Design Phase

The interpretation of the results from the previous phase led to the elaboration of strategic objectives during the second design phase. These objectives were grouped into three thematic clusters forming three transformative scenarios based on sustainable port development policies and frameworks (Fig. 2).

Scenario 1: Competitive Port.
Focusing on economic and industrial development, this scenario addresses energy transition issues and proposes the rethinking of port economies towards Blue Economy sectors. It includes 4 objectives and 11 actions:

- Objective 1.1 – Shift the energy sector to renewables
  - 1.1.a: Photovoltaic installations on industrial rooftops
  - 1.1.b: Development of a near-shore wind farm
  - 1.1.c: Electrification systems for port docks to reduce fossil fuel use by docked ships

- Objective 1.2 – Make the industrial hinterland sustainable
  - 1.2.a: Removal of high-impact energy industries
  - 1.2.b: Creation of sustainable economic zones for green and low-impact industries

- Objective 1.3 – Innovate port-related businesses
  - 1.3.a: Water surfaces for algae farming
  - 1.3.b: Centers for biofuel production and blue biotechnology
  - 1.3.c: Centers for marine robotics and technology research

- Objective 1.4 – Strengthen port activities
  - 1.4.a: Development of shipbuilding
  - 1.4.b: Expansion of logistics areas in the port hinterland
  - 1.4.c: Construction of new port yards for cargo handling

Scenario 2: Gate Port to the East.
Focused on tourism and intermodal infrastructure, this scenario proposes rethinking mobility as well as urban cultural attractors to increase urban vibrancy and tourism supply. It includes 6 objectives and 13 actions:

- Objective 2.1 – Develop intermodal transport

  2.1.a: Rail links between port, airport, and train station
  2.1.b: Enhanced bus connections among the same

- Objective 2.2 – Develop coastal tourism

  2.2.a: Cultural infrastructure network

2.2.b: Coastal areas equipped for beach and leisure services
2.2.c: Facilities for water sports
2.2.d: Soft mobility paths (cycling, trekking) for sustainable enjoyment of coastal and rural areas

- Objective 2.3 – Expand tourist port facilities

    2.3.a: Cruise terminals with proper services
    2.3.b: Moorings and facilities for recreational boating

- Objective 2.4 – Repurpose port buildings for hospitality functions

    2.4.a: Centers for migrant reception
    2.4.b: Cultural hubs to foster social interaction between residents and newcomers

- Objective 2.5 – Connect the port with city and region

    2.5.a: Public transport links along the historic waterfront
    2.5.b: Boat-based public transport routes
    2.5.c: Public transport services to connect the port with inland tourist attractions

Scenario 3: Green and Blue Infrastructure.
This scenario focuses on the environmental regeneration of the port, restoring its ecological components and cultural heritage, allowing citizens to recover from the impacts of pollution and reclaim access to the coastal landscape. It is divided into 6 objectives and 15 criteria:

- Objective 3.1 – Public use of the waterfront

    – 3.1.a: Remediation of contaminated or waste soils
    – 3.1.b: Creation of green waterfront areas for leisure, sports, events, and socializing
    – 3.1.c: Conversion of restricted areas into public spaces

- Objective 3.2 – Requalify historical heritage in port areas

    – 3.2.a: Restoration of anthropic and cultural assets
    – 3.2.b: Protection buffers for heritage conservation

- Objective 3.3 – Restore and protect the port's water systems

    – 3.3.a: Wetland restoration
    – 3.3.b: Re-naturalization of waterways and estuaries

- Objective 3.4 – Fight climate change

    – 3.4.a: Installation of desalination plants

- 3.4.b: Conversion of the gas power plant into a Hydrogen Valley

- Objective 3.5 – Enhance marine and coastal heritage

  - 3.5.a: Remediation of marine areas
  - 3.5.b: Re-naturalization of coastal areas
  - 3.5.c: Active protection of marine and coastal ecosystems

- Objective 3.6 – Develop the fishing economy

  - 3.6.a: Sustainable aquaculture facilities
  - 3.6.b: Devices to repopulate marine fauna
  - 3.6.c: Sustainable fishing and seafood processing centers

Pairwise comparisons of thematic scenarios identified conflicts and compatibilities among cluster objectives, enabling their recombination into three complex scenarios.

3.3 Valuation Phase

The three resulting complex scenarios have been evaluated to identify a preferable synthetic scenario using the SOCRATES tool, developed by the Joint Research Centre for ex-ante impact assessment. This method supports decision-makers in understanding the technical and social performance of alternative options [41].

First, the multi-criteria evaluation employed an impact matrix. The rows of the matrix represent the evaluation criteria, which are defined by the objectives within the three dimensions (i.e. the monothematic scenarios) that break down the decision problem. The columns of the matrix, on the other hand, correspond to the complex alternative scenarios, which are evaluated concerning their performance against the aforementioned criteria. Given the wide spatial scale of problem definition, this particular application of SOCRATES tool used a 7-point semantic scale [42], in order to offer an evaluation commensurate with the qualitative nature of alternative scenarios. The output identifies the most preferable alternative, which represents the solution that objectively maximises performance with respect to the assessment criteria.

Due to the multi-actor nature of the problem, the SMCE also includes two cycles of multi-group evaluation phase. A prior analysis of stakeholder power/interest was conducted, based on administrative competence (as defined by legislation) and observation of public meetings (e.g., PRP 2025 presentation) and unstructured interviews with stakeholders such as the Southern Adriatic Port Authority (AdSP MAM) and the Propeller Club Brindisi.

Stakeholders were divided into three groups according to their relative influence, reflecting the distribution of interest and power within the real decision-making problem. The weights have been assigned to the groups according to criteria of balance and proportionality, so that each group weighs half as much as the next and twice as much as the previous one, and in such a way that the achievement of a decision-making majority is bound to the establishment of alliances between the groups (Fig. 3).

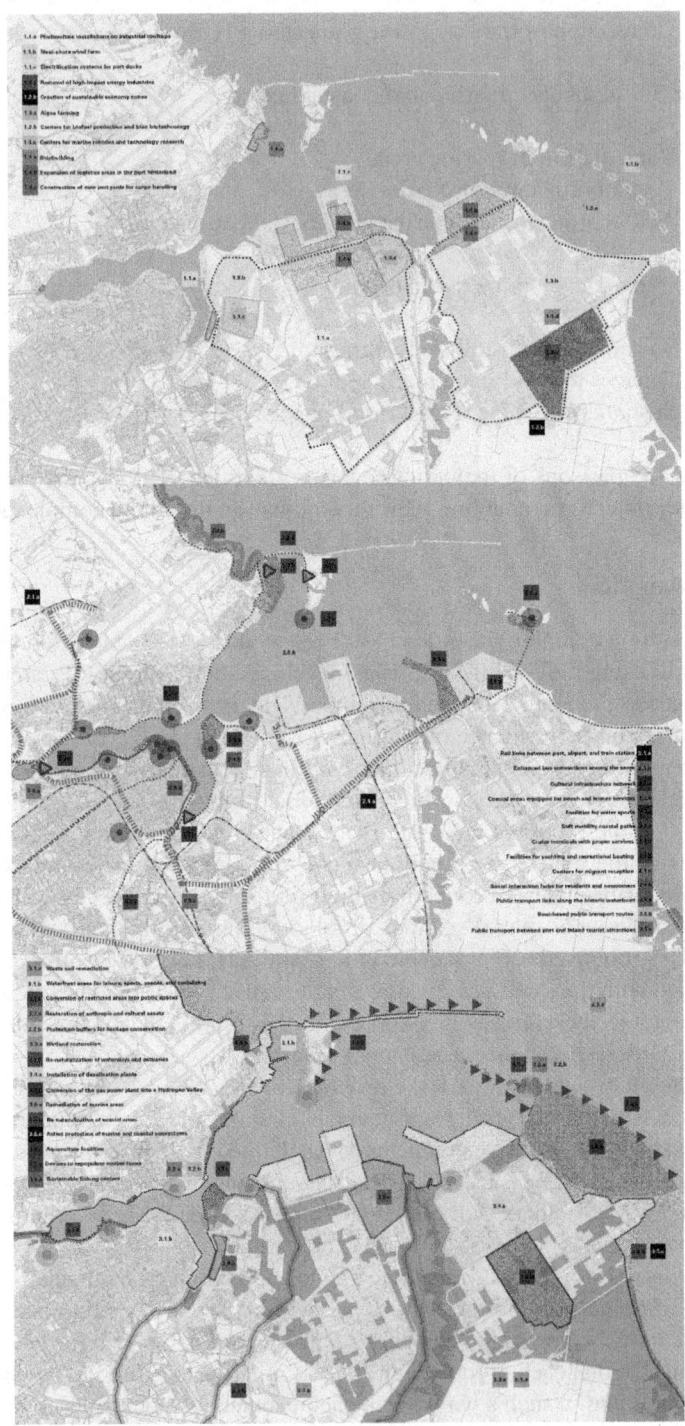

Fig. 2. Scenarios 1, 2, 3

- Cluster 1 – High influence (23%):

  - Port authorities (AdSP),
  - Public administrators (City of Brindisi, Apulia Region)

- Cluster 2 – Medium influence (12%):

  - Port workers,
  - Citizens,
  - Fishermen,

- Cluster 3 – Low influence (6%):

  - Activists,
  - students from the Nautical Technical Institute "Carnaro",
  - occasional users, such as visitors and tourists

This structure ensures decision-making balance and necessitates coalition-building while incorporating multiple stakeholder perspectives, including younger generations and tourists.

Next, a first multi-group analysis attempt was conducted, evaluating all three complex scenarios according to the perspectives expressed by the eight identified social groups, by employing an equity matrix. The results of this round revealed incompatibility with the results of the multi-criteria evaluation; therefore, a second round of multi-group analysis was conducted, which resulted in an unconventional iteration of the method compared to the standard protocol [41].

The repetition of the multi-group analysis is aimed at assessing the strategic objectives in a disaggregated form, and not aggregated into scenarios as in the first round, in order to highlight stakeholder preferences at a higher degree of definition thus increasing clarity and refinement of the evaluation. The second equity matrix, in which the alternatives considered are the individual strategic objectives initially identified, makes it possible to highlight the objectives for which social groups express a high degree of cross-party consensus, and thus to reintegrate them into the decision-making process, instead of discarding them in the selection of scenario clusters, arriving at a solution that reduces divergences and comes closest to the multi-criteria solution.

4 Results

The results presented in this section derive from the application of the Social Multi-Criteria Evaluation (SMCE) method, implemented through the SOCRATES tool, as outlined in the methodology. The evaluation phase was conceived as an integral complement to the design of alternative scenarios, with the aim of supporting a transparent and inclusive decision-making process. This approach enabled the comparison of complex, multidimensional development strategies by incorporating both quantitative criteria and the value preferences of diverse stakeholder groups. The evaluation process unfolded across three key steps, which are detailed below.

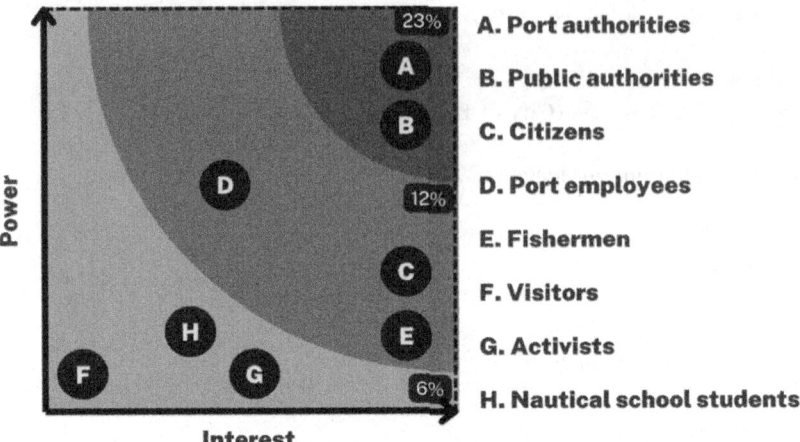

Fig. 3. Actors' map

4.1 Multicriteria Analysis

The multi-criteria evaluation identified the Green and Tourist Port scenario as the most preferable alternative. The global sensitivity analysis [41], conducted by varying the weights of each criterion, confirmed the robustness of this result, as Green and Tourist Port ranked first in 91.87% of the cases (Fig. 4).

The results from the impact matrix reflect the technical performance of the alternative in relation to the adopted evaluation criteria, highlighting how Green and Tourist Port emerges as the scenario most compatible with the dimensions of the decision-making problem. This is because it integrates ecosystem restoration strategies while also identifying economic activities capable of ensuring the port's economic development.

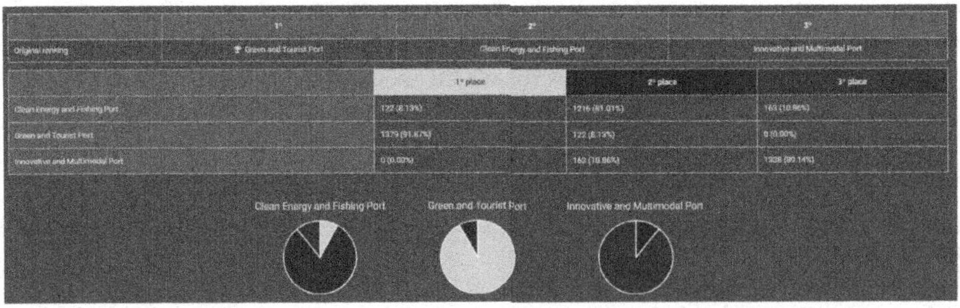

Fig. 4. Global Sensitivity analysis

4.2 Multigroup Valuation I

The first round of multi-group evaluation was carried out. The alternatives, consisting of the complex scenarios, were assessed based on the judgments expressed by the social groups involved in the decision-making process. The equity matrix enabled the creation of a coalition dendrogram (Fig. 5)–a graph that clearly illustrates convergence dynamics and alliances among the actors as they express a preference for one scenario over another.

The dendrogram reveals that Activists and Citizens are the first actors likely to ally, later joined by Fishermen and Visitors, all sharing a preference for the Green and Tourist Port scenario. At the same time, Port Administrators and Port Employees converge toward the Innovative and Multimodal Port alternative. Meanwhile, Public Authorities and Students of the Nautical Technical Institute lean toward the Clean Energy and Fishing Port, likely because it is perceived as a balanced scenario relative to the status quo. The civil cluster represented by G, C, E, and F is also inclined to support the Clean Energy and Fishing Port scenario, as it considers environmental values.

At the end of the process, actors A and D also manage to align with the other stakeholders, making Clean Energy and Fishing Port the socially preferable alternative, as it successfully reflects the value system shared by all actors involved.

After the first round of multi-group analysis, the results revealed a divergence between the technically most effective solution and the one preferred by the social groups. The best-performing scenario identified through the impact matrix prioritized environmental restoration and tourism development, whereas the ranking of social preferences favored the scenario that integrates clean energy and fishing.

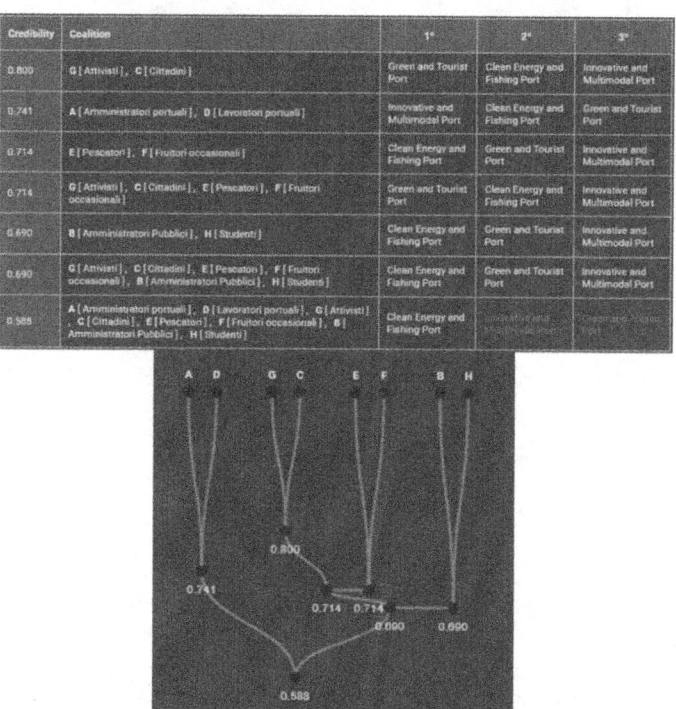

Fig. 5. Dendrogram of coalitions round I

4.3 Multigroup Valuation II

To resolve this inconsistency and determine a single, synthesized solution for the decision-making problem, a second multi-group analysis round was conducted. This phase directly compared the objectives underlying the scenarios with the stakeholder groups, identifying the true preferences of the actors involved at a more disaggregated and detailed level.

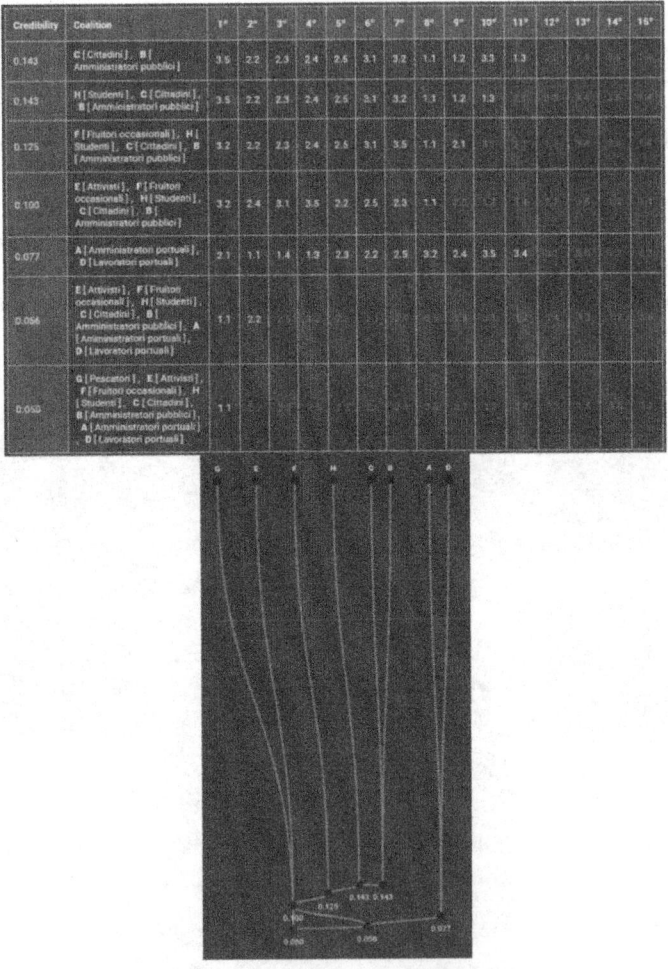

Fig. 6. Dendrogram of coalitions round II

The second dendrogram (Fig. 6) highlighted a tendency among the actors involved to polarize around two main interest coalitions. The first, composed of public authorities, citizens, visitors, and activists, shares a vision focused on environmental protection and the enhancement of the area's tourism potential. The second coalition brings together port authorities and port employees, who are primarily interested in strengthening the port's industrial, logistical, and energetic role to promote economic growth and job creation. Fishermen appear marginal in relation to the two main coalitions, although they maintain potential ties with both, as they represent both environmental and economic interests.

This particular iterative evaluation process made it possible to identify Objective 1.1, concerning the installation of wind and photovoltaic systems within the port area for production, and onshore power supply for breaking down docked ships' emissions, as the one goal capable of uniting all stakeholders.

The final scenario thus emerges as a synthesis between the technically preferred option, Green and Tourist Port, and Objective 1.1 (shifting the energy sector towards renewables) which was the most favored by the social groups.

5 Discussion and Conclusions

The evaluation process provided significant evidence of the advantage of integrating social perspectives with technical assessments in the development of port planning strategies. The multi-criteria and multi-group analyses revealed that, while the technically optimal scenario—focused on environmental restoration and tourism development—was favored by the impact matrix, the social evaluation leaned toward a scenario that emphasizes clean energy solutions. This divergence highlights a crucial transition: the general preference for renewable energy-based development marks a clear break from the past, which was characterized by polluting, high-impact economic models. Therefore, the case study is actively seeking a new balance, able to ensure alignment with international agendas and the achievement of sustainable development goals. The iterative evaluation process, which included successive rounds of multi-group analysis and the construction of equity matrices and coalition dendrograms, ultimately identified renewable energy production as the unifying goal that reconciles technical performance with social preferences. This finding illustrates that, when technical excellence is combined with social insights, it becomes possible to formulate strategies that are both innovative and reflective of community values. The final outcome of this integrated evaluation process is a robust, consensus-driven strategy that synthesizes environmental, social, economic and cultural objectives into a coherent port development model. This strategy not only connects diverse stakeholder interests but also marks a definitive move away from traditional business-as-usual policy-making practices, favoring bottom-up decision-making processes supported by an integrated and shared methodology. Moreover, the promotion of a tourism-based economy, which leverages both tangible and intangible cultural resources of the territory, is recognized as a vital element for reactivating port functions. However, this tourism development should also be guided by sustainable principles to ensure long-term resilience.

The results highlighted that the application of a multi-criteria and multi-group evaluation methodology to the definition of spatial planning strategies within the complex context of port cities not only enables the selection of preferable alternatives but also supports the progressive refinement of transformative strategies. These strategies integrate diverse objectives and foster shared ownership of planning decisions.

This contribution offers a test case for the application of SMCE within the decision-making process of a port city, highlighting the need for further development, particularly in enhancing and expanding public engagement. It opens the path for future research involving field-based participatory experiments, more extensive data collection through wider distribution of surveys, and more accurate and effective stakeholder analysis, with the aim of operationalising the outcomes of this initial simulation.

Indeed, the proposed methodology supports the definition of participatory and open decision-making processes, particularly in highly conflictual contexts marked by divergent viewpoints. In the specific case of port cities, it enables the reorientation of decision-making—typically dominated by economic objectives—towards a more shared and sustainable management and transformation of the territory. The process of selecting and refining the final preferred scenario facilitates the development of a planning strategy that can be implemented and further developed within the framework of public policies and planning instruments.

In conclusion, the proposed methodology offers policymakers a practical and replicable tool for intervention in complex and conflictual environments, while providing practitioners and evaluators with a scientific basis for integrating diverse values into participatory governance processes in port cities, transforming port planning from isolated, sector-specific interventions to an integrated, territorially oriented framework.

Acknowledgments. Conceptualization, G.C., S.S., M.C.; methodology, G.C., S.S. and M.C..; validation, M.C.; formal analysis, G.C., C.G.; investigation, G.C., C.G.; writing—original draft preparation, G.C. and C.G.; writing—review and editing, G.C., B.E., C.G., S.S. and M.C.; visualisation, G.C., C. G.; supervision, B.E., S.S., M.C. All authors have read and agreed to the published version of the manuscript.

Disclosure of Interests. The authors have no competing interests to declare that are relevant to the content of this article.

References

1. Hein, C., van de Laar, P.T.: The separation of ports from cities: the case of rotterdam. Presented at the (2020). https://doi.org/10.1007/978-3-030-36464-9_15
2. Pavia, R., di Venosa, M.: Waterfront: dal conflitto all'integrazione (2012)
3. Viana, M., et al.: Estimated health impacts from maritime transport in the Mediterranean region and benefits from the use of cleaner fuels. Environ. Int. **138** (2020). https://doi.org/10.1016/j.envint.2020.105670
4. Madhumitha, R., Rajakumari, S., Deepika, B.: Investigation of port intervention to coastal and nearshore dynamics: a GIS and AHP approach. Environ. Monit. Assess. **196** (2024). https://doi.org/10.1007/s10661-024-12472-x
5. Papaefthimiou, S., Sitzimis, I., Andriosopoulos, K.: A methodological approach for environmental characterization of ports. Marit. Policy Manag. **44**, 81–93 (2017). https://doi.org/10.1080/03088839.2016.1224943
6. Attardi, R., Bonifazi, A., Torre, C.M.: Evaluating sustainability and democracy in the development of industrial port cities: some italian cases. (2012). https://doi.org/10.3390/su4113042
7. Pugliano, G., Benassai, G., Benassai, E.: Integrating urban and port planning policies in a sustainable perspective: the case study of Naples historic harbour area. Plan. Perspect. **34**, 827–847 (2019). https://doi.org/10.1080/02665433.2018.1455068

8. Hein, C.: The Port Cityscape: Spatial and institutional approaches to port city relationships. https://repository.tudelft.nl/islandora/object/uuid%3A3e518ac3-5646-4dc8-bb69-116ec3bed422, (2019)
9. Lino, B.: Waterfront and transformation in contexts of conflict bt - the fluid city paradigm: waterfront regeneration as an urban renewal strategy. Presented at the (2016). https://doi.org/10.1007/978-3-319-28004-2_8
10. Sacco, S., Cerreta, M.: A decision-making process for circular development of city-port ecosystem: the east naples case study bt - computational science and its applications – ICCSA 2022 workshops. Presented at the (2022)
11. Hoyle, B.S.: The port—city interface: trends, problems and examples. Geoforum **20**, 429–435 (1989). https://doi.org/10.1016/0016-7185(89)90026-2
12. Jansen, M.: Ports as a Force for Positive Change? An ecosystems approach to inclusive port development (2025)
13. Cerreta, M., Muccio, E., Poli, G., Regalbuto, S., Romano, F.: City-port circular model: Towards a methodological framework for indicators selection. Lecture Notes Computer Science (including Subseries Lecture Notes Artificial Intelligence Lecture Notes Bioinformatics). 12251 LNCS, pp. 855–868 (2020). https://doi.org/10.1007/978-3-030-58808-3_61
14. Ettorre, B., Daldanise, G., Giovene di Girasole, E., Clemente, M.: Co-Planning port–city 2030: The InterACT approach as a booster for port–city sustainable development. Sustainability **15**, 15641 (2023). https://doi.org/10.3390/su152115641
15. AIVP: AIVP/ Our initiatives/ Commitment. https://www.aivp.org/en/commitment/. Accessed 30 May 2024
16. European Commission, European Climate Infrastructure and Environment Executive Agency: Sustainability criteria for the blue economy – Main report. Publications Office (2021). 10.2826/399476
17. Chamizo-Nieto, F.J., Nebot-Gómez de Salazar, N., Rosa-Jiménez, C., Reyes-Corredera, S.: Touristification and conflicts of interest in cruise destinations: the case of main cultural tourism cities on the spanish mediterranean coast. Sustain. **15** (2023). https://doi.org/10.3390/su15086403
18. Choi, H.S.C., Sirakaya, E.: Sustainability indicators for managing community tourism. Tour. Manag. **27**, 1274–1289 (2006). https://doi.org/10.1016/j.tourman.2005.05.018
19. Lozano-Oyola, M., Blancas, F.J., González, M., Caballero, R.: Sustainable tourism indicators as planning tools in cultural destinations. Ecol. Indic. **18**, 659–675 (2012). https://doi.org/10.1016/j.ecolind.2012.01.014
20. Nocca, F., Bosone, M., De Toro, P., Fusco Girard, L.: Towards the human circular tourism: recommendations, actions, and multidimensional indicators for the tourist category. Sustain. **15** (2023). https://doi.org/10.3390/su15031845
21. UNWTO: Statistical Framework for Measuring the Sustainability of Tourism (SF-MST): Final Draft (2024)
22. ESPO/ Our organization. https://www.espo.be/organisation. Accessed 8 May 2025
23. European Sea Port Organization: Code of Practice on Societal Integration of Ports (2010)
24. Moretti, B.: Investigating port spatiality: tools for a spatial approach to port clusters. Ocean Soc. **2** (2025). https://doi.org/10.17645/oas.9285
25. Cerreta, M., Poli, G., Regalbuto, S., Mazzarella, C.: A multi-dimensional decision-making process for regenerative landscapes: a new harbour for Naples (Italy). Presented at the (2019). https://doi.org/10.1007/978-3-030-24305-0_13
26. Panaro, S., Poli, G., Botte, M., Sacco, S., Cerreta, M.: Assessing the sustainability of the city-port transformations: multi-Criteria Decision Analysis (MCDA) for Alternatives Portfolio Selection. Valori e Valutazioni **2023**, 91–105 (2023). https://doi.org/10.48264/VVSIEV-20233208

27. Daldanise, G., Clemente, M.: Port Cities Creative Heritage Enhancement (PCCHE) scenario approach: culture and creativity for sustainable development of Naples Port. Sustain. **14** (2022). https://doi.org/10.3390/su14148603
28. Ciciriello, G., Sacco, S., Torre, C.M., Cerreta, M.: Port cities and evaluation: a literature review to explore their interplay in planning. Presented at the (2024). https://doi.org/10.1007/978-3-031-65273-8_13
29. Munda, G.: Social multi-criteria evaluation: methodological foundations and operational consequences. Eur. J. Oper. Res. **158**, 662–677 (2004). https://doi.org/10.1016/S0377-2217(03)00369-2
30. Di Tommaso, L., Daldanise, G., La Rocca, L., Panaro, S., Cerreta, M.: A co-governance process for the adaptive reuse of cultural heritage: the experience of St. Michael cloister in Anacapri. Presented at the (2024). https://doi.org/10.1007/978-3-031-65332-2_16
31. Joint Research Centre, European Commission: SOCRATES - Social multi-criteria assessment of European policies. https://knowledge4policy.ec.europa.eu/projects-activities/socrates-social-multi-criteria-assessment-european-policies_en
32. Ribezzi Petrosillo, V.: Guida di Brindisi : la storia, la città antica, il porto, il paesaggio costiero (1993)
33. De Leo, A.: Dell'antichissima città di Brindisi e suo celebre porto (1970)
34. Ministero dell'Ambiente e della Sicurezza Energetica: Home/ SIN schede/ Brindisi. https://bonifichesiticontaminati.mite.gov.it/sin-6/. Accessed 8 May 2025
35. Autorità di Bacino Distrettuale dell'Appennino Meridionale: Progetto di Piano di Gestione Acque - III Ciclo (2021–2027). https://www.distrettoappenninomeridionale.it/oldsite/index.php/piano-iii-fase-2021-2027-menu/progetto-di-piano-di-gestione-acque-iii-ciclo-2021-2027-menu
36. Redazione Shipping Italy: Approvato il nuovo Piano Regolatore Portuale del porto di Brindisi. https://www.shippingitaly.it/2025/01/31/approvato-il-nuovo-piano-regolatore-portuale-del-porto-di-brindisi/. Accessed 8 May 2025
37. Sanchez, C.: Unstructured interviews. In: Encyclopedia of Quality of Life and Well-Being Research, pp. 6824–6825. Springer Netherlands, Dordrecht (2014). https://doi.org/10.1007/978-94-007-0753-5_3121
38. Autorità di Sistema Portuale del Mare Adriatico Meridionale/Homepage. https://www.adspmam.it/. Accessed 8 Aug 2025
39. The International Propeller Clubs/ Port of Brindisi and Salento. http://propellerclubs.it/club/Port_of_Brindisi_and_Salento/4
40. Cerreta, M., Concilio, G., Monno, V. (eds.): Making strategies in spatial planning. Springer Netherlands, Dordrecht (2010). https://doi.org/10.1007/978-90-481-3106-8
41. Munda, G., Azzini, I., Cerreta, M., Ostlaender, N.: SOCRATES manual – Software manual for social multi-criteria evaluation, version November 2022. Publications Office of the European Union (2022). https://doi.org/10.2760/015604
42. Koo, M., Yang, S.-W.: Likert-type scale. Encyclopedia **5**, 18 (2025). https://doi.org/10.3390/encyclopedia5010018

Marginal Costs of Building Energy Retrofit

Sergio Copiello(✉) ⓘ, Carlo Grillenzoni ⓘ, and Pietro Bonifaci ⓘ

Department of Architecture and Arts, University IUAV of Venice, Santa Croce 191, 30135 Venice, Italy
{sergio.copiello,carlo.grillenzoni,pietro.bonifaci}@iuav.it

Abstract. The aim of decarbonizing the economy implies taking action in several areas, one of which is the building industry. Users are likely to benefit from the transition to green buildings in multiple ways, such as lower energy bills as well as higher healthiness and perceived comfort. Nonetheless, those benefits come at a cost. Indeed, property owners must incur substantial capital expenditures to build new high-efficiency constructions or to refurbish outdated ones. While the economic benefits of green buildings have been deeply addressed in the literature over the last two decades, much less attention has been paid to the related costs. This study aims to widen the knowledge about the marginal costs of improving energy efficiency in residential properties. Three detached houses and four to five energy efficiency measures are analyzed. Once the costs are computed through bills of quantities, the energy performance indices and the energy rating bands are identified. We find a substantial gap between the marginal cost curve drawn based on the latest figures and the same curve drawn according to a survey conducted in the late 2000s. The changes in technical standards for calculating building energy performance in the mid-2010s explain almost half the gap. The latest technical standard introduced the novelty of the so-called reference building, a fictitious building sharing the same overall shape but meeting minimum mandatory requirements. That approach has attracted criticism due to supposed flaws and side effects. Here, we show that it also makes building energy efficiency targets much less affordable.

Keywords: Building Industry · Energy Efficiency Measures · Marginal Costs

1 Introduction and Background Literature

Seeking energy efficiency in buildings brings with it several economic issues. Among these, two prominent concerns can be summarized as follows [1]. First, do high-performing buildings command a price premium, resulting in higher market values compared to traditional ones? Second, do high-performing buildings incur a cost premium, leading to greater capital expenses than ordinary ones? The answers to these questions are essential for identifying the cost-benefit balance and, therefore, the profitability of investing in energy efficiency measures for homes and workplaces.

While the first issue has been intensely investigated over the last two decades, the second issue still lacks extensive research and consistent empirical evidence. On the one hand, plenty of reliable market-based data has been published on the price and rent premiums for energy-efficient dwellings and offices. Accordingly, the first question has been chiefly answered since dozens of studies have investigated the real estate markets, finding consistent evidence over the last two decades that energy efficiency in buildings is rewarded with higher prices and rents. On the other hand, cost data for efficient residential and commercial buildings is uncertain, sparse, and scattered in the literature. Hence, the second question has yet to be fully answered because only a few works deal with it - namely, looking at potential economic shifts on the building industry's side - and their findings are contrasting at best.

1.1 A Brief Overview of the First Issue: The Price Premium for Energy-Efficient Buildings

Due to the wide availability of real estate market data, dozens of studies pointing to substantial price premiums for energy-efficient buildings have been published so far [2, 3]. Most of them deal with urban real estate markets in cities belonging to the European Union's (EU) member countries [4, 5], thanks to the Energy Performance Certificate system put forward by Directive 2010/31/EU [6–8], which enables to investigate the relationship between energy rating bands and property prices or rents when building units are sold or rented. Even so, other significant studies can be found concerning the United States [9, 10] and Eastern Asia [11, 12].

Comprehensive literature reviews on the topic can be found here [13] and here, too [14].

1.2 The Issue Still to Be Resolved: The Cost Premium for Energy-Efficient Buildings

Based on the empirical findings presented in several recent studies, high-efficiency buildings should be expected to cost more. A common way to improve efficiency, especially as far as consumption is concerned, is to substitute operating energy with embodied energy, as the two are known to be characterized by an inverse relationship (see Fig. 1, left panel) [13]. In turn, embodied energy has been shown to bear a positive - and likely nonlinear - relationship with construction cost (see Fig. 1, right panel) [15, 16]. Accordingly, the higher the energy performance, the higher the construction cost should be.

A literature review article analyzes seventeen early documents on the topic at hand [17], mainly trade publications and reports based on United States (US) data issued between 2000 and 2009, and a minority of papers in peer-reviewed journals, again with a predominance of US data, published between 2009 and 2014. The authors point out that the results are far from convergent. Two documents suggest there is no cost premium for LEED-certified buildings in the US, while a third paper [18] finds clues of higher construction costs for Green Star buildings compared to conventional ones in New Zealand, but the difference lacks statistical significance. A few documents find the cost premium for buildings that include green features and solutions to be low to moderate, that is to say, between 2 and 8%. Other sources set the bar of incremental costs for energy-efficient buildings higher: 11% for a residential project in the US [19],

17 to 18% for other residential buildings, up to 21% for the Platinum LEED certification of an office building, and a record high of 46% for school buildings [20].

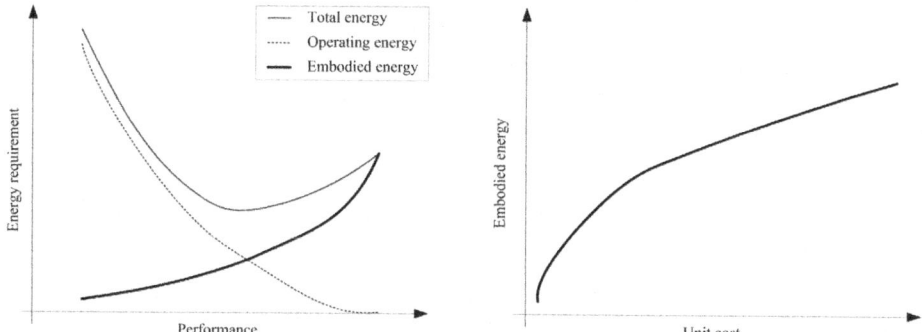

Fig. 1. Embodied energy and construction cost (sources: left panel – authors' study based on [13]; right panel – authors' study based on [15, 16]).

Just a few other studies dealing with the issue of additional upfront costs for green buildings have been published over the last fifteen years. One of them analyzes a sample of 160 LEED-certified buildings across the US, finding that the cost premium is about 4% on average and in the range of 2 to 9% [21]. Quite similarly, a study identifies a 7% additional cost for a Gold LEED-certified building and a 9% above-normal cost for a Platinum LEED-certified one [22]. Another work surveys 121 green building projects in Singapore and concludes that the cost premium lies between 5 and 10% [23]. A relatively recent study claims the cost premium is lower than the likely market premium as documented in the literature, the former being up to no more than 6.5% [24]. Finally, an investigation into the 6-Homestar certification documents shows that it attracts a 3-to-5% additional capital cost for ten detached and terraced houses in New Zealand [25].

1.3 Aim and Structure of This Study

The above literature review makes it clear that empirical findings on the cost side of green buildings are scarce and scattered. More importantly, their diverging results - from no to substantial cost premiums when comparing high-performing buildings to conventional ones - are at odds with the compelling need to understand how the economics of green buildings work on the cost side; they also cast a shadow on the ability to evaluate the economic viability and profitability of investing in the field. Under such a framework, this work aims to improve the knowledge about cost-side aspects of energy efficiency in buildings, as well as to investigate some possible reasons why large swings in the results characterize the few studies conducted so far. The analysis is meant to provide new and updated data concerning the marginal costs of energy efficiency measures usually adopted in dwelling retrofit and to compare them with previous data from European Union (EU) funded projects.

The remainder of this paper is organized as follows. Section 2 describes the method, starting with the cost theory in microeconomics and then identifying the marginal cost for energy efficiency in buildings. Section 3 presents the case studies, the analyzed energy retrofit measures, and the data sources. Section 4 discusses the results: first, a reliable marginal cost curve is traced, and then it is shown that marginal cost estimation largely depends on the method used to assess building energy performance, which changed over time, making it challenging to identify univocal marginal cost thresholds corresponding to increasing building performance. Finally, Sect. 5 draws conclusions and paves the way for further developments.

2 Method

The microeconomic theory of production identifies seven categories of short-run costs that characterize firms' activities. Six of these categories are as follows: variable costs (also known as direct costs in accounting), fixed costs (specifically, overhead expenses in accounting), their sum as total costs, and then average fixed, average variable, and average total costs (meaning the costs per unit of output). Out of all those categories, the most important one - as far as the identification of the optimal output level is concerned - is represented by the seventh: marginal costs, which are defined as the change in total cost resulting from the production of an additional unit of output [26, 27]:

$$MC = \Delta TC/\Delta Q \tag{1}$$

Marginal costs are of utmost importance in firms' decisions about the optimal output. In plain terms, production is worth expanding as long as the cost of each additional output unit (the marginal cost, as a matter of fact) is lower than the benefit of the same unit (the marginal benefit, indeed) so that each additional unit of output contributes to increasing and maximizing profit.

The above reasoning can be easily transferred to pursuing energy efficiency in buildings [28]. Let us assume that EPI_0 is the actual energy performance index of a building unit, EPI_1 represents the improved energy performance index of that same unit once an energy efficiency measure is implemented, and EPI_2 stands for the further improved energy performance index resulting from the adoption of an additional energy efficiency measure. Knowing the costs to be incurred for those measures (TC_1 and TC_2, respectively), the marginal costs can be calculated as follows (note the reversal of terms in the denominator since the energy performance index is bound to decrease as performance increases):

$$MC_1 = TC_1/(EPI_0 - EPI_1) \tag{2}$$

$$MC_2 = TC_2/(EPI_1 - EPI_2) \tag{3}$$

When it comes to constructing a new home or renovating an old one, how far is it worth pushing energy performance? Similarly to firms' decision-making process, energy efficiency is worth pursuing until the capital expenditure incurred to gain an improvement of one kWh/m^2 y in energy performance - namely, an additional energy saving unit - is lower than the corresponding benefit. Therefore, knowledge of marginal costs is a precondition for making viable and profitable decisions regarding the adoption of energy retrofit measures.

3 Case Studies and Data Sources

3.1 Case Studies for Updated Marginal Cost Data

Three detached houses are used as case studies. They are located on the outskirts of small-sized towns in Northeastern Italy, which means they fall within the E climate zone (from 2,101 to 3,000 degree days). One of the case studies was built in the early sixties, and two others in the early seventies; thus, they are characterized by the use of the same construction materials: hollow clay bricks for the walls, wood for slabs and roofs, and single-glazed windows. The gross floor area varies from 80 to 226 m^2, with heating volumes in the 274 to 901 m^3 range (see Figs. 2 and 3).

For each case study, four to five retrofit measures - to be implemented sequentially - are investigated. The first measure - adopted in the second and third case studies only - features replacing the heating system, limited to the boiler, with a new, state-of-the-art condensation one. The second focuses on the thermal insulation of the walls by installing a polyurethane foam coating layer, of which the thickness (10 to 14 cm) and placement (indoor or outdoor) depend on specific constraints. The third measure is to complete the thermal insulation of the building envelope by replacing the wooden roof and complementing it with a coating layer (14 cm thick). The fourth action is the installation of aluminum thermal break frames provided with triple-glazing windows. The fifth and last measure foresees the installation of solar photovoltaic panels on the roof combined with a heat pump.

Considering the building as-is, all three case studies are rated G, with energy requirements of about 358, 283, and 238 kWh/m^2 y, respectively. The costs of implementing each retrofit measure are calculated through bills of quantities (see Table 1), which include the cost of construction materials and systems, manpower, the cost of other goods and services required to run the building site, and overhead expenses of the construction company. The corresponding energy performance and the resulting energy saving are calculated according to the methodology adopted with the Inter-ministerial Decree 26.06.2015, which implements Directive 2010/31/EU.

3.2 Early Cost Data for Comparison Purposes

Early figures of marginal costs related to the refurbishment of residential properties are taken from Factor 4, an EU-funded project that dates back to the late 2000s (in full: "Program of actions towards Factor 4 in existing social housings in Europe"). Based on the information included in the deliverables of that project, three multi-family buildings located in Northern Italy (E climate zone) are selected as case studies. The properties were built in the mid-eighties, early fifties, and early nineties, respectively. The analyzed energy retrofit measures are as follows: insulation of the building envelope, separately for the walls and the roof; replacement of windows and frames; reduction of thermal bridges;

installation of a mechanical extract ventilation system. Building on energy audits, the marginal costs have been reconstructed and presented in a later conference paper [29] and further used for comparison with marginal benefits in a research article [14].

Fig. 2. Selected views of the case studies.

The construction cost indices provided by Istat, the Italian National Institute of Statistics, are used to update historical marginal cost data chronologically. Those indices are specific to the building industry, as they account for changes - on a monthly and yearly basis - in the costs of construction materials, manpower, and overhead expenses to run building sites [30].

Marginal Costs of Building Energy Retrofit 453

Case study 1

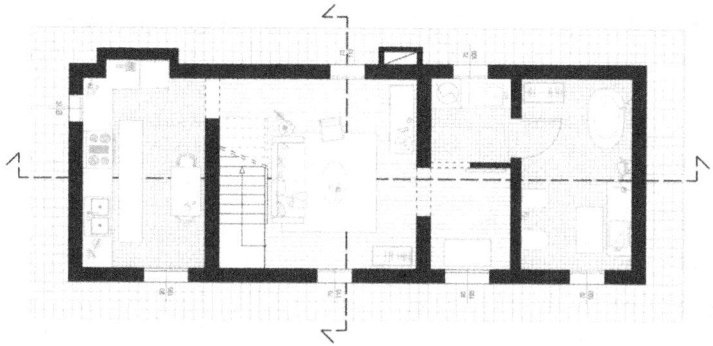

Case study 2

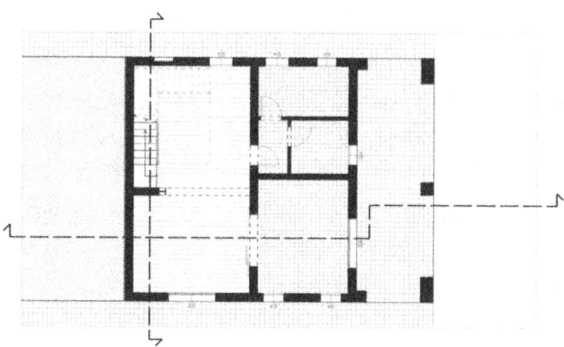

Case study 3

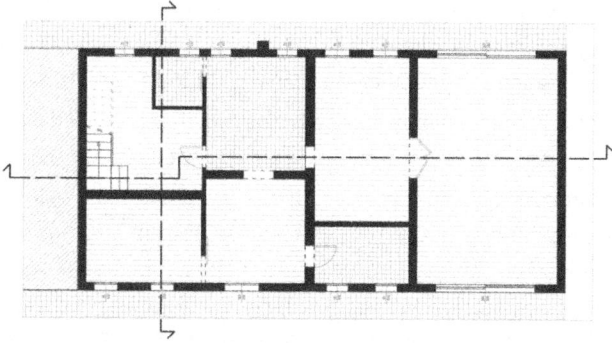

Fig. 3. Ground floor plans of the case studies.

Table 1. Excerpt from the bill of quantities for the third measure: coating layer of the roof.

Description of work	Unit (UoM)	Quantity	Rate (€/UoM)	Total (€)
Case study 1				
Removal of roof tiles	m^2	68.90	17.87	1,231
Replacement of wooden planks	m^2	68.90	19.14	1,319
Providing and laying in position insulation panels	m^2	68.90	67.28	4,635
Providing and laying in position new roof tiles	m^2	68.90	31.78	2,190
Scaffolding rental and erection/dismantling	m^2	169.83	17.92	3,043
Auxiliary construction worker	hrs	120.00	26.39	3,167
Skilled construction worker	hrs	40.00	33.42	1,337
General construction worker	hrs	–	–	–
Total				16,922
Case study 2				
Removal of roof tiles	m^2	145.44	17.87	2,599
Replacement of wooden planks	m^2	145.44	19.14	2,784
Providing and laying in position insulation panels	m^2	145.44	67.28	9,785
Providing and laying in position new roof tiles	m^2	145.44	31.78	4,622
Scaffolding rental and erection/dismantling	m^2	200.07	17.92	3,585
Auxiliary construction worker	hrs	168.00	26.39	4,434
Skilled construction worker	hrs	56.00	33.42	1,872
General construction worker	hrs	–	–	–
Total				29,680
Case study 3				
Removal of roof tiles	m^2	126.15	17.87	2,254
Replacement of wooden planks	m^2	126.15	19.14	2,415
Providing and laying in position insulation panels	m^2	126.15	67.28	8,487
Providing and laying in position new roof tiles	m^2	126.15	31.78	4,009
Scaffolding rental and erection/dismantling	m^2	201.52	17.92	3,611
Auxiliary construction worker	hrs	224.00	26.39	5,911
Skilled construction worker	hrs	56.00	33.42	1,872
General construction worker	hrs	112.00	31.67	3,547
Total				32,106

4 Results and Discussion

As expected, marginal costs are low for the first implemented retrofit measures, namely, the ones that provide a slight increase in energy performance (see Table 2).

Table 2. Energy performance, retrofit cost, and marginal cost calculation.

Energy efficiency measure	Additional investment cost	Energy performance index	Performance gain	Energy rating band	Marginal cost
	(€)	(kWh/m² y)	(kWh/m² y)		(€/kWh y)
Case study 1					
building as is	–	358.07	–	G	–
Boiler replacement	–	–	–		–
Wall insulation	12,810	222.44	135.63	F	1.19
Roof insulation	16,922	155.25	67.19	E	3.17
Windows replacement	6,249	142.86	12.39	E	6.34
Photovoltaic system	11,727	118.83	24.03	D	6.13
Case study 2					
building as is	–	282.56	–	G	–
Boiler replacement	2,505	235.28	47.28	G	0.37
Wall insulation	19,480	192.79	42.49	F	3.21
Roof insulation	29,680	142.11	50.68	E	4.11
Windows replacement	12,736	115.88	26.23	D	3.40
Photovoltaic system	13,063	111.32	4.56	C	20.08
Case study 3					
building as is	–	237.69	–	G	–
Boiler replacement	2,787	199.98	37.71	G	0.33

(*continued*)

Table 2. (*continued*)

Energy efficiency measure	Additional investment cost	Energy performance index	Performance gain	Energy rating band	Marginal cost
	(€)	(kWh/m² y)	(kWh/m² y)		(€/kWh y)
Wall insulation	28,867	165.96	34.02	F	3.76
Roof insulation	32,106	123.48	42.48	E	3.35
Windows replacement	20,719	103.24	20.24	D	4.54
Photovoltaic system	15,012	100.12	3.12	D	21.33

They are as low as 0.33–0.37 Euros/kWh for the replacement of the boiler and in the range of 1.19 to 3.76 Euros/kWh for the insulation of the walls, which let the case study buildings shift from the G to the F rating band. By contrast, marginal costs considerably grow when cumulating several retrofit measures and trying to push energy performance beyond given thresholds. They are likely to increase two to fivefold, with record highs of 6.34 Euros/kWh for the fourth measure and 21.33 Euros/kWh for the fifth, enabling them to reach the D and C rating bands.

Merging all the cost figures in the same diagram and searching for a reliable fitting function led to tracing an exponential curve (see Fig. 4, left curve). The fitting function - which has an R^2 index of 0.4815 - is as follows:

$$MC = 96.444e^{-0.022 EPI} \tag{4}$$

The implication is that the marginal costs of energy retrofit measures stay within five Euros/kWh when trying to reach an energy performance between 200 and 100 kWh/m² y. Still, approaching the threshold of 100 kWh/m² y, the marginal costs will likely increase sizably. The above results are less favorable than those found in early studies, where the bar for a steep increase in marginal costs is set at about 50 kWh/m² y [14, 31].

4.1 Changes in Costs Over Time

When tracing the marginal cost, early data derived from the source mentioned in Subsect. 3.2, an exponential fitting curve - whose R^2 index is 0.8412 - can be found again (see Fig. 4, right panel):

$$MC = 99.254e^{-0.060 EPI} \tag{5}$$

Based on early data, a surge in marginal costs is expected when aiming for a performance of about 50 kWh/m² y or less.

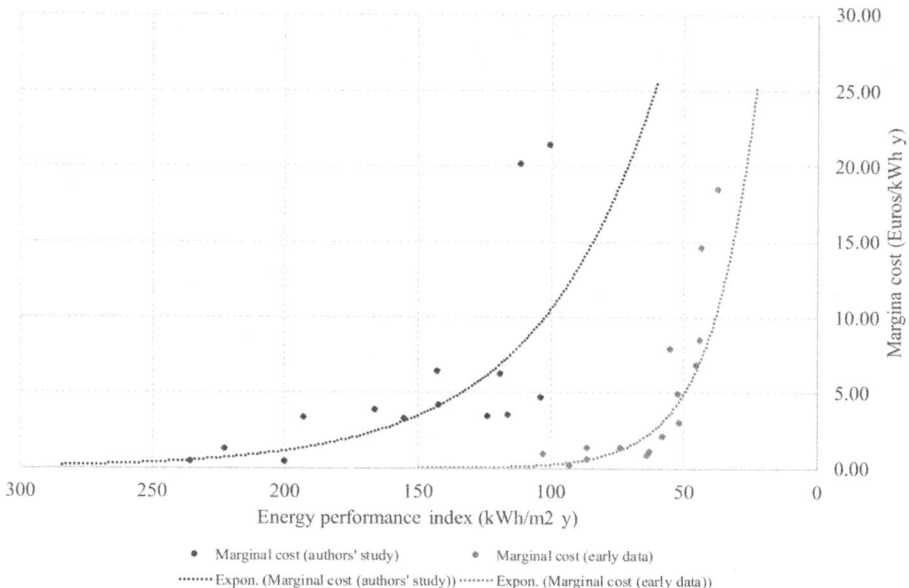

Fig. 4. Energy performance and marginal costs.

One could argue that the difference between Eqs. (4) and (5) is easily explained by the upward shift in construction costs over the last two decades, but that is not the case. All in all, the actual increase in costs the building industry experienced explains only a negligible fraction of that difference (see Fig. 5, the orange and green dotted lines).

4.2 Changes in Methods Over Time

The case studies are similar in terms of building typology and climate zone. Therefore, converging results would have been expected, provided the computational rules of building energy performance have remained the same. Actually, a significant change occurred in the method. In the second half of the 2000s, the building code (Legislative Decree 192/2005, implementing Directive 2002/91/CE) based the calculation of energy performance on two variables: degree days and heat transfer surface-to-volume ratio. Nowadays, the latest technical standard (Inter-ministerial Decree 26.06.2015, implementing Directive 2010/31/EU) features the novelty of the so-called reference building, namely, a fictitious building sharing the same overall shape but meeting minimum mandatory requirements.

By recalculating the latest figures of marginal costs using the building code previously in place, it can be easily noticed that the gap with older data narrows considerably (see Fig. 5, the blue dotted lines). The revised fitting function is as follows:

$$MC = 236.36 e^{-0.053 \text{EPI}} \qquad (6)$$

meaning the expected steep increase in marginal costs is likely to occur when approaching an energy performance between 80 and 50 kWh/m^2 y.

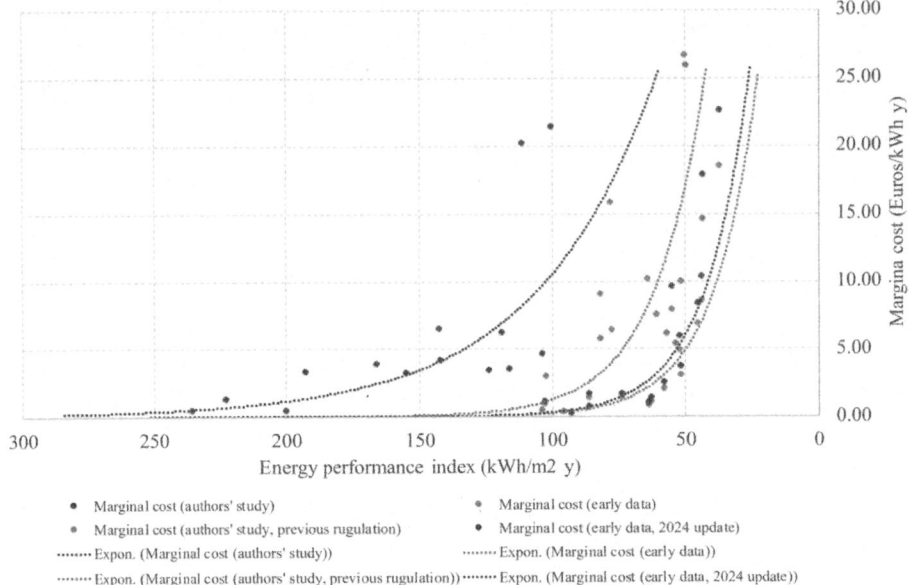

Fig. 5. Explaining the gap in marginal cost data.

5 Conclusions

Knowledge of the marginal costs of building energy efficiency measures is crucial to identifying their profitability by comparing them with their related marginal benefits, so that both policymakers and investors can identify energy retrofit projects that are economically viable. Yet, while marginal benefit estimation has attracted considerable interest and attention over the last two decades, the literature has neglected to analyze marginal costs.

This study provides updated figures concerning the marginal costs of energy retrofit measures in residential buildings. Even on a level playing field - meaning the same building typology and climate zone - those figures point to higher costs for achieving any given energy performance than previously known.

Data on the marginal costs of energy efficiency measures calculated before the mid-2010s are likely no longer helpful due to changes in the computational methodology for building energy performance. As far as the method changes are concerned, a few authors have come to criticize the so-called reference building approach for estimating energy performance [32], claiming that it might be prone to foster energy modeling and design that are characterized as poor, at best, if not even inefficient [33]. Here, we show that it is also likely to make building energy efficiency targets much less affordable as it shifts backward the performance threshold for which a steep increase in marginal costs has to be expected.

Future extensions of this research can help overcome its current limitations. In particular, the results presented here are based on a survey limited to three single-family buildings, all belonging to the same building typology and located in a uniform climate zone. It would be beneficial to extend the analysis by including additional buildings, not only detached houses, in a wider geographical area.

Acknowledgments. The authors thank E. Roncato and M. Robbi for their support in data gathering and processing.

Disclosure of Interests. The authors have no competing interests to declare that are relevant to the content of this article.

References

1. Copiello, S., Gabrielli, L., Micelli, E.: Building industry and energy efficiency: a review of three major issues at stake (2021). https://doi.org/10.1007/978-3-030-86979-3_17
2. Brounen, D., Kok, N.: On the economics of energy labels in the housing market. J. Environ. Econ. Manage. **62**, 166–179 (2011). https://doi.org/10.1016/j.jeem.2010.11.006
3. Copiello, S., Coletto, S.: The price premium in green buildings: a spatial autoregressive model and a multi-criteria optimization approach. Buildings **13** (2023). https://doi.org/10.3390/buildings13020276
4. Fuerst, F., McAllister, P., Nanda, A., Wyatt, P.: Energy performance ratings and house prices in Wales: an empirical study. Energy Policy **92**, 20–33 (2016). https://doi.org/10.1016/j.enpol.2016.01.024
5. McCord, M., Haran, M., Davis, P., McCord, J.: Energy performance certificates and house prices: a quantile regression approach. J. Euro. Real Estate Res. **13**, 409–434 (2020). https://doi.org/10.1108/JERER-06-2020-0033
6. Economidou, M., Todeschi, V., Bertoldi, P., D'Agostino, D., Zangheri, P., Castellazzi, L.: Review of 50 years of EU energy efficiency policies for buildings. Energy Build. **225**, 110322 (2020). https://doi.org/10.1016/j.enbuild.2020.110322
7. Gonzalez-Caceres, A., Lassen, A.K., Nielsen, T.R.: Barriers and challenges of the recommendation list of measures under the EPBD scheme: a critical review. Energy Build. **223**, 110065 (2020). https://doi.org/10.1016/j.enbuild.2020.110065
8. Pasichnyi, O., Wallin, J., Levihn, F., Shahrokni, H., Kordas, O.: Energy performance certificates — new opportunities for data-enabled urban energy policy instruments? Energy Policy **127**, 486–499 (2019). https://doi.org/10.1016/j.enpol.2018.11.051
9. Walls, M., Gerarden, T., Palmer, K., Bak, X.F.: Is energy efficiency capitalized into home prices? Evidence from three U.S. cities. J Environ Econ Manage. **82**, 104–124 (2017). https://doi.org/10.1016/j.jeem.2016.11.006
10. Kahn, M.E., Kok, N.: The capitalization of green labels in the California housing market. Reg. Sci. Urban Econ. **47**, 25–34 (2014). https://doi.org/10.1016/j.regsciurbeco.2013.07.001
11. Fuerst, F., Shimizu, C.: Green luxury goods? The economics of eco-labels in the Japanese housing market. J. Jpn. Int. Econ. **39**, 108–122 (2016). https://doi.org/10.1016/j.jjie.2016.01.003
12. Dell'Anna, F., Bottero, M.: Green premium in buildings: evidence from the real estate market of Singapore. J. Clean. Prod. **286**, 125327 (2021). https://doi.org/10.1016/j.jclepro.2020.125327
13. Copiello, S.: Building energy efficiency: a research branch made of paradoxes. Renew. Sustain. Energy Rev. **69** (2017). https://doi.org/10.1016/j.rser.2016.09.094
14. Copiello, S., Donati, E.: Is investing in energy efficiency worth it? Evidence for substantial price premiums but limited profitability in the housing sector. Energy Build. **251** (2021). https://doi.org/10.1016/j.enbuild.2021.111371

15. Copiello, S.: Economic implications of the energy issue: Evidence for a positive non-linear relation between embodied energy and construction cost. Energy Build. **123** (2016). https://doi.org/10.1016/j.enbuild.2016.04.054
16. Copiello, S., Bonifaci, P.: The relation between building costs and embodied energy: New insights. Int. J. Housing Sci. Appl. **41** (2017)
17. Dwaikat, L.N., Ali, K.N.: Green buildings cost premium: a review of empirical evidence. Energy Build. **110**, 396–403 (2016). https://doi.org/10.1016/j.enbuild.2015.11.021
18. Rehm, M., Ade, R.: Construction costs comparison between 'green' and conventional office buildings. Build. Res. Inform. **41**, 198–208 (2013). https://doi.org/10.1080/09613218.2013.769145
19. Kim, J.-L., Greene, M., Kim, S.: Cost comparative analysis of a new green building code for residential project development. J. Constr. Eng. Manag. **140** (2014). https://doi.org/10.1061/(ASCE)CO.1943-7862.0000833
20. Shrestha, P.P., Pushpala, N.: Green and non-green school buildings: an empirical comparison of construction cost and schedule. in: construction research congress 2012, pp. 1820–1829. American Society of Civil Engineers, Reston, VA (2012). https://doi.org/10.1061/9780784412329.183
21. Nyikos, D.M., Thal, A.E., Hicks, M.J., Leach, S.E.: To LEED or not to LEED: analysis of cost premiums associated with sustainable facility design. Eng. Manag. J. **24**, 50–62 (2012). https://doi.org/10.1080/10429247.2012.11431955
22. Uğur, L.O., Leblebici, N.: An examination of the LEED green building certification system in terms of construction costs. Renew. Sustain. Energy Rev. **81**, 1476–1483 (2018). https://doi.org/10.1016/j.rser.2017.05.210
23. Hwang, B.-G., Zhu, L., Wang, Y., Cheong, X.: Green building construction projects in Singapore: cost premiums and cost performance. Proj. Manag. J. **48**, 67–79 (2017). https://doi.org/10.1177/875697281704800406
24. Chegut, A., Eichholtz, P., Kok, N.: The price of innovation: an analysis of the marginal cost of green buildings. J. Environ. Econ. Manage. **98**, 102248 (2019). https://doi.org/10.1016/j.jeem.2019.07.003
25. Ade, R., Rehm, M.: Reaching for the stars: green construction cost premiums for Homestar certification. Constr. Manag. Econ. **38**, 570–580 (2020). https://doi.org/10.1080/01446193.2019.1640370
26. Frank, R.H.: Microeconomics and behavior. McGraw-Hill, New York (2008)
27. Frank, R.H., Bernanke, B.: Principles of microeconomics. McGraw-Hill, New York (2009)
28. Jakob, M.: Marginal costs and co-benefits of energy efficiency investments. Energy Policy **34**, 172–187 (2006). https://doi.org/10.1016/j.enpol.2004.08.039
29. Gabrielli, L., Copiello, S.: Marginal costs and benefits in building energy retrofitting transactions. In: Sustainable Built Environment Conference. pp. 836–845. ZEBAU – Centre for Energy, Construction, Architecture and the Environment GmbH, Hamburg (2016)
30. Canesi, R., Marella, G.: Residential construction cost: an Italian survey. Data Brief **11**, 231–235 (2017). https://doi.org/10.1016/j.dib.2017.02.005
31. Zalejska-Jonsson, A., Lind, H., Hintze, S.: Low-energy versus conventional residential buildings: cost and profit. J. Eur. Real Estate Res. **5**, 211–228 (2012). https://doi.org/10.1108/17539261211282064
32. Shen, P., Wang, H.: Archetype building energy modeling approaches and applications: a review. Renew. Sustain. Energy Rev. **199**, 114478 (2024). https://doi.org/10.1016/j.rser.2024.114478
33. Foroushani, S., Bernhardt, R., Bernhardt, M.: On the use of the reference building approach in modern building energy codes. Energy Build. **256**, 111726 (2022). https://doi.org/10.1016/j.enbuild.2021.111726

Author Index

A
Alonso, Francisco 54
Anelli, Debora 303, 320, 332, 346, 381, 393
Aversa, Clarastella Vicari 19

B
Barreca, Alice 177
Battisti, Fabrizio 131
Benedetti, Giacomo 3
Blečić, Ivan 199
Bollini, Letizia 72
Bonifaci, Pietro 447

C
Calabrò, Francesco 283
Carrus, Alessandro Sebastiano 199
Caviglione, Luca 3
Cerreta, Maria 429
Cerullo, Giuseppe 332
Charlier, Dorothée 410
Chimisso, Maddalena 145
Ciciriello, Giuseppe 429
Congiu, Eleonora 199
Copiello, Sergio 447
Coscia, Cristina 250

D
Dastoli, Priscilla Sofia 161
De Paola, Pierfrancesco 363
Del Giudice, Francesco Paolo 363
Dell'Ovo, Marta 268
Desogus, Giuseppe 199
Di Liddo, Felicia 303, 320, 346, 381
Donati, Edda 410

E
Ettorre, Benedetta 429

F
Faccin, Giulia 72

Falcone, Alberto 3
Fancello, Gianfranco 54
Fariello, Francesca 303, 320
Fazia, Celestina 19
Fečko, Miroslav 39
Felli, Annamaria 117
Ficco, Massimo 3

G
Gabaglio, Rossana 268
Giuffrida, Salvatore 232
Grandis, Carlotta 429
Grillenzoni, Carlo 447
Gron, Silvia 250
Guarascio, Massimo 3
Guarda, Teresa 106
Guarini, Maria Rosaria 393
Guerriero, Antonio 3

L
Lagarias, Apostolos 88
Locurcio, Marco 303, 320, 346, 381
Lorè, Immacolata 283

M
Malavasi, Giorgia 177
Manganelli, Benedetto 363
Marziali, Emilio 117
Minniti, Giovanna Emanuela 283
Miták, Ondrej 39
Montaldi, Cristina 117
Morano, Pierluigi 303, 320, 332, 346, 381, 393
Morente, Melania Arenas 332
Morgante, Federica Cadamuro 268

N
Nahiduzzaman, Kh Md 19
Nasca, Ludovica 232
Natoli, Cristina 19

P
Papazoglou, Angeliki 88
Perdonò, Melania 131
Pinna, Michele 54

R
Rebaudengo, Manuela 177
Rolando, Diana 177
Rossitti, Marco 216
Ručinská, Silvia 39

S
Sacco, Sabrina 429
Saiu, Valeria 199
Sayegh, John Cullen 268
Scorza, Francesco 161
Serra, Patrizia 54
Sortino, Federica 19
Staropoli, Rosa Maria 283
Stratigea, Anastasia 88

T
Tajani, Francesco 332, 363, 381, 393
Tatulli, Laura 346
Tiganea, Oana Cristina 268
Tomei, Vanessa 117
Torres, Washington 106
Torrieri, Francesca 216
Trovato, Maria Rosa 232

U
Useche, Sergio 54

V
Ventura, Vittoria 232
Vercellino, Enrico 250

Z
Zullo, Francesco 117

Made in the USA
Monee, IL
03 May 2026

49438663R00295